Central Publishing Company United States

Important events of the century

containing historical synopsis of the important events since the discovery of

America

Central Publishing Company United States

Important events of the century
containing historical synopsis of the important events since the discovery of America

ISBN/EAN: 9783744736596

Printed in Europe, USA, Canada, Australia, Japan

Cover: Foto ©ninafisch / pixelio.de

More available books at **www.hansebooks.com**

IMPORTANT

EVENTS OF THE CENTURY:

CONTAINING

HISTORICAL SYNOPSIS OF THE IMPORTANT EVENTS SINCE THE
DISCOVERY OF AMERICA.

ILLUSTRATIONS AND DESCRIPTIONS

OF THE

GREAT CENTENNIAL EXHIBITION

AT PHILADELPHIA;

PLACES OF REVOLUTIONARY FAME, PUBLIC BUILDINGS IN PRINCIPAL
CITIES, SKETCHES AND ILLUSTRATIONS OF THE PRESIDENTS;
ALSO, A CLASSIFIED AND ALPHABETICALLY AR-
RANGED LIST OF A LARGE NUMBER OF
LEADING BUSINESS HOUSES, GIV-
ING THE DATE OF THE ES-
TABLISHMENT OF
MANY FIRMS.

NEW YORK:
PUBLISHED BY THE UNITED STATES CENTRAL PUBLISHING COMPANY,
171 AND 173 GREENWICH STREET.
1877.
BENSON & RIPPEY, Managers.

CONTENTS.

Business Classifications.

	PAGE.
ALTON, Ill	234
ANDERSON, Ind	266
ANN ARBOR, Mich	280
ATCHISON, Kas	411
AURORA, Ill	224
BATTLE CREEK, Mich	272
BAY CITY, Mich	160
BELLEVILLE, Ill	240
BELVIDERE, Ill	465
BELOIT, Wis	464
BERLIN, Wis	246
BLOOMINGTON, Ill	240
BURLINGTON, Ia	302
CAMBRIDGE CITY, Ind	236
CEDAR RAPIDS, Iowa	430
CEDAR FALLS, Iowa	432
CHAMPAIGN, Ill	229
CHICAGO, Ill	465
CLINTON, Iowa	412
COUNCIL BLUFFS, Iowa	452
DANVILLE, Ill	192
DAVENPORT, Iowa	348
DECATUR, Ill	236
DES MOINES, Iowa	400
DIXON, Ill	458
DUBUQUE, Iowa	368
EAST SAGINAW, Mich	167
EAU CLAIRE, Wis	275
ELGIN, Ill	225
ELKHART, Ind	202
EVANSVILLE, Ind	137
EVANSTON, Ill	233
FLINT, Mich	462
FOND DU LAC, Wis	249
FORT HOWARD, Wis	275
FORT MADISON, Iowa	483
FORT WAYNE, Ind	121
FREEPORT, Ill	461
FULTON, Ill	412
GALENA, Ill	341
GALESBURG, Ill	422
GALVA, Ill	456
GRAND RAPIDS, Mich	320
GRAND HAVEN, Mich	287
GREEN BAY, Wis	273
HANNIBAL, Mo	421
HASTINGS, Minn	374
HUNTINGTON, Ind	200
INDIANAPOLIS, Ind	75
IONIA, Mich	283
IOWA CITY, Iowa	201
JACKSONVILLE, Ill	418
JACKSON, Mich	153
JANESVILLE, Wis	97
JEFFERSON, CITY, Mo	298
JOLIET, Ill	190
KALAMAZOO, Mich	217
KANKAKEE, Ill	224
KANSAS CITY, Mo	305
KENOSHA, WIS	200
KEOKUK, Iowa	383
KEWANEE, Ill	456
KOKOMO, Ind	254
LA CROSSE, Wis	332
LAFAYETTE, Ind	205
LANSING, Mich	284
LA PORTE, Ind	222
LASALLE, Ill	426
LAWRENCE, Kas	357
LEAVENWORTH, Kas	402
LEXINGTON, Mo	360
LINCOLN, Neb	453
LOGANSPORT, Ind	213
LYONS, Iowa	412
MADISON, Wis	270
MARSHALL, Mich	272
MENASHA, Wis	274
MENDOTA, Ill	459
MICHIGAN CITY, Ind	268
MILWAUKEE, Wis	318
MINNEAPOLIS, Minn	338
MISHAWAKA, Ind	268
MOLINE, Ill	343
MONMOUTH, Ill	196

Business Classifications.

	PAGE.
MORRIS, Ill	427
MUNCIE, Ind	256
MUSKEGON, Mich	286
MUSCATINE, Iowa	352
NEBRASKA CITY, Neb	420
NEENAH, Wis	275
NILES, Mich	267
OMAHA, Neb	446
OSHKOSH, Wis	290
OTTAWA, Ill	190
OTTUMWA, Iowa	462
PEKIN, Ill	423
PEORIA, Ill	413
PERU, Ind	270
PERU, Ill	426
PLYMOUTH, Ind	268
PRINCETON, Ill	459
QUINCY, Ill	436
RACINE, Wis	278
RED WING, Minn	308
RICHMOND, Ind	175
RIPON, Wis	245
ROCK FALLS, Ill	458
ROCKFORD, Ill	462
ROCK ISLAND, Ill	346
ROCHESTER, Ind	271
ROCHESTER, Minn	372
RUSHVILLE, Ind	261
SAGINAW CITY, Mich	174
SEDALIA, Mo	296
SHELBYVILLE, Ind	257
SHEBOYGAN, Wis	242
SOUTH BEND, Ind	262
SPRINGFIELD, Ill	391
STERLING, ILL	456
ST. LOUIS, Mo	15
ST. JOSEPH, Mo	396
ST. PAUL, Minn	376
TERRE HAUTE, Ind	106
TOPEKA, Kan	410
WATERLOO, Iowa	433
WATERTOWN, Wis	295
WAUKEGAN, Ill	194
WEST BAY CITY, Mich	166
WEST KANSAS CITY, Mo	314
WINONA, Minn	380
URBANA, Ill	226
YPSILANTI, Mich	205

Establishment of Business Houses.

BAY CITY, Mich	164
CHICAGO, Ill	492
DUBUQUE, Iowa	368
EAST SAGINAW, Mich	172
EVANSVILLE, Ind	152
FOND DU LAC, Wis	252
GRAND RAPIDS, Mich	337
INDIANAPOLIS, Ind	104
JACKSON, Mich	158
JEFFERSON City, Mo	302
KANSAS CITY, Mo	314
MILWAUKEE, Wis	328
OMAHA, Neb	452
PEORIA, Ill	418
QUINCY, Ill	446
ROCKFORD, Ill	463
SAGINAW, Mich	175
ST. JOSEPH, Mo	402
ST. LOUIS, Mo	74
TERRE HAUTE, Ind	121
WEST BAY CITY, Mich	167

Miscellaneous.

CHRONOLOGY OF HEROES OF THE REVOLUTION AND THE WAR OF 1812	361
FICTITIOUS NAMES OF STATES, CITIES, NOTED PERSONS, &c	383
IMPORTANT EVENTS IN THE U. S.	15
IMPORTANT EVENTS SINCE THE CHRISTIAN ERA	433
IMPORTANT INVENTIONS AND IMPROVEMENTS	330 & 377
SKETCHES AND ILLUSTRATIONS OF THE PRESIDENTS	301

INDEX TO ILLUSTRATIONS.

Centennial Buildings.

	PAGE.
AGRICULTURAL HALL	331
ARKANSAS STATE BUILDING	285
ART EXHIBITION HALL	89
BIRDS-EYE VIEW CENTENNIAL GROUNDS, Philadelphia, Pa	397
CALIFORNIA STATE BUILDING	163
CANADA LUMBER BUILDING	339
CARRIAGE BUILDING	335
CATHOLIC TOTAL ABSTINENCE FOUNTAIN	241
CONNECTICUT STATE BUILDING	215
DELAWARE STATE BUILDING	317
DEPARTMENT OF PUBLIC COMFORT	431
ENGLISH COMMISSIONERS' BUILDING	303
ENGLISH STAFF QUARTERS	129
FRENCH RESTAURANT	479
GERMAN EMPIRE BUILDING	361
GLASS BUILDING	327
HALL OF PHOTOGRAPHIC ART ASS'N	143
HORTICULTURAL HALL	245
ILLINOIS STATE BUILDING	393
INDIANA STATE BUILDING	69
IOWA STATE BUILDING	203
JAPANESE COMMISSIONERS' BUILDING	177
JUDGES' HALL	135
KANSAS & COLORADO STATE BUILDING	179
MACHINERY HALL	349
MAIN EXHIBITION HALL	375
MARYLAND STATE BUILDING	283
MASSACHUSETTS STATE BUILDING	219
MICHIGAN STATE BUILDING	341
MISSISSIPPI STATE BUILDING	315
MISSOURI STATE BUILDING	403
NEW HAMPSHIRE STATE BUILDING	217
NEW JERSEY STATE BUILDING	391
NEWSPAPER BUILDING	247
NEW YORK STATE BUILDING	27
OHIO STATE BUILDING	283
PHOTOGRAPHIC STUDIO	203
PENNSYLVANIA COM'RS' BUILDING	213
RHODE ISLAND STATE BUILDING	285
SHOE AND LEATHER BUILDING	425
SPANISH COMMISSIONERS' BUILDING	291
SWEDISH SCHOOL HOUSE	215
U. S. GOVERNMENT BUILDING	379
U. S HOSPITAL	223
VERMONT STATE BUILDING	303
W. VIRGINIA STATE BUILDING	43
WISCONSIN STATE BUILDING	191
WOMAN'S PAVILION	243

Miscellaneous Illustrations.

	PAGE.
BATTLE MONUMENT, Baltimore, Md	159
BATTLE SQUARE CHURCH, Boston. Mass.	353
BRIDGE between NEW YORK & BROOKLYN	97
BUNKER HILL MONUMENT. Charlestown	367
CARPENTERS' HALL, Philadelphia, Pa	259
CASINO CENTRAL PARK, New York	269
CHAMBER OF COMMERCE, Chicago, Ill	443
CHAMBER OF COMMERCE, Peoria, Ill	311
CHAMBER OF COMMERCE, St. Louis, Mo	83
CHICAGO WATER WORKS	417
CITY HALL, Baltimore, Md	151
CITY HALL, Boston, Mass	339
CITY HALL, Cleveland, O	415
CITY HALL, Detroit, Mich	183
CITY HALL, Louisville, Ky	183
CITY HALL, New York	91
CITY HALL, Philadelphia, Pa	297
CITY HALL, Pittsburgh, Pa	151
CITY HALL & MARKET HOUSE, St. Joseph	293
CITY HALL, St. Louis, Mo	41
COURT HOUSE, Bay City, Mich	227
COURT HOUSE, Bloomington, Ill	345
COURT HOUSE, Chicago Ill	455
COURT HOUSE, Cleveland, O	421
COURT HOUSE, Danville, Ill	139
COURT HOUSE & CITY HALL, Indianapolis	61
COURT HOUSE, Leavenworth, Kan	281
COURT HOUSE, Madison, Wis	319

Miscellaneous Illustrations.

	PAGE.
COURT HOUSE, Milwaukee, Wis	415
COURT HOUSE, Peoria, Ill	289
COURT HOUSE, Pittsburgh, Pa	85
COURT HOUSE, Quincy Ill	307
COURT HOUSE, St. Joseph, Mo	323
COURT HOUSE, St. Louis, Mo	37
EXPOSITION BUILDING, Chicago, Ill	487
FANEUIL HALL, Boston, Mass	353
FOUNTAIN PARK, Sheboygan, Wis	251
FORT INDUSTRY BLOCK, Toledo, O	279
HOME OF WASHINGTON'S ANCESTORS	219
ILLINOIS&ST.LOUIS RAILROAD BRIDGE ACROSS THE MISSISSIPPI RIVER	27
ILLINOIS UNIVERSITY, Urbana, Ill	229
INDEPENDENCE BELL, Philadelphia, Pa.	123
INDEPENDENCE HALL, Philadelphia, Pa.	101
INTERIOR VIEW OF INDEPENDENCE HALL, Philadelphia, Pa	49
INTERIOR VIEW OF MOODY & SANKEY TABERNACLE, Chicago, Ill	199
KANSAS CITY IN 1853	393
LAKE VIEW OF ERIE, Pa	447
LINCOLN MONUMENT, Springfield, Ill	187
MADISON, WIS., (Birds-Eye View)	77
MASONIC HALL, St. Louis, Mo	65
MASONIC TEMPLE, Cincinnati, O	407
MASONIC TEMPLE, N. Y	297
MASONIC TEMPLE, Philadelphia	309
MERCHANTS' EXCHANGE BUILDING, Kansas City, Mo	169
MERCANTILE LIBRARY, St. Louis, Mo	25
MISSOURI RIVER BEND, Kansas City, Mo	231
MT. VERNON, HOME OF WASHINGTON	131
NORMAL SCHOOL, Terra Haute	163
OLD ELM, Boston Common, Boston, Mass	273
OPERA HOUSE, Detroit, Mich	155
OPERA HOUSE, Evansville, Ind	123
OPERA HOUSE, Terra Haute, Ind	113
OPERA HOUSE (TOOTLES), St. Joseph, Mo.	299
PATENT OFFICE, Washington, D. C	409
PENN'S TREATY WITH THE INDIANS	117
PERRY'S FLAG SHIP LAWRENCE	237
POST OFFICE, Boston, Mass	339
POST OFFICE, Chicago, Ill	429
POST OFFICE, Cincinnati, O	291
POST OFFICE, Cleveland, O	413
POST OFFICE, Covington, Ky	317
POST OFFICE, Grand Rapids, Mich	109
POST OFFICE, Indianapolis, Ind	147
POST OFFICE, Milwaukee, Wis	165
POST OFFICE, New York	255
POST OFFICE, Philadelphia	119
POST OFFICE, St. Louis, Mo	21
POST OFFICE DEPARTMENT, Washington	459
PUBLIC LIBRARY, Detroit, Mich	155
SMITHSONIAN INSTITUTION, Washington, D. C	355
STATE CAPITOL, Columbus, O	139
STATE CAPITOL, Harrisburg, Pa	207
STATE CAPITOL, Indianapolis, Ind	57
STATE CAPITOL, Jefferson City, Mo	389
STATE CAPITOL, Lansing, Mich	259
STATE CAPITOL, Madison, Wis	173
STATE CAPITOL, Springfield, Ill	211
STATE CAPITOL, West Virginia	315
ST. LOUIS UNIVERSITY, St. Louis, Mo	53
STOCK EXCHANGE, Kansas City, Mo	451
SUSPENSION BRIDGE BETWEEN CINCINNATI AND COVINGTON	147
TUNNEL VIEW, Chicago, Ill	471
UNION MARKET, St. Louis, Mo	45
UNION PACIFIC DEPOT, Council Bluffs, Ia	371
UNITED STATES CAPITOL, Washington	439
UNITED STATES MINT, Philadelphia	263
VANCE BLOCK, Indianapolis, Ind	73
WASHINGTON ELM, Cambridge, Mass	381
WASHINGTON'S HEADQUARTERS AT VALLEY FORGE	105
WASHINGTON'S MONUMENT, Baltimore	159
WASHINGTON WHEN TOOK COMMAND OF THE CONTINENTAL ARMY	17

INDEX TO ADVERTISEMENTS.

Agricultural Implements.
	PAGE
DES MOINES PLOW CO., Des Moines, Ia...	398
PERKINS H. C. & Co., Chicago, Ill.........	417
RUMSEY L. M. & Co., St. Louis, Mo.......	116
SHELDON. S. L. Madison, Wis	173
TAYLOR, MACK & SMITH, Chicago........	17

Amusements.
ADELPHI THEATRE, Chicago, Ill.........	2
TIVOLI VAUDEVILLE THEATRE, St. Louis, Mo..............................	64

Architects.
ENOS V. B. & SON, Indianapolis, Ind......	147
LANDGUTH A. S. Milwaukee, Wis........	434
ROBINSON & BARNABY, Grand Rapids, Mich................................	108
SLICER, W. C., St. Louis, Mo...............	32

Attorneys at Law.
McFARLAND, DANIEL, Peoria, Ill.........	310
WARRICK, JAMES N., Indianapolis, Ind...	73

Baking Powders.
JUDD & DERRICK, Grand Rapids, Mich...	108
WOODRUFF JAMES E., Quincy, Ill........	307

Banks and Bankers.
LAWRENCE SAVINGS BANK, Lawrence, Kan..................................	179
KNOX JOHN D. & CO., Topeka, Kan......	179

Barbed Wire Fence.
ADAM MANUFACTURING CO., Joliet, Ill..	335
DILLMAN & STEVENS, Joliet, Ill.........	327
JOLIET WIRE FENCE CO., Joliet, Ill......	101

Battery Belt.
WITHERELL & KIRKHAM, Niles, Mich...	182

Billiard Parlors.
FRIEDRICHS HERMAN, Peoria, Ill........	298

Bill Posters.
HOLLEY JOEL & SONS, Bloomington, Ill...	138

Blacksmiths.
HURTUBISE A., Saginaw City, Mich.......	310

Boiler Manufacturers.
CLIFF & SON, Terre Haute, Ind...........	119
EVINSTON J. W., Milwaukee, Wis........	434
FULTON BOILER WORKS, Richmond, Ind.	80

Bolt Works.
ROCKFORD BOLT WORKS, Rockford, Ill...	470

Book Binders.
DAVIS & BRO., Fort Wayne, Ind...........	424
DONOHUE & HENNEBERRY, Inside front Cover..................................	
LUSK D. W., Springfield, Ill...............	210
ROKKER H. W., Springfield, Ill...........	210

Boots and Shoes.
BARNEY M. D., St. Louis, Mo.............	65
REDDEN A., St. Louis, Mo.................	129

Bottlers.
JOERGER JACOB, Springfield, Ill..........	186

Brass Foundry.
	PAGE
INDIANAPOLIS BRASS FOUNDRY, Indianapolis, Ind................................	60

Brewery.
GEISE C., Council Bluffs, Iowa.............	370

Burial Cases and Caskets.
POWERS & WALKER, Grand Rapids, Mich.	109

Business Colleges.
CRESCENT CITY COMMERCIAL COLLEGE, Evansville, Ind..................	49
CURTISS & HYDE, Minneapolis, Minn.....	128
JONES' COMMERCIAL COLLEGE, St. Louis, Mo...........................	125
NORTHWESTERN BUSINESS COLLEGE, Madison, Wis...........................	77
PARSONS W. B., Kalamazoo, Mich........	154

Butchers' and Mechanics' Tools.
DAEMICKE BROS., Chicago, Ill............	375
DAEMICKE L. C., Chicago, Ill.............	367

Butter Package.
FINNEGAN A. J., Minneapolis, Minn......	154

Carriages and Wagons.
BLACK & BACKUS, Indianapolis, Ind.....	60
BLOOM HENRY, Des Moines, Iowa........	389
GALE GEO. H., Jackson, Mich............	258
GIDDINGS JOHN W., Danville, Ill........	138
NEUMEISTER A., Rockford, Ill...........	470
WOOD, ARTHUR, Grand Rapids, Mich....	108

Carriage Springs.
CURTIS H. M. & CO., Ypsilanti, Mich......	183

Carriage and Wagon Material.
STEVENS & GARRIGUES, Leavenworth, Kan..................................	281

Cash Register.
HOOD, H. P., Indianapolis, Ind............	72

China, Glass & Queensware.
BERGUNDTHAL C., Indianapolis, Ind.....	68
WARREN JAMES M., Evansville, Ind.....	69

Chromos & Picture Frames.
NATIONAL ART AND CHROMO COMPANY, St. Louis, Mo..................	29
DURKEE ALBERT, Chicago, Ill............	434

Cigar Boxes.
BERNS F. G., Indianapolis, Ind............	146
HARTMANN & SUHR, Milwaukee, Wis....	163

Clairvoyant.
WITHEFORD, DR., Chicago, Ill............	119

Coffee & Tea Pots.
DEWALD, M. J. Chicago, Ill...............	442

Commission Merchants.
BLAKE, JACKSON & QUINIUS, Indianapolis, Ind.......................	68
LAWRENCE, A. V., Indianapolis, Ind.....	64
O'DONOGHUE, WILLIAM, St. Joseph, Mo.	293
SULLIVAN, JOHN E., Indianapolis, Ind...	116
TIVY & PURCELL, St. Louis, Mo..........	28
WALSH BROS., St. Louis, Mo.............	21
WILLIS, JOHN G., Omaha, Neb...........	277

INDEX.

Confectionery.
FOUTS, H. J. St. Louis, Mo 24
MIESSEN, J., Indianapolis, Ind.............. 340

Conservatory of Music.
YOUNG LADIES' ATHENÆUM,
Jacksonville, Ill........................... 186

Contractors and Builders.
KROEGER, B. H., Evansville, Ind........... 122
OWENS, G. C., DesMoines, Iowa............ 370

Cotton Batting.
EXCELSIOR COTTON BATTING CO.,
St, Louis, Mo.............................. 6

Driven Wells.
ROUSE, R. R., Indianapolis, Ind............ 81

Druggists.
COLEMAN, J. R., St. Louis, Mo............. 52
DONNELL MANUFACTURING CO.,
St. Louis, Mo.............................. 36

Dry Goods.
HODGES, D. H., Indianapolis, Ind........ 424
MILLER BROS., Evansville, Ind............ 123

Dyeing and Scouring.
PEEL, GEORGE W., Lawrence, Kas......... 230

Eclectic Heater.
SERVOSS, NORTHEN & CO., Chicago, Ill.. 428

Electric Manufacturing Company.
ST. LOUIS ELECTRIC MANUFACTURING
CO.. 438

Edge Tools.
RICHMOND EDGE TOOL MANUFACTURING CO., Richmond, Ind.................. 80

Engine Builders.
NICOL, BURR & CO., Peoria, Ill............ 289

Engravers.
BENZ & RICHES, St. Louis, Mo 73
CHANDLER. H. C., Indianapolis, Ind...... 72
HARRIS, J. G. & CO., St. Louis, Mo........ 28
REED, W. A. & CO., Grand Rapids, Mich.. 154
STILLMAN & CO., Cincinnati, Ohio........ 384

Fancy Cabinet Ware.
FURBISH, F. L., Grand Rapids, Mich 258
WENTER, F., Chicago, Ill.................. 258

Fancy Goods.
GRIFFITH, H. G., Springfield, Ill.......... 392

Flanging Flue-hole Machine.
REAGAN, E., Indianapolis, Ind............ 112

Flavoring Extract.
DAVIS' FLAVORING EXTRACTS............ 97

Foot Power Machinery
BARNES, W. F., & JOHN, Rockford........ 435

Fruits and Produce.
BLAKE, JACKSON & QUINIUS,
Indianapolis, Ind......................... 68
LAWRENCE, A. V., Indianapolis, Ind...... 68
SULLIVAN, JOHN E., Indianapolis, Ind.... 116

Furs.
LEWARK, JOSEPH, Indianapolis, Ind...... 56

Furniture.
BARSALOUX N., Chicago, Ill.............. 413
BEEMER BROS., Chicago, Ill.............. 388
BOURKE ULICK, Chicago, Ill.............. 425
GOODWINS INVALID BEDSTEAD,
St. Louis, Mo............................. 176
RICHTER HERMAN, Chicago, Ill.......... 177
RICKE S. & CO., Chicago, Ill.............. 385

Galvanic Belt.
PULVERMACHER GALVANIC CO.,
Cincinnati, O............................. 378

Galvanized Iron Cornice.
KLUGEL G. L., Danville, Ill............... 138

Gate Manufacturers.
WISELL, D. D., Ft. Wayne, Ind............ 4

Gents Furnishing Goods.
McELRATH A., St. Louis, Mo.............. 64

Glove Manufacturer.
JENSEN H., Chicago, Ill................... 379

Groceries.
DONNELL MANUFACTURING CO.,
St. Louis, Mo............................. 36
HALL & BANTA, Council Bluffs, Iowa..... 371
HULMAN & COX, Terre Haute, Ind....... 162
KELLER ROBT., Indianapolis, Ind........ 61
LIGHTHOLDER JAMES, St. Louis, Mo.... 28
NISBETT T P. & CO., Alton, Ill........... 210
THORNBURGH J, McC. & Co., St. Louis, Mo. 37

Grocers' Specialties.
WALSH BROS., St. Louis, Mo.............. 21

Gunsmith.
ABE AUGUSTUS, St. Louis, Mo............ 28

Hair Goods.
BOYCE MRS. E. L., Fort Wayne, Ind...... 57
GRIFFITH, H. G., Springfield, Ill.......... 392
HALL. J., Chicago, Ill., Center of Calendar...
THOME. M., Chicago, Ill., Center of Calendar

Hardware.
CAYLOR J., Indianapolis, Ind............. 424
EBERBACK C., Ann Arbor, Mich.......... 154
DAEMICKE BROS., Chicago Ill............ 375
BOSS, JAS. A., Indianapolis, Ind.......... 146
TYRING H. E. Chicago, Ill................ 454

Harness and Saddles.
BROWN L. G., Grand Rapids, Mich....... 182
HOLTHAUS AUGUST, St. Louis, Mo...... 36
OPFERGELT PH., Saginaw City, Mich.... 89

Hat and Bonnet Bleachers.
MURPHY & WADE, Springfield, Ill....... 392

Hides and Leather.
BECHAM JOHN, Des Moines Iowa........ 388
HASELTINE, WM. B., St. Louis, Mo 40

Heaters, Ranges and Furnaces.
MANNING JOHN N. & CO., Chicago, Ill... 424
SERVOSS, NORTHEN & CO., Chicago, Ill.. 428
WATSON GEO. H. & CO., Chicago, Ill..... 454

Horse Hoof Cooler and Expander.
DRAPER E. B., Chicago, Ill................ 1

Horse Hoof Paring Machine.
SCHAEFER G. W., St. Louis, No........... 438

Horse Protector.
PETER'S HORSE PROTECTOR, Chicago, 241

Horse Shoes.
HURTUBISE A., Saginaw City, Mich...... 340
O'NEILL P. H., St. Louis, Mo.............. 438
SCHAEFER G. W., St. Louis, Mo.......... 438

Hotels.
BARNUM'S HOTEL, Kansas City, Mo..... 450
BARRETT HOUSE, Burlington, Iowa..... 354
BIGGS HOUSE, Council Bluffs, Iowa..... 370
BRYANT HOUSE, Council Bluffs, Iowa... 370
BURDICK HOUSE, Chicago, Ill........... 1
CIRCLE HOUSE, Indianapolis, Ind....... 73
DOWNING HOUSE, Oskaloosa, Iowa..... 279
GOODWIN HOUSE, Beloit, Wis........... 470
GRAND HOTEL, Indianapolis, Ind....... 81
GRAND CENTRAL HOTEL, Omaha, Neb... 345
HURST'S HOTEL, St. Louis, Mo........... 64
LITTLE'S HOTEL, Indianapolis, Ind...... 61
MERCHANTS' HOTEL, Winona, Minn.... 162
METROPOLITAN HOTEL, Council Bluffs,
Iowa..................................... 371
OGDEN HOUSE, Council Bluffs, Iowa.... 371
PACIFIC HOUSE, Council Bluffs, Iowa... 371
PEABODY HOUSE, Eau Claire, Wis...... 261
ST. JAMES HOTEL, Kansas City, Mo..... 168
THE PALISADE HOTEL, Kansas City, Mo. 230
UNION HOTEL, Galesburg, Ill............ 273

House Furnishing Goods.
BOURKE, ULICK, Chicago, Ill............. 425

Hydraulic Motor.
TUERK BROS., Chicago, Ill................ 431

INDEX. 11

Ink Manufacturers.
ROKKER, H. W., Springfield, Ill............ 210
WOODMANSEE, FRANK A., Cincinnati.... 6

Invalid Bed Manufacturer.
GOODWIN'S INVALID BEDSTEAD,
St. Louis, Mo 176

Iron Works.
GARRETT, McDOWELL & CO.,
St. Louis, Mo............................... 28
GENESEE IRON WORKS, Flint, Mich...... 258

Insurance.
COREY & GRIFFIN, Omaha, Neb........... 269
GRUBB, PAXTON & CO., Indianapolis, Ind. 56
HAMLIN & BROWN, Minneapolis, Minn.... 135
HOWELL, SAM'L J., Omaha, Neb.......... 269
THE FRANKLIN LIFE INSURANCE CO.,
Indianapolis, Ind 57

Knitting Machines.
KALAMAZOO KNITTING CO.,
Kalamazoo, Mich 154

Lithographers.
BIRD & MICKLE, Jackson, Mich............ 258

Live Stock Commission.
IRWIN, ALLEN & CO., Kansas City, Mo.... 450
KINGSBERY & HOLMSLEY,
Kansas City, Mo............................ 450
WHITE & HOLMES, Kansas City, Mo...... 450

Livery and Sale Stables.
GALE, GEO. H., Jackson, Mich............. 258
KOLYER & KERR, Indianapolis, Ind....... 72

Machinery.
KERRICK & WINEGARDNER,
Indianapolis, Ind........................... 349
MANNING, JOHN N. & CO., Chicago, Ill... 424
STRANG, A. L., Omaha, Neb................ 281

Machinists.
KLEINSTEUBER, C. F., Milwaukee, Wis... 434
NICOL, BURR & CO, Peoria, Ill............. 289
REAGANS, E., Indianapolis, Ind............ 112

Manufacturer's Agent.
THORNBURGH, J. McC.& CO., St. Lous, Mo 37

Map Publishers.
BIRD & MICKLE, Jackson, Mich............ 258

Marble Works.
BROWER, H. O., Danville, Ill................ 138
DAVIS & CAMP, Davenport, Iowa 203
MOORE, W. B., Bloomington, Ill........... 138
NEAYER, C. L., Council Bluffs, Iowa...... 451

Medical Institute.
ACADEMY OF MEDICINE, St. Joseph, Mo. 322
LAFAYETTE EYE, EAR & THROAT DIS-
PENSARY, Lafayette, Ind.................. 117
MEDICAL HEALING INSTITUTE,
Chicago, Ill 105
MEDICAL AND SURGICAL INSTITUTE,
Grand Rapids, Mich....................... 109
PIERCE & GREEN, DRS., Kansas City..... 392

Millinery.
ATKINSON, A., Omaha, Neb................ 331
LEWANDOVSKA, MME, St. Louis, Mo..... 25

WALKER, JOSEPH, Bloomington, Ill....... 345

Mineral Spring Water.
BERTCHY & THAYER, Sheboygan, Wis.... 251

Music Dealer.
BARROWS, CHAS. S., Jacksonville, Ill..... 194

Newspapers.
CINCINNATI SATURDAY NIGHT......... 6
ILLINOIS STATE GAZETTE,
Springfield, Ill............................. 210
THE INVENTOR'S SCIENTIFIC & COM-
MERCIAL WORLD, Indianapolis, Ind... 354

Non-Explosive Fluid.
BEATTIE, A. F., St. Louis, Mo............... 40

Oils & Grease.
CROZIER, G. W., Indianapolis, Ind........ 182
WINSLOW, N. N., Bloomington, Ill........ 344

Opium Cure.
COLLINS, DR. S. B., LaPorte, Ind.......... 88

Painters.
DAUER, CHAS. W., Indianapolis, Ind...... 81

Paper Dealers.
SAWYER, F. O. & CO., St. Louis, Mo...... 41

Paper Hangings.
FITCH, B. F., Chicago, Ill................... 397

Patent Agency.
EMPIRE PATENT AGENCY, St. Louis, Mo. 408

Patent Solicitors.
KNIGHT BROS, St. Louis, Mo 408
LOTZ, WM. H., Chicago, Ill................. 408

Pattern & Model Makers.
KUPSCH, A., St. Louis, Mo.................. 409

Photographers.
CADMAN, A. W., Jacksonville, Ill.......... 186
JOSLIN & PHILLIPS, Danville, Ill......... 138
PIETZ, H., Springfield, Ill.................. 442
PENDEGRAST, Indianapolis, Ind.......... 112

Physicians.
AIKIN'S REMEDIAL INSTITUTE, Grand
Rapids, Mich............................... 96
BISHOP, GALEN E., St. Joseph, Mo....... 322
CARLTON, DR., Chicago, Ill................ 199
DECKER, DR. H. G., Chicago, Ill.......... 143
OLIN, DR. A. C., Chicago, Ill............... 199
PARSONS, E., Kewanee, Ill................. 288
PEKO, F. L., Chicago, Ill.................... 399
SMALL, A. E., Chicago, Ill.................. 187
VON TAGEN, CHAS. H., Chicago, Ill...... 187

Pickle Manufacturers.
WISWELL, W. H. & CO., Chicago, Ill...... 1

Planing Mills.
HERSCHBERGER, JOHN, Peoria, Ill...... 288
CAPITOL CITY PLANING MILL CO., Indi-
anapolis, Ind............................... 60
MEYERS, JACOB & BRO., Evansville, Ind.. 122

Plaster Company.
GRAND RAPIDS PLASTER CO., Grand Rap-
ids, Mich 341

Plasterers.
McCARTY, J. C. & G. VOGT, Chicago, Ill... 177

Plow Manufacturers.
DES MOINES PLOW CO., Des Moines, Iowa. 393

Plumbers and Gasfitters.
RUMSEY, L. M. & CO., St. Louis, Mo...... 116

Printers--Book and Job.
BLAKELY & BROWN, Chicago, Ill.......... 493
DAVIS & BRO, Fort Wayne, Ind........... 424
ROKKER, H. W., Springfield, Ill........... 210

Pump Manufacturers.
COMSTOCK, A. S., Indianapolis, Ind...... 68
MESSINGER, PHOSEUS & CO., Logansport, 80
RUMSEY, L. M. & CO., St. Louis, Mo...... 116
SPRINGER, THAYER & CO., Rockford, Ill. 447
STRANG, A. L., Omaha, Neb................ 281

Railroads.
HANNIBAL & ST. JOSEPH RAILROAD.... 292
CHICAGO, BURLINGTON AND QUINCY
RAILROAD................................. 416
INDIANAPOLIS, PERU & CHICAGO RAIL-
ROAD...................................... 202

Raisers and Movers of Buildings.
BAUMHARD & SHEELER, Indianapolis,
Ind... 56

Real Estate.
HAMLIN & BROWN, Minneapolis, Minn.... 135
NOHL, F. St. Louis, Mo..................... 32
WEBSTER, ED. H., Kansas City, Mo....... 450

INDEX.

Reapers and Mowers.
PERKINS, H. C. & CO., Chicago, Ill........ 417
Restaurants.
ENGLISH KITCHEN, The, St. Louis, Mo... 36
MATSON S., St. Louis, Mo.................. 44
MILLER'S RESTAURANT, Atchison, Kan... 179
SPRAGUE & BUTLER, St. Louis, Mo...... 45
THE "SAINT DENIS," St. Louis, Mo...... 24
VIENNA GARDEN AND RESTAURANT, Kansas City, Mo......................... 169
Regalia Manufacturer.
BUSH, JOHN A., Peoria, Ills............. 310
Renovating Works.
FLINT & COOK, Chicago, Ill.............. 265
Rheumatic Hospital.
MELLEN, DR. M., Oshkosh, Wis.......... 374
Roofing.
KLUGEL G. L., Danville, Ill............. 139
Saloons.
HENRY'S FIFTH ST. SALOON, St. Louis, Mo 85
MUEHLHAUSEN CHAS., St. Louis, Mo... 44
Sash, Doors and Blinds.
HERSCHBERGER JOHN, Peoria, Ill....... 288
Saw Manufacturer.
CURTIS & COMPANY, St. Louis, Mo...... 40
Scales.
HITCHCOCK, S. S., Des Moines, Iowa.... 370
Schools and Colleges.
ACADEMY OF ST. FRANCIS, Council Bluffs, Iowa.................................... 370
ILLINOIS FEMALE COLLEGE, Jacksonville, Ill................................ 195
JACKSONVILLE FEMALE ACADEMY, Jacksonville, Ill........................ 186
ST. LOUIS UNIVERSITY, St. Louis, Mo.... 53
ST. MARY'S ACADEMIC INSTITUTE, St. Mary's of the Woods, Ind.............. 134
Scrool Sawing and Turning.
CASE, F. F., St Joseph, Mo.............. 299
Seed Dealer.
FOOTE, J. A., Terre Haute, Ind.......... 113
Sewing Machines.
LARSEN, N. P., Chicago, Ill............. 1
THE NEW AMERICAN SEWING MACHINE, Omaha, Neb........................ 230
WRIGHT, S. A., Sedalia, Mo.............. 277
Shirt Manufacturers.
DEYO, A. H., East Saginaw, Mich........ 340
McELRATH, A., St. Louis, Mo............ 64
Show Case Manufacturers.
CLAES, C. & CO., St. Louis, Mo......... 44
LUTKE, R. G., Peoria, Ill............... 288
Silver Ware.
DURGIN, F. A., St., Louis, Mo........... 20
Soap and Candles.
WINSLOW, N. N., Bloomington, Ill....... 344
Spectacles.
WOLF, JOSEPH, Chicago, Ill............. 454
Spice Mills.
VERRIER, E. V., St. Louis, Mo.......... 41
Stamps and Stencils.
HARRIS, J. G. & Co., St. Louis, Mo..... 26
KLEINSTEUBER, C. F., Milwaukee, Wis... 434
Steamboats.
EAGLE PACKET CO........................ 133
GRAND REPUBLIC, (plys bet. St. Louis, Memphis and N. Orleans)............... 93
KEOKUK & NORTHERN LINE PACKET CO....................................... 198
Steam Heating Apparatus.
MANNING, J. N. & CO., Chicago......... 424

Stoves & Tinware.
BERTHOLD, H. & TROSSIN, Omaha, Neb.. 372
DAEMICKE, L. C., Chicago, Ill........... 367
ENSMINGER, S. F., Des Moines, Iowa.... 430
TYRING, H. E., Chicago, Ill............. 434
SERVOSS, NORTHEN & CO., Chicago, Ill.. 438
Stove Polish.
SKINNER, WM. A. & CO., St. Louis, Mo... 21
Tailors.
BUETOW & SCHRAEGER, Milwaukee, Wis. 319
CORBETT, JOHN, Ripon, Wis.............. 191
GATZ, ALOIS, Quincy, Ill................ 234
HEINIG, Frank, Chicago, Ill............. 442
NELSON, M. J., Chicago, Ill............. 143
PARKES, WM., St. Louis, Mo............. 33
TEALL, H. N., Jackson, Mich............. 97
ZALLEE, JOHN, St. Louis, Mo............ 59
Tape Worm Cure.
BIGGS, W. L., Council Bluffs, Iowa..... 370
Tea Dealers.
FITZHUGH, L. M. & CO., Indianapolis, Ind. 340
Tobacco & Cigars.
ANDREWS, L. M., Chicago, Ill........... 428
FITZHUGH, L. M. & CO., Indianapolis, Ind. 340
MEYER, CHRISTIAN, Indianapolis, Ind... 140
PEPER'S TOBACCO WORKS, St. Louis, Mo.................................... 100
RAUCH, J. & BRO, Indianapolis, Ind.... 146
Trunk Manufacturers.
BROWN L. G., Grand Rapids, Mich....... 183
GLENN, J. E., Chicago, Ill.............. 443
WEIL & SON, Evansville, Ind............ 113
Truss Manufacturers.
HOWE TRUSS CO., Council Bluffs, Iowa... 371
Turkish Baths.
ADAMS, G. F., M. D, St Louis, Mo....... 20
WRIGHT, MR. & Mrs., Galesburg, Ill.... 273
Undertakers.
DURFEE, ALLEN, Grand Rapids, Mich.... 108
VANCE, W. B., Peoria, Ill............... 311
Upholsterer.
HAASE, CONRAD, Evansville, Ind........ 379
Vinegar & Pickles.
GROSS, G. J., Chicago, Ill.............. 443
MEYER, JOHN C., Chicago, Ill........... 454
MISSISSIPPI VALLEY VINEGAR WORKS, Dubuque, Iowa.................. 242
NORTHWESTERN VINEGAR WORKS, Dubuque, Iowa........................... 248
WISWELL, W. H. & CO., Chicago, Ill.... 1
ZOPF & GILMORE, St. Louis, Mo......... 64
Watchmakers and Jewelers.
HERSHFIELD, R. N., Leavenworth, Kansas. 173
KNIGHTS, C. H. & CO., Chicago, Ill..... 428
REBER, G. F., Indianapolis, Ind........ 80
Water Heaters and Filters.
GARSTANG, RICHARD, St. Louis, Mo..... 20
Wall Paper and Shades.
FITCH, B F., Chicago, Ill............... 397
White Lead Manufacturers.
BOUCHER, LEON & CO, St. Louis, Mo.... 20
Wind Mills.
SPRINGER, THAYR & CO., Rockford, Ill.. 447
Wines and Liquors.
HULMAN & FAIRBANKS, Terre Haute, Ind 162
Wire Works.
LOCKWOOD & LYMAN, Rockford, Ill...... 470
SMITH, E. & CO., Chicago, Ill........... 455
VAN EPS, H. R., Peoria, Ill............. 310
Wood Carpet.
DUNFEE, J., Chicago, Ill................ 425
Wood Worker.
CASE, F. F., St. Joseph, Mo............. 299
Yeast.
WOODRUFF, JAS. E., Quincy, Ill......... 307

IMPORTANT EVENTS OF THE CENTURY.

ST. LOUIS.

AMUSEMENTS.

ESHER'S VARIETIES,

114 N. Fifth St., St. Louis, Mo.

Open every night with a First-class Company.

J. E. ESHER, - - - Prop.

TIVOLI VAUDEVILLE THEATRE, 110 & 112 N. 5th St. Rod. KORNBERGER, Prop.

ANNUNCIATORS.

HEISLER, CHAS., Hotel, House and Elevator ANNUNCIATORS, 309 Chouteau ave.

ARCHITECTS AND SUPERINTENDENTS.

GRABLE, A., Architect and Superintendent, 315 Olive street.

KIRCHNER, H. W., Architect & Superintendent. Granite blk, Fourth and Market sts, room 507.

MAURICE, JNO. H., Architect and Builder, 111 N. Seventh street.

PAULY, P. J. Jr., Architect and Contracting Agent, Fourth and Franklin ave.

SLICER, W. C., Architect and Superintendent, 720 Chestnut st, room 16.

JAMES STEWART,

ARCHITECT,

Rooms 38 and 39 Dr. McLean's Block,

N. E. Cor. Fourth and Market Sts.,

ST. LOUIS, MO.

ARTISTS' MATERIAL.

LOHMANN, WM., ARTISTS' and Architects' Drawing MATERIALS, 116 S. Fourth st.

ATTORNEYS AT LAW.

EDWARD CUNNINGHAM, JR.,

ATTORNEY AT LAW,

213 N. Third Street,

ST. LOUIS.

HALL, GEO. W., Attorney at Law, 209 Chestnut street.

WAKEFIELD, A. B., Attorney at Law, Grand Opera House, Market st.

1492.

Oct. 12.—Christopher Columbus discovers America. Columbus was born at Genoa, Italy, in 1435, and died neglected and in obscurity at Valladolid on the 20th of May, 1506. His body was buried in a convent, from which it was afterward taken to St. Domingo, and subsequently to Havana, in Cuba, where it now remains.

1497.

North America first discovered by Sabastian Cabot, a Venetian, in the service of England.

1512.

John Ponce de Leon, a Spanish soldier, discovered and named Florida, from its being discovered on Easter day, or feast of flowers.

1513.

Balboa, a Spaniard, crossed the Isthmus of Darien, and from the summit of the Andes, discovered the Pacific Ocean.

1517.

First patent for importing negroes to America granted by Spain.

1519-21.

Cortez, a Spaniard, conquered Mexico.

1520.

Magellan sailed round South America, discovered the southwest passage, and circumnavigated the globe.

1525.

Hops first used in malt liquors in England.
Tobacco first discovered by the Spaniards, near the town of Tobasco, in Mexico. It was introduced into England, from Virginia, by Mr. Lane, in 1536.

1528.

P. de Narvaez, with 400 men, lands in Florida, and attempts the conquest of the country. He is defeated by the natives.

1529.

The name of Protestant given to those who protested against the Church of Rome at the Diet of Spires in Germany.

1535.

Cartier, a Frenchman, first attempts a settlement in Canada.

1539.

Ferdinand de Soto, a Spaniard, landed in Florida, with 1,200 men, in search of gold. He penetrated into the country and discovered the Mississippi river in 1541.
Pins were first used in England by Cathrine Howard, Queen of Henry VIII.

1562.

Ribault, with a colony of French Protestants, began a settlement an the Edisto. It was abandoned.

ST. LOUIS—Continued.

AUCTION GOODS.
PAULDING, W. F., Dealer in Auction Goods, 1616 Broadway.

AWNINGS.
RIPPE, CHAS., Manufacturer of AWNINGS, Tarpaulins, etc., 111 and 113 Chestnut st.

BAKERY.
LEWIS, CHAS. & CO., Bread, Crackers, Biscuits, and Steamboat Supplies, 712 & 714 Morgan st.

BANKERS.
LOKER, G. H. & BRO., Bankers and Exchange Dealers, Cor. Pine and Second sts.

BARBERS.
KUEHNER, C., Hair Dressing Saloon, 503 Morgan street.
PHILLIPS, GEORGE, Shaving and Bathing Saloon, 117 Walnut st.

H. ZEIDLER,
SHAVING & HAIR-DRESSING
SALOON,
SHAMPOOING AND HAIR-CUTTING.
123 OLIVE STREET.

BARBERS' CHAIRS.
HENRY ARND & BRO.,
Manufacturers and Dealers in
DENTAL & BARBERS' FURNITURE,
Surgeons' Reclining and Easy Chairs
107 S. SECOND STREET,
Bet. Walnut and Elm Sts., ST. LOUIS.
☞ Send for Illustrated Catalogue.

BASE BALL GOODS.
G. McMANUS'
EMPORIUM FOR
Base Ball, Gymnasium & Cricket Goods,
320 NORTH SIXTH ST.,
St. Louis, - Mo.

BASKET MAKER.
MOORE, D. D., Basket Maker, 1530 Franklin avenue.

BELL-HANGERS.
HAMILTON & COOKE, Electric Bell-Hangers, 607 Market st.

BIRDS AND CAGES.
BIRDS AND CAGES.
SINGING BIRDS, PARROTS AND MONKEYS AND PET ANIMALS.
Bird Seed, and Mnfr. of Best Mocking-Bird Food.
AUGUST BOHNE 16 S. 5th St. St. Louis.

ST. LOUIS—Continued.

BITTERS.
E. SCHWARTZ,
Manufacturer of
VEGETABLE BITTERS,
WHOLESALE & RETAIL,
3201 Broadway, ST. LOUIS, MO.

BLACKSMITH.
FISCHER, F., Blacksmith, and Mnfr. of Stonecutters' & Quarrymasons' Tools, 1308 Carr st.

BLANK BOOK MANUFACTURERS.
KEIM & PAULI, Blank Book Manufacturers and Bookbinders, 311 Olive st.
MORITZ, CHARLES, Bookbinder and Blank Book Manufacturer, 302 N. Main st.

BOARDING HOUSE.
MRS. W. WRIGHT,
TABLE BOARD A SPECIALTY,
823 WASHINGTON AV.

BOOKS AND STATIONERY.
Established 1861.
American Baptist Publication
SOCIETY,
209 N. 6th St., St. Louis, Mo.
A General Theological and
SUNDAY SCHOOL SUPPLY STORE,
LEWIS E. KLINE, Agent.

JURGENS, ED., Bookseller, Stationer, News Dealer, etc., 711 Morgan st.

JOHNSON & MILES, Booksellers and Publishers, 602 N. Fourth st., St. Louis.

BOOKBINDERS' STOCK.
GRIFFIN, H., & SONS, Binders' Materials and Machinery, 304 N. Main st.

BOOT AND SHOE FACTORY.
EXCELSIOR SHOE FACTORY, Morris, Canning & Clinton, props., 303 Christy av.
REDDEN, A., Mnfr. of and Wholesale Dealer in English Shoes and Boots, 802 N. Fifth st.

D. A. TOWNE,
Manufacturer of Ladies', Misses' and Children's
Fine Shoes,
423 & 425 N. FIFTH ST.,
ST. LOUIS, MO.

Washington when he took Command of the Army.—This picture is supposed to illustrate how Washington appeared when he took command of the army, under the Old Elm, at Cambridge, Mass., June 3, 1775.

TAYLOR'S
One, Two and Four-Horse Sweep Powers

For running Corn Shellers, Fanning Mills, Feed Mills, Feed Cutters, Cider Mills, Grindstones, Circular and Drag Saws, Pumps, Churns, Lathes, &c.,

The Cheapest, Best & Simplest Power Invented.

Easily set up and quickly moved at pleasure.

Can be placed in a building or against it, with pulley of Power on the inside; or be set up independent of building.

Light One-Horse Power $40
Heavy One-Horse Power 50
Two-Horse Power 75
Four-Horse 100

Different sized Pulleys are furnished without extra charge, so that purchasers can attach to any machine.

Taylor, Mack & Smith, 189 LaSalle St. Chicago.
DEALERS IN AGRICULTURIAL IMPLEMENTS.

1563.
Potatoes first brought to England from America, by Hawkins, and introduced into Ireland in the year 1586, by Sir Walter Raleigh.

1572.
Modern masks and muffs, fans, false hair for women, were devised by the harlots of Italy, and brought to England from France.

1584.
Sir Walter Raleigh obtains a patent for making discoveries. Amidas and Barlow, in command of two ships, by order of Raleigh, landed on Wocoman and Roanoke. The country was taken possession of for the crown of England and named Virginia, in honor of the virgin Queen.

1585.
Sir Richard Grenville was sent with seven vessels and 107 men to settle Virginia. They settled at Roanoke in charge of Governor Lane, but returned to England the following year.

1586.
Sir Grenville left a second colony at Roanoke, which was destroyed by the Indians.

1587.
A third colony of 115 persons, under Gov. White, was left at Roanoke. Gov. White returned to England for supplies and additional number of colonists, but when he arrived at Roanoke, three years after he found no Englishman. It was evident they had been slain by the Indians or perished from hunger. The last adventurers were disheartened, and Gov. White returned to England.
Virginia Dare born—the first child of Christian parents born in the United States.

1602.
Bartholomew Gosnald sailed to America, named Cape Cod, discovered Martha's Vineyard and the adjacent islands; built a fort and store-house, but returned to England the same year.

1607.
Captain Newport arrived in Virginia, and began the first permanent British settlement in North America, at Jamestown, Virginia.

1608.
Chesapeake Bay first explored by Captain John Smith.
Canada settled by the French. Quebec founded July 3d.
John Laydon married to Ann Burras—the first christian marriage in Virginia, and in the United States.

1610.
Capt. Henry Hudson, an Englishman, in the service of the Dutch, discovers the Manhattan, now Hudson river.
Starving time in Virginia—of nearly 500 colonists, all perished but sixty in the course of six months.

1611.
Champlain, a Frenchman, discovered the lake which now bears his name.

1613.
Rolfe, an Englishman, married Pocahontas, daughter of Powhattan, the Indian King.
New York settled by the Dutch. The island where New York city now stands was purchased from the Manhattan Indians for $24.

St. Louis—*Continued.*

BOOTS AND SHOES.

CHARLES ADELMANN,
HAND MADE
BOOTS, SHOES, AND GAITERS,
1104 OLIVE ST., ST. LOUIS, MO.
Importer of French Leathers
All work guaranteed as represented.

ARNOLD, H., Manufacturer and Dealer in Boots and Shoes, 2306 Broadway.

BARNEY, M. V., Manfger's Agt. and Wholesale Dealer in Boots & Shoes, 618 Washington ave.

BATHGATE, J., Manufacturer and Dealer in Boots and Shoes, 419 Franklin ave.

BUTTERWORTH, J., Fashionable Boot & Shoe Maker, 316 N. Eighth st.

CLARK, THOMAS., Boots and Shoes, 823 Market street.

DIENSTBACH, WM., Boston Boot and Shoe Store, 1272 S. Fifth st., cor. Rutger.

DUERR, ADOLPH, Manufacturer of Fashionable Boots and Shoes, 623 Market st.

FRISCH, GEORGE, Boots and Shoes, 306 Walnut street.

GARSON, HENRY, Boots and Shoes, 1612 Broadway.

HECHLER, FRED., Boots and Shoes, 322 Walnut street.

JUNKER, FRED., Manufacturer and Dealer in Boots and Shoes, 704 Market st.

JOHN LEAHY,
BOOT AND SHOE MAKER,
1003 N. Fifth Street,
Near Wash.
ST. LOUIS, MO.,
INVISIBLE REPAIRING NEATLY DONE.

LIEBIG, GEO. P., Manufacturer of Boots and Shoes, 7 S. Sixth st.

MARKET, V., Manufacturer Custom Made Boots and Shoes, 1534 Broadway.

MARLOW, CHAS., Fashionable Boot and Shoe Maker, 213 S. Seventh st.

MUNK, J. W., Manufacturer and Dealer in Fashionable Boots and Shoes, 708 Market st.

H. H. NIEWOEHNER,
—DEALER IN—
Boots and Shoes,
823 O'FALLON ST.
HATS, CAPS, AND FURS,
825 O'FALLON ST.

SCHENK, JOHN C., Boots and Shoes, 1819 Market street.

SCHNEIDER, JOHN, Dealer in Boots and Shoes, 2110 Carondelet ave.

SCHNEIDER, M., Boots and Shoes, 1106 Market street.

SCHOENEPAUCK, G. H., Manufacturer and Dealer in Boots & Shoes, 1107 Wash st. Repairing.

VOGT, CHAS. & CO., Dealers in Boots & Shoes, 312 N. Fourth st.

IMPORTANT EVENTS OF THE CENTURY.

ST. LOUIS—*Continued.*

BRASS FOUNDERIES.

MESSMER, FRED., New Patent Self-Venting Beer Faucet, 513 Market st.

MORE, JONES & CO., BRASS FOUNDRY and Metals, 1608 N. Eighth st.

BROKER.

BARCLAY, D. ROBERT, Loans and Negotiations, 223 Pine st.

BRUSHES.

J. S. COSTELLO,
Manufacturer of
Superior Paint, Varnish, Sash, White Wash,
WHITENERS' AND PLASTERS'
BRUSHES.
1005 & 1005½ N. Fifth St.
BRUSHES OF ALL KINDS MADE TO ORDER.

Established 1847.

F. J. LAITNER & SON,
MANUFACTURERS AND IMPORTERS OF
BRUSHES,
All kinds of Steel Goods on hand.
105 S. Second St., - - ST. LOUIS.

BUSINESS COLLEGES.

BUSINESS EDUCATION.
Young men and boys specially prepared for business by an experienced accountant and first-class penman.

BUSINESS COLLEGE AND COUNTING ROOMS,
S. W. COR. 9th & FRANKLIN AVE.
S. J. GRIER & SON.
OBSERVE THE PLACE—900 FRANKLIN AV.

JONES' COMMERCIAL COLLEGE, Cor. Olive and Eleventh st.

BUTTER, CHEESE, AND EGGS.

IVY & PURCELL, BUTTER, CHEESE, EGGS, ETC., 424 N. Second st.

CANNED GOODS.

JOHN S. GIBBS & CO.,
Wholesale Dealers in
Canned Goods,
Fancy Groceries, Fruits, Etc.,
503 N. Second Street.

HOFMANN BROS., Butter, Cheese, CANNED GOODS, Dried Fruits, etc., 305 N. Second st.

CARPENTERS AND BUILDERS.

WM. H. GAFFNEY,
Carpenter and Builder,
1106 & 1108 Market St.
Jobbing Promptly Attended to.

1614.
The Dutch built a fort at Manhattan (near New York.)
Captain Smith made a fishing voyage to the northern part of America. Made a chart of the coast, which he presented to Prince Charles, who named the country New England.
Settlements commenced by the Dutch at Manhattan, now New York, at Albany, and in New Jersey.

1616.
Capt. Dermer was the first Englishman who sailed through Long Island sound.
Tobacco first cultivated by the English settlers in Virginia.

1617.
Pocahontas died in England, aged 22.

1618.
A great pestilence destroyed most of the Indians from Narragansett to Penobscot.

1619.
Twenty thousand pounds of tobacco exported from Virginia to England.

1620.
Plymouth settlers arrived at Plymouth Mass., December 22d.
Slavery first introduced into Colonies by the Captain of a Dutch vessel, who sold 20 negroes at Jamestown, Va.

1621.
Edward Winslow and Susannah White married—the first Christian marriage in New England.

1622.
The Indians massacred 349 of the Virginia colonists, March 22d.

1623.
First settlement of New Hampshire, at Dover, and at Little Harbor.
George Sandys, of Virginia, translated Ovid's Metamorphosis—the first literary production of the English colonists in America.

1624.
The first cattle brought into New England by Edward Winslow, agent for the Plymouth colony.

1627.
Delaware and Pennsylvania settled by the Swedes and Fins.

1629.
African slaves first brought into Virginia by a Dutch ship and sold to colonists.
Peregrine White, the first English child born in New England.

1630.
Charleston, Boston, Watertown and Dorchester settled by Gov. Winthrop.
July.—First house built in Boston.
Gov. Winthrop first abolished the custom of drinking healths.
John Billington executed for murder—the first execution in Plymouth Colony.

1632.
Magistrates of the colony of Massachusetts first chosen by the freeman in the colony.
The magistrates of Massachusetts ordered that no tobacco should be used publicly.
The general court at Plymouth passed an act that whoever should refuse the office of Governor should pay a fine of £20, unless he was chosen two years successively.

Established 1858. Established 1858.
F. A. DURGIN,
MANUFACTURER OF
Sterling Silver Ware
and Fine Electro Plate

From new, elegant and artistic designs. The only House in the West making a specialty of this class of goods.

No. 305 North 7th Street, Cor. of Olive,
ST. LOUIS, MO.

Turkish Bath Establishment,
311 N. 7th St., bet. Olive & Locust.

For both Ladies and Gentlemen.

GEO. F. ADAMS, M. D., Supt.

This is one of the finest Baths in the Country.

MOUND CITY WHITE LEAD AND COLOR WORKS.
LEON BOUCHER & CO.,
MANUFACTURERS OF
WHITE LEAD, PUTTY,
COLORS, ZINC, PAINTS,
——AND DEALERS IN——
Varnishes, Window Glass, Brushes, Paints, Oils and Naval Stores,
Nos. 704 & 706 North Second Street,
ST. LOUIS.

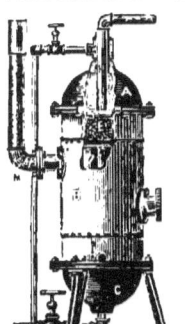

RICHARD GARSTANG'S
PATENT FEED
Water Heater and Filterer Combined

The most thorough Purifier of Feed Water for Steam Boilers before the public.

The only Double Acting Heater and also the only Heater supplied with a thorough Surface and Sediment Blower in the Market.

PATENTED JUNE 23, 1874.

Manufactured by RICHARD GARSTANG,
1245 to 1255 S. Second St., ST. LOUIS, MO.

New Post Office, St. Louis, Mo.—The excavation was commenced in the year of 1873; it is situated on the square bounded by Eighth, Ninth, Olive and Locust Streets. The site cost $400,000. The edifice is upon the parallelogram plan, 236 feet in length and 181 feet wide. The basement is of Iron Mountain red granite; above the basement the material used is Maine granite throughout. At the eastern end of the building the great Railway Tunnel passes from which the mails will be deposited direct into the basement of the building.

ALEXANDER B. WALSH.   DAVID T. WALSH.

WALSH BROS.,
MANUFACTURERS' AGENTS,
—DEALERS IN—

Grocers' Specialties,
—AND—
GENERAL COMMISSION MERCHANTS,
No. 219 North Second Street, St. Louis.

1633.

Virginia enacted laws for the suppression of religious sectaries.

Messrs. Cotton, Hooker and Stone, three eminent ministers, arrived at Boston, from England.

A specimen of rye first brought into the Court of Massachusetts as the first fruit of English grain.

The Dutch erect a fort on Connecticut river, in the present town of Hartford.

The Plymouth people erect a trading house, in the present town of Windsor, Conn.

1634.

Roger Williams, minister, of Salem, banished on account of his religious tenets.

First merchant's shop in Boston opened.

1635.

Great storm of wind and rain in New England; the tide rose twenty feet perpendicularly August 15.

1636.

The Desire, a ship of 120 tons, built at Marblehead—the first American ship that made a voyage to England.

The first court in Connecticut held April 26.

1637.

War with the Pequots in Connecticut; their fort taken by surprise and destroyed, May 26.

Ann Hutchinson holds lectures in Massachusetts for the propagation of her peculiar religious sentiments. She gains many adherents.

A Synod convened at Newtown, Mass., the first Synod held in America; they condemn eighty-two erroneous opinions which had been propagated in New England.

1638.

Two tremendous storms in August and December; the tide rose fourteen feet above the spring tide, at Narragansett, and flowed twice in six hours.

The ancient and honorable artillery company formed at Boston.

Three Englishmen executed by the government of Plymouth colony, for the murder of an Indian.

1639.

First general election in Hartford, Conn. John Hayes first Governor.

First Baptist Church in America formed at Providence, R. I.

Severe tempest and rain. Connecticut river rose twenty feet above the meadows, in March.

House of Assembly established in Maryland.

1640.

The general court of Massachusetts prohibited the use of tobacco.

1641.

Dutch trading house on the Delaware taken by the Swedes.

Severe winter; Boston and Chesapeake bays frozen; Boston bay passable for carts, horses, &c., for five weeks.

1642.

The Dutch fort at Hartford seized by the inhabitants of Connecticut.

Indian war in Maryland.

The New England ministers invited to attend the assembly of divines at Westminster, England, but they declined.

First commencement at Harvard College; nine candidates took the degree of A. B.

ST. LOUIS—*Continued.*

CARPENTERS AND BUILDERS.

PITCHER, HENRY, Carpenter and Builder, 517 and 519 S. Sixth st.

WILSON & BRUNSON, Contractors and Builders, 1003 M rgan st.

CARRIAGE MANUFACTURERS.

CARROLL, J. P., Manufacturer of Carriages and Buggies, 606 and 608 Cass ave.

Established 1863.

FRED YEAKEL,
Successor to JOST & YEAKEL,

Carriage Builder,
1336 & 1338 S. Second St.
Op. Lafayette Bank. **ST. LOUIS.**

MCAULIFF, WM. B. & BRO., Manufacturers of Buggies and Wagons, 2414 Franklin ave.

CHAIR MANUFACTURERS.

HELLER & HOFFMAN, Chair Manufacturers Cor. Eighth and Howard sts.

CHINA, GLASS, AND QUEENSWARE.

MISSOURI GLASS CO., Queensware, Glassware, Lamp Stock, etc., 217 and 219 N. Main st.

WELLS, RODNEY D. & CO., China, Glass and Queensware, etc., 516 N. Main st.

CLOTHING—WHOLESALE.

R. LEVY,
Manufacturer of Men's, Boys' and Children's
CLOTHING,
Oak Hall Building, 604 N. Fourth St.

MACK & CO., Manufacturers of Clothing, 717 and 719 Washington av.

J. & L. SEASONGOOD & CO.,
Manufacturers of Clothing,
IMPORTERS AND JOBBERS OF WOOLENS,
S. W. Cor. 5th & St. Charles Sts.,
ST. LOUIS, MO.

Cincinnati House, S. W. Cor. Third and Vine Sts.

STAHL, L. & CO., Manufacturers of Clothing, Shirts, Drawers and Overalls, 913 N. 4th st.

WHITE & ROSENTHAL, Mnfrs. and Jobbers of Men's Clothing, 707 Washington av.

COAL AND WOOD.

GODFREY, WM., Wholesale and Retail Dealer in Wood and Coal, 1829 N. Ninth st

STRATHMANN, A., Dealer in Wood and Coal, 809, 811 and 813 Carr st., bet. 8th and 9th sts.

COFFEE BROKERS.

BILLINGS, A. W., Merchandise Broker in Coffee, Sugar & Syrups, cor. Second & Vine sts.

GRIFFIN & PILLSBURY,
Manufacturers' Agents and
Merchandise Brokers,
501 N. Second St., ST. LOUIS.

COMMISSION MERCHANTS.

BROEDER & MILLER, Commission Merchants, 930 and 932 Broadway, St. Louis.

St. Louis—Continued.

COMMISSION MERCHANTS.

WILLIAM BEARD,
FRUIT AND PRODUCE
COMMISSION MERCHANT,
900 BROADWAY,
Cor. Cherry, ST. LOUIS.

A. B. BOWMAN & CO.,
Dealers in Foreign and Domestic
GREEN & DRIED FRUITS,
Produce Commission Merchants,
325 N. MAIN ST., - ST. LOUIS.

M. D. BURNES,
General Dealer in
Fruit, Produce, etc.
COMMISSION MERCHANT,
1009 BROADWAY, ST. LOUIS, MO.
All Orders promptly attended to.

FLINT, H. W. & CO., General Commission Merchants, 828 Broadway.

GERBER, SIGNAIGO & BRO.
(Successors to V. Gerber & Son),
FRUIT AND GENERAL
COMMISSION MERCHANTS,
818 BROADWAY.

Michael McGuirk,
DEALER IN
PROVISIONS,
1230 BROADWAY,
ST. LOUIS.

LOUIS HAKE & SON,
Commission & Produce Merchants,
And Dealers in Provisions.
827 Broadway, opp. Cherry St., and 824 N. Fourth St.

HEIL, JOS., & CO., Commission Merchants and Dealers in Fruit & Produce, 926 Broadway.

HOLLISTER, E. T., & CO., Commission Merchants, 805 Broadway.

JACOBSON, S., & CO., Hides, Wool and Furs, and Commission Merchants, 1027 Broadway.

KAUP & ELBRECHT, Commission Merchants. Consignments solicited. 1014 Broadway.

KEISKER BROS., Commission Agents and Mill Agents, 1105 and 1107 Broadway.

KNEHANS, H. W., & SONS, Commission Merchants, 1022 Broadway.

MOSS, CHAS. & CO., Commission and Produce Merchants, 22 N. Second st.

1643.
Union of the colonies of Plymouth, Massachusetts, Connecticut and New Haven for mutual defense.

1645.
Action between a New England ship and an Irish man-of-war.
Battle fought between the Dutch and Indians, near the confines of Connecticut; great numbers slain on both sides.

1646.
The Friends or Quakers first came to Massachusetts; laws passed against them; four executed in 1659.

1647.
First influenza mentioned in the annals of America.
Legislature of Massachusetts passed an act against the Jesuits.
First general assembly of Rhode Island.

1648.
Laws of Massachusetts first printed.
Margaret Jones of Charlestown, Mass., executed for witchcraft.
The "Cambridge Platform" and the "Westminster Confession of Faith" received by most of the New England churches. The Congregational church and its pastor ordered to depart from Virginia by the Governor of that colony.

1649.
The government of Massachusetts, with the assistants, signed a declaration against men's wearing long hair, as unscriptural.

1650.
Constitution of Maryland established.

1651.
The Legislature of Massachusetts passed laws against extravagance in dress.

1652.
The province of Maine taken under the protection of Massachusetts.
The first mint for coining money in New England erected.

1654.
The Dutch drive the Swedes from the Delaware.
Col. Wood, of Virginia, sent a company of men to explore the country of Ohio.

1657.
Disputes concerning baptism in New England.

1658.
Earthquake in New England.

1660.
At this time the colonies of Virginia, New England and Maryland, were supposed to contain no more than 80,000 inhabitants.

1661.
Society for propagating the gospel among the Indians of New England, incorporated by Charles II.

1662.
Charter of Connecticut granted by King Charles II.
The Legislature of Massachusetts appointed two licensers of the press.
The assembly of Maryland established a mint in that colony.

THE "SAINT DENIS"

French Cafe and Ice Cream Parlors,

Special attention given to Balls and Parties.

No. 317 NORTH FIFTH STREET,
SAINT LOUIS.

H. J. FOUTS, Proprietor.

Wm. A. Skinner & Co.'s
HUNGARIAN SELF-SHINING STOVE POLISH.

The only Polish that can be used with satisfaction to all without labor or the use of a brush. SHINES WHEN APPLIED.

A child ten years of age can Polish a Stove to a brilliant gloss equally as well as a grown person. We guarantee all we represent. Full instructions for using on every box.

In no branch of manufacture, perhaps, is there such a difference in the goods produced as in the manufacture of Stove Polish. The art (for it is an art) of Polishing Stoves is one that has always been considered very laborious and fatigueing to the performer. It has at last been brought to perfection in as much so that all labor and fatigue is entirely dispensed with. We are well aware there is such a thing as cheap Stove Polish, or in other words, that which does not claim to be of any great excellence. This is in a great measure attributable to the fact that the few concerns which are prepared to manufacture the finest qualities are so far in advance of those making the cheaper goods that any attempt at competition on the part of the latter would be futile, and consequently they content themselves by making the cheap article for the poorer class of trade. But such has been the improvement of our establishment that we can manufacture a superior class of goods and sell them as low as common goods can be sold which are manufactured by the common concerns. Our establishment, which is located at No. 1103 Morgan Street, manufactures and deals exclusively in *The Hungarian Self Shining Stove Polish* (the only genuine article in the market). Our firm first became established in Philadelphia in 1872. In consequence of the demand for our goods becoming so extensive throughout the West, we determined to establish a Manufactory and Depot in the city of St. Louis, through which to facilitate the supply demanded in the West. The beauty of our Polish is, no brush is required and no mixing, as it is applied with any woolen cloth and is used from the box it comes in. It will take off all grease and rust. It is more durable than any other. Saves labor. Will not burn off. It is free from all odor, and makes no dust. Will produce a brilliant Polish in less than five minutes time. Like all good articles put on the market, our Polish has imitations; therefore we caution the public. Buy none other but that having the signature on every box of the sole manufacturers (as there is none genuine without it). **WM. A. SKINNER & CO., 1103 Morgan St., St. Louis, Mo.**

ADVERTISEMENTS. 25

Mercantile Library, St. Louis, Mo.—Situated on the corner of Locust and Fifth Streets. The lot cost in 1851 $25,000. The cost of the building was estimated at $70,000, but amounted to considerable more when completed, was in part provided for by a loan and in part by contributions among which was the generous gift of $20,000 by Mr. Henry D. Bacon. The total number of volumes in the library is upwards of 42,000. Much credit is due Mr. John N. Dyer, who has held the position as Actuary and Librarian since 1862.

MILLINERY AND DRESS MAKING.

Mme. LEWANDOVSKA'S
FASHIONABLE
Millinery and Dress Making Emporium,

823 N. FIFTH STREET, under Mercantile Library Hall, St. Louis, Mo.

Is constantly receiving the latest importations in Elegant and Select Millinery Goods, including the choicest novelties—PATTERN HATS and BONNETS of exquisite taste, art and beauty. FLOWERS and BRIDAL WREATHS in perfect imitation of nature; also, hat and bonnet trimmings in all the new shades of color. Ornaments and Ostrich plumes in superb variety. Beautiful House, Street, Party and Bridal suits made in the latest Parisian styles, and equal to the most fastidious in taste. An elegant assortment of human hair, also the Demorest reliable patterns. PRICES MODERATE. Orders by mail will receive prompt attention.

1663.
Great earthquake in Canada and New England.

1664.
Elliott's Indian Bible printed at Cambridge, Mass., the first Bible printed in America.
A large comet seen in New England.
New York and Albany taken from the Dutch.

1665.
Sir J. Yeamans settled on the southern banks of Cape Fear river, with a colony from Barbadoes.
New Haven and Connecticut united into one colony.
At this time the militia of Massachusetts consisted of 4,400 men.
The government of Rhode Island passed a law to outlaw Quakers for refusing to bear arms.

1666.
The buccaneers of America began their depredations in the West Indies.

1669.
War between New York Indians and the Mohawks.

1672.
Laws of Connecticut printed; every family ordered to have a law book.

1673.
New England contained at this time about 120,000 inhabitants.
New York and New Netherlands taken by the Dutch—they were restored to the English the next year.

1675.
King Phillip's war commenced: action at Swanzey; Brookfield and Deerfield burnt; Captain Lathrop, with 80 men, surprised by Indians and almost every man slain.
Governor Winslow, with 1,000 men, attacked the Naragansetts (the allies of Phillip) in their fort; the fort destroyed and their country ravaged. December.
Virginia contained at this time about 50,000 inhabitants.

1676.
Lancaster burnt; Captain Pierce and his company slain; Capt. Wadsworth and about fifty of his men killed. Falls fight—the Indians surprised in the night—they lost 300 men, women and children, May 18; Hatfield and Hadley attacked—King Philip killed, August 12—which ends the war.
Bacon's insurrection in Virginia. Jamestown burnt.

1677.
Insurrection in Carolina; the insurgents exercised authority for two years in that colony.

1680.
New Hampshire separated from Massachusetts. The first assembly met at Portsmouth.
Great comet seen in New England; it occasioned much alarm.

1682.
William Penn held a treaty with the Indians.
M. de la Salle descended the Mississippi to its mouth, took possession of the country in the name of Louis XIV, the French King, and named the country Louisiana.

St. Louis—*Continued.*

COMMISSION MERCHANTS.

A. LANDAU & CO.,
COMMISSION MERCHANTS,
And Dealers in
Hides, Furs, Wool, Etc.,
1013 & 1015 Broadway,
ST. LOUIS, MO.

G. H. LITTLE,
GENERAL COMMISSION MERCHANT,
And Wholesale Dealer in
CRANBERRIES, BUTTER, BEANS, PROVISIONS AND DRIED FRUITS,
111 & 113 Pine St,
(Bet. Main and Second Sts,) ST. LOUIS.

REHBEIN, H. A. & CO., Produce Commission Merchants, 105 N. Main st.

SMITH & SAMUELS,
PRODUCE AND GENERAL
COMMISSION MERCHANTS,
701 BROADWAY, cor. B oadway & Bridge Sq.,
ST. LOUIS.
City References: Bank of St. Louis, Senter & Co., Dodson & Woods, Ex-Gov. E. O. Stanard.

STEINBERG, H., Commission Merchant, Dealer in Butter, Cheese, Eggs, etc., 930 Bro dway.

TIVY & PURCELL, General Commission Merchants, 424 N. Second st.

ZELLE BROTHERS, General Commission and Produce Merchants, 922 and 924 Broadway.

CONFECTIONERIES.

ADAM, P., Confectionery, Ladies' Restaurant and Ice Cream Saloon, 414 Market st.

FOUTS, H. J., Confectioner,
317 N. Fifth st.

Mrs. Josephine Gremore,
CONFECTIONERY,
AND NOTION STORE,
823 MORGAN STREET,
ST. LOUIS, • • • MO.

KENNEY, L., Confectionery, Ice Cream and Oyster Depot, 713 Chouteau ave.

LEONHARD, C. A., Confectionery, Ladies' Restaurant and Ice Cream Saloon, 320 Market st.

MARANESI, CHAS., Confectioner, original Mfr. of Pure Home-made Candies, 110 S. 4th st.

CORKS.

NICHOLAS JOST,
Manufacturer and Importer of
CORKS,
24 SOUTH SECOND ST.
All kinds of Machine and Hand-Cut Corks.
Corkwood, Imported Metallic Caps, &c.
Under Barnum's Hotel, **ST. LOUIS, MO.**
U. S. Regulation Life Preservers.

ST. LOUIS—*Continued*.

COSTUMER.

WOESE, CHAS., Costumer,
501 S. Fifth st.

COUNTRY PRODUCE.

ANDERSON, E. & CO., Apples, Butter, Eggs and Country Produce, 119 N. Second st.

CRACKER MANUFACTURER.

MANEWAL, LANGE & CO., Steam Cracker Manufacturers, Cor. Sixth and Cass ave.

CUTLERY AND GRINDERS.

CHARLES BROCH,

717 OLIVE ST., ST. LOUIS,
Manufacturer, and Dealer in

CUTLERY,

AND STEAM GRINDING IN GENERAL.

Always on hand a large assortment of Table and Pocket Cutlery, Fancy Hardware, Razors of the best makers, Razor Strops and Hones, Revolvers and Pistols, French Cook Knives, great variety of Fancy Articles. Patent Shears ground and set. Cutlery repaired. Country Orders attended to.

FRIEDMANN & LAUTERJUNG,

A. J. JORDAN, Sole Agent.

Manufacturers of CUTLERY,

Electric Razors, and Electric Shears,

91 Chambers and 73 Reade Sts., New York.
423 N. FIFTH ST., ST. LOUIS.

Steam Grinding.

AUGUST KERN,
912 N. Sixth Street, St. Louis.

All kinds of Knives and Razors kept on hand, best article only. Hollow Ground Razors, and all kinds of heavy and light work done at short notice. Orders from outside the city will receive prompt attention.

DENTISTS.

Centennial Dental Rooms.

TRADE 804 MARK 804

WASHINGTON AVENUE.

A Beautiful Set of Gum Teeth, only $5 00
Teeth extracted and an upper or lower set of S. S. White's Gum Teeth on Rubber. 9 00
Pure Gold Fillings and warranted... 1 50
Largest Size Platina Fillings.......... 1 00
Largest Silver Fillings, only......... 75
Extracting without Pain, with Gas only............................... 35
Extracting without Gas, only........ 25

All work warranted as contracted for or Money Refunded.

Be sure you Get in 804 WASHINGTON AVE. Sign of the Golden Tooth.

GREENE, C. R., Dentist,
408 Christy avenue.

1683.

The Governor of Virginia ordered that no printing press should be used in that colony, "on any occasion whatever."

1686.

First Episcopal Society formed in Boston.
Port Royal, Carolina, broken up by the Spaniards from St. Augustine.

1687.

Charter of Connecticut hid from Andros, in a hollow oak, and saved.
M. de la Salle, the discoverer of Louisiana, killed by his own men in mutiny.

1688.

New York and the Jerseys added to the jurisdiction of New England.
Andros appointed Captain-General and Vice-Admiral over the whole.
Opposition to Andros' administration in Massachusetts.

1689.

Williams and Mary proclaimed in the colonies. Andros is siezed and sent a prisoner to England.

1690.

Bills of credit issued by the government of Massachusetts, the first ever issued in the American colonies.
A body of French and Indians from Montreal burn Schnectady, and massacre the inhabitants, February 8.
Port Royal taken by Sir William Phipps; he makes an expedition against Quebec, but is unsuccessful.

1691.

Major Schuyler, with a party of Mohawks, attacks the French settlements on Lake Champlain.
The Assembly of Virginia obtain of the crown the charter of William and Mary College, so named from the English sovereigns.

1692.

Nineteen persons executed for witchcraft in Massachusetts.
Edmund Andros, the tyrant of New England, made governor of Virginia.
Sir William Phillips arrived as governor of Massachusetts under the new charter.

1694.

Legislature of Massachusetts caused the names of drunkards, in several towns, to be posted up in public houses, and imposed a fine for giving them entertainment.

1698.

Seat of government in Virginia removed to Williamsburg, the streets of which were laid out in the form of a W, in honor of the reigning King of England, William.

1699.

Assembly of Maryland removed to Aunapolis.

1700.

Legislature of New York made a law to hang every Papish priest who should come into the the province.
Two hundred and sixty-two thousand inhabitants in the American colonies at the beginning of this century.
Carolina infested with pirates.

W. N. TIVY. JOHN PURCELL.

TIVY & PURCELL,
Butter, Cheese and General Commission Merchants,
424 NORTH SECOND STREET, ST. LOUIS,

REFERENCES:

Henry Ames & Co., Pork Pks. | Fourth National Bank. | Wm. Barr & Co., Dry Goods,
Fath, Ewald & Co., Com. | Hon. E. O. Stannard. | And St. Louis Merchants generally,

CONSIGNMENTS OF ABOVE ARTICLES SOLICITED.

JAMES LIGHTHOLDER,
WHOLESALE AND RETAIL DEALER IN
Staple and Fancy Groceries, Wines and Liquors,
No. 612 N. Fourth St. and No. 611 N. Third St., (Opp. Bridge) St. Louis.

Goods delivered to all parts of the City, East St. Louis, Railroad Depots and Steamboat Landings free of charge.

J. G. HARRIS & CO.,
Successors to Proprietors of
HARRIS, HUGHES & CO. ST. LOUIS STAMP CO.

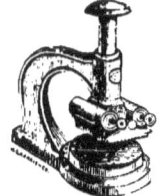

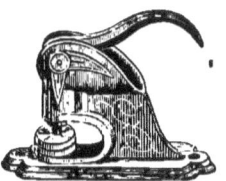

Ribbon Stamps. Seal Presses.

416 and 418 N. Second Street, St. Louis, Mo.
WOOD ENGRAVING IN ALL ITS BRANCHES.

Send for Illustrated Catalogue and Price List.

GARRETT, McDOWELL & CO.,
PIG IRON.
Northeast Corner Fourth and Washington Avenue,

SAINT LOUIS.

AUGUSTUS ABE,
GUNSMITH

—DEALER IN ALL KINDS OF—
Guns, Pistols, and Amunition,
1129 N. 5TH ST., (NEAR BIDDLE ST.) ST. LOUIS.
Repairing Neatly Done on Short Notice.

Illinois & St. Louis Railroad Bridge across the Mississippi River, at St. Louis, Mo. The first caisson on which the stone piers were built, was sunk on October 17th, 1869. It was sunk a depth of one hundred and thirty feet from the surface of the river, before the rock was reached. Each of the arches are over five hundred feet in length, the center of the middle arch is fifty-five feet above water level. The east approach is 1,136 feet in length, and that upon the western side 1,886 feet. Double lines of car tracks are constructed through the lower division of the bridge, which rest directly upon the arches, while the upper portion is forty-four feet wide, divided between horse car roads, carriage ways, and promenades. A tunnel from the west end of the bridge to the Union Depot, was constructed at a cost of about $1,000,000 or about one-tenth part of the cost of the bridge.

IRA STANBERY, JR.,
—*General Agent,*—

NATIONAL ART AND CHROMO CO.,

Publishers and Dealers in

Chromos, Engravings, &c., and Manufacturers of Gold Leaf, Walnut and Carved Frames.

807 WASHINGTON AVENUE, ST. LOUIS, MO.

1702.
Gov. Moore's expedition against the Spaniards at St. Augustine—it proves a failure.
First issue of paper currency in Carolina.
First Episcopal church in New Jersey and Rhode Island.

1703.
The Church of England established by law in Carolina.

1704.
First newspaper in America published in Boston called the Boston News Letter.
Deerfield burnt and most of its inhabitants carried captive by the French and Indians.

1706.
The Spaniards and French invade Carolina—they are defeated.

1707.
The New England troops make an unsuccessful expedition against Port Royal.

1708.
Haverhill surprised by the French and Indians.

1709.
First issuing of paper money currency in New York, New Jersey and Connecticut.

1710.
Twenty-seven hundred Palotines, from Germany, arrived and settled in New York and Pennsylvania.

1711.
Expedition against Quebec—failed by the loss of transports in the St. Lawrence.

1712.
War with the Tuscaroras in North Carolina—they are defeated.

1715.
A general conspiracy against the Carolinas by the Yemassees, Cherokees and other tribes. Governor Craven attacks and defeats them in their own camp.

1717.
Greatest snow-storm ever known in this country, February.
Yale College removed from Saybrook to New Haven.
Bellamy, a pirate, wrecked with his fleet on Cape Cod.

1718.
William Penn, the founder of Pennsylvania, died in England, aged 74.

1719.
First Presbyterian Church in New York founded.
Lotteries suppressed by the Legislature of Massachussetts.
Pensacola taken by the French from the Spaniards.

1721.
First innoculation for the small-pox, in America, at Boston.

1723.
Twenty-six pirates executed at Newport, R. I.
Paper currency in Pennsylvania first issued.
First settlement in Vermont.

1724.
Trenton, N. J., founded by William Trent.
The sect of Dunkers about this time took its rise in Pennsylvania.

St. Louis—*Continued.*

DENTISTS.

HUBERT, J. H., Zahnarzt Dentist, S. E. cor. Fourth and Market sts.

DESIGNER.

ZIMMERMANN, FRANK, Designer, Office, Granite Block, Room 510 Fourth and Market sts.

DRUGGISTS.

BARNARD H. C., Druggist,
Cor. Rock Road and Glendale ave.

DESHLER BEESON,
APOTHECARY and DRUGGIST,
COR. SIXTH AND CHESTNUT STS.
Agent for Liebig's Liquid Extract of Beef and Tonic Invigorator.

COLEMAN, JOHN R., Druggist.
Cor. Ninth and Christy ave.

WM. H. CRAWFORD,
DRUGGIST.
WHOLESALE AND RETAIL.
800 WASHINGTON AVENUE.

ROSEN-APOTHEKE.
OTTO D'AMOUR.
DRUGGIST,
N. W. Cor. Broadway and Chambers St.

DONNELL M'F'G CO., Grocers' and Druggists' Sundries. 316 N. Main st.

FOERG, HENRY, Druggist and Pharmacist, N. W. cor. Seventh and Spruce sts.

HARRIS, E. N., Druggist and Apothecary.
3139 Easton avenue.

KOCH, H., Druggist, N. E. cor. N. Market and Broadway, under Mound City Hotel.

MEYER BROS., Wholesale Druggists.
6, 8, 10 and 12 N. Second st.

MURISON'S Catarrh and Bronchial Cigarettes are a sure cure, and give perfect satisfaction.

PAULEY, F. C., Lion Drug Store, Easton and Campton avenues.

ROBINSON & SQUIRE, Drugs, Medicines, Perfumeries, etc., 416 Olive st.

WEBER, A. H. (Agt.) Wholesale Druggist, 231 N. Second st.

WEBSTER, M. R & CO., Druggists,
Eleventh and Chestnut sts.

DRY GOODS.

CRAWFORD, D. & CO., Dry Goods, 416 to 420 Franklin ave.

HARGRAVE, J., DRY GOODS, Hosiery, Notions, etc., 520 and 522 Elm st.

SCHUBERT, H., DRY GOODS, Ladies' and Gents' Furnishing Goods, 1515 Wash st.

J. H. TIEMEYER & CO.,
Staple & Fancy Dry Goods Dealers.
415 FRANKLIN AVENUE.

DYEING AND SCOURING.

SCHWARZ, JOS., Steam Dyeing and Scouring Establishment, 13 S. Sixth st.

IMPORTANT EVENTS OF THE CENTURY.

St. Louis—*Continued.*

DYEING AND SCOURING.

JOHN BECKER'S
Steam Dye House
704 Morgan Street.
Between Seventh and Eighth sts.

All kinds of Ladies' and Gents' Goods dyed and cleaned.

European Chemical Dye Works,
610 MORGAN STREET,
Four doors from S. W. cor. Sixth st., op. Union Market.

Special Attention Paid to Silk and Fancy Dyeing.

Also Gents' Clothing Dyed, Cleaned and Repaired at the lowest rates. Orders by Mail promptly attended to. Goods called for and delivered to all parts of the city. Has had 27 years' experience in Europe.

A. M. NORDFELDT.

THE PARIS
Dyeing and Scouring Emporium,
1428 Franklin Avenue.

JOSEPH MERKERT, PROP.

Gentlemen who desire their clothing Cleaned, Dyed, Repaired and Altered to the Latest Fashion, will find it to their advantage to give us a call,

WM. ULRICH,
DYER, CLEANER AND SCOURER,
CENTRAL DYE WORKS.
914 WASHINGTON AVE.

ELECTRIC MACHINERY.

E. A. FROECKMAN,
Manufacturer of
Electric & Telegraph Machinery,
MATHEMATICAL AND PHYSICAL INSTRUMENTS.
904 N. FOURTH ST.,

ELECTRIC PEN.

2,000
Or more Copies from a single writing.

ELECTRIC PEN.
Agency, 118 N. Second St.,
ST. LOUIS, MO.

EMPLOYMENT OFFICES.

J. L. KOHLER,
Female Employment Agency
8 N. SEVENTH ST.

If not in, inquire at Mr. Meyers', 621 Market st.

1725.
First newspaper printed in New York by William Bradford.
1727.
Great earthquake in New England, Oct. 29.
1728.
Drought and hurricane in Carolina; yellow fever in Charleston.
1730.
The Natchez Indians extirpated by the French.
1732.
Corn and tobacco made a legal tender in Maryland. Corn at 20 pence per bushel, and tobacco at one penny per pound.
1733.
First Masonic lodge held in Boston.
1737.
Earthquake in New Jersey.
1738.
College at Princeton, N. J., founded.
1740.
Hard winter; severe cold.
General Oglethorp with 2,000 men makes an unsuccessful expedition against St. Augustine.
1741.
The Moravians, or United Brethren, began the settlement of Bethlehem, Pa.
Four white persons executed; thirteen negroes burnt, eighteen hanged, and great numbers transported, for a conspiracy to burn the city of New York.
Expedition against Cuba.
1742.
Spanish expedition against Georgia—failed.
1746.
French expedition under Duke D'Anville, which threatened New England, failed by means of storms, sickness in the fleet, etc.
1747.
Saratoga village destroyed and the inhabitants massacred by the French and Indians.
1749.
Severe drought in New England; causes great distress; some of the inhabitants sent to England for hay.
1750.
Massachusetts enacts a law against theatrical entertainments.
1752.
New style introduced into Britain and America—September 2d, reckoned 14th.
Charleston, S. C., laid under water by a tempest.
1754.
Colonel Washington, with 400 men in Fort Necessity, surrendered to the French July 4.
1755.
Expedition against Nova Scotia—the French are subdued, the inhabitants brought away and dispersed among the colonies.
General Braddock defeated by the French and Indians, July 9.
Great earthquakes in North America.
1756.
Oswego taken by the French under Montcalm.

W. C. SLICER,
Architect & Superintendent,

S. E. COR. EIGHTH & CHESTNUT STS.,
Room No. 16, up stairs.   ST. LOUIS.

I have opened an office at the above place, where I am prepared to furnish Plans, Specifications, and Superintend all kinds of buildings, such as

Public Buildings, Churches, Stores, Warehouses, Dwellings, Country Houses, Stables, Etc.

I will also state that I can make arrangements to build for parties owning the ground, on one-third cash, balance in one and two years, at 8 per cent.

W. C. SLICER,
Architect and Superintendent.

F. NOHL,
Real Estate Agent

NOTARY PUBLIC AND CONVEYANCER,

No. 407 Walnut Street,

St. Louis.

WM. PARKES,
TAILOR & DRAPER,

Latest Styles made in the most correctly Fashionable manner.

The very best work guaranteed at reasonably low rates.

720 OLIVE ST.,
Bet. Seventh and Eighth Sts.   **St. Louis.**

CHAMBER OF COMMERCE, ST. LOUIS, MO.

1757.

Fort William Henry capitulated to the French, and many of the garrison massacred by the Indians.

1758.

Louisburg taken by the British.

Gen. Abercrombie defeated at Ticonderoga with great loss; Lord Howe killed.

Fort du Quesne abandoned by the French and taken by the English and named Pittsburgh, Nov. 25.

1759.

Niagara taken by the English; Gen. Prideaux killed.

Battle of Quebec; Gen. Wolf, the English commander, and Montcalm, the French commander, killed; the French defeated and Quebec taken. September.

Lotteries granted by the Legislature of Massachusetts for the benefit of Public Works.

1760.

Montreal capitulated to the English September, and Canada is subdued.

1762.

Severest drought ever known in America, no rain from May to September.

1764.

Spanish potatoes introduced into New England.

1765.

March 8.—Stamp act passed, which declared that no legal instrument of writing should be valid unless it bore a British stamp. The feelings of the people were so intense against this act, that in several cities mobs and violence ensued. The stamps were seized and burned, and the distributors, who were appointed by the Crown to sell them, were insulted and despised on the street, and, when the law was to take effect, there were no officials with courage enough to enforce it.

1766.

March 18.—Stamp act repealed. In London this was an occasion of great rejoicing; and in America bonfires and illuminations attested the feelings of the masses of the people.

June.—Mutiny act. British troops sent to America, and an act passed by Parliament providing for their partial subsistence on the colonies. The appearance of these troops in New York, and the order to feed and shelter them, occasioned violent outbreaks of the people in that city, and burning indignation all over the land.

1767.

June 29.—A tax imposed upon tea, glass, paper, painters' colors, etc., and a bill passed forbidding the New York Assembly to legislate until it should comply with the mutiny act of 1766. The people boldly resisted these acts of oppression. Circulars were issued to the Assemblies from Massachusetts asking their co-operation in obtaining a redress of grievances. The Governor of Massachusetts, in the King's name, was instructed to command the Assembly to rescind its actions, but in June, 1768, it unanimously voted *not* to rescind.

1768.

Jan. 20.—Petition of the Massachusetts Assembly to the King of England, against the late tax on trade in the American colonies.

St. Louis—*Continued*.

EMPLOYMENT OFFICE.

BASS, A., Female Employment Office, 617 Chestnut st.

ENGRAVERS.

418 N. 2nd St., SAINT LOUIS.

CHAS. STUBENRAUCH,
General Engraver & Die Sinker,

We make *Steel Seals* with *Solid Copper Counterdies*, which will last a lifetime, the extra charge being 25 per cent.

Also tastefully engrave

Dies, and Coin Medals, and Badges for Societies, Lodges and Clubs, Dating Stamps, Bank Stamps,

Wax Seals, Steel Stamps, Burning Brands and Name Plates, in the best style and at low rates.

213 MARKET ST.,
ST. LOUIS, MO.

FANCY GOODS AND NOTIONS.

EVANS, M. & CO., Jobbers of Hosiery, Fancy Goods and Notions, 917 N. Fifth st.

H. H HESS,
Jobber in
FANCY GOODS,
NOTIONS,

Gents' Furnishing Goods, Etc.,

1131 NORTH FIFTH ST.

J. JUDELL & PLATT,
Wholesale Dealers in
Fancy Goods, Notions,
619 NORTH FIFTH STREET.

FIRE ARMS.

FOLSOM, H. & CO., Shot Guns, Rifles and Ammunition, 620 and 622 N. Main st.

St. Louis—*Continued*.

FIRE ALARM.

HEISLER, CHAS., Manufacturer of City Fire Alarms, 309 Chouteau ave.

FLOUR AND FEED.

BAUR & REGEL, Flour Merchants and Millers' Agents, 833 Broadway and 828 N. Fourth st.

BERNARD & CO.,
(Formerly Switzer & Co.)

FLOUR
AND
COMMISSION MERCHANTS,
211 N. Second St., St. Louis, Mo.

BURR, CHAS. P. & CO., Flour Dealers, 119 and 121 N. Main st.

MEYER & STIPP, Wholesale and Retail Dealers in Flour and Feed, 1110 Cass ave.

SCHWARTZ, H., Dealer in Flour and Feed, S. E. cor. Fourteenth st. and Cass ave.

FLUID COOKING STOVE.

GANAHL, F. J., Manufacturer "Little Giant" Cook Stove, 209 S. Fifth st.

FURNITURE.

CLARKE, THOS. J., New & Second-hand Furniture, Tinware & Crockery, 1528 Franklin av.

GREAVES. A., Dealer in New and Second-hand Furniture, Stoves, etc., 806 N. Seventh st.

SMITH'S
IMPROVED SUSPENSION SPRING.
For Sale by the Furniture trade, and by
J. G. SMITH & Co., 821 N. 2d st., St. Louis.
Manufacturers of all kinds of
Mattresses, Spring Beds, Woven Wire Mattresses and Iron Beds.
Special attention given to furnishing Public Institutions. The very best inducements given to the Furniture trade.

St. George's Furniture House,
HOUSEHOLD & OFFICE FURNITURE.
(Building known as St. George's Church),
703, 705, 707 AND 709 LOCUST ST.

St. Louis Furniture Repairing Co.
J. W. PECKINGTON, PROP.,
117 and 119 N. Seventh St.,
Cabinet Making & Upholstering.
Packing and Shipping to all parts of United States.

ST. LOUIS.

1768.

First Methodist church in America built in New York.

May.—Commissioners of Customs, to collect duties, arrive in Boston. They are regarded with much contempt, and it was difficult to restrain the excitable portion of the population from committing personal violence.

June.—Arrival of sloop Liberty, at Boston, belonging to John Hancock (one of the signers of the Declaration of Independence), with a cargo of Madeira wine. The Commissioners demanded duties. It was refused, and they seized the vessel. The news spread over Boston, and the people resolved on resistance. The Commissioners were assailed by a mob, their houses damaged; and they were obliged to seek safety in Castle William, a small fortress about 3 miles S. E. from Boston.

Sept. 27.—British troops land in Boston, 700 strong, and with drums beating and colors flying, they marched to the Common.

1769.

Jan. 26.—British Parliament passes a bill requiring the arrest of offenders against the government to be sent to England for trial.

Dartmouth College, New Hampshire, received its charter. It was named from the Earl of Dartmouth, its benefactor.

American Philosophical Society, at Philadelphia, founded.

1770.

March 5.—Boston Massacre. A rope-maker quarreled with a soldier (March 2), and struck him. From this a fight ensued between several soldiers and rope-makers, in which the latter were beaten. A few evenings afterward (March 5), about 700 excited inhabitants assembled in the streets for the purpose of attacking the soldiers. A sentinel was attacked near the Custom House, when Captain Preston, commander of the guard, went to his rescue, with eight armed men. Irritated and assailed by the mob, the soldiers fired upon the citizens, killed three and dangerously wounded five. The mob instantly retreated, when all the bells of the city rang an alarm, and in less than an hour several thousand exasperated citizens were on the streets. Gov. Hutchinson assured the people that justice would be done in the morning, and thus prevented further bloodshed. Capt. Preston and six of his men were tried and acquitted by a Boston jury. Two other soldiers were found guilty of manslaughter, and the troops were removed to Castle William.

April 12.—All duties except on tea repealed.

Sept. 30.—George Whitefield, founder of the Calvinistic Methodists, died, aged 56 years.

1771.

Regulators formed in North Carolina to resist British taxation and oppression. In 1768 the people of North Carolina were taxed $75,000 by Gov. Tryon to build him a house at Newbern.

May 16.—The Regulators subdued and dispersed by Gov. Tryon, after hanging six of the leaders.

1772.

June 9.—Destruction of the British armed schooner Gaspe. This vessel was stationed in Narragansett Bay to assist the Com-

The English Kitchen,

D. S. RANDOLPH, PROP.

Open all day, and until 12 M.

FURNISHED ROOMS For single Gentlemen at $1.00 per day.

Number 105 N. Fifth Street, - - ST. LOUIS.

Empire Tonic Bitters,
Medicinal Blackberry Brandy,
Etherial Arnica Linament,
Flavoring Extracts & Essences,
Mucilage, Inks, Wash Blue, &c.,

DONNELL MANUFACTURING CO.,

GROCERS & DRUGGISTS' SPECIALTIES. 316 North Main St., St. Louis.

AUGUST HOLTHAUS.

Manufacturer of and Dealer in

Saddlery,
Harness,
Collars, &c.

1545 Broadway,
ST. LOUIS, MO.

☞ Send by mail for Price List.

ADVERTISEMENTS.

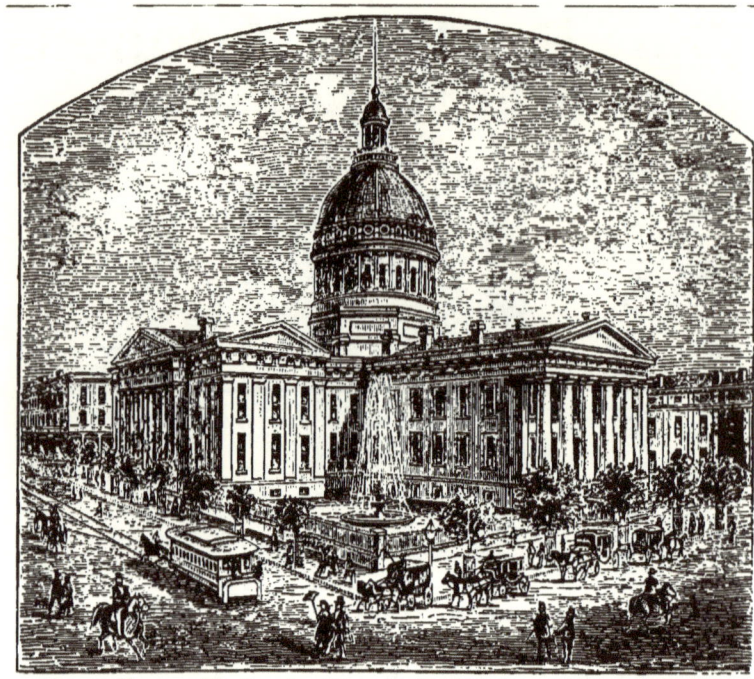

Court House, St. Louis, Mo.—Is situated on the square bounded by Fourth, Fifth, Chestnut and Market Streets. The building was commenced in 1826 to the original structure additions were made in 1839, and the building, as it now appears was not completed until 1862. The design of the edifice, which is modeled after the form of a Greek cross, includes an iron dome of fine proportions from the summit of the dome to which ascends an iron staircase, one gains a magnificent view far up and down the river, over church spires, parks, gardens, &c.

J. McC. THORNBURGH & CO.,
Manufacturers,
MANUFACTURERS' AGENTS,
—AND DEALERS IN—
Grocers' Sundries,
202 & 204 N. Second St., St. Louis, Mo.

Awarded First Premium

ST. LOUIS FAIR, 1874, 1875 and 1876.

ESTABLISHED, 1873.

1772.

missioners of Customs to enforce the revenue laws. The commander insisted that American navigators should lower their colors when they passed his vessel, in token of obedience, and, for refusing, a Providence schooner was chased until she grounded on a low sandy point; and on the same night 64 armed men went down from Providence in boats, captured the people on board the Gaspe and burned the vessel.

1773.

Dec. 16.—Tea thrown overboard in Boston harbor. It was a cold night and the citizens were just returning from several spirited meetings held at Faneuil Hall, when a party of about sixty persons, some disguised as Indians, boarded two vessels in the harbor, tore open the hatches, and, in the course of two hours, 342 chests of tea were broken open, and their contents cast into the water.

Daniel Boone settles in Kentucky.

1774.

The Shakers first arrived from England; they settled near Albany, N. Y.

March 7.—Boston port bill passed, ordering the port of Boston to be closed against all commercial transactions whatever, and the removal of the Custom House, Courts of Justice, and other public offices to Salem.

March 28.—A bill passed Parliament empowering Sheriffs appointed by the Crown, to select juries instead of leaving the power with the people. It prohibited all town meetings and other gatherings. It provided for the appointment of the councils, judges, justices of the peace, etc., by the Crown or its Representatives.

April.—Tea thrown overboard in New York Harbor.

Sept. 5.—First Continental Congress assembled in Carpenter's Hall, Philadelphia, in which all the States were represented except Georgia.

Dec. 25.—British tea ship forbidden to land at Philadelphia. The Shakers first arrived from England; they settled near Albany, N. Y.

1775.

April 19.—Battle of Lexington. Major Pitcairn, in command of 800 British troops, was sent by Gen. Gage to destroy some ammunition and stores at Concord, but when he reached Lexington, a few miles from Concord, he was met by eighty determined minute men. Pitcairn rode forth and shouted: "Disperse! disperse, you rebels! Down with your arms and disperse!" They refused to obey, and he ordered his men to fire, killing eight citizens and wounding several. This was the first blood of the Revolution. The British then pushed on and destroyed the stores at Concord; but they were so harrassed and annoyed by the minute men on their way that by the time they returned back to Bunker Hill they had lost in killed and wounded 273 men.

May 10.—Capture of Ticonderoga. Cols. Ethan Allen and Benedict Arnold, with a small company of volunteers, surprised this fortress. As Allen rushed into the sally-port, a sentinel snapped his gun at him and fled. Making his way to the commander's quarters, in a voice of thunder ordered him to surrender. "By whose authority?" exclaimed the officer. "In the name of the great Jehovah and the Continental Congress!" shouted Allen. No resistance was attempted. Large stores of cannon and

ST. LOUIS—*Continued.*

GENTS' FURNISHING GOODS.

M'ELRATH, A., Dealer in Gents' Furnishing Goods, 509 N. Sixth st.

GLASS CUTTER.

JAS. D. BERGEN,
GLASS CUTTER,
Flat Glass for Vestibule Doors and Cars. Gas and Kerosene Globes. Beveling. Odd work Cut to Order.
715 S. SIXTH ST., ST. LOUIS.

GLASS SIGNS.

VALLEY SIGN WORKS,
Glass Signs,
DRUGGISTS' & BARBERS' LABELS,
315 OLIVE STREET,
ST. LOUIS, : - MO.

GLASS WORKS.

ST. LOUIS GLASS WORKS, J. K. Cummings, Prop., 2301 to 2315 Broadway. Est'd, 1847.

GRAIN ELEVATORS.

FREEMAN, E. B. & CO., Grain Elevators, 514 Olive st.

GROCERS, WHOLESALE.

R. L. Billingsley,   J. H. Garth, Hannibal, Mo.

R. L. BILLINGSLEY & CO.,
WHOLESALE
Grocers,
513 & 515 NORTH SECOND ST.,
Bet. Vine St. & Washington Ave.   **ST. LOUIS.**

BUSCHMAN, C. L. & CO., Wholesale Grocers, 822 Broadway.

NAVE, GODDARD & CO., Wholesale Grocers, 522 and 524 N. Second st.

OBEAR, W. F., Wholesale Grocers, 511 N. Second st.

SHIELDS, JOHN & CO., Wholesale Grocers an Commission Merchants, 117 N. Second st.

SPAUNHORST & HACKMAN, Wholesale Staple and Fancy Groceries, 802 N. Second st.

GROCERIES.

ALTHAGE, F. W., Dealer in Groceries and Notions, 1119 Biddle st.

BECKER, G. H., Dealer in Staple and Fancy Groceries and Wines, 1101 and 1103 Wash st.

BERKLEY, M. H., Dealer in Staple and Fancy Groceries, 2300 Wash st.

BRANDES, WM., Dealer in Staple and Fancy Groceries, S. W. cor. Ninth and Biddle sts.

BUESCHER, WM. H., Dealer in Groceries, Wines and Liquors, 900 O'Fallon st.

G. F. GARLAND,
DEALER IN GROCERIES,
Provisions, and Commission Merchant,
No. 221 South Third Street.

KAISER, J. H. & CO., Wholesale Dealers in Groceries, Tobaccos, etc., 801 & 803 Wash st.

St. Louis—*Continued.*

GROCERIES.

KINDERMANN, H. H., Fancy and Staple Groceries, 1116 Carr st, cor. Twelfth st.

KOBES, FRANCIS J. & CO., Fancy GROCERIES, Oranges, Lemons, etc , 320 N. Second st.

LIGHTHOLDER, JAMES, Staple and Fancy Groceries, 612 N. Fourth st. Established 1866.

McCORMICK, J. & SON, Dealers in Staple and Fancy Groceries, 922 Cass ave.

OTTO, GEORGE H., Dealer in Groceries, 1701 Wash street.

PETERS, H., Staple and Fancy Groceries, S. W. cor. Twenty-first and Wash sts.

POWERS, W. M., Staple and Fancy Groceries, Wines and Liquors, 1027 Morgan st.

QUIGLEY, JAS. T., Staple and Fancy Groceries, Wines and Liquors, 801 Morgan st.

JOSEPH ROLFMEYER,
GROCER,
MERCHANT,
S. E. & S. W. Cor. Seventh and Hickory Sts.,
ST. LOUIS.

JOHN H. SHEPHERD,
Successor to JAMES FORTUNE,
WHOLESALE AND RETAIL
GROCER
WINES & LIQUORS.
624 BROADWAY, COR. CHRISTY AVE.
First cor. N. of Bridge.

STUMPF, LOUIS, Groceries, Mf'r Homemade Preserves, S. E. cor. Eleventh and Morgan sts.

THORNBURGH, J. McC. & CO., Manufacturers, Agents and Grocers, 400 & 402 N. Second st.

TURTON, W. C., GROCER and Commission Merchant, 605 Walnut st.

WALSH BROS., Manufacturers, Agents, Grocers' Specialties, 219 N. Second st.

WAELLE, C., Groceries and Provisions, 1228 N. Eighth street.

GUNS, PISTOLS, ETC.

ABE AUGUSTUS, Guns, Pistols, and Ammunition, 1129 N. Fifth st.

J. P. GEMMER,
Manufacturer, Importer and Dealer in
Guns, Rifles,
PISTOLS, AMMUNITION, ETC.
Only Manufacturer of the Hawken Mountain Rifle,
704 N. Third Street.
N. B.—Repairing promptly attended to with neatness and despatch.

HAIR DEALERS AND DRESSERS.

S. A. FERGUSON,
HAIR DRESSER,
816 Washington Avenue,
Makes a Specialty of all kinds of Hair Jewelry.

GORDON, MRS. BLANCH, HAIR WORKER, and Dress Maker, 307½ S. Fifth st.

1775.

ammunition were captured by the Americans, without the loss of a single man.

May.—First Declaration of Independence. The people of North Carolina assembled in convention at Charlotte, and by a series of resolutions absolved their allegiance from the British Crown, organized a local government and made provisions for military defense, virtually declaring themselves free and independent. This declaration of independence was made about 13 months previous to the general declaration made by the Continental Congress.

June 15.—George Washington appointed Commander-in-Chief of the Continental army, and took personal command at Cambridge, Mass., on the 3d of July.

June 17.—Battle of Bunker Hill. General Howe and Pigot, in command of 3,000 British troops, assisted by a heavy fire from ships of war, and a battery on Copp's Hill, attacked the redoubt at the foot of Breed's Hill, where lay 1,500 Americans awaiting their approach. Gen. Prescott ordered his men to aim at the waistband of the British and to pick off their officers, whose fine clothes would distinguish them; and when the British column was within ten rods of the redoubt he shouted FIRE! The British were repulsed and fell back in confusion, but were soon rallied for a second attack, and were again repulsed and scattered in all directions. Howe now was reinforced by Gen. Clinton, the fugitives rallied and they rushed up to the redoubt in the face of a galling fire. For ten minutes the battle raged fearfully, when the ammunition of the Americans became exhausted and the firing ceased. The British then scaled the bank and compelled the Americans to retreat, while they fought fearfully with clubbed muskets. The British took possession of Bunker Hill and fortified it, but withal could claim no great victory. The American loss from killed, wounded, and prisoners was about 450 men; while the loss of the British from the same cause was about 1,100. This was the first real battle of the Revolution and lasted about two hours.

June 17.—The first man killed at the battle of Bunker Hill was named Pollard, from Billerica. He was struck by a cannon ball from the battle ship Somerset.

Sept. 25.—Colonel Ethan Allen, with 80 men, attacked the British garrison at Montreal, under Gen. Prescott. Allen was defeated, and he was made prisoner and sent to England in irons.

Nov. 13.—Montreal surrendered to the Americans under Gen. Montgomery.

Dec. 31.—Americans assault Quebec and are repulsed. Gen. Montgomery was killed, and Colonel Arnold was wounded. The command then devolved upon Capt. Morgan, whose expert riflemen, with Lamb's artillery, forced their way into the lower town; but, after several hours' contest, he was obliged to surrender.

Peyton Randolph, first President of Congress, died, aged 52.

The first line of post-offices established; Dr. Franklin appointed postmaster.

Bills of credit, known as Continental money, issued by Congress.

Kentucky first settled by whites, near Lexington.

During this year Continental money depreciated so much that a hundred paper dollars were hardly equivalent to one dollar in silver.

CURTIS & COMPANY,

Saw Manufacturers,

—DEALERS IN—

Files, Mandrels, French Band Saws, &c.

SOLE MANUFACTURERS OF

Lockwood's Patent Slotted Circular Saw.

811 & 813 N. SECOND ST.,

St. Louis, Mo.

"The Question of the Hour."

How to Make Money Easily.

It has been done, and can be done again by purchasing a State or County interest in this fluid, in connection with the Burners and Cook Stove. The purchase of a County gives you the exclusive right to sell the goods. It makes a safe, beautiful light, requires no chimneys and no wick to trim. For removing grease or paint, cleaning kid gloves, destroying bugs, roaches, &c., it is unsurpassed in the world; it will penetrate to places you cannot introduce other material. Address

A. F. BEATTIE,

Jobber of Oil, Fluid, Summer Stoves and Lamp Goods,

802 Washington Ave., St. Louis, Mo.

AGENTS WANTED.

ESTABLISHED 1849.

WM. B. HASELTINE,

—DEALER IN—

Hides, Leather, Tanners' Oil,

—AND—

Shoemakers' Findings,

717 NORTH MAIN STREET, One Block above the Bridge, ST. LOUIS, MO.

THE HIGHEST MARKET PRICE PAID FOR HIDES.

City Hall, St. Louis, Mo.—Is situated on Eleventh Street, between Chestnut and Market Streets. The structure is a plain three-story brick building, which is only calculated for a temporary quarters for the city government. At some not far future day a more magnificent structure than this, no doubt, will be designed for a City Hall.

F. O. SAWYER & CO.,

WHOLESALE

PAPER DEALERS,

209 and 211 N. Second St.,

Depot of Globe Envelope Co.,

St. Louis, Mo.

Cash Paid for Rags.

E. V. VERRIER,

PROPRIETOR OF THE

Western & Mound City Spice Mills,

Manufacturer and Wholesale Dealer in

PURE GROUND SPICES,

Mustard, Cream of Tartar,

Roasted and Ground Coffee.

414 North Second Street,

St. Louis, Mo.

1775.
About $200,000,000 of Continental currency was now in circulation.

1776.
Jan. 1.—The Union flag was unfurled at Cambridge by Gen. Washington. This flag was composed of thirteen alternate red and white stripes, differing only from the present one by having on the blue corner a horizontal and perpendicular bar. Among the various flags borne by military companies was one from the men of Culpepper county, Va., bearing the significant device of a rattlesnake, and the injunction : *Don't tread on me!* It is said to the opposer : Don't tread on me; I have dangerous fangs !
British burned Norfolk.
At that time Norfolk contained a population of 6,000, and the loss by the conflagration was about $1,500,000.
March.—Silas Deane appointed to solicit aid for the Colonies, and succeeded in obtaining 1,500 muskets from France, and promises of men and money.
March 17.—British evacuate Boston, numbering 7,000 soldiers, 4,000 seamen, and 1,500 families of loyalists. Sailed for Halifax that day.
June 18.—Evacuation of Canada by the Americans.
June 28.—Fort Sullivan, at Charleston Harbor, attacked by land party, by the British, and, after a contest lasting ten hours, the British were repulsed, with a loss of 225 killed and wounded, while the garrison suffered a loss of only 2 killed and 22 wounded.
July 4.—Congress declared the thirteen United States free and independent. [Following this declaration, the statue of George III., in New York, was taken down, and the lead, of which it was composed, was converted into musket balls.]
July 8.—Declaration of Independence read to the people by John Nixon, in the Observatory State House yard, Philadelphia.
Aug. 27.—Battle of Long Island, in which 5,000 Americans were defeated by 10,000 British, under command of Cornwallis. Gowanus and Clinton. About 500 Americans were killed and wounded, and 1,100 made prisoners. The British loss in killed, wounded and prisoners, was 367.
Aug. 29.—Washington, under cover of a heavy fog, silently retreated from Long Island to New York. During the night a woman living near the present Fulton Ferry, where the Americans embarked, sent her negro servant to inform the British of the movement. The negro fell into the hands of the Hessians. They could not understand a word of his language, and detained him until so late in the morning that his information was of no avail.
Sept. 1.—Captain Nathan Hale, of Connecticut, was captured and executed as a spy by order of Sir William Howe.
Sept. 15.—New York City evacuated by the Americans, and taken possession of by the British.
Sept. 21.—A fire broke out in a small groggery near the foot of Broad street, N. Y., and about 500 buildings were destroyed. The British charged the fire upon the Americans, but it was proven to be purely accidental.
Oct. 11-12.—Battle on Lake Champlain. Retreat of Washington over the Hudson and across the Jerseys to Pennsylvania.
Oct. 28.—A severe engagement was

ST. LOUIS—*Continued.*

HAIR DEALERS AND DRESSERS.

MRS. J. BARRON,
Importer of
Millinery, Human Hair & Fancy Notions.
Combings or Tangled Hair Straightened, and made into any Style.
HAIR DRESSING A SPECIALTY.
616 FRANKLIN AVE., ST. LOUIS.

M. PETERSON,
Established, 1866.
Manufacturer and Wholesale Dealer in
HAIR AND FANCY GOODS,
AND IMPORTER OF HUMAN HAIR,
N. E. Cor. Fourth and Washington Avenue.
ST. LOUIS, MO.

HAME MANUFACTURERS.

WHERRY, JOHN & CO., St. Louis Hame Co., Mfg's Hames, etc., Eighth & Howard sts.

HARDWARE.

LINCK & HESS, Hardware and Hoop Iron, 2122 Carondelet ave.

HARNESS AND SADDLES.

John F. Hackmann,
MANUFACTURER AND DEALER IN
SADDLES, HARNESS,
COLLARS, BRIDLES, ETC.,
1007 N. Fifth St., St. Louis.
All orders promptly attended to. Repairing done at short notice.

HESSE, L., Manufacturer of Harness and Collars, 1411 Cass ave.

HOLTHAUS, A., Harness, Saddles, Collars, etc., 1545 Broadway.

SUMMERHAUSER, CHAS., Harness Maker and Shoe Repairing, 304 Walnut st.

H. H. TOENISKOETTER,
Mf'r, and Dealer in,
Saddles, Harness, Whips, Trunks, Etc., Etc.
3813 & 3815 Broadway, Cor. Bremen Ave.

HATS, CAPS, ETC., WHOLESALE.

WATKINS & GILLILAND,
Wholesale Dealers in
Hats, Caps, Straw Goods,
LADIES' TRIMMED HATS, GLOVES, ETC.,
606 Washington Ave.,
Op. Lindell Hotel.

HATS AND CAPS.

FALK, JOSEPH, Hatter, 318 Market street.

GOETTLER, M., Hats, Caps and Furs, 1260 S. Fifth st. Established 1853.

St. Louis—Continued.

HATS AND CAPS.

KLEVORN, H., Dealer in Hats, Caps, Furs and Straw Goods, 1533 Franklin ave.

S. F. SILENCE,

Wholesale and Retail Manufacturer of

Gents' Silk, Soft, Stiff & Cassimere
HATS,
ALSO KNIGHT'S TEMPLAR CHAPEAUX,

Hats retailed at wholesale prices. Old hats renovated.

714 Locust St., ST. LOUIS.

HOMŒOPATHIC PHARMACY.

MUNSON & CO.'S Western Homœopathic Pharmacy, 411 Locust st.

HORSE-HOOF PARING MACHINE.

SCHAEFER, GEO. W., Horse-Hoof Paring Machine, 616 N. Sixth st.

HORSE-SHOERS.

BLYHOLDER, J. B., Horse-shoer and Farrier, 2717 Franklin ave.

McCOY, HUGH, Practical Horse-shoer, 214 S. Third st.

LORENZEN, C. H., Practical Horse-shoer, 1418 Cass avenue.

O'NEILL, P. H., Horse-shoer, 1007 Broadway.

SCHAEFER, GEO. W., Horse-shoeing and Manufacturer, 616 N. Sixth st.

HOTELS.

Allemania House,
—BY—
FR. ERNST,
614 MARKET STREET, ST. LOUIS.
Between Sixth and Seventh Sts.

Best Accommodations for Travelers and Boarders.

BARNUM'S HOTEL, cor. Walnut and Second street.   L. A. PRATT, Prop.

Broadway Hotel

EDWARD WARD, PROP.
1025 BROADWAY,
ST. LOUIS, MO.

EVERETT HOUSE, Fourth st., bet. Locust and Olive.

HURST'S European Hotel and Restaurant, Fourth and Locust sts.

LACLEDE HOTEL, Chestnut st., bet. Fifth and Sixth sts.

LINDELL HOTEL, Washington ave., cor. Sixth st.

MONROE HOUSE, 600 & 602 Market st. Rooms 50 cents and upwards. W. C. HALL, Prop.

PLANTERS' HOTEL, Fourth st., bet. Pine and Chestnut sts.

ST. CLAIR HOTEL, cor. Third and Market sts. W. R. NEVIN & Co.

1776.

fought at White Plains, at which the Americans were driven from their position. Losses about equal—not more than 300 in killed, wounded and prisoners.

Nov. 26.—The British, 5,000 strong, capture Fort Washington, located between 181st and 186th streets, N. Y. In this engagement, the British lost more than 1,000 men, while the American loss in killed and wounded did not exceed 100. More than 2,000 Americans were made prisoners of war. [Nothing could exceed the horrors of those made prisoners. The sugar-houses of New York, being large, were used for the prisons, and therein scores suffered and died. But the most terrible scenes occurred on board several old hulks, which were anchored in the waters around New York, and used for prisoners. Of them, the Jersey was the most famous for the sufferings it contained, and brutality of its officers. From these vessels, anchored near the present Navy Yard at Brooklyn, almost 11,000 victims were carried ashore, during the war, and buried in shallow graves in the sand. Their remains were gathered in 1808, and put in a vault situated near the termination of Front street, at Hudson avenue, Brooklyn.]

Dec. 8.—The British squadron, defeated at Fort Sullivan, sailed into Narragansett Bay, and took possession of Rhode Island.

Dec. 12.—Congress, alarmed at the approach of the British to Philadelphia, adjourned to meet in Baltimore on the 20th inst.

Dec. 14.—Gen. Lee, while quartered in a small tavern at Baskingridge, New Jersey, remote from his troops, was surrounded and taken prisoner by English cavalry.

Dec. 25.—Washington crosses the Delaware.

Dec. 26.—Battle of Trenton. Rahl, the Hessian commander, was engaged at card-playing and wine-drinking, when a negro gave him a note from a Tory, warning him of the approach of the Americans. Being deeply interested in the game, and excited by wine, he thrust the note unopened into his pocket. By neglecting to read this note, he was taken completely by surprise, and a little after sunrise, and while rallying his troops in the streets of Trenton, he fell mortally wounded. Between 40 and 50 of the Hessians were killed and mortally wounded, and more than 1,000, with arms, ammunition and stores, were made prisoners.

1777.

Jan. 3.—Battle of Princeton. Washington attacks the reserves of Cornwallis in sight of Princeton, and just as the tide of battle was going in his favor, Cornwallis was aroused by the distant booming of cannon, and hastened to the assistance of his reserves. The Americans, who had not slept, nor scarcely tasted food, for thirty-six hours, were compelled, as the heat of the first battle was over, to contest with fresh troops or fly. Washington choose to fly, and when Cornwallis entered Princeton, not a "rebel" was found.

Jan. 7.—Americans attacked a party of Hessians, near Elizabethport, New Jersey, and killed between forty and fifty, and drove the remainder back to Staten Island.

March 1.—British were driven entirely out of the State of New Jersey, except New Brunswick and Amboy.

March 23.—British make a descent to destroy American stores at Peekskill, N. Y.,

CHAS. MUEHLHAUSEN'S SALOON.

Beer, Wines and Liquors, — ALSO — Finest Cigars always on hand.

Splendid Lunch Served Every Morning at 10 o'clock.

COLD LUNCH ALL DAY.

Cor. Third & Market Sts., (FORMERLY PRESCOTT HOUSE.) ST. LOUIS, MO.

MATSON'S
RESTAURANT,
No. 504 N. 6th Street,

Between Washington Avenue and St. Charles Street,

ST. LOUIS, MO.

All the delicacies of the season. Commutation Tickets issued.

C. CLAES & CO., Manufacturers of Show Cases and Store Fixtures.

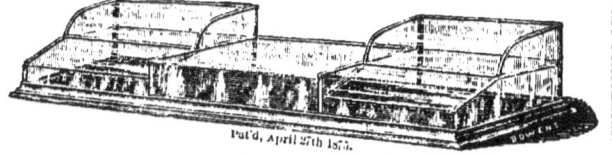

Send for Illustrated Catalogue.

First Premium at the Centennial.

Pat'd, April 27th 1875.

204 Market Street, St. Louis, Mo.

ADVERTISEMENTS. 45

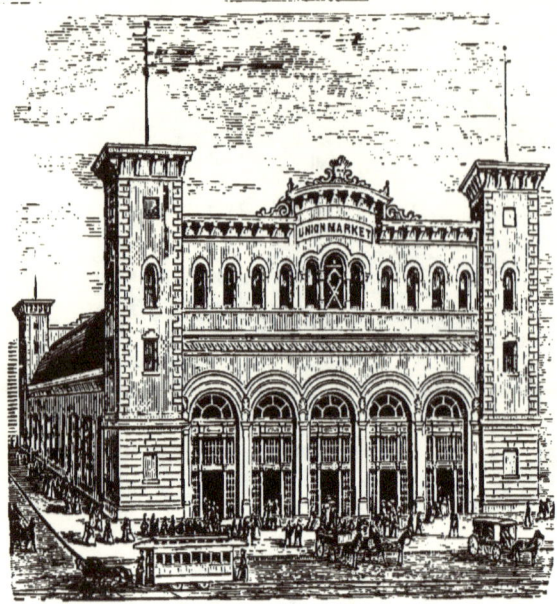

UNION MARKET, ST. LOUIS, MO.

ESTABLISHED 1862.

SPRAGUE & BUTLER'S
RESTAURANTS.

716 N. Fifth St., St. Louis, Mo.
OPEN DAY AND NIGHT.

321 Olive St., St. Louis, Mo.
OPEN DAY AND NIGHT.

1777.

but the Americans perceiving that defense would be futile, set fire to the stores and retired to the hills in the rear, while the British returned to New York the same evening.

April 26.—Danbury, Conn., was burned by order of Governor Tryon, destroying a large quantity of stores belonging to Americans, and cruelly treating the inhabitants.

May 23.—Col. Meigs attacked a British provision post at Sag Harbor, Long Island, and burned a dozen vessels, the store houses and contents, and secured ninety prisoners without losing a man.

June.—Congress resolved that the flag should carry as many stars and stripes as there were States. This resulted at last in a cumbrous flag with twenty stars and twenty stripes.

June 14.—Adoption of the American flag by Congress.

June 30.—British evacuate New Jersey.

July 5.—Burgoyne, with an army 10,000 strong, invested Fort Ticonderoga. The fort was garrisoned by about three thousand Americans under Gen. St. Clair. Owing to the immense advantage gained by the British, in planting a cannon on Mount Defiance, a hill 750 feet in height, the Americans were defeated and dispersed with a loss of a little over 300 in killed, wounded and missing; the British loss was reported at 183.

July 27.—Murder of Miss McCrea.

July 10.—Col. William Barton, with a company of picked men, crossed Narragansett Bay in whale boats, in the midst of the English fleet, and captured Gen. Prescott, while in bed, and carried him to Providence.

July 31.—Lafayette commissioned by Congress Major-General.

Aug. 3.—Lafayette introduced to Washington at a public dinner.

Aug. 16.—A party of marauders from Burgoyne's army were defeated at Bennington by the New Hampshire militia under command of Col. Stark. On the same evening, another party from Burgoyne's army were defeated by a Continental force, under Col. Seth Warner. The British lost by these expeditions almost 1,000 men, while the Americans lost but 100 men and as many wounded.

Sept. 11.—Battle of Brandywine. Gen. Howe, in command of 16,000 British troops, manoeuvres to take Philadelphia. Washington, with an army of 11,000, determines to defend the city, and takes a position at Chad's Ford, on the Brandywine. A portion of the British army succeed in getting in his rear, and he is compelled to retreat to Chester, and on September 12th to Philadelphia. American loss in killed, wounded, and prisoners, 1,200; British loss, near 800. During the engagement, Lafayette was wounded in the leg. He was conveyed to Bethlehem, Pa., where the Moravian Sisters nursed him during his confinement.

Sept. 19.—A severe but indecisive engagement was fought at Bemis' Heights, between the forces under General Burgoyne and General Gates. The number of Americans engaged in this battle was about 2,500; that of the British about 3,000. American loss in killed, wounded and missing, 319; British loss, about 500. [Bemis' Heights is about 4 miles north of the valley of Still Water, and 25 miles north of Albany.

Sept. 28.—General Wayne was surprised

St. Louis—*Continued.*

HOTELS.

ST. CHARLES HOTEL,

—| :o: |—.

S. E. Cor. Seventh and Morgan Sts.,

ST. LOUIS, MO.

—| :o: |—

Board per day, - - *$1.50*
Board per week, - *$4 to $6*

—:o: |—

T. B. RAYMOND, Proprietor.

ST. NICHOLAS HOTEL,
817 to 823 N. Fourth street.

ICE CHESTS.

WIEMANN & JANSEN,

Manufacturers of the

ZERO BEER,
—AND FAMILY—

Ice Chests

Store and Bar-room Fixtures, Counters etc.,
1528 & 1530 BROADWAY.

INSURANCE AGENTS.

BAKER, JAMES E., Universal Life Ins. Co., of N. Y., McLean's Block, Fourth & Market sts.

SOC. NEWMAN'S
Insurance Agency,
203 N. Second St., St. Louis.
All losses adjusted and paid by the Agent at St. Louis.

IRON DEALERS.

GARRETT, McDOWELL & CO., Pig Iron,
602 N. Fourth street.

JAPANNER.

CHAS. D. SMITH, JR.,
PLAIN AND ORNAMENTAL

Japanner on Tin, Wood, and Iron,
Sewing Machines, and all Kinds of Japanned Ware.
Tin for Signs a Specialty.
215½ CHESTNUT STREET, 2nd Floor.

LAUNDRIES.

Established 1876.

Bradford Turner,

LAUNDRY,

509 Morgan Street, St. Louis, Mo.

ST· LOUIS—Continued.

LAUNDRIES.

EMMERICH, CHAS. B., Domestic Steam Laundry, 25 S. Sixth st.

UNION STEAM LAUNDRY, 818 Morgan street.
W. M. BELSER, Prop.

LADIES' DRESS TRIMMINGS.

SCHACHT & BRO., Manufacturers, and Dealers in Ladies Dress Trimmings, 326 Market st.

LEATHER AND FINDINGS.

WM. B. HASELTINE,
717 N. MAIN ST., ST. LOUIS.

Dealer in Hides, Leather, Tanner's Oil, Shoe makers' Findings, etc. The highest market price paid for Hides. Established 1849.

JOHN DROZDA,
Importer and Dealer in LEATHER and FINDINGS, BOOT, SHOE, and GAITER UPPERS,
1619 Carondelet Ave.

LIVERY STABLES.

GRAY, C. W., Livery Stable,
613 and 615 Christy avenue.

KELSEY, L. E., Livery and Sale Stables, 914 & 916 Pine st. H. W. HANLEY, Manager.

LOOKING-GLASSES AND PICTURE-FRAMES.

DREY & KAHN, Looking-glasses, Mouldings, Window-glass, etc., 110 N. Second st,

MONDS, W., Looking-glasses and Picture-frames, 11 N. Seventh st.

RYCHLICKI, A., Importer and Dealer in Looking-glasses, etc., 911 N. Fourth st.

STANBERY, IRA Jr., General Agent National Art and Chromo Co., 807 Washington ave.

LUMBER DEALERS.

FLEITZ & GANAHL,
Pine, Poplar, Walnut, Oak and Ash

Lumber, Shingles, Lath,
FLOORING, SIDING, SASH, DOORS, &C.,
Office and Yard, 1320 Jackson Street.
Branch Yards, 2007 Carondelet Avenue.

MACHINISTS.

Central Iron Works,
GEO. J. FRITZ,

Manufacturers of Steam Engines, Boilers,
And Machinery in General.
Special attention given to Repairing. Send for Catalogue and Price List.
2026 & 2028 S. THIRD, Cor. JACKSON ST.

John T. Demoss, Pres't.   W. L. C. Brey, Sec'y.

A. K. HALTEMAN & CO.,
Manufacturers of

Steam Engines & Mill Supplies,
Wood Work for Flouring Mills,
IRON WORK IN GENERAL,
1610 & 1611 S. 3d St., and 510 & 512 Carroll St.

1777.

by a party of British and Hessians under General Gray, near Paoli Tavern, Chester county, Pa., and lost 300 men of his party. The bodies of 53 Americans, found on the field next morning, were interred in one broad grave, and 40 years afterwards, the Republican Artillerist, of Chester county, erected a neat marble monument over them.

Sept. 26.—The British, under Howe, march to Philadelphia without opposition.

Sept. 27.—Congress fled from Philadelphia to Lancaster, Pa.

Sept. 30.—Congress assembled in York, Pa., and continued in session there until the following summer.

Oct. 4.—Battle of Germantown. Washingtown attacked the British at Germantown, and caused the enemy to make a hasty retreat. Lieut. Col. Musgrave, in the retreat, in order to avoid the bayonets of his pursuers, took refuge in a stone house. This, together with a heavy fog, occasioned many mistakes among the Americans; and after a severe action, they were obliged to retreat with the loss of about 1,000 men in killed and wounded; while the British loss was about 800 killed and wounded.

Oct. 7.—Battle of Saratoga. Another battle was fought between Burgoyne and Gates on the same ground occupied September 19th, and, after a severe struggle, Burgoyne was compelled to fall back to the heights of Saratoga, leaving the Americans in possession of the field.

Oct. 13.—Kingston, N. Y., burned. General Clinton, who was to reinforce Burgoyne at Saratoga, sends marauding parties through the country, and burns Kingston. Being informed of Burgoyne's surrender, he retreats to New York.—[While the American forces were re-gathering, a man from the British army was arrested on suspicion of being a spy. He was seen to swallow something. An emetic brought it up, and it was discovered to be a hollow silver bullet, containing a dispatch from Clinton to Burgoyne written on thin paper. That bullet is yet in the family of George Clinton, who was the first Republican Governor of New York.]

Oct. 17.—Burgoyne surrenders his whole army, numbering 5,791, to Gen. Gates, at Saratoga, N. Y.

Oct. 22.—Fort Mercer, on the Delaware river, was attacked by 2,000 Hessian grenadiers, under Count Donop, and were repulsed by a garrison of 500 men, under Lieut. Col. Green. Hessians' loss, 400. Donop was terribly wounded, and was taken to the house of a Quaker near by, where he died. He was buried beneath the fort. [A few years ago his bones were disinterred and his skull was taken possession of by a New Jersey physician.]

Nov. 9.—Howe's army goes into winter quarters at Philadelphia.

Nov. 16.—American garrison abandon Fort Mifflin, and two days after, British ships sail up to Philadelphia.

Dec. 4.—Gen. Howe marched out to attack Washington, expecting to take him by surprise, but a Quaker lady of Philadelphia, who had overheard British officers talking about this enterprise at her house, gave Washington timely information, and he was too well prepared for Howe to offer his menaces. After some skirmishes, in which several Americans were lost, Howe returned to Philadelphia.

Dec. 11.—Washington goes into winter

ST. LOUIS—*Continued.*

MACHINISTS.

GARSTANG, R., Manufacturer of Steam Boilers, 1245 to 1255 S. Second st.

MACHINERY AND MILL SUPPLIES.

CORBY, F. P. & CO., Railway Equipments and Machinery Supplies, 709 N. Second st.

MANUFACTURERS' AGENTS.

MORE & CO., Agents and Jobbers in Nails, Virginia Tobacco, 415 and 417 N. Second st.

MARBLEIZER.

READER, C. H., Marbleizer and Enameller of Grates, 817 Pine st.

MARBLE WORKS.

NORDMAN'S MARBLE WORKS.

GEO. NORDMAN,
—Manufacturer of and Dealer in—

Italian and American MARBLE,

Monuments, Gravestones, Tablets, &c.,
323 N. MARKET ST., ST. LOUIS, MO.

ROSEBROUGH, R. L. SONS, Marble Works, 1421 Broadway.

WM. SULLIVAN & CO.'S

MARBLE WORKS,

Monuments, Mantles and Grates,
Manufacturers of every description of
SLAB WORK, TILING, ETC.,
1119 OLIVE STREET,
ST. LOUIS, MO.

MATTRESS MANUFACTURERS.

KAISER & MUELLER, Manufacturers of Mattresses and Bedding, 114 Market st.

MEAT MARKETS.

BUSCHMANN, H., Dealer in Fresh and Salt Meat, 2736 Franklin ave.

DRAUDE, CHAS., Dealer in all kinds of Meat and Vegetables, 3119 Easton ave.

FITZPATRICK, MICHAEL, Daily Meat Market, 1416 N. Eighth st.

GURGEN, JOHN, Meat Market, 613 Walnut st.

MOERSCHEL & OELLERMANN, Fresh and Salt Meats, 117 N. Seventh st.

SCHAEFFER, J., Daily Meat Market, 600 Wash st. Established, 1877.

SMITH, A. G., Meat Market, 823 Walnut st.

ZEIGLER, A., Meat and Vegetable Market, 814 N. Eighth st.

MILL PICKS.

James J. McCabe,
Manufacturer and Dresser of

MILL PICKS,
819 SOUTH THIRD ST.,
Cor. Lombard, ST. LOUIS.

ST. LOUIS—*Continued.*

MILLINERY, WHOLESALE.

WEISELS, J. & CO., Wholesale Millinery, 704 N. Fifth st.

MILLINERY AND DRESSMAKING.

CLARK, MRS., Fashionable Millinery, 1917 Broadway.

LEWANDOVSKA'S, MME., Millinery and Dressmaking Emporium, 323 N. Fifth st.

MRS. A. McDONALD,

Fashionable Dress and Cloak Making,

929 NORTH FIFTH ST.,
ST. LOUIS.

MUSICAL INSTRUMENTS.

LEBRUN, N., Manufacturer and Dealer in Musical Instruments, 207 S. Fifth st.

NEWSPAPERS.

ST. LOUIS DAILY AND WEEKLY JOURNAL, Wolcott & Home Co., pub'rs, 111 N. Fifth st.

NEWSDEALERS AND BOOKSELLERS.

NIXON, W. T., Book, News and Stationery Dealer, cor. Ninth st. and Washington ave.

REGAN, STEPHEN, News-stand, Cigars and Tobacco, e. Ill. and St. Louis Bridge (west end).

JOHN A. STICKFORT & CO.,
Wholesale and Retail

Newsdealers and Booksellers,

20 NORTH FOURTH ST.,
Opp. the Courthouse, ST. LOUIS, MO.

Orders from the country promptly attended to.

NON-EXPLOSIVE FLUID.

BEATTIE, A. F., prop. Beattie's Non-Explosive Crescent Fluid, 802 Washington ave.

OILS.

MAXWELL, E. & CO., Oils, 719 N. Main st.

PAINTERS.

HUGO BARTELS.

FRESCO, HOUSE AND SIGN

PAINTER,

SIGNS OF EVERY DESCRIPTION.

313 MARKET ST.

EVANS, J. W., House and Sign Painter, 1811 N. Ninth st.

HERTWIG, G., Carriage and Wagon Painter, 2131 Franklin ave.

HUNN, JOHN, House and Sign Painter, 519 St. Charles st.

M'GINNESS & RUDOLPH, House, Sign and Ornamental Painter, 214 N. Seventh st.

PHILLIPPS & PRASSE, Carriage Painters, 2204 Broadway.

INTERIOR VIEW OF INDEPENDENCE HALL, PHILADELPHIA.

G. W. RANK, Principal.

Crescent City Commercial College,
Cor. Main & First, Evansville, Ind.

Life Scholarship $30. P. S.---Send 25cts. and stamp for first lessons in short hand.

1777.

quarters at Valley Forge. This was a gloomy winter for the Patriot army. Continental money was so depreciated in value that an officer's pay would not keep him in clothes. The men were camped in cold comfortless huts, with little food or clothing. Barefooted, they left on the frozen ground their tracks in blood. Few had blankets, and straw could not be obtained. Soldiers, weak from hunger and benumbed by cold, slept on the bare earth, with no change of clothing and no suitable food; sickness soon followed, and with no medicine to administer to their complaints, many found relief from their sufferings in death.

Dec. 16.—Independence of the United States acknowledged by France.

Dec. 18.—Constitution of North Carolina adopted.

During this year Vermont was claimed by both New York and New Hampshire, as a part of their territory, but the people met in convention and proclaimed themselves free, independent, and separate States. After purchasing the claims of New York, for $30,000, Vermont was admitted into the Union, February 18, 1791.

1778.

Feb. 6.—Treaty of alliance was formed with France, by which the French and Americans became united against the British Government.

March 20.—American Commissioners were received at the Court of France as the representatives of a sister nation; an event which was considered in Europe, at that time, as the most important which had occurred in the annals of America since its first discovery by Columbus.

May 7.—Salutes were fired by the army at Valley Forge, in honor of the event of the treaty of alliance with France, and, by order of Washington, shouts and huzzas were proclaimed for the King of France.

June 18.—Howe's army evacuate Philadelphia, and retreat towards New York.

June 28.—The battle of Monmouth was fought on a Sabbath day. It was one of the most sultry ever known when the two armies met in conflict, which raged from 9 A. M. until dark. Many soldiers on both sides fell from the excessive heat of the day, and when night came they were glad to rest. The British were commanded by Gen. Clinton and the Americans by Washington. The Americans intended to renew the fight on the morning of the 29th, but found the enemy's camp deserted. The British left about 300 killed on the field of battle, and a large number of sick and wounded. American loss in killed, wounded, and missing, 228. Many of the missing returned to the army, and the killed was less than 70.

July 5.—Massacre of Wyoming. About 1,600 Indians and Tories, under command of Butler and Brant, appeared on the banks of the Susquehanna, and compelled two of the forts nearest to the frontier to surrender to them. The savages spared the women and children, but butchered the rest of their prisoners without exception. They then surrounded Fort Kingston, and to dismay the garrison, hurled into the place 200 scalps still reeking with blood. The garrison was overpowered by the savages, and compelled to surrender. The prisoners, composed of men, women, and children, were then enclosed in houses and barracks, which were set on fire, and the miserable

St. Louis – *Continued.*

PAINTERS.

WILSON, L. R., House and Sign Painter, 1015 Locust st.

PAINTS AND OILS.

BARSTOW & WHITELAW, Oils, Paints, Naval Stores, Heavy Drugs, etc., 617 N. Second st.

BOUCHER, LEON & CO., Paints, Oils, Varnishes, etc., 704 and 706 N. Second st.

PARTRIDGE, GEO. & CO., Railway, Machinery, Burning Oils and Paints, 712 N. Main st.

PAPER COLLAR CO.

MERCHANTS' PAPER COLLAR COMPANY, Isaac Swope, prop., 124 N. Main st.

PAPER DEALERS.

GRAHAM, H. B. & BRO., St. Louis Paper Warehouse, 113 N. Second st.

SAWYER, F. O. & CO., Wholesale Paper Dealers 209 and 211 N. Second st.

PAPER-HANGERS.

J. J. RYAN & BRO.,
Plain and Decorative Paper-hangers,
And Dealers in
Paper-Hangings and Window Shades,
1111 MORGAN ST.,
ST. LOUIS, MO.

PATENT SOLICITORS.

BRYAN, J. E., Patent Agency, 602 N. Fourth st.

KNIGHT BROS., Patent Solicitors, 317 Olive st.

PATTERN AND MODEL MAKERS.

KUPSCH, A., Pattern and Model Maker, Illinois St Louis Bridge (west approach).

LORD, SIMEON, Pattern and Model Maker, 821 N. Second st.

E. SPANGENBERG & CO'S
Machine, Pattern and Model Shop,
And Manufacturers of Patented Articles,
ILLINOIS & ST. LOUIS BRIDGE BLD'G,
ST. LOUIS, MO.

STRAWBRIDGE, D., Pattern and Model Maker, Illinois and St. Louis Bridge, west end.

PATENT INVALID BEDSTEAD.

NIDELET, S. L. & J. C. & CO., Invalid Bedstead, 927 N. Fifth st.

PHOTOGRAPHERS.

THE AVENUE GALLERY,
N. W. cor. Seventh and Franklin Ave.
ALL STYLES OF PICTURES TAKEN IN CLOUDY OR CLEAR WEATHER.
Promenade Pictures a Specialty. Copying and Enlarging to any size and finished in Crayon, India Ink, Oil or Water Colors. Pictures of Deceased Persons taken.
Negatives preserved. *J. A. SEIBERT.*

ST. LOUIS—Continued.

PHOTOGRAPHERS.

BENECKE, ROB., Photographer, S. E. corner Fourth and Market sts.

BOEHL & KOENIG, Photograph and Art Gallery, 707 N. Fourth st.

CRAMER, GROSS & CO., Photographers and Art Gallery, 1001 S. Fifth st.

PHYSICIANS.

BATEMAN, THOMAS, Physician and Surgeon. Chronic Diseases a Specialty. 621 N. 5th st.

LOUGEAY, C. I., Homœopathic Physician, 410 Washington ave.

VAUGHN, DR. R. A., Office, 523 Chestnut st. Hours, 8 to 11 A.M., 2 to 4 P. M., 7 to 9 P.M.

PIANOS AND ORGANS.

HOLTZ, C., Pianos, Organs bought, sold or exchanged, 1513 Franklin ave.

PLUMBERS AND GAS FITTERS.

J. P. GALLAGHER,
PLUMBER & GAS FITTER
Manufacturer of Gallagher's Patent
Hydrant & Three-Way Fire Plug,
1133 N. FIFTH ST., ST. LOUIS.

SCHIES, J., Plumber and Gas Fitter, 2001 Franklin ave.

POWDER.

LAFLIN & RAND POWDER CO., Mnfrs. Sporting, Mining and Blasting Powder, 218 N. 2d st.

PRINTERS.

THE HOBART MNFG. & PRINTING CO., Alex. J. Brand, Jr., General Agent, 615 Chestnut st.

PRODUCE AND FRUITS.

HORSTMAN & CALDWELL, Dealers in all kinds of Produce and Fruits, 811 Broadway.

PROPRIETARY MEDICINES.

THE DR. HARTER MEDICINE CO., Proprietary Medicines, 213 N. Main st.

PUMP MANUFACTURERS.

RUMSEY, L. M. & CO., Pump Manufacturers, 811 N. Main st.

RAILROAD TICKETS.

MANTZ & CO., Railroad Tickets bought and sold, 508 Chestnut st.

REAL ESTATE AGENTS.

A. JUDLIN & CO.,
House, Real Estate & Financial Agents,
COLLECTORS OF RENT, &c.,
215 N. Eighth St., St. Louis, Mo.
Particular attention paid to Collecting Rents and Negotiating Loans on Real Estate security.

NOHL, F., Real Estate and Notary Public, 508 Market st.

1778.

wretches were soon consumed by the flames. The whole Wyoming valley, consisting of eight towns on the Susquehanna, suffered the same destruction of life and property, and none escaped but a few women and children, and these dispersed and wandered about through the forests without food and without clothes until starved to death.

July 8.—Count D'Estaing, of the French navy, arrives in the Delaware with a large fleet, causing Howe to retreat with his vessels to the waters of Amboy or Raritan bay.

Aug. 12.—Count D'Estaing sailed out of Newport harbor, Rhode Island, to engage the British fleet in command of Howe, but a terrible storm arose and disabled both fleets, and the French squadron returned to Newport and sailed to Boston for repairs. [Very old people of Rhode Island used to speak of this gale as the great storm. So violent was the wind that it brought spray from the ocean a mile distant, and incrusted the windows of the town with salt.]

Aug. 29.—Battle of Quaker Hill, Rhode Island, in which the Americans lost 30 killed and 172 wounded and missing. British loss about 220.

Sept. 22.—Paul Jones' naval battle. The engagement lasted from seven in the morning until ten at night. The contest was fierce and desperate. Paul Jones, in command of the American flotilla, finding the enemy's guns longer than his, brought his ships so close, until the muzzles of his guns came in contact with those of the enemy. The magazine of the British ship Serapis blew up, set fire to the vessel and communicated the flames to Jones' vessel. In the midst of this the American frigate Alliance came up, and mistaking her partner, fired a broadside into the vessel of Jones; but soon discovered her mistake and turned her guns upon the enemy. The British crew were all killed or wounded, the Serapis on fire, (but the flames were afterward subdued) and the frigate Countess of Scarborough captured by the Americans. Paul Jones came off victorious. His vessel (the Goodman Richard) was so badly crippled that it soon sunk; and of the crew of 365, only 68 were left alive. Jones, after this victory, wandered with his unmanageable vessel for some time, and at length, on the 6th of October found his way into the waters of the Texel.

Nov. 11.—Cherry Valley, New York, attacked by Indians and Tories. Many of the people were killed and carried into captivity, and for an area of a hundred miles around the village, desolation, ruin, and destruction prevailed for months.

Dec. 29.—Savannah captured. General Howe, the American officer, defended the city with about 1,000 men, while he was attacked by Col. Campbell of the British forces with 2,000 veterans. Through the treachery of a negro, Campbell was informed of a private path to the right of the Americans, through which his troops marched and gained the rear of Howe's army. Howe finding himself attacked in front and rear ordered a retreat, pursued by the enemy. The Americans lost 100 killed, 38 officers and 415 privates made prisoners. The whole loss of the British was 7 killed and 19 wounded.

1779.

Jan. 9.—Fort Sunbury, about 28 miles

 # John Zallee,

(Successor to JOHN G. SHELTON,)

MERCHANT TAILOR,

NO. 606 OLIVE STREET, ST. LOUIS, MO.

Premium Awarded at Paris L'Exposition Universelle, 1867, & at Vienna, 1873,

FOR FINEST MADE SUIT OF GENTS' CLOTHING.

The oldest Merchant Tailoring Establishment in St. Louis, established in 1834, when St. Louis contained only 4,000 inhabitants.

Orders solicited from Gentlemen in distant localities. Send measure taken by your tailor, and give your weight and height and photograph if convenient.

LIVER CORRECTIVE

THE GREAT FAMILY REMEDY OF THE AGE

For Diseases of the Liver, Blood, Stomach

It has no equal.

Contains no Aloes,

No Alcohol,

---AND IS NOT A STIMULANT---

A prompt and efficient remedy for *Biliousness, Derangement of the Liver, Constipation of the Bowels, Headache, Dyspepsia, Boils, Pimples,*

Bilious Colic, Bilious Diarrhœa, Neuralgia, Rheumatism, Catarrh or Fresh Cold, and Derangements of the System Generally.

J. R. COLEMAN, Apothecary, 9th and Christy av.
 Dear Sir: I have examined your "Anti-bilious Bitters and Liver Corrective," and consider it the best preparation of its kind ever offered to the public for those complaints for which you recommend it. I consider it a mild and safe medicine.
JOHN J. O'BRIEN, M. D.,
March 20, 1875. Sutter av., St Louis Co.

ST. LOUIS, January 18, 1875.
J. R. COLEMAN, Apothecary, 9th and Christy av.
I have used your Anti-bilious Bitters, and take pleasure in recommending it as the best family medicine for all derangements of the system.
Yours truly, BENJ. R. TYLER, M. D.

I have used Coleman's Anti-bilious Bitters, and it has given me satisfaction.
LEVIN H. BAKER.
St. Louis, Sept. 22, 1875.

J. R. COLEMAN, St. Louis.
I think your Bitters has done more good toward the healthy condition of our country than all other patent medicines combined.
Yours very respectfully,
FRANCIS H. ULLRICH,
Alton, Ill., Sept. 8, 1874. Apothecary.

Prepared by J. R. COLEMAN,

CHEMIST & DRUGGIST, ST. LOUIS.

N. W. Cor. 9th St., and Christy Ave.,
and S. E. Cor. 4th and Christy Ave.

ST. LOUIS UNIVERSITY, ST. LOUIS, MO.

ST. LOUIS UNIVERSITY,

Corner Ninth and Washington Avenue,

ST. LOUIS, MO.

This Literary Institution, under the direction of the Jesuit Fathers, was established in 1829, in what was then the neighborhood of St. Louis, but is now at the very heart of the city. It is situated a few blocks from the Union Depot, only two blocks from the Lindell Hotel, and it is, consequently, of easy access to parents and students who come from a distance. Though in the center of a large city, the College enjoys to a certain extent the advantages of the country, its play-ground being so spacious as to afford ample room for out-door exercise. The College possesses a villa or country seat, easily reached by street cars, where the students may spend their weekly holy days and summer vacation.

The St. Louis University by its charter, granted in 1832, has the power to confer degrees and academical honors in all the learned professions, but for many years past it has limited itself to the Classical and Commercial branches of a thorough education.

There are two distinct courses of study, the Classical and the Commercial. French and German are optional in either course, and form no extra charge.

For further particulars, address

President St. Louis University, St. Louis, Mo.

1779.

southward from Savannah, captured by the British.

Feb. 14.—While a band of Tories, under Col. Boyd, were on their march to join the Royal troops, and desolating the Carolina frontier, they were attacked by Colonel Pickens, at the head of a body of militia. Boyd and 70 of his men were killed, and 75 made prisoners. Pickens lost 38.

March 3.—General Ashe, in command of near 2,000 Americans at Brier creek, about 40 miles below Augusta, Ga., was surprised by Gen. Prevost and lost almost his entire army by death, captivity, and disappearance. About 150 killed and drowned, 80 made prisoners, and a large number who were dispersed, did not take up arms again for several months.

March 11.—General Prevost, commanding the British forces, demands the surrender of Charleston, but, receiving a prompt refusal, he spent the remainder of the day in preparing for an assault. That night was a fearful one for the citizens, for they expected to be greeted at dawn with bursting bomb-shells and red-hot cannon balls. But Prevost had been informed of the approach of Lincoln, and at midnight retreated to Savannah.

March 26.—Governor Tryon went with 1,500 British regulars and Hessians to destroy some salt works at Horseneck, N. Y., and attack an American detachment under General Putnam at Greenwich. The Americans were dispersed, but Putnam rallied his troops at Stamford, pursued the British on their return to New York the same evening, capturing a lot of plunder and 38 prisoners.

May 9.—Sir George Collier entered Hampton Roads with a small fleet, bearing General Matthews with land troops, and from thence they carried destruction and desolation on both sides of Elizabeth river, from the Roads to Norfolk and Portsmouth.

June 20.—The British were attacked at Stone Ferry, 10 miles southwest from Charleston, by a part of Lincoln's army, but after a severe engagement, and the loss of almost 300 men in killed and wounded, they repulsed the Americans, whose loss was greater.

July. 4.—Collier's vessels conveyed Gov. Tryon and 2,500 troops to the shores of Connecticut, where they plundered New Haven and laid East Haven, Fairfield, and Norwalk in ashes, and cruelly treated the defenseless inhabitants. This destruction was completed from the 4th to the 12th of July.

July 15.—Stony Point, 40 miles north of New York on the Hudson, captured by General Wayne. Wayne attacked the fort in the rear with ball and bayonet at two separate points, in the face of a heavy cannonade from the garrison. Wayne, though wounded in the head wrote to Washington, "The fort and garrison, with Col. Johnson, are ours." The British loss in killed, wounded, and prisoners, about 600; the loss of Americans was 15 killed and 83 wounded.

July 19.—Major Henry Lee surprised the British garrison at Paulus Hook (now Jersey City) opposite New York, and killed thirty soldiers and took one hundred and sixty prisoners.

Oct. 9.—A combined assault by the Americans and French was commenced on the British works around Savannah, by General Lincoln and Count D'Estaing, and after five hours hard fighting there was a truce for the purpose of

St. Louis—*Continued.*

RESTAURANTS.

J. BICKELL'S
Restaurant and Coffee House,
515 MORGAN ST.

MATSON, S., Restaurant,
504 N. Sixth st.

MARKET ST. RESTAURANT, 812 Market st., August Schroeck, prop.

RANDOLPH, D. S., prop. of the English Kitchen, 105 N. Fifth st.

SCHAFER, WM., Restaurant,
N. Third st.

§. 11.
Apollo Theater
RESTAURANT & SALOON
JULIAN SCHROEDER, PROP.
S. E. cor. Fourth and Poplar sts.,
ST. LOUIS,   -   -   MO.

SPRAGUE & BUTLER, Restaurants, 716 N. Fifth st., and 321 Olive st.

RUBBER STAMPS.

ST. LOUIS RUBBER STAMP CO., Mnfr. of Ribbon and Hand stamps, 414 Washington ave.

SADDLERY HARDWARE.

BURNS & WEGNAN, Saddlery and Saddlery Hardware, 509 N. Main st.

MARSHEL, JAMES H., Saddlery and Saddlery Hardware, 412 N. Main st.

MEYER, BANNERMAN & CO., Saddlery and Saddlery Hardware, 418 N. Main st.

SALOONS.

Jos. Apprederis,
Columbia House and Saloon.
1448 *BROADWAY*,
St. Louis.

BOELLING, CASPAR, Wine and Beer Saloon, 1701 S. Seventh st.

CHARLES J. BREMER'S
Wine & Beer Saloon,
Fine Liquors & Cigars always on hand.
314 MARKET STREET,
ST. LOUIS, MO.

CABINET SALOON, N. E. cor. Sixth and Elm sts.   JOHN & CHARLEY, Proprietors.

ERDER, JA., Wine and Beer Saloon,
2307 Franklin avenue.

St. Louis—Continued.

SALOONS.

PETER CLEVER'S
BANK SALOON,
211 N. THIRD ST., Op. Post Office.

Choice Liquors and Mixed Drinks a Specialty. Finest Imported Cigars, and Ice Cool Beer on draught. Warm Meals and Coffee served at all hours.

Everett House
=BAR,=
Choice Wines and Liquors Always on Hand.
306 & 308 N. Fourth St.
L. T. HARTMAN, (Formerly of John Bennett's,) PROP.

Peter Fix,
WINE & BEER SALOON,
1547 BROADWAY,
S. W. cor. Mullanphy st.,
ST. LOUIS, MO.

CHARLES FOLEY,
WINE and BEER SALOON,
1001 BROADWAY,
St. Louis, Mo.

FLORAL HALL,
—AND—
SALOON,
—JOHN BOECHER, Proprietor.—

700 S. FOURTH ST., ST. LOUIS.

R. B. GINOCHIO,
Wine and Beer Saloon.
Choice Wines, Liquors & Cigars always on hand.
220 S. FOURTH STREET.

GITTERMANN, FERD., Wine and Beer Saloon, S. W. cor. Fourteenth and Wash sts.
HAQUETTE & LEAMAN, Prop's Olympic Theatre Saloon, 111 S. Fifth st.
HAUSMANN, JOHN, Wine and Beer Saloon, 1434 Broadway.
HENRY'S SALOON, 108 N. Fifth street. THEODORE BRUEGGESTRADT, Prop.

1779.

burying the dead. Nearly 1,000 of the French and Americans had been killed and wounded. A renewal of the assault was proposed by General Lincoln, but he was compelled to give up the idea when he felt sure of victory, on account of the opposition of the French Commander.

Oct. 25.—British troops evacuate Rhode Island, leaving behind them all their heavy artillery and a large quantity of stores.

1780.

Murder of Mrs. Caldwell.—While the British were plundering through the State of New Jersey, in the vicinity of Elizabethtown, they came upon the residence of Rev. Mr. Caldwell. Mrs. Caldwell was sitting on the bed with her little child by the hand, and her nurse, with her infant babe by her side, when she was instantly shot dead by an unfeeling British soldier, who had come around to an unguarded part of the house, with an evident design to perpetrate the deed. Her murderer was never punished.

April 14.—General Tarleton, commanding the British, defeated Col. Huger on the head-waters of the Cooper river, near Charleston, S. C., and killed 25 Americans.

May 6.—A party under Col. White, of New Jersey, were routed at a ferry on the Santee, with a loss of about thirty in killed, wounded, and prisoners.

May 12.—Surrender of Charleston. After three days of heavy cannonade from two hundred guns, and all night long the bursting of destructive bombshells, and at one time a fire in five different places, the city of Charleston was surrendered to the British, under Gen. Clinton. Gen. Lincoln and his troops, with a number of citizens, were made prisoners of war. Altogether the captives amounted to between 5,000 and 6,000, and four hundred pieces of cannon.

[Among the American detachments which hastened towards Charleston to assist Lincoln, and retreated when they heard of his fall, was that of Col. Buford, commanding 400 infantry and a small troop of cavalry, with two field pieces. He retreated, and when near the Waxhow Creek, some 60 miles further north, he was overtaken and supprised by Tarleton. They gave no quarters, but massacred or maimed the larger portion of Buford's command. His loss in killed, wounded, and prisoners was 313. He also lost his artillery, ammunition, and baggage.]

May 19.—Dark days. Darkness commenced between the hours of 10 and 11 A. M., and continued until the middle of the next night. Its extent was from Falmouth, Maine, to New Jersey. The darkness was so great in some part of Massachusetts, New Hampshire, Maine, Rhode Island and Connecticut, that persons were unable to see to read, or manage their domestic business, without lighting candles, and everything bore the appearance and gloom of night.

June 7.—British take possession of Elizabethtown and burn Connecticut farms.

June 12.—Clinton, commanding British forces, endeavors to draw Washington into a general battle or to capture his stores at Morristown, but fails in both.

June 23.—In a skirmish at Springfield, N. J., the British were defeated by the Americans under Gen. Greene. After setting fire to

CONRAD BAUMHARD,   HARVEY SHEELER,
Cor. Market and Miss. Sts., Indianapolis, Ind.   No. 307 Aberdeen St., Chicago, Ill.

BAUMHARD & SHEELER,
RAISERS AND MOVERS OF BRICK AND FRAME BUILDINGS,
COR. MARKET & MISSISSIPPI STS. INDIANAPOLIS, IND.

The undersigned wish to inform the public that we are prepared to Raise, Lower, and Move Brick and Stone Buildings of any size, in any part of the country accessible by rail or water. We possess advantages superior to our competitors in shipping tools. Indianapolis being a great railroad center, by which we can reach all parts of the country with less expense, in consequence we are able to reduce first cost. We have successfully completed several difficult jobs for the following parties, to whom we refer:

INDIANAPOLIS:

Murphy, Johnston & Co., Cor. Meridian and Maryland streets.
Hervey Bates, Esq., corner Home avenue and Delaware street.
Rev. S. T. Gillett, I S Massachusetts avenue.
Flouts May, Rooms 3 and 6 Glenn Block.
D. Gibson & Co., Millers.
Defees Bros., Iron Founder, 290 Pennsylvania street.
Smith & Hanneman, Virginia avenue.
And others too numerous to mention.

CHICAGO:

Chief Marshall Fenner, Chicago Fire Department.
D. E. Eddy, 54 North Clark street.
C. E. Holmes, 60 Clinton street, for whom we lowered two Brick Stores, Nos. 603 and 670 State street.
Mr. F. Morrison, with Carson, Pirie, Scott & Co., corner Madison and Franklin streets.
S. J. Toy, Secretary Commercial Bureau, 22 Major Block.
Jas. L. Campbell, Alderman Thirteenth Ward.

HEADQUARTERS FOR INSURANCE.

GRUBB, PAXTON & CO.,
INSURANCE AGENTS AND ADJUSTERS,
29 and 31 Circle Street, INDIANAPOLIS, IND.
Over $40,000,000 Represented!

Firms having large lines of Insurance are solicited to place control of it with us. Insurance furnished on all insurable interests, at all desirable points throughout the West. Orders by mail receive prompt attention. You will find it to your interest to send orders to the office direct. Correspondence solicited.

JOSEPH LEWARK,
Dealer in all kinds of
RAW FURS,
Muskrat, Opossum, Raccoon, Red Fox, Grey Fox, House Cat, Wild Cat, Skunk, Sheep Pelts,
MINK AND OTTER.
(Highest Market Price paid for Furs.)
No. 14 W. PEARL STREET, INDIANAPOLIS, IND.

STATE CAPITAL, INDIANAPOLIS, IND.

MISS E. L. BOYCE
15 Calhoun Street,
Over Graff's Jewelry Store,
FORT WAYNE, - - INDIANA.
MANUFACTURER OF AND DEALER IN
FINE
HAIR GOODS,
WIGS,
Switches, Curls, Frizzettes,
And Invisible Fronts
For Young and Old Ladies, made to order.
☞ Special attention paid to Theatrical Work.
Combings rooted, and made up in the most approved manner. Warranted to give satisfaction.
Hair Dressing for Weddings and Parties.
N. B. Human Hair Bought and Sold.

The Franklin Life
INSURANCE COMPANY.
INDIANAPOLIS, IND.
The only Home Company in the State.
SECURE,
MUTUAL,
LIBERAL.

Its best friends are among the principal business men of Indianapolis—men who know it best. Its funds loaned only to policy holders.

A. D. LYNCH, President.
A. G. PETTIBONE, Vice-President.
L. G. HAY, Secretary.
W. E. HARVEY, Actuary.
FREDERICK BAGGS, Treasurer

1780.

the village, the enemy retreated, and passed over to Staten Island.

July 10.—A powerful French fleet, under Admiral Ternay, arrives at Newport, Rhode Island, bearing 6,000 troops, under the Count de Rochambeau. This had a tendency to restrain Clinton from any further advances towards enticing Washington to fight.

Aug. 6.—Battle of Camden. After a desperate struggle with an overwhelming force, the Americans, under command of Gen. Gates, were defeated and routed with a loss of killed, wounded and prisoners, of about 1,000 men, besides all of their artillery and ammunition and a portion of their baggage and stores. The British loss was 325. Among the American officers killed was Baron de Kalb, whose remains yet lie under a monument at Camden.

Sept. 4.—Benedict Arnold's treason discovered.

Sept. 28.—Major Andre was captured by three militiamen named John Paulding, David Williams, and Isaac Van Wart.

Oct. 2.—Major John Andre, an adjutant general in the British army, was hanged as a spy at Tappan, on the Hudson river, New York.

Oct. 7.—Battle of King's Mountain, South Carolina. This was a severe engagement, in which the British were defeated with a loss of 300 men in killed and wounded, and the death of Major Patrick Ferguson, their commander. The spoils of victory, which cost the Americans only 20 men, were 800 prisoners and 1,500 stand of arms.

Nov. 20.—Gen. Sumter engages the British general Tarleton at Blackstocks's plantation on the Tyger river, in a Union district. The British were repulsed with a loss in killed and wounded of about 300. The American loss was only 3 killed and 5 wounded. Sumter was among the latter, and he was detained from the field for several months, by his wounds.

1781.

Murder of Mr. Caldwell (husband of Mrs. Caldwell, killed in 1780). Mr. Caldwell was escorting a lady from New York, up town, in Elizabethtown. She was carrying a small bundle tied up in her handkerchief, when a British sentinel said the bundle must be seized for the State. Mr. Caldwell immediately left the lady, saying he would deliver the bundle to the commanding officer, who was present; and, as he stepped forward to do so, another soldier told him to stop, which he immediately did. The soldier without further provocation shot him dead on the spot. The villain who murdered him was seized and executed.

Jan. 1.—Mutiny of Pennsylvania Line. The pay of officers and men of the Continental army had been so long in arrears, and money askd for in vain, that finally 1,300 troops of the Pennsylvania Line left the camp at Morristown, with the avowed determination of marching to Philadelphia, and in person, demand justice of the National Legislature. When the mutineers reached Princeton they were met by British emissaries from New York, who came to seduce them by bribes to enter the King's service. Indignant at the implied suspicion of their patriotism, the insurgents seized the spies and delivered them to Gen. Wayne for punishment. When Gen. Wayne, who was sent by Washington to bring the insurgents back, first placed himself before the insurgents

St. Louis—*Continued.*

SALOONS.

Robert Hilbert,
WINE and BEER SALOON,
313 MARKET ST.,
ST. LOUIS, MO.

Jacob Huether,
SALOON,
No. 412 OLIVE STREET,
ST. LOUIS, - - MO.

H. HUMMERT,
Boarding House and Saloon,
1587 Broadway.

JOQUEL & MOTTE, Wine and Beer Saloon, 319 S. Seventh st.

KLEINE, F., Wine and Beer Saloon, 720 Broadway.

CHAS. E. KOERNER,
Fine Old Bourbon Whisky,
(*BRIDGE SALOON,*)
606 N. THIRD ST.

LANG, P., Wine and Beer Saloon, 2413 Franklin ave.

FRED. LOEHR,
Liquors, Champagne Wines
—AND—
IMPORTED CIGARS,
110 N. Third Street, and 1 N. Main Street. Op. Main Entrance Merchants' Exchange.

MERCHANTS' SALOON,
702 BROADWAY,
ST. LOUIS.

WM. T. CALVERT, Prop'r.

PAUL OBERGFELD,
WINE & BEER SALOON,
126 OLIVE STREET,

St. Louis—*Continued.*

SALOONS.

MUEHLHAUSEN, CHAS., Saloon,
  Cor. Third and Market sts.

NAEHAR, E. H., Saloon and Billiard Hall, 717 Morgan st.

FRED. POHLMANN,
WINE, BEER,
—AND—
LIQUOR SALOON,
S. E. Cor. Fifth & Christy Ave.,
St. Louis.

SCHOCH, CHAS. T., Wine and Liquor Saloon, cor. Seventh and Rutger sts.

SCHULZE, FRED., Wine and Lager Beer Saloon. 216 Market st.

SICKINGER, JOHN, Wine and Beer Saloon, S. W. cor. Morgan and Third sts.

JOHN M. WOLF,
Wine and Beer Saloon,
Choice Cigars and Liquors always in stock.
1020 Broadway.

SALT DEALERS.

PRIESMEYER, W.'H., Dealer in Coarse, Fine and Dairy SALT, 1003 and 1013 Carr st.

SASH, DOORS AND BLINDS.

GRAVE, JAMES & SON, Manufacturer of Sash, Doors, Blinds, etc., 107 S. Seventh st.

HAFNER, JOS., Wholesale Dealer in SASH, DOORS, BLINDS, and Glazed Windows, Moulding and Building Paper, 604 S. Seventh st., St. Louis, Mo.

SAUSAGE MANUFACTURER.

John Boepple's
Cincinnati Steam Sausage Manufactory,
FIRST PREMIUM.
615 & 617 S Second St.

SAW MANUFACTURERS.

CURTIS & CO., Saw Manufacturers,
  811 and 813 N. Second street.

SCALES.

PEARSON, A. B., Improved Shallow Pit, Wagon, Stock and Floor Scales, 212 S. Second st.

SCHOOL.

ST. LOUIS UNIVERSITY,
  Christy ave., bet. Ninth and Tenth sts.

SEWING MACHINES.

WHEELER & WILSON Sewing Machine Co., Fitch & Moore, City Agents, 415 N. Fifth st.

SHOW-CASE MANUFACTURER.

CLAES, C. & CO., Show-Case Manufacturers, 204 Market st.

SIGN MANUFACTURER.

UNION SIGN WORKS, ALEX. S. MANN, Proprietor. Manufacturer of Signs of every discription. Attractive Glass Signs, and Engraved Metal Signs a Specialty. 412 Locust st.

1781.

with loaded pistols, they put their bayonets to his breast, and said: "We love and respect you, but if you fire you are a dead man. We are not going to the enemy; on the contrary, if they were now to come out, you should see us fight under your orders with as much alacrity as ever." They were met also by a deputation from Congress, who relieved their wants, and gave them such satisfactory guarantees for the future, that they returned to their duty.

Jan.—The Bank of North America, the first ever established in the United States, about this time came into existence in Philadelphia. It was under the charge of Robert Morris, to whose superintendence Congress had intrusted the public Treasury.

Jan. 5.—Benedict Arnold, traitor, now in the employ of the British, penetrates up the James river, and destroys a large quantity of public and private stores at Richmond. [Great efforts were made to seize Arnold. Sergeant Champs, one of Major Lee's dragoons, went in disguise to New York, enlisted in a corpse over which Arnold had command, and had almost consummated a plan for abducting him to the Jersey shore, when the traitor was ordered to the Southern expedition. Instead of carrying Arnold off, Champs, himself, was taken to Virginia with the corps in which he had enlisted. There he escaped and joined Lee in the Carolinas.]

Jan. 17.—Defeat of the British at Cowpens, S. C., by Gen. Morgan. The enemy lost near 300 men in killed and wounded, 500 were made prisoners, and a large quantity of arms, ammunition, and stores were captured.

Jan. 18.—A mutiny occurred among a portion of the Jersey line, at Pompton. Washington sent General Robert Howe, with 500 men, to suppress it, and, after hanging two of the ringleaders, the remainder quietly submitted.

March 15.—Battle of Guilford, N. C. The Americans were repulsed and the British were left masters of the field, though the victory so completely shattered Cornwallis' army that it was almost as destructive to him as a defeat. American loss, in killed and wounded, about 400, besides almost 1,000 who deserted to their homes. The loss of the British was over 600, including Lieut.-Col. Webster, one of the most efficient officers in the British army.

April 25.—Battle near Camden, S. C. While Gen. Greene was breakfasting at a spring on the eastern slope of Hobkirk's Hill, S. C., and while some of his men were cleaning their guns, and others washing their clothes, they were surprised and defeated by the British, under Rawdon. American loss in killed, wounded and missing, 266 men. The British lost 258. Greene conducted his retreat so well, that he carried away all his artillery and baggage, with 50 British prisoners.

May 10.—Gen. Rawdon, alarmed at the prospective increase in Greene's army, set fire to Camden, and retreats to Nelson's Ferry, on the Santee.

June 4.—Gen. Tarleton, in command of a British marauding party, captured seven members of the Virginia Legislature. Gov. Jefferson narrowly escaped capture by fleeing from his house to the mountains.

June 5.—Surrender of Augusta, Ga., to the Americans, under Gen. Lee, after a siege of eleven days. American loss 51 in killed

J. B. MANY, President.   J. L. AVERY, Secretary and Treasurer.   C. J. MANY, Superintendent.

CAPITAL CITY
Planing Mill Company,
Manufacturers of

Doors, Sash, Blinds, Stairs, Stair Railing, Balusters, Posts, &c.
AND DEALERS IN

LUMBER, LATH, SHINGLES, ETC.,
317 to 327 Massachusetts Ave., Indianapolis, Ind.

CHAS. H. BLACK.   VICTOR M. BACKUS.
BLACK & BACKUS,
—MANUFACTURERS OF—

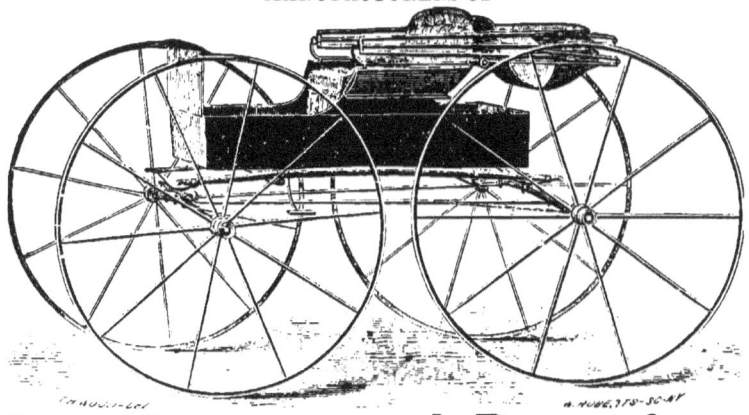

Carriages and Buggies,
OF EVERY STYLE AND DESCRIPTION,
Nos. 36, 38 and 44 East Maryland Street, INDIANAPOLIS.

An Illustrated Catalogue containing all the latest styles and prices furnished gratis on application.

H. STACEY, Proprietor.   JOHN SCHNEIDER, Superintendent.
INDIANAPOLIS
BRASS FOUNDRY,
106 & 108 South Delaware, Corner Georgia Street,
MANUFACTURERS OF ALL KINDS OF

BRASS CASTINGS
For Machinists, Plumbers, Steam and Gas Fitters.
Railroad Car and Machine Brasses a Specialty. Also Manufacturers of Stacey's Automatic Gas Burner.

ADVERTISEMENTS. 61

Court House and City Hall, Indianapolis, Ind.—It is built in the modern French Renaissance style of Architecture, situated on the public square, bounded by Washington, Market, Delaware and Alabama Sts. The building is 278 feet in length, 137 feet in breadth, 86 feet in heighth and 235 feet to the apex of the main tower. The two end pavilions are 124 feet and 96 feet to the apex of the roof. The building is constructed of drab limestone from Ellettsville, Monroe Co., Ind., while the columns are of polished Scotch Granite. The building is the only one of the kind in the state. In the tower is a clock with four dials, ten feet in diameter, and will be illuminated and regulated by electricity, which can be seen for miles.

1877.   1877.
LITTLE'S HOTEL,
Cor. New Jersey & Washington Sts.
INDIANAPOLIS, IND.
The Old Reliable Hostelrie

Has been thoroughly renovated throughout, with comfortable and airy beds, and a table well supplied with the choicest edibles of the season, equal to the best hotels of the country—all for the living price of *$1.25 per day.*
No better establishment can be desired.
JOSEPH FITZGERALD, Prop'r.
Joseph Wright, Clerk.

ROBERT KELLER,
125 East Washington Street,
INDIANAPOLIS, IND.
Importer of and Dealer in Fine

Groceries,

French Mustard, | Swiss, Limberger
Holland Herrings, | Holland & Sap Sago,
Russ. Sardines, | CHEESE.
Germ. Prunes, Pears | Olive Oil, Table Sauce
Farina, Pease, etc. | Catsup, Chow Chow,
etc. | etc.

1781.

and wounded. British loss 52 killed, and 334 (including wounded) were made prisoners.

Sept. 6.—Arnold lands at the mouth of the Thames, attacks Fort Trumbull, and burns New London (his native town), Connecticut. Another division of this expedition went up on the east side of the Thames, attacked Fort Griswold, at Groton, and after Col. Ledyard had surrendered it, he, and almost every man in the fort were cruelly murdered or badly wounded.

Sept. 8.—Battle of Eutaw Springs, S. C. This was a severe battle, which resulted in the British being driven from their camp by Gen. Greene. But while the Americans were scattered among the tents of the enemy, indulging in drinking and plundering, the British unexpectedly renewed the battle, and, after a bloody conflict of about four hours, the Americans were obliged to give way. That night, the British retreated to Charleston, and the next day, Greene took possession of the battlefield. American loss in killed, wounded and missing, 555. British loss, 693.

Oct. 19.—Surrender of Cornwallis at Yorktown. For ten days, the Americans kept up a heavy cannonade upon the British works at Yorktown, and hurled red-hot balls among the English shipping, and burned several vessels. Cornwallis, despairing of receiving any aid, and perceiving his fortifications crumbling one by one under the terrible storm of iron from a hundred heavy cannon, attempted to escape by crossing to Gloucester, break through the French troops stationed there, and, by forced marches, reach New York. When the van of his troops embarked on York River, a storm arose as fearful and as sudden as a summer tornado, dispersed the boats, compelled many to put back, and the attempt was abandoned. Cornwallis surrendered 7,000 British soldiers to Washington, and his shipping and seamen into the hands of DeGrasse.

Oct. 24.—Congress, and the loyal people throughout the United States, join in rendering thanks to God for the great victory at Yorktown—the surrender of Cornwallis.

1782.

First English Bible printed in America by Robert Aiken, of Philadelphia.

British flee from Wilmington, N. C., at the approach of Gen. St. Clair.

Clinton and his army blockaded in New York by Washington.

March 4.—British House of Commons resolve to end the war.

April 8.—The United States vessel, Hyder Ally, carrying only sixteen guns, captured by the British ship, General Monk, with twenty-nine guns.

May 3.—George Washington indignantly refused to be made king.

May.—Arrival of Sir Guy Carleton to treat for peace.

July 11.—British evacuate Savannah in accordance with a resolve of the British House of Commons to end the war and cease hostilities.

First war ship constructed in the United States at Portsmouth, N. H.

Oct. 8.—Independence of the United States acknowledged by Holland.

Nov. 30.—A provisional treaty acknowledging the independence of the United States signed by England, at Paris.

William IV., son of George III., came to the

ST. LOUIS—*Continued.*

SILVER PLATERS.

DURGIN, F. A., Sterling Silverwaer, 305 N. Seventh street.

EATON & GREEN, SILVER PLATERS, Mf's Carriage & Saddlery Hardware, 305 N. 7th st.

PELTON BROS., & CO., SILVER PLATED and Britannia Ware Mfg's, 717 S. Sixth st.

SPICE MILLS.

VERRIER, E. V., Western and Mound City Spice Mills. 414 N. Second st.

STAIR BUILDERS.

FISHER, JAS. A., Stair Builder, 1430 N. Eighth st. Country orders promptly attended to.

FRANTZ, W. H., *STAIR BUILDER.* Rails, Newels and Balusters constantly on hand. Country orders a specialty. Send for Price List, Second and Mound sts., St. Louis, Mo.

HASSFURTHER, EDW. J., Stair Builder. 1430 N. Eighth st. Country orders promptly attended to.

REES, JOHN B., Stair Builder, 1433 N. Eighth st. Stairs neatly finished and orders promptly attended to.

STEAMBOATS.

EAGLE PACKET CO., Wharf, Boat foot of Vine street.

GRAND REPUBLIC, W. H. THORWEGEN, Commander.

KEOKUK NORTHERN LINE PACKET CO., W. F. DAVIDSON, Pres.; P. S. DAVIDSON, General Supt.; F. L. JOHNSTON, Sec.

STEREOTYPERS AND ELECTROTYPERS.

Strassburger & Drach,

STEREOTYPERS
—AND—
ELECTROTYPERS,

N. W. Cor. Chestnut and Second Sts.

STOCK DEALERS.

W. P. WALTON & CO.,

Live Stock Commission Merchants,

UNION STOCK YARDS. St. Louis. Office No. 17. NATIONAL STOCK YARDS, East St. Louis, Ill.

Live Stock Agents Keokuk and Northern Line of Packets. All communications should be addressed to main office, Union Stock Yards. We will sell stock at any yard in the city, or East St. Louis.

STOVES, RANGES AND TINWARE.

ALLEN, J. B., Dealer in New and Second Hand Stoves, etc.. 803 N. Seventh st.

BOLTE, FRED., Wholesale and Retail Dealer in St. Louis Mfg'd Stoves, etc., 1310 Broadway.

BLUTHARDT, J. G., STOVES, TINWARE and Plumbing Goods, 202 N. Twelfth st.

KREYLING, D., Dealer in Stoves, Tinware. 2427 Franklin ave.

St. Louis—Continued.

STOVES, RANGES AND TINWARE.

C. HEINZ,
Manufacturer, and Wholesale Dealer in

STOVES,

Tin, Stamped & Japan Ware.

506 N. Main Street.
Bet. Washington avenue and Vine street.

NISCHWITZ, F., Dealer in Stoves and Tinware, 1406 Carondelet ave. Established 1853.

ROCKWELL, E., Dealer in Stoves and Tinware, 2321 Franklin ave.

N. M. SIMONDS,
Manufacturer of

Simond's Patent Hotel and Family RANGES,

Broilers, Carving Tables, Coffee Urns, Laundry Stoves, etc. Send for circular.

WELCKER, F. & CO., Dealers in Stoves and Tinware, 16 S. Third st.

STOVE POLISH.

SKINNER, WM. A. & CO., Hungarian Stove Polish, 1103 Morgan st.

TAILORS.

BENJAMIN, M., Merchant Tailor, and Dealer in Gents' Furnishing Goods, 710 Market st.

Henry Camien,

TAILOR,

Dyeing, Cleaning and Repairing
Done in the best manner,

414 Morgan Street.

DENEKE, FRED., Merchant Tailor, 705 Morgan street.

JOHNSON, J. L., Tailor, Residence, 1115 Wash street.

H. KONERT,

Merchant Tailor,

914 Market Street.

☞ PERFECT FIT WARRANTED. ☜

LORENZEN, M., Merchant Tailor, 113 Vine street.

M. NENNSTIEL,

TAILOR,

928 N. Sixth Street.

Cleaning, Dyeing and Repairing.

1782.

United States as a midshipman, in a fleet sent over to conquer us as a rebellious colony. An attempt was made to capture him while his vessel was lying off New York, but the scheme failed.

Dec. 14.—British evacuate Charleston, S. C.

1783.

Jan.—Bank of North America opened in Philadelphia.

Jan. 19.—Society of Cincinnatus formed by many of the officers of the Continental army at Newberg, N. Y., for the purpose of promoting cordial friendship, and refreshing the memory, by frequent reunions, of the great struggles they had passed through.

Slavery abolished in Massachusetts.

Jan. 20.—French and English Commissioners sign a treaty of peace.

Sept. 3.—A definite treaty of peace signed at Paris, and England acknowledged the independence of the United States; allowed ample boundaries extending northward to the great lakes, and westward to the Mississippi.

Nov. 3.—Continental army disbanded and return to their homes. Of the two hundred and thirty thousand Continental soldiers, and the fifty-six thousand militia, who bore arms during the war, scarcely any survive at the present day. Great Britain sent to America during the war 112,584 troops for the land service, and more than 22,000 seamen. Of this host, not one is known to be living. One of them (John Battin) died in the city of New York, June, 1852, at the age of 100 years and 4 months.

Nov. 25.—British evacuate New York, and on the same day, General Knox entered the city with a small remnant of the Continental army, and took possession of the city. Before evening, the last British soldier passed from the shores of America.

Dec. 4.—Washington takes an affectionate farewell with his officers at New York.

Dec. 23.—Washington, in the city of Annapolis, Maryland, resigns his commission in the army.

During the war, the English employed to aid them in the subjection of the country over 11,000 Indians, whose mode of warfare was to take scalps, not prisoners, and to massacre women and children. As an evidence of this fact, Captain Gerrish, of the New England militia, captured on the frontier of Canada eight packages of scalps, properly cured and dried, which were to be sent to England as a present from the Seneca Indians to George III. The packages contained 43 scalps of soldiers, 297 of farmers, 88 of women, 190 of boys, 211 of girls, 22 of infants, and 122 assorted, making a total of 973 scalps.

1784.

First voyage of an American ship to China from New York.

New York Chamber of Commerce founded.

Jan. 1.—Treaty of Paris ratified by Congress.

1785.

John Adams, first American Ambassador to England, has an audience with the King.

First Federal Congress organized in York.

First instance of instrumental music in the Congregational churches at Boston.

HURST'S HOTEL
ON THE EUROPEAN PLAN,
Cor. 4th and Locust Sts., ST. LOUIS, MO.

Splendid Sample Rooms for Commercial Travelers. Elegant Rooms, .75, $1.00 and $1.50 per day.

150 ROOMS. 75, $1.00 AND $1.50 PER DAY.

Street Cars run direct from Union Depot to this House. A First-Class Restaurant in Connection with THE HOTEL.

J. H. HURST, Proprietor.

GLOBE VINEGAR AND PICKLE WORKS.

ARMIN ZOTT.   W. C. GILMORE.

ZOTT & GILMORE,
Manufacturers of all kinds of

VINEGAR.

Packers of Sourkrout, Plain and Mixed Pickles, Chow Chow, Spiced Pigs Feet, Tongues, Tripe, Bologne and Ham Sausage. A specialty made of the manufacture of English Malt Vinegar and Barsaloux's Globe Table Sauce. No. 207 NORTH MAIN STREET, ST. LOUIS, MO.

A. McELRATH,
MAKER OF THE GUARANTEE

FITTING SHIRT,
AND DEALER IN
Men's Fine Furnishing Goods,
No. 509 North 6th Street, ST. LOUIS.

TIVOLI VAUDEVILLE THEATRE,
110 & 112 N. Fifth Street, ST. LOUIS, MO.

Open every Evening. Matinee every Saturday afternoon. First-Class Talent always in reserve. New Stars Weekly.

RUDOLPH KORNBERGER, Proprietor.

MASONIC HALL, ST. LOUIS, MO.

M. D. BARNEY, General Agent and Wholesale Dealer in BOOTS AND SHOES,

Janesville Shoe M'f'g Co.—Women's, Misses' and Children's Machine and cable sewed and pegged custom work. Janesville, Wis. **E. D. Mullin & Co.**, Celebrated Philadelphia Children's Fine Shoes, Slippers, &c. Philadelphia, Pa. **James J. Evans**, Celebrated Rochester Men's Women's and Misses' Fine Boots and Shoes, Rochester' New York.

618 WASHINGTON AVENUE, Opp. Lindel Hotel, St. Louis.

1786.

Jan. 25.—Universalist church founded in Boston.

Shay's insurrection in Massachusetts. Heavy taxes, decay of trade, and debts due from individuals to each other, were the primary cause of the insurrection. Daniel Shay, at the head of 1,100 malcontents, threatened the peace of the State by attempting to intimidate the courts. He approached Springfield for the purpose of taking possession of the barracks, when he was met by the militia under Gen. Sheyhard. The artillery was leveled at the malcontents, and three were killed and one wounded. They then dispersed, taking refuge in the neighboring States.

1787.

May 25.—The first cotton mill in the United States was built at Beverly, Mass. A convention to amend articles of confederation, composed of all the States, except Rhode Island, met in Philadelphia.

July.—Northwestern territory, embracing the present States of Ohio, Indiana, Illinois, Michigan and Wisconsin, established.

July 20.—James Whittaker, first Shaker preacher, died at Enfield, Conn., aged 36 years. "Elder Whittaker" may be considered the John Wesley of American Shakers.

Sept. 28.—The Constitution of the United States submitted to Congress and that body sent copies of it to the several legislatures, and it was ratified by the States in the following order. Delaware, Dec. 7, 1787; Pennsylvania, Dec. 12, 1787; New Jersey, Dec. 18, 1787; Georgia, Jan. 2, 1788; Connecticut, Jan. 9, 1788; Massachusetts, Feb. 6, 1788; Maryland, April 28, 1788; South Carolina, May 23, 1788; New Hampshire, June 12, 1788; Virginia, June 26, 1788; New York, July 26, 1788; North Carolina, Nov. 21, 1789; Rhode Island, May 29, 1790.

1788.

Quakers of Philadelphia emancipate their slaves. Cotton first planted in Georgia, by R. Leake. "The Doctor Riot" in New York, as it was called, originated from some indiscreet exposure of portions of a human body. The doctors were mobbed and their houses invaded.

April 7.—Marietta, Ohio, founded; the first white settldment within the limits of the present State of Ohio.

1789.

March 4.—The old Continental Congress expired and Federal Constitution ratified by the requisite number of States, and becomes the organic law of the Republic.

March 11.—Philadelphia incorporated a city.

April 6.—Washington elected President of the United States, by the unanimous vote of the electors, and John Adams was made Vice-President. Washington on his way to the inauguration, from Mount Vernon, was greeted with ovations from the people throughout the whole country.

April 30.—Washington was inaugurated first President of the United States. He appeared on the street gallery of the old City Hall, corner of Wall and Broad streets, New York, and there, in the presence of a large concourse of people, the oath of office was administered to him by Chancellor Livingstone.

Sept. 29.—First Congress adjourned after a session of almost six months in New York.

ST. LOUIS—*Continued.*

TAILORS.

JOHN A. NIES,
MERCHANT TAILOR,
814 MARKET STREET,
ST. LOUIS.

Established 1852.

PARKES, WM., Merchant Tailor,
720 Olive street.

ZALLEE, JOHN C., Merchant Tailor,
606 Olive street.

TEAS, COFFEES, ETC.

FORBES BROS., & CO., Wholesale TEAS.
506 N. Second street.

REIBELL, G., Wholesale and Retail Dealer in Teas and Coffees. 2413 Broadway.

TELEGRAPH MACHINERY.

HEISLER, CHAS., Telegraph Machinery, Insulated Wires and Supplies, 309 Chouteau ave.

TIN AND SHEET IRON WORK.

KRAATZ & BRO., Manufacturers of COPPER, TIN & SHEET IRON Ware, 2114 Broadway.

POCOCK, J. H., Mf'r TIN CANS, Iron Tanks, & Iron-clad Milk Cans, 113 to 119 Cherry st.

TOBACCO AND CIGARS.

BRANT, S., Cigar Factory,
2425 Franklin avenue.

LIZZIE A. BUCKEY,
420½ N. SIXTH STREET,
THE CHEAPEST

CIGAR STORE
IN THE CITY.
Fiagros, 3 for 10 cents. Try it and see.

DAUBERD, WM., Dealer in Cigars and Tobacco, 1526 Broadway.

DIETERICH, L. A. Dealer in Tobaccos, Cigars and Snuff, 814 Franklin ave.

FRAHM H., Manufacturer, and Dealer in Havana and Domestic Cigars, 500½ Market st.

T. J. GUNDRICH,
Cigar and Tobacco
MANUFACTURER,
803 Morgan Street, St. Louis,

WM. KUPFERLE,
(Successor to R. W. DURKAN,)
—Wholesale and Retail Dealer in—
Cigars and Tobacco,
125 Olive Street.
ST. LOUIS, MO.

St. Louis—Continued.

TOBACCO AND CIGARS.

HYNES, GEO. A. & CO., Wholesale Dealers in Imported Key West and Domestic Cigars, 309 N. Fifth st.

KAUB, E. & CO., Retail Dealers in Cigars and Tobaccos, 421 Walnut st.

Wm. Mestemacher,
Manufacturer, and Dealer in
IMPORTED AND DOMESTIC

CIGARS,
115 N. Fifth St., and 1110 Market St.
Est. 1858.   St. Louis, Mo.

MICHAEL HEIN,
Manufacturer, and Dealer in

Imported and Domestic Cigars,
SMOKERS' ARTICLES, ETC.,
1204 Broadway, St. Louis.

PEPER CHRISTIAN, Tobacco Works, Cor. Main and Morgan sts.

PUSCH, C., Mf'r and Dealer in Havana and Domestic Cigars, 1414 Market st.

M. Rabinowich,
Only Manufacturer, and Retail Dealer of
'FUTURE GREAT'
STRAIGHT, PURE HAVANA FILLER
5 CENT CIGAR,
Sold only at
804 Washington Avenue.

CHARLES REHFELDT,
Manufacturer, and Dealer in
HAVANA AND DOMESTIC

CIGARS,
914 Broadway.
Op. Franklin ave.   Est. 1873.

Lucas Schottmueller,
Manufacturer, and Dealer in
CIGARS AND TOBACCO,
PIPES, ETC.,
1008 BROADWAY.
Bet. Wash and Carr sts.

SPILKER, A., Wholesale and Retail Dealer in Cigars and Tobacco, 803 N. Fourth st.

STERNE, MAX, Wholesale Tobacco, Cigars, Pipes, etc., 116 N. Second st.

AMEDEE VEIL,
Importer of Cigars,
111 N. FIFTH STREET.

IMPORTANT EVENTS OF THE CENTURY.

1789.
Convention of Episcopal clergy in Philadelphia; the first Episcopal convention in America.

Dr. Carrol, of Maryland, consecrated bishop of the Roman Catholic Church—the first Catholic bishop in the United States.

1790.
From a report of the Register of the Treasury at this date, the entire cost of the war for Independence was estimated at $130,000,000, exclusive of the vast sums lost by individuals. The Treasury payments amounted to $93,000,000; the foreign debt amounted to $8,000,000, and the domestic debt, due chiefly to officers and soldiers of the Revolution, was more than $30,000,000.

Gen. Harmer, with a strong force, penetrates the country north of Cincinnati and destroys Indian villages and crops.

District of Columbia ceded to the United States by Maryland and Virginia.

A United States ship circumnavigated the globe.

April 17.—Death of Benjamin Franklin, aged 84 years.

May 29.—Rhode Island adopts the Constitution, being the last of the thirteen original States to do so.

Aug. 12.—Congress adjourns to New York, and December 6th meets in Philadelphia.

Oct. 22.—Near the present city of Fort Wayne, Indiana, Gen. Harmer, in an engagement with the Indians, was defeated with considerable loss.

Captain Robert Grey in the ship "Columbia," completed the first American voyage around the globe.

1791.
The first census of the inhabitants of the United States was completed this year. The population of all sexes and color was 3,929,000. The number of slaves was 695,000.

Nov. 4.—Gen. St. Clair, while in camp near the northern line of Darke county, Ohio, was surprised and defeated by the Indians, with a loss of about six hundred men.

Vermont admitted as a State. City of Washington founded. First bale of cotton exported to England since the Revolution.

June 21.—Philadelphia and Lancashire Turnpike Company chartered. Road opened in 1795—the first turnpike in the United States.

City of Washington laid out.

1792.
The first mint went into operation in Philadelphia, and remained the sole issuer of coin in the United States until 1835, when a branch was established in each of the States of Georgia, North Carolina and Louisiana.

Yellow fever in Philadelphia. It commenced in August, and lasted until about the 9th of November, during which time 4,000 persons died out of a population of 60,000; as many as 119 dying in a single day. More than one-half of the houses were closed, and about one-third of the inhabitants fled the city. The streets were almost entirely deserted, except by a few persons who were in quest of a physician, a nurse, a bleeder, or the men who bury the dead.

John Hancock, Roger Sherman and John Manly died this year.

June 1.—Kentucky admitted into the Union.

C. Bergundthal,

DEALER IN

GLASS & QUEENSWARE,

Bar Glassware a Specialty.

68 N. Illinois Street,
INDIANAPOLIS, IND.

ESTABLISHED 1830.

A. S. COMSTOCK,

MANUFACTURER OF THE

Genuine Durbon Pump,

197 & 199 S. Meridian St.,   INDIANAPOLIS, IND.

A. V. LAWRENCE,

GENERAL

Commission Merchant,

173 W. WASHINGTON ST., Indianapolis, Ind.

Dealer in Fruits, Vegetables, and Shipper of Western Produce. Eggs, Butter, Poultry and Game a Specialty.
All Orders Promptly Filled.

JOHN G. BLAKE,   THOMAS B. JACKSON,   JOHN G. QUINIUS.
Firm of Van Camp & Jackson.

Blake, Jackson & Quinius,

Successors to G. C. Van Camp & Son, and Prather & Blake,
WHOLESALE FRUIT, PRODUCE, AND

General Commission Merchants,

Fruit, Produce, Poultry, Game, Hides, Feathers, etc., a specialty.

75 W. WASHINGTON STREET, Indianapolis, Ind.

REFERENCES. { John C. New, Vice Pres. First National Bank, Indianapolis,
Aquilla Jones, Sr., Pres. Indianapolis Rolling Mill Co.
Merrill, Hubbard & Co., Booksellers and Stationers.

Consignments and Correspondence Solicited.   Prompt Returns Guaranteed.

Indiana State Building, Centennial Exposition, Philadelphia.
—This building is constructed of a combination of wood and other building materials, a frame of wood being the support of the building and roof, to which an outer wall of brick, stone, terra-cotta, iron and coal can be attached. The assembly hall is a grand auditorium for miscellaneous gatherings. It is in the form of an irregular cross, 55 feet at its longest angle, and has about 1,400 feet of floor. From the level of the ceilings of the side rooms it is spanned by a truss-arched roof at a height of 24 feet above the center of the hall. It is lighted by the rotunda above, and an ornamental fountain plays in the center below. On the walls are 200 tablets, of which number, 92 are used by the counties of the State for the general statistics of each county, and the remainder are given to individuals or firms. The entire cost of the building was $10,000.

JAMES M. WARREN,

DIRECT IMPORTER OF

QUEENSWARE, CHINA

AND GLASSWARE,

NO. 118 FIRST ST. - EVANSVILLE, IND.

1793.

Erection of the Capitol at Washington commenced.
Lehigh, Pa., coal mines discovered.
Cotton gin invented by Eli Whitney.
May 30.—The "Democratic Society" formed. First introduction of the word into American politics.

1794.

Whisky insurrection in Pennsylvania. A law was passed in 1791, which imposed duties on domestic distilled liquors, and when officers of the Government were sent to enforce it among the Dutch inhabitants of western Pennsylvania, they were resisted by the people in arms. The insurrection soon became general in all the western counties, and in the vicinity of Pittsburgh many outrages were committed. Buildings were burned, mails were robbed, and Government officers were insulted and abused. It was thought that the insurgents at one time numbered 7,000. The President ordered a large body of malitia, under Gen. Henry Lee, to the scene of these troubles, and the insurrectionists were dispersed and obedience to the laws enforced.
Congress appropriates seven hundred thousand dollars for the purpose of organizing a navy. This was the first movement of the United States in establishing a navy.
Feb.—Bank of United States incorporated with a capital of $10,000,000. Prior to this, the whole banking capital in the United States was only $2,000,000, invested in the Bank of North America, at Philadelphia; the Bank of New York, in New York City; and the Bank of Massachusetts, in Boston.
April 19.—John Jay was appointed by the United States envoy extraordinary to the British Court, to adjust all complaints growing out of the Revolutionary war, such as the British violating the treaty of September 3, 1783, by holding military posts on the frontiers; that British emissaries incited the Indians to hostilities; that no remuneration had been made for plantations plundered and negroes sold into the West Indies at the close of the war; and also to remonstrate to the English government against capturing neutral vessels and impressing our seamen into their service.

1795.

Nov. 28.—A treaty of peace was made with the Dey of Algiers, by which an annual tribute was given by the United States, for the redemption of captives. Between the years 1785 and 1793, the Algerine pirates captured and carried into Algiers fifteen American vessels, and made 180 officers and seamen slaves of the most revolting kind. By this treaty the United States agrees to pay $800,000 for captives then alive, and in addition, to make the Dey, or governor, a present of a frigate worth $100,000. An annual tribute of $23,000, in maritime stores, was also paid. This was complied with until the breaking out of the war of 1812.
June 24.—A treaty, concluded by Mr. Jay, with the British government, was ratified by the Senate. This treaty was not very satisfactory. It provided for the collection of debts here by British creditors, which had been contracted before the revolution, but procured no redress for those who lost negroes. It secured indemnity for unlawful captures on the

---

St. Louis—*Continued.*

TOOLS.

BATH, T. H., Dealer in New and Second-hand Tools, 1436 Broadway.

TURKISH BATHS.

ADAMS, GEO. F., Turkish Baths,
311 N. Seventh st.

TURNING SHOP.

Established 1864.

North St. Louis Turning Shop,
—AND—
Furniture Manufactory,

H. KRIEGSHAUSER & CO.,
2519 N. Ninth Street.

Stone Cutters' Mallets, Stair Ballusters and Newel Posts always on hand. All kinds of turning done on the shortest notice. All orders promptly filled.

UPHOLSTERERS.

CURELL & FRANCOIS, Upholsterers and Repairers. 117 and 119 S. Seventh st.

KOHRNMEL, L., UPHOLSTERER, Mattresses and Bedding, 1917 Franklin ave.

KRUSE, C. F., Practical Upholsterer,
1213 Olive street.

J. A. MADDEN & CO.,
Cabinet Makers and Upholsterers,

Leave orders to have your

Furniture, Mattresses, Bedding, etc., etc., Cleaned, Upholstered and Repaired.

715 MORGAN STREET.

☞ Packing and Shipping at shortest notice.

WM. WARMBOLD,
Upholsterer,

Mf'r, Wholesale and Retail Dealer in
Hair, Moss, Shuck and Spring Mattresses,
2607 FRANKLIN AVE.

VINEGAR AND PICKLES.

ZOTT & GILMORE, Vinegar and Pickles,
207 N. Main st.

WATCHES, CLOCKS AND JEWELRY.

GRAWE, H. C., Dealer in Fine Jewelry, Watches, Clocks, etc., 827 N. Fourth st.

Fred. Herkstroeter,
Dealer in
Watches, Jewelry, Guns,
PISTOLS, &C.,
1009 Cass Avenue.

Between 10th and 11th sts.

ST. LOUIS—*Continued.*

WATCHES, CLOCKS AND JEWELRY.

R. JAEGERMANN & CO,
Practical Watch Makers,
218 N. FOURTH STREET.

☞ All kinds of Watch Repairing done at very low prices, and on short notice.

M. JOSEPH,
Dealer in
Watches, Jewelry and Optical Goods,
306 N. Fourth Street.
Under Everett House.

Watches & Jewelry Skillfully and Promptly Repaired.

R. R. Tickets Bought and Sold.

KOETKAMP, E. H., Watch-maker and Jeweler, 514 Franklin ave.

MAUCH, H., Watch-maker and Jeweler, 407 Franklin ave., and 3201 S. Seventh st.

STUDLER, J. P., Dealer in Watches and Clocks, 2023 Franklin ave.

WHITENERS.

Chas. Hall & Co.,
Whiteners
—AND GENERAL—
Jobbers,
930 N. SIXTH STREET.
Bet. Franklin ave., and Wash st.

PRETABOIR, SAMUEL & CO., Whiteners and Plasterers, N. E. cor. Sixth and Spruce sts.

WILLOW WARE.

ERNST BEHNE,
Manufacturer, Wholesale and Retail Dealer in
PLAIN AND ORNAMENTAL
WILLOW WARE,
OF ALL DESCRIPTIONS,
714 & 716 Market Street.

WINDOW GLASS.

VOIGT, EDWARD & CO., WINDOW GLASS, Paints, Dye-stuffs, etc., 323 N. Main st.

WINES AND LIQUORS.

HUBER, J. G. & CO., California Wines and Brandies, 212 S. Fourth st.

STERN, SOL. & CO., Wines and Liquors, Cased Cigars a specialty, 203 N. Main st.

1795.

seas and the evacuation of the forts on the frontier.

Aug. 3.—Commissioners of the United States meet the Indian chiefs of western tribes at Greenville, Ohio, and conclude a treaty of peace, by which the United States obtains a large tract of land in the present States of Michigan and Indiana.

Yellow fever pestilence in New York.

1796.

June.—Tennessee admitted into the United States, making the number of States in the Union sixteen.

Louis Phillippe, King of France, arrived in Philadelphia. He makes a tour through the country; returns again to the United States in 1800, thence to France, and dies in England in 1848.

Credit of the Government re-established, and all disputes with foreign powers, except France, adjusted.

Sept. 17.—Washington issued his farewell address.

1797.

John Adams inaugurated President of the United States; Thomas Jefferson, Vice-President.

May 15.—An extra session of Congress was convened to consider our relations with France. Our government had been insulted by the French minister here, the American minister ordered to leave France, and the French authorized depredations upon our commerce. Three envoys, appointed by Congress to proceed to France to adjust difficulties, were refused an audience unless they would pay a tribute to the French treasury, and, upon refusal, were ordered out of the country.

Nov.—Congress convened, and preparations were made for war with France.

1798.

Alien and sedition laws adopted by the United States. The first authorized the President to expel from the country any person not a citizen, who should be suspected of conspiring against the Republic. The sedition law authorized the suppression of publications calculated to weaken the authority of the government.

May.—Quite a large standing army was authorized by Congress, and in July Washington was appointed its Commander-in-Chief. The army was never summoned to the field.

1799.

Jan.—Lafayette returns to France.

Feb.—Hostilities commenced on the ocean between the United States and France, and the U. S. frigate Constellation captures the French frigate L'Insurgente.

Feb. 26.—Three commissioners proceed to France to negotiate for peace. When they arrived in France they found the government in the hands of Napoleon Bonaparte. He promptly received the commissioners, concluded a treaty of peace September 30, 1800, and gave such assurances of friendly relations that the provincial army of the United States was disbanded.

Dec. 14.—Washington died at Mount Vernon, at the age of sixty-eight years. At the recommendation of Congress, the wearing of crape on the left arm for thirty days, was pretty generally complied with.

RIPLEY'S
Cash Register,
For Recording
CASH SALES
Saves
TIME AND MONEY!
Is simple and Practical.

Does away with paper slips,
And is a
PERFECT
PROTECTION
against mistakes and discrepancies in retail cash accounts.

H. P. HOOD,
Sole Manufacturer,
INDIANAPOLIS, IND.
Send for Circular.

KOLYER & KERR'S

Livery, Sale & Feed Stables,
163 & 202 W. Washington St., Indianapolis.
Boarding a Specialty. Horses and Buggies Bought and Sold. Give us a call.

ADVERTISEMENTS. 73

JAS. W. WARRICK,
Attorney at Law.

ROOM 28.

VANCE BLOCK,
Indianapolis.

VANCE BLOCK, INDIANAPOLIS, IND.

Geo. Rhodius, *Proprietor.*   F. Lindner, E. Kitz, A. Orsbach, *Clerks.*

CIRCLE HOUSE,
On the European Plan.

No. 15 North Meridan St., Indianapolis, Ind.

The Circle House is centrally situated in the midst of the business portion of Indianapolis, and close to the Union Depot. The Rooms are fine, large and airy.
THE SAMPLE ROOMS, for Merchants to display their Goods, are the finest of any Hotel in the West. A First-class RESTAURANT is attached to the Hotel, where Meals are served up at all hours of the day. The rates are regulated by the Bill of Fare. A First-class BARBER SHOP is connected with this Hotel, where Hot and Cold Baths may be taken.
The English, German and French Languages are spoken by the Clerks, and the Traveling Public are well accommodated and served.
REGULAR RATES TO SUIT THE TIMES, $2.00 PER DAY.

Benz & Riches,
WOOD AND SEAL ENGRAVERS
No. 118 N. Third St., St. Louis, Mo.

1800.

Feb. 1.—The U. S. frigate Constellation had an action with the French frigate La Vengeance, but escaped capture, after a loss of 160 men killed and wounded.

Removal of the Capitol from Philadelphia to Washington.

A second census was taken, and the population of the Union was found to be 5,319,762, an increase of 1,400,000 in ten years. The revenue, which amounted to $4,771,000 in 1790, now amounted to $13,000,000.

The inoculation of the kine pock introduced into America by Professor Waterhouse of Cambridge, Mass.

1801.

Repeal of the act imposing internal duties. The enforcement of this law is what caused the whisky insurrection in Western Pennsylvania in 1794.

March 4.—Thomas Jefferson inaugurated President of the United States, and Aaron Burr Vice-President. When the electors counted the votes Jefferson and Burr had an equal number. According to the provisions of the Constitution the vote was then transferred to the House of Representatives. Mr. Jefferson was finally chosen President after 35 ballots, and Burr proclaimed Vice-President.

June 10.—Tripoli declares war against the United States. Prior to the declaration of war (1800) Capt. Bainbridge arrived at Algiers, in the frigate George Washington. The Dey demanded the use of his vessel to carry an ambassador to Constantinople. Bainbridge remonstrated, when the Dey haughtily observed: "You pay me tribute, by which you become my slaves, and therefore I have a right to order you as I think proper." Bainbridge was obliged to comply, for the castle guns would not allow him to pass out of the harbor.

1802.

April.—Ohio admitted as a State, with a population of 72,000.

Yellow fever ravages in Philadelphia.

Merino sheep introduced into the United States by Mr. Livingston and General Humphreys.

Military academy founded at West Point, on the Hudson.

1803.

Com. Preble sent to humble the Algerine pirates. After bringing the Emperor of Morocco to terms, his squadron proceeded to Tripoli. One of his vessels (the Philadelphia) struck on a rock while reconnoitering, and was captured by the Tripolitans. The officers were treated as prisoners, but the crew were made slaves.

April.—Louisiana purchased of France for $15,000,000, and divided into Territory of New Orleans and the District of Louisiana. It contained a mixed population of about 85,000, and 40,000 slaves at this time.

Jerome Bonaparte, nineteen years of age, arrived in New York. He visits Baltimore, falls in love there with a Miss Patterson and marries her. In 1805 he returns to France, leaving his wife to follow. The Emperor forbids her to enter France, and had the marriage annulled by the French Council. Jerome then married the daughter of the King of Wurtemberg, and six days after was made King of Westphalia.

Louisiana purchased from the French government for fifteen million dollars.

St. Louis Business Houses,
When Established.

ABE, A., Gunsmith, 1869.
BARNEY, M. V., Boots and Shoes, 1873.
BEATTIE, A. F., Crescent Fluid, 1875.
BERNARD & CO., Flour and Commission Merchants, 1837.
BOUCHER, LEON & CO., Paints and Oils, 1867.
BRYAN, J. E., Patent Agency, 1877.
CURTIS & CO., Saw Manufacturers, 1854.
DURGIN, F. A., Silverware, 1853.
FRITZ, GEO. J., Iron Works, 1872.
GALLAGHER, J. P., Plumber, 1859.
GARRETT, M'DOWELL & CO., Pig Iron, 1868.
GARSTANG, R., Boiler Mf'r, 1863.
GIBBS, J. S. & CO., Canned Goods, 1872.
HACKMANN, JOHN F., Saddles and Harness, 1874.
HARRIS, J. G. & CO., Engravers, 1868.
HASELTINE, W. B., Leather and Findings, 1849.
JAEGERMANN, R. & CO., Watch-makers, 1871.
JONES' COMMERCIAL COLLEGE, 1841.
JOSEPH, M., Jeweler, 1874.
JOST, N., Corks, 1872.
KOHLER, J. L., Employment Agency, 1869.
LAITNER, F. J. & SON, Brushes, 1847.
LEWANDOVSKA, MME., Millinery, 1855.
M'CABE, JAMES J., Mill Picks, 1862.
M'CANN & CO., Carriage Mf'rs, 1876.
M'ELRATH, A., Gents' Furnishing Goods, 1872.
RANDOLPH, D. S., English Kitchen, 1861.
REDDEN, A., Boots and Shoes, 1875.
SAWYER, F. O. & CO., Wholesale Paper, 1859.
SCHAEFER, GEO. W., Horse-shoer, 1861.
SLICER, W. C., Architect, 1870.
SPRAGUE & BUTLER, Restaurant, 1862.
STANBERY, IRA, JR., Agt. Cromos, 1875.
ST. LOUIS UNIVERSITY, 1829.
THORNBURGH, J. M'C., & CO., Grocers' Sundries, 1873.
TIVY & PURCELL, Gen'l Commission Merchants, 1856.
VERRIER, E. V., Spice Mills, 1841.
WALSH BROS., Grocers' Specialties, 1877.
WATKINS & GILLILAND, Hats and Caps, 1877.

INDIANAPOLIS.

ABSTRACTS OF TITLE.

WM. C. ANDERSON,
ABSTRACTS OF TITLE,
TO
Real Estate in Marion Co., Ind.
Moore's Block.
86 E. Market St., INDIANAPOLIS, IND.

AGRICULTURAL IMPLEMENTS.

PRIER, H. J., Agricultural Implements, 177 E. Washington st.

ARCHITECTS.

Bohlen & Roth,
ARCHITECTS,
BRANDON BLOCK,
INDIANAPOLIS, IND.

R. M. COSBY,
Practical Architect,
ROOM 65, VANCE BLOCK,
Indianapolis, Ind.

ENOS, B. V. & SON, Architects, 33 and 34 Talbott's block.

I. HODGSON,
ARCHITECT,
INDIANAPOLIS, - IND.
—:o:—
Established, 1856.

EDWIN MAY,
ARCHITECT & SUPERINTENDENT,
Plans furnished for
Fire-proof Court Houses, "May's Patent Jail," Residences, Stores, School Buildings, Churches, &c.,
Office, 5 and 6 Glenn's Block.

ASSESSOR.

BROUSE, D. W., Township Assessor, office in Court House.

ATTORNEYS AT LAW.

COULON, CHAS., Attorney and Counselor at Law, Notary Public, 27½ S. Delaware st

DOWNEY, A. C. & SONS, Attorneys at Law, Washington and Meridian sts.

1804.

Feb. 3.—Lieut. Decatur, with only 76 men, sails into the harbor of Tripoli, boards the Philadelphia, killed and drove into the sea all the Tripolitans defending her, set fire to the vessel, and returned to the American squadron without losing a man.

July 12.—Alexander Hamilton killed in a duel by Aaron Burr. The difficulty grew out of a political quarrel. Burr had been informed of some remarks made by Hamilton in public, derogatory to his character, and he demanded a retraction. Hamilton considered his demand unreasonable, and refused compliance. Burr challenged him to fight, and Hamilton reluctantly met him on the west side of the Hudson, near Hoboken, N. J., where they fought with pistols. Hamilton discharged his weapon in the air, but Burr took fatal aim, and his antagonist fell. Hamilton died the next day.

Brown University, R. I., established.

A large fire occurred in New York on Wall, Front, and Water streets. Forty or fifty houses were destroyed.

1805.

The Pennsylvania Academy of Fine Arts founded.

Michigan created into a Territory.

June 3.—The Pasha of Tripoli makes terms of peace.

Yellow fever pestilence in New York.

1806.

Cause of War in 1812.—England insists upon continuing the right to search American vessels for suspected deserters from the British navy. American seamen were thus forced into the British service, under the pretense that they were deserters. The British in persisting in this outrage upon American seamen brought on the war of 1812.

Treason of Burr.—During the summer of this year Aaron Burr organized military expeditions in the west, and the secrecy with which he carried on his operations, led the government to suspect that he designed to dismember the Union, and establish an independent empire west of the Alleghenies, with himself at the head.

1807.

Feb.—Aaron Burr arrested on the Tombigbee river, in the State of Alabama, on the charge of treason. He was tried at Richmond, Va., but the testimony showed that his probable design was an invasion of Mexican provinces, and then to establish an independent government. He was acquitted.

June 22.—The Chesapeake fired upon by the British frigate Leopard. The British demanded four seamen from the commander of the Chesapeake, claiming them as deserters from the British ship Melampus. Commodore Barron, not suspecting danger, and unprepared for an attack, surrendered the Chesapeake after losing three men killed and eighteen wounded.

July.—Proclamation issued ordering all British armed vessels to leave the waters of the United States, and forbidding any to enter until full satisfaction is given for the outrage on the United States frigate Chesapeake, and security against future aggressions should be made.

Nov. 11.—British in council issue an order prohibiting neutral nations trading with France, excepting upon paying a tribute to Great Britain; and France retaliates by issuing a

INDIANAPOLIS—Continued.

ATTORNEYS AT LAW.

J. ROSS DUBBS,

Attorney & Counselor

AT LAW,

Room 8, Fletcher & Sharp's Bank Bl'g,

Cor. Pennsylvania & Washington Sts.,

INDIANAPOLIS, IND.

GREEN & PEARSON, Lawyers, Room 4, Etna Building, 17 N. Pennsylvania st.

KELLOGG, JUSTIN A., Attorney at Law, 20½ N. Delaware st.

PARMELEE & NORTON, Attorneys at Law, Room 17, Hubbard's block.

S. L. ROWAN,

Authorized

U. S. CLAIM ATTORNEY,

36 W. Washington Street,

INDIANAPOLIS, IND.

WARRICK, JAMES W., Attorney at Law, Room 28, Vance block.

ARTIFICIAL LIMBS.

Artificial Limbs and Braces for Deformities.

172 EAST WASHINGTON ST.
Circulars sent free.

BAG MANUFACTURERS.

BUTLER, E. Y. & CO., Paper Bag Manufacturers, 215 E. Washington st.

BAKING POWDER.

CHURCHMAN & CO.,
Mnfrs. of Imperial Baking Powder,
Flavoring Extracts, Cream of Tartar, &c.
Est'd. 1875.   54 S. PENNSYLVANIA ST.

BARBERS.

BECKER, CHAS. T., Barber Shop.
13 Indiana ave.

INDIANAPOLIS—Continued.

BARBERS.

CIRCLE HOUSE BARBER SHOP, Brand & Harms, props., 19 N. Meridian st.

HARRIS, THOS. F., Barber and Hairdresser, 315 Indiana ave.

HILL, J. T. V., Barber Shop.
86 Indiana ave.

THE ENTERPRISE SHAVING & HAIRDRESSING Saloon, H. Jaeckel, prop., 84 Mass. ave.

PATTERSON, G. C., Barber Shop,
410 Indiana ave.

SUESS BROTHERS,
SHAVING PARLOR
153 E. Washington Street.
Ladies' and Children's Hair Shampooed and cut in the latest style at the shop or their residence. The Hair can be saved in straight and separate braids, and without loss in length.

TURNER, A., Shaving and Hairdressing Saloon, 51 Kentucky ave. Established, 1835.

BILL POSTERS.

HARBISON & ABRAMS,
CITY BILL POSTERS,
Large stands in all prominent parts of city.
OFFICE, Journal Building, Indianapolis.
Orders sent by mail or express to our address, promptly attended to.

BLACKSMITHS AND HORSESHOERS.

G. W. FORSHEE,
Blacksmithing, Horseshoeing
Plow & Wagon Repairing, Manufacturing, &c.,
Est'd 1864.   *32 S. Tennessee St.*

G. W. VAN ANTWERP,
Horseshoeing Shop!
302 E. Washington St., Indianapolis, Ind.
Established, 1862.

WOOD, CHAS. T. & CO., Blacksmithing and Horseshoeing, 281 W. Washington st.

BOARDING HOUSES.

BEVEL, MRS. SARAH, Boarding House, 271 W. Washington st.

MORGAN, MRS. SADIE M., Day Boarding House, 167 W. Washington st.

BOILER MANUFACTURER.

REAGAN, E., Boiler Manufacturer, 305 W. Washington st.

BOOKS AND STATIONERY.

BARTH & PRESTON, Stationery, Periodicals, Cigars, Tobacco and Fruits, 10 W. Louisiana st.

GOLDHAUSEN, FRANZ, German Bookseller and News Agent, 195 E. Washington st.

BOOTS AND SHOES.

CAMPLIN, DARROW & CO., Whole ale Boots and Shoes, 78 S. Meridian st. Est'd 1873.

ADVERTISEMENTS. 77

We constantly keep  on hand the celebrated
"H. M. WILMOT GOLD AND STEEL PENS,"
Which for Flexibility, Durability, Smoothness of Action, and Proper Shape, are not excelled by any other Pen manufactured. For Price List, etc., address, WILMOT, DEMING & BOYD, Madison, Wis.

Northwestern Business College.
INSTITUTE OF PENMANSHIP, TELEGRAPHY, AND CLASSICAL ACADEMY.

BIRDSEYE VIWE OF MADISON, WISCONSIN.—*Population in 1875, 11,500.*

Located in the city of Madison, Wisconsin, is one of the LEADING COLLEGES IN THE U. S. The Course taught is thorough and practical. For College Journal, containing full information, call upon, or address, WILMOT, DEMING & BOYD.

MADISON—Capital of the State of Wisconsin, and County seat of Dane Co. The city is pleasantly situated on an isthmus about three-fourths of a mile wide, between lakes Mendota and Monona, in the centre of a broad valley, surrounded by heights from which it can be seen at a distance of several miles. Lake Mendota lies northwest of the town, is six miles long, and four miles wide, with clean, gravelly shores, and a depth sufficient for steamboat navigation (estimated at about 60 feet).

78 IMPORTANT EVENTS OF THE CENTURY.

1807.

decree December 17, forbidding all trade with England or her colonies, and authorizing the confiscation of any vessel found in French ports which had submitted to English search, or paid the exacted tribute. These retaliating war measures between England and France almost destroyed American shipping trade abroad.

Dec. 22.—Congress decreed an embargo, which detained all vessels, American and foreign, in our ports, and ordered American vessels home immediately, that the seamen might be trained for war.

The first steamboat built in the world by Robert Fulton, in New York. It was named "Clermont," and made its first trip during this year from New York to Albany.

1808.

Jan. 1. - The importation of African slaves into the United States, prohibited by Congress. Commodore Barron, of the Chesapeake, tried and sentenced to be suspended for five years, on account of surrendering his vessel to the British in 1807.

1809.

March 1.—Congress repeals the embargo on shipping, and at the same time passes a law forbidding all commercial intercourse with England and France until their obnoxious restrictions on commerce shall be rev   ed.

March 4.—James Madison augurated President of the United State   nd George Clinton as Vice-President.

General Harrison concludes a treaty with the Miami Indians, by which the United States gets possession of a large tract of land on both sides of the Wabash.

1810.

Third census of the United States. Population, 7,239,814.

March 23.—France issued a decree which declared every American vessel which had entered French ports since March, 1810, or that might thereafter enter, as forfeited, and authorized the sale of the same, together with the cargoes, and money to be placed in the French treasury. Bonaparte justified this decree on the plea that it was made in retaliation for the American decree of non-intercourse.

May.—Congress offers to resume commercial relations with either France or England, or both, on condition that they repeal their obnoxious orders and decrees before March 3, 1811. France feigned compliance, and the United States resumed commercial intercourse with that nation. But American vessels continued to be siezed by French cruisers, and on March, 1811, Napoleon declared the obnoxious laws to still exist, and America thereafter ceased intercourse with that nation.

1811.

April 16.—Engagement between the American frigate, President, Commodore Rogers commanding, and the British sloop-of-war, Little Belt, Captain Bingham. The Little Belt was preying upon American merchantmen when hailed by Rogers, of the President, and received a cannon shot in reply. A brief action ensued, when Captain Bingham, after losing eleven men killed and twenty-one wounded, gave a satisfactory answer to Rogers. At this time, the American navy numbered only twelve large vessels of war; the British near nine hundred.

May 19.—A fire broke out near the corner

INDIANAPOLIS—*Continued.*

BOOTS AND SHOES.

J. W. Strong.   George Schopp.

CO-OPERATIVE
FASHIONABLE
Boot and Shoe Makers,
42 W. Maryland St., Indianapolis.
Repairing neatly and promptly done.

WM I. FISHER,
Custom
BOOT AND SHOE MAKER,
15 MASSACHUSETTS AVE.,
Indianapolis,   -   Indiana.
—:o:—
W. I. Fisher, formerly with Joseph Wert.

J. FOX,
Fashionable
BOOT AND SHOE MAKER,
175 SOUTH TENNESSEE ST.,
Repairing a Specialty.   Established 1873.

HART, C. H., Mf'r Boots and Shoes, 411 Indiana ave. All work warranted.

LUFT, WM. Manufacturer of Boots and Shoes, 264 W. Washington st.

MILLER, W. W., Dealer in Boots and Shoes, Washington and Illinois sts.

M. J. Murphy,
—PRACTICAL—
Boot and Shoe Maker,
59 INDIANA AVENUE.

Established 1871.

J. D. Nelson,
Manufacturer of
LADIES' AND GENTS' FASHIONABLE
Boots, Shoes and Gaiters,
Lasts made to order, a specialty.
21 Circle Street.

NOLAN, EDWARD, Boot and Shoe Store, 23 Indiana ave.

NUGUE, A., Boot and Shoe Maker, and Dealer in Cigars, 114 Illinois st.

L. PETERSON,
Manufacturer of
First-Class BOOTS
AND SHOES TO ORDER,
13 Madison Avenue.
Satisfaction Guaranteed.

INDIANAPOLIS—Continued.

BOOTS AND SHOES.

SCHULTE, JOHN, Custom Boot and Shoe Maker, 283 E. Washington st.

UPDEGRAFF, GEO. W., Boot and Shoe Maker, 235 E. Washington st.

WALTER, WM., Manufacturer of Boots and Shoes, 30 Kentucky av. All work warranted.

WEBB, GEO., Auction and Commission Merchant in Boots & Shoes. 61 S. Meridian st.

WEHLE, LUCAS, Manufacturer, and Dealer in Boots and Shoes. 194 E. Washington st.

BRASS FOUNDERS AND FINISHERS.

INDIANAPOLIS BRASS FOUNDRY, 106 and 108 S. Delaware st.   H. STACEY, Prop.

NEUBACHER, L., BRASS FOUNDER and Finisher, 90 E. Georgia st.

Rudolph Droessler,

Brass   Finisher,

96 S. DELAWARE ST.,

Indianapolis.

BUTTER, EGGS AND PRODUCE.

JONES, G. E., Dealer in Butter, Eggs, and Poultry, 24 Indiana ave.

STUART BROS., Dealers in Butter and Eggs, 37 Mass. ave. Cash paid for Country Produce.

CAR-WHEEL MANUFACTURERS.

Thomas May & Co.
Manufacturers of the Standard

Car
—AND LOCOMOTIVE—
Wheels,
Spoke Engine Truck Wheels a Specialty.
Cor. Tenth and Sheldon Sts.

CARPET DEALERS.

HAWKES, P. C., Manufacturer, and Dealer in Rag and Listing Carpets, 90½ Mass. Ave.

HOFFMAN & HUTCHINSON, Manufacturers and Dealers in Carpets, 14 E. Washington st.

CARPENTERS AND BUILDERS.

CHAMBERLAIN, J. H., Contractor and Builder, 223 N. Noble st. Est. 1857.

FULTON & VANCE, Plain & Fancy Fly-Screens for Doors and Windows, 241 & 243 Mass. ave.

JINKINS, JOHN, CARPENTER and Cabinet Maker, 26 E. South st.

Thomas Richards,
CONTRACTOR
—AND—
BUILDER,
129 E. Maryland Street,
Est. 1835.

IMPORTANT EVENTS OF THE CENTURY. 79

1811.
of Chatham and Duane streets, N. Y., and destroyed nearly one hundred buildings on both sides of Chatham street.

Nov. 11.—Battle of Tippecanoe. At four o'clock in the morning, the Indians attacked the American camp, commanded by Gen. Harrison, but after a bloody battle, lasting until dawn, the Indians were repulsed. The battle of Tippecanoe was one of the most desperate ever fought with the Indians, and the loss was heavy on both sides.

The British government declare the attack on the Chesapeake to have been unauthorized, and promised pecuniary aid to the families of those who were killed.

Dec. 27.—Burning of the Theatre at Richmond, Va. There were about 600 persons in the audience when the fire was first discovered. There was but one door for egress, and men, women and children were pressing upon each other to get out, while the flames were surging upon those behind. It is supposed there were 61 persons burned to death.

During this year, British orders for searching American vessels and impressing American seamen were rigorously enforced; insult after insult was offered the American flag, and the British press insolently boasted that the United States "could not be kicked into a war." A continuation of these outrages brought .the war of 1812.

1812.

War of 1812.—Congress passed an act empowering the President to enlist 25,000 men, accept 50,000 volunteers, and to call out 100,000 militia. Henry Dearborn appointed commander-in-chief.

British Government declared the whole American coast to be in a state of blockade, except that of the New England States. The apparent sympathy of these States with Great Britain caused the enemies of our country to think that they would secede from the Union; but, as the war progressed, it proved that their patriotism was was too stroog to admit of such a catastrophe.

June.—Mob in Baltimore. A newspaper, called the *Federal Republican*, was destroyed by a mob for uttering sentiments of censure on the conduct of the Government. Shortly after this affair, the paper made its appearance again, containing severe allusions to the mayor, police, and people of Baltimore for the depredations that had been committed upon the establishment. The office was again mobbed, and during the frequent discharge of muskets, Dr. Gale was killed, when the party in the office were finally escorted by the military to the county jail for protection against further violence. Shortly after dark, the mob assembled at the jail, carried the mayor away by force, and compelled the turnkey to open the door. General Lingan was killed: eleven were beaten and mangled with such weapons as stones, bludgeons, sledge-hammers, etc., and thrown as dead into one pile. Mr. Hanson, editor of the paper, fainting from repeated wounds, was carried away by a gentleman of opposite political sentiments, at the risk of his life. No effectual inquiry was ever made into this violation of the law, and the guilty escaped punishment.

First house in Rochester, N. Y., built.

April 8.—Louisiana admitted as a State.

April 12.—Death of George Clinton, Vice-President of the United States.

G. F. REBER,
Watch Maker and Jeweler,
AND DEALER IN
Watches, Clocks, Jewelry and Spectacles.
84 Virginia Avenue, Indianapolis.
Special attention given to all work done. All Goods sold Engraved free of charge.

RICHMOND EDGE TOOL MANUFACTURING COMPANY,

MANUFACTURERS OF THE CELEBRATED
RICHMOND EDGE TOOLS
One Square West of Union Depot, RICHMOND, IND.
Repairing promptly attended to. SPECIALTIES—Axes, Hatchets, Butchers' and R. R. Tools.

FULTON BOILER WORKS,
ESTABLISHED 1876.
JERRY COWHIC, Proprietor.
(Late Foreman Boiler Maker of Robinson Machine Works.)
North of Union Depot, RICHMOND, IND.
Steam Boilers of every Description,
Lard Tanks and Coolers, Smoke Stacks and Brichings, Plate Iron Work of all Kinds. Second-Hand Boilers bought and sold. Repairing promptly attended to, at hard-pan prices.

Estimates furnished on application.   Send for Circular.

| J. B. MESSINGER. | R. A. PROSEUS. | J. A. HERMAN. |

MESSINGER, PROSEUS, & CO.,
ESTABLISHED 1862.
Manufacturers and Wholesale and Retail Dealers in the
Improved Stone Cylinder Pump,

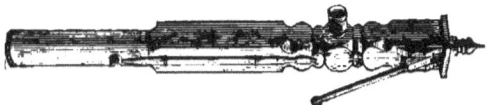

Porcelain Lined and the Old Style Wood Pump. Well and Drain Pipe Furnished to Order.
Factory, Cor. Elm and Duret Sts., LOGANSPORT, IND.

GRAND HOTEL,
Indianapolis, Ind.

T. Baker.
T. B. Wightman.   **T. BAKER & CO.**

The only Hotel in the City with Passenger Elevator and all Modern Improvements. **Rates reduced to $3.00 per day.** Extra for Rooms with Bath.

Charles W. Dauer,
House, Sign and Ornamental

PAINTER,

Paper Hanging, Decorating, Calsomining, Wall Tinting, Graining, Glazing, Varnishing, &c.

No. 127 East Maryland Street,
INDIANAPOLIS.

R. R. ROUSE,
Inventor of Improved Driven Wells,
And Agent for all Kinds of

Well, Cistern, Lift and Force Pumps, Tubing Filter Points, and all Improved Tools for Well Drivers,

Steam Fittings, Rubber Hose and Packing, Niagara Steam Pumps and Engines.

Store, No. 19 W. Maryland St., Indianapolis, Ind.

STRATA VIEW OF DRIVEN WELL.

1812.

June 4.—War with England. A bill declaring war to exist between the United States and Great Britain, passed the House of Representatives, by a vote of 79 to 49. On the 17th, it passed the Senate by a vote of 19 to 13, and on that day it received the signature of the President. He issued his war manifesto two days afterward.

July 12.—Gen. Hull crosses the Detroit river to attack Fort Malden. He encamped at Sandwich, and by this fatal delay, lost every advantage which an immediate attack might have secured.

July 17.—Fort Mackinaw, one of the strongest posts of the United States, was surprised and captured by an allied force of British and Indians.

Aug. 5.—Maj. Van Horne, while escorting a supply party to camp, was defeated by some British and Indians, near Brownstown, on the Huron river.

Aug. 7.—Gen. Hull retires from Canada and takes his post at Detroit.

Aug. 13.—The Essex, Captain Porter, captures the Alert, the first vessel taken from the British during that war.

Aug. 16.—Hull surrenders Detroit to the British. The English were commanded by Brock, consisting of 700 troops and 600 Indians.

Aug. 19.—U. S. frigate, Constitution, Commodore Isaac Hull, captures the British frigate, Guerriere. The contest lasted about forty minutes when the commander of the Guerriere surrendered his vessel, which was so completely wrecked that she was burned. The Constitution suffered little damage and was ready for action the following day.

Sept. 10—Perry's victory on Lake Erie.

Oct. 13.—Queenstown Heights on the Canada frontier, captured by 225 Americans under command of Col. Van Renselear. Van Renselear was wounded at the landing, and Capt. Wood took command and successfully assaulted and took possession of the Heights.

Oct. 13—Gen. Brock, with 600 British troops, from Fort George, attempted to regain the battery at Queenstown Heights but was repulsed and Brock was killed. In the meantime Gen Stephen Van Renselear was using his utmost endeavors to send reinforcements, but only 1,000 undisciplined troops could be induced to cross the river. These were attacked by fresh troops from Fort George and nearly all killed or made prisoners, while at least 1,500 of their companions in arms cowardly refused to cross to their aid.

Oct. 18.—U. S. sloop-of-war, Wasp, Capt. Jones, captures the British brig Frolic, after a very severe conflict for three-quarters of an hour. Only three officers and one seaman, of 84 of the crew of the Frolic remained unhurt. The Wasp lost only ten men. The same afternoon the British ship Poictiers, carrying 74 guns, captured the Wasp.

Oct. 25.—The frigate United States, Commodore Decatur, captures the British frigate Macedonia. The fight lasted near two hours. The British lost more than 100 in killed and wounded, and Decatur lost only five killed and seven wounded. The frigate United States was very little injured.

During this year, it is estimated that upwards of 50 British armed vessels and 250 merchantmen, with an aggregate of more than

INDIANAPOLIS—*Continued.*

CARRIAGE AND WAGON MAKERS.

BLACK & BACKUS, Carriages and Spring Wagons, 36, 38 and 44 E. Maryland st.

BREMERMAN, F. & CO., Carriages and Farm Wagons, 86 and 88 E. New York st. Est. 1862.

DREW & WADDELL, Carriages, Buggies and Phaetons, 123 and 125 N. Delaware st.

Fred. Gessert,

Manufacturer of

CARRIAGES & WAGONS,

AND

BLACKSMITHING.

353 Madison Avenue.

Prompt attention to Repairing and General Jobbing. Horse-shoeing promptly done. Est. 1854.

HELFER, A. A., Carriages, Buggies and Spring Wagons, 26-30 Tennessee st.

SCHWEIKLE, & PRANGE, Manufacturers of Carriages & Wagons, 424 & 426 E. Washington st.

Carl H. Wehling,

BLACKSMITH

—AND—

WAGON-MAKER,

326 S. DELAWARE STREET.

Particular attention paid to Horse-shoeing, and General Jobbing and Repairing. Est. 1857.

CASH REGISTER.

HOOD, H. P., Manufacturer CASH REGISTER and Novelties, 84 W. Market st.

CHINA, GLASS AND CROCKERY.

BERGUNDTHAL, CHARLES, Glass and Queensware, 68 N. Illinois st.

HOLLWEG & REESE, China, Glass, and Queensware, 96 and 98 S. Meridian st. Est. 1868.

CIGAR-BOX MANUFACTORY.

BERNS, F. G., Manufacturer of Cigar Boxes, 247 E. Morris st.

CLOTHING.

THE WHEN CLOTHING STORE, 5 and 6 Bates Block, N. Penna. st.

COMMISSION MERCHANTS.

BLAKE, JACKSON & QUINIUS, Commission Merchants, 75 and 77 W. Washington st.

BUDD, J. R. & CO., Commission Merchants in Butter, Eggs, etc., 25 W. Pearl st. Est. 1869.

COMINGORE & CO.,

Wholesale Dealers in

Feathers, Rags, Beeswax & Produce.

Commission Merchants,

21 W. MARYLAND STREET.

LAWRENCE, A. V., General Commission Merchant, 173 W. Washington st.

IMPORTANT EVENTS OF THE CENTURY. 83

INDIANAPOLIS—*Continued.*

COMMISSION MERCHANTS.

Poor & Bliebel,

COMMISSION MERCHANTS

72 S. Delaware St.

Established, 1870.

S AEIVAY, H. J., Oat Meal, Pearl Barley and Wheat Flour, etc., 163 Mass. ave.

S ULLIVAN, JOHN E., Produce and Commission Merchant, 23 Circle st.

S YERUP, HENRY & SON, Commission Merchants in Fruits, Vegetables & Produce, 23 S. Del. st.

Samuel Woodruff,

COMMISSION MERCHANT,

BUTTER, EGGS, POULTRY, GAME, ETC.,

137 Massachusetts Ave.

Correspondence Solicited. All Letters of Enquiry promptly answered.

CONCERT SALOONS.

JOHN H. GRUENERT,

Billiard and Concert Hall,

Choice Wines, Liquors and Cigars,

68 East Washington Street,

INDIANAPOLIS, IND.

City Garden Varieties!

156 E. Washington St.

INDIANAPOLIS.

JACOB CRONE, Prop.

⁂ First-class Entertainment Every Evening.

CONFECTIONERS.

Bidwell's Trade-mark.

"Father, I can't tell a lie."

Bidwell's Wild Cherry Cough Candy!

25 Cents a Box.

Is perfectly harmless, contains no drugs, and will cure a Night Cough in ten minutes.

Retail Department, 42 N. Pennsylvania St. Opposite Post Office.

M IESSEN, JULIUS, Wholesale and Retail Confectionery, 180 Virginia ave.

S HANNAN, MRS. L. S., News Depot, Dealer in Tobacco and Cigars, 119 Massachusetts ave.

1812.

3,000 prisoners, and a vast amount of booty, were captured by the Americans.

Dec. 29.—Commodore Bainbridge, commanded the frigate Constitution, after three hours fighting, captured the British frigate Java, off San Salvador. The Java had 400 men on board, of whom almost 200 were killed or wounded, and she was so badly crippled that Bainbridge, finding her incapable of floating, burned her three days after the action. The Constitution was very little damaged.

1813.

Jan. 17.—The British frigate Narcissus captured the United States schooner Viper.

Jan. 22.—Americans defeated at Frenchtown, about 25 miles south of Detroit. A combined force, under Proctor, of 1,500 British and Indians, fell upon the American camp, commanded by Gen. Winchester, at dawn. After a severe battle and heavy loss on both sides, Winchester, who was made prisoner by the Indians, surrendered his troops on condition that ample protection should be given. Proctor, fearing the approach of Harrison, immediately marched for Malden, leaving the sick and wounded Americans behind, who were afterwards murdered and scalped by the Indians.

Feb. 22.—Ogdensburg, N. Y., taken by the British.

Feb. 24.—United States sloop-of-war, Hornet, Capt. Lawrence, engages the British brig, Peacock, off the mouth of Demara river, South America. The Peacock surrendered after a conflict of fifteen minutes, and a few moments afterward she sunk, carrying down with her nine British seamen and three Americans. The loss of the Peacock in killed and wounded was 37; of the Hornet only 5.

April 25.—Mobile taken by a body of the American army.

April 27.—Americans capture York (now Toronto). The Americans landed about two miles west of the British works, and in the face of a galling fire from regulars and Indians, under Gen. Sheaffe, drove them back to their fortifications. The British retreated from the fort, but laid a train of wet powder to the magazine, and set fire to it, and while Gen. Pike, was pressing forward, the fort blew up, causing great destruction of life among the Americans. Gen. Pike was mortally wounded, but he lived long enough to know that the American flag floated in triumph over the fort at Toronto. Gen. Sheaffe escaped with the principal part of the troops, but lost all his baggage, books, papers, and a large amount of public property.

May 2.—British repulsed at Fort Sandusky, Ohio. The garrison of the fort consisted of 150 young men, commanded by Major Croghan, was assaulted by 500 regulars and 800 Indians, under Gen. Proctor. The British recoiled, panic-stricken, and fled in confusion, leaving 150 of their killed and wounded. American loss, 1 man killed and 7 wounded.

May 3.—Havre de Grace, Md., burned by the British blockading squadron.

May.—Unsuccessful seige of Fort Meigs, on the Maumee river, by the British. Gen. Clay, commanding 1,200 men, arrived with reinforcements for the fort and dispersed the enemy, but imprudently pursuing the fugitives, was surrounded and captured. Proctor returned to the siege, but his Indian allies under Tecumseh, becoming impatient, deserted him, and the siege was abandoned.

INDIANAPOLIS—Continued.

COPPERSMITH.

Established 1868.
WM. LANGSENKAMP,

COPPERSMITH,

And Manufacturer of all kinds of
COPPER WORK FOR BREWERS, DISTILLERS, CONFECTIONERS, HOTELS AND DYE WORKS,
Soda Fountains, Generators and Apparatus on hand.

96 S. DELAWARE ST.

CORNICE WORKS.

KLUGEL & HINKLEY, Indianapolis Cornice Works, 198 S. Pennsylvania st.

CRADLE AND SCYTHE SNATHS.

E. W. TUCKER,
Manufacturer of

Grain Cradles, Scythe Snaths

Etc., Etc.

NORTH INDIANAPOLIS, IND.

CUTLERS AND GRINDERS.

H. KNECHT,

Dealer in Cutlery,

All kinds of

Grinding and Repairing of Edge Tools,

99 EAST WASHINGTON ST.

PISCATOR, AUGUST. Steam Grinding Establishment, Delaware and Georgia sts.

DENTIST.

SUTHERLAND, W. H., Dentist. Laughing Gas used. Established 1865. 70 N. Illinois st.

DIAMOND SETTER.

L. SCHAFER,

Diamond Setter

And Manufacturing Jeweler,

83 1-2 E. WASHINGTON ST., Second Floor.

REPAIRING NEATLY DONE.

DRUGGISTS.

CARTER & FLETCHER, Drugs and Medicines, 300 Massachusetts ave.

W. M. HAAG'S
PHARMACY,
82 MASSACHUSETTS AVE.,
INDIANAPOLIS.

—o—

☞ Prescriptions a Specialty.

INDIANAPOLIS—Continued.

DRUGGISTS.

POWELL & ALLEN, Druggists, cor. Illinois and Market sts.

TRAUB, GEO. F. & CO., Apothecaries, 252 W. Washington st.

DRY GOODS.

BYRAM, CORNELIUS & CO., Wholesale Dry Goods and Notions, 101-105 S. Meridian st.

HODGES, D. J., Dry Goods, Notions and Fancy Goods, 298 Massachusetts ave.

DYEING AND SCOURING.

CINCINNATI
DYEING, CLEANING & REPAIRING HOUSE

31 EAST CIRCLE ST.,

INDIANAPOLIS, - - - IND.

Wm. Goebler, Prop.

All work warranted and done in the best manner.

EDGE TOOL MANUFACTURER.

I. ALTHOUSE,

Manufacturer of Edge Tools,

Such as Planing, Carriage Maker's and Shingle Knives, Moulding Bits, Carpenter's and Cooper's Tools.

Mill Picks and Axes made and repaired in the best manner. All work warranted.

FACTORY, 191 South Meridian St.

ELECTROTYPE FOUNDRY.

INDIANAPOLIS

NEW JOURNAL BUILDING.
KETCHAM & WANAMAKER PROPRIETORS.
Entrance on Circle Street.

ELECTRICITY.

D. KITSON,

Electricity for Medical Use.

Rooms at 31 Kentucky Avenue.

GUARANTEED TO CURE CHILLS & FEVER.

It cures Rheumatism, Toothache, Headache, Neuralgia, and all diseases arising from Nervousness, Skin Diseases, etc.

ENGINEERS AND SURVEYORS.

FATOUT, H. B., County Surveyor and Civil Engineer, New Court House.

HOSBROOK, D. B. & J. A., Civil Engineers, Room 16, Hubbard block.

ADVERTISEMENTS. 85

Court House, Pittsburgh, Pa.—This is a handsome building, situated at the corner of Fifth Avenue and Grant Street. It is built of solid stone, with a columned portico, surmounted with a dome.

Fifth Street Henry's Free Lunch,
108 N. FIFTH ST., near Chestnut, ST. LOUIS, MO.

SOUP.
Whalebone.   Lampwick.   Cork.   Sponge.
FISH.
Blind Herring.   Red Herring.   Cross-eyed Herring.
COLD DISHES.
Broken Ice.   Ice Berg.   Raw Ice.   Cold Ice.
ROAST.
Chickens 48 years old.   Scared Crow.   Goose.
GAME.
Tiger. Smut. Old Maid. Don Pedro. Seven Out. Pitch. Keno. Euchre. Pool. Poker. Casino.
TONGUE.
Vinegar Sauce.   Mother-in-Law Tongue.
Son-in-Law's Sass.
ENTREES.
Spider Toes.   Locusts on the Half Shell.
Raked Chignons.   Horse Blankets, Fricaseed.
Hair Pins on Toast.
VEGETABLES.
Tight Boot Corns.   Hard Corns.   Soft Corns.
Corn Cobs.
PASTRY.
Leather Pies, with Buckles.   Sponge Pies, Cut Bias.   Sawdust Pudding, a la Pine Sauce.
DESERTS.
Yeast Cakes.   Door Jam.   Grind-Stone Ice Cream.
FRUITS, NUTS, ETC.
Hog's Foot Gum Drops.   Raw Onions.
Boiled Acorns.   Horse Chestnuts.   Osage Oranges.
LIQUIDS.
Mississippi River Water.   St. Louis Water.
Salt Water.   Soda Water.   Hard Water.
Soft Water.   N-Ice Water.   Congress Water.

ITS MANY ADVANTAGES.
:0:

THE HENRY SALOON, is the most respectful part of the city, has been refitted for the accommodation of the citizens and traveling public.

On entering the Saloon, each gentleman will be asked how he likes the location, and if he says HENRY'S SALOON ought to have been placed somewhere else, the location will be immediately changed. The most comfortable seat in the room for each gent; daily papers from all parts of the country; piano and telegraph in each corner of the Saloon; drinks every minute if required; consequently no time lost; waiters of every nationality and color if desired; every waiter furnished with a librette button-hole bouquet, full dress suit of ball tablers and his hair parted in the middle. Every patron of HENRY'S SALOON will have the best seat and the best waiter in the Saloon.

Any gent not getting his drinks red hot or ice cold as desired or experiencing a delay of ten seconds after giving his order will please mention the fact to the proprietor, and the bar-keepers and waiters will be blown from the mouth of a cannon in front of HENRY'S SALOON at once.

A discreet porter who belongs to the Masons, Odd Fellows, Sons of Malta, Knights of Pythias and Ku Klux, and who was known to tell the truth or the time of the day, has been employed to carry Milk Punches, Hot Toddies and Lemonades to the Ladies in any part of the town.

The bar-keeper has been carefully selected to please everybody, and can lead to song, play draw poker, shake or drinks at any hour of the day or night, play billiards, good waltzer, can dance the German, and make a fourth at euchre, repeat the Beecher trial from memory, is a good judge of horses, and as a railroad reference, is far superior to Appleton's or any other man's guide, will flirt with any young lady and not mind being cut to death when "Pa comes around" and dont mind being damned any more than the Mississippi river, can eat forty guests at once, and give every gentleman the best drink in the house, and answer all questions in Greek, Hebrew, Choctaw, Sioux, Irish, German, or any polite language at the same moment without turning a hair. Dogs allowed to lie on the Brussels carpet or in the w(h)ine room.

Gentlemen can drink, smoke, swear, chew gum, gamble, tell shady stories, stare at strangers, or any innocent amusement common in saloons.

The proprietor will always be happy to hear that some other saloon is the best in the country.

Special attention given to parties who can give information as to how nicely and differently things are set up at other places.

This Card is good for the best drink at the bar on payment of the usual price.

THEODOR BRUEGGESTRADT,
108 N. Fifth St., near Chestnut,
St. Louis, Mo.

1813.

May 27.—Fort George, on the western shore of Niagara river, near its mouth, surrendered to the Americans.

May 29.—British repulsed at Sackett's Harbor. Sir George Prevost and 1,000 soldiers landed in the face of a severe fire from some regulars stationed there. Gen. Brown, commander, rallied the militia, and their rapid gathering so alarmed Prevost, that he hastily re-embarked, leaving almost the whole of his wounded behind.

June 1.—"*Don't give up the ship!*" Capt. Lawrence, now in command of the frigate Chesapeake encountered the British frigate Shannon, about 30 miles from Boston. A furious action commenced which lasted only fifteen minutes. In that short time the Chesapeake lost 48 killed and 98 wounded; the Shannon 23 killed and 56 wounded. Lawrence, with his second officer in command, Ludlow, were among the slain at the beginning of the action; and, when Lawrence was carried below, he issued those brave and ever memorable words : "Don't give up the ship." During the contest the two vessels became entangled, and the British boarded the Chesapeake, and, after a desperate hand-to-hand struggle, hoisted the British flag. The remains of Lawrence, together with Ludlow's, were carried to Halifax and buried with the honors of war.

June 6.—British attack American camp at Stony Creek, Canada West, and were repulsed. It was very dark, and in the confusion both of the American generals (Chandler and Winder) were made prisoners. American loss in killed, wounded and missing, 154.

June 23.—Admiral Cockburn defeated at Craney Island.

June.—Gen. Dearborn, on account of ill-health, retires from commander-in-chief of the army, and is succeeded by General Wilkinson.

Aug. 14.—British sloop-of-war Pelican captures the American brig Argus.

Aug. 30.—Fort Mimms, on the Alabama river, surprised and captured by a large body of Indians, under Tecumseh, who massacred about 300 men, women, and children.

Sept. 5.—British brig Boxer, Captain Blythe, encounters American brig Enterprise, Lieut. Burrows, and after an engagement of forty minutes, off the coast of Maine, the Boxer surrendered. Both commanders were slain, and their bodies were buried in one grave at Portland.

Sept. 10.—Perry's victory on Lake Erie. The carnage of this engagement, was very great. The Lawrence, Perry's flag ship, was soon disabled and became unmanageable, having all her crew, except four or five, killed or wounded. Perry then left her, in an open boat, and hoisted his flag on the Niagara. With this vessel he passed through the enemy's line, pouring broadsides right and left at half pistol-shot distance. The American loss, 27 killed and 96 wounded. The British lost about 200 in killed and wounded, and 600 prisoners. The British were commanded by Commodore Barclay.

Sept. 29.—Detroit evacuated by Proctor, and taken possession of by the Americans.

Oct. 5.—Battle of the Thames in Canada. Gen. Harrison, with 3,500 men, overtook Proctor in his retreat from Detroit, about 80 miles from that city. A desperate battle ensued.

INDIANAPOLIS—*Continued.*

FANCY GOODS AND NOTIONS.

BARGAIN STORE.

S. CROMBACH,
Cheap Notions & Fancy Goods,
50 INDIANA AVENUE,
Corner Tennessee St.

BOOTH, WM., Manufacturer of Stockings, Shirts and Drawers, 145 N. Delaware st.

OPDYCKE, TERRY & STEELE, White Goods, Laces, etc., 375 Broadway, N. Y. Represented by Geiger, Finney & Co., 112½ S. Meridian st.

FLOUR AND FEED.

HARTMANN & CO., Flour, Feed and General Commission, 216 S. Meridian st.

Edmund B. Noel.   Wood Noel.

NOEL BROS.,
Wholesale and Retail Dealers in

FLOUR, MEAL AND FEED,
Brands, White Rose & New Process,

47 & 49 North Tennessee St.,
Corner Market.

City Agt's for Gibson's Celebrated Flour

RHOADES, H. C., Flour and Feed Store, 254 Massachusetts ave.

WEST END FEED STORE, Catt & Co., props., 263 W. Washington st.

FURNITURE.

M^cCLAIN, J. A., New and Second-hand Furniture, 83 E. Washington st.

GROCERS.

BARCKDALL, D., Staple and Fancy Groceries, 255 W. Washington st.

BROWN, J. G., Groceries and Provisions, 300 N. New Jersey st.

BURNS, WM., Groceries and Provisions, 206 W. Walnut st.

DAVIS, J. E., Tea and Grocery Store, 169 E. Washington st.

KELLER, ROBERT, Grocery and Provision Dealer, 125 E. Washington st.

MALEY, JAS., Groceries and Provisions, 306 W. Washington st.

OWSLEY, W. A. & SON, Staple and Fancy Groceries, 300 W. Washington st.

SYFERS, M'BRIDE & COOK, Wholesale Grocers 131 S. Meridian st.

"ROLLING MILL GROCERY,"

C. WATERMAN,
Dealer in

Groceries, Flour and Feed,
Cor. *South and Tennessee Sts.*

ZIMMER, PETER, Groceries, Provisions and Saloon, 299 S. Delaware st.

INDIANAPOLIS—*Continued.*

HARDWARE AND CUTLERY.

CAYLOR, J., Hardware and Cutlery, 296 Massachusetts avenue.

HANSON, VAN CAMP & CO., Hardware, Cutlery and Iron, Steel, etc., 80 S. Meridian st.

ROSS, JAMES A., Hardware and Cutlery, 179 Indiana ave.

HARNESS AND SADDLES.

ARNHOLTER, H., Harness & Saddles, Bridles, Collars, whips, etc., 578 Virginia ave.

FETTY, A. H., Dealer in Saddles and Harness, 248 W. Washington st.

J. M. HUFFER,
(MANAGER,)
Manufacturer, and Dealer in
HARNESS and SADDLES,
23 S. Meridian Street.
Established 1862.

M. E. KING & CO.,
Manufacturers, and Dealers in
Harness, Saddles, Etc., Etc.
231 MASS. AVENUE.
Repairing promptly attended to.

F. M. ROTTLER,
Manufacturer, and Dealer in
Harness, Saddles and Horse Clothing.
All work warranted.
18 N. DELAWARE STREET.

SCHULTZ, H. C., Harness and Saddlery, 15 S. Meridian st. Est. 1873.

HATS AND CAPS.

REYNOLDS, C. E., Hats, Caps and Men's Furnishing Goods, 196 E. Washington st.

HOTELS.

BROADWAY HOUSE,
35 WEST GEORGIA STREET,
One Block N. of Union Depot,
· J. C. Clawson, Proprietor.

☞ This house has been renovated and newly furnished throughout. Good Sample rooms, and rates reasonable.

CARNEY HOUSE, 272 W. Maryland st. Est. 1865. J. R. CARNEY, Prop.

CIRCLE HOUSE, European Plan. 15 N. Meridian st. GEO. RODIUS, Prop.

GRAND HOTEL, cor. Illinois and Maryland sts., T. BAKER & Co., Prop's.

LITTLE'S HOTEL, New Jersey and Washington sts. J. FITZGERALD, Prop.

M'KAY, SAMUEL, HOTEL and Restaurant, 6 and 8 Louisiana st.

1813.

Tecumseh was slain, and his followers, who fought furiously, broke and fled. Almost the whole of Proctor's command were killed or made prisoners, and the General himself narrowly escaped with a few of his cavalry.

Nov. 3.—Gen. Coffee, with 900 men, surrounds an Indian camp near where the village of Jacksonville, Benton county, Alabama, now stands, and killed 200 of them. Not a warrior escaped.

Nov. 5.—Americans again invade Canada, 7,000 strong, with the intention of co-operating with about 4,000 troops under Hampton, in an attack on Montreal.

Nov. 11.—Battle of Chrysler's Field, about ninety miles above Montreal, on the St. Lawrence river. This battle was fought by a detachment under General Brown, who was sent to disperse the British at Williamsburg, and cover the descent of boats carrying American troops on the St. Lawrence. Americans lost more than 300 men in killed and wounded, and the British about 200.

Dec. 10.—General McClure, commanding at Fort George, burnt the Canadian village of Newark, and two days after was compelled by the British to abandon the fort.

Dec. 19.—Fort Niagara captured by a strong force of British and Indians, and, in retaliation for the burning of Newark, set fire and destroyed Youngstown, Lewistown, Manchester (now Niagara Falls), and the Tuscorora Indian village, in Niagara county.

Dec. 30.—Buffalo and the little village of Black Rock laid in ashes, and a large amount of public and private property destroyed.

The remains of Captain James Lawrence, who died from wounds received on board of the United States frigate, Chesapeake, in 1813, were removed from Halifax and interred in Trinity church yard, N. Y., with imposing ceremony.

Power loom introduced in the United States.

During the spring and summer Admiral Cockburn, with a small squadron, carried on a distressing warfare on the coast between Delaware Bay and Charleston. The shipping in the Delaware was destroyed, and Lewistown cannonaded; Frenchtown, Havre de Grace, Georgetown, and Frederickstown, on the Chesapeake, were plundered and burned.

1814.

March 27.—General Jackson attacked and defeated the Indians at the Great Horse-Shoe Bend, on the Tallapoosa river. The Indians had assembled there, in a fortified camp, 1,000 warriors strong, with their women and children, determined to make a desperate defense. They fought bravely, and almost 600 of his warriors were killed, as they refused to surrender. Only two or three were made prisoners, with about 300 women and children. Among those who bowed in submission was Weathersford, their greatest leader. He appeared suddenly before Jackson, in his tent, and standing erect said: "I am in your power; do with me what you please. I have done the white people all the harm I could. I have fought them bravely. My warriors are all gone now, and I can do no more. When there was a chance for success I never asked for peace. There is none now, and I ask for it for the remnant of my nation."

March 28.—United States frigate Essex,

OPIUM

3000

Testimonials of Persons CURED.

Send for Magazine and Test of Time Mailed Free.

I REFER TO A FEW OUT OF THE MANY HUNDREDS WHOM I HAVE CURED.

ILLINOIS.
Mary A. Badger, Waukegan, March 9th, 1873.
J. Ed. Clark, Grayville, Oct. 27th, 1873.
S. P. Guin, Jacksonville, Nov. 29 h, 1872.
Charles Green, Tallula, January 8th, 1877.
Amy S. Green, Dwight, December 26 h, 1876.
George C. Howe, Knoxville.
Mrs. L. D. Hitchcock, Ottawa, October 10, 1872.
S. H. Jillson, Freeport, May 29th, 1872.
Thomas Moss, Grayville, August 20th, 1872.
H. N. Stoddard, Joliet, May 3d, 1872.
Wm. Sanderson, Prophetstown, Dec. 5th, 1872.

VIRGINIA.
James M. Brown, M. D., Suffolk.
C. H. Williams, Portsmouth, Sept. 6th, 1875.

MISSOURI.
John Donaldson, Ironton, Nov. 11th, 1872.
John B. Howard, M. D., St. Joseph, Jan. 20, 1870.
E. H. Spalding, Kansas City, Sept. 6th, 1874.

OHIO.
Jacob Ambrosier, Sulphur Springs, April 24, 1874.
Jennie D. Bracken, Jersey, Jan. 2d, 1877.
B. B. DePeyster, Kent, Jan. 20th, 1874.
Wm. Sheffield, Napoleon, Dec. 10th, 1874.
J. J. Will, Piqua, Oct. 28th, 1875.

PENNSYLVANIA.
Mrs. H. S. Brown, Factoryville, Sept. 8th, 1873.
Mrs. E. A. Hamilton, Brookland, May 19th, 1875.

MISSISSIPPI.
W. L. Towner, Lake Station, Nov. 21st, 1872.

RHODE ISLAND.
Elisha C. Clarke, Kingston, Feb. 1st, 1874.

KANSAS.
Mrs. J. F. Cummings, Topeka.

NORTH CAROLINA.
James W. Davis, Mount Airy.
James Hatsell, Mount Airy.

CANADA.
John Darling, Wallaceburg.

MICHIGAN.
Joseph C. Darrow, Adrian, April 18th, 1860.
Carlie Edson, Hart, Dec. 15th, 1873.
Daniel Munger, Grass Lake, Oct., 29th, 1875.

CALIFORNIA.
Mrs. George Hobson, San Jose, Nov. 6th, 1875.
R. F. Scott, San Francisco, Oct. 4th, 1872.

LOUISIANA.
Jacob Hardy, Cotile Landing, Red River, Feb. 4, '74.

TENNESSEE.
W. Y. C. Hannum, Marysville, Nov. 10th, 1872.
J. R. Leonard, Jalapa.
H. Zellner, Brentwood, April 10th, 1874.

ARKANSAS.
J. R. Henry, M. D., Noark, Jan. 30th, 1877.

INDIANA.
T. M. Endicott, Shelbyville, Jan. 31st, 1874.
James Hart, Greensburg, Feb. 6th, 1873.
Luman Jones, Marietta, Nov. 28th, 1872.
D. J. Jackson, Rensselaer, July, 30 h, 1873.
John McLain, Union Mills, June 1st, 1875.
Robert McNeil, Pierceton, Nov. 7th, 1873.
Harriet Townsley, Crawfordsville, Jan. 20th, 1874.
T. M. Worthington, Lafayette, Dec. 20th, 1876.

GEORGIA.
Mollie E. Duke, Franklin, Jan. 20th, 1875.
J. T. Allen, Carr's Station, Jan. 7th, 1877.

WISCONSIN.
D. M. Loy, Depere.
Sophronia Palmer, Evansville, April 8th, 1874.

TEXAS.
H. D. Phillips, Atlanta, Feb. 20th, 1876.
W. A. Tuttle, Canton, November 18th, 1875.

IOWA.
B. B. Reynolds, De Soto.
L. S. Spitler, Danville, June 3d, 1876.
Joseph Coler, Nashua, February 21st, 1874.

VERMONT.
Lorenzo Fassett, West Enosburgh, May 25th, '76.
James Whitney, Bristol, January 1st, 1876.
H. Williams, Wallingford, Feb. 10th, 1873.

INDIAN TERRITORY.
James S. Price, Tahlequah, July 25th, 1873.

WEST VIRGINIA.
A. G. Pickett, Parkersburg, July 25th, 1876.

NEW YORK.
Chas. Beardsley, New Berlin, Jan. 28th, 1873.
Julia A. Caster, Rochester, Aug. 6th, 1874.
Nash Dyke, West Bangor, April 30th, 1874.
R. C. Hall, Groton.
David McClure, Franklinsville, Dec. 30th, 1875.
Mrs. Levi McNall, Allegany, Dec. 29th, 1876.
Mrs. M. M. Smith, Albion, July 8th, 1875.
Marcus P. Norton, Troy, Jan. 10th, 1874.

CONNECTICUT.
J. B. Blair, 28 Crown St., New Haven, Dec. 9, '74.

KENTUCKY.
Susan A. Bibb, Greensburg, Jan. 6th, 1877.

MASSACHUSETTS.
Joseph Cooper, Braytonville, March 2d, 1873.

ALABAMA.
B. F. Cannon, Marion, October 26th, 1874.
J. W. Morland, Brush Creek, Sept. 6th, 1875.

ADDRESS

DR. S. B. COLLINS,

LAPORTE, IND.

ADVERTISEMENTS.

Art Exhibition Hall, Centennial Exposition, Philadelphia.—The building is in the modern form. The materials are granite, glass and iron. No wood is used in the construction. The building is 365 feet in length, 210 feet in width, and 59 feet in height. The dome is 150 feet from the ground. It is of glass and iron, and of a unique design. It terminates in a colossal bell, from which the figure of Columbia rises with protecting hands. A figure of colossal size stands at each corner of the base of the dome. These figures typify the four quarters of the globe. The building will remain as a permanent exhibition hall on the grounds. The cost of the building was $1,500,000.

Ph. OPPERGELT,

Corner Cass and Hamilton Sts., **SAGINAW CITY, MICH.**, Manufacturer of and Dealer in

Harness, Saddles, Collars, Bridles, Whips, Robes, Blankets, Brushes, Combs, Trunks, Valises, &c.

All kinds of Repairing neatly done on short notice. Also dealer in UNCLE SAM's HARNESS OIL.

1814.

Captain Porter, was captured in the harbor of Valparaiso, by the British frigate Phœbe, and sloop-of-war Cherub. It was a desperate battle, the Essex loosing 154 men killed and wounded. Captain Porter, in acknowledging the defeat to the Secretary of the Navy, says: "We have been unfortunate but not disgraced."

April 21.—The United States sloop-of-war Frolic was captured by the British frigate Orpheus and schooner Shelbourne.

April 29.—The Peacock captured the British brig Epervier, off the coast of Florida.

May 5.—Battle of Oswego. A British squadron, carrying 3,000 men, attacked Oswego, by land and water. The town was defended by about 300 men, under Captain Mitchell, and a small flotilla, under Captain Woolsey. They defended the place for two days, when they were compelled to yield to superior force. The British loss was 235 men in killed and wounded; the Americans lost 69. The object of the British in this expedition was to destroy or capture a large quantity of stores at Oswego Falls, but the determined resistance they met with caused them to abandon the project.

July 3.—Generals Scott and Ripley cross the Niagara river into Canada, and capture Fort Erie.

July 5.—Battle of Chippewa. General Brown met the British in the open fields at Chippewa, and repulsed the enemy with a loss of about 500 men; American loss, about 300. The British retreated to Burlington Heights, where they were reinforced by troops under Lieut.-Gen. Drummond, who assumed command.

July 25.—Battle of Niagara Falls. The British force, under Drummond, was about one-third greater than Brown's. The battle commenced at sunset, and ended at midnight, when the Americans had lost 858 men in killed and wounded, and the British 878. The Americans were left in possession of the field, but were unable to carry away any of the spoils which they had captured. Generals Scott and Brown were wounded. The Americans retired to Fort Erie, where General Gaines took chief command.

Aug. 9-14.—Com. Hardy makes an unsuccessful attack on Stonington.

Aug. 15.—Gen. Drummond, in command of 5,000 British, made an assault on Fort Erie, but was repulsed with a loss of almost 1,000 men.

Aug. 24.—Battle of Bladensburg. Capture of Washington, burning of the White House, and other public and private buildings. Ross, the British commander, first attacked Gen. Winder and Com. Barney at Bladensburg, in command of 3,000 undisciplined militia, sea men and marines. The militia fled, and the marines and seamen were made prisoners. Ross was in command of 5,000 men. He then pushed on to Washington, completed his destruction there, and retreated to his shipping on the 29th of August. In these exploits the British loss in killed, wounded and by desertion, was almost 1,000 men: that of the Americans, about 100 killed and wounded, and 20 prisoners. The President and his Cabinet were at Bladensburg when the British approached, but returned to the city when the conflict began, and narrowly escaped capture.

Sept. 11.—Battle of Plattsburgh. The

INDIANAPOLIS—*Continued.*

HOTELS.

MERIDIAN HOUSE,

106 & 108 N. Meridian St.,

Furnished and Unfurnished Rooms.

DAY BOARDING, $4 PER WEEK.

Transient guests accommodated.

Single Meals 25 cents.

Est. 1876. Mrs. A. J. SHELLEY,

St. Nicholas Hotel,
And Restaurant.

Kept on the European Plan. Meals at all hours, day or night, for 25 cents. Lodging, 25 to 50 cents. This hotel is on the cor. Meridian and Louisiana sts., op. N. E. cor. Union Depot.

J. LONG,   -   Proprietor.

HOUSE RAISERS AND MOVERS.

BAUMHARD & SHEELER, Raisers and Movers of Buildings, Market and Mississippi sts.

JOHN S. MILLIKAN,

RAISE, LOWER, AND MOVE

Brick or Frame Houses

ACCESSIBLD BY LAND OR WATER,

In City or Country.   Safes and Heavy Machinery Moved with care.

255 S. Tenneesee Street.

INSURANCE.

ÆTNA FIRE INSURANCE CO., Room 1, Ætna Building, 19 and 21 N. Penn'a st.

THE
Charter Oak Life Ins. Co.,
Hartford, Conn.

L. C. BURT, General Agent,

Indianapolis, Ind.

The Equitable
Life Assurance Society of the United States,
120 Broadway, N. Y.
D. B. SHIDELER, Gen. Agt. Rooms 1 & 2 Vajen block, 66 N. Pennsylvania Street.

INDIANAPOLIS—Continued.

INSURANCE.

Berkshire Life Insurance Company,
Pittsfield, Massachusetts.
INCORPORATED 1851.
JAMES GREENE, Gen. Agt.
10 Martindale's Block.

THE FRANKLIN LIFE INSURANCE CO., Kentucky ave., and Illinois st.

GRIFFITH, W. C., Manager Ætna Life Ins. Co., Room 4, Ætna Building, 17 N. Penn'a st.

GRUBB, PAXTON & CO., Insurance Agents, and Adjusters, 29 and 31 Circle st.

LIFE ASSOCIATION OF AMERICA, A. C. Hartwell, Secretary, 34 E. Market st.

LEATHER BELTING.

HIDE, LEATHER AND BELTING CO., 125 S. Meridian st. G. W. SNIDER, Manager.

LEATHER AND FINDING.

DIETZ & REISSNER, Hides, LEATHER, OILS, and FINDINGS, 21 and 23 S. Delaware st.

LINEN GOODS.

O'DONNELL, P., Irish and Scotch Linens, 50 S. Tennessee st. Est. 1865.

LIVERY AND SALE STABLES.

DREW, JOHN A., Livery and Boarding Stables, Circle st. Established 1863.

FAUCETT, WM., & CO., Proprietors Empire Livery and Sale Stables, 72 W. Market st.

HOLLINGSWORTH, ZEPH, Livery, Feed and Boarding Stable, 277 W. Washington st.

KOLYER & KERR, Livery and Sale Stables, 163 and 202 W. Washington st.

LONG, M., Livery, Feed and Sale Stable, 13 Circle street.

LOAN OFFICE.

DUCAS, ED., Capitol Loan Office. Money advanced on all articles of value, 115 W. Washington street.

MATHEMATICAL INSTRUMENTS.

BILLING, A., Mf'r Mathematical Instruments, Delaware and Georgia sts.

MEAT MARKET.

NUETZEL, JOHN, Fresh and Salt Meats, and sausage, 319 W. Washington st.

THOMPSON, W. K., Dealer in Fresh and Salt Meats, 170 Indiana ave.

VOLLMER, D. G., Meat Store. Chas. H. Zollner, Clerk, 290 W. Washington st.

MERCHANDISE BROKER.

REYMER, GEORGE, Merchandise Broker, 70 N. Illinois street.

MINCE MEAT.

DANVERS, C. F., Mince Meat and Fruit Butter, 74½ N. Delaware st.

OIL DEALER.

CROZIER, G. W., Lubricating and Carbon Oils, 212 S. Meridian st.

1814.

British, 14,000 strong, in command of Prevost, marched to Platsburg, where, in conjunction with the navy, a battle ensued. The Americans, 1,500 strong, commanded by Gen. Macomb, and a large body of militia, under Gen. Mooers, retired to the south side of the Saranac. The land forces fought until dark, and every attempt of the British to cross the Saranac was bravely resisted. In the evening, Prevost retreated, leaving his sick and wounded, and a large quantity of military stores, behind him. The British loss, from the 6th to the 11th of September, in killed, wounded, and deserted, was about 2,500; that of the Americans, 121.

Sept. 11.—McDonough's victory on Lake Champlain. After an engagement of two hours and forty minutes, the British fleet, under Com. Downie, surrendered. The Americans lost in killed and wounded 110; the British 194, among whom was Commodore Downie, whose remains lie under a monument at Plattsburg.

Sept. 12.—The British make an unsuccessful attack on Baltimore, were Gen. Smith was in command. Ross, with 8,000 British troops, was pressing forward, when he was met by Gen. Stricker; a slight skirmish ensues, in which Gen. Ross is killed. He is succeeded in command by Col. Brooke. A battle now commenced, which lasted an hour and a quarter, when the Americans fell back towards the city. Both parties slept on their arms that night. On the following morning the British advanced as if to attack the city. In the meantime a bombardment had been kept upon the fort, whose garrison, under command of Major Armisted, made a gallant defense. No less than 1,500 shells were thrown. On the morning of the 14th the British re-embarked, and silently withdrew from the city. It is estimated that the enemy lost between six and seven hundred in these engagements.

Sept. 13.—Key composes "The Star Spangled Banner."

Sept. 15.—British attack Fort Bower (now Fort Morgan) at the entrance to Mobile Bay. They are repulsed by Major Lawrence, with the loss of one ship and many men.

Sept. 17.—A successful sortie was made from Fort Erie, and the advanced works of the besiegers destroyed and the enemy driven toward Chippewa. Gen. Drummond then retired to Fort George, on the northwestern shore of the Niagara river, near its mouth.

Oct. 29.—First steam war vessel was launched, and named The Fulton.

Nov. 5.—Americans abandon and destroy Fort Erie, cross the river and go into winter quarters at Buffalo, Black Rock, and Batavia.

Nov. 7.—Gen. Jackson, with 2,000 Tennessee militia and some Choctaw warriors, stormed Pensacola, Fla., drove the British to their shipping, and finally from the harbor. and made the Governor beg for mercy and surrender the town and all its military works unconditionally. Jackson then returned to Mobile.

Dec. 2.—Gen. Jackson arrives at New Orleans and declares martial law.

Dec 14.—British capture a flotilla of American gun-boats in Lake Borgne. The attack was made by the enemy in about forty barges, conveying 1,200 men. American loss in killed and wounded about 40; the British about 300.

INDIANAPOLIS—Continued.

OYSTERS AND FISH.

IRWIN, J. L., Oysters, Fruit, Fish, and Game, 218 E. Washington st.

OYSTER DEALER.

J. SCHAFFNER'S

OYSTER BAY,

60 E. WASHINGTON STREET.

PAINTERS.

BAUGHMAN, J. A., CARRIAGE PAINTER and Trimmer. 36 S. Pennsylvania st.

T. V. COOK, THE SIGN PAINTER.

N. E. cor. Washington and Meridian Sts.
☞ Banner and Ornamental work a specialty.

DAUER, CHARLES W., House and Sign Painter, 127 E. Maryland st.

DRAKE & GLOVER, "The Inimitable" Sign Writers, 40 W. Maryland st.

FRANK FERTIG,

House, Sign and Fresco Painter,

24 S. Meridian Street.

W. T. Kennedy,

Sign Painter,

Banner, Glass and Ornamental Work a Specialty.

S. E. cor. Washington & Meridian Sts.

J. M. SINDLINGER,

House, Sign,
—AND—
Ornamental Painter,

23 N. Delaware Street.
Est. 1863.   INDIANAPOLIS.

PHOTOGRAPHERS.

CLARK, D. R., Vance Block Photographic Art Gallery, Virginia ave., and Washington st.

FOWLER'S

Gallery of Photography,

22, 24, 26 and 28 E. Washington St.

Entrance 24½.

PENDERGAST, W.J., Photographer, 212 E. Washington street.

INDIANAPOLIS—Continued.

PHOTOGRAPHERS.

POTTER, W. H., Photographer, op. Hotel Bates, Illinois and Washington sts.

SALTER, W. H., Photographer, 64 and 68 N. Pennsylvania st.

PHYSICIANS.

CORLISS, DR. C. T. Homœopathist, 5 Miller's Block, Illinois and Market sts.

DUFF, DR. O., Cronic, Virulent and Special Diseases, 39 Kentucky ave.

FARR, DR. H. G., Physician, 30 ane 32 Hubbard Block, Washington & Meridian sts. Est. 1858.

DR. D. NEFF,
(OF INDIANA AVENUE,)

Has now opened an Office at 306 Virginia Avenue.

A No. 1 Chronic Physician, and warrants a cure very cheap. Piles, $3 to $10. Other cures very cheap; also Fever and Ague. Seventy-five cents for traveling trade east of the Union Depot. Three squares is the street-car line, direct to the office, —five cents.

PICKERILL, GEO. W., M. D., Office 66 W. Market st.

WOETZER, MADAME GEORGE, ASTROLOGIST and never-failing healing Medium, 118 N. Illinois st.

YOUART, JOHN M., M. D., Surgeon, 62 N. Illinois street.

PICTURE FRAMES.

KIEL, C., Superintendent Moulding and PICTURE FRAME CO., 600 to 606 Madison ave.

PLANING MILL.

CAPITOL CITY PLANING MILL CO., 317 to 327 Massachusetts ave.

PLATER, GOLD, SILVER, ETC.

A. W. SNOW,
ELECTRO GOLD,

Silver and Nickel Plater,

10 W. MARKET STREET.

PRINTERS.

BUTTERFIELD BROS., Practical Job Printers, Room 7, 36 W. Washington st. 2d Floor.

PROPRIETORY MEDICINES.

ROHER'S NEW REMEDY, For the Throat and Lungs, 347 S. Meridian st. Mrs. E. Roher, and J. P. Beeler, Proprietors.

PUBLISHERS.

DOUGLASS, ROBERT, Publisher, and Wholesale Dealer in Subscription Books, N. E. cor. Washington and Meridian sts.

TILFORD, N. E. & CO., Publishers of Indianapolis City Directory, Circle and Meridian sts.

PUMP MANUFACTURER.

BIDDLE, STEPHEN, Wooden, Iron and Chain Pumps, 70 W. Market st.

COMSTOCK, A. S., Genuine Durbon Pump, 197 and 199 S. Meridian st.

EVANS, A. & CO., Wooden, Iron and Chain Pumps, 3 Massachusetts ave.

ADVERTISEMENTS. 93

City Hall, New York.—Constructed of white marble, 216 feet long and 105 feet wide. Commenced in 1803, and was eight years in building, and for many years was the most elegant structure in America. The tower surmounting the edifice formerly contained a bell weighing 9,000 pounds, and was removed several years ago.

St. Louis to New Orleans.
Memphis to New Orleans.
VIA MISSISSIPPI RIVER.

The Largest and Finest Steamboat on the Mississippi River.

GRAND REPUBLIC.
W. H. THORWEGEN, Commander,

Plies regularly in the trade from Memphis to New Orleans during the Cotton Season, from October 1st to March 1st, leaving Memphis on every alternate Wednesday, and New Orleans every alternate Friday. Also, regular packet from St. Louis to New Orleans, March 1st to August 1st, leaving St. Louis every third Saturday, and New Orleans every third Tuesday.

The boat is 350 feet long and 100 feet wide, and has a cabin 300 feet long, 30 feet wide and 18 feet high; has 50 staterooms, and accommodations for 150 cabin passengers. She has capacity for 4000 tons of freight, and has carried 8210 Bales of Cotton—the largest amount ever taken on one boat to New Orleans; and can store 12,000 Bales Uncompressed Cotton. Two fine Bridal Chambers (extra large), and every convenience to be found the same as at home. Every modern improvement for safety—fire escapes, fire extinguishers, etc., etc., and is the Fastest Steamer in the St. Louis and New Orleans trade.

Post Office address, Steamer Grand Republic, St. Louis, Memphis, New Orleans.

1814.

Dec. 15.—Hartford Convention. This convention consisted of delegates from Massachusetts, Connecticut, and Rhode Island, and two members from New Hampshire, and one from Vermont. These last were appointed at county meetings. The object of the convention was opposition to the war, and a threaten of secession of the New England States, but failed to amount to anything.

Dec. 23.—Gen. Jackson attacked, in the night, about 2,400 of the enemy, on the Mississippi, 9 miles below New Orleans. After killing or wounding 400 of the British he withdrew. The American loss was about 100.

Dec 24.—Treaty of peace between the United States and Great Britain, signed at Ghent. The articles of the treaty chiefly related to the disputes respecting boundaries, for the determination of which it was agreed that commissioners should be reciprocally appointed.

Gen. Wilkinson repulsed on Canada frontier and superseded by Gen. Izard.

Hull tried for cowardice and treason at Albany, N. Y., for the surrender of Detroit. He was found guilty of cowardice and sentenced to be shot, but was afterward pardoned by the President.

The Wasp, Capt. Blakely, made a successful cruise, but after capturing thirteen prizes disappeared and was never heard of again. Probably lost in a storm.

1815.

Jan. 8. Battle of New Orleans.—Gen. Jackson, in command of 6,000 militia, concentrated his forces about four miles below the city within a line of entrenchments a mile long, extending from the river far into the swamp. He was attacked in this position by 12,000 British, under command of Gen. Packenham. As the British approached, a terrible cannonade was opened from the American batteries, yet they continued to advance until within rifle range, when volley after volley of deadly storm of lead poured into the ranks of the invaders. The British column soon wavered, Gen. Packenham fell, and the entire British army fled in dismay, leaving 700 dead, and more than 1,000 wounded on the field. The Americans were so safely entrenched that they lost only 7 killed and 6 wounded.

Joseph Bonaparte, brother of the Emperor, came to the United States as Count de Survilliers, and purchased 1,500 acres of land in Bordentown, N. J., and settled down to the life of an opulent gentleman. In 1830 he returned to France, and died in Florence in 1844.

Feb. 18.—Peace proclaimed by the President of the United States, and a day of thanksgiving to the Almighty was observed throughout the Union.

Feb. 20.—The Constitution, Commodore Stewart, had a severe action with the British frigate Cyane and sloop-of-war Levant, and captured both.

Feb. 24.—Robert Fulton, inventor of steam navigation, died in New York, aged fifty years.

April.—Massacre of American prisoners at Dartmoor, England.

April 10.—The United States Bank rechartered for twenty years, with a capital of $35,000,000. The existence of the bank expired with this character in 1836.

April 17.—Commodore Decatur cap-

INDIANAPOLIS—*Continued.*

RAW HIDES AND FURS.

BAUGHER, F. W., Hides, Tallow, Furs and Buffalo Robes, 10 W. Pearl st.

LEWARK, JOSEPH, Dealer in Raw Furs, 14 W. Pearl street.

REAL ESTATE.

ARDEN, J., Real Estate Broker, 12½ N. Delaware street.

BREEDLOVE, T. J., Real Estate Agent, 17½ W. Washington st.

J. B. Cleveland & Co.,

Real Estate and Insurance Brokers,

CHARLES F. CLEVELAND, Notary Public.

76 E. Market Street.

M'CLELLAN, JOHN, Real Estate & Rental Agt. Loans Negotiated. Notary Public, 83½ E. Washington st.

SAILORS, H. C., Real Estate and Loan Broker, 34 E. Washington st.

E. H. SABIN. M. SABIN.

SABIN & CO.,

Real Estate and Loan Brokers,

2½ W. WASHINGTON ST.

ROOM No. 2.

City property, Lands, and Farms bought, sold and exchanged.

STROBLE, JOHN, Dealer in Real Estate, Room 1, 83½ E. Washington st. Negotiates Loans, buys and sells Real Estate, Rents Houses, etc.

JOHN M. TODD & CO.,

BROKERS,

24½ E. WASHINGTON ST.

Sell and Negotiate Real Estate. Specialties.—Negotiating the sale of Stocks and Personal Interests, and organizing Manufacturing and Mining Corporations.

RECORDER.

DARNELL, CAL. F., Recorder Marion County, office in Court House.

REGALIA AND SOCIETY GOODS.

REEVES, J. N. D., Manf'r of Regalia and Society Goods, 10 N. Pennsylvania st.

RESTAURANTS.

BOSS

Oyster House and Restaurant,

79 S. ILLINOIS ST.,

JOHN C. GUISEY, Prop.

GOLLADAY, J. G., Dining, Oyster and Lunch Rooms, 14 N. Delaware st.

INDIANAPOLIS—Continued.

RESTAURANTS.

MOZART HALL,
RESTAURANT, SALOON AND BILLIARDS.
Public Hall Rented for Amusements.

JOHN GROSCH, Proprietor,
(Est'd 1867.)   37 and 39 S. Delaware st.

PEARCE, E. J., Restaurant and Lunch Room, 72 N. Delaware st.

TROW'S
RESTAURANT,
25 N. ILLINOIS ST.,
Established 1873.   INDIANAPOLIS.

WEINBERGER, H., Restaurant and Saloon, 10, 12 and 14 W. Louisiana st.

ROOFING MATERIAL.
Established 1864.

SIMS & SMITHER,
Manufacturers and Dealers in

Roofing and Sheathing Felt,
Pitch, Naptha, Dead Oil, Paving Cement and Rosin.

OFFICE, 169 W. MARYLAND ST.

SALOONS.

BENDER, TOBIAS, Wine and Beer Saloon, 191 E. Washington st.

"THE STORE."
(SALOON.)

GEO. M. BLAKE, Prop.,
10 WEST PEARL ST.

Established 1876.

BUENNAGEL, FRED, Saloon and Boarding House, 145 E. Washington st.

COBLE, GEO., JR., Saloon, 156 and 284 W. Washington st.

COLEMAN, HENRY, Wine and Beer Saloon, 131 W. Washington st.

CITY HALL EXCHANGE, 176 E. Washington st., Nessler & Walter, Props.

80 HOUSE OF LORDS. 80
WEST WASHINGTON STREET.
Established 1863.

The Best Imported and Domestic

Wines, Liquors & Cigars.
Lunch from 9 to 12 A.M. and 9 to 11 P.M.

1815.
tures two Algerine vessels and six hundred prisoners.
June 30.—The Dey of Algiers signs a treaty of peace, agreeing to restore all American prisoners to liberty, pay indemnity for all property destroyed, and to relinquish all claims of tribute from the United States.
July.—Commodore Decatur demanded and received $46,000 from the Bashaw of Tunis, in payment for American vessels he allowed the English to capture in his harbor. A demand of $25,000 and restoration of prisoners was made upon the Bashaw of Tripoli, which was complied with. This cruise to the Mediterranean gave full security to American commerce in those seas, and left the United States at peace.
Sept. 9.—John Singleton Copley, American historical painter, died, aged 78 years.

1816.
Bank of the United States, with a capital of thirty-five millions of dollars, incorporated in April.
The first pugilistic encounter between trained men occurred in the United States between Jacob Hyer (father of Tom Hyer) and Tom Beasley. The match was declared a draw.
Extremely cold season, hickory wood selling in New York for $23 per cord, and oak for $15. There was frost every month of the year.
The Republican party in New York city adopts, for the first time, the title of Democrats.
Dec.—Indiana admitted into the union of States.

1817.
United States suppresses two piratical slave dealing establishments, one at the mouth of the St. Mary, Florida, and the other at Galveston, Texas.
Trouble with the Seminole Creek Indians and runaway negroes, who commenced murderous depredations upon the frontier settlements of Georgia and the Alabama territory. General Gaines sent to suppress these outrages.
March 4.—James Monroe inaugurated President at Congress Hall, Washington city, the capitol having been destroyed by the British.
July 4.—Ground was broken for the Erie canal.
July 8.—Remains of General Montgomery, after resting 42 years at Quebec, were brought to the city of New York and placed in a monument in front of St. Paul's church.
Nov.—United States troops take possession of Amelia Island, the rendezvous of the pirates on the Florida coast.

1818.
The present flag was established by law—thirteen stripes and as many stars as States, arranged in a circle on a blue ground, a star being added on the Fourth of July after the admission of a new State. And on the whole it is a very graceful and picturesque standard.
Provision is made for the support of the surviving soldiers of the Revolution and their families.
American citizens are accorded by Great Britian a share in the Newfoundland fisheries.

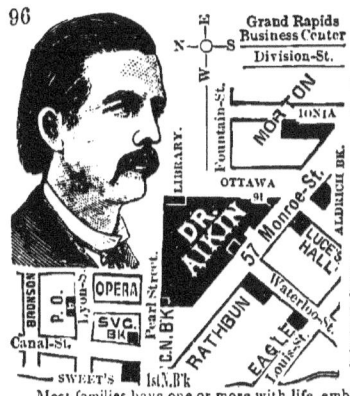

READ THIS! HE
What is Wealth, or Fame,

Dr. Aikin's Rer
FOR THE
Eye, Ear, Throat, Lung
Surgical

The Doctor's location i
and conve
Opposi
57 Monroe St, opposit
a few doors from the Union Tic
91 Ottawa St. (Hall ex
Pa
rooms for the convenience of all
abroad should come at once to tl
and arrange treatment before ot
Office Hours, from 9 00 A. M. to

Most families have one or more with life embittered by needless suffering—conscious of diseases or disability. Yet they can be cured by the skilful Speciali
☞ Established here in extensive practice since 1869 (at St. Louis in '65; San
a wide and merited reputation as a most successful Physician, and having thoro
aptness for the Healing Art, with a complete supply of instruments, appliance:
remedies known to the Profession, a constant succession of cures still attends l
quently the number of his patients is ever on the increase.

DR. AIKIN,
*The well known Specialist, now permanently located in Grand Rapids, Mich
Treatment have made him Celebrated for his Extraordinary Success. All cla.
Equal care and Skill. Hundreds attest the Great Efficacy of the Treatment.
Lung, Throat, and other Chronic Diseases cured; and Broken Down constitutio
Serious, complicated Diseases, that for Many Years Resisted the Treatment
Speedily cured by Dr. Aikin.*

A DOCTOR TO HAVE FA
A lady writes to Dr. Aikin: "I am so soon and easily well by your treat
bounded, and shall recommend you to all my friends as a most reliable physicia
or go insane I concluded," writes a man of 26, in poor health for years, who,
Aikin, further states: "Your remedies are having a remarkable effect. I can
and my health is improving in all respects." DR. AIKIN has given the public suf
most skeptical and incredulous that his method of treatment is peculiarly success
Great Specialties, especially such cases as have defied the skill of other and ju
ONE SHOULD DESPAIR that is afflicted with seemingly incurable disease, but che
suffering, if not entirely cured, by his experienced skill and care.

BLINDNESS! DEAFN!
All Diseases and Affections of the Eye and Ear successfully treated by mild 1
ened. Artificial Eyes inserted that look natural. No pain.

CATARRH, CONSUMP
Asthma, Bronchitis, and all Throat and Lung Complaints (which, in thi
mies to Health and Life,) when change of climate and all else fails, are cured by
and Constitutional Restorative Treatment.

LINGERING OR CHRONIC, AND SURGIC
Scrofula, Rheumatism, Dyspepsia, Piles, Goitre, Dropsy, Gravel, Consti
eases, Cancers, Tumors, Fistula, Hare Lip, Club-Foot, etc., remedied by the m

St-Stuttering, Stammering, and Impediments in speech that daily an
make one a laughing-stock through life, permanently cu
practical method—the cause removed, and cure permanent and positive.

LADIES Married or single, confidently consult the Doctor on any delicat
is doubtless the most skilful Ladies' Physician in the World. I
ness, Whites, Ulceration, Suppression, or other diseases, and drag out a miseral
of easy, safe, and speedy cure in any case by applying to DR. AIKIN.
Stirpiculture— few, healthy children, or none. Trusses, Supporters, Prevent
EPILEPSY, Palsy, Chorea or St. Vitus Dance, Neuralgia, etc.,

GENTLEMEN! YOUNG, MIDDLE-AGED
Suffering the sad effects on body and mind of Self-Abuse, Excesses, Disease, or
tored in vain, let not despair or false modesty be your ruin, but call, or send c
tional lasting cure for Spermatorrhœa, Seminal Weakness, Nervous Debility, Ir
deception. Friendly advice and reliable aid. It is well known that Dr. A. alway
includes ALL—you need never look elsewhere. Those about to marry should n
SURE, quickest, and mild remedies for all private diseases or old symptom
Defects, Phimosis, Hydrocele, Varicocele, etc., radically cured. No mercury used
prescriptions." Travelers promptly supplied. While many innocent victims suff
diseases neglected or badly treated by physicians in general (they should not
it is right and proper to use plain terms that the indiscreete or unfortunate may l
offense can be taken by pure minded persons—See Titus I-15.

CONFIDENTIAL.
Every patient (either sex) may freely state all particulars of their case to D
letter, reposing to his trust any delicate personal, or family matter, and can alw
fidence and secrecy. ☞ DR. AIKIN guarantees better, safer treatment (and,
Cases than can be had elsewhere. He is easily accessible from all points.

The Most Difficult Cases Solicited.—*Consultation Fre
Come prepared to arrange needful, thorough treatment. Satisfaction Guara
nished.* Patients, visited, in city, or any distance, in serious cases.

Life is too Short to be Miserable.—If YOU have any serious, obstinate di
ter how discouraged or how often disappointed, stop useless doctoring and dosing and apply to th
time be cured in a few weeks. All the afflicted who come to him will find the aid they seek.

Cured at Home.—Persons at a distance may be cured at home by addressing letter
length of time the disease has continued, and have medicine promptly forwarded, free from dam
country, with full and plain directions for use, by enclosing $10 in registered letter. P. O. order, or
Call, or address **N. J. AIKIN, M. D., 57 Monroe St.,**

Remember, DR. AIKIN is the only qualified, experienced, reliable specialist here; tr
choicest remedies, is a regular graduate in medicine, universally owned the most successful and is t

ADVERTISEMENTS. 97

Bridge between New York and Brooklyn.—Total length, 5,878 feet; total height above highhide, 268 feet. The bridge is now in course of construction. The first wire was stretched across the river, August 14th, 1876, and the prospects indicate a vigorous prosecution of the work. It will be finished probably in a few years.

DAVIS'
FLAVORING EXTRACTS,

True, Rich Flavors of Lemon, Vanilla, Rose, Almond, Orange, Celery, &c.

Davis' Crystal Baking Powder,

Full Strength, Pure and Wholesome. Used and recommended by the leading Hotels.

Mr. MORRO: None but Superior Goods bear my name.

JOHN DAVIS, Chemist.

H. N. TEALL,
MERCHANT TAILOR.

A Selected Stock of

French, English, German and Scotch Cloths.

Vestings and Doeskins of all Shades and Colors.

Orders promptly attended to, and a fit guaranteed

**210 MAIN STREET, N.E. Cor. Mechanic St.,
JACKSON, MICH.**

1818.

General Jackson pursues the Indians into Florida, takes Pensacola and banishes the Spanish authorities and troops. At St. Mark he captured Alexander Arbuthnot and Robert C. Ambrister, who were tried and found guilty of being the principal emissaries among the southern Indians, inciting them to hostilities. They were both executed.

1819.

Florida ceded by Spain to the United States.
Steamer named the Savannah first crossed the Atlantic.
First lodge of Odd Fellows opened in the United States.
Territory of Arkansas formed
Aug. 23.—Commodore Perry dies in the West Indies.
Dec.—Alabama admitted as a State.

1820.

Napoleon Murat, nephew of Napoleon I., arrived in the United States. He was of a scientific turn of mind, and took great interest in our educational institutions. He married a grand niece of George Washington, and died in Tallahassee, in 1847.
Fourth census of the United States. Population 9,638,190. National debt, $89,987,427.
Maine admitted as a State.
James Monroe re-elected President.
First mariner's church erected in New York.
March 22.—Stephen Decatur, an American Naval officer, was killed in a duel with Commodore Barron.

1821.

Aug. 21.—Missouri admitted as a State, with the famous "compromise," under which it was resolved that in future no slave State should be erected north of the northern boundary of Arkansas.
Streets of Baltimore lighted with gas.

1822.

Conspiracy of the blacks at Charleston, S. C. The blacks of Charleston had arranged an extensive plot for the indiscriminate massacre of the whites on the night of the 16th of June. This information was conveyed to the Governor, who had the city patrolled on that night with a large military force. The conspirators finding this the case, no revolt was attempted. About 131 of the conspirators were afterwards arrested; 35 of them were executed; 51 acquitted, and the rest were sentenced to be transported.
March 19.—The independence of the South American Government acknowledged by the United States.
Piracy in the West Indies suppressed by the United States.
Boston, Mass., incorporated as a city.
March 8.—United States acknowledges the independence of South America.
Oct. 3.—Treaty with Columbia.

1823.

President Monroe promulgates the doctrine that the United States ought to resist the extension of foreign dominion or influence upon the American continent.

1824.

Aug. 15.—Lafayette re-visits the United States.

INDIANAPOLIS—*Continued.*

SALOONS.

K ISTNER, FRED M., Wine and Beer Saloon, 168 W. Washington st.

LOUIS LANG,

SALOON,

And Dealer in

BOTTLED GOODS & CIGARS,

24 N. DELAWARE STREET.
Established 1857.

M ATZ, JOHN & SON, Saloon, 286 W. Washing ton st.

M ANDREWS, W., Saloon, 251 W. Washington st.

M BRIDE, DANIEL, Saloon, 282 W. Washington st.

M NELIS, P. H., Saloon, 143 W. Washington st.
Established 1872.

JOHN NORTON,
FARMER'S SALOON

Choice Wines, Liquors and Cigars
Constantly on hand.

161 WEST WASHINGTON STREET.

J. O'LEARY,
Concert Hall,
WINES, LIQUORS & CIGARS

17 N. ILLINOIS ST., Opp. Hotel Bates.
Established 1862.

Q UINN, J. P., Saloon, 298 W. Washington st.

HERBERT REINHOLD,
WINE & BEER SALOON,

Cor. Illinois Street and Indiana Ave.

S HAMROCK SALOON, M. Crosby, prop., 139 S. Illinois st.

S TEFFAN, WM., Saloon and Boarding House, 323 W. Washington st

W ACHTSTETTER, JOHN, Wine and Beer Saloon, 439 W. Washington st.

SAW WORKS.

I NDIANAPOLIS SAW WORKS, T. Farley, prop., 189 S. Meridian st.

SCALES.

S. B. MORRIS,
Agent for the sale of the

Buffalo Scales,
9 SOUTH ALABAMA ST.
All kinds of Scales repaired.

INDIANAPOLIS—Continued.

SCALES.

GALLUP, WM. P., Agent Fairbanks' Standard Scales, 26 S. Meridian st.

SCREW-PLATES.

E. J. CHAPIN,
Manufacturer of
SCREW-PLATES,
Taps and Dies of every description
And of Superior Quality, as the Teeth are Tempered and Bodies left Untempered.
90 EAST GEORGIA STREET.

SEWING MACHINES.

STEPHENS, R. E., Sewing Machine Agent. Machines Repaired. 19 Massachusetts ave.

SHIRT MANUFACTURERS.

COOK, C. H., Shirt Mnf'r. Perfect Fit and Lowest Prices. 60 N. Illinois st.

GRAUMAN, MRS. M., City Shirt Mnf'y, and Masquerade Costumes for Rent. 108 S. Ill. st.

INDIANAPOLIS
CUSTOM SHIRT FACTORY,
WE GIVE OUR CUSTOMERS FITS
"Perfect Fit or No Pay."
"Shirts Made to Order."
F.M. TAGUE
36 EAST OHIO ST.

SHOOTING GALLERY.

BONA, G. L., The Flying Bird Shooting Gallery. 109 S. Illinois st.

STENCILS AND STAMPS.

COX, CHARLES H., Seal Engraver, Stencils, Stamps, etc, 27 S. Meridian st.

STOVES AND TINWARE.

HOOVER, J. J., Mnfr. and Dealer in Stoves and Tinware, 453 S. Delaware st.

MYERS, JOHN A., Stoves and Tinware, 157 W. Washington st.

1825.

March 4.—John Quincy Adams inaugurated President.
Civil war threatened in Georgia. The Federal Government, in consideration of Georgia releasing her claims to portions of the Mississippi territory, agreed to purchase for that State Indian lands within the borders of Georgia. The Indians refused to sell their lands, and the Government of Georgia was about to drive them out, when the Federal Government interfered on behalf of the Indians. The Indians finally removed to the wilderness of Mississippi.
Napoleon Lucien Charles, nephew of Napoleon I., came to America and married a Yankee school-mistress. He went to France in 1848, and reccieved the title of Prince of the Imperial Family.
Erie Canal completed. It was one of the most stupendous important public improvements, at that time, ever undertaken in the United States.
Corner-stone of Bunker Hill Monument laid by Lafayette.
Lafayette leaves for France in the frigate Brandywine.

1826.

Anti-Mason party and Morgan excitement. William Morgan, of Western New York, announced his intention to publish a book, in which the secrets of Masonry were to be disclosed. He was suddenly seized at Canandaigua, one evening, placed in a carriage, and was never heard of afterward. Some Free Masons were charged with his murder, and the report of an investigating committee appointed by the Legislature of New York confirmed the suspicion. An Anti-Mason party was formed, and in 1831 an Anti-Masonic convention was held in Philadelphia, which nominated William Wirt, of Virginia, for President of the United States. Although the party polled a large vote, it soon afterward disappeared.
Feb. 13.—American Temperance Society instituted at Boston.
July 4.—Death of John Adams and Thomas Jefferson, almost at the same hour. They were both members of the committee who had framed the Declaration of Independence; both signed it; both had been Foreign Ministers; both had been Vice-Presidents and then Presidents of the United States. Together with their death, it was a singular coincidence.

1827.

A national convention was held in Harrisburg, Pa., to discuss the subject of protective tariffs. Only four of the slave States sent delegates. They memorialized Congress for an increase of duties on woolen and cotton fabrics.
The first railroad built in the United States from Quincy, Mass., used with horses.

1828.

May.—Congress passes a tariff bill imposing heavy duties on British goods. It is denounced by the Southern people as oppressive and unconstitutional.
The title of "Democrats" adopted generally by the Republican party.

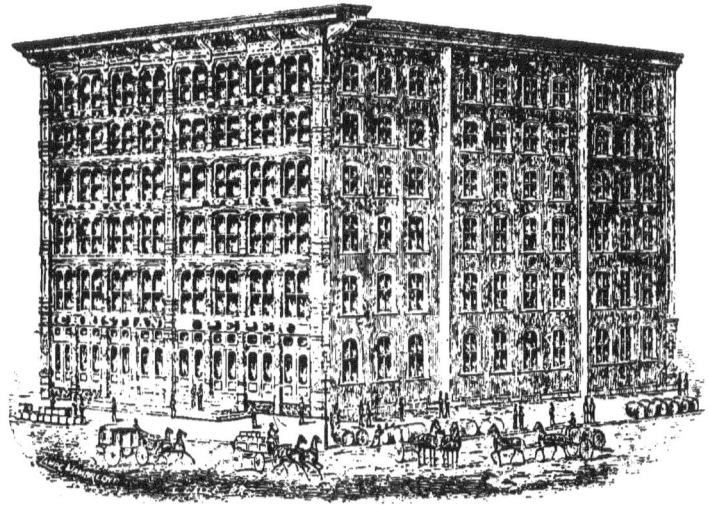

721, 723, 725 & 727 North Main Street St. Louis, Mo.

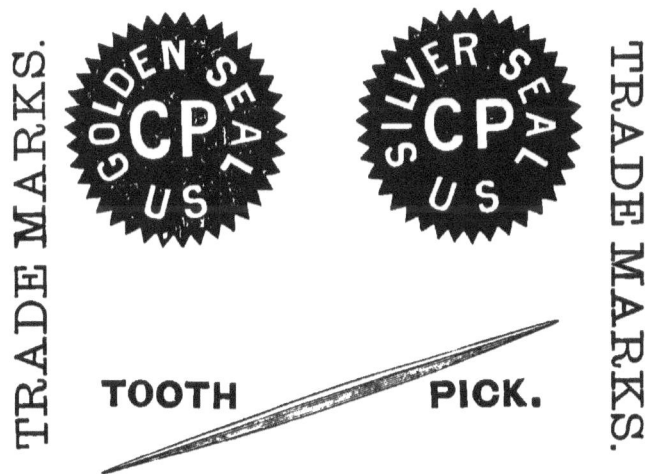

ADVERTISEMENTS. 101

INDEPENDENCE HALL, PHILADELPHIA.

H. B. Scutt, President.   J. R. Ashley, Secretary.   W. S. Brooks, Treasurer.

JOLIET WIRE FENCE CO.

Manufacturers of the Original and justly Celebrated Four-pointed

Steel Barbed Cable Fence Wire,
CHEAP, DURABLE AND EFFICIENT.

A Sure Cure for Breachey Stock. More than twenty thousand miles now in use, and pronounced by all who have tested it, "The greatest improvement of the age."

JOLIET, ILLS.

1829.

March 4.—Inauguration of General Andrew Jackson as President, and John C. Calhoun as Vice-President.

June 4.—United States steam frigate Fulton blown up at New York; between 30 and 40 persons killed.

Aug. 8.—The first locomotive engine run upon a railroad track was the Stourbridge Lion, on the Delaware and Hudson Canal Company's railroad, at Honesdale.

1830.

First American locomotive built by Peter Cooper, and run on the Baltimore & Ohio railroad.

Treaty with the Ottoman Porte.

Workingman's party originated in New York city.

Fifth census of the United States—population 12,866,020.

Jan. 6.—Daniel Webster made his great speech in the United States Senate in answer to Mr. Hayne, of South Carolina.

May 27.—President Jackson vetoes the Maysville Road bill.

Oct. 5.—The President issued a proclamation declaring the ports of the United States open to British vessels from the West Indies.

1831.

June 10.—King of the Netherlands renders his decision on the boundary question between Maine and the British possessions. Rejected by both parties, and question settled in 1842 by the treaty of Washington.

July 4.—James Monroe dies.

Sept. 21, 22, 23.—Riots in Providence, R. I. Five sailors started out for a cruise, and when they arrived at the foot of Olney's lane, about 8 o'clock in the evening, they met six or seven steamboat men, who said they had a row with the darkies, and asked the sailors to go up and aid them. This party greatly increased, proceeded up the lane, where they were received with stones thrown from the houses of the blacks. Stones were then thrown by the crowd against the houses. During the melee the darkies fired upon them, killing one man and wounding two others. As soon as it was discovered the following day that that a white man was killed by the blacks, it occasioned great excitement, and a mob assembled, when the Sheriff arrested seven and committed them to jail, but in three or four instances the mob made a rescue. On the 23d the mob renewed their attack at Snowtown, stoning and destroying houses. The military were called out to preserve order, but were met with defiance from the mob. Stones were hurled at them with such force by the mob, as to split the socks of several muskets, and, as a matter of self-protection they were compelled to fire. Four of the rioters were killed and the mob dispersed. A committee of the citizens of Providence appointed to investigate the matter were unanimous in their opinion that the infantry was justified in firing, and that it was strictly in defense of their lives.

Insurrection and massacre in Southampton county, Va. In August about sixty or seventy slaves rose upon the white inhabitants and massacred fifty-five men, women, and children.

Oct. 13.—Anderson, an English vocalist, was driven from the stage of the Park theatre, New York, for disrespectful remarks concerning the United States.

INDIANAPOLIS—*Continued.*

STOVES AND TINWARE.

W. F. KIRKWOOD,
Tin Shop and Stove Store,

Manufacturer of Sheet Iron & Copper-ware.

Also Prompt Attention Given to Out-door Work and Job Work of all kinds.

176 INDIANA AVENUE.

M. B. MOORE,
Dealer in

Hardware, Stoves,
AND TINWARE,

133 VIRGINIA AVENUE.

—o—

Special attention paid to Roofing, Spouting, Repairing, and all kinds of Job Work.

SURGICAL APPLIANCES.

DAVIS & LINGENFELTER, Surgical Appliances and Apparatus for Physical Deformities, 195 S. Illinois.

TAILORS.

COOPER, H., Custom Tailor, 11 Indiana ave.

GILMORE, A. C., West End Tailor Shop, 270 W. Washington st.

I. HURRLE,
Merchant Tailor,

170 E. Washington Street.

KELLY, P., Merchant Tailor, 193 S. Illinois st.

LEADLEY, WILLIAM, Custom Tailor, 77½ N. Delaware st.

MUELLER, L., Union Dye House and Custom Tailor, 62 S. Illinois st.

NILIUS, CHARLES, Merchant Tailor, 188 S. Illinois st. Est. 1865.

T. R. PORTER,
MERCHANT TAILOR,

24½ W. WASHINGTON ST.

Next door to Trade Palace.

ROSENBERG, JOHN, Merchant Tailor, Hats. Caps and Furnishing Goods, 198 E. Washington st.

JOSEPH STAUB,
MERCHANT TAILOR,

No. 2 Odd Fellows' Hall,

WASHINGTON ST.

INDIANAPOLIS—*Continued.*

TAILORS.

SYMERS, A. F., Tailor,
21 S. Meridian st.   Est. 1875.

H. W. WHITE,
MERCHANT TAILOR
60 N. Illinois Street.

WILKINSON, J., Tailor. Reasonable Terms; all work warranted, 64 W. Market st.

TEAS AND COFFEES.

H. B. M'CUNE.   J. T. M'CUNE.

McCune & Son,
TEAS, COFFEES & SUGARS
100 N. Illinois St.   230 E. Washington St.
53 N. Washington Street.

TELEGRAPH COMPANY.

BUTLER, M. D., Manager Western Union Telegraph Co., 11 S. Meridian st.

TOBACCO AND CIGARS.

H. J. T. Arbuthnot,
Dealer in
Cigars, Tobacco and Pipes,
54 Kentucky Avenue.

BEHRENDT, ALBERT, Havana and Domestic Cigars, 138 S. Illinois st.

Clemens Back,
Manufacturer and Wholesale and Retail Dealer in
Cigars, Tobacco, Pipes, &c.,
209 E. WASHINGTON ST.

T. C. CLIFTON,
Dealer in
Fine Cigars, Tobacco, etc.,
157 E. Washington St.

DONAHUE, THOS., Cigars and Tobacco, Wholesale and Retail, 11 Massachusetts ave.

FITZHUGH, L. M. & CO., Dealers in Teas, Tobaccos, and Cigars, 66 S. Meridian st.

HAUG, CHARLES, Cigars and Tobacco, 151 E. Washington st.

Maas & Kiemeyer,
Wholesale and Retail Dealers in
CIGARS AND TOBACCO,
141 E. WASHINGTON ST.

MEYER, C., Cigars. Mfr of Cigars, Wholesale and Retail, 26 Indiana ave.

1832.

Congress passes a bill rechartering the United States Bank, but on July 10 Jackson vetoes the bill, and the charter expired, by limitation, in 1836.

The tariff act of 1828 produces discontent among the Southern States, and South Carolina declares it null and void, and threatens to resist the collection of duties in the port of Charleston with arms, and secede from the Union if the government persists in enforcing the law.

Black Hawk War.—After several skirmishes the Indians were driven from Illinois to beyond the Mississippi. Black Hawk was captured and taken to Washington City, and there to impress his mind with the strength of the nation he had foolishly made war with, he was conducted through several of the Eastern States. This ended the Black Hawk war.

The Morse system of electro-magnetic telegraphy invented.

Cholera in the U. S.—The epidemic first appeared in New York, June 27. The number of deaths from the 1st of July to the middle of October, when the pestilence ceased, is reported at 4,000. During this time the population was reduced from 225,000, by removals, to 140,000. The ratio of deaths to cases was 1 to 2, and the greatest number of dying in one day was 311, on the 21st of July. The first case appeared in Philadelphia, July 5th, and the number of cases to September 13 was 2,314; the number of deaths 935. In Baltimore the number of deaths to September 29, 710; in Norfolk, to September 11, 400; in Cincinnati, from May 1 to August 7, 1833, 307; in Nashville, from March 27 to July 12, 27 whites and 50 blacks. The disease appeared in New Orleans October 27, 1832, and raged with great severity among the blacks, occasioning a pecuniary loss to slave owners of nearly four million dollars.

Dec. 10.—President Jackson issues a proclamation denying the right of any State to nullify any act of the Federal Government, and warned the people of South Carolina that the laws of the United States would be strictly enforced by military power, if necessary, and South Carolina was obliged to yield.

1833.

Feb. 12.—Tariff dispute settled by the passage of a bill, introduced by Henry Clay, which provided for a gradual reduction of the obnoxious duties during the succeeding ten years.

March 4.—President Jackson inaugurated for a second term.

Oct. 4.—Political riots in Philadelphia. The President removes the public funds ($10,000,000) from the Bank of the United States. The effect produced was sudden and widespread commercial distress, paralyzing the whole business of the country.

Opponents of Andrew Jackson first call themselves the Whig party.

1834.

Cholera again rages in New York.

The President sent General Wiley Thompson to Florida to prepare for a forcible removal of the Seminole Indians if necessary. The tone and manner of Osceola displeased Thompson, and he put him in irons and in prison for a day. The chief feigned penitence, and was released, but his wounded pride called for revenge, and

INDIANAPOLIS—Continued.

TOBACCO AND CIGARS.

RAUCH & BRO., Manufacturers and Dealers in Tobacco and Cigars, 160 and 162 Indiana ave.

REINKEN, HENRY, Mf'r and Dealer in Cigars and Tobacco, 290 E. Washington st.

STEFFEN, ANDREW, Manufacturer and Dealer in Cigars and Tobacco, 224 E. Washington st.

TRUNKS AND BAGS.

SHILLING, R. W., Trunks and Treveling Bags, 39 S. Illinois st.

UNDERTAKERS.

E. HEDGES,
Undertaker,
And Wholesale and Retail Dealer in
METALIC BURIAL CASES, CASKETS AND WOODEN COFFINS, and Undertakers' Goods Generally.
66 W. Maryland St., Second Door W. of Illinois St.
Established 1876.

HERRMANN, F. J. & SON., Undertakers, 26 S. Delaware st. Est. 1854.

RENIHAN, LONG & HEDGES, Undertakers, Metalic Burial Cases, Caskets and Wooden Coffins. 15 Circle st.

WATCHES, CLOCKS AND JEWELRY.

GREINER, LOUIS, Watchmaker and Jeweler, 190 W. Washington st.

HEINRICH, CHARLES, Watchmaker and Jeweler, 195 E. Washington st.

REBER, G. F., Watchmaker and Jeweler, 34 Virginia ave.

WOLVERTON & CONNOR, Watchmakers, 216 E. Washington st.

WELL DRIVERS.

ROUSE, R., Drive Wells, 19 W. Meridian st.

WINES AND LIQUORS.

BAAS, JACOB, Choice Liquors, Wines and Cigars, 234 S. Delaware st.

BRINKMEYER, J. C. & CO., Wholesale Dealers in Kentucky Whiskies, 43-45 N. Tennessee st.

California Wine House.
Thomas J. Barlow, Prop.
22 N. Delaware St.
Established 1867.

CHAPIN & CORE,
Importers and Wholesale Dealers in
Fancy Groceries,
Fine Whiskies,
IMPORTED WINES, LIQUORS & CIGARS.
30 & 32 N. ILLINOIS ST.
Est. 1875.   Capt. A. S. STEWART, Manager.

INDIANAPOLIS—Continued.

WINES AND LIQUORS.

W. W. ELLIOTT,
Wholesale Dealer in
KENTUCKY WHISKIES,
Office, 23 S. Tennessee St.
Established 1877.

WOOD ENGRAVERS.

CHANDLER, H. C., Wood Engraver. 28½ E. Market st.

WOOD TURNER.

LOUIS KOLB,
Plain and Ornamental
JOB TURNER,
23 E. SOUTH STREET.
Between Pennsylvania & Meridian Sts.

WOOD WORKING MACHINERY.

KERRICK & WINEGARDNER, Wood Working Machinery, 63 & 65 W. Maryland st.

INDIANAPOLIS, IND.
BUSINESS HOUSES.
When Established.

BAUMHARD & SHEELER, House Movers, 1876.
BERGUNDTHAL, Glass and Queensware, 1876.
BERNS, F. G., Cigar Boxes, 1875.
BLACK & BACKUS, Carriage Mf'rs, 1871.
BLAKE, JACKSON & QUINIUS, Commission Merchants, 1861.
BRADFORD, C., Solicitor of Patents, 1876.
CAPITOL CITY PLAINING MILL, 1873.
CAYLOR, J., Hardware, 1876.
CHARTER OAK LIFE INS. CO., 1850.
CIRCLE HOUSE, 1857.
COMSTOCK, A. S., Durbon Pump, 1830.
CROZIER, G. W., Oils, 1876.
ENOS, B. V. & SON., Architects, 1865.
FITZHUGH, L. M. & CO., Teas, 1873.
THE FRANKLIN LIFE INS. CO., 1866.
GRAND HOTEL, 1875.
GRUBB, PAXTON & CO., Ins. 1869.
HODGES, E. J., Dry Goods, 1876.

WASHINGTON'S HEADQUARTERS, VALLEY FORGE.

The Medical Healing Institute

PROFESSOR M. M. GRAY,
CLAIRVOYANT, MAGNETIC PHYSICIAN, Proprietor,
233 W. Madison St., Chicago, Ills.

PROF. GRAY has had a varied experience in the Healing Art for twenty-eight years, followed by a reco d of the most remarkable success, having the **Gift of Healing** by the **Magnetic Life Force,** or "Laying on of hands." He seldom fails to give the most speedy and permanent relief in the most obstinate cases of all classes of diseases and pains, without the use of medicine. **Incurable Cases** (so-called) **solicited.**

1834.

fearfully did he pursue if the following year. McCormick's reaper patented.

1835.

July 12.—Negro riots in Philadelphia. Democrats first called the the "Locofoco" party.

Dec. 16.—A very disastrous fire occurred in New York, destroying 674 buildings in the lower part of the city. Loss estimated at $20,000,000.

War with Seminole Indians, led by Osceola, in Florida.

Dec. 28.—While Major Dade was marching at the head of 100 men for the relief of Fort Drane, in the interior of Florida, he was attacked, killed, and all but four of his attachment massacred. On the same day, and only a few hours before, with a small war party, Osceola killed General Thompson and five of his friends who were dining at a store a few yards from Fort King. Osceola scalped General Thompson with his own hands, and thus enjoyed the revenge for the indignity he had suffered in 1834.

1836.

March 29.—Pennsylvania newly incorporates the Bank of the United States.

June 15.—Arkansas admitted as a State. National debt paid off.

Charles Louis Napoleon, the late Emperor of the French, was banished to the United States for attempting to gain the throne of his uncle, the First Consul, by revolutionary means. He landed at Norfolk, in March, 1827, and then came to New York, where he remained until May, when he sailed for Switzerland to see his dying mother.

The Creek Indians aid the Seminoles in their war. They attack mail carriers, stages, steamboats, and finally villages in Georgia and Alabama, until thousands of white people were fleeing for their lives from place to place. The Creeks were finally subdued by General Scott, and several thousand of them were removed to beyond the Mississippi.

1837.

March 4.—Martin Van Buren inaugurated President, and Richard M. Johnson, of Kentucky, Vice-President.

The banks suspend specie payment, and a general panic prevails in business circles. During the months of March and April the failures in New York alone amounted to more than $200,000,000. The effect of these failures was felt all over the Union, and credit and confidence destroyed.

March 6.—Osceola and several chiefs appeared in General Jessup's camp, and signed a treaty of peace, and guaranteed instant departure of the Indians to their new home beyond the Mississippi. Osceola during the summer broke this treaty, and hostilities were again resumed.

Oct. 21.—Osceola, with several chiefs and 70 warriors, appeared the second time in Jessup's camp, under the protection of a flag. They were seized and confined. Osceola was sent to Charleston, where he died of a fever, while confined in Fort Moultrie.

June 25.—Michigan admitted as a State.

Sept. 4.—An extra session of Congress was convened to devise measures to relieve the financial embarrassments of the country, and after a session of 42 days it did but little, ex-

INDIANAPOLIS—*Continued*.

LEADING BUSINESS HOUSES.

HOOD, H. P., Novelties, 1870.
INDIANAPOLIS BRASS FOUNDRY, 1876.
KERRICK & WINEGARDNER, Wood Working Machinery, 1874.
LAWRENCE, A. V., Commission Merchant, 1857.
LEWARK, JOSEPH, Fur Dealer, 1837.
MIESSEN, J., Confectioner, 1874.
MEYER, CHRISTIAN, Cigar Mf'r, 1873.
PENDERGRAST, J. W., Photographer, 1875.
ROUCH, J. & BRO., Cigars and Tobacco, 1870.
REAGAN, E., Boiler Maker, 1876.
REBER, G. F., Jeweler, 1876.
ROSS, JAMES A., Hardware, 1874.
ROUSE, R. R., Driven Wells, 1868.
STUART BROS., Commission Merchants, 1876.
SULLIVAN, JOHN E., Commission Merchant, 1876.
WASON, J. A., Carriage Painter, 1870.

TERRE HAUTE, IND.

AGRICULTURAL IMPLEMENTS.

F. J. HESS,
Dealer in all kinds of

AGRICULTURAL IMPLEMENTS,
TERRE HAUTE, IND.

Terre Haute Implement Co.,
Wholesale and Retail Dealers in all kinds of

Machinery and Agricultural Implements.

Machinery of all kinds Stored and Transferred at Reasonable Rates.

20 SOUTH THIRD ST.
E. R. CRITES, Secretary.

AGUE CURE.

SWISS AGUE CURE.

THE SPRINGS OF LIFE,
Liver Regulator and Blood Purifier.

Thousands of People have found permanent Health by the use of it.

JULES HOURIET, Prop.
MANUFACTURED

Cor. Third & Walnut Sts.,
TERRE HAUTE.

IMPORTANT EVENTS OF A CENTURY. 107

TERRE HAUTE—*Continued.*

ARTESIAN BATHS.

Terre Haute Pool of Siloam; or
ARTESIAN BATHS.
Recommended by the Highest Medical Authorities as Wonderfully Efficacious in Rheumatic Complaints and all Diseases of the Skin. The Most Powerful Alterative Bath known.
RIVER, between WALNUT and POPLAR STS.
MILLER & CONANT, Props.

ATTORNEYS AT LAW.

H AVENS, B. F., Attorney at Law,
503½ Main st.

C. E. HOSFORD,
ATTORNEY at LAW
Cor. MAIN AND FOURTH STS.
TERRE HAUTE, IND.

R OYSE, GRIMES & ROYSE, Attorneys at Law, Real Estate and Loan Brokers, 503 Main st.

HARVEY D. SCOTT,
Attorney at Law,
Terre Haute, Vigo Co., Ind.
—:o:—
General Collecting Agent for Claims in Western Indiana and Eastern Illinois.

BAKERS AND CONFECTIONERS.

FRANK HEINIG,
Crackers, Bread, Cake and Candy,
128 and 130 Lafayette St. Goods delivered Free of Charge. Established 1866.

F. A. HEINIG,
Bakery, Confectionery & Notions,
1142 MAIN STREET.

JOHN H. CHAPMAN & CO.,
BAKERY & DINING ROOM,
124 & 126 SOUTH FOURTH ST.

BARBERS.

S PENGLER, PHILLIP, Barber and Hairdresser, 649 Main st.

V OGES, HENRY, Hairdresser and Shaving Saloon, 649 Main st.

W ELDLE, GEO., Barber and Hairdresser, 28 N. Third st.

BLACKSMITHS AND HORSESHOERS.

B URNETT & WATSON, for Horseshoeing and General Blacksmithing. Cherry st., north side, bet. Third and Fourth. Will guarantee to cure by Shoeing:
Corns, Quarter Cracks, Hoof Bound, Contraction of the Heel, and Interfering.

K IDD & NICHOLSON, Horseshoeing and General Blacksmithing, 231 N. Fourth st.

W ELLS, GEO., Blacksmithing and Horseshoeing, cor. Seventh & Lafayette sts. Est. 1872.

1837
cept the passage of a bill authorizing the issue of Treasury notes not to exceed the amount of ten million dollars.
Revolutionary movements in Canada, and many Americans assist the insurgents. The steamboat Carolina was set fire by the British, near Schlosser, east of Niagara, on United States territory, and she went over the great cataract in full blaze.
Nov. 7.—Riot at Alton, Ill.; E. P. Lovejoy killed.
Dec. 25.—Col. Taylor (afterward Gen. Taylor and President of the United States), in command of 600 troops, repulsed a large body of Indians on the northern border of Macaco Lake, sometimes called Big Water Lake.

1838.
April 18.—Destructive fire in Charleston, S. C.
Proclamation by the President against American citizens aiding the Canadians.
The steamship Sirius, the first to make the western transatlantic passage, arrives at New York from Cork, Ireland, and is followed, on the same day, by the Great Western, from Bristol, England.
The Wilkes exploring expedition to the South Sea sailed.

1839.
A treaty was made which appeared to terminate the Indian war, but murder and robberies continued, and it was not until 1842 that peace was finally secured. This war lasted seven years, and cost the United States many valuable lives, and millions of treasure.
Another financial panic, and in October banks suspend specie payment.

1840.
July 4.—The Sub-Treasury bill becomes a law. This bill established an independent treasury for the safe keeping of the public funds, and their entire and total separation from banking institutions.
Railroad riots in Philadelphia.
St. Mary's Academic Institute, St. Mary's of the Woods, Vigo Co., Indiana, founded by the Sisters of Providence, from Ruille, in France.

1841.
Feb. 4.—United States Bank failed and other banks suspended specie payment.
March 4.—William Henry Harrison inaugurated President, and died April 4th.
April 6.—John Tyler, Vice-President, was inaugurated President.
Aug. 9.—Sub-Treasury act repealed and a general bankruptcy bill passed.
Oct. 14.—Alexander MacLeod implicated in the burning of the Caroline in 1837, tried for murder and arson at Utica, N. Y., and acquitted.
Nov. and Dec.—Affair of the United States brig, Creole, which leads to a dispute with England. This vessel, an American, was on her voyage to New Orleans with a cargo of slaves; they mutinied, murdered the owner, wounded the captain, and compelled the crew to take the ship to Nassau, New Providence, where the Governor, considering them as passengers, allowed them, against the protest of the American consul, to go at liberty.

1842.
Return of the United States exploring expedition from the great Southern ocean. The

JUDD & DERRICK,

MANUFACTURERS OF

Magic Baking Powder,

No. 28 South Division Street,

GRAND RAPIDS, MICH.

ROBINSON & BARNABY,

Architects and Superintendents,

GRAND RAPIDS, MICH.

Designs and Specifications prepared for Churches, School and County Buildings, Hotels and Residences. Interior finish of Stores and Banks a specialty. Full size details supplied in all cases. Established 1865.

ESTABLISHED 1871.

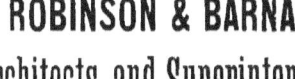

Furnishing Undertaker,

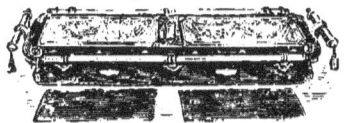

Embalming a Specialty.
No. 103 Ottawa Street, GRAND RAPIDS, MICHIGAN.

ARTHUR WOOD,

Manufacturer of

Carriages, Sleighs,

PLATFORM

SPRING BUGGIES
—AND—
Market Wagons.

37 WATERLOO ST.,
GRAND RAPIDS, Mich.

☞ Send for cuts and prices. ☜

POST OFFICE, GRAND RAPIDS, MICH.

MEDICAL AND SURGICAL INSTITUTE.
Dr. H. C. STEPHENSON & BRO.

29 Monroe Street, Grand Rapids, Mich.,

Manufacturers of Stephenson's Patent Trusses, Supporters, Artificial Limbs and Surgical Appliances for Deformities of the Spine, Hips, Knees, Ankles and Feet.

All those afflicted will do well to call at this Institute.

WM. H. POWERS.   JOS. H. WALKER.

POWERS & WALKER,
WHOLESALE MANUFACTURERS OF

Wood Burial Cases & Caskets,

Office and Factory, 83, 84, 85, 86, 87 and 88 South Front Street,

GRAND RAPIDS, MICHIGAN.

1842.

expedition made a voyage of about 90,000 miles, equal to almost four times the circumference of the globe.

The Croton aqueduct, which conveys water from Croton river, in Westchester county, in the city of New York, a distance of forty miles, was completed.

Prince de Joinville, of France, brother-in-law of Dom Pedro, of Brazil, arrived in New York.

Aug.—Treaty defining the boundaries between the United States and the British American possessions and for suppressing the slave trade, and for giving up fugitive criminals, signed at Washington.

Aug. 1.—Abolition riots in Philadelphia. Churches burned.

1843.

Jan. 11.—"Weavers' Riots" in Philadelphia.

Feb. 28.—A gun on board the steamship Princeton, while on an excursion on the Potomac bursted, killing Abel P. Upshur, Secretary of State, and Mr. Gilmer, Secretary of the Navy, and several other distinguished gentlemen. The President and many ladies were on board. Among the killed was Mr. Gardiner, of the State of New York, whose daughter the President soon afterwards married.

Suppression of threatened insurrection in Rhode Island, known as the Dorr Rebellion. Thomas Dorr was elected Governor by the "Suffrage party," and the "Law and Order" party chose Samuel W. King. Dorr was finally arrested, tried, and convicted of treason, and sentenced to imprisonment for life. He was afterwards released, but deprived of all the civil rights of a citizen, and finally these disabilities were removed.

June 9.—Washington Allston, painter, born in South Carolina, died at Cambridge, Mass., aged 64 years.

Nov. 10.—John Trumbull, painter, born in Connecticut, died in New York, aged 87.

1844.

April 12.—The Texans conclude a treaty with the United States for the annexation of Texas to the Union.

June 25.—Joseph Smith, founder of Mormonism, died, aged 39 years.

July 6.—The United States recognizes the independence of the Sandwich Islands.

Treaty of commerce with China.

May and July.—Riots and Catholic churches burned in Philadelphia.

May 27.—Anti-Rent riots in New York. The tenants on some of the old "patroon" estates had refused to pay rent. It consisted of only "a few bushels of wheat, three or four fat fowls, and a day's work with horses and wagon, per year." The anti-renters considered it illegal, and, disguised as Indians, tarred and feathered those tenants who paid their rents, and even killed officers who served warrants upon them. The disturbances were finally suppressed by the military.

Telegraphic communication established between Baltimore and Washington.

1845.

March 1.—The Republic of Texas admitted into the Union.

March 3.—Florida and Iowa admitted as States.

TERRE HAUTE—Continued.

BOILER MANUFACTURERS.

CLIFF & SON, Boiler Manufacturers, First st., bet. Walnut and Poplar.

BOOKBINDERS.

LANGFORD, M. F. & CO., The Bartlett Bindery, 524½ Main st.

BOOTS AND SHOES.

W. H. GREINER & CO.,
Hoosier Shoe Store,
COR. FOURTH & OHIO STS.

FRESEE, JOHN, Manf'r Boots and Shoes, 911 Chestnut st.

J. G. KRETZ,
Manufacturer of
BOOTS & SHOES,
472 N. FOURTH STREET.

J. P. MATHENY,
Boot and Shoe Maker,
807½ MAIN STREET.

JOHN R. MILLER,
Manufacturer of Boots and Shoes,
23 NORTH FOURTH ST.

TAYLOR, GEO. A., Manf'r of Boots and Shoes, 937 Poplar st.

WATKINS, A., Muf'r of Boots and Shoes, 937 Poplar st.

BREWERS.

Established 1856.

A. MAYER,
Lager Beer Brewer
Cor. POPLAR & NINTH STS.

No. 1 Lager Beer constantly on hand.
All Orders from abroad promptly attended to.

BUILDER.

WILLIAM SHELDON,
CONTRACTOR & BUILDER
SHOP, 125 OHIO ST.,
Bet. First and Second Streets, first door west of Pence's Drug Store.

CABINET MAKER.

TRICHE, CHARLES, Cabinet Maker, Walnut st., bet. Fifth and Sixth.

CARRIAGE MANUFACTURER.

FRED L. MEYER,
Carriage Manufacturer & General Blacksmithing,
COR. FIFTH AND CHERRY STS.

IMPORTANT EVENTS OF THE CENTURY.   111

TERRE HAUTE—*Continued.*

CHINA, GLASS AND CROCKERY.

RICHARDSON, H. S. & CO., China, Glass and Queensware, 318 Main st.

COAL AND WOOD.

HIXON, J., Coal, Wood, Lime, etc., at crossing of 5th st. and Indianapolis & St. Louis R.R.

COMMISSION MERCHANT.

JOS. H. BRIGGS,
Produce & Commission Merchant
And Dealer in Hides, Pelts, Rags, Butter, Eggs, &c., cor. of Fourth and Cherry sts.

DENTISTS.

Dr. L. H. BARTHOLOMEW

DENTIST,

DENTAL ROOMS,

523 1-2 MAIN STREET, NEAR SIXTH.

LINCOLN, DR. C. O., Dentist,
681½ Main st.

DRESSMAKERS.

THE MISSES BELSER,
Fashionable Dress and Cloak Makers,
634½ MAIN STREET.

MRS. KESTER, FASHIONABLE

DRESS AND CLOAK MAKER,
642½ MAIN STREET.

Mrs. Oosley & Miss Jones,
Fashionable Dress and Cloak Makers,
920½ MAIN STREET.

DRUGGISTS.

Established 1871.
BUNTIN & ARMSTRONG,

Druggists, Manufacturing Pharmacists
And Dealers in Surgical Instruments,
No. 600. Cor. Main & Sixth.

GROVES & LOWRY, Druggists, Perfumery, etc., cor. Third and Main sts.

GULICK & BERRY,
Wholesale Druggists,
COR. FOURTH & MAIN STS.

MUREW, W. E. & CO., Druggists and Pharmacists, cor. Third and Walnut sts.

SALE, ED. T., Druggist,
131 Lafayette st.

FANCY GOODS.

FECKHEIMER, I., Ladies' Popular Fancy Bazar, 20 Fourth st. Established 1870.

FLOUR AND FEED.

BAKER, JOHN, Dealer in Flour, Feed and Produce, 101½ Main st.

BURNS, PHILIP, Flour and Feed Store, cor. Third and Poplar sts.

8

1845.

March 4.—James K. Po'k inaugurated President.
Treaty with Great Britain fixing the northwestern boundary, by which it was settled that Oregon was a part of the territory of the United States by right of first discovery.
March 6.—Mexican minister protests against the admission of Texas into the Union and demanded his passport.
April 10.—Great fire at Pittsburgh, burning over a space of 56 acres, entailing a loss of property of over five millions of dollars.
July—The President, aware of the hostile feelings of the Mexicans, sent Gen. Taylor, with a force of 1,500, for the defence of Texas. At the same time a squadron, under command of Commodore Connor, sailed for the Gulf of Mexico, to protect American interests there.
July 19.—Great fire between Broadway, Exchange place, Broad and Stone streets, New York. Loss, $5,000,000.
The Mexican government, by continued depredations upon American vessels and the confiscation of the property of the Americans within her border, brought on a crisis that required a settlement. The United States remonstrated, but the Mexicans continued their depredations, until the amount appropriated by them reached more than $6,000,000. The Mexican government finally acknowledged the debt, and agreed to pay it in installments of $300,000 each. Only three of the installments were paid, and the Mexican government refused to decide whether she would pay the remainder.

1846.

April 24, War with Mexico.—First blood of the war shed. Gen. Taylor, being informed that the Mexicans were crossing the Rio Grande, above his encampment, sent Capt. Thornton, with 60 dragoons, to reconnoitre. They were surprised and captured. Sixteen Americans were killed, and Capt. Thornton escaped by an extraordinary leap off his horse.
May 3.—Fort Brown, on the Rio Grande, attacked by the Mexicans. After suffering a bombardment of 160 hours, the garrison was relieved, and the Mexicans trembled for the safety of Matamoras. Major Brown (in whose honor the fort was named) was mortally wounded.
May 8.—Battle of Palo Alto. Gen. Taylor, with a little over 2,000 troops, met, in battle array, 6,000 Mexicans, under Gen. Arista. For five hours, a hot contest was maintained, when the Mexicans gave way and fled. American loss in killed and wounded, 53. Among the wounded was Capt. Page, of Maine, who afterwards died on the 12th of July; and Major Ringgold, commander of Flying Artillery, who died four days afterward. The Mexicans lost about 600.
May 9.—Battle of Resaca de la Palma. This was a short and bloody conflict, but the Americans were again victorious. American loss in killed and wounded, 110; Mexican loss was at least 1,000. Gen. La Vega and 100 men were made prisoners. This was the second battle of the war fought between Gen. Taylor and Gen. Arista. Arista saved himself by solitary flight, and made his way alone across the Rio Grande.
May 18.—Before the battle of Palo Alto

WM. CLIFF. [Established 1865.] HENRY CLIFF.

CLIFF & SON,
—*MANUFACTURERS OF*—

LOCOMOTIVE, STATIONARY AND MARINE BOILERS,

Tubular and Cylinder, Iron Tanks, Smoke Stacks, Breeching, Sheet Iron Work, Etc. Particular attention paid to all kinds of Jail Work.

ALSO BLAST FURNACE WORK.

Shop on First St., bet. Walnut & Poplar, Terre Haute, Ind.

REPAIRING done in the most substantial manner at short notice, and as liberal in price as any establishment in the State. Orders solicited and punctually attended to.

REAGAN'S PAT. for FLANGING FLUE-HOLES in BOILER HEADS.

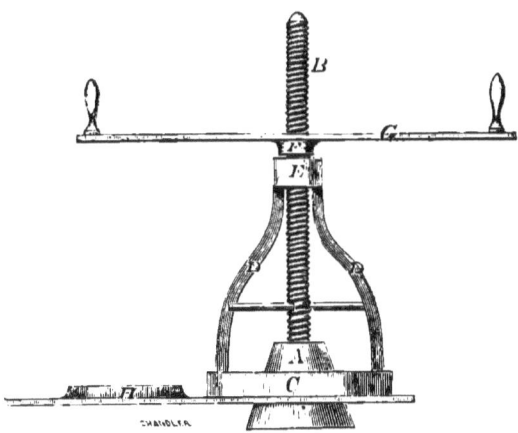

THIS INVENTION re ates to a device by which to turn a Flange to the Flue Holes in Boiler Heads, and consists in a cone shaped Die, the base of which is of the size of the external diameter of the Flue. This Flanging device is used in the following manner: The Boiler-head H having been pierced with suitable holes, and heated to a workable temperature, is laid upon trestles or other supports, and is prevented from being turned in operating the device, by inserting a pin throu h one of the Flue-holes into the support below. The Bracket, with the Screw hanging therein by the Nut F in Lever G, is then set over the hole to be flanged, and the Die attached to the lower end of the Screw from below the Boiler-head. By turning the Lever G, the Screw C and Die D are drawn upward; the Die forces up and forms the Flange I around the hole in the Boiler-head.

THIS MACHINE IS CLAIMED TO BE THE BEST IN USE,

And will illustrate its own merits by trial.
After the Iron is Hot, the Flue can be formed for General Use in the space of Two Minutes.

Machines, and State, County and Shop Rights, for Sale by EDWARD REAGAN, PATENTEE.

All communications should be addressed to EDWARD REAGAN, 132 S. Tennessee St., Indianapolis, Ind. Factory, 305 W. Washington St.

J. W. PENDERGAST,
LANDSCAPE AND PORTRAIT PHOTOGRAPHER,
ALL KINDS OF

Viewing and Copying promptly attended to.

A Full Assortment of Stereoscopic Views of the Principal Streets and Business Blocks o this City. Also Birds' Eye Views taken from the New Court House steeple, 175 to 200 feet high, giving a good View of the City, always for sale at Gallery,

212 WEST WASHINGTON ST., INDIANAPOLIS, IND.

A Liberal Discount to Dealers and Agents.

Opera House, Terre Haute, Ind.—Was built in 1869-'70. The building is located on the corner of Fourth and Main streets; is 80 feet front by 148 feet in depth, and cost exclusive of the ground $140,000. It has a seating capacity of 1,400; and a stage complete, in machinery and scenery. It ranks as one of the most elegant, convenient and comfortable houses in the country.

J. A. FOOTE,

IMPORTER AND DEALER IN

SEEDS

AND

Horticultural Goods,

No. 512 Main-st., Terre Haute, Ind.

ESTABLISHED IN 1866.

The only complete Seed Store in the State.

RELIABLE SEEDS SOLD.

Accurate information as to relative value of varieties.

New varieties introduced from year to year.

Seed Catalogue issued in January.
Bulb　　　"　　　"　　September.
Fancy Goods "　　 "　　April.

☞ Catalogues free to all applicants.

L. WEIL & SON,

TRUNK

Manufacturers,

—AND—

REPAIRERS.

No. 321 Upper 1st St.,

EVANSVILLE, IND.

All kinds of Trunks and Sample cases made to order.

1846.

and Resaca de Palma were known in the United States, Congress authorized the President to raise 50,000 volunteers, and appropriated $10,000,000 towards carrying on the war.

May 18.—Gen. Taylor drives the Mexican troops from Matamoras and takes possession of the town.

May 30.—Gen. Taylor, as a reward for his skill and bravery, *brevetted* Major-General.

July.—Americans in California declare themselves independent, and place Gen. Fremont at the head of their affairs.

July 7.—Commodore Sloat bombards and takes possession of the city of Monterey.

July 9.—Commodore Montgomery takes possession of San Francisco.

Aug. 15.—Col. Fremont and Commodore Stockton take possession of Los Angeles, California.

Aug. 18.—Gen. Kearney takes possession of Santa Fe, the capital of New Mexico. The Governor and 4,000 Mexican troops fled at his approach, and the people, numbering about 6,000, quietly submitted.

Aug. 22.—Annexation of New Mexico to the United States.

Sept. 21.—Gen. Taylor, now in command of 6,000 men, commenced the siege of Monterey. The city was defended by Gen. Ampudia, and 9,000 troops. The conflict lasted four days, a part of the time within the streets of the city, where the carnage was fearful. Ampudia surrendered. American loss in killed, wounded and missing, 561. The number lost by the Mexicans was never ascertained, but it was supposed to be more than 1,000.

October.—Tobasco and Tuspin captured by Com. Perry.

Nov. 14.—Tampico surrenders to Com. Conner.

Nov. 15.—Gen. Worth took possession of Saltillo, capital of Coahuila.

Dec. 22.—Col. Doniphan, in command of 1,000 Missouri volunteers, while on his march to Chihuahua to join Gen. Wool, met a large force of Mexicans at Braceti, in the valley of the Rio del Norte, under Gen. Ponce de Leon. He sent a black flag to Doniphan with the message, "We will neither ask nor give quarters." The Mexicans then advanced and fired three rounds. The Missourians fell upon their faces, and the enemy, supposing them to be all dead, rushed forward for plunder. The Americans suddenly arose, and delivering a deadly fire from their rifles, killed 308 Mexicans and dispersed the remainder in confusion.

Dec. 29.—Gen. Taylor took possession of Victoria, capital of Tamaulipas.

1847.

Jan. 19.—A revolt in Mexico against the United States government: Gov. Bent and many other Americans murdered at Fernando de Taos, and massacres occurred in other portions of the country.

Ten thousand Mormons from Illinois, under the leadership of Brigham Young, entered Desert, now called Utah, and founded Salt Lake city.

Jan. 23.—Col. Price, with 350 men, defeated the insurgents at Canada, and finally dispersed them at the mountain gorge called the Pass of Embudo.

Feb. 23.—Battle of Buena Vista. Gen. Taylor's forces at this battle were only 5,000, while that of the enemy under Santa Anna,

TERRE HAUTE—*Continued.*

FLOUR AND FEED.

MAYS & CUMMINGS, Flour and Feed Store, cor. Third and Cherry sts.

FLOURING MILLS.

THOMPSON, R. L., Merchant Mills. Cash paid for Wheat. Poplar and First sts.

FURNITURE.

FISHER, J. R., Dealer in Furniture, etc., 106 S. Fourth st.

R. FORSTER & SON,

—Dealers in New and Second-hand—

FURNITURE AND STOVES,

103 N. Fourth st. Upholstering done to order.

DENNIS SULLIVAN,

Second-hand Furniture, Stoves,

Clothing, etc. Cash paid for all kinds.
101 NORTH FOURTH ST.

W. P. WILSON,

Dealer in

New & Second-hand Furniture & Stoves,

29 NORTH FOURTH ST.

GROCERIES.

W. F. BRISCOE,

Family Grocer,

N. W. Corner Third and Park sts. Est. 1865.

BYERS BROS., Dealers in Groceries, 111 S. Fourth st.

ECKHOFF & ZIMMERMAN, Groceries and Provisions, 208 S. Fourth st.

Motto: Not to be Undersold.

GWYN & NAYLOR, (successors to D. H. Alvey,) Cash Dealers in Choice

Teas, Groceries & Provisions,

121 N. 4th st. Highest prices paid for Produce, &c.

HULMAN & COX, Wholesale Grocers and Liquor Dealers, cor Fifth and Main sts.

PATTON BROTHERS,

Dealers in

Fancy and Staple Groceries,

Fre-h Meat, Vegetables, etc.,
116 South Fourth st., bet. Ohio and Walnut.

A. & E. REIMAN,

Dealers in

Provisions, Groceries, Flour

AND BUILDING MATERIAL,

Delphi and Greencastle Lime, Newark and Michigan Plaster, Lath, Fire Brick, Fire Clay, Plastering Hair, Etc.,

MAIN STREET,

Bet. Eighth and Ninth.

SHALEY, F. W. & CO., Groceries and Provisions, cor. Eighth and Poplar sts.

HARNESS AND SADDLES.

P. H. KADEL, MANUFACTURER OF

Harness, Saddles, Collars, Trunks, Valises, &c.

Main st., near Ninth, South side.
Repairing promptly attended to.

TERRE HAUTE—*Continued.*

HARNESS AND SADDLES.

G. HANDWERK,
Manufacturer of and
WHOLESALE AND RETAIL

Dealer in Harness and Saddles,
29 S. SECOND ST.

HATS, CAPS AND FURS.

SYKES, JOHN H., Dealer in Hats, Caps, Furs and Straw Goods.

HOTELS.

FELBECK HOUSE.
HERMAN SCHERRER, PROP.,
COR. FIFTH AND CHERRY STS.

NEW BRONSON HOUSE,
DAVID BRONSON, - - Proprietor.
COR. TENTH & SPRUCE STS.
Newly furnished throughout and First-Class in every appointment. Nearest Hotel to both Depots. Free Bus to Guests to and from all Trains. TERMS, $2.00 PER DAY. Nearest Hotel to Union Depot.

INSURANCE.

HAVENS & FARIS, General Insurance Agents, 103½ Main st.

JEWELRY AND SILVER WARE.

TRASK, O., Jewelry, Silver Ware, etc., 618 Main st.

LIVERY AND SALE STABLES.

D. B. ARNOLD,
Livery & Boarding Stable,
209 & 211
S. Third St.,
TERRE HAUTE.

J. H. HOLMES,
Livery and Boarding Stable,
1126 & 1128 Main st., bet. Eleventh & Twelfth.

LIVERY AND COMMISSION
SALE STABLES.
Horses, etc., Bought and Sold.
The Best Rigs for Hire in the City.
AUCTION SALES EVERY SATURDAY, AT 2 P.M.
FOUTS & HUNTER, Props.,
123 & 125 S. THIRD STREET.

1847.
numbered 20,000. The Mexican General, assuring Gen. Taylor that he was surrounded, ordered him to surrender within an hour. Taylor refused, and both armies prepared for battle. It was a desperate and bloody battle, commencing at sunrise and lasting until sunset; but finally the Mexicans fled in confusion, leaving their dead and wounded behind, and the Americans were left masters of the field. Americans lost 267 killed, 456 wounded, and 23 missing. The Mexicans lost almost 2,000. They left 500 of their comrades dead on the field.

Feb. 8.—Gen. Kearney proclaimed the annexation of California to the United States.

Feb. 23.—Captain Webster, with a small party of Americans, drove Gen. Minon, with 800 cavalry, out of Satillo.

Feb 28.—Col. Doniphan, when within 18 miles from Chihuahua, was met by 4,000 Mexicans. These he completely routed, losing in killed and wounded only 18 men, while the Mexicans lost about 600. He then pressed forward to the city, entered it in triumph, and raised the American flag upon its citadel (March 2) amidst a population of 40,000, and took possession of the province in the name of government.

March 27.—Surrender of Vera Cruz and Castle of San Juan de Ulloa to Gen. Scott and Com. Perry, with 5,000 prisoners and 500 pieces of artillery. The Americans lost 47 killed, and about the same number wounded. It is supposed 1,000 Mexicans were killed, and a great number of them wounded. During the siege it is estimated that 6,700 shot and shell were thrown by the American batteries, weighing in the aggregate more than 4,000 pounds.

April 18.—Battle of Cerro Gordo. This place was defended by Santa Anna, and 12,000 Mexicans, in a strongly fortified position, and many pieces of cannon. Gen. Scott, with 8,000 Americans, assaulted the enemy, and drove the Mexicans from their position. Santa Anna himself narrowly escaped capture by fleeing upon a mule taken from his carriage. More than 1,000 Mexicans were killed or wounded, and 3,000 made prisoners. Americans lost in killed and wounded 431.

April 21.—Battle of Churubusco. Gen. Scott advanced on Churubusco, where Santa Anna was in command of the main body of the Mexican army. The enemy were defeated, and Santa Anna abandoned the field and fled to the City of Mexico. This defeat of the Mexicans was the final destruction of an army 30,000 strong, by another about one-third its strength in number. Full 4,000 of the Mexicans were killed or wounded, 3,000 made prisoners, and 30 pieces of cannon taken. Americans lost in killed and wounded about 1,100.

April 22.—Gen. Worth takes possession of the castle of Perote. This was considered one of the strongest fortresses in Mexico, yet it was surrendered without resistance. Fifty-four pieces of cannon and mortars were captured here, and a large quantity of munitions of war.

May 15.—Americans take possession of the city of Puebla, a city of 80,000 inhabitants, without opposition.

Aug. 21.—Gen. Scott was now within three miles of the city of Mexico, when Santa Anna sent a flag of truce, asking for an armis-

JOHN E. SULLIVAN,

Produce and Commission Merchant

FOREIGN & DOMESTIC FRUITS,

28 - CIRCLE STREET - 28
INDIANAPOLIS, IND.

ADVERTISEMENTS. 117

Penn's Treaty with the Indians.—Although historians differ as to the precise locality where this treaty took place, it is pretty generally conceded to have occurred under the great elm tree at Shakamaxon, in the vicinity of Philadelphia, in the year 1682. This treaty was never broken for a period of forty or fifty years, and during all that time the scalping knife and tomahawk was sheathed in peace with the white men of Penn's treaty.

LAFAYETTE
Eye, Ear & Throat Dispensary.

DR. A. BURKE,

The Surgeon of this establishment, was formerly first assistant to the celebrated oculist, Professor L. Von Wecker, and acted in the same capacity in the Throat Dispensary of Professor Chas. Fauvel, the highest authority in Europe, on all Catarrhal and Lung Complaints. These titles on the public opinion, are all certified by the American Embassy from Paris, and can be seen in the Doctor's Office. Address,

161 Main St., La Fayette, Ind.

ADVERTISEMENTS.

TERRE HAUTE—Continued.

LIVERY AND SALE STABLES.

C. P. STAUB, Proprietor of

Livery, Sale and Feed Stable,
N. Third st., bet. Main and Cherry. Proprietor and Author of Staub's Complete Horse Farrier.

MACHINIST.

J. A. PEABODY,

Patentee and Manufacturer of Peabody's

Improved Rotary Mortising Machine,

Model Maker and Machinist,

Etab. 1865.   **1119 N. Second St.**

MARBLE WORKS.

City Marble Works,

M. HANRAHAN,

Manufacturer and Dealer in

American and Italian Marble,

AND SCOTCH GRANITE,

Monuments, Tomb Stones, Urns, Vases, Garden Figures and Statuary.

SHOP—On Third St., bet. Ohio & Walnut.
One Door South St. Charles Hotel.

MARBLE WORKS.

Barnett, Palmer & Swift,

Importers and Dealers in

Rose and Gray Scotch Granite,

And Italian Marble Monuments, Tombs, Head Stones, Vaults, Mantels, etc.,
East Main St, bet. Twelfth and Thirteenth Sts.,
All work warranted to give Satisfaction.

MILLINERY.

MARY A. CRONIN,

Dealer in Millinery, Fancy Goods, Embroideries, Laces, and Variety Goods,
Stamping done to order.
18 S. FOURTH ST.

Mrs. Fanny Mautz,

MILLINERY,

10 S. FOURTH STREET.

Work done to order.

PRAIRIE CITY EMPORIUM, E. B. Cole, MILLINERY, and Ladies' Furnishing Goods, 324 Main st.

NOTARY PUBLIC.

E. MONTGOMERY,

Notary Public,

AND GENERAL AGENT.

Office with H. D. SCOTT, Esq., Attorney.
517½ South side Main, bet. 5th and 6th Sts.
Established 1876.

TERRE HAUTE—Continued.

OYSTERS AND FISH.

M. C. RAFFERTY'S

Fulton Oyster & Fish Market,

Wholesale and Retail Dealer in and Shipper of

Can and Bulk Oysters, and Fresh Fish
OF ALL KINDS.

Poultry and Game Depot, 617 and 619 E. Main St.

PAINTERS.

WILLIAM ALDER,

HOUSE & SIGN PAINTER,

501 Ohio St.

Calhoun Bros.,

CARRIAGE PAINTERS,

1311 E. Main St.

JACKSON & AUBLE.

House & Sign Painters

No. 25 S. Sixth St., Opp. P. O.

MANN, CHAS. H., House and Sign Painter, 126 North Fifth St.

MANNING, W. H., Carriage and Sign PAINTER, Cor Fifth and Cherry Sts.

STUCKINSCH & WOLFE, House and Sign Painters and Paper Hanging, 7 Ohio st.

PRINTERS.

RUPE & WHITAKER, The Gem Job Printing Office, Pences Block.

PRODUCE DEALERS.

BAISLER & WINTERSTEIN, Produce, Vegetables, Fruits etc., 653 Main St.

RESTAURANT.

C. H. ROUSER'S

Grand Restaurant and Dining Rooms,

No. 610 Main St., N. Side. Open day and night.

RUSTIC WORK.

FRIDLEY & BRO.,

Manufacturers and Dealers in all kinds of

FANCY HICKORY RUSTIC WORK, CHAIRS,
Settees, Flower Stands, Hanging Baskets, &c.
Cor. 7th and Poplar sts.

SALOONS.

JOHN F. O'REILLY,

Wine and Beer Saloon,
12 N. SECOND ST.

NEW POST OFFICE, PHILADELPHIA.—The new, elegant and vast edifice, now in the course of erection, is to occupy the entire front on the west side of Ninth street, from Chestnut to Market Streets, and is to face almost one-half of the square on Chestnut and Market streets, and is to have an extensive passage for mail wagons, from Tenth street, entering into a vast court yard, provided with spacious and uninterrupted facilities for dispatching and receiving mails. The building will probably cost $6,000,000.

DR. WITHEFORD,
MATERIALIZING MEDIUM
231 W. Madison St., Chicago, Ill.

Public seances every evening, private consultations daily. Spirit voices are heard, names given, spirit hands, faces and full forms are seen and recognized, also messages written out by spirit hands, full name signed, &c., IN THE LIGHT.

1847.

tice, preparatory to negotiations for peace. It was granted, but the propositions of the United States were spurned and scorned, and Santa Anna treacherously violated the armistice by strengthening the defenses of the city.

Aug. 21.—Battle of Contreras. General Smith attacked the Mexicans at sunrise, and, after a brief and sanguinary conflict, the Americans were victorious. Eighty officers and 2,000 private soldiers were made prisoners, and thirty-three pieces of artillery were captured. The Mexican force engaged was 6,000, under General Valencia.

Sept. 8.—Battle of El Molinos del Rey. About 4,000 Americans attacked 14,000 Mexicans, under Santa Anna, near Chapultepec. The Americans were first repulsed with great slaughter, but, returning to the attack, they fought desperately for an hour, and drove the Mexicans from their position. Both armies suffered dreadfully. The Mexicans lost about 1,000 dead on the field, and the Americans about 800.

Sept. 13.—Battle of Chapultepec. This was the last place to be defended outside the suburbs of the City of Mexico. The Americans, under Gen. Scott, made a furious assault and routed the enemy with great slaughter, and unfurled the Stars and Stripes over the shattered castle of Chapultepec. The Mexicans fled to the city, pursued by Gen. Quitman to its very gates. That night Santa Anna and his army, with the officers of government, fled the doomed city.

Sept. 14.—American army, in command of Gen. Scott, enter the City of Mexico without resistance.

1848.

May 29.—Wisconsin admitted as a State, Gen. Scott superseded in Mexico by Gen. William O. Butler.

July 4.—Peace proclaimed between the United States and Mexico. By this treaty, the United States came into possession of California and New Mexico. The treaty stipulated the evacuation of Mexico by the American army within three months; the payment of $3,000,000 in hand and $12,000,000, in four annual installments, by the United States to Mexico, for the territory acquired by conquest; and, in addition, to assume debts due to certain citizens of the United States to the amount of $3,500,000, it also fixed boundaries.

The corner-stone of the Washington Monument was laid in the national capital.

July.—News of the discovery of gold in California reached the States.

Postal convention between the United States and Great Britain.

Mormons (founded by Joseph Smith in 1827) settle near Great Salt Lake, Utah.

Sept. 9.—Large fire in Albany, N. Y.

Dec. 8.—First deposit of California gold in mint.

1849.

March 4.—"Wilmot Proviso" passed by Congress.

March 5.—Gen. Zachary Taylor inaugurated President.

May 15.—Great fire in St. Louis, Mo.

March 30 to Sept. 8.—Philadelphia depleted by cholera.

June 15.—James K. Polk dies.

Aug. 11.—The President of the United States publishes a proclamation against the

TERRE HAUTE—*Continued.*

ALOONS.

Delmonico Billiard Hall,
WINE & BEER SALOON,
FINE WINES, LIQUORS AND CIGARS.

Julius Blumenberg, Prop..
Main st., bet. Sixth and Seventh.

SIBLEY, W. W., Wine and Beer Saloon, 12 S. Fifth st.

ROBERT HIGDON,
CONCERT HALL,

WHOLESALE & RETAIL DEALER IN LIQUORS
24 NORTH SECOND ST.

SAUSAGE MANUFACTURER.

GEORGE H. WOLF,
Butcher and Steam Sausage Manufacturer,
27 N. FOURTH ST., bet. Main & Cherry sts.

SEED DEALER.

FOOTE, A. J., Seed Merchant,
512 Main st.

SEWING MACHINES.

BRANCH OFFICE OF THE
HOWE SEWING MACHINE CO..
320 Main st., bet. Third and Fourth sts.
T. D. OLIN, AGENT.

STOVES AND TINWARE.

H. P. TOWNLEY & CO.,
STOVES, TINWARE
House Furnishing Goods, Main st., bet. 4th & 5th.

TOBACCO AND CIGARS.

SEEMAN, C. H., Manufacturer of and Dealer in Cigars and Tobacco, 643 Main st.

HENRY C. UCHTMAN,
Manufacturer of and Dealer in
Foreign and Domestic Cigars,
Also the Best Brands of Chewing and Smoking Tobaccos, 177 Main st., bet. Sixth & Seventh.

CHARLES WEIDEL,
Manufacturer of
Cigars and Dealer in Tobacco.
19 SOUTH FOURTH ST.,

Furnishes Cigars to Secretary of Navy.

WALL PAPER AND SHADES.

J. W. ROBERTS, Dealer in
WALL PAPER, WINDOW SHADES,
Paints, Glass, Oils, Varnishes, etc.,
825 MAIN STREET.

IMPORTANT EVENTS OF THE CENTURY. 121

TERRE HAUTE—*Continued.*

WINES AND LIQUORS.

ALEXANDER & CO., Wholesale Dealers in Liquors, Cigars, Oysters, etc., 615 Main st.

JOHNSON, E. W., Wholesale Dealer in Liquors, Cigars, etc., 613 Main st.

Terre Haute Business Houses.
WHEN ESTABLISHED.

BARNETT, PALMER & SWIFT, Marble Works, 1867.
CLIFF & SON, Boiler Manufacturers, 1865.
FOOTE, A. J., Seed Merchant, 1866.
HULMAN & COX, Grocers and Liquors, 1850.
MAYER, A., Brewery, 1856.

FORT WAYNE, IND.

ARCHITECTS.

TOLAN, T. J. & SON, Architects. Court Houses and Jails a specialty. Armory Hall.

Geo. Trenam,

ARCHITECT

160 West Main St.

Residence : 162 West Main St.

ATTORNEYS AT LAW.

BITTENGER, J. R., Prosecuting Attorney, 38th Judicial Circuit, N. W. Cor. Calhoun & Main.

Law and Collection Offices.

Graham & Gotshall,

17 E. MAIN ST.

Collections made in all parts of the United States and Canada.

HOAGLAND, JOHN R., Attorney at Law and Justice of the Peace, 12½ E. Main St.

JENISON, WM. T., Attorney and Counselor at Law, over First National Bank.

TAYLOR & MORRIS, Attorneys at Law, 34 East Bery St.

WILKINSON & GRAHAM, Attorneys at Law and Notaries Public, N. W. cor. Main & Calhoun.

BARBERS.

KINSEY, J. J., American House Shaving and Hair Dressing Saloon, 17 W. Columbia St.

BOOK BINDERS.

DAVIS & BRO., Book Binders and Blank Book Manufacturers, 78 and 80 Clinton St.

1849.

marauding expedition of General Lopez to Cuba. Notwithstanding this proclamation, Lopez landed 600 men at Cuba, and after a short struggle took the town of Cardenas from the Spaniards.
Fearful rage of the cholera in New York; 5,071 died from the disease.
Sept. 1.—California adopts a Constitution excluding slavery from the territory.

1850.

Treaty with England for a transit way across the Isthmus of Panama.
Immense immigration of gold-seekers to California.
Seventh census of the United States; population, 23,191,074.
Violent debates between the Pro-slavery and Free-soil parties in Congress, over the proposed admission of California.
March 31.—John C. Calhoun dies.
April 19.—The Bulwer-Clayton treaty between England and the United States, relative to the establishment of a communication by ship canal between the Atlantic and Pacific Oceans, was signed at Washington, April 19, and ratifications were exchanged there July 4, 1850.
May 17.—Gen. Lopez conducts another marauding expedition against Cuba for the purpose of annexing that Island to the United States, but is repulsed at Cardenas by the Spanish authorities.
May.—The Grinnell expedition, in search of Sir John Franklin, leaves New York.
Territory of Utah organized.
July 9.—President Taylor dies.
Great fire in Philadelphia.
July 10.—Vice-President, Millard Fillmors, assumes the Presidency.
Aug. 13.—Admission of California into the United States.
Sept. 9.—Passage of Henry Clay's Omnibus Bill; one of the stipulaitons of this bill was the abolishing of slavery in the District of Columbia, and a law providing for the arrest, in the northern or free States, and return to their masters, of all slaves who should escape from bondage.
Sept. 18.—Fugitive Slave Bill passed by Congress. This bill imposed a fine of $1,000 and six months' imprisonment on any person harboring fugitive slaves, or aiding in their escape. Repealed June 13th, 1874.

1851.

Jan. 27.—John James Audubon, American naturalist, died, aged 71 years.
May 8.—A "Southern Rights" convention assembles at Charleston, S. C.
Resolutions passed for a dissolution of the Union.
Survey of the coast of the United States completed.
May 3.—Great fire in San Francisco.
Letter postage reduced to three cents to all parts of the United States, excepting California and the Pacific Territories.
Minnesota purchased from the Upper Sioux Indians, for $305,000, to be given when they should reach their reservation in Upper Minnesota, and $68,000 a year for fifty years. By this purchase the Government came in possession of 21,000,000 acres of land.
United States purchases a large tract of land from the Lower Sioux, paying $225,000 down,

SOUTHERN PLANING MILL.
JACOB MEYERS & BRO.,

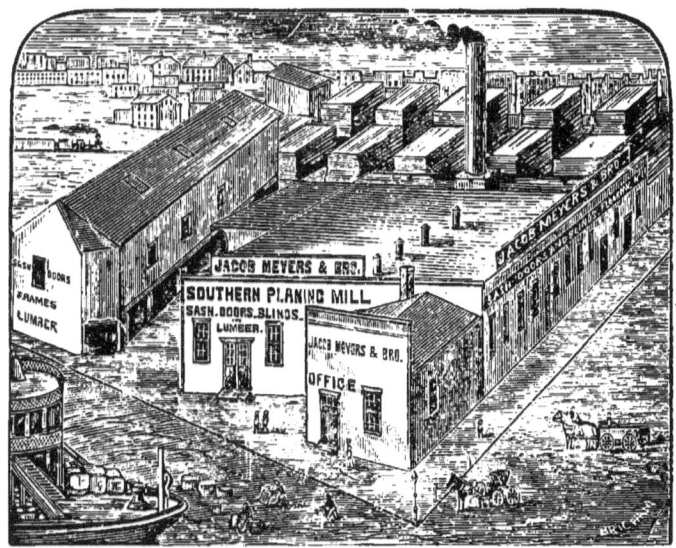

Manufacturers, Wholesale and Retail Dealers in
ALL KINDS OF BUILDING MATERIALS,
Cor. Water and Goodsell Streets, EVANSVILLE, IND.
All orders promptly filled. Send for Price List.

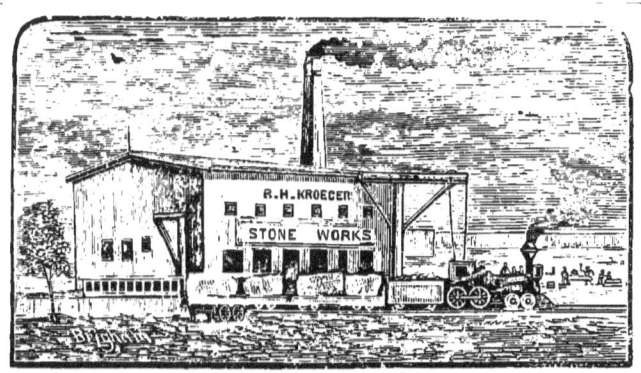

B. H. KROEGER,
CONTRACTOR AND BUILDER IN STONE WORK.
Steam Mill and Yard: COR. EDGAR AND PENNSYLVANIA STREETS, EVANSVILLE, IND.
All kinds of Stone Work for Buildings, Fences, &c., done to order.
All orders from a distance promptly attended to.

ADVERTISEMENTS. 123

Opera House, Evansville, Ind.—Was built in the year 1868, at a cost exclusive of ground, of $126,000. Has a frontage of 50 feet, and is 130 feet deep by about 50 feet high. Is built of pressed brick with sand stone front. The entrance is unusually broad, with wide stairway to second story diverging from box office on either side to the main hall. It is the only strictly first-class place of amusement in the city, and has been lately entirely remoddled, refitted and enlarged with 666 elegant folding opera chairs. The family circle and gallery will accommodate 600, making a total seating capacity of 1266.

MILLER BRO.'S
THREE STORES
113, 115, 221 and 717 Main St., Evansville, Ind.
The largest retail business in our line in the State.
General Dry Goods,
Silks & Fine Goods a Specialty.
Best quality at lowest prices.

FORT WAYNE—*Continued.*

BOARDING HOUSE.
JOSEPH LANGARD,
Proprietor

French Boarding House,
And Dealer in
Wines, Liquors and Cigars.
No. 70 Columbia St.

BOOTS AND SHOES.

FORTRIED, LOUIS, Manufacturer of Boots and Shoes, 32 W. Main st.

HUSER, L. P., Boot and Shoe Maker.
178 Broadway.

CARNAHAN, HANNA & CO., Wholesale dealers in Boots and Shoes, 30 & 32 E. Main st.

CARRIAGE AND WAGON MANUFACTURERS.
JOHN BAKER,

Old Fort Carriage Works,
16 & 18 Lafayette st.

J. B. GILBERT,
Manufacturer of
CARRIAGES, WAGONS, ETC.,
Also a fine Stock of Light Harness kept on hand, or made to order.
Corner of West Main and Fulton Sts.

Fred. Rolsener,
WAGON AND BUGGY MANUFACTURER,
102 WEST MAIN ST.

STANLEY & BIEBER,
CARRIAGE MANUFACTURERS
106 West Main St.

H. STHAIR,
Manufacturer of
Carriages, Buggies and Spring Wagons,
11 East Jefferson St.

CLOTHING.

NIRDLINGER, S. F., Clothing, 53 E. Main & 33 Calhoun Sts.

THIEM, E. J. G. & BRO., Merchant Tailors and Clothiers, 37 E. Columbia St.

COMMERCIAL COLLEGE.
FORT WAYNE

COMMERCIAL COLLEGE.
—(AND)—
Institute of Penmanship,
THOS. POWERS, Principal.
Cor. E. Main & Court Sts.

FORT WAYNE—*Continued.*

CONSERVATORY OF MUSIC.
FORT WAYNE

Conservatory of Music,
INCORPORATED, 1871.
For Catalogue and particulars, address,
C. F. W. MEYER, Principal.

DENTIST.

LOAG, G. W., Dentist,
7 W. Columbia St.

DRY GOODS.

GEO. DWALD & CO.,
Wholesale and Retail dealers in

Staple and Fancy Dry Goods,
No. 1 COLUMBIA ST.

DYERS AND SCOURERS.

B. A. LEWIS,

CITY DYE HOUSE
59 W. Water St.
ESTABLISHED, 1851.
Goods received and returned by express.

NIERMANN, M., Renovating,
43 W. Water st.

EXPRESS COMPANIES.

UNITED STATES EXPRESS CO., C. L. Smith, Agt, 28 E. Main st.

FURNITURE AND UPHOLSTERING.

F. BAUS,
Upholstering and Furniture Shop.
Furniture made to order. Repairing neatly done. Furniture repaired and varnished. Chairs caned.
NO. 143 CALHOUN STREET.

GRIEBEL & SON, manufacturers of all kinds of Furniture, 44 E. Main St.

H. TEGEDER & CO.,
Manufacturers of and dealers in all kinds of

FURNITURE,
Repairing Promptly done.
213 CALHOUN ST.

ADVERTISEMENTS. 125

INDEPENDENCE BELL.—The bell, originally cast in England in 1751, at a cost of one hundred pounds sterling, was ordered to be of 2,000 pounds weight. Before it was properly hung it was cracked by a stroke of the clapper to try the sound, and was recast by Paris & Stow of Philadelphia. It was hung again in June, 1753. It contains the following inscription : "By order of the assembly of the Province of Pennsylvania, for the State House in the City of Philadelphia, 1752;" also, "Proclaim Liberty throughout all the land, and unto all the inhabitants thereof." The most important event connected with the bell is, that it rang to proclaim the birth of a nation, and the freedom of the American people from British oppression. It was broken in ringing.

JONES' COMMERCIAL COLLEGE
309 North Fifth St., St. Louis, Missouri.

This Institution is one of the oldest of its kind in the United States. It maintains a full Board of Teachers throughout the year, and Young Gentlemen can register themselves as Students at any time they may choose. For Circulars call at the office as above, or address, **JONATHAN JONES, St. Louis, Mo.**

1851.

and an annual payment of $30,000 a year for fifty years.

Steamer Cleopatra seized by the United States authorities in New York, on suspicion of preparing to invade Cuba, and many respectable gentlemen arrested on the same charge.

Louis Kossuth, the Hungarian patriot, arrives in New York.

July 4.—President laid the corner-stone for additional buildings to the National Capitol.

August.—Lopez's second expedition to Cuba. He sailed from New Orleans with about 480 men. He left Colonel Crittenden, with 100 men, on the northern coast of Cuba, who were captured, carried to Havana, and on the 16th were shot. Lopez and six of his followers were captured and executed on the 1st of September.

Oct.—Return of the Grinnell expedition from the search of Sir John Franklin, without accomplishing its object.

Dec. 24.—Capitol at Washington partly destroyed by fire.

1852.

United States expedition to Japan, under command of Commodore Perry, a brother of the hero of Lake Erie.

June 29.—Henry Clay dies in Washington, aged 75 years.

Oct. 24.—Daniel Webster dies.

Nov.—Spanish authorities at Havana refuse to receive the United States mails and passengers from the American steamship Crescent City, plying between New York and New Orleans.

England and France propose a treaty with the United States, binding the latter to disclaim "now and forever hereafter all intention to obtain possession of the island of Cuba," and "to discountenance all such attempts to that effect on the part of any power or individual whatever." The treaty was rejected by the United States.

1853.

March 2.—Washington territory created out of the northern part of Oregon.

March 4.—Franklin Pearce inaugurated President.

May.—Second expedition leaves in search of Sir John Franklin, under the command of Dr. E. K. Kane.

Four vessels, under Captain Ringgold, leave on an exploring expedition to the Northern Pacific Ocean.

Four expeditions start to explore as many different routes for a railway to the Pacific coast. One under Capt. Gunnison was attacked by the Indians, and Gunnison and several of his party were killed.

July 2.—Capt. Ingraham upholds the rights of American citizenship. Martin Kaszta, while in business at Smyrna, was seized by order of the Austrian consul, and taken on board of an Austrian brig as a rebel refugee, notwithstanding he had proclaimed allegiance to the United States. Capt. Ingraham claimed Koszta as an American citizen, and on the refusal of the Austrian authorities to give up the prisoner, Ingraham cleared his vessel for action, and threatened to fire on the brig, if he was not delivered up within a given time. The Austrians yielded, and Koszta was placed in the custody of the French consul to

FORT WAYNE—*Continued.*

GATE MANUFACTURER.

WISELL, D. D., Patent Gate,
34 Calhoun st.

GROCERS.

BLEEKMAN, J. & CO., Staple and Fancy Groceries, 25 W. Columbia st. Established 1877.

DIDIER, J. C., Established 1865. Groceries and Provisions, 66 E. Columbia st.

MILLER, W. H. & CO., Groceries, Crockery, Glassware and Provisions, 24 Harrison st.

JOHN RAAB,

Pork Packer and Dealer in Groceries and Provisions,

18 E. COLUMBIA ST.

☞ Established 1850.

GUN AND LOCKSMITH.

MAX. G. LADE,

Practical Gunsmith,

Locksmith and Engraver.

Dealer in
Cutlery, Guns, Revolvers, Gun Materials,
Etc., Etc.,
Manufacturer of

Breech-Loading Guns & Rifles.

Stencil-cutting done to order a specialty.

58 East Main St.

HARNESS AND SADDLES.

KUNTZ, G. H., Manf'r of Harness, and Dealer in Saddles, Collars, &c., Main & Harrison sts.

HORSE DEALER.

FRED BRIEL,

Dealer in

Horses,

Will Buy at all times for Eastern and Southern Market.

19 W. Columbia St., Fort Wayne.

HORSE COLLAR MANUFACTURERS.

(Established 1867.)

A. RACINE,

—Manufacturer of—

HORSE COLLARS

Of all kinds. Also Patentee and Manufacturer of the **COMBINED PAD & COLLAR FASTENER,**

Cor. FIRST and CASS STS., North Side.

Orders solicited and promptly filled.

FORT WAYNE—*Continuud.*

HORSE COLLAR MANUFACTURERS.

F. L. RACINE,
Wholesale Manufacturer of

HORSE COLLARS
Shop, 36 North Cass Street,
Near Saginaw Depot, Corner of Alley.

HORSESHOERS.

ED. FOGERTY,
Practical Horseshoer,
Cor. Harrison and Pearl Sts.

Shoeing for all Diseases of Horses' Feet, such as

Corns, Contracted Feet, Quitters, Sand Cracks, Etc.,

Will be attended to by the most scientific workmen, and executed with neatness and despatch, on the most improved principles of Veterinary practice.

Advice given on Proper Treatment of all Diseases of Horses' Feet.

Residence, cor. Harrison & Pearl Sts.

A. VIZARD,
PRACTICAL

HORSESHOER,
94 E. Columbia St.

Established 1870.

HOTELS.

THE GRAND HOTEL, J. H. Buckls, prop., Columbia and Harrison sts.

HEDEKIN HOUSE, A. Freeman, prop., 25 Barr st.

MAYER HOUSE, Dr. J. M. Rhoads, prop., Calhoun and Main sts.

THE ROBINSON HOUSE,
JAS. H. ROBINSON, Prop.,
The Best $2.00 per day House in the State.

Central, Commodious & Attractive.

Cor. Harrison and Columbia Sts.

HUMAN HAIR DEALERS.

BALDWIN, MISS ANNIE, Ladies' Hair Dresser, 30 E Columbia st.

BOYCE, MISS E. S., Ladies' Hair Dresser, 15 Calhoun st.

LAUNDRY.

KELSEY & CO.,
CENTRAL CITY LAUNDRY,
All work done to Order. Lace and fine work a specialty. 114 W. Wayne st.

9

IMPORTANT EVENTS OF THE CENTURY. 127

1853.

await the action of the respective governments. He was finally given up to the United States.

July 14.—"Crystal Palace," or World's Fair, in New York, was formally opened for the reception of visitors.

Oct.—The fishery question settled by mutual concession of Great Britain and the United States.

1854.

Feb. 28.—Seizure of the American steamship Black Warrior in the harbor of Havana.

March 7.—Homestead bill passed, which provides that any free white male citizen, or one who may have declared his intentions to become one previous to the passage of this act, might select 160 acres of land on the public domain, and on proof being given that he had occupied and cultivated it for five years, he might receive a title to it, in fee, without being required to pay anything for it.

March 9.—Ostend Conference—a conference held by American ministers in Europe, recommending the purchase of Cuba by the United States, and also asserted the right to take Cuba by force, if Spain refused to sell.

March 31.—Commercial treaty with Japan concluded by Com. Perry.

May.—Passage of the Kansas-Nebraska bill, which created those two territories, and left the people of every territory, on becoming a State, free to adopt or exclude the institution of slavery. A few days after the passage of the bill a riot occurred in Boston over the arrest of a fugitive slave. A deputy marshal was shot dead. United States troops from Rhode Island and the local militia were called out to sustain the government. The fugitive slave was finally returned to his master in Virginia without further violence.

June 7.—Reciprocity treaty between Great Britain and the United States respecting international trade, fisheries, etc.

July 13.—Bombardment of Greytown, Central America, by a United States manof-war, in retaliation of an insult offered to the American consul by the Spaniards.

Col. Fremont and party exploring the Rocky Mountains. They suffered terribly. For fortyfive days they fed on mules meat, which from want of food could go no further, and were killed and eaten, every particle even to the entrails. They were met and relieved by another party 19th of February.

Death of J. Harrington, last survivor of the battle of Lexington.

1855.

Gen. Harney chastises the Sioux Indians. Serious troubles in Kansas over the slavery question.

Wm. Walker, an adventurer from California, with an army of filibusters, takes possession of Nicaraugua and establishes a government there.

Dispute with England over enlistment of soldiers for Crimean war. The British minister at Washington and the British consuls at New York and Cincinnati dismissed by the United States for sanctioning the enlistments.

June 28.—Railroad from Panama to Aspinwall opened.

Dec. 23.—British Arctic vessel Resolute

128 ADVERTISEMENTS.

Young and Middle-aged men and women prepared for business.

MINNEAPOLIS BUSINESS COLLEGE.

C. C. CURTISS, A. M. AND C. W. G. HYDE, PROPRIETORS.

Address CURTISS & HYDE, MINNEAPOLIS, MINN. Box 299.

English Staff Quarters, Centennial Exposition, Philadelphia.—The Staff Quarters, which has an area of 1,200 feet, is used as the residence of the Staff of the British portion of the exhibition. The building is of the picturesque half-timber style of architecture, so much in vogue during the sixteenth century.

A. REDDEN,
Manufacturer and Wholesale Dealer in
Men's Fine Boots and Shoes,
802 N. Fifth St., St. Louis, Mo.

The English Walking Shoe,
A dirt Excluder, and perfectly Water Tight to the top.

The Alexis,
A Perfect Fitting Shoe, and Warranted in every respect.

ESTABLISHED IN 1875.

With more than twenty years' previous experience in the management of the largest manufactories in the United States.

All orders promptly filled, whether large or small.

1855.

found and brought to New London by an American whaler.

1856

Feb. 2.—N. P. Banks, Jr., of Massachusetts, elected Speaker of the House of Representatives of the United States, after a contest of nine weeks, by a plurality of votes.

May 22.—Senator Sumner, of Massachusetts, assaulted by Preston S. Brooks, of South Carolina. The former was so severely injured that he could not resume his seat in the Senate for three years.

May 28.—The British envoy to the United States ordered to quit Washington.

June 21.—The President of the United States recognizes the filibuster, General Walker, as President of Nicaraugua.

Nov. 4.—James Buchanan, the pro-slavery candidate, elected President of the United States, after a close contest with Colonel Fremont, the anti-slavery candidate.

1857.

Jan. 4.—Kansas rejects the Lecompton Constitution.

William Walker driven out of Nicaraugua by the Costa Ricans and Nicarauguans.

Feb. 12.—George Peabody donates $300,000 to establish a free literary and scientific institute at Baltimore.

March 4.—James Buchanan inaugurated President and John C. Breckinridge Vice-President.

March 6.—The Dred Scott decision delivered by Chief Justice Taney. Dred Scott and his wife were slaves belonging to a surgeon in the army. They were taken by him from a slave State into a territory where slavery was forever prohibited, and they claimed their freedom by the act of their master, on the ground that he had taken them into free territory. The decision of the court was against their claims, and they were continued slaves.

Aug. 24.—Beginning of financial panic, which culminates in an almost entire suspension of the banks.

Sept. 8.—Loss of the Central America and 450 lives, off Cape May.

Sept. 23.—Commencement of great religious revivals in the United States.

Dec. 8.—Father Theobald Matthew died, aged 67. He was better known as Father Matthew, Apostle of Temperance. He was a Roman Catholic, born in Ireland, and arrived at New York June 29, 1849. He was received by the Board of Aldermen, and introduced and welcomed by an address from Wm. F. Dodge and Mayor Woodhull. He was escorted through the city by a large procession.

Commercial failures this year amount to 5,123. Liabilities, $291,757,000.

1858.

Feb. 14.—United States army defeats the Mormons in an engagement at Eco Cañans.

March 28.—Nicaraugua places herself under the protection of the United States.

May 23.—Minnesota admitted as a State.

June.—President Monroe's remains were removed from New York city to Richmond, Virginia.

Aug. 2.—Kansas again rejects the Lecompton Constitution.

FORT WAYNE—Continued.

LEATHER AND FINDINGS.

FREIBURGER, S. & BRO., Dealers in Leather and Findings, 24 E. Main st.

LIME MANUFACTURER.

M. BALTES,

Manufacturer of WHITE LIME, PLASTER, Etc.,
3 HARRISON ST.

LIVERY AND SALE STABLE.

FLETCHER, J. F., Livery, Feed and Sale Stable, 32 Barr st.

LUMBER DEALERS.

HOFFMAN BROS.,
Manufacturers of
BLACK WALNUT LUMBER
200 WEST MAIN ST.

MARBLE WORKS.
Established A. D. 1847.

Underhill & Congdon,
Monumental, Gravestone, Marble,
AND GRANITE WORKS,
74 & 76 W. MAIN ST.

W. C. YOUNG,
Practical

Marble Worker and Monumental Designer.

Will furnish all kinds of Cemetery Work at reduced prices. Those wishing anything in my line will find it to their advantage to give me a call before purchasing. Fine Carving and Sculptor Work a specialty. Office and Shop, 171 W. Washington st., near Broadway.

MATTRESS MANUFACTURER.

BECKEL, F. H., Manufacturer of Spring Mattresses and Lounges, 21 Court st.

MILLINERY AND DRESSMAKING.

MRS. J. SCHEFFER.
Established 1870,

Millinery and Dressmaking,
26 CLINTON STREET.

FLETCHER, MRS. M. A., Dressmaker,
65 E. Main st.

MINERAL WATER MANUFACTURERS.

H. BARGUS & ROBBE,
(Successors to J. Laurent & Son,) Dealers in
FOREIGN AND DOMESTIC

WINES AND LIQUORS,
And Manufacturers of
MINERAL WATER & GINGER ALE,
29 & 31 BARR STREET.

FORT WAYNE—*Continued.*

NEWSPAPERS.

FORT WAYNE MORNING GAZETTE,
25 W. Main st.

FORT WAYNE WEEKLY JOURNAL, C. Fairbank
& Co., props., Court st., over Post Office.

FORT WAYNE DAILY NEWS,
Page, Taylor & Co., props.

OYSTERS AND FISH.

HASKELL, W., Oysters, Fish, Game, etc., 65 E.
Columbia st. Established 1865.

L. E. K'KEE,
Dealer in

OYSTERS, FISH & GAME,
Also Butter, Eggs & Poultry,
152 CALHOUN ST.

PAPER BOX MANUFACTURERS.

DAVIS & BRO., Wood and Paper Box Manufacturers, 78 and 80 Clinton st.

PIANOS AND ORGANS.

TAYLOR BROS.,
Dealers in the

Hallett, Davis & Co. and Schomaker

PIANOS,
Also the STERLING ORGAN,
15 WEST WAYNE STREET.

PHOTOGRAPHERS.

SHOAFF, J. A., Photographer,
7 W. Columbia st.

CARL SOMMER,
PHOTOGRAPHER,
30 CALHOUN STREET,
FORT WAYNE, IND.

C. E. WALLIN,
The Leading Photographer,
Sole Proprietor of the CARBON PROCESS
for this State.

18 WEST BERRY ST.

BROADWAY
PHOTO. GALLERY
E. W. POSTON, Proprietor.
108 NEAR REMMEL'S BLOCK, BROADWAY.

1858.
Aug. 5.—Atlantic telegraph cable laid. President Buchanan's message to Queen Victoria sent on the 16th, but cable proves a failure.

1859.
Oregon admitted as a State.
June 25.—Commodore Tatnall, of U. S. navy, in Chinese waters, makes his famous utterance: "Blood is thicker than water."
July 4.—A. H. Stephens, of Georgia, advocates the formation of a Southern Confederacy.
Nov. 28.—Death of Washington Irving, American novelist and historical writer.
Oct. 17.—A negro insurrection breaks out at Harper's Ferry. John Brown, with a score of followers, crossed the Potomac at Harper's Ferry and entered Virginia, where he incited the slaves to take up arms against their masters. After a short time, Brown was captured and tried for treason, found guilty, he bore his misfortune with the greatest composure, and when asked upon the scaffold to give a sign when he was ready, he answered, "I am always ready." He died in the midst of slaves and slave owners—his countrymen—and now no countryman of his can look at his place of execution and call himself a slave owner or a slave.
Oct.—J. Y. Slidell, U. S. Minister to France, died at Paris.
Nov.—Gen. Scott sent to protect American interests in San Juan.
Deaths in the U. S. this Year.—George W. Doane, Episcopal bishop of New Jersey, poet, etc., aged 60 years. Rufus Choate jurist, advocate, and Senator, aged 60 years. Horace Mann, statesman and educationist, aged 63 years.

1860.
Eighth census of the United States; population, 31,443,332.
Feb. 1.—Pennington, of New Jersey, elected Speaker of the House of Representatives, after balloting nearly two months.
From February, 1820, to this year, there arrived in the United States from foreign countries, 5,062,414 emigrants.
March 27.—Japanese Embassy, first to leave Japan, arrive at San Francisco. Received at Washington, D. C., by President Buchanan, and afterward have public receptions in Baltimore, Philadelphia, and New York, departing from the latter city in the frigate Niagara, June 29.
May 17.—Abraham Lincoln nominated for President at Chicago, by the Republicans.
June 28.—Steamship Great Eastern first arrives at New York.
July 7.—Dr. Hayes' arctic expedition sails from Boston.
Aug. 23.—A Democratic Convention assembled in Charleston, S. C., to secure the election of Stephen A. Douglass, President of the U. S.
Sept. 21.—Prince of Wales arrives at Detroit visiting the United States, and subsequently goes to Philadelphia, New York, Boston, and many of the western cities, embarking for home October 20, at Portland, Me.
Nov. 6.—Abraham Lincoln, of Illinois, and Hannibal Hamlin, of Maine, elected Presi-

FORT WAYNE—Continued.

PHYSICIANS.

T. J. DILL, M.D.,
Practice limited to
DISEASES OF THE EYE AND EAR,
20 WEST BERRY STREET.

A. GOERIZ, M. D.,
Office, 30 Columbia St., residence, cor. Lafayette and LaSalle sts.

Makes all Acute and Chronic Diseases a Specialty. Also all manner of Delicate and Private Diseases, treated with success and privacy. Long practice enables him to do justice to all who may entrust themselves to his care. Those who cannot come themselves may send a vial of urine with a description of their disease.

GREEN, MRS. M. F., Physician.
139 W. Main st.

T. S. VIRGIL,

Physician and Surgeon,

Also, Electric and other baths given, at

70 & 72 HARRISON STREET.

PLUMBER AND GAS FITTER.

OGEDEN, ROBERT, Plumber and Gas Fitter, 125 Calhoun st.

REAL ESTATE AND INSURANCE.

ISAAC D'ISAY,

Real Estate and Insurance,

Land Agent Missouri, Kansas and Texas R. R.,

FORT WAYNE, IND.

FISHER & TONS, Insurance, Real Estate and Loan Agency, 32 E. Berry st.

JONES, L. M., Real Estate Agent,
26 Court St.

RESTAURANTS.

Don't fail to stop at the

Fort Wayne House.

JOS. WILKISON, Pro.

$1 per day. No better to be had in the city. Give me a call. Meals at all hours for 25 cts. Good clean beds and tables.

258 Calhoun Street.

P. G. Tompkins,

Restaurant & Confectionery,

Warm meals at all hours.

278 CALHOUN ST.

FORT WAYNE—Continued.

SALOONS.

ATLANTIC GARDEN,

28 Columbia St.

PETER ZIEGLER, Proprietor.

The finest and most elegantly appointed Saloon in the West. Best Cincinnati lager Beer, Liquors, Cigars, etc., etc.

BON "TON" Wine and Billiards, R. McDonnald, Prop., 35 E. Main st.

BRIEL, FRED., Billiard Saloon. Wines and Liquors, 19 W. Columbia st.

F. X. GOODMAN,

Billiard Saloon,

Choicest wines and Liquors constantly on hand.

ESTABLISHED, 1852.

KABISCH, JULIUS, Wine and Beer Saloon, 12 W. Main.

A. LAZZARINI,
European

Restaurant & Saloon,

Meals and Lodging, twenty-five cents.
First-class in every respect.

NO. 74 EAST COLUMBIA STREET.

L. M. NEUENSCHWANDER,
Wholesale and Retail Dealer in

SCHWEIZER & LIMBURGER CHEESE

also, Wine and Beer Saloon,

46 COLUMBIA ST.

STOTZ, ULRICH, Wine, Beer and Billiard Rooms, 21 and 23 E. Main st.

STRODEL, M., Union Saloon,
10 E. Berry st.

SEWING MACHINES.

The World Renowned

Howe Sewing Machines,

Are the oldest established of any in the world, they being the first Sewing Machines ever made, and having been manufactured continuously under the supervision of the original inventor, Elias Howe, Jr, since their first introduction in 1845. Every Machine is fully warranted and satisfaction guaranteed in every case. Remington & Holcomb, 10 Court St., General Agents for Allen Co.

STOVES AND TINWARE.

METSKER, S. R. & CO., Stoves, Tinware, second hand goods, etc., 61 E. Main st.

Mount Vernon Home of Washington.—Is situated about sixteen miles down the Potomac from Washington, D. C. The mansion fronts the river. The center was built by Lawrence Washington, half brother of the President, from whom he inherited the estate. The more modern portions were constructed by the General. Here are deposited the remains of George and Martha Washington. The Ladies' Mt. Vernon Association own the mansion and contiguous ground. Their endeavor is to restore them to the same condition they were in during the life of Washington.

J. R. WILLIAMS, Pres.   HENRY LEYHE, Gen. Supt.   G. W. HILL, Sec'y.   J. M. EAREL, Gen. Agt.

EAGLE PACKET CO.

St. Louis, Madison, Alton, Jersey, Portage DeSioux and Grafton.

Daily Packet--Champion of the Waters,

SPREAD EAGLE,

HENRY LEYHE, Master.   Leaves from Wharf Boat foot of Vine, at Three o'clock p. m.   N. MOREHEAD, Ed. YOUNG, Cl'ks.

Steamers Spread Eagle, Eagle, Grey Eagle, Little Eagle, Little Eagle No. 2 and Barges. DeSmet.

Steamer Eagle, J. R. Williams, Master, Daily Packet, between Quincy and Keokuk, landing at all intermediate points. Steamer Little Eagle and Barges, Wm. Leyhe, Master, doing general towing and jobbing business between Keokuk and St. Louis, with headquarters at Quincy. Steamer Grey Eagle, D. M. Morris, Master, Daily Packet between Peoria and Henry, touching at Spring Bay, Chilicothe and Lacon on Illinois River.

J. A. Bruner, Agent, Alton, Ill.   Hunter B. Jenkins, Agent,
Office: Wharf Boat, foot of Vine Street,   **St. Louis.**

Company's Gen'l Office at Quincy, Ill.--H. Leyhe, Supt.

St. Mary's Academic Institute

ST. MARY'S OF THE WOODS, VIGO CO., IND.

This noble Institution was founded in 1840, by the Sisters of Providence, from Ruille in France. The little band which undertook the arduous task of opening an educational establishment in the Western wilds of Indiana, was composed of six Sisters, including Mother Theodore, the foundress, whose name is held in veneration by all who had the happiness of knowing her. Many and great were the difficulties to be overcome in a new and uncivilized country, in which the resources were few, the language, customs, and manners entirely strange. But the zealous laborers, aided by those who came to join in the good work, struggled on, and before the lapse of many years, St. Mary's Institute attained the well-earned reputation of being a first-class Academy. The present Academic building is pronounced, by all who visit it, to be one of the finest in the United States. It is located four miles west of Terre Haute, near the Indianapolis & St. Louis R. R. It is spacious, well ventilated, convenient, and furnished with all modern improvements. It is liberally supplied with philosophical and astronomical apparatus, charts, globes, and everything conducive to the attainment of knowledge. The pupils have access to a well-filled library of choice and standard works. Every facility is afforded for attaining proficiency in music, painting in oil and water colors, etc. Special attention is paid to forming the morals and manners of the pupils. Simplicity of dress is enforced by rule. The extensive grounds surrounding the institute, are beautifully laid out, and offer every inducement to the young ladies to engage in healthful exercises.

Parents may rest assured that pupils placed under the Sisters' care, receive all the attention that kindness can suggest.

For further information, address

Sister Superior,
ST. MARY'S INSTITUTE,
VIGO CO., INDIANA.

ADVERTISEMENTS. 135

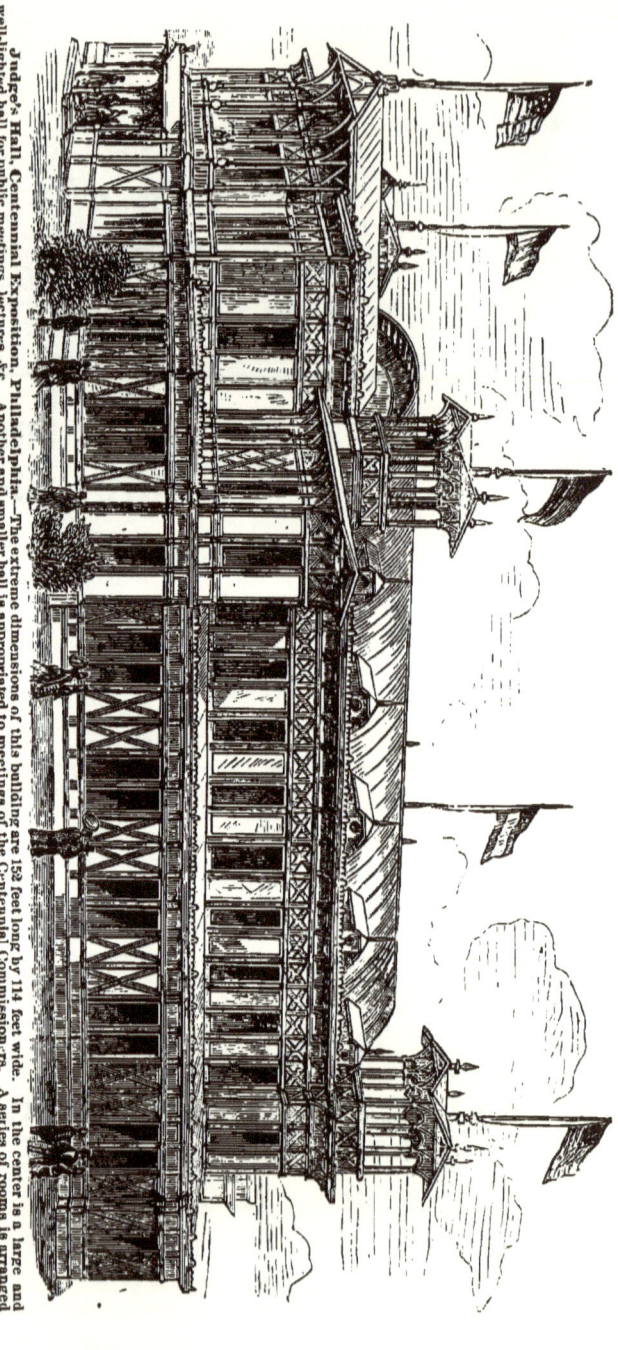

Judge's Hall, Centennial Exposition, Philadelphia.—The extreme dimensions of this building are 182 feet long by 114 feet wide. In the center is a large and well-lighted hall for public meetings, lectures, &c. Another and smaller hall is appropriated to meetings of the Centennial Commissioners. A series of rooms is arranged for the accommodation of the judges. It was bought by the Permanent Exhibition Company for $1,500. The building cost $11,000.

HOBART O. HAMLIN, with Gale & Co. 11 years. ZELORA E. BROWN.

HAMLIN & BROWN,

REAL ESTATE, LOAN AND INSURANCE AGENTS, P. O. Box 461, MINNEAPOLIS, MINN.

References by permission: Gov. John S. Pillsbury; Hon. Chas. E. Vanderburgh, Judge of District Court; H. G. Sidle, Esq., Cashier First National Bank; T. A. Harrison, Esq., Prest. State National Bank; T. B. Walker, Esq.; Hon. H. T. Welles; E. S. Jones, Esq., Prest. Hennepin County Savings Bank.

Persons desirous to purchase, sell or exchange houses and lots in the City, or land in the County, will find it to their advantage to call on us. The appraisement of Real Estate in Minneapolis and vicinity a specialty. *TAXES PAID FOR NON-RESIDENTS.*

1860.

dent and Vice-President of the United States, by the votes of all the northern States except New Jersey, which chose 4 electors for Douglas and 3 for Lincoln. This election is made the pretext for rebellion and secession of the cotton States.

Nov. 7.—The news of Mr. Lincoln's election received at Charleston, South Carolina, with cheers for a Southern Confederacy. The "Palmetto Flag" hoisted on the vessels in the harbor.

Nov. 9.—An attempt to seize the arms at Fort Moultrie.

Nov. 10.—A bill was introduced into the South Carolina Legislature to raise and equip 10,000 men. The Legislature also ordered the election of a convention, to consider the question of secession. Jas. Chester, United States Senator from South Carolina, resigned.

Nov. 11.—Senator Hammond, of South Carolina, resigned.

Nov. 18.—Georgia Legislature appropriated $1,000,000 to arm the State. Major Anderson sent to Fort Moultrie to relieve Colonel Gardner.

Dec. 18.—United States Senate rejects the "Crittenden compromise," settling the difference between the North and the South.

Dec. 20.—South Carolina secedes from the Union.

Dec. 26.—General Anderson evacuates Fort Moultrie, Charleston, and occupies Fort Sumter.

Dec. 30.—President Buchanan declines to receive delegates from South Carolina.

Deaths this Year.—Samuel G. Goodrich, ("Peter Parley," author, aged 67 years. Chauncey A. Goodrich, scholar and divine, aged 70 years. Theodore Parker, Unitarian clergyman and author, aged 50 years. J. Addison Alexander, theologian and commentator, aged 51.

The Great Rebellion. Dec. 1.—Florida Legislature ordered the election of a convention. Great secession meeting in Memphis.

Dec. 3.—Congress met. The President denied the right of a State to secede, and asserted the right of the general government to coerce a seceding State.

Dec. 10.—Howell Cobb, Secretary of the Treasury, resigned. Senator Clay, of Alabama, resigned.

1861.

Jan. 23.—Georgia members of Congress resigned.

Jan. 24.—The Confederates siezed the United States arsenal at Augusta Georgia.

Jan. 26.—The Louisiana Legislature passed secession ordinance by a vote of 113 to 17.

Jan. 30.—North Carolina Legislature submitted the convention question to the people. This was the first instance of the will of the people being consulted in regard to the question of secession.

The revenue cutters, Cass, at Mobile, and McLelland, at New Orleans, surrendered to the Confederate authorities.

FORT WAYNE—*Continued.*

TAILORS.

CLARK, JOS. M., Merchant Tailor, 34 E. Berry st.

JOHN RABUS,

Fashionable Merchant

TAILOR,

61 Wells St., (Bloomingdale.)

SCHMALZ, CHAS., Tailoring and Repairing of all kinds, 108 Harrison st.

TOBACCO AND CIGARS.

CARL, JOHN, Wholesale and Retail dealer in Tobacco and Cigars, 39 Calhoun st.

C. NEWCOMER,

SAMPLE ROOM,

NO. 230 CALHOUN STREET,

Where you can buy

Cigars, Tobacco and Nose Paint.

WEBER, FRED, Wholesale and Retail dealer in Cigars & Tobacco, Calhoun & Maumee sts.

UMBRELLAS AND PARASOLS.

Thos. Miller,

Umbrella Manufacturer,

Umbrellas and Parasols repaired on short notice and at low rates.

174 Calhoun Street.

UNDERTAKER.

Charles Fink.

UNDERTAKER

CRAIN, BREED & CO'S

BURIAL CASES OF THE LATEST IMPROVED STYLE.

All kinds of wooden cases, also, Shrouds and Shrouding. Hearses and carriages at short notice, and on the most reasonable terms.

55 W. MAIN STREET.

WATCHES, CLOCKS AND JEWELRY.

CAPS, J. E. & CO., Watches, Clocks and Jowelry, Fort Wayne.

MAYER, GEO. J. E., Watchmaker and Jeweler, 19 E. Main.

EVANSVILLE, IND.

ARCHITECTS.

J. K. FRICK & CO.,
Architects & Superintendents,
320 Upper First st.

H. MURSINNA,

ARCHITECT,
3 Chandler's Building, cor. First and Locust.

WOOD & M'KENNON, Architects, Room 2, Chandler's Building.

ATTORNEYS AT LAW.

GARVIN, THOS. E., Attorney at Law, 314 Upper Third st.

S. E. SMITH,
ATTORNEY AT LAW,
328 UPPER THIRD ST.

C. H. WESSELER,
ATTORNEY AT LAW,
AND NOTARY PUBLIC,
OFFICE WITH WESSELER & BUSH, REAL ESTATE AGENTS,
326 1-2 Upper Third St.

BAG MANUFACTURER.

EVANSVILLE HOMINY MILLS.
Established 1876.

J. B. HARRISON,
Manufacturer of Hominy, Meal, Grits, Burlap Bags, Cotton Flour Sacks, Salt Sacks, And Dealer in Seamless Grain and Gunny Bags,
314 Upper Water St., Evansville, Ind.

BAKERIES.

A. W. BENTZ,
Bakery and Confectionery,
523 Main st. Established 1876.

CHRIST, A. & W., Steam Bakery, 325 Main and 315 Fourth sts.

DOESCHER, CHRIST, Confectioner and Fancy Cake Baker, 306 2d st., bet. Main & Locust.

FRED HOFMANN,
BAKERY & CONFECTIONERY,
424 Upper Fourth st. Established 1865.

ROETTGER, FERDINAND, New York Bakery and Confectionery, 629 Main st.

JACOB SCHMITZ,
BAKERY AND CONFECTIONERY,
704 Fifth street.

STADLER, FRED, Bakery, cor. Fourth ave. and Delaware st.

IMPORTANT EVENTS OF THE CENTURY. 137

1861.

Feb. 1.—Texas Convention passed an ordinance of secession by a vote of 166 to 7, to be submitted to the people.
The Louisiana authorities seized the Mint and Custom House at New Orleans.

Feb. 4.—Delegates from the seceded States met at Montgomery, Alabama, to organize a Confederate government.
Peace Congress met at Washington; ex-President Tyler was chosen President. A stormy session soon followed, accomplishing no good result.

Feb. 8.—The United States arsenal at Little Rock surrendered to Arkansas.

Feb. 9.—Jefferson Davis and A. H. Stevens were elected Provisional President and Vice-President of the Southern Confederacy.

Feb. 13.—The electoral vote counted. Abraham Lincoln received 180 votes; Stephen A. Douglas, 12; John C. Breckenridge, 72; and John Bell, 39.

Feb. 19.—Fort Kearney, Kansas, seized by the Confederates.

Feb. 23.—Gen. Twiggs surrendered Government property in Texas, valued at $1,200,000, to the Confederacy.

March 1.—Gen. Twiggs expelled from the army.

March 4.—Inauguration of Lincoln, President of the United States.
The ordinance of secession passed by the Texas Convention, and submitted to the people, having been adopted by a majority of 40,000, the Convention declared the State out of the Union.

March 5.—Gen. Beauregard took command of the troops at Charleston.

March 6.—Fort Brown on the Rio Grande, was surrendered by special agreement. The Federal troops evacuated the fort and sailed for Key West and Tortugas.

March 28.—Vote of Louisiana on secession made public. For secession, 20,448; against, 17,926.

March 30.—Mississippi Convention ratified the Confederate Constitution by a vote of 78 to 70.

April 3.—South Carolina Convention ratified the Confederate Constitution by a vote of 114 to 16.

April 7.—All intercourse between Fort Sumter and Charleston stopped by order of Beauregard.
The steamer Atlantic sailed from New York with troops and supplies.

April 12.—Bombardment of Fort Sumter commenced by the Confederates.

April 13.—The bombardment of Fort Sumter continued; early in the day the officers' quarters were fired by a shell; by noon most of the wood work was on fire; Sumter's fire was almost silenced when Gen. Wigfall came with a flag of truce, and arrangements were made for evacuating the fort.

April 14.—Major Anderson and his men sailed for New York.

April 15.—The President issued a proclamation commanding all persons in arms against the United States to disperse within twenty days; also calling for 75,000 volunteers. The New York Legislature authorized the rais-

JOSLIN & PHILLIPS,
PHOTOGRAPHERS
85 S. W. Cor. Public Square,
DANVILLE, ILL.

JOHN W. GIDDINGS,
Manufacturer of
Carriages & Buggies,
High Street, near Main, DANVILLE. ILL.

H. O. BROWER,
MARBLE WORKS,
South of Puplic Square — — — — — DANVILLE, ILL.
RED SCOTCH GRANITE MADE A SPECIALTY OF.
His prices are such that he is receiving many o ders from adjoining counties for this most excellent and durable material.

G. L. KLUGEL,
Western Union Cornice Contractor
Manufacturer and Dealer in
Galvanized Iron Cornices, Slate and Tin Roofing, and Sheet Metal Work in all its Branches,
Work done in any part of the United States. Designs for Cornices made to Order.
Cor. Main & Walnut — — — — DANVILLE, ILL

JOEL HOLLEY & SONS,
—THE ONLY CITY—
BILL POSTERS,
Owners of all the Boards in the City.
Have the Exclusive Right of the City, and only Licensed Bill Posters.
205 West Front Street, Opposite New Post Office.
All Orders Promptly Attended to }
Address P. O. Box 800.   }   BLOOMINGTON, ILL.

W. B. MOORE,
MANUFACTURER AND DEALER IN

Marble and Granite Monuments, Grave Stones,
Mantles, Grates, Hearths, Shelving, Etc.
Stone Work furnished for Cemetery Lots and Buildings.

311 West Washington St.   BLOOMINGT, ILL.

COURT HOUSE, DANVILLE, ILLS.

1861.

ing of $3,000,000 for their equipment and support.

April 16.—The Governors of Kentucky, Virginia, Tennessee, and Missouri, refused to furnish troops under the President's proclamation. The Confederate Government called for 32,000 men.

April 17.—Virginia Convention adopted secession ordinance in secret session by a vote of 60 to 53, to be submitted to the people on the fourth Thursday in May. Forces were sent to seize the U. S. arsenal at Harper's Ferry, and the Gosport Navy Yard. Jefferson Davis issued a proclamation offering letters of marque and reprisal to all who wished to engage in privateering.

April 18.—U. S. arsenal at Harper's Ferry destroyed by Lieut. Jones to prevent its falling into the hands of the enemy. Colonel Coke, with 400 men of the 25th Pennsylvania regiment arrived in Washington. These were the first troops to enter the city for its defense.

April 19.—Steamer Star of the West seized by the Confederates at Indianola, Texas.
The 6th Massachusetts regiment, while passing through Baltimore, was attacked by a mob; two soldiers were killed. The troops fired upon the mob, killing 11 and wounding many. President Lincoln issued a proclamation declaring the ports of South Carolina, Florida, Georgia, Mississippi, Louisiana and Texas in a state of blockade.

April 20.—The U. S. arsenal at Liberty, Mo., seized by the secessionists, and the arms distributed among the surrounding counties. The Gosport Navy Yard destroyed by General McCauley, to keep it from the Confederates; the war vessels Delaware, Pennsylvania, Columbia, Germantown, Merrimac, Raritan, Dolphin, and United States were scuttled and set on fire; the Cumberland was towed out.
The 4th Massachusetts regiment arrived at Fortress Monroe.

April 21.—Federal Government took possession of the Philadelphia and Baltimore Railroad. Senator Andrew Johnson of Tennessee mobbed at Lynchburg, Virginia. Harper's Ferry arsenal burned by its garrison.

April 22.—U. S. arsenal at Fayetteville, N. C., seized by the Confederates. Arkansas seized the arsenal at Napoleon.

April 24.—Fort Smith, Arkansas, seized by the Confederates under Senator Boland.

April 25.—Major Libby surrendered 450 U. S. troops to the Confederate Colonel Van Dorn, at Saluria, Texas.
Governor Letcher proclaims Virginia a member of the Southern Confederacy.

April 27.—The blockade extended to the ports of North Carolina and Virginia. All officers of the army were required to take the oath of allegiance.

April 29.—The Maryland House of Delegates voted against secession, 63 to 13.

May 1.—North Carolina Legislature passed a bill calling a State Convention to meet on the 20th of May. The Legislature of Tennessee passed an act in secret session, authorizing the Governor to form a league with the Southern Confederacy.

EVANSVILLE—*Continued.*

BARBERS.

HENRY KOHL,
SHAVING & HAIRDRESSING SALOON
—ALSO—
SHAMPOOING & HAIRCUTTING,

Second St., bet. Main & Sycamore.

SCHMIDT, ALBERT F., Barber Shop. Also Music furnished for Balls and Parties. 104 Upper Water st.

BOARDING HOUSE.

CORA HARRIS,
LADIES' BOARDING HOUSE,
26 LOWER THIRD ST.

BOOKBINDERS.

MEYER & RAHM,
BINDERS, PAPER BOX
And Blank Book Manuf'rs, 310½ Upper First st.

BOOKSELLER.

PRINCE, JOSEPH, Bookseller and Picture Frames, 207 Upper Fourth st.

BOOTS AND SHOES.

JOHN M. APP,
Manufacturer of
CUSTOM MADE BOOTS AND SHOES,
2 LOWER THIRD ST.

CRONBACH, MARCUS, Boots and Shoes, 711 Main st. Established 1850.

ELBERT, CHAS., Manufacturer of Boots and Shoes, 708 Main st.

STEPHEN ENZ,
Manufacturer Fine Boots and Shoes.
206 Third Street.

Fred. W. Harnishfeger,
Manufacturer of

Boots & Shoes,
120 LOCUST STREET.
Bet. First and Second.

HAST, JOHN, Boots and Shoes. 108 Upper Water st.

LOUIS LOETZERICH,
Manufacturer of Fashionable Boots & Shoes
All work warranted. 316 Upper Second st.

EVANSVILLE—*Continued.*

BOOTS AND SHOES.

SCHENTRUP, HENRICH, Boots and Shoes, 426 Upper Fourth st.

MAGNUS SIEGEL,
Manufacturer of
Boots and Shoes,
All Work Warranted.
114 Locust st., bet First and Second.

SCHMIDT, FRANK A., Custom Boots and Shoes, 104 Upper Water st.

THALMUELLER, EMIL, Boots and Shoes, 117 Locust st.

H. L. WITTMER,
Manufacturer Boots and Shoes,
812 MAIN STREET.

BOTTLERS.

AUMILLER & NEU, keep constantly on hand a
Large Supply of Evansville XX Ale,
Also Madison XX Ale and Porter,
18 HIGH STREET.

BERNARDIN, A. & CO., Manufacturers of Ginger Ale, Selters Water, etc., 712 and 714 Main st.

BREWERY.

COOK & RICE, City Brewery,
214 Seventh st.

BUILDERS.

LEHNHARD & EARL,
Contractors and Builders,
Manufacturers and Dealers in
DOORS, SASH, BLINDS AND ALL KINDS OF BUILDING MATERIAL.
Stairs and Hand Railing a Specialty.
Planing Mill, cor. Canal and 6th Sts.

CANDIES, TOYS, ETC.

HASSLER, JOHN, Candies, Toys, Foreign Fruits, etc., 308 Upper First st.

CARRIAGE AND WAGON MANUFACTURERS.

F. ALTHOFF,
Manufacturer of
Carriages & Spring Wagons
Family Carriages, Open & Top Buggies,
SULKIES, ETC.,
Manufactory, cor. Second Ave. and Ingle St.

BECKER & BRO., Manufacturers of
Wagons & Steamboat Blacksmiths,
816 Pennsylvania street.
Established 1855.

EAGLE CARRIAGE WORKS.
F. HAMMERSTEIN,
Manufacturer of
FIRST-CLASS CARRIAGES,
BUGGIES, SPRING WAGONS, &c.,
Cor. 4th & Locust Sts. None but the best workmen employed.

1861.

President Lincoln called for 42,000 three years volunteers; 22,000 troops for the regular army, and 18,000 seamen.

May 4.—Gen. McClellan placed in command of the department of Ohio, comprising the States of Ohio, Indiana and Illinois.

May 5.—Gen. Butler took possession of the Relay House, Maryland.

May 6.—Arkansas Convention passed an ordinance of secession, by a vote of 69 to 1. Tennessee Legislature adopted secession ordinance in secret session, to be submitted to a vote of the people.

May 11.—Blockade of Charleston, S. C., established by the steamer Niagara.

May 13.—Queen Victoria's proclamation of "neutrality" in the American conflict.

May 16.—General Scott ordered the fortification of Arlington Heights.

May 18.—Military Department of Virginia created, comprising Eastern Virginia, North and South Carolina; headquarters at Fortress Monroe; commander, General Butler.

May 20.—Telegraphic dispatches were seized throughout the North by order of the Government. North Carolina secession ordinance adopted. Governor Magoffin proclaimed the neutrality of Kentucky.

May 21.—Tennessee secedes.

May 22.—Fortifications of Ship Island destroyed to keep them from the enemy.

May 24.—Thirteen thousand troops crossed the Potomac into Virginia. Alexandria occupied by Federal troops. Colonel Ellsworth shot by Jackson; the murderer was instantly killed. Arlington Heights occupied by Union troops.

May 26.—The port of New Orleans was blockaded by the sloop-of-war Brooklyn. All postal service in the seceded States suspended.

July 1.—Lieut. Tompkins, with 47 men, attacks the Confederates at Fairfax Court House, killing Capt. Marr and several others. Union loss, two killed.

The steamers Freebon and Anacosta engaged the batteries at Aquia Creek the second time.

June 3.—Col. Kelly defeated the Confederates at Phillippi, Va., killing 15; Col. Kelly was severely wounded.

Hon. S. A. Douglass, died in Chicago. Born at Brandon, Vt., April 23, 1813.

Gen. Beauregard arrived and assumed command of the Confederate forces at Manassas Junction, Va.

June 10.—Battle of Big Bethel. Three regiments of Union troops, under the command of General Pierce, were defeated with a loss of sixteen killed, among them Major Winthrop, and forty one wounded.

Neutrality in the American conflict proclaimed by Napoleon III.

June 14.—Confederates evacuated Harper's Ferry after destroying all available property.

June 15.—Brig Perry arrived at New York with the privateer Savannah.

June 17.—Wheeling Convention unanimously declared Western Virginia independent of the Confederate portion of the State. General Lyon defeated the Confederates at

EVANSVILLE—Continued.

CARRIAGE AND WAGON MANUFACTURERS.

LANNERT & BARENFANGER,

CARRIAGE BUILDERS,
MANUFACTORY:
Cor. Sycamore & Fifth Sts.

CARRIAGE HARDWARE.

BABCOCK & VIELE,
WHOLESALE CARRIAGE HARDWARE,
Trimmings and Fancy Horse Goods,
210 NORTH FIRST ST.

CHINA, GLASS AND CROCKERY.

ICHENHAUSER, LOUIS, Lamps, Glassware, etc. 7 U. per First st.

WARREN, JAS. M., China and Glassware, 118 First st.

CIGAR-BOX MANUFACTURER.

J. A. SPALDING,
Cigar-Box Manufacturer,
And Dealer in Cigar-Box Labels and Nails.
409 EIGHTH STREET.

COAL DEALER.

INGLE, MORRIS & CO., Coal Dealers, 200½ Upper Water st.

COMMERCIAL COLLEGE.

CRESCENT CITY COMMERCIAL COLLEGE, G. W. Rank, Pr ncipal, cor First and Main sts.

CUTLER AND GRINDER.

BORRER, AUG., Cutlery, and Razor Concaving, 321 Locust st.

DENTIST.

HERMAN WILDE'S
DENTAL ROOMS,
222 1-2 MAIN STREET,
Over the People's Savings Bank.

All Operations in our "Specialty" will receive Prompt, Careful and Successful Attention.

DRUGGISTS.

BEARD, JAS. A., Druggist, 720 Ingle st.

L. W. DEUSNER,
DRUGGIST,
Cor. Second and Sycamore Sts.
PURE DRUGS AND CHEMICALS,
Paints, Oils, Perfumery, Window Glass, Patent Medicines and a full line of Druggists' Fancy Goods. Prescriptions filled at all hours, day or night.

EPMEIER, W. F., Prescription Druggist, 129 Upper Third st., cor. Sycamore.

EVANSVILLE—Continued.

DRUGGISTS.

HUT, C. H., DRUGGIST and APOTHECARY, Dealer in Drugs, Chemicals, Dye Stuffs, Fine Perfumery, Brushes and Toilet Articles. Prescriptions Carefully Compounded at all hours, day or Night.
COR. SIXTH AND OAK STREETS.

WM. WEBER,
Pharmacist & Dealer in Drugs, Medicines, Etc., Cor. Main and Seventh Sts. Est. 1871.

DRY GOODS.

JAQUESS, BRO. & CO.,
Wholesale Dealers in Dry Goods and Notions,
110 N. First street.

MILLER BROS., General Dry Goods, 113 and 115, 221 and 717 Main st.

Miller, Gardner & Co.,
WHOLESALE
DRY GOODS & NOTIONS
114 Upper First St.

DYE WORKS.

WILLIAMS, W. W., Steam Dye works, 220 Locust st.

ENGINEERS AND SURVEYORS.

BATEMAN, CHAS. B., Civil Engineer and Surveyor, 200½ Upper Water st.

Jas. D. Saunders, Sr.,
CIVIL ENGINEER
AND
Surveyor,
412 UPPER 3d ST.

FLORIST.

CARMODY, J. D. & CO., Floral Gem Bouquets, Decorations, etc., Water & Chestnut sts.

GROCERS.

ALTHEIDE, AUGUST, Groceries, Cor. 8th & Mulberry sts.

JOEST, N. & J., Established 1874, Fancy and Staple Groceries, 621 Upper 6th st.

WM. KOELLING,
Dealer in Staple & Fancy
Groceries,
NO. 138,
Corner Third Avenue and Pennsylvania Street.

KOESTER & KORFF, Wholesale Grocers, Eighth st. bet. Chestnut & Cherry sts.

ADVERTISEMENTS. 143

Hall of the Photographic Art Association, Centennial Exposition, Philadelphia.—The dimensions of this building are 240 feet long by 75 feet wide, and 20 feet is the height of the walls. In order that there may be plenty of light, the roof is composed entirely of glass. It cost $26,000, which was contributed by the photographers of America. The building is devoted exclusively to the exhibition of American and foreign photographic art. It was bought by H. Crouse, of Reading, Pa, for $1,500.

Dr. H. G. Decker

Cures all cases of Consumption; all chronic cases of the Liver, Lungs and Kidneys, also gives particular attention to Female Weakness. Perfect cure or no pay. Consultation by mail, and medicine sent by mail or express. Address,

H. G. Decker,
226 Blue Island Ave., Chicago.

P.S.—$500 reward for any disease undertaken by me that I fail to cure.

Račte se povšimnouti!

DR. DECKER,
226 Blue Island Avenue.

Hojí veškeré neduhy souchotin, všecky chronické neduhy jater, plic a sleziny, zvláštní pozornost věnuje neduhům pohlaví ženského.

Dokud nevyhojí, nechce plat. Douška: $500 onměny nabízí kdyby podnikne vybojiti nemoc a kdyby se mu jediný případ nevydařil Račtež si toto vystřihnouti.

M. J. NELSON,
TAILOR,
201 West Madison St.,
CHICAGO.

10

1861.

Booneville, Mo., with a loss of about 30 killed and 50 wounded; Union loss, 2 killed and 9 wounded.

June 20.—General McClellan assumed command in person of the army in Western Virginia.

June 23.—Forty-eight locomotives belonging to the Baltimore and Ohio Railroad, valued at $400,000, were destroyed by the Confederates.

June 24.—The United States gunboat Pawnee attacked the Confederate battery at Mathias Point. A spy arrested at Washington, with full details of the number of troops and batteries, and best plan of attack on the city.

June 26.—The President acknowledged the Wheeling government of Virginia.

June 27.—The steamers Pawnee, Resolute, and Freeborn made a second attack on the Confederate battery at Mathias Point; Captain Ward, commanding the Federal force, was killed.

June 29.—The Confederate privateer, Sumter, escaped from New Orleans. The Confederates made a dash at Harper's Ferry, destroying several boats and a railroad bridge.

July.—First War Loan of the United States Government, $250,000,000.

July 2.—General Patterson defeated the Confederates at Falling Water, Va.; Union loss, 3 killed and 10 wounded.

July 4.—Congress met in extra session.

July 5.—Battle of Carthage, Mo. Confederates were commanded by Governor Jackson; the Federal troops, numbering 1,500, by Col Sigel. Colonel Sigel retreated to Springfield. Union loss, 14 killed and 31 wounded.

July 6.—General Fremont appointed to the command of the Western Department, consisting of the State of Illinois and the States and territories west of the Mississippi and east of the Rocky Mountains. Headquarters at St. Louis.

July 10.—Skirmishes at Laurel Hill, Virginia; Confederate defeated. Union loss, 2 killed and 2 wounded.

July 11.—J. M. Mason and R. M. Hunter, of Va.; T. L. Clingham and Thomas Bragg, of North Carolina; L. T. Wigfall and J. C. Hemphill, of Texas; C. B. Mitchell and W. K. Sebastian, of Arkansas, and O. A. S. Nicholson, of Tennessee, expelled from the United States Senate.

July 12.—Battle of Rich Mountain. The Federal troops, under command by Colonel Roscecrans, defeated the enemy under Colonel Pegram. Confederate loss, 150 killed and wounded, and 800 prisoners.

July 13.—The Confederates, under General Garnett, were defeated at Garrick's Ford, Virginia. The Confederate General Garnett was killed. Union loss, 2 killed and 10 wounded.

Battle of Screytown, Va. The Federals under Colonel Lowe were defeated with a loss of 9 killed and 40 wounded and missing.

July 16.—Tilgram, a negro, killed three of a Confederate prize crew on the S. J. Warring, and brought the vessel into New York.

EVANSVILLE—*Continued.*

GROCERS.

Schlensker & Woehler,
Retail Dealers in

Groceries ⊛ Produce,

COR. 8th & CHESTNUT STS.

SCHWEITZER, F., Fancy Groceries,
Cor. 8th & Powell sts.

VIELE, STOCKWELL & CO., Wholesale Grocers.
Cor. 1st & Sycamore Sts.

H. A. WENDT & CO.,
Dealers in
GROCERIES AND DRY GOODS,
800 E. Pennsylvania St.

GUN AND LOCKSMITHS.

EMIG, NIC., Locksmith and Bell-hanger,
Cor. 6th & Main sts.

GUSTAVE HOSSE,

Gun and Locksmith,
Manufacturer and Grinder of
CUTLERY AND EDGE TOOLS.
302 Ingle St.

PHILIP KRUG,
Manufacturer of

Cutlery, Surgical Instruments and

TOOLS OF ANY KIND.
GUN AND LOCKSMITH AND GRINDER,
124 Locust St.

HAIR DEALER AND DRESSER.

Miss. B. Scherer,

LADIES' HAIR DRESSER,
And manufacturer of
Switches, Front Braids, Puffs, Curls, Frizzes, etc.
311 UPPER SECOND ST.

HARDWARE.

BOETTICHER, KELLOGG & CO., General Hardware, 122 Upper First st.

PIERSON & ROCK, General Hardware.
11 Upper First st.

SONNTAG, GEO. S. & CO., General Hardware, 123 & 125 Upper First st.

HOES AND MILL PICKS.

SMITH, J. C. & J. G., Hoes and Mill Picks, Factory, foot of Bayless st.

HORSESHOEING.

RAYMOND, C. W., Shoeing Shop,
Cor. Fourth & Locust sts.

EVANSVILLE—*Continued.*

HOTEL.

SHERWOOD HOUSE,

Cor. 1st & Locust Sts.,

J. W. BOICOURT, Proprietor,

Evansville, Ind.,

CHOICE

Sample Rooms For Commercial Agents.

IRON AND SLATE MANTLES.

A. P. BELL,

Manufacturer and dealer in

ENAMELED and MARBELIZED

Iron and Slate Mantles,

ENAMELED GRATES, ETC.,

613 Upper Seventh Street.

JUSTICES OF THE PEACE.

BURKE, PATRICK, Justice of the Peace,
206 Locust st.

DAY, SAM., Justice of the Peace,
Cor. Locust & 3d st.

LEATHER AND FINDINGS.

KERTH, THOMAS, Leather and Findings,
219 Main st.

LIME AND CEMENT.

EDGAR D. MILLS.   GEORGE W. MILLS.

MILLS BROS.,

(Successors to Lockhart & Co.)

DEALERS IN

LIME, CEMENT, HAIR AND PLASTER,

409 8th St., bet. Locust and Walnut.

LIVERY AND BOARDING STABLE.

CAVENDER & JONES.

Livery, Sale and Boarding Stable,

408 & 410 UPPER SECOND ST.,

Bet. Locust and Walnut.

MEAT MARKETS.

EMRICH, W., Meats and Vegetables,
Cor. 5th & Chestnut sts.

SCHNIEP, A. & CO., Meat Market & Sausage Factory, 9th & Division and cor. 4th & Main sts.

1861.

President Lincoln authorized to call out the militia and accept the services of 500,000 men.

July 18.—Fight at Blackburn Ford. The Federal troops under command of General Tyler made the attack, but after three hours' fighting were ordered back to Centerville; their loss was 19 killed and 64 wounded and missing.

The department of Maryland created, and Gen. John A. Dix placed in command; headquarters at Baltimore.

July 19.—Gen. Banks superseded General Patterson; headquarters in the field.

July 20.—The Confederate Congress met at Richmond.

July 21.—Battle of Bull Run. The army of the Potomac, about 45,000 strong, under command of Brigadier General McDowell, which left Washington July 17, attacked the Confederates, about equal in numbers, at Manassas, Va., where they occupied a strong position. The chances were at first in favor of the Federals, but the Confederates receiving large reinforcements under General Johnson, the scale was turned. Panic seized upon the Union troops, and they commenced a disorderly retreat towards Washington. The Union loss was, 481 killed, 1,011 wounded, 1,216 missing. Confederate loss, as reported by General Beauregard, 269 killed and 1,843 wounded.

July 22.—General McClellan took command of the army of the Potomac.

Three-months volunteers began to return home.

Aug. 1.—The Confederates retreated from Harper's Ferry to Leesburg.

Aug. 2.—General Lyon defeated the Confederates at Dug Spring, Missouri. Union loss, 8 killed and 30 wounded.

The vessels engaged in a contraband trade with the Confederates of Virginia and North Carolina were destroyed in Pocomoke Sound.

Aug. 3.—Congress passed a bill for raising $20,000,000 by direct taxation, and the Confiscation bill.

Aug. 5.—Commodore Alden bombarded Galveston, Texas.

Aug. 6.—The extra session of Congress closed.

Aug. 7.—The village of Hampton, Virginia, destroyed by the Confederates. The privateer York burned by the United States gunboat Union; crew taken prisoners.

Aug. 10.—Gen. Lyon with 5,000 troops attacked a Confederate force double that of his own at Wilson Creek, near Springfield, Mo. After a hard fight of six hours, Gen. Lyon being killed, the Union troops under the command of Col. Sigel and Maj. Sturgis, retired to Springfield.

Aug. 12.—President Lincoln appointed the 30th of September as a fast day.

Aug 14.—General Fremont declared martial law in St. Louis.

Aug. 16.—Gen. Wool took command at Fortress Monroe.

President Lincoln interdicts all commercial relations with the seceded States.

Aug. 26.—The 7th Ohio regiment, 660 strong, were surprised at Summerville, Virgi-

J. RAUCH & BRO.,
MANUFACTURERS AND JOBBERS OF
FINE CIGARS,
160 Indiana Avenue, INDIANAPOLIS, IND.

FINE CUT, PLUG AND SMOKING TOBACCOS A SPECIALTY. ALSO,
Manufacturers of the Two Brothers Cigars.

CHRISTIAN MEYER,
Manufacturer and Wholesale and Retail Dealer in
CIGARS & TOBACCO
No. 26 Indiana Avenue,
INDIANAPOLIS, IND.

F. G. BERNS,
MANUFACTURER OF ALL KINDS OF
CIGAR BOXES
I give my Work Personal Attention and Guarantee every Satisfaction. Factory,
247 East Morris Street, - - INDIANAPOLIS, IND.

Established 1876.
JAMES A. ROSS,
DEALER IN
Hardware, Cutlery, Doors,
Sash, Blinds, Nails, Glass, Edge Tools,
Etc., Etc., Etc.
179 INDIANA AVENUE,
INDIANAPOLIS. - INDIANA.

POST OFFICE AND CUSTOM HOUSE, INDIANAPOLIS, IND.

B. V. Enos & Son,
ARCHITECTS. [Established 1865.

Superintendents of the above building. Rooms 33 and 34 Talbot's Block,
Cor. *PENNSYLVANIA* and *MARKET STREETS*. - - *INDIANAPOLIS, IND*

Suspension Bridge between Cincinnati & Covington.—The bridge connecting Cincinnati and Covington, was constructed by John A. Roebling, at a cost of $1,800,000. The distance between the towers is 1,057 feet, and including approaches, it is 2,252 feet in length and 36 feet in width. The towers are 200 feet in height, with the turrets 230. The main cables are a foot in diameter and contain 10,360 wires, weighing 16,300 pounds. The bridge is 103 feet above low water mark. It was opened to the public on the 1st of January, 1867.

1861.

nia, but fought their way out with a loss of six officers. The Hatteras expedition sailed.

Aug. 29.—Capture of Forts Hatteras and Clark, N. C.; Confederate loss about 1,000; Federal loss none.

Sept. 1.—Fight at Boonville, Virginia; the Confederates were defeated and the town destroyed. Union loss six wounded.

Sept. 6.—Gen. Grant took possession of Paducah, Ky.

Sept. 10.—Gen. Rosecrans with 4,500 troops attacked the Confederates under Floyd near Carnifex Ferry. After several hours' fighting, darkness put an end to the contest. During the fight Floyd retreated, burning the bridge over Gauley river.

Sept. 11.—President Lincoln modified General Fremont's emancipation proclamation.

Sept. 12.—Fight at Cheat Mountain. Col. J. A. Washington, proprietor of Mount Vernon, was killed. Union loss, 9 killed and 12 wounded.

Sept. 18.—Maryland legislature closed by provost marshal; secession members sent to Fort McHenry.

Sept. 21.—John C. Breckenridge fled from Frankfort, Ky., and joined the confederates. Gen. Lane defeated a confederate force at Papinsville, Missouri. Federal loss, 17 killed.

Sept. 23.—Capture of Lexington, Missouri, by the Confederates after a siege of four months.

Oct. 3.—Gen. Reynolds made an armed reconnoissance of the enemy's position at Greenbrier. The Confederates evacuated Lexington, Mo.

Oct. 5.—The steamer Monticello shelled the Confederates at Chicamacomico, under Barlow and drove them to their boats.

Oct. 7.—The Confederate iron-clad steamer Merrimac made its first appearance within sight of Fortress Monroe.

Oct. 9.—Confederates made an attack on Santa Rosa Island, but were defeated. Union loss was 13 killed and 21 wounded.

Col. Geary, with 400 Pennsylvania troops, crossed the Potomac at Harper's Ferry and captured 21,000 bushels of wheat.

Oct. 11.—Confederate steamer Theodore escaped from Charleston, S. C., with Mason and Slidell on board.

Oct. 21.—Fight at Fredericktown, Missouri. The Confederates defeated. Union loss, 6 killed and about 60 wounded.

Battle of Ball's Bluff. Union forces commanded by Col. Baker. Gen. Stone failed to cross the Potomac to his support, and after a severe fight, in which Col. Baker was killed, the Federals retreated. Union loss was, 223 killed, 266 wounded and 455 prisoners, including 100 wounded.

Gen. Zollicoffer, with 6,000 Confederates, attacked the Unionists at Camp Wild Cat, Laurel county, Ky., and was repulsed. Union loss, 4 killed and 21 wounded.

Oct. 22.—Skirmish at Buffalo Mills, Mo. Confederates lost 17 killed and 90 prisoners.

Oct. 25.—General Kelly defeated the enemy at Romney, Virginia.

EVANSVILLE—*Continued.*

MEAT MARKETS.

C. SCHWENTKER & CO.,
Proprietors of

Meat and Vegetable Market,

5 LOWER THIRD ST.

Established 1872.

WEIL, THEODORE, Meat Market, Poultry and Vegetables, 713 Main st.

MILLINERY AND DRESS MAKING.

DUNLEVY, MRS. M. J., Millinery, 510 Main st.

J. E. DUTCHER,

MILLINERY,
Straw and Fancy Goods,
506 MAIN ST.

MRS. S. E. ELLISON,
Fashionable

MILLINER
—(AND)—

Dressmaker,

112½ MAIN ST., OVER M. LYON.

SCHWENTKER, MRS. & BAUR, MISS L., Millinery and Notions. 502 Main st.

MRS J. G. SEESSENGUT,

Millinery & Hair Goods.
WIGS MADE TO ORDER.
120 Main St.

NOTIONS.

GRUHN, A., Hosiery, White Goods, Notions and Gents' Furnishing Goods, 417 Main st.

PAINTS AND OILS.

BURBANK & JOHNSON, Paints, Oils, Window Glass. etc . 14 Main st.

PAINTERS.

RICHARDSON, J. V., House and Sign Painter, 204 Upper 4th st.

F. S. Zumstein,
FRESCO, HOUSE AND SIGN PAINTER,
118 NORTH FOURTH STREET.
Established 1862.

PAPER DEALER.

JOHN WYMOND,

Wholesale Stationery,
BAGS, WRAPPING PAPERS, WALL PAPER, ETC.

PHYSICIANS.

EHRMAN, DR. E. J., Homeopathist, Office, 323 Upper 2d st.

PILOTO, MADAME, Astrologist and Clairvoyant Physician. Locust & 3d sts.

POLLARD, DR. W. S., Office, 312½ Upper 3d st., also, U. S. Pension Examiner.

EVANSVILLE—Continued.

PLANING MILL.

MYERS, JACOB & BRO., Planing Mill and Lumber, 301 Lower Water st.

PRINTER.

GROVES, THOS, J., Book & Job Printer.
312 Upper 1st st.

PROPRIETORY MEDICINES.

AKIN, G. L. & CO., Proprietory Medicines, 16 Upper 1st st.

PUMP MANUFACTURERS.

Eames & Co.,
Manufacturers of the
NONESUCH PUMPS,
Improved Rubber Bucket, Wood & Iron PUMPS,
511 & 513 FOURTH ST.

RESTAURANT.

JEWELL, R. C., Grand Central Dining Rooms, 319 Upper 1st st.

SALOONS.

John Albecker,
Proprietor of

APOLLO SALOON
—(AND)—
Pleasure Garden,
408 Upper 3d St, bet. Locust and Walnut.
Agent for Aurora Lager Beer.

GREEN, WM., Proprietor Katie Saloon, Choice Liquors and Fine Cigars, 302 Upper Water st.

LORENZ, GEORGE, Rhine & French Wines, etc., Cor. 2d & Division sts.

Robert Lohse,
WINES, LIQUORS, CIGARS
And Lager Beer,
318 UPPER SECOND STREET.

MAGNOLIA SALOON,
P. N. Jarvis & Son,
PROPRIETORS,
118 Upper Water Street.

RUHL, CHAS., Saloon, Best Wines, Liquors and Cigars, 312 Upper Second st.

C. SIHLER,
Wines, Liquors, Cigars, Etc.,
CINCINNATI BEER.
211 Upper Second Street.

1861.

Oct. 26.—Gallant charge of Maj. Zagonyi, with 150 of Fremont's body guard, on a large force of Confederates near Springfield, Mo. The enemy was routed with a loss of 106 killed and 27 prisoners.
Gen. Lane captured a Confederate transportation train near Butler, Mo.

Oct. 29.—The second naval expedition, consisting of 80 vessels and 15,000 men, sailed from Fortress Monroe. The naval force was commanded by Commodore Dupont; the land forces were commanded by Gen. Sherman.

Nov. 1.—General Scott resigned as commander-in-chief of the armies of the United States. Gen. McClellan was appointed in his place.
Gen. Benham defeated the Confederates at Gauley Bridge, Va.

Nov. 2.—Gen. Hunter superseded Gen. Fremont in the command of the Western department.
The Confederate schooner, Bermuda, ran the blockade at Savannah.

Nov. 7.—The naval and military forces under command of Commodore Dupont and Gen. Sherman, captured Forts Walker and Beauregard at Port Royal entrance. They also took possession of the town of Beaufort and Hilton Island. The Union loss was 8 killed and 25 wounded.
Gen. Grant, with a force of 2,800, attacked a Confederate camp at Belmont, Mo., driving the enemy out, destroying the camp and taking a quantity of arms; but, reinforcements arriving at Columbus, the Federals were compelled to retreat; their loss was 84 killed, 288 wounded and 235 missing.

Nov. 11.—Guyandotte, Va., burned by the Unionists.
Gen. Halleck takes command of the western department.

Nov. 15.—The U. S. frigate San Jacinto, Capt. Wilkes, arrived at Fortress Monroe with Mason and Slidell, the confederate commissioners to Europe, taken from the British mail steamer Trent, Nov. 8.

Nov. 18.—Confederate Congress met.

Nov. 21.—The U. S. vessel Santee captured the privateer Royal Yacht, off Galveston, Texas.

Nov. 23.—Fort Pickens and the United States war vessels Niagara and Colorado bombarded the confederate fortifications at Pensacola.
Port of Warrenton burnt.

Nov. 27.—Gen. McClellan directed the observance of the Sabbath in all the camps of the U. S. army.

Nov. 30.—Lord Lyons, the British minister at Washington, receives instructions from Earl Russel to leave America within seven days, unless the United States government consent to the unconditional liberation of Messrs. Mason and Slidell.
Jefferson Davis elected President of the Confederate States.

Dec. 3.—Congress met.

Dec. 4.—John C. Breckenridge expelled from the United States Senate.

Dec. 5.—Engagement between the confederte gunboats and Federal vessels at Cape Hatteras. According to the reports of Secre-

EVANSVILLE—Continued.

SALOONS.

PETER ROESNER
Proprietor Central Stock Yard
AND
DROVERS' EXCHANGE,
Cor. Ingle St. & Second Ave.

WM. WEIDNER,
Proprietor of Sportsman Hall,

Saloon & Restaurant,
Cor. Third and Sycamore Sts.
Formerly Prop. of Prescott House, St. Louis, Mo.

JOHN WIEGAND,
Wine and Lager Beer Saloon,
201 East Pennsylvania St.

SEWING MACHINES.

K OHL, B., Howe Machine.
Office, 304 Upper Second st.

T. E. MARTIN,
Manufacturer of Cripple Apparatus. All kinds of Sewing Machine Repairing,
413 Locust St., bet. Fourth and Fifth Sts.

STONE WORKS.

K ROEGER, B. H., Contractor and Builder in Stone Work, Cor. Edgar & Pennsylvania sts.

FRANZ R. CADEN,
Successor to Albaker & Caden,
Proprietor of the
EMPIRE STONE WORKS,
No. 100 Upper Fourth St.
Stone Fronts and other elaborate work executed according to Drawings and Specifications.

STOVES AND TINWARE.

Blemker, Tillman & Co.,
EXCELSIOR
STOVE WORKS,
Wholesale Manufacturers of
Stoves, Castings, Hollow-Ware, Mantles, Grates, Tin-Ware, and Dealers in Tinners' Stock.
Sample Room, No. 213 Second Street.

B LISS, J. L., STOVES AND TINWARE,
121 Locust Street.

Evansville Foundry Association,
Wholesale Manufacturers of
STOVES, CASTINGS,
HOLLOW-WARE,
—House Fronts, Grates and Tin-Ware—
Office, Warerooms and Foundry,
Corner Read and Pennsylvania Sts.

EVANSVILLE—Continued.

STOVES AND TINWARE.

FELDHACKER & SANDERS,
Manufacturers and Dealers in
Tin, Copper, Sheet Iron & Japanned Ware
Established, 1853. No. 411 Main Street.

S CHMITT, AUGUST, Stoves, Tinware, House Furnishing Goods, 605 Main Street.

TAILORS.

B OLEN, The Tailor,
211 Locust Street.

E LIKOFER, FRIED, Tailor,
119 Locust Street.

E. C. MEYER,
Merchant Tailor,
No. 721 Main Street,
Bet. Seventh and Eighth Sts.

CHAS. SCHERER,
MERCHANT TAILOR
317 Sycamore St., bet. Third and Fourth.

S CHMITS, G. H., Merchant Tailor, and Dealer in Dry Goods, 100 Upper Third Street.

J. H. SCHRICHTE,
TAILOR,
FINE CUSTOM WORK,
124 MAIN STREET.

F. W. SCHULTZ,
Merchant Tailor,
213 Seventh Street.

JOSEPH THORBECKE,
Merchant Tailor and Dealer in Gents' Furnishing Goods,
427 Main Street, bet. Fourth and Fifth sts.

TOBACCO AND CIGARS.

K ESTNER & HEYDEN, Manufacturers of and Dealers in Tobacco & Cigars, 100 Upper 8th st.

TRUNKS AND VALISES.

D. BAER,
Manufacturer of
Trunks and Valises,
Factory and Salesroom,
No. 21 Main Street,
A Fine Assortment of Traveling Bags Constantly on hand. Repairing done on Short notice.

W EIL, L. & SON, Trunks, Valises, etc.,
321 Upper First Street.

ADVERTISEMENTS. 151

City Hall, Baltimore, Md.—The corner stone of this building was laid October 18th, 1867. It is one of the most elegant structures in the United States, occupying the entire square on which it is erected. The length of the building is 239 feet, the width 149 feet, covering an area including pavements, of 50,500 feet. It is built of stone, marble and iron. It is four stories high, the entire height from the base to the finial being 250 feet.

City Hall, Pittsburg, Pa.—The building fronts on Smithfield Street, near Fifth Avenue facing eastward. The corner stone was laid May 5th, 1869. A leaden box was enclosed in the corner stone, containing the following: copies of the Pittsburg Daily of May 5th, 1869, copy of the City Code, Map of Pittsburg, 1875, Map of Pittsburg, 1869, Report of Board of Trade, giving statistics of the city, Paper containing names of all city officials, Paper containing names of members of the building commission and the builders. Specimens of United States Currency. The building has a frontage of 120 feet and is 110 feet deep, the main walls are 72 feet high, the extreme height of the tower is 175 feet, with a large clock in the observatory. On the 23d day of May, 1872, the building was dedicated with appropriate ceremonies, and the city government thereupon took permanent possession. The total cost of the building and grounds $600,579.00.

1861.

taries of War and Navy the Union forces numbered 640,537 volunteers, 20,334 regular soldiers, and 22,000 seamen.

Dec. 9.—The Confederate Congress passed a bill admitting Kentucky into the Southern Confederacy.

Freestone Point, Va., shelled by the National gunboats and captured.

Dec. 13.—Engagement at Camp Allegheny, Va., in which Gen. Milroy defeated the confederates under Col. Johnson. Union loss, 21 killed and 107 wounded.

Dec. 17.—Fight at Munfordsville, Ky. Drawn battle. Union loss, 10 killed and 17 wounded.

General Pope captured 360 secessionists at Osceola, Mo.

Dec. 18.—Gen. Pope captured 1,300 confederates, a number of horses and wagons, and 1,000 stand of arms at Milford, Mo. Union loss, 2 killed and 17 wounded. Stone fleet sunk in Charleston harbor.

Dec. 20.—Battle of Drainsville, Va., in which the confederates were defeated by the Union troops under Gen. McCall. Union loss, 7 killed and 61 wounded.

Dec. 23.—Troops despatched to Canada by the British government as a precaution against aggression by the U. S.

Dec. 30.—The New York banks suspend cash payments.

1862.

Jan. 1.—Mason and Slidell left Fort Warren for England in the British steamer Rinaldo.

Jan. 4.—Gen. Milroy defeated the confederates at Huntersville, Va., and captured $80,000 worth of stores.

Jan. 7.—Confederates defeated at Romney.

Jan. 8.—Gen. Palmer defeated the Confederates at Silver Creek, Mo. Union loss, 4 killed and 18 wounded.

Jan. 10.—Col. Garfield defeated the confederates under Humphrey Marshall at Prestonburg, Ky.

Jan. 11.—The Burnside expedition sailed from Fortress Monroe. Naval engagement on the Mississippi between the Union steamers Essex and St. Louis, and four Confederate boats; the latter were compelled to seek protection under the batteries at Columbus.

Simeon Cameron resigned his position as Secretary of War, and E. M. Stanton was appointed in his place.

Jan. 19.—Battle of Mill Spring, Ky. This battle was fought between 3,000 Union troops under Gen. Schoep and Confederates under Gen. Zollicoffer. The enemy were defeated and Gen. Zollicoffer killed. Union loss, 39 killed and 127 wounded.

Feb. 3.—The Federal government decided that the crews of the captured privateers were to be considered as prisoners of war.

Feb. 5.—Jesse D. Bright expelled from the U. S. Senate.

Feb. 6.—Commodore Foote with 7 gunboats attacked Fort Henry on the Tennessee river. The Confederate commander General Tilghman made an unconditional surrender.

EVANSVILLE.—*Continued.*

UNDERTAKERS.

SCHAEFER, JOS., Undertaker,
11 Lower Fifth St.

R. SMITH,
Undertaker and Dealer in Metallic Cases, Caskets, and Walnut Coffins.
——No. 425 MAIN STREET.——

UPHOLSTERER.

HAASE, CONRAD, Upholsterer,
719 Main st., bet. Seventh and Eighth.

WATCHES, CLOCKS AND JEWELRY.

ARTES, CHAS. F., Watches, Jewelry, etc., 130 Main st.

OTTO, C. H., Jewelry and Gold Pens,
210 Locust st.

WADE, CHARLES, Watchmaker and Jeweler, 210 Locust st. Established 1832.

WINES AND LIQUORS.

David Heimann.   Abraham Heimann.

DAVID HEIMANN & SON,,
Wholesale Dealers in
Liquors, Fine Kentucky Whiskies,
BRANDIES, WINES, ETC.,
22 SYCAMORE STREET.

OHIO VALLEY WINE CO., F. W. Cook, Pres.; A. Bernardin, Sup't. Office, 214 Upper Seventh st.

MUSCO COX,
Wines and Liquors,
214 Locust Street.

WOOLENS.

H. Brommelhaus.   H. Feldmann.
H. Brommelhaus & Co., Importers & Jobbers of
Foreign and Domestic Woolens,
105 Upper First street.

WOOLEN MILLS.

EVANSVILLE WOOLEN MILLS, Henke & Lemcke, 329 Main st.

EVANSVILLE LEADING BUSINESS HOUSES.

WHEN ESTABLISHED.

ALTHOFF, F., Carriage Manufacturer, 1874.
BAER, D., Trunks and Valises, 1863.
BOYD & BRICKLEY, Architects, 1859.
ELLISON, MRS. S. E., Milliner, 1875.
HAASE, CONRAD, Upholsterer, 1860.
HAMMERSTEIN, F., Carriage Manufacturer, 1855.
HARNISHFEGER, FRED. W., Boots and Shoes, 1874.
HEIMANN, DAVID & SON, Wholesale Liquors, 1876.
KROEGER, B. H., Contractor, 1868.
KRUG, PHILIP, Locksmith, 1857.

EVANSVILLE.—Continued.

LEADING BUSINESS HOUSES.

LEHNHARD & EARL, Builders, 1872.
MEYER, E. C., Merchant Tailor, 1867.
MILLER, GARDNER & CO., Dry Goods, 1864.
MILLS BROS., Lime and Cement, 1866.
SCHLENSKER & WOEHLER, Groceries, 1873.
SCHRICHTE, J. H., Merchant Tailor, 1849.
SMITH, R., Undertaker, 1865.
WEIL L. & SONS, Trunks, 1875.

JACKSON, MICH.

ARTISTS.

ROBISON & WALLACE, Portrait Artists, cor. Main and Mechanic sts. Est. 1870.

ATTORNEYS AT LAW.

GEO. F. ANDERSON,

Attorney and Counselor at Law.

Collections Promptly Made.

Office, 214 Main Street.

BLISS, A. A., Attorney at Law,
201 Main st.

GOULD, JAMES, Attorney at Law. Collections made in all parts of the State. 230 Main st.

J. C. LOWELL,
ATTORNEY at LAW
Real Estate, Loan and Insurance Agent,
214 MAIN STREET.

THOMAS A. WILSON,

ATTORNEY,

Office, 212 Main Street.

Special Attention given to Collections.

BARBER.

TAYLOR, ALFRED, Barber and Taxidermist, 189 Main st.

BREWERY.

G. FREY, Proprietor of

Jackson Brewery and Bottler of Frey's Celebrated Lager Beer,

Cor. Park and Water Sts.

1862.

Feb. 8.—Gen. Burnside captured six forts on Roanoke Island, taking about 3,000 small arms and destroying all the Confederate fleet except two vessels. Union loss was 50 killed and 212 wounded. 2,500 prisoners and a large quantity of ammunition were captured.

Feb. 10.—Elizabeth City, N. C. surrendered to Gen. Burdside. The Federal gunboats ascended the Tennessee river as far as Florence, Ala., capturing three and destroying six Confederate boats.

Feb. 13.—Gen. Curtis took possession of Springfield, Mo.

Feb. 14.—Com. Foote attacked Fort Donelson with the gunboats, but was compelled to withdraw.

Feb. 15.—The attack on Fort Donelson renewed by the land forces under Gen. Grant, numbering 40,000.

Bowling Green evacuated by the Confederates.

Feb. 16.—Gen. Buckner made an unconditional surrender of Fort Donelson and the troops under his command. Between 12,000 and 15,000 prisoners, 40 cannon, and a large amount of stores were captured. Union loss was 321 killed, 1,046 wounded, and 150 missing.

Skirmish at Independence, Mo.

Feb. 21.—Desperate fight at Fort Craig, New Mexico, between the Union troops under Col. Canby, and the Texans. The Federals were defeated with a loss of 62 killed and 162 wounded.

Feb. 22.—Jefferson Davis inaugurated President and A. H. Stephens Vice-President of the Southern Confederacy.

Feb. 24.—Nashville, Tenn., occupied by the Union troops.

Feb. 27.—Columbus evacuated by tthe Confederates.

March 1.—Fight at Pittsburg Landing between two Union gunboats and a Confederate battery.

March 4.—Brunswick, Ga., Fort Clinch, Fernandini, and St. Mary's, Fla., were captured by Com. Dupont.

Andrew Johnson appointed military governor of Tennessee.

Pike's Opera House, Cincinnati, destroyed by fire.

March 6.—President Lincoln proposes a plan of pecuniary assistance for the emancipation of the slaves in such States as should adopt an abolition policy.

March 8.—Battle of Pea Ridge. Total defeat of the enemy. Union loss was 212 killed and 920 wounded. The Confederate steamers, Merrimac, Jamestown and Yorktown, attacked the Federal fleet at Hampton Roads, destroying the Cumberland and Congress, and damaging several other vessels.

March 9.—Battle between the Confederate iron-clad, Merrimac, and the Federal floating battery, Monitor; the former compelled to retire. This—the first contest between iron-clads which the world had ever seen—was studied by the naval departments of all civilized powers, and a reaction took place against wooden vessels.

March 11.—Gen. McClellan took command of the army of the Potomac; Gen Fre-

ADVERTISEMENTS.

BUSINESS COLLEGE
Writing & Telegraph Institute
KALAMAZOO, MICH.

Send for Journal. Agents wanted to sell our Copy Slips of Business and Ornamental Penmanship. Send 50 cents for sample set.

Established 1874.
Kalamazoo Knitting Co.,
Manufacturers of the Celebrated

Home - Made Woolen Socks,
WITH DOUBLE HEELS AND TOES.

Kalamazoo, Mich.

Established 1876. | **C. EBERBACH,**
DEALER IN
Hardware, Stoves,
Coal, Iron, Nails, Glass, Cutlery, Felloes, Hubs and Spokes.
Manufacturer of **Tin, Sheet Iron and Copper Ware.**
23 and 25 MAIN STREET, ANN ARBOR, MICH.

W. A. Reed & Co.,
DESIGNERS & ENGRAVERS
ON WOOD.
Satisfaction always Guaranteed.

25 CANAL STREET, GRAND RAPIDS, MICH.

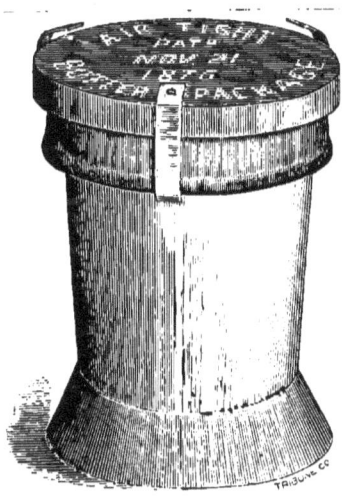

AIR TIGHT
BUTTER PACKAGE
Is warranted to keep
Butter Sweet and Fresh
FOR YEARS.

A. J. FINNEGAN,
310 Hennepin Ave.,
MINNEAPOLIS, MINN.
Patentee and Manufacturer.

Send for Circular.

ADVERTISEMENTS. 155

Public Library, Detroit, Mich.—Is situated on Central Park. The construction of this building was commenced in April, 1875, and completed in November, 1876. It has a front of 95 feet, with a rear of 100 feet, 60 feet of which is the Library proper. It is built of iron, glass, brick and stone, with iron trusses supporting glass roof. It has capacity for 200,000 volumes, arranged in 20 alcoves, 12 feet square and 14 feet high. The building is 61 feet to top of main cornice, 116 feet to top of dome, and 150 feet to top of figure. Cost of Library room, $135,000; when complete, will cost $175,000. Designed and superintended by Henry T. Brush, architect, Detroit, Mich.

Opera House, Detroit, Michigan.—Was built in the year 1869, at a cost of $200,000. It is 160 feet high, with a front of 100 feet, extending back 156 feet. The first story has an iron front, and the lobby is built entirely of brick. Its seating capacity is 2,000.

1862.

ment, of the Mountain department; Gen. Halleck, of the department of the Mississippi. Manassas occupied by Union troops.

March 12.—Com. Dupont took possession of Jacksonville, Fla.

The Confederates driven from their works at Paris, Tenn.

March 13.—The Confederates evacuated their works at New Madrid, Mo., in such haste as to leave 25 pieces of artillery and a large quantity of military stores valued at $1,000,000.

March 14.—Gen. Burnside attacked the Confederates in their fortification at Newbern, N. C. After a fight of four hours, the enemy retreated, leaving a large quantity of ammunition, provisions and stores in the hands of the victors. The Union loss was 91 killed and 466 wounded.

March 16.—Commodore Foote commenced the attack on Island No. 10. Confedfederates defeated at Cumberland Mountain, Ky.

March 18.—Confederate fortifications at Acquia Creek evacuated.

Confederates defeated at Salem, Ark.

March 23.—Battle of Winchester, Va. The Confederates were defeated and retreated to Strasburg, leaving their dead and wounded upon the field. The Union loss was 103 killed and 466 wounded.

March 28.—Fight at Pigeon Ranch, between 3,000 Union troops under Col. Hough and 1,100 Texans. The battle was a drawn one.

April 6.—Battle of Shiloh. The Confederates under Gens. Johnson and Beauregard attacked Gen. Grant's army at Pittsburgh Landing. The Union forces were driven back to the river and a number of prisoners captured.

April 7.—The battle of Shiloh renewed. Gen. Buell arrived during the night with reinforcements. The battle lasted throughout the day with varied success, but the Confederates were finally defeated and driven to their fortifications at Corinth. The Federal loss was 1,644 killed, 7,721 wounded, and 3,956 missing. The Confederate Gen. Johnson was killed.

April 8.—Island No. 10 captured; 5,000 prisoners, 100 siege guns, 24 pieces field artillery, 5,000 stands of small arms, 2,000 hogsheads of sugar, and a large quantity of clothing, tents, and ammunition.

April 11.—Fort Pulaski, commanding the entrance to Savannah, surrendered after a bombardment of thirty hours. Gen. Mitchell occupied Huntsville, Ala., taking 200 prisoners, 15 locomotives and a large number of cars. Congress passed the bill abolishing slavery in the District of Columbia.

April 12.—Gen. Mitchell captured 2,000 prisoners at Chattanooga.

April 18.—The Confederates attacked Gen. Smith's division at Yorktown, but were repulsed.

April 19.—Fight between Gen. Burnside's troops and the enemy near Elizabeth City, N. C. The latter were defeated. Union loss, 11 killed. Gen. Reno, with 2,000 Union troops, defeated the enemy at Camden, N. C.

April 25.—Com. Farragut arrived at

JACKSON.—*Continued.*

BLACKSMITHS AND HORSESHOERS.

TIFT & WESLEY, Blacksmiths and Horseshoers, Cortland st.

BOOTS AND SHOES.

HATCH & WARREN, Dealers in Boots and Shoes, 214 Main st.

BOTTLING WORKS.

CONKLIN BOTTLING WORKS, D. M. Conklin prop., 12 Pearl st.

BROOM FACTORY.

JACKSON CITY BROOM FACTORY, Manufacturer of Extra Family, Store, Mill, Railway, Boat and Brewery

Brooms and Whisks,
39 Cortland St.   JOHN F. MACK.

CABINET MAKER.

EATON, F., Cabinet Maker. Furniture Repaired and Varnished. 26 Pearl st.

CARRIAGES AND WAGONS.

JACOB BIEBER,

Carriage and Wagon Maker,
Cor. Cortland and Mill Streets.

COPPS, C. N., Carriage Maker and Blacksmith, Mechanic st.

FOGG, L. B., Carriage Making and Repairing, 11 Pearl Street.

CARRIAGE TOPS.

A. E. BALL,
Manufacturer of

Fine Carriage Tops,

AND ALL KINDS OF

Carriage Trimmings at Bottom Prices,
at No. 11 PEARL ST.

CIGAR MANUFACTURER.

EBERBACH, WM., Cigar Manufacturer. Established, 1874.   121 Mechanic Street.

CIGAR BOX FACTORY.

W. F. STEVENS & CO.,
JACKSON CITY

Steam Cigar Box Factory,
And Manufacturers of all kinds of Boxes,
Cor. Clinton and Jackson Sts.
New Brands, Labels, Edgings, Tacks, etc., constantly on hand.

COAL AND WOOD.

SMITH BROS., Dealers in Coal and Wood. Cor. Main Street and M. C. R. R. Crossing.

CONTRACTORS AND BUILDERS.

DIAMOND, GEORGE, Contractor and Builder. 100 Mechanic Street.

JACKSON.—*Continued.*

DENTIST.

DORRANCE, W. H., Dentist,
254 Main Street, Jackson.

DYER AND SCOURER.

DONALDSON, JOHN, Steam Dyer and Scourer,
Established, 1862.   102 Mechanic Street.

GROCERIES.

HOBART, C. D. & CO., Grocers and Dealers in Foreign and Domestic Goods, 260 Main st.

KENNEDY, F. A., General Groceries,
Cor. Pearl and Jackson sts.

PAYNE, C. W., Groceries and Provisions,
161 Mechanic street.

SHEARER, R., Groceries and Provisions,
Jackson and Cortland streets.

GUNS AND SPORTING GOODS.

LINDERMAN, LOUIS, Dealer in Guns, Pistols and Rifles, 127 Mechanic street.

GEO. A. SMITH,
Wholesale and Retail Dealer in

Guns, Ammunition & Sporting Goods

All Repairing done in the best possible manner. Guns bored to shoot close and hard and warranted every time.

Store 35 Mill St., opp. Keystone Block.

N. B.—Any description of Gun, either Breech-Loading or Rifle, furnished on the shortest notice and at lowest prices.

HOTELS.

HIBBARD HOUSE, Jackson, Mich.,
J. M. Bradley, Proprietor.

HURD HOUSE,
Smith & Hurd, Proprietors.

LAUNDRY.

SHEARER, A. M., Jackson Steam Laundry, 50 Cortland st.

LITHOGRAPHERS.

BIRD & MICKLE, Lithographers and Map Publishers, cor. Maine & Mechanic sts.

LIVERY AND SALE STABLE.

GALE GEO. H., Livery & Sale Stables,
Mechanic st., opp. Post Office.

MACHINISTS.

DENNIS, E. & CO., Founders and Machinists and Machinery Supplies, 48 Jackson st.

MEAT MARKET.

E. M. Evans,
Proprietor

PEOPLE'S MARKET,

129 & 131 MECHANIC ST.

Jackson, - - Mich.

MEDICAL INSTITUTES.

BAIRD, DR. A. H., Medical Dispensary and Institute, 223 Main st., up stairs.

1862.

New Orleans, and took possession of the city. Fort Macon, Georgia, surrendered after a bombardment of eleven hours. Gen. C. F. Smith died at Savannah, Tennessee.

April 28.—Forts Jackson and St. Philip surrendered.

April 29.—Gen. Mitchell defeated the Confederates at Bridgeport, Ala.

May 3.—The Confederates evacuated Yorktown, Jamestown, and Mulberry and Gloucester islands, leaving ammunition, camp equipage, and 100 guns behind.

May 5.—Battle of Williamsburgh, Va. The Union troops were commanded by Gens. Hancock and Hooker. The Confederates were defeated, and retreated in the night towards Richmond.

May 7.—Battle of West Point, Va. Gens. Franklin and Sedgwick, with a force of 20,000 men, were attacked by Gen. Lee. The Confederates were defeated. Union loss about 300 killed and wounded.

May 8.—Gen. Milroy attacked the enemy at McDowell's, Va. After a fight of five hours he was forced to withdraw.

May 9.—The Confederates evacuated Pensacola, and destroyed the Navy Yard.

May 10.—The Federal forces took possession of Norfolk, Va. Gosport Navy Yard destroyed by the Confedeartes. Gunboat fight on the Mississippi, near Fort Wright; the Confederates were repulsed, losing two vessels.

May 11.—The Confederates blow up their iron-clad Merrimac, to prevent its capture by the enemy.

May 12.—Natchez, Miss., surrendered to Com. Farragut.

May 16.—The Union Gunboats repulsed at Fort Darling.

May 17.—Confedeates driven across the Chickahominy, at Bottom Bridge.

May 23.—Confederates defeated at Lewisburg, Va.

May 24.—Col. Kenley, commanding the Federal troops at Front Royal, Va., was attacked by large force of the enemy and defeated with a heavy loss.

May 25.—General Banks defeated at Winchester, Virginia, and driven across the Potomac.

May 27.—Confederates defeated at Hanover, Virginia. Union loss, 35 killed and 220 wounded.

May 29.—Confederates evacuated Corinth, Miss.

May 31.—The Confederates under General Johnson attacked the left wing of the Army of the Potomac, commanded by General Casey, at Fair Oaks. Union forces were driven back.

Corinth taken.

June 1.—Battle of Fair Oaks was renewed. Confederates repulsed. Union loss, 890 killed, and 4,844 wounded.

June 6.—After a naval battle, Memphis surrendered to the Union troops.

June 8.—Battle of Cross Keys, Va., between Gen. Fremont's army and the Confederate army, commanded by Gen. Jackson. The latter were defeated.

JACKSON.—Continued.

MEDICAL INSTITUTES.

Dr. A. DeLafayette Angell,

MEDICAL INSTITUTE
AND
RUPTURE or HERNIA CURE,
Also manufacturer of the Excelsior Elastic Trusses, Abdominal Supporters, etc.

PAINTERS.

BUTCHER, E., General House Painting and Papering, Mechanic & Cortland sts.

John H. Reimers,
FRESCO PAINTER
AND
SCENIC ARTIST,
100 Mechanic st.

ROOT, ORWILL, Sign Writer and Scenic Painter, Mill st.

WEST END PAINT SHOP.
F. L. Shurragar,
Practical

SIGN WRITER and PAPER HANGER,
Graining, Kalsomining and General Painting,
280 MAIN ST., DOWN STAIRS.

Geo M. Wright,
HOUSE & SIGN PAINTER,
Rear of 85 Jackson Street.
Graining and Glazing, Store and Office Painting, Signs and Banners, Kalsomining and Paper Hanging.

PAPER DEALER.

HUNT, EDWARD S., Paper Dealer, 32 Cortland st.

PATENT AGENCY.

The Only Reliable
MICHIGAN PATENT AGENCY.
JAMES HAMMILL,   W. G. GILBERT,
Attorney at Law.   Eng'r and Dr'htsman.
Drawings, Specifications and Assignments. We also prepare and file Caveats, procure Design Patents, Trade-marks and Re-issues. We have no Sub-Agents, but do our business direct with the Commissioner of Patents.
Office, 239 Main St., Up Stairs.

PORK PACKER.

CARL DETTMANN,
Pork-Packer,
Wholesale and Retail dealer in Fresh, Salt and Smoked Meats and Lard,
202 MAIN ST.

PHYSICIANS.

CALVERT, W. J., M. D., Homeopathic Physician and Surgeon, 296 Main st.

JACKSON.—Continued.

PHYSICIANS.

GIBSON, W. A., M. D., Homeopathic Physician and Surgeon, Main & Jackson sts.

A. S. GREGORY, M. D.,
Eclectic Physician and Surgeon,
Removes and cures Cancers and Tumors (in all curable cases,) without the knife or loss of blood, with little pain and no debility of the system. The treatment consists in the use of Chemical Cancer Antidotes. Specific in character, efficient in action and superior to all other methods now in use. Throat and Lung difficulties and Nasal Catarrh successfully treated with the most approved system of medicated inhalations. Rheumatism and Hemorrhoids or Piles readily yield to Dr G.'s new system of treatment. Office, 198 Main st., Jackson, Michigan. Address, with stamp, A. S GREGORY, M. D.

PRINTER.

REYNOLDS' SPECIALTY PRINTING HOUSE.
Letter, Note and Bill Heads, Statements, Blanks, Envelopes, Cards, &c., &c., Printed and promptly delivered to any part of the United States or Canadas.
AT WONDERFULLY LOW PRICES.
Send 3ct Stamp for Circular and liberal terms to Agents.
198 MAIN ST.

RESTAURANT.

RUST, F. W., Reform Club Restaurant and Saloon, 165 Mechanic st.

ROOFER.

Thos. McGraw.
SLATE & METAL ROOFER,
And Manufacturer of Galvanized Iron Cornice Window Caps, Chimneys, Etc., Etc. Also dealer in Slating, Nails, Felt and Zinc.
P. O. BOX 445, JACKSON, MICH.

TAILORS.

TEALL, H. N., Merchant Tailor, 210 Main st.

JACOB WEIS,
TAILOR & CUTTER.
New Garments made to order. Clothing Cleaned and Repaired.
KEYSTONE BLOCK, MILL STREET.

WATCHES AND JEWELRY.

CHILD, W. W., Watches, Jewelry, Solid Silver, French Clocks, Bronzes, etc, 276 Main st.

Jackson, Mich., Business Houses,
WHEN ESTABLISHED.

ANDERSON, GEO. F., Attorney, 1874.
ANGELL, DR. A. DeLAFAYETTE, 1871.
BIRD & MICKLE, Lithographers, 1871.
DETTMANN, CARL, Meat Market, 1865.

Washington Monument, Baltimore, Md.—The corner stone was laid on the 4th of July, 1815, and the Statue, representing Washington resigning his commission, was placed in position October 19, 1829. The Monument is a graceful Doric Column, built of white marble. The base is 50 feet square and 24 feet high, and the column is 164 feet in height. The whole structure rises to an elevation of over 280 feet above tide-water.

Battle Monument, Baltimore, Md.—This Monument stands on Calvert street, between Fayette and Lexington streets. It was erected in honor of the memories of the heroes who fell at the battle of North Point, September 12, 1814. The corner-stone was laid in 1815, and the expenses were defrayed by individual subscription.

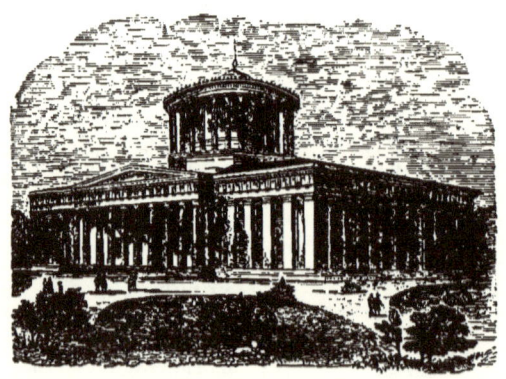

STATE CAPITOL, COLUMBUS, O.

1862.

June 9.—The United States Senate decrees the abolition of slavery in all the territories of the Union.

June 16.—Fight on James Island, near Charleston, S. C. Federals defeated.

June 17.—Col. Fitch destroyed a Confederate battery at St. Charles, Ark. 125 were killed by an explosion on one of the Federal gunboats.

June 18.—Union troops occupied Cumberland Gap.

June 26.—General Pope assigned to the command of the Army of Virginia. Commencement of the six days' fight before Richmond. The Confederates attacked McClellan's right wing at Mechanicsville. Battle undecided.

June 27.—Bombardment of Vicksburg commenced. Gen. Fremont relieved of his command. Battle before Richmond renewed; the Federals were driven back; loss heavy on both sides. White House evacuated by the Union troops.

June 28.—Incessant fighting all day between the right wing of the Union army on the Chickahominy, and the left wing of the Confederates; the enemy were repulsed. In the evening the Unionists were ordered to fall back.

June 29.—Battle before Richmond renewed by an attack on the Union forces at Peach Orchard; the Confederates were driven back, but late in the evening made another attack at Savage's Station. The fight continued until nine at night. The wounded fell into the hands of the enemy.

June 30.—Battle of White Oak Swamp; heavy loss on both sides.

July 1.—Battle of Malvern Hill, and last of the Richmond battles. The Confederates were repulsed at every point. The Union loss during the six days' fighting before Richmond was 1,561 killed, 7,701 wounded and 5,958 missing. President Lincoln calls for 300,000 additional volunteers.

July 11.—Gen. Halleck appointed commander of all the land forces of the United States.

July 13.—Fight at Murfreesboro, Tenn.; Union troops surrendered. General Morgan captured Lebanon, Kentucky, burned part of the town and robbed the bank.

July 17.—President Lincoln sanctions a bill confiscating the property and emancipating the slaves of all persons who shall continue in arms against the Union for 60 days.

July 19.—Severe skirmish at Memphis, Tennessee; Union loss, 6 killed and 32 wounded.

July 21.—John S. Phelps appointed military Governor of Arkansas.

July 22.—The siege of Vicksburg abandoned.

July 28.—Confederates defeated at More's Hill, Mo.

Aug. 3.—The Confederate General Jeff Thompson defeated near Memphis, Tennessee. General Halleck ordered Gen. McClellan to evacuate the Peninsula of Va.

EVANSVILLE.—*Continued.*

LEADING BUSINESS HOUSES.

EVANS, E. M., Meat Market, 1860.
FREY, G., Brewer, 1865.
LOWELL, J. C., Real Estate, 1868.
McGRAW, THOS., Roofer, 1876.
MICHIGAN PATENT AGENCY, 1859.
REYNOLDS, JOHN, Printer, 1876.
SHURRAGER, F. L., Sign Writer, 1870.
SMITH, GEO. A., Gunsmith, 1876.
STEVENS, W. F. & CO., Cigar Boxes, 1876.
TEALL, H. N., Merchant Tailor, 1872.
WILSON, THOS. A., Attorney, 1866.
WRIGHT, GEO. M., Painter, 1869.

BAY CITY, MICH.

ARCHITECTS.

LEVERETT A. PRATT,

Architect and Superintendent,

OFFICE,

Room No. 5, Bank Bl'g, Center St.

ATTORNEYS AT LAW.

HOLMES, COLLINS & STODDARD, Attorneys and Counselors, Watson block.

WILSON & WEADOCK,

Attorneys, Counselors and Solicitors.

Proctors in Admiralty, 3 and 4 Watson Block.

BARBERS.

CORWIN, W. S., Barber Shop, 110 Water st. Establi-hed 1869.

H. E. SUSAND & CO.,

Barbers,

CENTER ST. & 315 WATER ST.,

BAY CITY, MICH.

SUSANDS LEAD THE TRADE.

BOTTLING WORKS.

NETT & PARTENFELDER,

Proprietors of the

Bavarian Lager-Beer Bottling

WORKS,

CORNER WATER & SEVENTH.

BAY CITY—*Continued.*

BREWERY.

BAY CITY BREWERY.
C. E. YOUNG.
Celebrated Lager Beer.
Cor. Water & Twenty-second Sts.

CARRIAGE AND WAGON MANUFACTURERS.

HANDRICKS & M'DONALD, Carriage Makers and General Blacksmiths, Harrison & 33d sts.

HEMBLING'S CARRIAGE WORKS. All kinds of BUGGIES AND CUTTERS made to order.
Horseshoeing & Jobbing a Specialty.
THIRD STREET.

O'BRIEN BROS.,
Wagon & Carriage Makers,
AND
GENERAL BLACKSMITHS.
Saginaw St., bet. 2nd & 3rd.
Established 1872.

DENTIST.

MAXON, C. W., Dentist,
Opera House block.

DRUGGISTS.

Established 1865.
JOHNSON, LEWIS & CO.,
Dealers in Groceries & Provisions, Drugs & Medicines,
Water st., bet. Thirtieth and Thirty-first sts.

LORANGER & CHAPIN,
DRUGGISTS,
211 Third street. Prescriptions carefully compounded, day or night.

FORCE PUMP MANUFACTURER.

FURMAN, L., Force Pump Manufacturer, Eighth and Water sts. Established 1876.

GROCERIES.

ASHLEY, A. J., Groceries and Provisions, Water st., bet. 22d and 23d sts. Est. 1873.

D. BAUMGARTEN,
Dealer in
Staple and Fancy Groceries,
Provisions, Foreign & Domestic Fruits,
CENTER STREET, COR. ADAMS.

GUNS AND SPORTING GOODS.

BASCOM, H. C., Guns, Ammunition, Sporting Apparatus and Fishing Tackle.

IMPORTANT EVENTS OF THE CENTURY. 161

1862.

Aug. 4.—The Secretary of War ordered a draft of 300,000 men. The Confederate ram Arkansas destroyed by her crew.

Aug. 5.—Gen. Robert McCook murdered by the Confederates while wounded and riding in an ambulance. The Confederate General J. C. Breckenridge made an unsuccessful attack on Baton Rouge, La.

Aug. 9.—Confederates under Gen. Jackson attack General Banks at Cedar Mountain. The contest was short but severe. General Banks held his position, while the enemy fell back two miles and did not renew the fight.

Aug. 16.—Gen. McClellan evacuated Harrison's Landing.

Aug. 19.—Gen. Wright placed in command of the department of the Ohio.

Aug. 25.—Confederates made an unsuccessful attack on Fort Donelson.

Aug. 26.—The Confederate General Ewell drove the Union troops from Manassas.

Aug. 29.—Battle of Gainsville or Groveton, Va. The Battle was opened by General Sigel early in the morning. Gens. Reno and Kearney arrived with reinforcements. The fight continued until 6 P. M., when the enemy retired.

Aug. 30.—Battle of Richmond, Ky. Union troops under General Manson defeated, with a loss of about 200 killed, 700 wounded, and 2,000 prisoners. Confederates defeated at Bolivar, Tenn.

Aug. 30.—Second battle of Bull Run. The Federal forces under General Pope defeated.

Sept. 1.—Fight at Britton's Lane. Tenn. Confederates retired, leaving their dead on the field. Union loss, 5 killed, 78 wounded, and 92 missing.
Fight at Chantilly, Va. The Union troops were commanded by Gens. Hooker, Reno and Kearney. The Confederates retired, leaving their dead and wounded on the field. This was the last fight in which General Pope's army was engaged.

Sept. 2.—Gen. McClellan appointed to the command of the troops for the defense of Washington.

Sept. 5.—Confederates began crossing the Potomac into Maryland.

Sept. 7.—General Banks assigned to the command of the fortifications in and around Washington. General McClellan took the field at the head of the Army of the Potomac.

Sept. 12.—Fight at Middletown, Maryland. Union loss, 80 killed and wounded.

Sept. 14.—Gen. McClellan overtook the enemy at South Mountain, Md. A general engagement took place. The fight was severe, and the loss heavy on both sides, the Unionists losing 443 killed and 1,806 wounded. Gen. Reno was among the killed. The Confederates retreated towards the Potomac.

Sept. 15.—Harper's Ferry surrendered after two days' fighting, to the enemy, with all the garrison, consisting of 8,000 men.

Sept. 17.—Battle of Antietam, Md. This battle was fought on Antietam creek, near Sharpsburg; it began early in the morning and

HULMAN & COX,
Wholesale Grocers
—: AND :—
LIQUOR DEALERS,
TERRE HAUTE, IND.

HERMAN HULMAN.   CRAWFORD FAIRBANKS.

Hulman & Fairbanks,
DISTILLERS OF
M^cGREGOR,
and Phœnix Bourbon and White Corn Whiskies,
OFFICE :
COR. MAIN AND FIFTH STREETS,
TERRE HAUTE.

MERCHANTS' HOTEL, WINONA, MINN.

Centrally located, nearest hotel to Post Office and Philharmonic Hall.

Within one Block of Leading Wholesale Houses and Banks.

Terms $2.00 per Day.   **J. SCHWEITZER, Pro.**

This Hotel is new and elegantly furnished throughout, and is first-class in every particular.

IMPORTANT EVENTS OF THE CENTURY. 163

California State Building, Centennial Exposition, Philadelphia.—The building is rather different in structure from the other State Centennial buildings on the ground. It is constructed entirely of wood, with an oval roof surmounted with a dome. The interior of the building is sealed with finished lumber from California, and inlaid with fancy colored woods from the same state, altogether making it present a very handsome appearance inside as well as outside.

NORMAL SCHOOL, TERRE HAUTE.

ADVERTISEMENTS.

BAY CITY.—*Continued.*

HOTELS.

EVERETT HOUSE, A. J. Gilson, prop., Harrison and Thirty-second sts. Est. 1875.

MANSION HOUSE,
Wm. Ferris & Son, Props,
$1.50 PER DAY.
602 WASHINGTON STREET.

MOULTON HOUSE, Peter Van Horn, prop., Fourth and Saginaw sts. Established 1876.

Portland House
FRANK LEFEVRE, Prop.,
Cor. First & Washington Sts.
Travelers Stopping at this House will receive Courteous Attention.

SCHINDEHETTE HOUSE, John Schindehette, prop., Fourth and Saginaw sts.

LIVERY STABLES.

HANLIN, JOHN, Livery and Sale Stable, Fourth and Washington sts. Established 1870.

MEAT MARKETS.

LOUIS BERTCH,
Wholesale and Retail Dealer in

FRESH & SALTED MEATS
Particular Attention Given to Supplying Boats.
112 & 114 CENTER ST.

GEO. W. MANSFIELD,
Wholesale and Retail Dealer in

Fresh and Salted
MEATS,
HAMS, SAUSAGES, ETC.,
Taylor and Rose Block.
COR. THIRD & WASHINGTON STS.

FRED. SIMON,
Dealer in Fresh and Salted
MEATS,
OF ALL KINDS.
MANUFACTURER OF ALL KINDS OF SAUSAGES.
Dried, Smoked, Spiced and Corned Beef constantly on hand.

CENTER ST., next to the Opera House Block.

BAY CITY.—*Continued.*

PAINTERS.

A. BAUMBACH & CO.,
Carriage, Sign & Ornamental
PAINTERS,
Cor. Eighth and Water Sts.

PHOTOGRAPHER.

COLBURN, E. J., Photographer, Griswold block.

PLUMBERS AND GAS FITTERS.

JOHN STYNINGER,
PLUMBER, GAS AND STEAM FITTER
COPPERSMITH,
AND HEAVY SHEET IRON WORK,
117 WATER STREET.

SULLIVAN & FINN, Plumbers, Steam and Gas Fitters, Center st.

SAWS.

WILLIAM WARD,
Saw Repairer & Furnisher
All kinds of Mill Saws Gummed and Straightened, and made good as new.
—Agent for American Saw Company—
302 SOUTH WATER ST.
All Orders promptly filled. When sending Circular Saws, it is necessary to mark the Log Side of the Saw or send instructions in regard to it.

TAILORS—MERCHANT.

OCTAVIUS BOUCHER,
Custom Tailor, Fancy Dyer and Clothes Cleaner,
Water Street, opp. Grow Bros.

W. E. TEALL,
MERCHANT TAILOR
The Boss $5.00 Pants. 118 Water Street.

TEALL, W. R., Merchant Tailor, Harrison st., bet. 33d and 34th sts.

TOBACCO AND CIGARS.

H. SCHINDEHETTE,
Dealer in Wines, Liquor, Ale, Lager, Pipes, Tobacco and Cigars,
No. 115 Water Street.

Bay City, Mich., Business Houses.
WHEN ESTABLISHED.

BAUMBACH, A. & CO., Painters, 1877.
BAUMGARTEN, D., Groceries, 1869.
BAY CITY BREWERY, 1872.
BERTCH, LOUIS, Meat Market, 1868.
MANSFIELD, GEO. W., Meat Market, 1872.

POST OFFICE, MILWAUKEE.

LOUIS L. HARTMANN.   HENRY SUHR.

HARTMANN & SUHR,

MANUFACTURERS OF

CIGAR BOXES,

Labels, Edgings, Brands,

LACES, TRIMMINGS, COLORED PAPER, &c.

74 Biddle St., cor. Market,

MILWAUKEE, - - WISCONSIN.

1862.

continued until evening. Armies each numbering 100,000 men. During the night the Confederates retreated, leaving 3,500 prisoners, 39 stands of colors and 13 guns in the hands of the victors. The Union loss was 2,010 killed, 9,416 wounded and 1,043 missing. Confederate loss, 14,000.

Cumberland Gap evacuated by the Federals.

Sept. 18.—The Confederates recrossed the Potomac into Virginia, having been in Maryland two weeks. Evacuated Harper's Ferry.

Sept. 19.—Gen. Rosecrans commenced an attack on the Confederate forces at Iuka, Miss. Confederates evacuated the place during the night. The Union loss was 135 killed and 527 wounded.

Sept. 21.—Gen. McCook recaptured Munfordsville, Ky.

President Lincoln's Emancipation Proclamation issued.

Sept. 25.—Habeas corpus suspended by the United States Government.

Sept. 27.—Fight at Augusta, Ky. The Union garrison 120 strong surrendered after a gallant defense.

Sept. 29.—Gen. Nelson was shot by Gen. Jeff. C. Davis, at Louisville, Ky.

Oct. 4.—Battle of Corinth, Miss. The Confederates were defeated with heavy loss. The Union loss was 315 killed and 1,802 wounded.

Oct. 6.—Confederates attacked Gen. Palmer's brigade at Lavergne, Tenn., but were defeated.

Oct. 8.—Battle of Perryville, Ky. The advance of Buell's army was attacked at Perryville, Ky., by a superior force of the enemy under Gens. Jackson and Terrel. The Confederates retreated during the night. Union loss was over 3,000 killed and wounded.

Oct. 10.—The Confederate cavalry under Gen. Stuart entered Chambersburg, Pa., and captured a quantity of small arms and clothing.

Oct. 18.—The Confederate, Gen. Morgan, occupied Lexington, Ky.

Oct. 19.—The Confederate, Gen. Forrest, defeated near Gallatin, Tenn.

Oct. 22.—Confederate salt works in Florida destroyed.

Gen. Blunt defeated the Confederates at Maysville, Ark., capturing all their artillery. Fight at Pocotaligo, S. C.

Oct. 28.—Gen. Herron defeated the Confederates near Fayetteville, Ark.

Oct. 30.—Gen. Rosecrans assumed command of the army of the Cumberland.

Gen. Mitchell died at Port Royal, S. C.

Nov. 5.—Gen. McClellan relieved of the command of the army of the Potomac, and Gen. Burnside succeeds him.

Nov. 11.—Gen. Ransom defeated the Confederates under Woodward, near Garretsburg, Ky.

Nov. 16.—President Lincoln enjoined on the United States forces the orderly observance of the Sabbath.

Nov. 17.—A cavalry fight took pleace near Kingston, N. C.

BAY CITY.—Continued.

LEADING BUSINESS HOUSES.

NETT & PARTENFELDER, Bottling Works, 1874.
O'BRIEN BROS., Carriage Makers, 1872.
PORTLAND HOUSE, 1874.
PRATT, LEVERETT A., Architect, 1872.
SIMON, FRED., Meat Market, 1863.
STYNINGER, JOHN, Plumber, 1870.
WARD, WILLIAM, Saw Maker, 1862.

WEST BAY CITY, MICH.

BILLIARD HALL AND RESTAURANT.

JOHN GARY NICKEL,

Billiard Saloon

And Restaurant,

Midland St., near Linn.

CARRIAGE MAKERS.

PAJOT, J. J. & CO., Carriage Makers and Blacksmiths, River street.

DRUGGISTS.

DAVIS, JOHN, Druggist,
Linn street, West Bay City.

J. T. Travers,

PRACTICAL

DRUGGIST and CHEMIST,

Cor. Linn and John Streets.

A full line of Drugs, Medicines and Toilet Articles of every description always on hand.

GROCERIES.

R. GREEN,

DEALER IN

Groceries and Provisions,

Game, Oysters and Fresh Fish,

TEAS A SPECIALTY.

West Bay City.

HOTEL.

WELLS HOUSE, A. Wells, Proprietor.

LIVERY STABLES.

R. H. RICH'S

Livery Stable

Fine Carriages. Rates reasonable.

Stable: West Side of Linn Street.

WEST BAY CITY.—*Continued.*

LIVERY STABLES.

W. M. GREEN,
Proprietor Green's Livery, Boarding and Sale Stable. First Class Horses and Carriages at all hours.

Linn Street, North of Midland.

MEAT MARKET.

J. A. BEHMLANDER,
Wholesale and Retail Dealer in all kinds of

Fresh & Salt Meats,
Lard, Sausages, etc.,

—LINN STREET.—

PAINTER.

SMITH, E. C., House and Sign Painter, Established. 1870. River Street.

PERFUMERY.

DAVIES, JOHN, Extracts and Toilet Articles. Linn Street.

WATCHMAKER AND JEWELER.

S. SWART,
PRACTICAL

Watchmaker & Jeweler,
And Dealer in Watches, Clocks & Jewelry, Repairing promptly attended to. All work warranted. Terms cash.

Linn Street, opposite Wells House.

West Bay City, Michigan, Business Houses,
WHEN ESTABLISHED.

BEHMLANDER, J. A., Meat Market, 1873.
DAVIS, JOHN, Druggist, 1868.
GREEN, R., Grocer, 1877.
GREEN, W. M., Livery Stable, 1868.
RICH, R. H., Livery Stable, 1869.
SWART, S., Jeweler, 1869.
TRAVERS, J. T., Druggist, 1876.

EAST SAGINAW, MICH.

ARCHITECT.

V. BUDE,
ARCHITECT,
Cor. Emerson and Franklin Sts.,

Plans furnished for Buildings of every description, and satisfaction guaranteed.

1862.

Nov. 22.—All political State prisoners released.

Nov. 28.—Battle of Crane Hill, Ark. The Union army, numbering 1,000 men, was commanded by Gen. Blunt. The Confederates were defeated with a heavy loss, and retreated to Van Buren.

Dec. 6.—Gen. Banks' expedition sailed for New Orleans.

Dec. 7.—Battle of Prarie Grove, Ark. The Union army was commanded by Gens. Blunt and Herron. The Confederates were defeated with heavy loss and retired during the night.

Dec. 11.—The city of Fredricksburg bombarded by the Union troops, under cover of which they crossed the Rappahannock.

Dec. 13.—Battle of Fredricksburgh, Va. Confederate works were attacked by the Union troops in three divisions, under Sumner, Hooker and Franklin, who were repulsed. Federals lost 1,512 killed, 6,000 wounded and 100 prisoners.

Dec. 14.—Gen. Banks superseded Gen. Butler at New Orleans.

Dec. 16.—Gen. Burnside's army removed to the north side of the Rappahannock. Gen. Foster defeated the Confederates at White Hall, N. C.

Dec. 17.—The Union troops occupied Baton Rouge, La.

Gen. Foster defeated the Confederates at Goldsboro, N. C., destroying the railroad bridge.

Dec. 19.—The Confederates recaptured Holly Springs, Miss., taking the garrison prisoners.

Dec. 23.—The Confederates repulsed by by Gen. Sigel at Dumphries, Va.

Dec. 27.—Gen. Sherman attacked the advance works of the enemy about 6 miles from Vicksburg, at the same the gunboats attacked the Confederate batteries on Haines' Bluff.

Dec. 28.—Second attack on Vicksburg. The Federals drove the Confederates from the first and second lines of defense and advanced to within two and a half miles of Vicksburg.

Gen. Blunt entered Van Buren, Ark., capturing four steamboats laden with provisions.

Dec. 29.—The Confederates attacked Gen. Sherman with their whole force, and drove him back to the first line of defense.

Dec. 31.—Battle of Murfreesboro, or Stone River. The Union army, numbering 45,000 men under Gen. Rosecrans. Gen. McCook's division was driven back four miles and lost 26 guns, but reinforcements being sent from the left and centre, the enemy was in turn repulsed and the lost ground regained.

West Virginia admitted into the Union as a State.

Deaths in the U. S. in 1862.—Cornelius C. Felton, scholar and critic, President of Harvard University, aged 55 years. Theodore Frelinghuysen, statesman, aged 75 years.

1863.

Jan. 1.—Gen. Sullivan defeated the Confederates under Van Dorn, at Hunt's Cross Roads, near Lexington, Tenn. The Union garrison and the steamer Harriet Lane captured at Galveston, Texas.

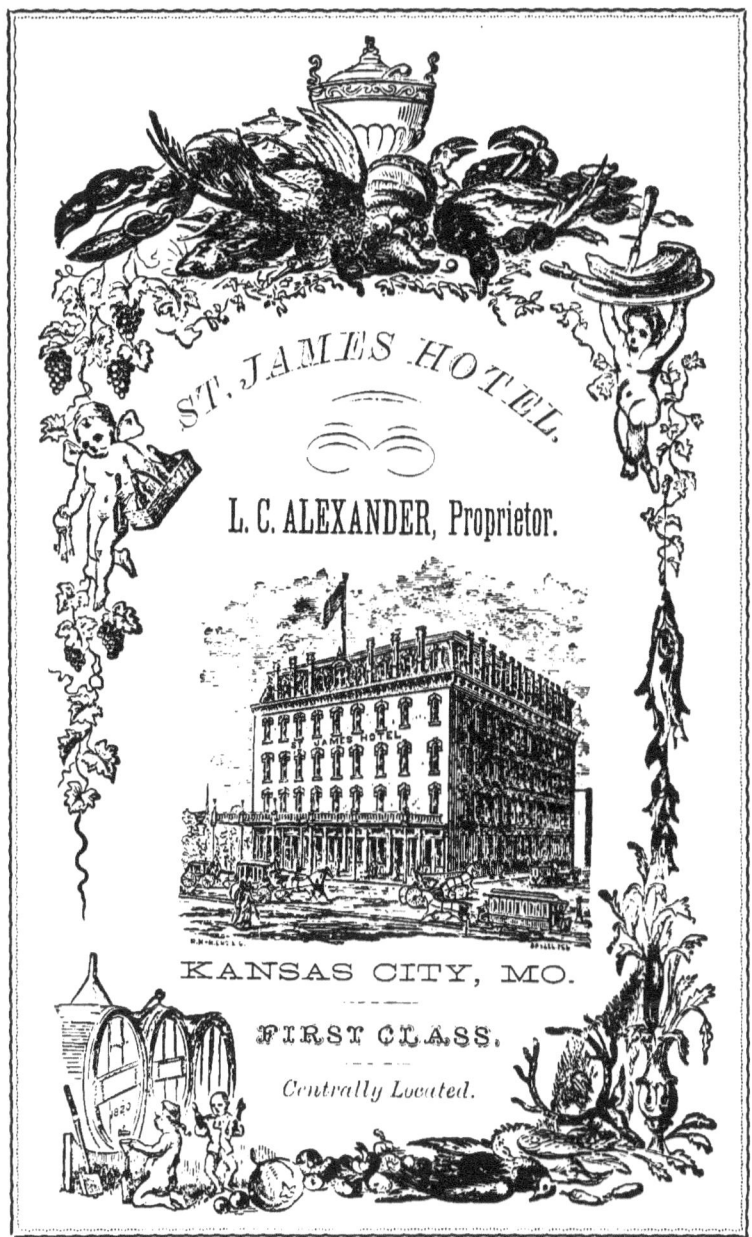

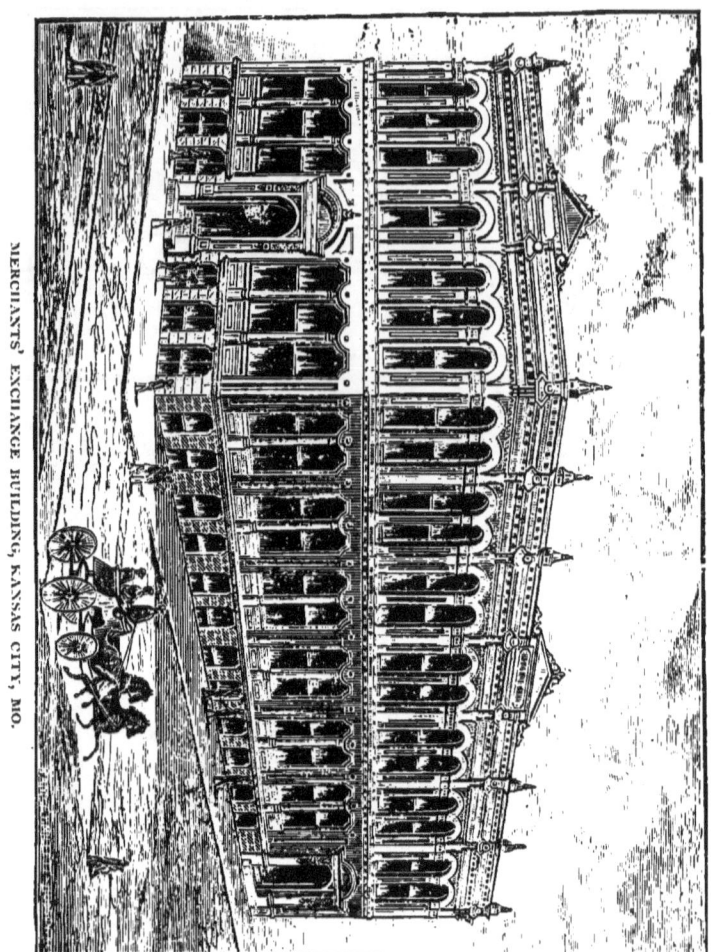

VIENNA GARDEN
RESTAURANT,
S. W. Cor. Missouri Ave. & Walnut St.
KANSAS CITY.

Meals can be had at all Hours. Travelers and Transient Visitors can find the Best of entertainment here. Boarding by the Day or Week.

S. CARO, Supt.

Grand Concert Every Wednesday and Saturday Evening by a Full Band.

170 IMPORTANT EVENTS OF THE CENTURY.

1863.

The Westfield destroyed to keep it from falling into the hands of the enemy. Commodore Renshaw perished with his vessel.

President Lincoln publishes a proclamation confirming his manifesto of Sept. 22, 1862, and declares all the slaves in the Confederate States free, and under the military protection of the United States.

Jan. 3.—Since the hard battle of Dec. 31, fighting had been going on between the two armies at Murfreesboro. On the night of Jan. 3, the rebels commenced their retreat. The following is the official statement of the Union loss at the battle of Stone river: killed, 1,997, wounded, 6,425, and 3,550 missing.

The Federal army withdrew from before Vicksburg. The Union loss in the second attack on Vicksburg was about 600 killed, 1,500 wounded, and 1,000 missing.

Jan. 10.—Battle of Arkansas Post. The attack was commenced Saturday night by the Mississippi squadron under Admiral Porter. On the following day, the land forces under Gen. McClernand joined in the fight, and before night all the fortifications were taken. About 7,000 prisoners and a large quantity of ammunition was captured. The Union loss was about 200 killed and wounded.

Jan. 20.—The Morning Light and Velocity, blockading Sabine City, Texas, were both captured by the Confederates.

Jan. 22.—Third attack on Vicksburg. After the capture of Arkansas Post, Gen. McClernand returned to Vicksburg and resumed the siege of that place.

Jan. 28.—Gen. Burnside relieved of the command of the army of the Potomac, and Gen. Hooker appointed in his place.

Gens. Sumner and Franklin relieved from duty in the army of the Potomac.

Jan. 31.—The Confederate General Pryor made an attack on the Union troops, under Gen. Peck, at Blackwater, Va. The Confederates were repulsed.

Feb. 2.—The Federal ram Queen of the West ran the blockade at Vicksburg, but was captured a few days after by the Confederates.

Feb. 27.—The Confederate steamer Nashville, while attempting to run the blockade, got aground near Fort McAllister and was destroyed by the blockading fleet.

March 7.—Gen. Minty attacked a Confederate cavalry force at Unionville, Tenn., capturing their wagons, horses, and tents, and about 60 prisoners.

March 9.—A band of Confederate cavalry passed through the Union lines, entered Fairfax, Va., and captured Gen. Stoughton and a few privates.

March 17.—Two hundred cavalry under command of General Averill crossed the Rappahannock near Kelly's Ford, where but a single horseman could cross at once, and in the face of a most terrible fire from sharpshooters charged the Confederates in their entrenchments, killing or capturing nearly the whole force. They then encountered Stuart's cavalry, and after a desperate hand-to-hand encounter for five hours, routed them with great slaughter, capturing 80 prisoners.

March 20.—John Morgan with 4,000 men

EAST SAGINAW.—*Continued.*

BAKER AND CONFECTIONER.

D EISLER, A., Baker and Confectionery, Jefferson st., near Tuscola. Established 1873.

BARBER.

GO TO
Robinson's Barber Shop
For Good and Quick Work at Reasonable Prices.
HE KEEPS FIVE FIRST-CLASS WORKMEN ALWAYS ON HAND.
314 Genesee Ave.

BOOTS AND SHOES.

M ERGER, M., Dealer in Boots and Shoes, Jefferson st., bet. Genesee & Tuscola. Est. '63.

CARRIAGE MAKERS.

H OFF & BINGHAM, BLACKSMITHS AND WAGON MAKERS, and Manufacturers of **Hurd & Puller's Celebrated Centennial Wagon,**
East Saginaw, Mich. Box 1100.

H OUGHTON, W. S., Carriage Maker, cor. German and Franklin sts. Established 1871.

COMMISSION MERCHANT.

SPENCER BARCLAY,
COMMISSION MERCHANT,
PORK & BEEF PACKER,
And Curer of Extra Sugar Cured Hams,
204 & 206 NORTH WATER ST.

DENTIST.

W HITING, L. C., Dentist,
11 Hess block.

DRUGGISTS.

B RUSKE, R., Dealer in Drugs, Medicines, Perfumery, etc., Jefferson st. and Genesee ave.

D AVIS, T. W., Drugs, Medicines, Perfumery and Patent Medicines, S. Saginaw.

M. B. Liddell. W. S. Jones.
LIDDELL & JONES,
Druggists,
POTTER STREET,
Opposite F. and P. M. Depot.

NATIONAL DRUG STORE,
G. S. LEYERER,
PROPRIETOR,
Cor. Park and Lapeer Sts.

DRY GOODS.

O 'DONNELL, J., Dry Goods, Boots, Shoes, Hats, Caps, Groceries, Hardware, &c., S. Saginaw.

EAST SAGINAW.—*Continued.*

GROCERIES.

PETER BAUM'S
Grocery Store and Meat Market,
Cor. Washington Ave. & Hoyt St.
A full assortment of Choice Groceries and Family Supplies. Also all kinds of Fresh and Salt Meats constantly on hand, and for sale cheap for cash. Established 1870.

HARDWARE AND TINWARE.

E. JOCHEN & BRO., Dealers in
HARDWARE, TINWARE & STOVES
Mnf'rs of Tin, Copper and Sheet Iron Ware,
S. SAGINAW.

HORSESHOERS.

DOLLIVER, C. A., Practical Horseshoer, Franklin and German sts. Established 1867.

MOXLEY, E., PRACTICAL AND FANCY HORSESHOER, corner of Cass and German sts. I received
THE FIRST PREMIUM FOR THE BEST SHOD HORSE AT THE MICHIGAN STATE FAIR. Established 1875.

HOTELS.

EVERETT HOUSE,
LEW B. CLARK,
PROPRIETOR.
$2.00 PER DAY.
EAST SAGINAW, MICH.

LLOYD HOUSE,
NEWKIRK & LLOYD, Prop's.
Cor. Franklin & German Sts.

LAUNDRY.

LAUNDRY,
ROBERT SMITH,
JEFFERSON ST.,
Between Genesee Ave. and Tuscola Sts.,
East Saginaw, - - Mich.

MEAT MARKETS.

BAUM, W. Y., Dealer in all kinds of Fresh Meats, Genesee and Webster sts.

JACOB MEIER,
Dealer in
FRESH & SALT MEATS,
And Manufacturer of
Pork, Ham, Frankfort, Liver and
BOLOGNA SAUSAGES,
408 GENESEE AVE.

1863.

was totally defeated near Milton, Tenn., by Col. Hall with 1,400 mounted men.
The negro brigade took Jacksonville, Florida.
Major General Burnside appointed to command the department of the Ohio.
March 22.—Confederates under Clark captured Mt. Sterling, Ky.
April 6.—Gen. Mitchell, with 300 cavalry, dashed into a Confederate camp near Nashville, on a sabre charge, capturing 5, killing 15, and capturing all their tents, arms, horses, and equipments.
April 7.—Attack on Charleston. The Federal fleet was composed of nine iron-clad vessels under the command of Commodore Dupont. The fight began in the afternoon of April 7, and lasted about two hours. The Keokuk was so badly damaged that she sunk in a few hours. Several other vessels were temporarily disabled. The fleet was then withdrawn.
April 10.—Gen. Van Dorn's forces attacked Gen. Granger at Franklin, Tenn., and were driven back with loss.
April 17.—Gen. Banks' command left Baton Rouge, fought three battles, two on land and one on Grand Lake, capturing 2,000 prisoners. Our loss was 700.
Six vessels of Porter's fleet ran by the Confederate batteries at Vicksburg.
April 18.—Fayetteville, Ark., attacked by 3,000 Confederates with four pieces of artillery; Union forces numbered but 2,000. The Confederates were repulsed. Our loss was 5 killed and 17 wounded.
April 22.—The ram, Queen of the West, was captured in Grand Lake with Capt. Fuller and all her officers and crew, numbering 90.
April 30.—Col. Mulligan repulsed by the Confederates at Fairmont, West Va., and the B. & O. R. R. bridges blown up at Fairmont and Cheat river.
May 1.—Gen. Carter with 5,000 men attacked the Confederate forces at Monticello, under Pegram, driving them from the field.
Battle of Port Gibson, Gen. Grant defeated Gen. Bowen, with a loss of 1,550 men and 5 pieces of artillery.
May 2.—On the morning of the 17th of April, 1863, the 6th and 7th Illinois cavalry, 900 strong, under command of Col. Grierson, of the 6th Illinois, set out from Lagrange, Tenn., marched through the center of Mississippi, destroying as they went railroads, bridges and stores of all kinds belonging to the Confederates, in immense quantities. They reached Baton Rouge, La., on the evening of the 2nd of May. They had traveled nearly 800 miles in 16 days. At several points the enemy made great attempts to capture them, but failed. They brought into Baton Rouge over 1,000 horses and a large number of cattle; 500 negroes followed them.
May 3.—Battle of Fredericksburg. The second attempt to capture the Confederate fortifications at Fredericksburg, Va., was made by the army of the Potomac under Gen. Hooker, and failed. Severe skirmishing took place on Friday and Saturday, May 1 and 2, but the main battle was fought on Sunday, May 3, resulting in the defeat of the Federal troops. In the meantime Gen. Sedgwick had

EAST SAGINAW.—*Continued.*

PAINTERS.

DOBSON & HARTZELL, Painters, Kalsomining, Graining, Glazing, Paper-hanging, etc., etc., 130 Cass st.

PIANO-FORTE PEDAL ATTACHMENT.

Piano-Forte Pedal Attachment,

L. C. WHITING, Sole Prop.,

EAST SAGINAW, MICH.
— 0 —

This enables children to use the Piano Pedal with the same ease and facility as grown persons.

PHOTOGRAPHERS.

GOODRIDGE BROS.,
Practical, View & General Business

PHOTOGRAPHERS
THE

Largest First-Floor Gallery in the State.

221 E. WASHINGTON AVE.

Established 1863.

MACOMBER, A. D., Boston Gem Gallery, 316 Genesee st. Established 1873.

PHYSICIAN.

THE SHOEMAKER'S CURE FOR RHEUMATISM.

This medicine is undoubtedly one of the most valuable discoveries of the age. Having been a sufferer for ten years with that most distressing of all diseases, RHEUMATISM, which baffled all the efforts of the most skillful physicians, and after using many remedies, and spending hundreds of dollars without the least benefit, I at last concluded that as I had some botanical knowledge, I would try and see if I could not find a remedy somewhere in nature's vast garden, in which I believe there is a remedy for every disease that man is heir to. After many experiments, and many failures, at last success crowned my efforts; I found the cure for which I had so long been searching. After using this remedy I was restored from a deformed cripple on crutches to perfect health. Since then nearly seventeen years have passed, and I have known no such thing as Rheumatism. I have furnished this remedy in hundreds of cases since my own cure, and not one has failed to receive a cure that have used the medicine according to directions. I do not blame the public for being skeptical about medical advertisements in general, but would say to all those who are afflicted with Rheumatism, no matter in what form, you can be soundly cured. If you want testimonials I can furnish the address of reliable parties who are ready and willing to testify to the truths contained in this card. This medicine is to be had only of

W. B. GRESS, 129 N. Washington St., East Saginaw, Mich.

PLUMBERS.

CANNON, J. C. & CO., Plumbers, Gas and Steam Fitters, Cass st., bet. Genesee and German.

SHIRT MANUFACTURER.

DEYO, A. H., Manf'r of French Yoke Dress and Night Shirts, Collars, Cuffs, etc., Washington st.

EAST SAGINAW.—*Continued.*

STOVES AND TINWARE.

JOHN ELWERT,
STOVES, TINWARE,

Galvanized Iron Cornices, Roofing,
Spouting and all kinds of Job Work done to order.

GENESEE & WEBSTER STS.

TAILORS, MERCHANT.

BOERGERT & KOSANKE, Merchant Tailors, Jefferson st. Established 1873.

H. HEINLEIN,

MERCHANT TAILOR,
305 LAPEER ST.

CHARLES MATTHAEY,

MERCHANT TAILOR,
On Tuscola St., bet. Franklin & Cass Sts.

ALL KINDS OF GENTLEMEN'S CLOTH CUT AND MADE TO ORDER.

Also Ladies' Sacks and Cloaks cut and made to order by the Latest Style.

ZEIGIN, KASPAR, Tailor. Imported and Domestic Cloths, Cassimeres and Vestings.

UPHOLSTERER.

Charles Fuerstenau,
UPHOLSTERER

And Manufacturer Lambrequins.

Upholster Work, Curtain Hanging and Carpet Laying of all kinds done to order.

Robinson Block, Genesee Ave.

WATCHMAKER AND JEWELER.

BROWN, GEORGE, Watchmaker and Jeweler, Jefferson st., near Genesee.

WINES, BEER AND LIQUORS.

H. HEINLEIN,

WINE & BEER SALOON

Billiard Hall and Bowling Alley, 307 Lapeer st.

O'BRIEN, M., Wholesale and Retail Dealer in Wines, Liquors and Cigars, 103 Cass st.

East Saginaw, Mich., Business Houses
WHEN ESTABLISHED.

BUDE, V., Architect, 1850.
DEYO, A. H., Shirt Manufacturer, 1867.
GRESS, W. B., Rheumatism Cure, 1860.
LEYERER, G. S., Druggist, 1875.

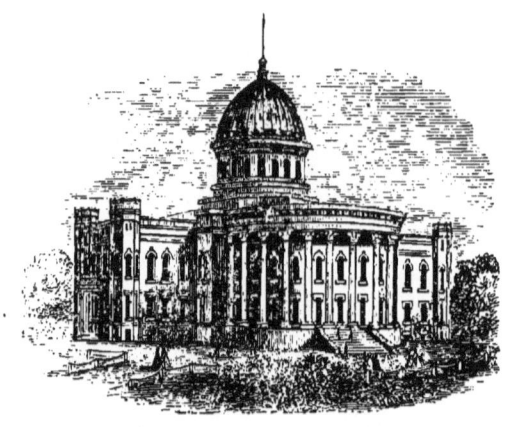

State Capitol, Madison, Wis.—The building is a beautiful stone structure standing on an eminence 70 feet above the level of the lakes, in the centre of a public park of 14 acres, and contains the very valuable State Historical Library, the State Library, and collections of the Academy of Science, Arts and Letters. (Its cost was $500,000.)

S. L. SHELDON,

—DEALER IN—

Meadow King Mowers,

LEADER AND LITTLE CHIEFTAIN REAPERS,

All Standard Threshing Machines,

SULKY RAKES,

—AND ALL KINDS OF—

AGRICULTURAL MACHINERY

MADISON, WISCONSIN.

1863.

crossed the Rappahannock and occupied Fredericksburg. He too was defeated and compelled to retire to the northern bank of the river. Hooker's army recrossed the river on the night of May 5. The loss on each side was about 15,000 killed, wounded and prisoners. "Stonewall" Jackson mortally wounded. While the fight was going on near Fredericksburg, Gen. Stoneman, with a large cavalry force, crossed the Rapidan east of Orange Court House, and made a bold and partially successful raid into the enemy's country.

May 8.—Col. Streight's command of 1,700 men captured by Forrest's cavalry, two miles from Cedar Bluff, Ga., after severe fighting. The Confederate general, Van Dorn, killed by Dr. Peters in Manny county, Tenn.

May 9.—Col. Jacobs routed a guerrilla force near Horse Shoe Bend on the Cumberland river.

May 10.—The Confederate general, Stonewall (Thos. J.) Jackson, died at Richmond, Va., of wounds and pneumonia.

May 12.—Gen. McPherson attacked Raymond, Miss., and took the town after a hard fight.

May 13.—Grant defeated Joseph F. Johnston and captured Jackson, Miss., with 7 cannon and large quantities of military stores, besides 400 prisoners. The State capitol was destroyed by fire.

May 15.—Battle of Baker's Creek, Miss. The Confederate army under Gen. Pemberton, and the Union forces under Gen. Grant. About 25,000 men were engaged upon each side. The Confederates met with a disastrous defeat, losing 2,600 in killed and wounded, 2,00 men prisoners, and 29 pieces of artillery.

May 17.—Battle of Big Black River. Grant again attacked Pemberton, and defeated him with a total loss of 2,600 men and 17 cannon.

May 18.—Investment of Vicksburg by the Federals under Gen. Grant and Admiral Porter.

May 25.—Confederate navy yard destroyed at Yazoo City.

May 27.—Gen. Banks commences the siege of the forts at Port Hudson, Miss.

June 1.—Gen. Hunter removed from the command of the department of the South. Gen. Gilmore succeeds him.

June 11.—Forrest, with 5,000 cavalry and two batteries of artillery, attacked the Union cavalry at Triune, Tenn., under command of Col. R. B. Mitchell. The Confederates were defeated.

June 14.—Gen. Ewell defeated Gen. Milroy at Winchester, Va., with a loss of 2,000 men, and drove him to Harper's Ferry.

June 17.—The ram Atlanta captured off the coast of South Carolina, after a brief fight, by the Weehawken, commanded by Capt. John Rodgers.
A division of our cavalry under Col. Kilpatrick encountered Gen. Fitzhugh Lee's cavalry brigade near Aldie, Va., and a desperate hand-to-hand encounter followed, ending in a hasty retreat of the Confederate forces; 100 prisoners were captured.

June 21.—Gen. McClernard removed by Grant, and Gen Ord succeeds him.

SAGINAW CITY, MICH.

ARCHITECT.
FRED W. HOLLISTER,

ARCHITECT,
Office, Jerome Block, Court St. Est. 1869.

ATTORNEYS AT LAW.

CLARK, WM. A., Law and Collection Office, Newell block.

WOOD, N. S., Attorney at Law and Solicitor in Chancery, Court st.

BAZAAR.

NEW YORK NINETY-NINE CENT BAZAAR, T. Goldsmith, prop., Wisner block.

BOOKBINDERS.

F. BUSCH & CO.,
Plain and Fancy

BOOKBINDERS
—AND—
BLANK BOOK MANUFACTURERS,
E. C. Newell's Block,
Bet. Court and Adams.

CARRIAGE MANUFACTORY.

WM. D. LEWIS,
Carriage Manufactory,
COR. MONROE AND BOND STS.

New Work, Light and Heavy, made to order. Repairing done promptly.

DENTISTS.

E. L. BAKER,
SURGICAL & MECHANICAL DENTIST,
Beech Block, Court St.,
Bet. Hamilton and Washington Streets.

MORGAN, W. P., D.M.D., Dentist, Washington st., near Court. Established 1871.

DRUGGISTS.

WILLIAM MOLL,
Dealer in
Drugs, Medicines Perfumery
Pure Wines and Liquors for Medicinal Uses.
PAINTS, OILS, VARNISHES, ETC.
Cor. of Court & Hamilton Sts.
Branch Store cor. of Washington St. & Cross Road.

IMPORTANT EVENTS OF THE CENTURY. 175

SAGINAW CITY—*Continued.*

DRUGGISTS.

E. RINGLER,
Dealer in
Drugs, Medicines, Chemicals,
PERFUMERY & PATENT MEDICINES,

HAMILTON STREET.

JAY SMITH,
Dealer in
Drugs, Medicines
PAINTS, OILS,
Pure Wines and Liquors for Medicinal Use.

HARNESS, SADDLES, TRUNKS, ETC.

OPFERGELT, PH., Harness, Saddles, Trunks, Collars, etc., Hamilton and Cross sts.

RICHARDSON, J. W., Harness, Saddles, Bridles, Whips, Collars, etc., Hamilton st.

HORSESHOER AND BLACKSMITH.

HURTUBISE, ALEX., Champion Horseshoer, & Blacksmith, cor. Hamilton & Mackinaw.

LIVERY STABLES.

MARTIN, J. S., Livery and Sale Stables, Adams st., bet. Washington and Hamilton sts.

LOG INSPECTOR.

VANCE, H., Log Inspector, Court st., bet. Hamilton and Washington sts.

SAGINAW, MICH., BUSINESS HOUSES
WHEN ESTABLISHED.

HURTUBISE, ALEX., Horseshoer, 1872.
LEWIS, WM. D., Carriage Manufacturer, 1869.
MOLL, WM., Druggist, 1863.
OPFERGELT, PH., Harness and Saddles, 1862.
RINGLER, E., Druggist, 1867.
SMITH, J., Druggist, 1852.

RICHMOND, IND.

AGRICULTURAL IMPLEMENTS.

MITCHELL, W. M., with Briggs & Co., Richmond, Ind.

ATTORNEYS AT LAW.

CHIPMAN, D. C., Attorney at Law and Notary Public, Rooms 2 & 4 Odd Fellow's Bldg.

FOX, H. C., Attorney at Law, 236 Main st.

12

1863.

June 23.—Battle of Big Black River, Missouri. Confederates under Johnston attacked Osterhaus' division and were defeated with great slaughter.

June 25.—Another fight at Liberty Gap between a Confederate division under Clayborne, and Willich, Wilder and Carter's brigades. The Confederates fled in disorder.

June 26.—Rear Admiral Foote died in New York City.

June 29.—Gen. Hooker was relieved of his command of the army of the Potomac at his own request, and Gen. Meade succeeded him.

July 1.—Battle of Gettysburg, Penn. Gen. Meade attacked the Confederates near Gettysburg, and after a three days' battle drove them from the field, leaving 5,000 killed and wounded in our hands. Meade took 20,000 prisoners. Maj. Gen. Reynolds, commanding the first corps of the Union army, was killed.
Missouri passed the Ordinance of Emancipation.
Rosecrans drove Bragg from Tullahoma.

July 4.—Gen. Prentice defeated the Confederates under Holmes, at Helena, Ark.
The siege of Vicksburg by the Union army under Gen. Grant commenced May 18th and was pressed forward with vigor until July 4th, when Pemberton surrendered to Gen. Grant 27,000 prisoners, 132 cannon and 50,000 stand of arms.

July 8.—In the month of May Gen. Banks invested Port Hudson. Two grand attacks were made by land and water on the 27th of May and 14th of June, in which portions of the enemy's works were taken. At last, on the 8th of July, the commander, Major General Gardiner, surrendered with 7,000 prisoners, 60 cannon, and 10,000 stands of arms to General Banks.
Morgan's raid into Indiana and Ohio; crossed the river into Harrison county, Ind., and marched rapidly through the southern part of the State into Ohio, committing numerous depredations. On the 18th he lost his artillery and 1,300 prisoners. With a mere fragment of his command he retreated to Columbiana county, Ohio, where on the 20th he surrendered to Gen. Shackleford.

July 13-16.—Riots take place in New York, Boston, and other Union cities, in consequence of the enforcement of a conscription decree.

July 13, 14, 15.—Draft riots in New York city. Mobs had possession of the city for three days. Offices where the draft was going on were demolished, and the buildings were burned. The mob directed their fury particularly against negroes, several of whom were murdered. The colored orphan asylum on Fifth Avenue was pillaged and burnt down. Collisions between the mob and military frequently occurred. Many persons were killed during the prevalence of the riot. The city paid above $1,500,000 as indemnity for losses that occurred during the riot.

July 17.—Gen Sherman attacked Jackson, Miss., routed Johnston and occupied the city. Large stores were captured, and also 40 locomotives, and all the rolling stock of three railroads. Gen. Ransom captured Natchez with a large quantity of ammunition, 13 cal.

GOODWIN'S
INVALID BEDSTEAD.

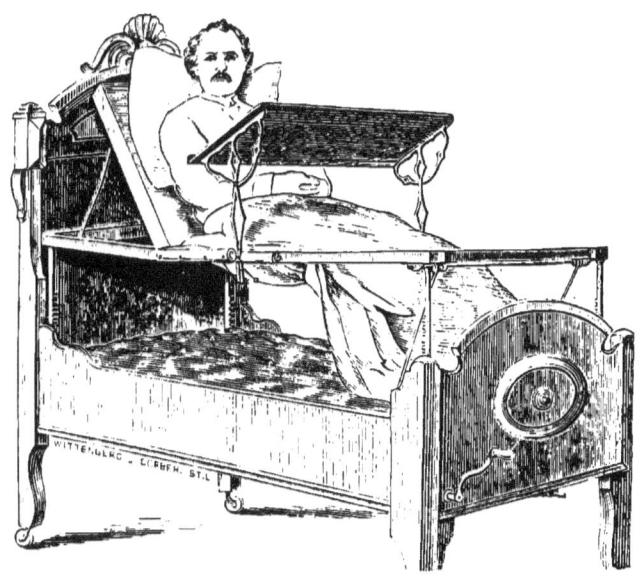

THE WONDER OF THE AGE.

This bedstead is now being manufactured in St. Louis, where its intrinsic merits are recognized, and its superiority over any other invention of the kind is attested by eminent medical gentlemen who have witnessed its operation.

By means of a small crank, which can be easily worked by any attendant, the patient can be placed in numerous positions without manual assistance. He can be turned in bed, have his sheets changed, his mattress removed and turned over, be placed upon a stool chair, and have his body inclined in whatever posture he may desire.

A light table, 3 feet 3 inches in length by 15 in breadth, is readily attached to the frame, enabling the patient to eat his food in the same posture as if in health, and by the turn of a small screw it can be converted into a writing table or reading desk, upon which book or pamphlet can be read without the discomfort of having to hold it.

In fine, without the removal of the patient or the slightest discomfort to himself, the bed can be formed into a Lounge, Ordinary Chair, Stool Chair, or Fracture Bed, and by raising and setting aside the frame, which requires but a moment, it can be used as an ordinary bedstead.

Prices range from $40.00 upward, according to style, and finish of bed. Send for Circular.

S. L. & J. C. NIDELET & CO.,
927 N. 5th St., St. Louis, Mo.

ADVERTISEMENTS. 177

Japanese Commissioners' Building, Centennial Exposition, Philadelphia.—This building is regarded as the finest piece of carpenter-work ever seen in this country. The wood of which it is built is most beautifully grained, and as smooth as satin. Every portion of the building is most carefully fitted together, and the carving is truly wonderful.

J. O. McCARTY & G. VOGT,
Ornamental Plasterers.
No. 571 STATE STREET, Near Twelfth, CHICAGO.

Manufacturers of Center Pieces, Brackets, Etc., of the Latest New York Patterns. Orders by mail promptly attended to. Will guarantee against serious breakage in transportation.

HERMAN RICHTER,
MANUFACTURER OF
PARLOR SUITS,
SOFAS, LOUNGES, MATTRESSES, &c., AT WHOLESALE.

75 Clybourn Avenue, - CHICAGO, ILL.

Established 1856. Established 1856.

R. N. HERSHFIELD
Successor to Hershfield & Mitchell.

Manufacturing Jeweler,
AND JOBBER OF
WATCHES, CLOCKS, MATERIALS, ETC.
LEAVENWORTH, - KANSAS,

RICHMOND—Continued.

ATTORNEYS AT LAW.

HARRIS, F. B., Counselor and Attorney at Law, Est. 1874, 225 Main st.

POPP, JOHN H., Attorney and Notary Public, Richmond, Ind.

JOHN C. WHITRIDGE,
Attorney at Law and Notary Public,
Office, Fifth & Main sts.
References: Second National Bank, Richmond; Gaar, Scott & Co., Richmond.

BAKERIES.

BELLINGER, CHARLES, South 6th st. Bakery, No. 93

D. J. Hoerner's
Pearl Street

STEAM BAKERY,
13 S. Pearl St.
Established 1858.

MASON, JOHN, Bakery & Confectionery, 166 Main st.

ZELLER & CO., Steam Cracker Bakery, 357 & 359 Main st.

BANK.

FIRST NATIONAL BANK, J. F. Reeves, Cashier, Main & Franklin sts.

BARBERS.

BURROWS, G. W., Shaving Saloon, 218 Ft. Wayne ave.

Warren N. Carter,
SHAVING AND HAIR-DRESSING PARLORS,
Dealer in Choicest Cigars,
265 Main St.

SCHRAMM & CO., Fashionable Hair-dressers, Saloon, Huntington House block.

STAUBER, ALBERT, Shaving & Hairdressing Saloon, 301 Main st.

BLACKSMITHS AND HORSESHOERS.

BARTEL, C. A., Horseshoeing & General Job Work, 43 s. Marion st.

RICHMOND—Continued.

BLACKSMITHS AND HORSESHOERS.

E. W. Evans & Co.,
The CHAMPION SHOEING SHOP
Of Indiana.
Diseased Feet and Track Shoeing a
Specialty,
11 NORTH 6th ST.

THOMAS & GORMON, Pioneer Shoeing Shop, 118. Fifth st.

VETERAN SHOEING SHOP.
Rentschler & Nischwitz,
BLACKSMITHING, SHOEING AND GENERAL
JOBBING,
22 NORTH MARION STREET.

BOILER WORKS.

FULTON BOILER WORKS, Jerry Cowbig, Proprietor, Est. 1876, North Union Depot.

BOOKS AND STATIONERY.

J. H. MOORMANN.

Books, Stationery,
WALL PAPER, ETC., ETC.,
Also dealer in
Groceries and Provisions,
236 & 238 MAIN ST.

BOOTS AND SHOES.

ABLEY, EDWARD, Manuf'r and dealer in Boots & Shoes, Main st., second door from eighth.

CUNINGHAM, J. A., Dealer in Fine Boots and Shoes, est. 1865, 241 Main st

FRANK TAYLOR & CO.,
Manufacturers and dealers in
BOOTS AND SHOES,
269 MAIN ST.

NOLTE & QUATZ, Manf's and dealers in Boots & Shoes, 234 Main st.

SCHELL, HENRY, Manufacturer of Boots and Shoes, 199 Ft. Wayne ave

Kansas and Colorado State Building, Centennial Exposition, Philadelphia—Occupies a plot of ground 132 by 132 feet. The building is an ornamental cottage, with a large circular hall in the centre. Commodious apartments radiate in four directions from the central room, with numerous large private offices at their intersections.

ENOCH HOAG, President. JOHN K. RANKIN, Cashier.

Capital Stock $100,000.

Lawrence Savings Bank,
No. 52 Massachusetts Sts.,
Lawrence, Kansas.

General Banking and Savings Institution.

JOHN D. KNOX & CO.,
BANKERS.
TOPEKA, KANSAS.

Do a General Banking Business. Interest paid on time Deposits, from 6 to 8 per cent., according to time. Collections made and remitted promptly. Money loaned on Real Estate security at 10 per cent. Semi-annual interest, without cost to the lender. School, Township, and other 10 per cent Bonds for sale. Some good lands and farms for sale. Taxes paid for non-residents. Correspondence solicited, and satisfaction guaranteed.

MILLER'S RESTAURANT,
211 Commercial Street,
(Opposite OTIS HOUSE.)
ATCHISON, KANSAS.

Meals, 35 cents; Lodgings, 50 cents; Transient, $1.50 per day.

1863.

non, 2,000 head of cattle, and 4,000 hogsheads of sugar. A severe fight occurred on Elk Creek, Ark., between Gen. Blunt and the Confederate Gen. Cooper; the former was victorious. Union loss 40, that of the Confederates 184.

July 22.—Col. Wilder of Rosecrans' advance shelled Chattanooga. Brashear City, La., recaptured by the Union gunboat Sachem.

July 23.—A gallant fight occurred near Manassas Gap, in which 800 men of Gen. Spinola's brigade utterly routed twice their number of Georgia and North Carolina troops with 17 cannon. Kentucky again invaded. Kit Carson with a part of the first New Mexico regiment defeated the Navajoe Indians in a severe fight beyond Fort Canby.

July 31.—The Union forces in Kentucky, under Col. Saunders, thoroughly routed the Confederate troops under Scott and Pegram. Martial law in Kentucky.

Aug. 2.—A severe though indecisive cavalry fight occurred at Culpepper, Va., between Buford and Stuart, in which 100 prisoners were captured by the Union troops.

Aug. 7.—President Lincoln rejects the demand for the suppression of the conscription in the State of New York.

Aug. 17.—Lieut. Col. Phillips of the 9th Illinois Mounted Infantry attacked the Confederate forces at Grenada, Miss., consisting of 2,000 men under command of Gen. Slimmer, and drove them from the place. He then destroyed all the ordnance and commissary stores, burnt the depot and machine shop, tore up the railroad track, and destroyed 57 locomotives and more than 400 cars.

Aug. 20.—The town of Lawrence, Kansas, was surprised in the middle of the night by 300 guerrillas under the leadership of Quantrell. The town was set on fire and 182 buildings burned to the ground, and $2,000,000 worth of property destroyed. 191 persons were killed, many of whom were helpless women and children; 581 were wounded, many of them mortally. About 80 of the murderers were killed.

Aug. 22.—Gen. Blunt with 4,500 men attacked Gen. Cooper with 11,000 Confederate troops in the Indian Territory and compelled him to retreat to Red River.

Aug. 29.—The Confederate army in Arkansas under General Price severely pushed by the Union forces under Gen. Steele.

Sept. 1.—Gen. Blunt defeated the Confederate forces in Arkansas under Cooper and Cobell, and captured Fort Smith. The Confederates evacuate Little Rock.

Sept. 4.—Burnside occupied Knoxville, Tenn., and was hailed with delight by the inhabitants.

Sept. 9.—General Crittenden's division of Rosecrans' army entered Chattanooga.

Sept. 10.—Gen. Burnside captured Cumberland Gap with 2,000 prisoners, and 14 pieces of artillery under command of Major General Frazer. Gen. Steele took possession of Little Rock, Ark.

Sept. 15.—President Lincoln suspends the Habeas Corpus act.

Sept. 19.—Chickamauga. The battle

RICHMOND—*Continued.*

BREWERY.

RICHMOND BREWERY

Emile Mink, Proprietor.

Cash Paid For Barley.

CARRIAGE MANUFACTURERS.

STRATTAN, S. S., Carriages,
158 & 160 Ft. Wayne ave.

We beg to inform you that we have opened a

New Carriage Shop,

on South Fifth street, where we are prepared to build

FIRST-CLASS CARRIAGES.

All kinds of repairing done promptly.

P. SCHNEIDER & CO.,
10 & 12 S. 5th st.

CHINA, GLASS AND CROCKERY.

Established 1873.

RALPH W. NYE,
Wholesale and Retail

QUEENSWARE,

French China, Glassware, Lamps, Chandeliers, Table Cutlery, Silver-plated Ware, Shelf Ornaments, &c.,
277 MAIN STREET.

CONFECTIONERS.

SAUER, J. A., Cigar and Fruit Stand,
Cor. 5th & Main sts.

VAN SANT, R. R., Manufacturing Confectioner,
23 N. 5th st.

CONTRACTORS AND BUILDERS.

KIDDER & BEETLE, Contractors and Builders,
11th & Sassafras sts.

CONSERVATORY OF MUSIC.

RICHMOND
Conservatory of Music,

Musical instruction in all branches of Vocal and Instrumental Music.

Send for Circular.
AUGUST RHU, Director.

DENTIST.

JAY, J. W., Dentist,
300 Main st.

IMPORTANT EVENTS OF THE CENTURY. 181

RICHMOND—Continued.

DINING ROOMS.

Central Dining Rooms,

294 Main st., next door to Quaker City Bakery,

Z. E. HINSHAW, Proprietor.

Warm Meals at all Hours.   Call and see Me.

DRUGGISTS.

BOPPART, A., Druggist,
365 Main st.

MULLER, B., Druggist,
Est. 1866, cor. Main & Marion sts.

ROSS, W. H., Druggist & Apothecary,
314 Main st.

DYERS AND SCOURERS.

UNDE, AUGUST, Steam Dyer,
West of National Bridge. Est. 1861.

EXPRESS CO.

HYATT, D. P., Agent for United States Express Co., 305 Main st.

FANCY GOODS AND NOTIONS.

BARTEL & SCHAEFER, Wholesale & retail dealers in Notions, 243 Main st. Est. 1877.

FIRE DEPARTMENT.

DOUGAN, I. G., Chief Fire Department, Richmond, Ind.

FLOUR, FEED AND GRAIN.

DILKS, G. R., Feed Store & Mills, dealer in Flour, Grain, Hay, &c., 10 N. 5th st.

GRIFFITH, JOHN, Est. 1875, Flour & Feed,
175 Ft. Wayne ave.

FLOUR, FEED AND GRAIN.

SCHWEGMAN, CHRIS., Flour and Feed,
141 S. Front st. Established 1876.

FURNITURE.

F. WEISS & SON,
MANUFACTURERS OF

Chairs and all kinds of Furniture,
163 S. MARION ST.

A large stock of well-made Chairs and Furniture of all kinds at the lowest prices.

GRAIN ELEVATOR.

VAN FRANK, H. M., Proprietor Depot Grain Elevator, Richmond, Ind.

GROCERIES.

CUTTER, HENRY, Groceries, Flour, Feed, Sugar, Cured Hams, &c., Front and Mill sts.

DOUGAN, GEO. B., Grocer,
197 Fort Wayne Ave.

1863.

was commenced by Gen. Bragg in the morning and continued all day. At night both armies occupied nearly the same position that they did in the morning. On the next day the battle was renewed by the Confederates and lasted until dark. The Union army was defeated and driven back to Chattanooga. The Federal loss was about 1,800 killed, 9,500 wounded, and 2,500 prisoners.

Oct. 9.—Wheeler's Confederate cavalry defeated with considerable loss at Farmington, Tennessee, and again near Shelbyville.

Oct. 20.—The departments of the Cumberland and Mississippi were consolidated and placed under the command of General Grant. Gen. Rosecrans removed and Gen. Thompson appointed in his place.

Nov. 5.—Brownsville, Texas, captured.

Nov. 25.—The Confederate army under Bragg was badly whipped near Chattanooga, losing about 6,000 prisoners and 52 guns. The Union loss was between 3,000 and 4,000 in killed and wounded.

Nov. 29.—An unsuccessful attempt of the Confederates to carry Knoxville by storm.

Nov.—The first Fenian convention assembled at Chicago. According to tradition the Fenians or Finians were a national militia established in Ireland by Fin or Fionn, the son of Cumbal.

Dec. 4.—Gen. Longstreet commenced the siege of Knoxville, Nov. 17th. On the 29th there was a severe fight, in which he was defeated. This, with the defeat of Bragg at Chattanooga, compelled Longstreet to raise the siege.

1864.

Feb. 1.—President Lincoln orders a draft for 500,000 men.

Feb. 9.—A large number of prisoners, including Colonel Streight, escaped from Libby Prison, Richmond.

Feb. 15.—Gen. W. T. Sherman with his command arrived at Meridan, Miss., on his great raid into the heart of the enemy's country. Returned to Vicksburg with immense booty.

Feb. 20.—The advance into Florida of the Union forces about 5,000 strong, under General Seymour, was repulsed near Olustee with a loss of 1,200. Confederate loss, about the same.

Feb. 22.—A heavy reconnoitering force sent out from Chattanooga by General Grant, met and defeated the enemy at Tunnel Hill.

Feb.—Kilpatrick and Dahlgren's raid on Richmond.

March 8.—Gen. Grant was formally presented by the President with his commission as Lieutenant General, and on the 12th was assigned to the command of the armies of the United States.

March 15.—The Union forces under General A. J. Smith captured Fort De Russey, Louisiana, on Red river, with 325 prisoners and an immense amount of ammunition and stores.

March 25.—About 5,000 Confederates

L. G. BROWN,

MANUFACTURER OF AND DEALER IN

Harness, Trunks, Bags,

WHIPS, COLLERS, ETC.

75 Waterloo St., - Grand Rapids, Mich.

BETWEEN RATHBUN HOUSE AND EAGLE HOTEL.

☞ REPAIRING PROMPTLY DONE. ☜

T. P. WITHERELL.   J. KIRKHAM.

WITHERELL & KIRKHAM,
NILES, MICHIGAN.

Manufacturers of the Celebrated

BATTERY BELT,

Recommended by all the Medical Faculty for the cure of Epilepsy, Rheumatism, Neuralgia, Lameness in the Back and Limbs and General Decline of the System. Also for Female Complaints in General.

PRIVATE CORRESPONDENCE RESPECTFULLY SOLICITED AND PROMPTLY ATTENDED TO.

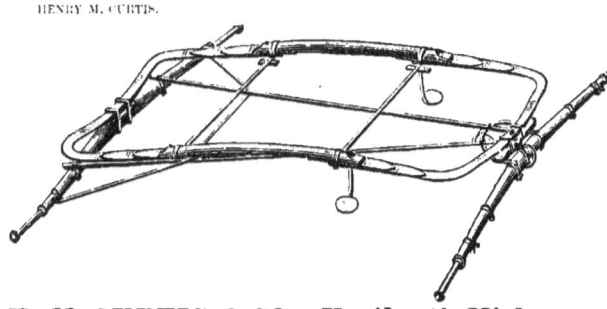

HENRY M. CURTIS.

H. M. CURTIS & CO., Ypsilanti, Mich.

F. P. BOGARDUS.
Manufacturers of CURTIS' PAT.

END

AND

SIDE BAR

Springs,

And Curtis' Pat,
WOOD FENDERS
FOR
Phætons & Carriages

Established 1870.

G. W. CROZIER,

Wholesale and Retail Dealer in

Rail-Road Oils, and Axel Grease.

ALSO, WINTER PRESSED PARAFFINE AND

CARBON OILS.

212 South Meridian st., - Indianapolis, Ind.

New City Hall, Detroit.—The site of the new City Hall is on Campus Martius. The building is 200 feet long on Woodward avenue and Griswold street, and 90 feet wide on Fort street and Michigan avenue. It is three stories above the basement. The height from street to cornices at roof is 66 feet, and to the top of the tower 180. On the several sides of the first section of tower, are figures representing "Justice," "Industry," "Arts," "Commerce." In this section is the clock, and above that the general fire alarm bell, and over it the lookout. The building was completed in July, 1871. The whole cost, including furniture, outside improvements, etc., was about $600,000.

City Hall, Louisville, Ky.—This building at present covers an area of 200 feet on Sixth street and 100 feet on Jefferson, but it is designed in the future to extend the front on Jefferson street about 150 feet, covering the space now occupied by the jail and Engine house, and thus complete the principal facade, which it is intended shall front on Jefferson street, the present completed portion being that of a pavillion to the entire building. As it is now occupied, the building cost about $460,000. This building was commenced on the 14th day of August, 1870, and was completed and occupied in the early part of 1873; its architecture is that of the Italian Rennaissance.

1864.

under Forrest captured Paducah, Ky., and fired the place.

April 8.—The advance of Gen. Banks' expedition up Red river, under the direction of Gen. Stone was repulsed near Shreveport, La.; but on the following day our men defeated the enemy. Our loss was about 2,000 and the enemy's the same.

April 12.—Gen. Forrest captured Fort Pillow, and immediately after commenced an indiscriminate massacre of our wounded soldiers, both colored and white, not excepting women and children who had taken refuge in the fort.

April 23.—The Governors of Ohio, Illinois, Iowa, Wisconsin, and Indiana offer to raise for the general Government 85,000 men for one hundred days.

April 26.—Government accepted services of one-hundred-day-men, and appropriated $20,000,000 for their payment.

May 5.—Draft ordered in Massachusetts, New Jersey, Ohio, Minnesota, Kentucky and Maryland.

Gen. Butler lands on the south side of the James.

May 6.—Gen. Grant crossed the Rapidan, and Lee fell back towards Richmond. Battle of the Wilderness.

May 7.—Grant still advances, driving Lee's forces before him.

May 8.—Sherman occupied Dalton.

May 9.—After three days hard fighting, Lee's forces retreated, leaving 3,000 killed and 10,000 wounded on the field in possession of the Union army.

May 12.—Battle at Spottsylvania. Union troops victorious. They capture 4,000 prisoners and 25 pieces of artillery.

May 13.—Gen. Sheridan, with cavalry, reached the rear of the enemy near Hanover Junction, breaking two railroads, capturing several locomotives, and destroying Lee's depot for supplies at Beaver Dam, containing over 1,000,000 rations.

May 15.—Sherman forced Johnson to evacuate Resaca after two days' fighting.

Union defeat at Newmarket, Va.

May 19.—Nathaniel Hawthorne, American novelist, died, aged 55 years.

May 23.—Army of the Potomac flanked the Confederates under Lee, and forced them to evacuate their fortifications near Spottsylvania Court House.

John Morgan enters Kentucky with 4,000 men.

May 27.—Grant crossed the Pamunkey, and occupied Hanovertown.

May 28.—Battle near Dallas, Ga.

May 30.—Gen. Grant reached Mechanicsville.

June 3.—Battle of Coal Harbor, in which the Confederates are routed; heavy loss.

June 5.—Sherman flanked Johnson, and captured Ackworth Station.

June 7.—General Hunter defeats the Confederate General Jones, near Staunton, Virginia.

RICHMOND—*Continued.*

GROCERIES.

Meyer & Kraas,
Staple & Fancy Groceries,
254 MAIN.

NESTOR, THOMAS & CO., Grocers and Butter and Egg Packers, 179 Main st. Estab. 1855.

TULLIDGE, ALFORD, Groceries and Provisions, Wines and Liquors, 179 Fort Wayne ave.

HAIR DEALERS AND DRESSERS.

OUTLAND, P., Hair Dresser, 1 South 5th st. Established 1869.

WEAVER, JAMES N., Hair Work done to order in the latest styles, 5 S. 5th st. Estab. 1870

HARNESS AND SADDLES.

KEYS, CHARLES A., Harness Manufacturer, 268 Main street.

NEIREITER, C. B., Harness and Saddle Maker, 237 Main st. Established 1876.

WIGGINS & CO., Harness, Saddles and Bridles, 221 Main st. Established 1830.

HOTELS.

AVENUE HOUSE,
S. D. MEREDITH, Proprietor,
RICHMOND, IND.

COMMERCIAL HOUSE, Chas. Peck, proprietor, 200 Main st

European Hotel and City Dining Rooms.
WARM MEALS AT ALL HOURS.
PRICES LOW. Street Cars pass the Door.
NOBLE ST., Near Union Depot
GILL, SARVENT, Manager

GITHENS' HOTEL, J. H. GITTENS, prop., Main st.

HOTEL, GERMAN, 12, 14 & 16 South Pearl st. Established 1860. B. BESCHER, Prop.

HUNTINGTON HOUSE.
O. HUNTINGTON, Prop.
The Best Hotel Accommodations in the City.
Newly furnished throughout. Good sample rooms on the first floor.
RATES, TWO DOLLARS PER DAY.

REYNOLDS HOUSE, No. 131 North Fifth st., C. R. PERRY, Proprietor.

RICHMOND—Continued.

HOTELS.

RICHMOND TEMPERANCE HOUSE, 91 North Front st. J. G. COLLINS, Prop. Est. 1873.

ICE DEALER.

BRANNON & HAWKINS,
268 Fort Wayne Ave.,
Wholesale and Retail Dealers in Ice.

INSURANCE.

GRAFFORT, EVANS & CLINGERMAN,
General Fire and Life

Insurance Agents,
Representing First-class Non-Board Companies.
No. 2 North 5th St.

LIVERY AND SALE STABLES.

LAFLIN & BURNS, Livery, Feed and Sale Stable Main and Walnut sts. Established 1874.

PICKENS, THOS., Livery, Sale and Boarding Stable, Nos. 135 & 137 Fifth st.

LUMBER.

HOPKINS & FARNHAN, Hard and Soft Wood Lumber, Noble st., bet. 7th & 8th.

MACHINIST.

DILLE & McGUIRE, Fort Wayne ave. Machine Shop, Richmond.

MARBLE WORKS.

STACE & CANDLER,
Manufacturers and Dealers in
Marble Monuments and Tomb Stones,
Scotch and American Granite Monuments,
190 Fort Wayne Ave.
Designs and plans furnished and Work executed in the best style of Art.

MEAT MARKET.

PAXSON, I. H., Avenue Meat Market, No. 181 Fort Wayne ave.

MILLINERY AND DRESSMAKING.

BROWN, MRS. E. A., Dress and Cloak Maker, 323 Main st.

FOULKE, LIZZIE A., Millinery Trimmer, 237 E. Walnut st.

WEDEKIND, JENNIE, Millinery, 233 Main st. Established 1867.

WEDEKIND, M. E., Millinery and Fancy Goods, 291 Main st.

TIGNER, MRS. M., Dress and Cloak Maker, 369 Main st.

ZONBRO, M. H., Dress and Cloak Making, 12 S. Franklin st

IMPORTANT EVENTS OF THE CENTURY. 185

1864.

June 8.—Abraham Lincoln and Andrew Johnson nominated for President and Vice-President. Morgan defeated by Gen. Burbridge, near Lexington, Ky.

June 12.—Gen. Hancock drove the Confederates from Bottom Bridge at the point of the bayonet.

June 15.—Gen. Smith attacked with a force of 15,000 men.

June 16.—Battle of Lost Mountain, Georgia.

June 19.—The Confederate cruiser Alabama sunk by the U. S. frigate Kearsage, in the English Channel.

June 23.—Confederates attack Wright and Hancock, capturing three full regiments, after which they are repulsed.

June 27.—Sherman made an unsuccessful attack on the enemy's position, losing from 1,000 to 3,000 men.

June 28.—Left wing of Grant's army take possession of the Weldon railroad.

June 30.—Secretary Chase resigned, and Hon. Wm. P. Fessenden was appointed to fill the vacancy.

July 5.—The Confederates under Early invade Maryland.

July 13-15.—The Confederates under Gen. Forrest defeated in five different battles, near Pontotoc, Mo.

July 17.—The Confederate army was driven within the fortifications at Atlanta.

July 20.—The enemy assaulted General Sherman's lines three times, but were repulsed each time with severe loss. General Averill defeated the enemy near Winchester, Va.

July 22.—A great battle was fought before Atlanta, resulting in the complete defeat of the Confederates.

July 30.—A mine containing six tons of powder, under a Confederate fort at Petersburg, exploded, destroying the fort and garrison. Chambersburg, Penn., burned by the Confederates.

Aug. 5.—Commodore Farragut's fleet passed Forts Morgan and Gaines. The Confederate ram Tennessee was captured and several other vessels destroyed. Shortly after Fort Gaines surrendered and Fort Powell was evacuated.

Aug. 7.—Gen. Averill defeated the enemy at Morefield, Va.

Aug. 15.—The Confederate Gen. Wheeler repulsed at Dalton, Ga.

Aug. 18.—The Weldon railroad seized by Gen. Grant.

Aug. 23.—Fort Morgan surrendered.

Aug. 25.—Gen. Hancock, who held the Weadon railroad south of Ream's Station, was attacked several times, but repulsed the enemy each time.

Sept. 1.—Gen. Sherman defeated the enemy at Jonesboro, Ga.

Sept. 2.—The Federal troops took possession of Atlanta.

Sept. 4.—Morgan's forces were routed at Greenville, Tennessee, and 100 of his men were

JACKSONVILLE FEMALE ACADEMY,

ESTABLISHED 1830.

The Oldest Institution in the West,

For the Education of Young Ladies. Departments of Study include Preparatory, Collegiate, Musical, and Fine Art.

Instruction in all Departments Thorough and Complete. For Catalogues, or any desired information, address

E. F. BULLARD, Principal,

Jacksonville, Ills.

JACOB JOERGER,

BOTTLER, and Dealer in

Bottled Beer and Ale,

No. 617 East Monroe Street, Between 6th and 7th,

(Opposite NEW POST OFFICE,)

SPRINGFIELD, ILL.

A. W. CADMAN'S

Photograph Ferrotype Studio,

AND EXHIBITION ROOMS,

South Main Street, JACKSONVILLE, ILL.

Orders taken for Enlarged Work of all kinds.

ESTABLISHED 1864.

EDUCATION, MUSIC, ART,

The Young Ladies' Athenæum

A UNIVERSITY FOR YOUNG LADIES, AND THE

Illinois Conservatory of Music,

The Great Western College of Music, with its ART DEPARTMENT, offer unsurpassed facilities for either solid or ornamental culture. For Circulars address Jacksonville, Ill.

W. D. SANDERS, Superintendent.

ADVERTISEMENTS. 187

LINCOLN'S MONUMENT, SPRINGFIELD, ILLS.

Chas. H. von Tagen, M. D.
(Graduate 1858. Professor of Operative Surgery.)

SURGEON.

OFFICE HOURS: 7 to 10 A. M., 2 to 5 P. M., and 7 to 10 P. M.
N. B.--Available at all hours of the night.

Gives Special Attention to the operative branch and treatment of Surgical affections in general—EMBRACING ALL THE KNOWN *Specialties.* After an extended and practical experience in both *Civil and Military Service* as a *Collegiate* and *Clinical Instructor* and successful operator and practitioner for more than twenty years past, he confidently offers his services to the UNITED STATES PUBLIC IN GENERAL.

Consultations and Calls will be promptly responded to, by letter or in person, at home or abroad.

Unexceptional References as to ability and skill will be furnished whenever required.   ADDRESS,
Room No. 8 Kentucky Building, No. 201 Clark St., cor. Adams,
CHICAGO, ILL.

A. E. SMALL, M. D.,

At Residence, 583 Wabash Ave.,   At Office, Room 7, Kentucky Block, 201 S. Clark St.
8 to 9 A. M.   7 to 8 P. M.   10 to 11 A. M.   2½ to 5 P. M.

CHICAGO, ILL.

Having had the advantage of more than thirty-five years' experience as a Physician and Surgeon, and from the fact that his present position of being the PRESIDENT OF HAHNEMAN MEDICAL COLLEGE, OF CHICAGO, PROFESSOR OF THEORY AND PRACTICE OF MEDICINE, brings him extensively into professional relations, DR. SMALL respectfully offers his services in consultation.   He also devotes much time to

Catarrhal and Consumptive Diseases,
——AND OTHER——
CHRONIC AFFECTIONS,
in which he has realized satisfactory results.

1864.

captured, including his staff, and 75 of his men killed. General Gillem commanded the Union forces.

Sept. 7.—The Confederate General John Morgan was killed near Greenville, Tennessee.

Sept. 7.—A force of 2,000 Confederates defeated at Readyville, Tenn.

Sept. 19.—Gen. Sheridan gained a complete victory over the enemy in the Shenandoah valley.

Sept. 22.--Battle at Fisher's Hill; the Confederate army defeated.

Sept. 28.—Gen. Grant advanced his lines on the north side of the James river to within seven miles of Richmond. The Confederates under Gen. Price invaded Mo.

Oct. 5.—The Confederates attacked Allatoona, Georgia, but were repulsed with a severe loss.

Oct. 7.--The pirate vessel Florida captured by the United States steamship Wachusett.

Oct. 8.--The Confederates in Shenandoah valley are again defeated by Sheridan.

Oct. 19.--Gen. Sheridan gained his fourth victory over the Confederates under Early at Cedar creek, Va.

Oct. 23.--The Confederate Gen. Price defeated at Blue river, Mo.

Oct. 27.--Engagement at Hatcher's Run.

Oct. 28.--Gen. Blunt defeated the Confederates under Price at Neosho, Mo.

Oct. 30.—Gen. Hood made three attacks on Decatur, Alabama, but was repulsed each time.

Oct. 31.—Union troops recaptured Plymouth, N. C.

Nov. 3.—The Confederate ram Albemarle destroyed by Lieut. Cushing.

Nov. 8.- The Presidential election took place. Lincoln and Johnson received 212, McClellan and Pendleton twenty-one electoral votes.

McClellan resigns his command in the army.

Nov. 16.—General Sherman left Atlanta and began his great march to the Atlantic.

Nov. 30.- General Hood attacked the Union troops under General Schofield at Franklin, Tennessee, but was repulsed with great loss.

Dec. 13.--Fort McAllister captured by Gen. Sherman's army.

Dec. 16.--General Thomas defeated the enemy at Nashville, Tennessee, with heavy loss, capturing a large number of guns and prisoners.

Dec. 20.—The Confederates under Gen. Breckenridge defeated in southwestern Virginia, and the salt works destroyed.

Dec. 21.--Gen. Sherman entered the city of Savannah, capturing 150 cannon, 30,000 bales of cotton, and a large amount of munitions of war.

Dec. 24.--First bombardment of Fort Fisher.

RICHMOND—*Continued.*

MINERAL WATER.

H. W. Rosa & Son,
Manufacturers of

Mineral Water & Vinegar,

Also Dealers in Cider and Walker's XX Ale and Porter. No. 199 South Front st.

NEWSPAPERS.

DAILY AND WEEKLY INDEPENDENT, J. G. McKee, Editor. Fred. Maag & Co., Prop.

DAILY AND WEEKLY PALLADIUM, Jenkinson, Cullaton & Reeves, Ed's & Pubs.

PAINTER.

HART, WM., House Painter and Grainer, No. 10 North Green st.

PHYSICIANS.

FISHER, BENJAMIN, Magnetic Physician, 317 Main st.

HANNBERG, DR. JULIUS, Physician, Richmond, Ind.

HARRIMAN, DR. S. B., Physician and Surgeon, 16 North Pearl st. Established 1846.

PLUMBER AND GAS FITTER.

H. H. Meerhoff,
Plumber, Gas & Steam Fitter.

Dealer in Gas Fixtures, and all kinds of Iron and Wood Pumps, Iron and Lead Pipe, Drive Wells, Sewer Pipe, Lightning Rods, &c.

Nos. 7 & 9 South 6th St.

PUMP MAKER.

G. H. WEFEL,
Practical Pump Maker,

Iron Wells, Sinks and Iron Pumps, Wood Pumps, Wood Sinks, &c. Repairing done promptly and charges reasonable.

No. 10 South 6th St., near Main.

REAL ESTATE.

FETTA, H. H., Real Estate and Patent Broker.

Established 22 Years.

Richmond Real Estate, Loan and General Agency.

WILLIAM E. BELL,
(Successor to WILLIAM BELL,)
Real Estate, Loan and Insurance Agent, Notary Public and Conveyancer.
S. E. Cor. Main & Fifth Sts.

RICHMOND—*Continued.*

REAL ESTATE.

S. C. MENDENHALL & CO.
Real Estate & Loan
Office, Room No. 1, Up stairs Odd Fellows Building.

RUSSELL, J. J., Real Estate and Insurance Agent, 304 Main st.

SALOONS.

BESSELMAN, FRED, Wholesale and Retail Liquor Store, 34 S. Marion st.

KENNEPOHL, B. A., Wine and Beer Saloon, 18 S. Marion st.

LICHTENFELS, THOS. C., Wine and Beer Saloon, 20 and 22 S. Marion st.

MACKE & MACKE, Dealers in Wine, Beer and Whisky, 12 N. Marion st.

MOREL, EUGENE, Wine and Beer Saloon, 187 Main st.

STAUFER & FORBES, Wholesale Dealers in Liquors and Wines, Ft. Wayne ave. & Fifth st.

THE GROTTO PARLORS,
BILLIARDS,
Wines, Liquors and Cigars.
365 MAIN STREET.
DOC. J. W. IRISH, Prop.

SEWING MACHINES.

THOMPSON, D., Sewing Machines. Repairing a specialty. 291 Main st.

STAMPS AND STENCILS.

SMITH, W. J., General Stencil Works and Novelty Shop, 13 S. Marion st.

STONE WORKS.

SIMMONS, G. W., Asbestine Stone, Stone Steps, Window Caps and Stone Walks, 194 Fort Wayne ave.

STOVES AND TINWARE.

CHASE, J. J., Tin, Copper and Sheet Iron Ware. Also Rags, Metals, etc., Lock Box 1114.

HOFFMAN, FRED, Stoves and Tinware, 206 Main st.

TAILORS.

M'PHERON, NANNI H., Tailoress, 24 Marion st.

PELTZ, JOHN E., Merchant Tailor, 298 Main st.

SCHIEFNER, T., Renovator of Clothing. Suits made to order. 19 S. Marion st.

WERNER, JOSEPH, Merchant Tailor, 341 Main st.

TOBACCO AND CIGARS.

FETTA, L., Manfr. and Dealer in Cigars and Tobaccos, cor. Ft. Wayne ave. and Fifth st.

HANER, J. F., Manufacturer and Wholesale Dealer in Cigars, 299 Main st.

1864.

Dec. 29.—Hood's army crossed the Tennessee river, thus ending the Tennessee campaign.

1865.

Jan. 3.—Massachusetts ratified the Constitutional amendment.

Jan. 8.—General Butler removed from the command of the army of the James, and succeeded by Gen. Ord.

Jan. 11.—Beverly, Va., was attacked by a Confederate force under Gen. Rosser. The town and a large portion of the force defending it were captured.

Jan. 15.—Edward Everett, American statesman and distinguished orator, died, aged 71 years.

Jan. 16.—Fort Fisher, near Wilmington, North Carolina, captured with all its equipments.

Jan. 20.—Confederates evacuate Corinth.

Jan. 27.—Confederate incendiaries set fire to the city of Savannah.

Feb. 1.—Congress abolishes slavery in the United States.

Illinois ratified the constitutional amendment.

Feb. 2.—Maryland, Michigan, New York, and Rhode Island ratified the Constitutional amendment.

Feb. 4.—Illinois black laws repealed.

Feb. 7.—Maine ratified the Constitutional amendment.

Feb. 12.—Gen. Sherman occupied Branchville, S. C.

Feb. 13.—Indiana ratified the Constitutional amendment.

Feb. 17.—Louisiana ratified the Constitutional amendment.

Gen. Sherman's victorious columns entered Columbia, S. C., and burned the city.

Feb. 18.—Gen. Lee assumes supreme command of the Confederate armies, and recommends arming of the blacks.

Charleston, S. C., evacuated and taken possession of by Gen. Gilmore. Six thousand bales of cotton destroyed. Ammunition stored in the railroad depot exploded, and many lives were lost. Gen. Gilmore hoisted the old flag over Fort Sumter.

Feb. 19.—Fort Anderson, N. C., taken.

Feb. 21.—Wisconsin ratified the Constitutional amendment. Fort Armstrong, N. C., taken.

Feb. 22.—Confederate Congress decrees that the slaves shall be armed.

Wilmington captured by General Schofield.

Feb. 23.—Raleigh, N. C., captured. Governor Vance captured.

March 2.—Gen. Sheridan fought and captured the Confederate, General Early, with 1,800 men, between Staunton and Charlottesville.

March 4.—Inauguration of Abraham Lincoln and Andrew Johnson as President and Vice-President of the United States.

March 10.—Gen. Bragg attacked Gen. Cox near Kingston, N. C., but was defeated.

RICHMOND—Continued.

TOBACCO AND CIGARS.

HARVEY, JAMES, R., Cigar Manufactory, Noble st., opposite Depot.

A. Drifmeyer.   Wm. Drifmeyer.
Established 1856.

A. DRIFMEYER & BRO.,
Manufacturers of

CIGARS,
259 MAIN STREET.

King Bee Cigar Factory,
Manufacturer of Fine Cigars.
S. M. BUCKLEY, PROPRIETOR,
228 Main st.

SPIEKENHIER, J., Cigar Manufacturer, Main and Front.

TOOL MANUFACTURERS.

RICHMOND EDGE TOOL CO. Established 1876. One square west of Depot.

UMBRELLA MANUFACTURERS.

SAYMAN, MRS. & SON, Umbrella Manufacturers, 8 S. Pearl st.

VETERINARY SURGEONS.

COMER, WM., Veterinary Surgeon. Residence, Main st., bet. Fifteenth and Sixteenth.

WEEKS, C. A., Veterinary Surgeon, Richmond, Ind.

WATCHES, CLOCKS AND JEWELRY.

C. A. DICKINSON,
Dealer in
Diamonds, Watches, Clocks, Jewelry,
Sterling Silver and Plated Ware,
306 Main St., opposite Odd Fellow's Hall.
Watches, Clocks and Jewelry repaired and warranted. Engraving done to order. Sole Agent for the Celebrated Paul Breton Watch. Est. '35.

WINES AND LIQUORS.

S. H. LIPINSKY, Wholesale Dealer in
PURE BOURBON WHISKIES,
Importer of Wines and Liquors, 257 Main street.

WHELAN & MORMAN, Wholesale and Retail Liquor Dealers, 11 N. Fifth st.

WOODEN WARE.

DETCH, GEO., Manfr of Patent and Staff Churns, Tubs and Butter Firkins, 227 Main st.

JOLIET, ILLS.

COAL DEALERS.

FREY, FRANK P., Hard & Soft Coal, Coke and Wood, office & yard, Scott & Washington sts.

KING, J. Q. A., Agent for the leading varieties of Coal, Jefferson st. & St. Louis R. R. Depot.

JOLIET—Continued.

COAL DEALERS.

SHAFFNER, B. & SON, Coal Coke & Wood, Scott & Washington sts.

COFFEE AND SPICE MILL.

ARNOLD & BOWEN, Joliet Steam Coffee & Spice Mills, Wholesale dealers in Coffees and Spices. Coffees roasted for the trade. Office and Mills: Nos. 27, 29 & 32 Bluff st.

HORSE SHOERS.

HAGEN, H. H., Horseshoer & manuf'r of Stonecutters' & Marble-workers' tools, 91 N.Bluff st.

STANTON, JOSEPH, Plough Repairing, Horseshoeing & General Jobbing, 27 Washington st.

MILLINERY GOODS.

BUTLER, MRS. ELLA, Choice Millinery,
Centennial Block.

PAINTER.

YOUNG, E. H., House, Sign and Ornamental painter, 40 Jefferson st.

SASH, DOORS AND BLINDS.

MASON & PLANTS, Lumber, Sash, Doors, Blinds, etc., Desplaines & Cass sts.

SMUT MILLS.

WALLACE EMERY STONE SMUT MILL MANUfacturing Co., and Pearl Barley Mills.

WAGONS AND CARRIAGES.

McMILLAN, F., Manf'r and repairer of Wagons, Carriages, etc., 7 Washington st.

WIND MILLS.

L. LEACH,
Manufacturer of
WIND MILLS,
And
Earth Augers for Boring
Wells, also, Drive-well Supplies. Send for descriptive circular and price list.
Address, BOX 135, Joliet, Ills.

WIRE FENCES.

JOLIET WIRE FENCE CO., Manfactu's of Patent Barbed Wire Barbs, etc.

THE ADAMS MANUFACTURING CO., Manuf's of Barbed Cable Fence Wire.

THE STEVENS ORIGINAL LOCKSTITCH BARB, all Steel, Fence Wire.

WATKINS, WM., Inventor & Manf'r of Cable Barbed Fence, P.O.box 492, res 91 Herkimer st.

OTTAWA, ILLS.

ATTORNEY AT LAW.

JOHNSTON, JAMES B., Attorney at Law,
Office, N. W. cor. Public Sq.

WISCONSIN STATE BUILDING, CENTENNIAL EXPOSITION, PHILA,

JOHN CORBETT,
MERCHANT TAILOR

EVERY VARIETY OF

FRENCH, ENGLISH and DOMESTIC CLOTHS,

Kept Constantly on Hand.

SPECIAL ATTENTION PAID TO CUSTOM TRADE.

A FULL STOCK OF

GENTS' FURNISHING GOODS, HATS, CAPS, ETC.

ALWAYS ON HAND.

GREENWAY BLOCK,
RIPON, - WISCONSIN.

1865.

Gen. Sherman occupied Fayetteville, N. C.

March 13.—Gen. Schofield occupied Kingston.

March 16.—Confederate Gen. Hardee defeated at Averysboro, N. C.

March 17.—Confederate Congress adjourned. "sine die."

March 19.—Confederate Gen. Johnson defeated at Bentonville, N. C.

March 21.—Goldsboro, N. C., occupied.

March 25.—Confederates attack Gen. Grant and get severely defeated.

April 1.—Victory of Five Forks, Va.

April 2.—Lee's lines at Petersburg carried.

April 3.—Richmond taken.

April 9.—Surrender of Gen. Lee and his whole army at Appomattox Court House, Va.

April 12.—The Union flag hoisted at Fort Sumter.

Mobile, Ala., captured.

April 13.—Drafting and recruiting stopped.

April 14.—President Lincoln shot by J. Wilkes Booth in Ford's Theatre, Washington; Mr. Seward and his son wounded.

April 15.—Death of President Lincoln. Vice-President Johnson sworn in as President of the United States.

Mr. Stanton's letter to Charles Francis Adams, Minister to England: "Washington, April 15th. Sir—It has become my distressing duty to announce to you that his Excellency Abraham Lincoln was assassinated, about the hour of half-past ten o'clock, in his private box at Ford's Theatre, in this city. The President, about eight o'clock, accompanied Mrs. Lincoln to the theater. Another lady and gentleman were with them in the box. About half-past ten, during a pause in the performance, the assassin entered the box, the door of which was unguarded, hastily approached the President from behind, and discharged a pistol at his head. The bullet entered the back of his head and penetrated nearly through. The assassin then leaped from the box upon the stage, brandishing a large knife or dagger, and exclaimed, 'Sic semper tyrannis!' and escaped in the rear of the theatre. Immediately upon the discharge the President fell to the floor insensible, and continued in that state until twenty minutes past 7 o'clock this morning, when he breathed his last.'"

April 26.—Gen. Johnson surrendered.

April 27.—Booth, the murderer of President Lincoln, mortally wounded and captured.

May 4.—General Dick Taylor surrenders.

May 10.—Jefferson Davis captured at Irwinville, 75 miles southwest of Macon, Ga., by the 4th Michigan cavalry, under Col. Pritchard, of Gen. Wilson's command; also, his wife, mother, Postmaster-General Regan, Col. Harrison, private secretary, Col Johnson and other military characters.

May 19.—Confederate Gov. Watts, of Alabama, arrested.

May 21.—Confederate Gov. Letcher, of Virginia, arrested.

OTTAWA—Continued.

FURNITURE.

RUGG, GEO. H., Wholesale & retail dealer in Furniture, 1st door West of City Drug Store.

BESTMANN, F., Furniture repairing and Picture framing, 2 doors South of Park House.

HARDWARE.

COWLES & BURTISS, Hardware & House Furnishing Goods, 31 LaSalle st.

IRON FOUNDRY.

BENZ, J., Ottawa Ornamental Works. Fences a Specialty. P. O. Box, 1022.

MARBLE WORKS.

McNIHILL, E., Marble Ornaments, Headstones, etc., opposite Postoffice.

MUSIC—BAND.

BACH'S CITY BAND, Music at short notice. E. Bach, P. O. drawer, 1851.

PAINTERS.

HOSSACK & CLARK, House & Sign Painters, Paperhanging, &c, Columbus & Jefferson sts.

PHYSICIAN.

STOUT, J., Physician and Surgeon, over Kneussl's Drug Store, res. Paul & Lafayette sts.

DANVILLE, ILLS.

ATTORNEYS AT LAW.

Law and Collection Office
—OF—
YOUNG & PENWELL,
Collections a specialty.
DANVILLE, - - - *ILLINOIS.*

References : Vermillion Co. Bank, First National Bank; Geo. Dillon, Circuit Clerk; Danville Banking and Trust Co.

BARBERS.

LUTES, JACOB, Shaving and Hairdressing Rooms, 140 E. Main.

MILLER, FRANK, Barber, under Ætna House, Vermillion st.

BLANK BOOK MANUFACTURERS.

ILLINOIS PRINTING CO., Blank Book Manufacturers, Stationers and Book Binders.

BOOTS AND SHOES.

P. J. WALKER & CO.,
(Est. 1874.)
Proprietors

BOSTON SHOE STORE,

114 Main Street,
DANVILLE, ILLS.

IMPORTANT EVENTS OF THE CENTURY. 193

DANVILLE—*Continued.*

CARRIAGES AND BUGGIES.

DANVILLE CARRIAGE FACTORY, Wm. H. Whitehill, Proprietor, 27 W. Main st.

GIDDINGS, J. W., Manfr of Carriages & Buggies, Hazle st. near Main st.

CONTRACTORS AND BUILDERS.

DANVILLE
Contracting & Building Company,

Contractors of Brick-Work, Stone-Work, and Plastering; also, dealers in Lime, Hair, Cement and Plaster Paris.

JOHN A. LEWIS, Superintendent.
WEST MAIN ST.

Established 1877.
GLASS & BURLEIGH,
CONTRACTORS & BUILDERS,
Co. North & Hazle sts.

HANKEY, C. F., Contractor & Builder,
W. Main st.

CORNICE WORKS.

KLUGEL, G. L., Western Union Cornice Contractor, Main & Walnut sts.

DENTIST.

DWIGHT, C. R., Dentist,
Short's Block, Main st.

DRUGGIST.

E. C. WINSLOW,
Est. 1859.
Dealer in Strictly

PURE DRUGS, CHEMICALS,

Druggists' Sundries, etc., Paints, Oils, Glass and Brushes,
107 Main Street, Danville, Ills.

GROCERS.

Geo. F. Eaton & Co.,
WHOLESALE GROCERS,
AND
Commission Merchants,
Opera House Block,
DANVILLE, - - - - ILLINOIS.

PIERCE, J. C., Groceries, Hardware and Agricultural Implements, Ridge Farm, Ills.

HAIR DEALERS AND DRESSERS.

HENRY & ROSS,
Ladies' Hair Dressers.
Hair Work of all kinds done to order.
73 Vermilion st.

HATTER AND FURRIER.

MILLIS, J. H., Hatter, Furrier, Gents' Furnisher, 72 Main st.

1865.

May 24.—Grand Review of Gen. Sherman's army at Washington.
Jefferson Davis indicted for treason.
May 26.—Kirby Smith surrendered. The last armed Confederate organization has succumbed.
May 31.—Confederate Gen. Hood and staff surrendered.
COST OF THE WAR.—In the Union armies probably 300,000 men were killed in battle, or died of wounds and disease, while doubtless two hundred thousand more were crippled for life. If the Confederate armies suffered as heavily, the country thus lost one million able-bodied men. The Union debt, Jan. 1, 1866, was nearly $2,750,000,000. At one time, the daily expenses reached the sum of $3,500,000. During the last year of the war, the expenses were greater than the entire expenditures of the Government from Washington to Buchanan. The Confederate war debt was never paid, as that Government was overthrown.
June 22.—President Johnson rescinds order requiring passports from all travelers entering the United States, and opens Southern ports.
July 7.—Execution of Payne, Atzerott, Harold and Mrs. Surratt, for complicity in the assassination of President Lincoln.
Oct. 11.—Pardon of Alexander Stephens and other Southern officials.
Nov. 9.—Confederate privateer Shenandoah surrenders at Liverpool, having destroyed about 30 vessels; crew released.
Nov. 10.—Execution of Wirz, the Confederate prison-keeper, for cruelty to Union prisoners.

1866.

Jan. 28.—Hon. Thomas Chandler dies. Queen Emma, widow of a former King of the Sandwich Islands, arrived in San Francisco, and after making a thorough inspection of our institutions and religious and educational systems, she went to England *via* New York.
Feb. 19.—President vetoes Freedmen's Bureau bill. This bill required the Government to take care of the emancipated slaves and destitute whites of the South.
March 14.—Jared Sparks, historian, dies.
March 27.—President Johnson vetoes Civil Rights bill. This bill guaranteed the same rights to the negro, in every particular, as those enjoyed by the white man.
April 2.—President Johnson issues a proclamation declaring that the insurrection which heretofore existed in the States of Georgia, South Carolina, North Carolina, Virginia, Tennessee, Alabama, Louisiana, Arkansas, Mississippi, and Florida, is at an end, and henceforth to be so regarded.
April 9.—Civil Rights bill passed over the President's veto.
April 12.—Hon. Daniel S. Dickinson dies.
May 16.—President Johnson vetoes the admission of Colorado as a State.
May 29.—Death of General Winfield Scott, aged 80 years.
June 2.—Fort Erie, in Canada, occupied

CONSERVATORY MUSIC STORE.
CHARLES S. BARROWS,
DEALER IN

SHEET MUSIC,

MUSIC BOOKS, VIOLINS, FLUTES, GUITARS, ETC.
STRINGS A SPECIALTY.

JACKSONVILLE, - - - - ILLINOIS.

CATALOGUES SENT FREE ON APPLICATION.

DANVILLE—*Continued.*

HOTELS.

FINEST SAMPLE-ROOMS in the City.

Rates only $2 per Day.

CENTENNIAL HOTEL.
CRANE, McCORMACK & CO., Props.
Cor. Main and Walnut Sts.

JUSTICE OF THE PEACE.

STANSBURY, J. W., Justice of the Peace and Collecting Agent, 78 Main st.

LIVERY STABLES.

KUYKENDALL & CO., City Livery, Feed and Sale Stable, 33 Hazle st., near Main.

TINDALL & HARBESON, Livery, Sale and Feed Stable, W. Main st.

MARBLE WORKS.

BROWER, H. O., Marble Works, south of Public square.

VERMILION MARBLE WORKS, H. L. Payne, prop., 22 Walnut st.

MILLINER AND DRESSMAKER.

CHENOWETH, MRS. P. S., Milliner and Dressmaker, 31 S. Vermilion st. Established 1876.

NEWSPAPERS.

DANVILLE DAILY AND WEEKLY TIMES, A. G. Smith, editor.

ORGAN WORKS.

MILLER & SON, Beethoven Organ Works, E. Main st.

PHOTOGRAPHERS.

F. A. HARTWELL,

Photographer,

112 Main st. Established 1873.

JOSLIN & PHILLIPS, Photographers, 85, S. W. cor. Public square.

DANVILLE—*Continued.*

SEWING MACHINES.

AGNEW & MARTIN, Agents for No. 8 Wheeler & Wilson Sewing Machine.

TOBACCO AND CIGARS.

WORTMAN, F. H., Cigars, Tobacco and Smokers' Articles, 34 Vermilion st.

UNDERTAKERS.

KIMBALL, N. A., Undertaker, 59 Main st.

WATCHMAKER AND JEWELER.

BLANKENBURG, AUGUST, Watchmaker and Jeweler, 60 Vermilion st.

WAUKEGAN, ILLS.

BROOMS AND BRUSHES.

DICKINSON, A. E., Manufacturer of Brooms and Brushes. Established 1863.

DENTIST.

CLARKSON, R. W., Dentist. Office over Steele's store. Established 1846.

HOTEL.

WHEN YOU GO TO WAUKEGAN,

STOP AT THE CITY HOTEL.
First Class. Prices Moderate.
JOHN H. O'HARA, Proprietor.
Good Stabling. Good Sample Room.

KITCHEN CABINET.

W. V. SMITH,
Manufacturer of the

Celebrated Kitchen Cabinet.

Housekeepers who have used it all concur in recommending it as one of the most economical, convenient and useful articles ever invented for the Kitchen. Send for Circular.

M. B. SMITH, Patentee.

ADVERTISEMENTS. 195

REV. W. F. SHORT, President.

Illinois Female College, Jacksonville, Illinois,

Established 1849.

ILLINOIS FEMALE COLLEGE
—AND—
ACADEMY OF MUSIC AND ART.

A full Board of Instruction, including Primary, Preparatory, Scientific, Classical, Music, Painting, Drawing, German, French, Calisthenics, Æsthetics and Etiquette. The Buildings, Board, Discipline, Course of Study, and Instruction in each Branch, unsurpassed in any School for Young Ladies and Misses in the West. Young Ladies wishing to prepare themselves for teaching in our Public Schools or for teaching Music, Painting and Drawing, will find rare advantages in this Institution.
☞ Send for Catalogue and Information to

Rev. W. F. SHORT, President.

1866.

by a party of Fenians under Col. O'Neill, May 31; they are defeated and O'Neill killed.

June 7.—President Johnson issues a proclamation against the Fenian movement in the United States. Fenians from the United States make a raid into Canada.

June 17.—Hon. Lewis Cass dies.

July 13-27.—The Atlantic Telegraph successfully laid between Great Britain and America.

July 16.—Freedmen's Bureau bill becomes a law.

July 30.—Major-General Lysander Cutler dies.

Aug. 14.—National Union Convention assembles in Philadelphia wigwam.

Sept. 1.—Southern Unionists' Convention assembles in Philadelphia.

Sept. 7.—Matthias W. Baldwin, pioneer in American locomotives, dies.

Oct. 13.—"Prince" John Van Buren, son of Martin, dies.

Dec. 13.—Congress passes a bill giving negroes the right to vote in the District of Columbia.

Dec. 26.—Major-General Samuel R. Curtis dies.

1867.

Jan. 9.—Virginia rejects the Fourteenth Amendment. This amendment guaranteed civil rights to all, regardless of race or color.

Jan. 10.—Congress passes a bill providing for "universal suffrage" in the territories.

Jan. 29.—President Johnson vetoes the bill to admit Nebraska.

Feb. 6.—Delaware and Louisiana reject Constitutional amendment.

Feb. 8.—Nebraska admitted as a State.

Feb. 25.—Tenure of Office bill passed over President's veto. This bill makes the consent of the Senate necessary before the President can remove any person from a civil office.

Feb. 30.—Announced at Washington that Russia cedes Alaska to the United States.

April 11.—Site conveyed to the United States government for post-office in New York city.

May 3.—Eight-hour riots in Chicago.

May 9.—General strike of workingmen throughout the States.

May 13.—Jefferson Davis admitted to bail at Richmond, Va.

June 3.—Gen. Sheridan removes Gen. Welles, of Louisiana, and on the 6th appoints B. F. Flanders, Governor.

July 11.—Reciprocity treaty between the United States and the Hawaiian Islands.

July 24.—New York States Constitutional Convention rejects the proposition of woman suffrage.

July 30.—General Sheridan removes Governor Throckmorton, of Texas.

Aug. 5.—Secretary Stanton is requested by the President to resign, but refuses.

Aug. 12.—Stanton suspended, and Gen-

WAUKEGAN—*Continued.*

HORSESHOEING.

DUNLAY & RAFTIS, Horseshoeing and General Job Work, Washington st.

PAINTER.

B. H. MORRELL,
House, Sign, Carriage and Ornamental

PAINTER,
Dealer in
PAINTS, OILS, VARNISHES, PUTTY, GLASS, ETC.,

Shop, First Door North of Waukegan House

PUMP MANUFACTURERS.

POWELL & DOUGLASS, Manufacturers of the Celebrated Star Pump.

SICKLE GRINDER.

The Boss Sickle Grinder.
[TRADE-MARK PATENTED.]
Every Farmer should Have One. Simplest, most durable and perfect Sickle Grinder in the World. A boy can run it. Can be changed from an oscillating to a stationary Stone in a moment. Is the best Grindstone in use for all purposes. For Sale by all dealers. Good Agents and canvassers wanted. POWELL, STEVENS & DOUGLAS, Waukegan, Illinois.

TAILOR.

MERCHANT, JAMES, Merchant Tailor, Genesee st. Established 1877.

MONMOUTH, ILLS.

ATTORNEY AT LAW.

WILLITS, ELIAS, Attorney at Law, south side Square.

BANK.

FIRST NATIONAL BANK, cor. Broadway and Public square.

BARBER.

SCHIEBEL, M., Bathing and Hairdressing, cor. Main and Public square.

GUNSMITH.

HAYDEN, D. S., Gunsmith,
S. Main st.

HOTEL.

THE NEW
BALDWIN HOUSE,
ESTABLISHED 1856.
MONMOUTH, ILLS.

MONMOUTH—Continued.

MEAT MARKET.
G. KOBLER,
Pioneer Meat Market,
S. MAIN ST., MONMOUTH, ILLS.

PHOTOGRAPHERS.
FOSTER, J. C. & CO., Photographers, south side Square.

SEWING MACHINES.
ALVIN M. BRUNER, General Repair Shop. Sewing Machine Repairing a Specialty. Dealer in Sewing Machines Attachments, Oils, Needles, Parts, etc., etc.,
First Door North of National Hotel.

WASHING MACHINE.
MERRILL, J. M., The Best Washing Machine, Broadway.

JANESVILLE, WIS.

BARBERS.
BROWN, A., Barber and Hairdresser, 37 Milwaukee st., over Davis Bros.

RIEBE, ROB'T (successor to Wieglef), Barber Shop, W. Milwaukee st., over Carle's grocery.

GENERAL REPAIR SHOP.
PALMERTER, C. N. C., Magic Coal Sifter and Broom Holder. General Repair Shop, Franklin st.

FURNITURE.
M. HANSON & CO.,
Manufacturers of
FURNITURE
OF ALL KINDS.

HARNESS AND SADDLES.
M'ALPIN, ALEXANDER, Manufacturer of Harness, Saddles, Collars, etc., 77 N. Main st.

INSURANCE AND REAL ESTATE.
WHITAKER, F., Insurance and Real Estate Agent, over Gazette office.

LIVERY STABLE.
CARTER & PARKER, Livery Stable, Franklin st., near Corn Exchange.

MARBLE WORKS.
BENNETT, F. A., Monuments, Tombstones, etc., east side of Corn Exchange square.

PUMPS.
CALF, E., Driven Well and Deep Well Pumps, Franklin st.

SALOON.
BUCKINGHAM, W. H., Arcade Saloon, Wines, Liquors and Cigars, 54 Main st.

1867.

eral Grant appointed Secretary of War ad interim.

Aug. 17.—General Sheridan relieved at New Orleans.

Aug. 19.—National Labor Congress meets at Chicago.

Sept. 8.—President issues amnesty proclamation.

Sept. 30.—Negro riots in Savannah, Georgia.

Oct. 3.—Whisky riot in Philadelphia.

Nov. 2.—General Sherman announces Indian war at an end.

Nov. 14.—Denmark concludes a treaty, ceding and selling the islands of St. Thomas, San Juan, and Santa Cruz to the United States.

Nov. 22.—Jefferson Davis returns to Richmond, Va.

Dec. 7.—Resolution of Judiciary Committee to impeach President Johnson, voted down in the House—102 to 57.

1868.

Jan. 2.—Governor Flanders of Louisiana resigned, and Joshua Baker was appointed his successor by Gen. Hancock.

Jan. 5.—United States Military Asylum at Augusta, Me., destroyed by fire.

Jan. 6.—Congress met. The President censured in the House for removing General Sheridan.

Gen. Meade assumed command of the third military district, consisting of Alabama, Georgia and Florida.

House of Representatives passes bill making eight hours a day's work for Government laborers.

Jan. 10.—Secretary Seward announced to the House that 21 States had ratified the 14th article of the amendment to the Constitution.

Jan. 11.—The Chinese Government appointed Anson Burlingame, formerly United States Minister in Pekin, its special envoy to all the treaty powers, at a salary of $40,000.

Jan. 13.—The U. S. House of Representatives passed a bill declaring that five members shall constitute a quorum of the Supreme Court, and that a concurrence of two-thirds of all the members shall be necessary to a decision adverse to the validity of any law passed by Congress.

The Senate reinstates Stanton.

Jan. 14.—The Virginia Constitutional Convention declared that Virginia shall forever remain in the Union and that slavery is forever abolished in the State.

General Grant vacates War Office in favor of Secretary Stanton.

Jan. 15.—Gen. Pope assigned to the command of the Department of the Lakes with headquarters at Detroit.

Jan. 24.—Fifty thousand American breech-loading rifles ordered by the Spanish Minister of War.

Jan. 29.—The President instructed Gen. Grant in writing not to obey any orders from

Keokuk Northern Line

PACKET COMPANY

Daily Line of Steamers
—BETWEEN—

ST. LOUIS & ST. PAUL!

One of the following Side-Wheel Passenger Steamers leaves

St. Louis Daily at 4:00 P. M.

RETURNING LEAVES

St. Paul Daily at 9:00 A. M.

Connecting at all intermediate points with Railroads for all points East, West, North and South.

NAMES OF STEAMERS:

GOLDEN EAGLE, MINNEAPOLIS,
WAR EAGLE, DUBUQUE,
CLINTON, NORTHWESTERN,
ALEX. MITCHELL, MINNESOTA,
RED WING, BELLE of La CROSSE,
ROB ROY, LAKE-SUPERIOR.

These Steamers are First-Class in every respect; are large and commodious (from 225 to 275 feet in length; cabins full length. Upper Decks exclusively for use of passengers. Rooms large and well ventilated; beds clean and comfortable. The tables are supplied at all times with the best the market affords. Every facility is given Excursionists to see the many points of interest along the route.

Through Tickets for Sale at all Principal Points.

MOODY AND SANKEY TABERNACLE, CHICAGO.

DR. A. G. OLIN'S
PRIVATE HOSPITAL,
187 East Washington Street, CHICAGO, ILL.

For the cure of all Chronic and Confidential Diseases of either sex, particularly those of a long standing and complicated character, those having failed to find relief elsewhere specially invited to call or write; private board for patients at reasonable charges.

Marriage Guide, 275 pages. Information for the young and middle-aged, a valuable treatise for the married and those contemplating marriage, everybody should get this book that desires to be healthy and happy in the marriage relation. Sent to any address sealed on receipt of 50 cents. Address

DR. A. G. OLIN.

OPIUM
AND MORPHINE

HABITS absolutely and speedily cured; painless and no publicity. Send two stamps for particulars, with book on Opium-eating and guide to health. **DR. CARLTON, 187 East Washington Street, CHICAGO, ILL.**

1868.

the War Department, unless authorized by himself.

Feb. 5.—Congress passed a bill authorizing the Secretary of War to employ counsel to defend Generals or other persons entrusted with reconstruction in cases brought against them for their acts under the reconstruction laws.

Thermometer 51 degrees below zero in Wisconsin.

Feb. 13.—Another attempt to impeach President Johnson.

Feb. 18.—Senate bill passed for the reduction of the army.

Feb. 20.—New Jersey Legistature withdrew ratification of proposed Fourteenth Constitutional Amendment.

Feb. 21.—The President ordered the removal of Secretary Stanton from the war office, and authorized Gen. Thomas to act as Secretary of War *ad interim*. Stanton decided to retain personal possession of the office until action in the matter be taken by the Senate. The Senate disapproved the action of the President, declaring it to be unconstitutional.

Feb. 22.—Adjutant-General Thomas arrested for violation of the tenure of office bill on complaint of Secretary Stanton. He is released on $10,000 bail.

Feb. 23.—Conclusion of a treaty between the North German Confederation and the United States, concerning the nationality of persons emigrating from one of the two countries to the other.

Feb. 24.—The United States House of Representatives resolve by a vote of 126 to 47, that "Andrew Johnson, President of the United States, be impeached of high crimes and misdemeanors." The President sent a message to the Senate vindicating his position.

Feb. 25.—The Committee of the House appointed Boutwell, Stevens, Bingham and Wilson a sub-committee to take evidence and prepare articles of impeachment.

The House informed the Senate and presented their action in regard to the impeachment of President Johnson.

Governor Ward, of New Jersey, vetoed resolution of Legislature withdrawing ratification of Fourteenth Amendment.

The Florida Convention adopted the new Constitution.

Feb. 26.—General L. Thomas discharged from arrest and began a suit against Secretary Stanton for false imprisonment and malicious prosecution, setting his damages at $150,000.

An amendatory reconstruction bill passed Congress, providing that any election in the Southern States should be decided by a majority of the votes actually cast.

March 2.—The Senate adopted a code of procedure for an impeachment trial.

The House adopted nine articles of impeachment and appointed seven managers of the impeachment trial.

March 5.—New Jersey Senate passes over Gov. Ward's veto as to amendment; lower House does the same.

March 6.—President Johnson summoned

JANESVILLE—*Continued.*

STOVES, HARDWARE, ETC.

BENNETT, W. S. & CO., Stoves, Hardware, Farming Tools, etc., 17 W. Milwaukee st.

TAILOR.

PENTON, GEORGE, Merchant Tailor, N. Main st.

TOBACCO AND CIGARS.

KNUDSON & SUCHANEK, Cigar Manufacturers and Tobacconists, N. Main st.

VETERINARY SURGEONS.

DR. J. BROWN & SON,
VETERINARY SURGEONS,
East End Court St. Bridge.

WAGON MAKER.

WHIFFEN, ISAAC A., Wagon and Carriage, Jobbing and Repair Shop, Franklin st.

WATCHES AND CLOCKS.

HORN, GEORGE, Watch and Clockmaker, also Dealer in Jewelry, 46 Main st.

KENOSHA, WIS.

BOOTS AND SHOES.

Established 1860.

LYMAN & SON,
Dealers in
FINE BOOTS & SHOES,
Cor. Main & Market Sts.,
KENOSHA.

C. L. ELY, Dealer in
FINE BOOTS AND SHOES
90 MAIN ST. Established 1845.

DRY GOODS, ETC.

Established 1862.

SETH DOAN,
Dealer in
DRY GOODS & NOTIONS,
MAIN STREET.

Established 1861.

BENDT & HANSEN,
Dealers in
DRY GOODS, GROCERIES,
CROCKERY,
GLASSWARE & YANKEE NOTIONS
KENOSHA, WIS.

KENOSHA—Continued.

DRY GOODS, ETC.
CRANEY, M., Dealer in Dry Goods and Clothing, 62 Main st. Established 1870.

DRUGGIST.
CLARK, H. E., Druggist,
Main st.

GENERAL STORE.
CAMERON, D., General Store,
Main st.

HARDWARE.
P. BECKER & SON, Dealers in Hardware, Stoves and Agricultural Implements, MAIN STREET.

HOTEL.
CITY HOTEL, T. J. Meyers, Prop.,
Market st. near Main st.

WATCHES AND JEWELRY.
MILLER, M. A., Dealer in Jewelry & Watches,
Main st.

IOWA CITY, IOWA.

BAKERY AND CONFECTIONERY.
VICTOR, GEO. F., Avenue Bakery, Confectionery & Cigars, City ave. near Dubuque st.

BARBER.
REESE, C., Boston Barber Shop,
Dubuque st. near College st.

BLACKSMITH.
PORCH, L. D., Blacksmithing, Repairing and Horseshoeing, College & Capitol sts.

BOOKS AND STATIONERY.
ALLIN, WILSON & SMITH,
Wholesale and retail dealers in
Books & Stationery,
And General Agents for Iowa City Paper Mills,
Clinton St., opposite University.

BOOTS AND SHOES.
BRUCE & SPENCER, Manufac's of Boots & Shoes Repairing done, Dubuque st. near avenue.

FLANNAGAN, JOHN S., Manf'r of Boots & Shoes, Dubuque st. near College st.

FRIAUF, V., Manufacturer of Boots & Shoes, City Avenue near Dubuque st.

KRAMER, JACOB, Manufac'r of Boots & Shoes, Dubuque st.

LEIBROCK, D., Manufacturer of Boots & Shoes, College st. near Clinton st.

CARRIAGES AND WAGONS.
STIMMEL, D. J., Carriages, Wagons, Open & Top Buggies, etc., College st. near Capitol st.

1868.

to appear before the courts of impeachment, on the 18th of March.

March 12.—The House passed the bill to abolish the tax on manufacturers. Trial of Jeff Davis postponed until April 14th.

March 13.—The President asked forty days' time to prepare his answer to the articles of impeachment. The Senate extended the time till March 23.

March 18.—The House passed the bill providing that in case of the death or removal of the Chief Justice, the senior Associate Justice of the Supreme Court shall perform the duties of Chief Justice.

Admiral Farragut received by the Pope of Rome.

March 23.—The High Court of Impeachment opened for the trial of President Johnson. The President filed his answer to the articles of impeachment. His counsel asks for further delay.

March 26.—The Senate passed the Habeas Corpus appeal bill over the President's veto. They also ratified the treaty with the North German Confederation, recognizing the rights of naturalized citizens.

March 27.—The House passed the Supreme Court bill over the President's veto.

March 28.—A new indictment found against Jeff. Davis by the United States Grand Jury at Richmond.

March 30.—G. A. Ashburn, a member of the Constitutional Convention, assassinated at Columbus, Ga.

Gen. B. F. Butler of Massachusetts, opened in the Court of Impeachment, the prosecution on the part of the managers.

April 2.—North German Parliament passes the naturalization treaty with the United States.

April 4.—The case for the prosecution in the Court of Impeachment closed. General Schofield appointed Henry H. Wells Governor of Virginia.

April 6.—Michigan votes against negro suffrage.

April 9.—The counsel for President Johnson opened the argument for the defense in the Court of Impeachment.

April 20.—Evidence in the impeachment case closed.

April 23.—Charles Dickens left the United States.

April 24.—A treaty of peace concluded with the Sioux Indians.

May 6.—Argument in the impeachment trial closed.

May 21.—U. S. Grant nominated by the Republicans at Chicago as candidate for President and Schuyler Colfax for Vice-President.

May 22.—Arrival of Chinese Embassy in New York.

May 26.—Impeacnment trial concluded, and the President found not guilty.

May 30.—The Grand Army of the Republic decorated with flowers the graves of the Union soldiers in the cemeteries throughout the country.

Indianapolis, Peru & Chicago
RAILWAY,
—FOR—
CHICAGO AND THE NORTH-WEST,
Indianapolis and the South.

The Most Direct Route

FROM INDIANAPOLIS TO

Ft. Wayne, Toledo and Detroit,

—AND THE—

Great Lumber and Salt Regions

—OF THE—

SAGINAW VALLEY.

Shortest Line from Chicago,
VIA KOKOMO,

And the Only Line Running Through to Indianapolis, From Michigan City and La Porte,

WITHOUT CHANGE.

Woodruff Parlor and Sleeping Cars on all Night Trains.

F. P. WADE, Gen. Pass. & T'k't Ag't.

Iowa State Building, Centennial Exposition, Philadelphia.— Is built entirely of wood, with portico supported by four columns. It is two stories high, divided off into rooms for the reception of visitors, ladies' parlor, and the keeping of matters of special interest to the state. It was numerously visited during the Centennial by persons from all parts of the country, and especially from Iowa. At the close of the Exhibition it was sold for $575 to Mr. Bower, of New Jersey, who intends removing it to his farm, about 10 miles from Camden, N. J.

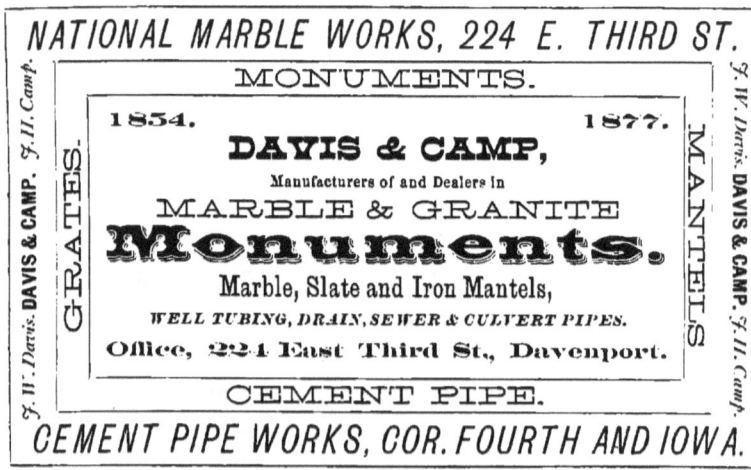

1868.

June 1.—Ex-President James Buchanan dies.

June 3.—Trial of Jeff. Davis again postponed till November.

June 4.—Ex-President Buchanan buried at Wheatland, Penn.

June 10.—The Senate passed a bill for the admission of the Southern States with only five negative votes.

June 12.—Reverdy Johnson confirmed as Minister to England.

June 16.—Governor Humphreys, of Mississippi, removed by General McDowell, and General Ames appointed military governor in his stead.

June 19.—The House passed the Senate bill, giving thanks to Secretary Stanton.

June 20.—The House passed the bill for the admission of Arkansas over the President's veto without debate.

June 22.—King of Belgium reviews United States squadron under Farragut off Ostend.

June 24.—The Senate ratified the Chinese treaty. The House passed a bill for the immediate reorganization of the States of Virginia, Mississippi and Texas.

June 25.—The Freedman's Bureau bill passed over the President's vote.

July 4.—President Johnson issued a proclamation of general amnesty and pardon to all engaged in the late rebellion except those already indicted for treason or other felony.

July 11.—Com. James F. Miller died at Charleston, Mass., aged 76 years.

July 17.—The Senate passed the bill appropriating $7,200,000 in coin for the payment of Alaska.

Moses Yale Beach, American journalist, for many years proprietor of the New York *Sun*, died, aged 68 years.

July 21.—Congress passed a resolution declaring the 14th article ratified. The Senate passed a resolution appealing to the Turkish government in behalf of the Cretans.

July 24.—President orders Secretary of War to withdraw military forces from Southern States represented in Congress.

July 27.—Jefferson Davis and family sail from Quebec for England.

The government of Germany stopped all prosecutions against adopted citizens of America, of German birth.

Aug. 1.—General Jeff. C. Davis assigned to the command of the Military district of Alaska.

Aug. 3.—Mr. Washburn indignantly denied the charge of conspiracy against President Lopez.

Failure of Atlantic cable of 1866.

Charles G. Halpine, better known as "Miles O'Riley," died at New York, aged 39 years.

The first colored jury impanneled in Tenn., at Nashville.

Aug. 11.—Thaddeus Stevens, M. C. from Penn., died at Washington, aged 75 years.

Gen. Gillem assumed the command of the department of Mississippi.

IOWA—*Continued.*

CLOTHING.

GOLDSCHMIDT & SAWYER, Chicago One Price Clothing House, Clinton st.

DENTIST.

PEARCE, I. D., Dentist,
Clinton st.

GROCERIES AND PROVISIONS.

MAHER, DENNIS, Groceries Provisions & Family Supplies, Dubuque st. near College st.

LAUNDRY.

SAGER, J. A., City Laundry,
Cor. Linn st. & Iowa ave.

MARBLE WORKS.

IOWA CITY MARBLE WORKS.

B. S. HOLMES,
Manufacturer of
FOREIGN & AMERICAN MARBLE,
Clinton st., opposite Court House,
IOWA CITY, IOWA.

MILLER, J. U., Manf'r of all kinds of Marble Work, College st. near Dubuque st.

PAINTS AND OILS.

MAHANA, R. B. & CO., Paints, Oils, Glass & Wall Paper, Washington st.

PHRENOLOGISTS.

MRS. M. DEUELL,
CLAIRVOYANT and PHRENOLOGIST,
BURLINGTON STREET,
One door East of Clinton st., near Phinney House.

D. R. S. PRYSE.
Philosophical Phrenologist,
Lecturer and Practical Delineator of Character.
Graduated at the American Phrenological Institute of Fowler & Wells, N. Y., Class 68.
The best of references.
IOWA CITY.

SALOONS AND RESTAURANTS.

BAUMER, J. B., Milwaukee Lager Beer Saloon, Iowa ave., East of P. O.

DEHNER, JOSEPH, Wine & Oyster Parlor,
Washington st.

SEWING MACHINES.

TAYLOR, L. G., Ag't. for Singer Sewing Machines & Wood's Organs, Clinton st. opp. University.

STOVES AND TINWARE.

Established 1867.
WM. LOUIS & BRO.,
Dealers in
STOVES, TINWARE,
And all kinds of Pumps,
DUBUQUE STREET, NEAR AVENUE.

IOWA CITY—Continued.

VINEGAR.

HAM, D., Sells Pure Cider Vinegar and buys Country Produce, Dubuque st.

WATCHES AND JEWELRY.

STICKLER, VAL., Watchmaker & Jeweler, Clinton st., opposite University.

YPSILANTI, MICH.

CARRIAGES AND SPRINGS.

BEACH CARRIAGE MANUFACTURING CO.,
Owners and exclusive manufacturers of the
Beach Patent Shifting Seat Carriage Bodies,
Also Phæton, Yacht, Piano and Hearse Bodies of all kinds, and Shifting Seat, Swell Body, Portland and Square-box Sleighs, Wood-work unfinished to Carriage Makers. Send for price list.
S. M. CUTCHEON, President.   H. BATCHELDER, Secretary.

CURTIS, H. M. & CO., Mant's of End and Side Bar Springs for Phætons and Carriages.

DRUGGIST.

Wm. Grossman,

CHEMIST & PHARMACIST,
Drugs, Medicines, Fine Chemicals, Fancy and Toilet Articles.

DEPOT DRUG STORE.
CROSS STREET.

HAIR WORK.

HAIR WORK MANUFACTURED AND FOR SALE by Jane Harris and Norah Cary, Post Block

PHOTOGRAPHER.

PARSONS, MRS. J. H., Photographer, Post Block. Business and Furniture for sale.

TAILORING AND CLEANING.
E. ELLIOTT,
CLOTHES MADE, CLEANED AND REPAIRED,
Huron st. opposite Freeman's Hall.
Established 1876.

WINE AND BILLIARD SALOON.

STERNBERG, DAVID, Billiards & Wine, Beer & Liquor Palace, Congress st.

LAFAYETTE, IND.

ATTORNEYS AT LAW.

DE HART, R. P., Attorney at Law, Lafayette, Ind.

JONES & MILLER, Attorneys at Law, 64½ Main st.

1868.

Aug. 13.—Terrible earthquake in South America. A large number of towns in Ecuador and Peru entirely destroyed. Great damage done to the buildings in Quito. The loss of life estimated at 30,000.
The U. S. ship Fredonia, at Arica, Peru, was dashed to pieces and her crew lost. The man-of-war Wataree was carried half a mile inland by a tidal wave.

Sept. 9.—Chinese Embassy sail for Europe.

Sept. 18.—Gen. Hindman assassinated at Helena, Arkansas.
Death of Seba Smith, author of "Major Jack Downing's Letters," aged 76.

Oct. 7.—Death of Gen. Adam J. Slemmer, at Fort Laramine.
Randolph, a negro preacher and a member of the South Carolina Senate, assassinated at Cokesville.
James Hind, member of Congress from Arkansas assassinated.

Nov. 3.—Iowa and Minnesota vote in favor of negro suffrage, and Missouri against it.

Nov. 23.—Gen. Howard issued an order for the discontinuance of the Freedmen's Bureau after January 1st, except the educational department and the collection of money due to soldiers.

Dec. 25.—President Johnson issued a universal amnesty proclamation.

Dec. 29.—Mosby Clark, a revolutionary soldier, died at Richmond, Va., at the advanced age of 121 years.

Dec. 31.—Gen. Sheridan captured the Indian chiefs, Santanta and Lone Wolf.
The U. S. House of Representatives passed a resolution relative to amendments to the naturalization laws by a vote of 125 to 32; the bill regulating the duties on imported copper and copper ores by a vote of 105 to 51; also a bill providing for the transfer of the Indian Bureau from the Department of the Interior to the War department, by 116 to 33.
The House passed the bill repealing an act prohibiting the organization of militia in all the reconstructed States except Georgia; also a resolution allowing women in the government employ the wages of men for the same work
The Senate denounced the views of President Johnson on the national debt; also passed a resolution disapproving the President's financial recommendations.
The Secretary of the Navy accepted the transfer of League Island by the city of Philadelphia to the Government for a navy yard.

1869.

Jan. 1.—General Grant holds a public reception in Independence Hall, Philadelphia.

Feb. 20.—Martial law declared in Tennessee.

Feb. 22-26.—Congress passes Fifteenth Amendment. Kansas is the first State (Feb. 27), to ratify it, though imperfectly, and Delaware the first to reject it.

March 25.—Pennsylvania ratifies Fifteenth Amendment.

LAFAYETTE—Continued.

ATTORNEYS AT LAW.

Oscar D. Kirk,
Attorney at Law,
Collections a specialty.   7 N. Third St.

BAKERY AND CONFECTIONERY.

K AHL, JOHN, (Established 1872.) Bakery and Confectionery, 69 Ninth st.

J. B. Ruger.   Geo. Rogers.

Ruger & Rogers,
(Established 1861.)
MANUFACTURING
CONFECTIONERS & BAKERS,
Jobbers of Canned Goods, Fruits, Spices, Cheese, Nuts, &c.
13 North 5th & 90 Main St.

BARBERS.

ALDRICH, H. A., (Established 1877.) Barber, No. 71 N. 9th st.

LORCHER, JOHN, Bath House and Hair Dressing Rooms, 83 Columbia st.

TOOTLE, GENERAL, Shaving and Hair Dressing Saloon, No. 16 S. 5th st.

BLACKSMITHS AND HORSE SHOERS.

BAUGHER & WEGNER,
Plough and Wagon Manufacturers,

General Blacksmiths
AND HORSE SHOEING.
No. 14 S. SECOND ST.

J. W. Fullenlove,
Practical Horse Shoer.

SPECIAL ATTENTION GIVEN
TO DISEASED FEET.
Established 1862.   No. 31 SOUTH ST.

ODEL & THIES, (Established 1877.) General Blacksmithing and Horse Shoeing, 8 S. 8th st.

RANK, G. W., General Blacksmithing and Horse Shoeing, 20 S. 2nd st. Established 1851.

BOOTS AND SHOES.

Wm. W. Comstock & Co.
Manufacturers and Wholesale Dealers in
Boots & Shoes,
LAFAYETTE, IND.

NOYES, F. H., Manufacturer and Dealer in Boots and Shoes, 134 Main st.

LAFAYETTE—Continued.

BUSINESS COLLEGE.

Star City Business College
AND
TELEGRAPH INSTITUTE.
P. W. Kennedy, Principal,
BALL'S BLOCK, COLUMBIA ST.

DENTISTS.

FAHNESTOCK, J. W., Dentist, Cor. 5th & Main sts.

McCORMACK, E. A., Dentist, 92½ Columbia st.

DRESS AND CLOAK MAKING.

HASKETT, MRS. M., Dressmaker, 120½ Columbia st.

PLATT, MRS. M., Dressmaker, 68 N. 4th st.

WEITZEL, MRS. J., Dress and Cloak Making, 63 N. 6th st.

DRUGGISTS.

McCLURE & BROUILLETTE, Druggists, 81 Columbia st.

B. H. BOYD, M. D.,
DRUGGIST
AND MANUFACTURING CHEMIST,
PROPRIETOR OF
Boyd's Chloroform Elixir,
Boyd's Ague Remedy, Boyd's Cough Syrup,
AND THE
Mexican Mustang Condition Powder
68 MAIN ST., OPPOSITE ARTESIAN WELL.

DRY GOODS.

GERNON, G. D., Staple and Fancy Dry Goods, Notions, &c., 86 Columbia st.

FLORISTS.

JAS. CHAMBERS & CO.
FLORISTS,
Greenhouse, cor. 6th & North Sts.
Bouquets, Cut Flowers, Floral Baskets, and Wire Designs for Cut Flowers in every Variety, Greenhouse and Bedding Plants at all times. Fine Commercial Work, Wedding and Ball invitations, in the execution of which we are unequaled. No business transacted on the Sabbath, except for funeral occasions.

GROCERS.

NELSON, O., & CO., Family Groceries and Provisions, 109 Columbia st.

State Capitol, Harrisburg, Pa.—On the 31st of May, 1819, the corner-stone of the Capitol was laid by Governor Findlay. The building was completed in 1821, and first occupied by the General Assembly on the 3d of January, 1822.

1869.

April 13.—Senate rejects Alabama treaty with Great Britain.

May 13.—Woman Suffrage Convention in New York city.

May 19.—President Grant proclaims that there shall be no reduction in Government laborers' wages because of reduction of hours.

June 18.—Hon. Henry J. Raymond, of N. Y. Times, dies.

July 13.—Completion of Atlantic cable from Brest to St. Pierre; thence to Duxbury, Massachusetts.

Aug. 16.—National Labor Convention, Philadelphia.

Sept. 1.—National Temperance Convention, Chicago.

Sept. 8.—Hon. William Pitt Fessenden, dies.

Sept. 10.—Hon. John Bell dies.

Sept. 16.—Hon. John Minor Botts dies.

Sept. 24.—Black Friday.

Oct. 8.—Virginia ratifies Fourteenth and Fifteenth Amendments.

Ex-President Franklin Pierce dies.

Nov. 4.—George Peabody dies.

Nov. 6.—Admiral Charles Stewart dies.

Nov. 24.—National Woman-suffrage Convention, Cleveland, Ohio, and Henry Ward Beecher chosen President.

Dec. 10.—National Colored Labor Convention, Washington.

Dec. 24.—Hon. Edwin M. Stanton dies.

1870.

Jan. 21.—Prince Arthur, third son of Queen Victoria, arrived in New York. Three days later he was introduced to President Grant by the British Minister, and was honored with a grand ball in the Masonic Temple in Washington.

Jan. 26.—Virginia readmitted into the Union.

Feb. 9.—U. S. Signal Bureau established by Act of Congress.

Feb. 17.—Mississippi re-admitted into the Union.

Feb. 23.—Hon. Anson Burlingame dies.

March 28.—Major-General George H. Thomas dies.

March 29.—Texas re-admitted to representation in Congress, thus completing the work of reconstruction.

March 30.—President Grant announces the adoption of the Fifteenth Amendment.

July 12.—Admiral John A. Dahlgren dies.

Aug. 14.—Admiral David G. Farragut dies.

Aug. 15.—National Labor Congress, Cincinnati.

Aug. 22.—President Grant issues a proclamation enjoining neutrality as to war between France and Prussia.

Aug. 23.—Irish National Congress convenes, Cincinnati.

Oct. 4.—Second Southern Commercial Convention, Cincinnati.

LAFAYETTE—*Continued.*

GROCERS.

C. PAIGE & CO.,
(Established 1866,)

Groceries, Flour and Feed,
Cor. 9th & Cincinnati Sts.

R ONAN, JOHN, Groceries, Provisions, Flour, Wines and Liquors, 188 N. 6th st.

Wm. Schilling. John B. Ruger.

WM. SCHILLING & CO.
Commission Merchants
AND
GROCERS,
122 MAIN ST. Fruits. Produce. Game. &c.

HARDWARE.

B ENNEWITZ, C. & BRO., Hardware, Stoves and Tinware, 177 Main st.

E. W. Straubinger & Co.
(Successors to HEATH & CO.)
WHOLESALE
HARDWARE
132 Main & 9 N. 6th St.

HOTELS.

G ERMANIA HOTEL, South and 2nd sts. Rates, $1.50 per day. J. P. Welschbillig, Prop.

St. Nicholas Hotel
LaFayette, Indiana.
NICHOLAS GRIBLING,   TOM B. SEELY
Proprietor.   CRIS GRIBLING
  Clerks.

LIVERY AND FEED STABLES.

B AIRD, JAMES W., (Established 1865,) Exchange, Livery and Boarding Stable, So. & 3d.

T AYLOR, S. O., (Established 1861,) Livery, Feed and Sale Stable, 63 & 65 S. 3rd st.

LOOKING GLASS AND FRAMES.

G RIEVE, HENRY, Manufacturer of Picture Frames and Looking Glasses, 46 Main st.

MEAT MARKETS.

B ONNER, GUST. & WM., Dealer in Fresh and Salt Meats, 207 Main st.

M UELLER, DANIEL, (Established 1865,) Union Meat Market, 67 N. 9th st.

LAFAYETTE—Continued.

MILLINERY AND DRESSMAKING.

Miss Nellie M. Bohan,

Fashionable Millinery and Dressmaking

115 Columbia St.

Miss F. M. Carson,

Millinery & Dressmaking

No. 11 North 5th St.

JORDAN & ELDRIDGE, Millinery and Fancy Goods, No. 9 North 5th st.

NEWSPAPERS.

DAILY AND WEEKLY DISPATCH, J. C. Dobelbower, Editor and Proprietor, 5th & Main sts

SUNDAY LEADER, F. E. D. McGinley & Son, Proprietors, 5th & Main sts.

PAINTERS.

Chas. A. Davis,
(Established 1872.)

House & Sign Painter

80 Ferry Street.
Graining, Paper Hanging and Decorating neatly executed at reasonable rates.

PHOTOGRAPHERS.

WRIGHT, C. C., Photographer, 90½ Main st.

PRINTERS AND STATIONERS.

SPRING & ROBERTSON, (Established 1843,) Wholesale and Retail Printers and Stationers.

PHYSICIANS.

BURKE, DR. A., Eye, Ear and Throat Dispensatory, 161 Main st.

YOUNT, DR. S. T., Physician, No. 93 Main street.

SALOONS.

BRILLIANT SALOON, Wm. Fitzgerald, Proprietor, 103 Columbia st.

John Leuther,

Wine & Beer Saloon,

193 E. Main Street.

SCHAIBLE, GEORGE, Wine, Beer and Billiard Hall, 87 Columbia st.

1870.

Oct. 12.—Death of General Robert E. Lee.

Oct. 25.—Convention in Cincinnati for the purpose of removing the National Capital from Washington to some point west.

1871.

Jan. 1.—Cabral, the Dominican Chief, denounced President Grant as the "gratuitious enemy" of Dominican liberty, and called upon all Dominicans to oppose the sale and annexation of the island to the United States.

Jan. 6.—Immense meetings of Catholics to protest against Italian occupation of Rome, held in Boston, and Cleveland, Ohio.

Jan. 20.—Motion to strike out the word "male" in the section of the Fourteenth Amendment giving the elective franchise to all male citizens; defeated in the House of Representatives; vote, 55 to 117.

O'Denovan Rossa and other Fenian exiles arrived in New York.

Jan. 25.—Miss Vinnie Ream's statue of President Lincoln unveiled in the Rotunda of the Capitol at Washington.

Jan. 26.—The income tax repealed.

Jan. 28.—Eighty persons killed by the explosion of the steamboat, W. R. Authur, near Memphis, Tenn.

Feb. 1.—House of Representatives abolishes the test oath.

A destructive fire in Virginia City, Nevada; two men burned to death.

Feb. 3.—The Kensington National Bank of Philadelphia robbed of $100,000 by thieves disguised as policemen.

Feb. 4.—The Adelphia Theatre in Boston burned.

Feb. 5.—The Catholics of Brooklyn in their churches denounced Italian occupation of Rome.

Feb. 18.—The town of Halena, Arkansas, almost destroyed by a tornado.

General Cabral, in a letter to Vice-President Colfax, denounces the union of Dominica and Hayti

Feb. 22.—Arrival in New York of the British members of the Joint High Commission.

Feb. 23.—A large meeting to congratulate Italy on the completion of her unity held in Boston.

Capt. E. S. Jenkins, Deputy Revenue Collector and U. S. Deputy Marshall, assassinated at New Madrid, Mo.

March 3.—The Pennsylvania coal Riots; Mr. Hoffman killed and his house blown up by miners, at Mt. Carmel, Pa.

March 5.—Riot by Chinamen in San Francisco.

March 6.—Judge Bramlette shot in court by a negro named Tyler, at Meridian, Miss. A riot occurred in the courtroom, during which two negroes were killed. Tyler having escaped from custody, was pursued and killed by the sheriff and posse. The sheriff and his men, while executing an order to disarm the negroes of the town, rere resisted, resulting in the shooting of several of the negroes.

March 9.—Fight between whites and

H. W. ROKKER,
Printer, Binder, Stereotyper,
BOOK PUBLISHER,
—AND—
Blank-Book Manufacturer.

Writing and Copying Inks---all Colors,
MY OWN MANUFACTURE.

Express Companies are adopting our Inks in their principal offices.

No. 309 South Fifth Street, SPRINGFIELD, ILLS.

ILLINOIS STATE GAZETTE.
D. W. LUSK,
State Printer and Binder.

Book and Job Printing, Ruling and Binding, Blank-Books of all kinds made to order.

618 Washington St., Springfield, Ill.

T. P. NISBETT & CO.,
WHOLESALE AND RETAIL GROCERS,
AND DEALERS IN

Fine Teas, Coffees, Sugars, Best Brands of Family Flour, Canned Goods, &c.

SECOND ST., opp. CITY HALL,
ALTON, ILLS.

STATE CAPITOL, SPRINGFIELD, ILL.

1871.

negro militia near Chester, S. C.; a number of negroes were killed, and the remainder were driven for refuge into a Federal camp.

An illicit distiller named Zacharius Young shot by U. S. Deputy Marshall Looper, near Pickens Court House, S. C, Looper received a shot in return, from the effects of which he also died.

March 24.—President Grant, by proclamation; ordered certain bands of armed men in South Carolina to disperse within twenty days.

March 30.—Grand parade of the colored people in New York to commemorate the proclamation of the Fifteenth Amendment.

April 1.—The Troy Opera House, and the P. E. Church of the Messiah, Greene and Claremont avenues, Brooklyn, destroyed by fire.

April 7.—The coal riots occur at Scranton, Pa.; the rioters destroy the facilities for working several mines, and attack the miners employed in them. Governor Geary called out the military.

A fire in Albany destroyed the large printing establishment of Weed, Parsons & Co.; loss about $500,000.

April 10.—Grand celebration for German unity and the return of peace in New York. Wm. Marby stoned to death by rioters at Tivoli, Duchess county, N. Y.

April 19.—Kleon Rangabe, Greek Minister at Washington, married in New York City to Miss De Gerolt, daughter of the Prussian Minister at Washington.

April 26.—The United States Supreme Court decides that the general Government can not tax the salaries of State officials.

April 29.—Sharon Tyndale, Ex-Secretary of the State of Illinois, murdered in Springfield, Ill.

April 30.—The Apache tribe of Indians in Arizona attacked; 120 braves, squaws, and children massacred.

The Ku-Klux-Klan destroy a newspaper office in Rutherfordton, N. C., and brutally maltreat Mr. Justice, a prominent Radical.

June 12.—Fearful storm in Galveston, Texas; houses prostrated and vessels blown ashore or to sea and others sunk.

June 13.—A hurricane devasted the coast of Labrador, some of the settlements totally destroyed, and the vessels in the harbor blown ashore and wrecked; 300 lives lost.

June 16.—Catholic celebration on the completion of the twenty-fifth year of the Pontificate of Pius IX.

June 17.—The ratification of the treaty of Washington exchanged in London.

June 19.—An earthquake shock felt in New York and vicinity.

June 24.—Corner stone of the Capitol laid in Albany.

July 1.—Bust of Washington Irving unveiled in Prospect Park, Brooklyn.

July 4.—President Grant proclaims the complete ratification of the Treaty of Washington.

July 10. Supt. Kelso issued an order forbidding a proposed parade of Orange societies in New York on the 12th July.

LAFAYETTE—*Continued.*

SALOONS.

Mason House

GEORGE BOLICH, Prop.

SALOON & RESTAURANT,

Nos. 165 & 167 E. Main St.

SEWING MACHINES.

THE HOWE MACHINE CO. H. C. Brunson, Agent, 117 Main st.

THE SINGER MANUFACTURING CO. Wm. B. King, Manager, cor. 5th & Columbia sts.

SODDER OF YARDS.

HEALEY, JAMES, Yards Laid with Grass Sods, 14 Oakland Hill.

TAILORS.

KIRCHHOF, FRANK, Gents' Outfitter, 130 Main st.

WINDER, J. A., Merchant Tailor, Cleaning and Repairing, 93 Columbia.

TOBACCO AND CIGARS.

FLUCK, J. D., (Established 1877,) Cigar Manufacturer, 9th & Brown sts.

UNDERTAKER.

SCUDDER, C. R., Undertaker, 110 Main st.

WATCHES AND JEWELRY.

C. H. Ankeny & Co.

DIAMONDS,

Watches, Clocks, Jewelry and Silverware,

East Side of Public Square.

Special attention given to the Repairing and Regulating of Fine Watches.

E. M. CARR,

Practical Watchmaker,

No. 206 E. Main St.

WINES AND LIQUORS.

AYLWARD, THOS., Foreign and Domestic Liquors, No. 11 Purdue's Block, 2nd st.

GAGEN, T. F., & BRO., Straight Kentucky Sour Mash Whiskies, 39 S. 2nd st.

LOGANSPORT, IND.

BARBERS.

J. H. LINDSEY,
Shaving and Hairdressing
SALOON,
Market St., near Burnett House.

BLACKSMITHS.

KISER & CRAIN,
Blacksmithing and General Job Shop,
TABERTOWN.

BOARDING.

TRAIN, MRS. G. W., First-Class Boarding at reasonable rates, Second and Railroad sts.

BOOTS AND SHOES.

BOSTON BOOT AND SHOE STORE, 42 Fourth st., J. Kauffman, manager.

MERRITT, T. C. & CO., Manufacturers of Boots and Shoes, 75 Sixth st.

CARRIAGE AND WAGON MAKERS.

BOERGER, FREDRICK, Wagon Maker, Tabertown. Established 1857.

ESMUS, ENGLISH & TRUMAN,
Carriage & Wagon Manufacturers,
SIXTH STREET,
Opp. Forest Mills.

ESTABLISHED 1867.

Grusenmeyer & Barrett,
CARRIAGE & WAGON MANUFACTURING
And General Repair Shop,
TABERTOWN. Established 1862.

C. F. HAMAKER,
Manufacturer of
Wagons, Carriages
And Light Vehicles of every description.
☞ Carriage Repairing a Specialty.
THREE DOORS EAST OF MARKET ST. ON EEL ST.

W. M. KREIDER & SON,
CARRIAGE AND WAGON
MANUFACTURERS,
Cor. SIXTH & RACE STS.
Established 1849.

1871.

Mrs. E. G. Wharton arrested in Baltimore, charged with having poisoned her husband, Col. H. W. Wharton, her son and daughter, and Gen. Wm. Scott Ketchum.

July 11.—Gov. Hoffman issues a proclamation giving permission and protection to all persons desiring to peacefully parade on the 12th July. Supt. Kelso revokes his order of the 10th inst.

July 12.—Orangemen riot. On the occasion of a procession of Protestant Orangemen in New York, they were maliciously attacked by the Roman Catholic Irish. Threats of assault having been given, the Orangemen were protected by the military. Stones, pistols, and guns being discharged at the militia, several were killed and wounded, when an order was given to the soldiers to fire on the rioters. Five soldiers and about a hundred rioters were killed.

July 13.—Mrs. Lovel killed by lightning while praying at the bedside of her children, near St. Joseph, Mo.

July 19.—The crew of the Atlanta Club of New York beat the Harvard University crew in a race on the Connecticut river, at Holyoke, Mass.

July 22.—A powder magazine at the Arsenal in Washington, D. C., explodes, and destroys much property.

July 25.—Thieves gag a driver of a wagon of the U. S. Express Company, and rob him of $90,000 in money and bonds in St. Louis, Mo.

July 30.—The Westfield horror. The steamer's boiler explodes; 40 persons killed outright, and 63 injured—subsequently died.

Aug. 15.—Religious riot in Ogdensburg, N. Y.; a lecturer against Catholicity assaulted and his hearers dispersed by the rioters.

Aug. 20.—Forty buildings burned in Williamsport, Pa., loss, $225,000.

Aug. 21.—Dr. Helmbold attempts to commit suicide at Long Branch, N. J.

Aug. 27.—A piratical band of Mexicans attacks the American bark Brothers off Santa Anna. After some fighting, Capt. Thurston and crew abandon the vessel. The crew were subsequently picked up by the bark Harvest Home, which had also been attacked, but unsuccessfully, by the same band of pirates.
Political riots in La Messilla, New Mexico, 7 men killed and 30 injured.

Sept. 1.—International scull race at Halifax, N. S.; J. H. Sadler, of England, the victor.

Sept. 6.—The mare Goldsmith Maid trots a mile in 2 minutes and 17 seconds at Milwaukee, Wis.

Sept. 9.—Great fire in Bloomington, Ill.; loss $300,000.
Major L. Hodge, Assistant Paymaster-General of the United States army, declares himself a defaulter of the government in $500,000.

Sept. 13.—Great demonstrations in New York of workingmen in favor of the eight hour labor system.

Sept. 14.—A fire destroys the Park Place and Columbia Hotels, and other buildings at Saratoga; loss, $200,00.

Sept. 16.—Pioche, Nevada, burned; loss,

ADVERTISEMENTS.

LOGANSPORT—*Continued.*

CARRIAGE AND WAGON MANUFACTURERS.

HENRY HARTMAN,
WAGONMAKER, TIBERTOWN
Established 1865.

DENTISTS.

BUDD, J. W., Dentist,
85 Broadway.

DEHART, WILL. M., Dentist,
47 Fourth st.

MASLONE, H. T., Dentist,
44 Fourth st.

DETECTIVE AND COLLECTING AGENCY.

GALLAGHER & FLANAGAN,
DETECTIVES,
AND COLLECTING AGENCY.
Office, cor. Fourth & Broadway
(McTaggart's Block).
All Business Strictly Confidential.

DRESSMAKERS.

BEACH, MRS. KATIE C., Dressmaker,
61 Broadway.

GRAHAM, MRS. & SISTER, Dressmaking, 43 Fourth st.

HURNES, MRS. M. M., Dressmaking,
42 Fourth st.

DRUGGIST.

Druggist and Pharmaceutist.
L. W. REDD,
51 Market St., near Bridge,
Fine Drugs, Chemicals, Toilet Articles, Perfumery, etc.
Prescriptions carefully compounded. Night Calls promptly answered.

DRY GOODS.

KERN BROS. & CO., Staple and Fancy Dry Goods, 70 Broadway.

FLOUR AND FEED.

CRONISE, C. T., Grain, Flour, Feed and Produce, 53 Sixth st. Established 1873.

GROCERIES AND PROVISIONS.

KRATLI, J. G. & CO., Groceries and Provisions, 58 Sixth st. Established 1873.

HARNESS AND SADDLES.

HENRY TUCKER,
Manufacturer and Dealer in
Harness, Saddles, Collars,
BRIDLES, WHIPS, ROBES,
Blankets, Brushes, Fly Nets, Etc.,
88 MARKET ST.
Repairing promptly attended to.

LOGANSPORT—*Continued.*

HAIR DEALER.

TURNER, MRS. KATE, all kinds of Hair Work done to order. Broadway.

INSURANCE.

SAMUEL M'GUIRE,
LIFE AND FIRE INSURANCE AND LOAN AGENT,
Fourth st., opp. Court House.

LAUNDRIES.

LOGANSPORT CUSTOM LAUNDRY, Geo. W. Crump, prop., Barnett House.

THOMAS, LUCY, Laundry, near cor. Sixth and North sts.

LIVERY AND SALE STABLE.

N. E. BOIES,
FEED & SALE STABLE,
—ALSO—
Veterinary Surgeon,
40 SIXTH ST. Established 1847.

MACHINIST.

LOGANSPORT BOILER AND MACHINE WORKS. A. U. McAllester, prop., at Lock Foundry Works.

MESSINGER, PROSEUS & CO., Manfrs of Stone Cylinder Pump, Elm & Durest sts. Est. '62.

TUCKER & HOWE,
GENERAL MACHINISTS
And Manufacturers of
Plow, Carriage and Wagon Wood Work,
LOGANSPORT, IND. (Est. 1867.)

MEAT MARKET.

THOS. BECKER,
BUTCHER SHOP
All kinds of Meat kept on hand.

MARKET STREET.

MILLINERY.

MRS. S. A DILLIE & SISTER,
MILLINERY,
42 Fourth st.

JOLLEY, MRS. H. C., Millinery and Dressmaking, 87 Broadway.

M'MAHON, J. F., MILLINERY AND DRESSMAKING,
SHROUDS, HABITS AND BURIAL ROBES OF ALL KINDS.
Corner Fourth and Broadway.

Connecticut State Building, Centennial Exposition, Phila.— Is of the Dutch Colonial style; 30 feet front by 40 feet deep, with a wing 10 feet by 20. The lower part of the outside of the building is constructed of scollop-fashioned shingles, and the upper part is lathed and plastered. A massive stone chimney protrudes from the roof, and the front is relieved by an old-fashioned porch.

Swedish School House, Centennial Exposition, Philadelphia. This building was erected by the government of Sweden. It is composed entirely of wood, either polished or oiled, and was brought from Sweden prepared to be put together upon the grounds. The most singular part of it is that is impossible, on the exterior, to discover a nail or screw. The boards are beveled and so joined together that no seams are visible. It is intended to keep school there during the summer; genuine Swedish youths of both sexes, with teachers, will be brought over for that purpose.

IMPORTANT EVENTS OF THE CENTURY.

1871.

$300,000; during the fire gunpowder explodes and kills six persons.

Sept. 19.—Fire in Virginia City, Nevada; loss, $75,000.

Sept. 21.—A statue of President Lincoln unveiled in Fairmount Park, Philadelphia.

Sept. 24.—Fire in San Francisco; $100,000 worth of property destroyed.

Sept. 27.—Chief Justice McKean, of Utah, decides against Mormons serving as grand jurors in Federal courts.

Gen. Joseph H. Clanton shot and killed by Col. D. M. Nelson, in Knoxville, Tenn.

Sept. 30.—Professor Wilbur unexpectedly descends from his balloon and is instantly killed, at Paoli, Indiana.

Oct. 2.—Brigham Young arrested by the United States Marshal for Mormon proclivities.

Oct. 3.—Daniel H. Wells, Mayor of Salt Lake City, and a Mormon bishop, arrested by the United States Marshal for Mormon proclivities.

Oct. 5.—A special conference of the Mormon Church held in the New Tabernacle in Salt Lake City; the Federal authorities denounced as "tools of the devil."

Oct. 7.—The first of the great fires in Chicago breaks out; loss, $300,000. General O'Neill's filibusters seize the Canadian Custom House and Hudson Bay Post at Pembina, Manitoba; they are thereupon attacked by the United States troops, and General O'Neill and his men made prisoners.

Oct. 8.—The great fire by which Chicago was desolated breaks out at 10 o'clock at night; loss, $190,526,000.

The great forest fires; Peshtigo, Wisconsin, destroyed by fire, 600 of its inhabitants perish; Manistee, Williamsonville, Menekaunee, Marinette, and Brussels, Wis., burned; a number of inhabitants perish.

Oct. 9.—The great Chicago fire continues to rage and destroy.

Oct. 10.—An election riot between negro and white roughs in Philadelphia, four men killed and many wounded; attempt to destroy the *Press* newspaper office by the roughs frustrated.

Oct. 12.—President Grant summons the Ku-Klux-Klan of South Carolina to disband and deliver up their arms and ammunition.

Oct. 17.—President Grant suspends the writ of *habeas corpus* in nine counties of South Carolina.

Oct. 24.—Riot in Los Angeles, Cal., a mob attacks the Chinese quarter, and captures and hangs eighteen Chinamen.

Oct. 26.—A warrant is issued for the arrest of Wm. M. Tweed, Jas. H. Ingersoll, A. J. Garvey, and E. A. Woodward, at the suit of Attorney-General Chamberlain.

Oct. 27.—Wm. M. Tweed arrested and bailed.

Oct. 28.—Mayor D. H. Wells, ex-Attorney-General Hoza Stout, and Wm. H. Kimball arrested on a charge of murder in Salt Lake City.

Nov. 2.—City Treasurer, James T. Marcer, and C. T. Yerkes, banker, of Philadelphia,

LOGANSPORT—*Continued.*

MILLINERY.

MISS A. WEASA,

Millinery,

MARKET STREET.

Logansport, - - Ind.

MUSICAL INSTRUMENTS.

BRIDGE & STANTON, dealers in all kinds of Musical Instruments, 87 Broadway.

NEWSPAPERS.

EVENING NEWS, Z. Hunt, Editor & Proprietor.

PRATT & CO., Publishers of Daily and Weekly Journal.

PHYSICIANS.

HALL, PROF. R. R.—M. & Ph'd—Chronic Diseases a Specialty, cor. 6th & North sts.

POWELL, J. Z., M. D., office and residence, 71 Sixth street.

REAL ESTATE.

G. W. DOWELL,
Office, 78 Broadway.

Real Estate, Collection,
INSURANCE AND RENTAL AGENCY.
Southern and Western Lands for Sale or Trade.
COLLECTIONS A SPECIALTY.

M'NARY & LEEDY,
Attorneys-at-Law.

Real Estate & Insurance Ag'ts
70 Broadway.
COLLECTIONS A SPECIALTY.

TOBACCO AND CIGARS.

SEBASTIAN BROS., Manf's of Havana, Yara and Connecticut Cigars, 57 Fourth st.

WATCHES, CLOCKS AND JEWELRY.

CHURCH, C. H., Dealer in Fine Watches, Jewelry, Silver-ware, Clocks, etc., 98 Broadway. Practical Watchmaker, Jeweler and Engraver. All work warranted. Particular attention paid to repairing Fine Watches.

C. E. GRIDLEY,
PRACTICAL WATCH-MAKER,
And dealer in
Watches, Clocks and Jewelry.
☞ Repairing promptly attended to. ☜
51 MARKET ST.

IMPORTANT EVENTS OF A CENTURY. 217

LOGANSPORT—*Continued.*

WOOLEN MILLS.

FOREST MILLS, Established 1834, Czil & Wilson Proprietors, Race and 6th st.

NASH & LaROSE, Established, 1862, Woolen Mills, Tabertown.

KALAMAZOO, MICH.

ART SCHOOL.

Established 1870.

Kalamazoo Art School,

117 MAIN STREET.

Branches taught: Portrait, Landscape and India Ink. Portraits finished, any size, in Oil or India Ink, and satisfaction guaranteed. GEO. W. REED, Artist.

ARCHITECT.

LAKEY, A. L., Architect,
83 Water st.

ATTORNEYS AT LAW.

BEESE & STEARNS, Attorneys & Counselors at Law, 100 Main st.

BRIGGS & BURROWS, Law Office,
152 Main st. Established 1860.

BURKE, LAWRENCE N., Attorney & Counselor at Law, 114 Main st.

DAVIS, JAMES M., Attorney at Law & Circuit Court Commissioner, 21 N. Burdick st.

MASON H. GERMAIN,
ATTORNEY, SOLICITOR,
AND COUNSELOR,
148 Main Street. Corner Rose.

JUDSON, R. F., Attorney at Law,
21 N. Burdick st.

HAMPDEN KELSEY,
Established 1871.

ATTORNEY AT LAW,
Kalamazoo, Mich.
Over First National Bank.

MAY, POWERS & DANIELS, Attorneys and Counselors at Law, 140 Main st.

SEVERENS, BOUDEMAN & TURNER, Attorneys at Law, 160 Main st.

SWAN, W. L., Attorney at Law
21 N. Burdick st.

TRUMBULL, T. D., Attorney at Law,
122 Main st.

BOOTS AND SHOES.

ISBELL, HENRY, Fine Boots & Shoes,
83 Main st. Established 1861.

1871.

arrested for defalcation and embezzlement of $478,000 from the city's funds.

Nov. 5.—In the African Baptist Meeting-house, in Louisville, Ky., the flooring gives way, and eleven women and children are trampled to death in the panic that follows.

Nov. 7.—Apache Indians attack a stage near Wickenburg, Arizona, and kill six of its passengers, one of whom was F. W. Loring, the author.

Nov. 12.—An incendiary fire destroys a block and a half of buildings in Chattanooga, Tenn.

Nov. 17.—Fire in Kit Carson, Nevada, loss $100,000.

Nov. 18.—Russian frigate Svetlana, with the Grand Duke on board, arrived off Sandy Hook late at night.

Nov. 19.—Grand Duke Alexis, son of the Czar of Russia, arrived in New York. His reception was of a dual character, first as an officer of the Russian navy, and then as the son of an imperial father. He was treated to an exciting buffalo hunt by Gen. Sheridan.

Nov. 21.—Grand civil and military reception of the Grand Duke Alexis, of Russia, in New York.

Nov. 22.—The Grand Duke Alexis arrives in Washington. Steamboat City of New London burned on the river Thames, near Norwich, Ct., seventeen lives lost.

Nov. 23.—Grand Duke Alexis formally received by President Grant.

Nov. 26.—Two young ruffians named Joseph Forbish and William Chenoweth, outraged and murdered a child four years old at Mulberry Creek, Ark. They were arrested, and having attempted to escape while being taken to jail, were both shot dead by their captors.

Nov. 30.—Prize fight between Jim Mace and Joe Coburn, near New Orleans; twelve rounds, occupying almost four hours, were fought without a decisive result.

Dec. 3.—Seventeen immigrants frozen to death in Saline county, Nebraska.

Dec. 6.—Great fire in Hagerstown, Md.; the court house and other buildings burned. Loss, $83,000.

Dec. 11.—Grand Duke Alexis gives $5,000 to the poor of New York city.

Dec. 14.—The American steamer Florida sails from St. Thomas, and is followed and overhauled by the Spanish man-of-war Vasco de Nunez; but her papers being found correct, she was allowed to proceed on her voyage.

Dec. 15.—A band of negroes took possession of Lake City, Ark., and shot three residents whom they charged with murdering a negro lawyer. Wm. M. Tweed arrested on a charge of felony, but confined in the Metropolitan Hotel.

Dec. 18.—The Fourth National Bank of Philadelphia thrown out of the Clearing House, and placed in the hands of a receiver.

Dec. 21.—President Grant issues proclamation abolishing discriminating duties on merchandize imported from Spain.

Dec. 23.—Tom McGehan acquitted of the murder of Thomas S. Myers, at Dayton, Ohio.

Dec. 25.—Outbreak of Ku-Klux at Marshall, Missouri.

KALAMAZOO—*Continued.*

BOOTS AND SHOES.

ISAAC DeBOW,
Established 1874.

Manufacturer of

BOOTS and SHOES,

COR. MAIN & PORTAGE STS.

SPRAGUE, A. P., Fine Boots & Shoes,
79 Main st. Established 1860.

BUSINESS COLLEGE.

PARSONS, W. F., Business College,
Main & Burdick sts.

CARRIAGE MAKERS.

NEWTON & FLYNN,
Established 1874.

Carriage Makers,
25 PORTAGE ST.

SHIELDS, R., Manuf'r of Carriages, Wagons and
Sleighs. Water & Edward sts.

E. G. TIERNEY,

Carriage Maker,

AND

GENERAL BLACKSMITH,

Repairing neatly done.
32 Pitcher St., bet. Main and Water Sts.

CHINA, GLASS AND CROCKERY.

COBB, T. S. & SON, Jobbers & retailers of
Crockery, Glassware, Lamps, &c., 102 Main st.

CONFECTIONER.

PELGRIM, I. C., Manuf'r of Plain & Fancy Confectionery. Established 1873. 71 Main st.

DENTIST.

HOLMES, A. J., Dentist.
116 Main st.

JAMES, DR. R. P., Established 1873. Dentist.
113 Main st.

DRUGGIST.

SORG, ANDREW, Chemist and Druggist, 81 Main
st. Established 1876.

DRY GOODS.

BIGELOW, A. L., Dry Goods and Notions, 8
Union Hall block. Established 1869.

Established 1840.

L. L. CLARK & CO.,
Dealers in

DRY GOODS,

|KALAMAZOO, MICH.

———o———

L. L. Clark.   Chas. S. Clark.   L. M. Lester.

KALAMAZOO—*Continued.*

FURNITURE.

M'KEE, JOHN, Parlor, Chamber and Common
Furniture and Undertakers' Materials, 45
N. Burdick st.

GROCERS.

HICKS, LEWIS, Groceries, Teas, Fruits, etc., 67
Main st. Established 1871.

TROWBRIDGE & CROSBY, Wholesale and Retail Grocers, 104 Main st.

HARDWARE.

DE VISSER, JOHN & CO., Hardware, Tin, Copper and Sheet Iron Ware, 36 S. Burdick st.

HOTELS.

AMERICAN HOTEL,

Opposite G. R. & I. R., and near L. S. & M. S.
R.R. Depots.

FRED HOTOP, Prop.

RATES, $1.50 PER DAY.

BURDICK HOUSE, H. F. Badger, prop., Kalamazoo, Mich.

CITY HOTEL.

Strictly Temperance House.

70 N. BURDICK ST.

Newly Furnished and Fitted Up. Rates,
$1.00 Per Day.

T. B. SMITH, PROP.,

Formerly of the Eureka Hotel.

INTERNATIONAL HOTEL,
De Forest Davis, prop.

INSURANCE.

1860 **E. W. DE YOE,** 1877

Insurance, Real Estate, Conveyance,

Collecting & Loan Agency,

Office over Amer. Express Office, 5 S. Burdick Street.

Representing Ten First-Class Reliable Non-Board Companies.

MACHINIST.

GODFREY J. BREMER,

BRASS FOUNDRY,

PRACTICAL MACHINIST,

MODEL AND TOOL MAKER,

57 North Burdick Street.

MARBLE WORKS.

EXCELSIOR MARBLE WORKS, Johnson &
Peck, prop's, 88 N. Burdick st.

SWEETLAND, HUNN & SMALL, Manf'rs and Importers of Monuments, Tablets and Headstones, 96 N. Burdick st.

IMPORTANT EVENTS OF THE CENTURY. 219

The Home of Washington's Ancestors.—The Manor House, Sulgrave, Northamptonshire, which was held of the Priory of St. Andrew, was surrendered to the Crown upon the dissolution of the Monasteries, and in the 30th of Henry VIII, (1529), it was granted to Lawrence Washington, gent of Northampton. Robert Washington, his son and heir, conjointly with his eldest son Lawrence sold the manor in 1610 to Lawrence Makepeace, gent of the Inner Temple, London. Lawrence Washington, after the sale of his estate, retired to Brington, where he died; and his second son, John Washington, emigrated to America about the middle of the 17th century, and was grandfather of the great American patriot and father of his country, George Washington.—[Extract from Wm. W. Nellan & Co.'s History of Northamptonshire.]

Massachusetts State Building, Centennial Exposition, Phila.
—Built after the style of houses that were common in colonial times. The building is one and a half stories high, with dormer windows, and light fancy verandahs. It is 85 by 70 feet in dimensions. The buiding was sold for $1500 to a gentleman of that State who will remove it to a place near Boston.

1871.

Dec. 27.—J. D. Miner acquitted of a charge of counterfeiting, in the U. S. Circuit Court in New York city.

Dec. 28.—Great fire in Little Rock, Ark.; loss, $100,000.

Dec. 30.—Destructive fire in Monroe, La.; loss, $580,000. A negro named Howard outrages and attempts to murder a little girl near Rochester, N. Y. An intense excitement was created among the people by the horrible crime.

1872.

Jan. 2.—Brigham Young returns to Salt Lake City and surrenders to an indictment for the murder of Richard Yates; bail is refused, and he is ordered into the custody of the law officers.

A mob in Rochester threaten to attack the jail and lynch the negro Howard, charged with an outrage upon a little girl. The military fire upon them, and two men are killed.

Jan. 4.—The negro Howard is convicted in Rochester of the outrage on the little girl named Oehs; sentenced to 20 years' imprisonment.

Jan. 6.—James Fisk, Jr., shot by Edward S. Stokes on the private staircase of the Grand Central Hotel, New York.

Dr. Merryman Cole murdered by an unknown person in his office on Exter street, Baltimore.

Jan. 7.—James Fisk, jr., dies of the wound inflicted by Edward S. Stokes.

Jan. 16.—Fire in Reading, Pa.; loss $250,000.

Jan. 17.—Benjamin Franklin's statute unveiled in Printing-House square, New York.

Jan. 24.—Mrs. E. G. Wharton acquitted of the charge of murdering General Ketchum, in Annapolis, Md.

Jan. 31.—U. S. District Attorney Bates, with the permission of Attorney-General Williams, applies for the release on bail of Mormons charged with murder. Chief Justice McKean refuses to grant the application.

Feb. 10.—The Grand Jury of the Court of General Sessions of New York city present indictments against Mayor A. O. Hall, R. B. Connolly, Wm. M. Tweed, Nathaniel Sands, and others.

Feb. 15.—Ex-Speaker Carter, of the Louisiana Legislature, and Chief of Police Badger, of New Orleans, fight a duel with rifles at Bay St. Louis, Mississippi. Nobody hurt.

Feb. 16.—The Lowery gang of outlaws enter the town of Lumberton, N. C., and rob the sheriff's office and other places.

Feb. 29.—The Japanese Embassy arrives in Washington.

March 2.—Judge Cardoza sustains the validity of the indictment found against Edward S. Stokes for the murder of James Fisk, jr.

March 4.—President Grant receives the Japenese Embassy.

Jayne's "Granite Block" in Philadelphia almost destroyed by fire; loss, $478,000.

The ship Great Republic abandoned in a sinking condition, off Bermuda.

KALAMAZOO—*Continued.*

MEAT MARKET.

BARNES, WM. T., Meat Market, 67½ Main st. Established 1876.

RICHMOND, J. & BRO., Meat Market, 14 N. Burdick st. Established 1877.

MILLINERY AND DRESSMAKING.

CAPEN, C. C., Wholesale and Retail Dealer in Millinery, 107 Main st. Established 1866.

Established 1871.

MRS. ANNA M. LUMBARD,

DRESSMAKING,

Rooms over Scott's Clothing Store,

105 MAIN ST.

SMITH, MRS. M. A., Dealer in Millinery Goods.

VANCE, K. MRS., Dressmaker, Main and Portage sts. Established 1871.

MUSICAL INSTRUMENTS.

PHILLIPS, DELOS, Manf'r of the Celebrated Star Organ, and Dealer in Musical Merchandise, 142 Main st.

NEWSPAPER.

SHAKESPEARE, A. J., Publisher of the Kalamazoo Gazette, 99 Main st.

PAINTERS.

WALTER GREGG,

Carriage and Wagon

PAINTER,

Cor. Water & Edwards Sts.

Repainting of Carriages and Sleighs a Specialty.

Terms Reasonable. Established 1874.

SMITH, R. & SON, Paints and Oils, House and Sign Painting, 144 Main st.

PHOTOGRAPHERS.

PACKARD, C. C., Photographer, 103 Main st. Established 1865.

M. H. PORTER,

Solar Printing for the Trade,

On Paper or Canvas.

118 Main st. Send for Circular.

VAN SICKLE'S NEW GALLERY, 108 Main st. Makes all the latest styles of Pictures.

W. S. WHITE,

ARTIST PHOTOGRAPHER,

116 Main st.

PHYSICIAN.

HATFIELD, DR. D. S., Homœopathic Physician, office, 41 N. West st.

KALAMAZOO—Continued.

PICTURE FRAMES.

CHAS. P. RUSSELL,
Manufacturer of

Picture Frames & Window Cornice.
A full line of
Pictures, Engravings and Chromos
ON HAND.
POST OFFICE BUILDING.

PRINTERS.
Established 1874.

JAS. M. VERITY & CO.,
"*STAR*" *JOB*

PRINTERS,
Cor. Main and Portage Sts.,
KALAMAZOO,   -   -   MICH.

SHIRT MANUFACTURER.

UNDERWOOD SHIRT MANUFACTORY, Manf'rs of Shirts, Night Shirts, Collars and Cuffs, 29 and 31 N. Burdick st.

SHOWCASES.

GOODALE, J. C., Showcases and General Undertakers, cor. Main and Burdick sts.

SOCIETY REGALIAS.

FRANK HENDERSON,
Manufacturer of

Society Uniforms & Regalias,
Military, Firemen and Band Equipments,

104 MAIN ST.

STOVES AND TINWARE.

BROWNELL & VAN MALE, Stoves, Ranges and Tinware, 180 Main st.

KAUFFER, H. P., Manufacturer of Tin and Sheet Iron Ware, 94 Water st.

TAILORS.

BASEMANN, LOUIS, Tailor. Repairing neatly done. 113 Main st. Est. 1866.

KERSTENE, HERMAN, Tailoring and Repairing neatly done, Main and Burdick sts.

WINES AND LIQUORS.

WM. T. HOTOP & BRO.,

BILLIARD HALL,
110 MAIN STREET.

Best of Wines, Liquors and Cigars always on hand.

LILIENFIELD, D. & BRO., Wholesale Tobacconists, Importers of Wines and Liquors, 112 Main st.

1872.

March 6.—Six steamboats burned at Cincinnati; loss, $250,000.

March 22.—The outlaw Hildebrand shot dead by a police officer, in Pinckneyville, Illinois.

March 26.—An earthquake in California. Through the valley of the Sierras, a chasm, varying in width, and thirty-five miles in length, opens in the earth. During four hours the earth is shaken. A large number of people are killed.

March 30.—A tornado throws down a large market-house in St. Louis.

April 8.—The Mormon Conference re-elects Brigham Young President of the Church.

April 10.—"Lord" Gordon is arrested in the Metropolitan Hotel, New York, at the suit of Jay Gould, on a charge of embezzling. Phillip Klingon Smith, of Lincoln county, Nevada, a former Mormon bishop, charges the Mormons with the "Mountain Meadow Massacre" of immigrants in 1857, and exonerates the Indians.

April 11.—The boiler of the steamer Oceanus explodes on the Mississippi river, and kills 70 persons. The boiler of the tug-boat Davenport, on the North river, explodes and kills five persons.

April 15.—The counsel of the U. S. and the English arbitrators on the Alabama claims meet in Geneva, Switzerland. The "cases" are exchanged, and the British consul presents a protest against the claims for indirect damages. The British authorities at Kingston, Jamaica, seize the American steamer Edgar Stuart as a Cuban privateer. Deadly encounter between outlaws and a United States marshal's posse at Indian Court House, Indian Territory. A sheriff and seven deputy marshals killed, and three outlaws.

April 19.—Indians and renegades massacre its escort, and plunder and destroy a government supply train, near Howard's Wells, Texas.

April 22.—A party of disguised men take Isaac Vaniel, an old man from his house in Williamson county, Ill., and hang him.

April 24.—A mob stops a train near Holden, Mo., and assassinates on it Judge Stevenson, and Messrs. Cline and Dutro.

April 25.—Brigham Young released on a writ of *habeas corpus*.

April 26.—The U. S. war vessel Kansas releases the American steamship Virginius from blockade by the Spanish man-of-war Pizarro, in the port of Aspinwall.

April 29.—A party of five armed men enter the town of Columbia, Ky., and rob the deposit bank after killing the cashier.

May 2.—Steve Lowery and Andrew Strong, two "Swamp Angels," murder Capt. M. Wishart near Shoe Heel, North Carolina.

May 2.—Niblo's Garden Theater destroyed by fire. The painters in New York and vicinity strike for the eight hour system, and are subsequently joined by the other trade societies.

May 16.—A rain-storm floods the town of Easton, Kansas, and four persons are drowned.

May 18.—Extensive forest fires prevail in the northern part of New York State, north-

222 ADVERTISEMENTS.

KALAMAZOO—Continued.

WINES AND LIQUORS.

JOHN MALOY,
Wholesale Dealer in
WINES, LIQUORS & CIGARS
87 MAIN STREET,
Opp. Kalamazoo House. Est. 1874.

WOOLEN MANUFACTURERS.

KALAMAZOO KNITTING CO., Manf'rs of Woolen Hosiery, Leggings, Gents' Scarfs and Yarns.

KANKAKEE, ILLS.

AGRICULTURAL IMPLEMENTS.

SHAFFER, J. H., Agricultural Implements and Seeds, 43 Court st. Established 1857.

AUCTION AND COMMISSION.

NICHOLS, A. B., & CO., Auction and Commission, 1 Court st. Established 1853.

BOOTS AND SHOES.

GIRARD, ISRAEL, Custom-Made Boots and Shoes, West ave. Established 1872.

MERTENS, M., Boots, Shoes, &c.,
East ave. Established 1865.

RICKEY, JOSEPH, Boots and Shoes,
34 Court st.

WHITCOMB, WM., Custom-Made Boots, Shoes and Gaiters, 1st Nat. Bank Bld'g. Est. 1854.

CARRIAGE MANUFACTURERS.

BERGERON, NAPOLEON, Carriage Manufacturer, Station st. & Schuyler ave. Established 1866.

SCHREMPF, PHILIP, & SON, Carriage Manufacturers, Station st. & Schuyler ave. Est. 1866

DENTISTS.

AMES, DR. AARON, Dentist,
8 Court st. Established 1855.

CUTLER, DR. ANDREW S., Dentist,
Cor. Court st. & Schuyler ave. Estab. 1867.

DRY GOODS.

DORION, T., Dry Goods,
16 Court st. Established 1860.

ROUDY, JOHN, Dry Goods and Notions,
40 Court st.

SWANNELL, F., & SON, Dry Goods, Carpets, Trunks and Wall-Paper, 30 & 32 Court st.

FURNITURE.
(Established 1857.)

A. BABST,
New and Second-Hand
FURNITURE
Of every Description constantly on Hand. UNDERTAKING attended to. Monthly Payments taken. West ave., Kankakee, Ills. I invite attention to my styles and prices.

KANKAKEE—Continued.

HARDWARE.

BABST, LAWRENCE, Hardware, Cutlery and Agricultural Implements, 13 East av. Est. '69

HOTEL.

EXCHANGE HOTEL.
Only First-Class House in the city.

JUSTICES OF THE PEACE.

COFFIN, JAMES M., Justice of the Peace, Collecting Agent, Knecht's Block. Est. 1868.

DURFEE, OTIS, Justice of the Peace,
Collecting Agent, Knecht's Block. Est. 1854.

LIVERY AND BOARDING STABLE.

OLIVER VINING,

 Livery, Sale & Boarding Stable

STATION ST., Rear EXCHANGE HOTEL.

Established 1875. KANKAKEE, ILLS.

MEAT MARKET.

OTT, GEORGE K., Meat Market,
East ave. Established 1877.

PHYSICIAN.

DR. JULES N. FRASER,
Physician & Surgeon

Graduate of Laval University, Quebec; Licentiate of the College of Physicians and Surgeons, Quebec. OFFICE HOURS: Any time of day or night.
13 Court St., Kankakee, Ills.

PHOTOGRAPHER.

KNOWLTON, CHARLES, Artist Photographer,
56 Court st. Established 1874.

REAL ESTATE AND INSURANCE.

DALE, JOHN, Real Estate and Insurance. Taxes Paid for Non-residents. Established 1856.

SALOONS.

FENA, PETER, Saloon and Billiards,
22 Court st. Established 1854.

POIRIER, HONORE, Saloon and Sample Room,
Court st., near Schuyler ave. Estab. 1871.

RADEKE, ERNST, Proprietor Schiller Hall,
East ave., S. Exchange Hotel. Estab. 1875.

*SOAP WORKS.

STANTON SOAP WORKS,
Manufacturers of
LAUNDRY & TOILET SOAPS.

P. O. Box 345. N. Harrison Ave., Kankakee, Ills

IMPORTANT EVENTS OF THE CENTURY. 223

United States Hospital, Centennial Exposition, Philadelphia.—This building contains an exhibition of the medical department of the army, to-wit: hospital supplies employed in the care of sick and wounded soldiers. It is 125 feet front, surrounded by a piazza 10 feet wide, and consists of a central administration building with two wings, in each of which is a ward 45 by 25 feet, intended for twelve beds. All the other rooms are occupied with the exhibition of army and navy hospital supplies of every description.

1872.

eastern part of Pennsylvania, and northern counties of New Jersey.

May 19.—The Jayne building on Dock street Philadelphia, destroyed by fire, loss $475,000.

Great Roman Catholic celebration in honor of the convention of the Catholic benevolent societies, in Dayton, Ohio.

May 23.—Shakespeare's monument in Central Park unveiled.

May 25.—A severe storm destroys life and property in Morgan county, Mo.

May 27.—The balloon of Prof. Atkins descends into the Tennessee River, near Decatur, Alabama, and the Professor is drowned.

May 29.—Canadian authorities sieze the American fishing schooner, Enola C., for violating the fishery laws.

May 30.—"Decoration Day;" impressive honors paid to the dead soldiers of late war.

June 4.—Captain Colvocoresses, of the United States Navy, murdered and robbed in Bridgeport, Conn.

June 6.—Great storm along the New England coast; much damage done to shipping.

The United States Minister at Madrid demands the release of Dr. Howard.

June 7.—A delegation of Sioux Indians, headed by Red Cloud, have a reception at Cooper Institute.

June 8.—William H. Bumsted, a Jersey city official, sentenced to State prison for nine months, for conspiring with others to defraud the city.

An Ecclesiastical Court pronounces the charges of immorality not proven against the Rev. Dr. Huston, of Baltimore, Md.

June 9.—Comanche Indians massacre the Leo family, of seven persons, near Fort Griffin, Texas

June 10.—The London (England) Rowing Club crew beats the crew of the Atlanta Club, of New York, on the Thames.

June 15.—The members of the Tribunal of Arbitration assemble in Geneva (Switzerland) and organize; after a short session, the tribunal adjourns until the 17th inst.

June 17.—The World's Peace Jubilee opens in Boston.

June 18.—Mexican soldiers at Matamoras fire on and arrest the American occupants of a pleasure boat, on the Rio Grand, between that city and Brownsville, Texas.

The Canadian cutter, Stella Marie, siezes the American fishing schooner, James Bliss, for violating the fishery laws; the American flag is insulted by being turned union down under the Dominion flag on the captured vessel.

June 19.—The trial of Edward S. Stokes, for the murder of James Fisk, Jr., begun.

June 20.—The bodies of Confederate soldiers killed and buried at Gettysburg removed and conducted through Richmond, Va., by a mournful procession.

June 26.—A jury is sworn on the Stokes trial; District Attorney Garvin opens the case.

Ellis Ward beats J. J. O'Leary in a three-

AURORA, ILLS.

ATTORNEY AT LAW.

CLAPSADDLE, D. M., Attorney and Counselor at Law, No. 28 South Broadway.

BREWERY.

AURORA BREWERY. Philip Bonte, Proprietor. End of Union st.

CLOTHING AND FURNISHING GOODS.

HIRSH, L., Clothing, Hats, Caps and Furnishing Goods, 13 Broadway.

DENTISTS.

ROBINSON, F. H., Surgeon Dentist. Established 1869. West Aurora, Ills.

WILLSON, O. D. D. S., Surgeon Dentist, Coulter Opera House Block.

DRUGGISTS.

HOLMES BROTHERS,
Bitter Wine of Iron

The World's Tonic. GERMAN OIL, for Rheumatism, Neuralgia, &c.

26 MAIN ST., AURORA, ILLS.

FURNITURE AND BURIAL CASES.

DENNEY BROTHERS,
Dealers in all kinds of

Furniture & Burial Cases

Nos. 27 & 29 Broadway, Aurora, Ills.

GROCERIES.

O'DONNELL BROS., Staple and Fancy Groceries. 15 Main st. Established 1866.

HARDWARE.

REISING & KENDALL, Hardware & Crockery, 19 & 21 Broadway.

LADIES' FURNISHING GOODS.

CARPENTER, MRS. B. C., Ladies' Furnishing & Fancy Goods, 30 Main st. Established 1867.

LIVERY AND OMNIBUS STABLES.

VAN VLEET, A., Livery & Omnibus Stables, 5, 7 & 9 N. LaSalle st.

LOCKSMITH.

ZIEGLER, M., Locksmith Brass Foundry & Stove repairer, opposite Fitch House.

MACHINIST.

NOVELTY MACHINE WORKS.
M. S. HENDRICK, Proprietor,
Builder of Stationery Engines and manfa'er of Machine Tools. Est. 1872. Send for circulr and price list. Cor. Galena & Lake sts.

AURORA—*Continued.*

NEWSPAPER.

THE AURORA DAILY NEWS
Is not
The Only Advertising Medium in the World,
It is
ONLY ONE OF THEM.
And being the only daily newspaper published in Southern Kane County, it reaches more readers than can here be reached through any other medium.   SIEGMUND & HAWKINS,
Aurora, Ills.

PHOTOGRAPHER.

PRATT, D. C., Portrait & Landscape Photographer, 48 Broadway.

PHYSICIANS.

BRIGHAM, L. R., M. D., Physician,
Room 5, Opera House.

JURDEN, W. E., Inventor of the Celebrated Painless Cancer Plaster, 12 S Broadway.

SASH, DOORS AND BLINDS.

ALLEN & CORSAIR, Manf'rs & dealers in Sash, Doors, Blinds, &c., 4 N. LaSalle st.

TONSORIAL ARTIST.

FICKENSHER, H., Tonsorial Artist.
Established 1850. 9 S. Broadway.

ELGIN, ILLS.

ATTORNEY AT LAW.

LOVELL, E. C., Attorney at Law, Public Administrator of Kane Co., Real Estate & Loans.

BAKERY AND CONFECTIONERY.

BENNETT, C. R., Bakery, Confectionery & Cigars, 10 Douglas ave. Established 1877.

BOOK-KEEPER.

MANN, M., Book-keeper. Manf'r of Mann's Compound Cathartic & Blood Purifier. Agents wanted.

BUTTER AND CHEESE.

MANN & SHERWIN,
Wholesale dealers in
Butter and Cheese,
Salt, Factory and Dairy supplies.
CHEESE A SPECIALTY.
Agents for Higgins' Liverpool Salt. Established 1872.
HOAGLAND'S BLOCK.
Reference: First National Bank, Elgin, Ill.

CAN MANUFACTORY.

ELGIN CAN COMPANY, Manufacturers of Elgin Kerosene Cans.

DRY GOODS, ETC.

FEHRMAN, F., Dry Goods & Groceries,
17 Douglas ave. Established 1872.

IMPORTANT EVENTS OF THE CENTURY. 225

1872.
mile scull race on Lake Quinsigamund, Mass.; time, 21 min. 38 sec.

July 2.—Judge John H. McCunn, of the Supreme Court, removed from the bench by the Court of Impeachment at Albany.

July 7.—Samuel J. Browne, an octogenarian, murders a youth named Frank Schik, in Cincinnati, Ohio.

July 8.—Absalom and Jacob Kimball and Alexander McLeod, who outraged and murdered a young girl named Secor, are taken from jail, in Celina, Ohio, by a mob, and Absalom Kimball and McLeod are hanged at the scene of their crime.

The Cuban privateer, Pioneer, captured by the U. S. revenue cutter, Moccasin, off Newport, R. I., and brought into that port.

Two men, named Hale and Tucker, are shot and killed while in custosy of a sheriff's posse, near Dover, Arkansas; the Republican officials are charged with the murders for political effect; an unparalleled state of anarchy and assassination results.

-July 11.—An earthquake shock felt on Long Island and in Westchester county.

July 12.—Columbus and Govan Adair executed in Hendersonville, North Carolina, for the murder of Silas Weston and three children.

July 13.—Burglars take Charles Wesson, the teller of the Blackstone National Bank at Uxbridge, Mass., from his home at night, and compel him to open the bank's safe, from which they take $14,000.

July 15.—The jury in the Stokes trial fail to agree on a verdict, and are discharged.

July 16.—The great Longfellow and Harry Bassett race at Saratoga won by the latter; Longfellow is injured during the race, to which is attributed his defeat.

July 19.—Tom Lowery, Swamp Angel outlaw, shot and killed by Robert Wishart, near Moss Neck, N. C.

July 22.—Hugh Marra shoots Alderman Wm. McMullen, in Philadelphia.

July 24.—The college boat regatta on the Connecticut river, won by the Amherst College crew, the Harvards second.

July 29.—A riot occurs between negroes and whites in Savannah, Ga., and several on each side are injured.

July 30.—A destructive fire occurs at Hunter's Point, L. I.; it originates on a canal boat, and spreads to an oil-yard, the buildings thereon, and a number of ships, canal boats, lighters, and scows.

July 31.—B. Hetzeler kills his divorced wife's paramour and then commits suicide in Rochester, N. Y.

Aug. 3.—The Cuban privateer Pioneer is formally seized by the U. S. Marshal, at Newport, R. I., for violation of the neutrality laws.

Aug. 8.—Geo. H. Evans, a West Point graduate, shoots and kills a burglar, named Hoegerling, in Pittsburg, Pa.

Aug. 9.—Newton Chandler hanged for rape, robbery, and arson, in Charlotte, North Carolina.

Aug. 10.—Mr. Alexander, a merchant,

ADVERTISEMENTS.

ELGIN—Continued.

DRY GOODS, ETC.

STOLT, FRED, Dry Goods & Millinery, 20 Douglas ave. Established 1858.

DYE WORKS.

ELGIN & CHICAGO STEAM DYE WORKS, Car-line Bros., Proprietors, 48 River st.

HARNESS, SADDLERY, ETC.

SCHROEDER, C. & CO., Harness, Sadd'ery, Collars, Blankets, etc., cor. Milwaukee & River sts. Established 1874.

SCOTT. E. D., Harness, Saddles, Bridles & Collars, River st. Established 1869.

H. MUNTZ,
SADDLER AND HARNESS MAKER.
Cor. Brook & Division sts.
Established 1872.

HOTELS.

COMMERCIAL HOTEL
GOOD SAMPLE ROOMS.
Centre of the city.
Elgin, Ills.　　　　　　　　W. F SHAW, Prop.

LIVERY STABLES.

SWAN & SMITH, Livery, Feed & Sale Stables, Milwaukee st. Established 1875.

PAINTER.

John G. Day:
Painter, Glazier, Graining, Sign-Writing and Carriage Painting.
Established 1871. Shop at Bierman's Agricultural Works,
RIVER ST.

RESTAURANTS AND SAMPLE ROOMS.

SAMPLE AND BILLIARD ROOM, COMMERCIAL HOTEL.
Elgin, Illinois.
Established 1876.　　　GEO. W. SHAW, Prop

William Saunders.

RESTAURANT
—(AND)—
Sample Room,
Established 1874.　　　　14 Chicago St.

URBANA, ILLS.

ATTORNEY AT LAW.

J. O. Cunningham,
ATTORNEY AT LAW,
Particular attention given to Real Estate and Probate matter.
2 W. MAIN ST., OPP. COURT HOUSE.
Urbana,　　-　　-　　-　　Ills.

URBANA—Continued.

BAKERY AND CONFECTIONERY.

TIERNAN, M., Bakery, Confectionery & Ice Cream Parlor, 13 Main st.

BOOKS AND STATIONERY.

FOX, O. W., Books, Stationery & Musical Instruments, 1 N. Market.

BOOTS AND SHOES.

JOHN CAIN,
Manufacturer of Boots and Shoes,
11 MAIN STREET.

DRUGGISTS.

CUSHMAN, E. H. & CO., Drugs, Chemica , Paints, Oils, &c., Cor. Main & Race sts.

HUNT & WHELDON,
DEALERS IN
DRUGS, BOOKS, STATIONERY, WALL PAPER, AND A General assortment of Fancy Articles, Sheet Music, etc., etc.　　20 MAIN ST.

DRY GOODS AND NOTIONS.

RILEY, N. A., Dry Goods & Notions,
27 Main st.

FLOUR AND FEED.

A. W. SAINT,
FLOUR and FEED STORE,
49 Main St. Established 1875.

GROCERIES.

TIERNAN, F., Groceries, Country Produce, Queensware, etc., 16 Main st.

HARDWARE AND TINWARE.

LITTLE, J. S., Hardware, Stoves, Tinware, etc., Main st.

HOTELS.

COMMERCIAL TRAVELERS' HOTEL,
45 & 46 West Main Street.
URBANA,　　-　　-　　-　　ILLS.
EXCLUSIVELY FOR COMMERCIAL MEN.
Three good Sample Rooms on ground floor.
A good table, clean and airy chambers.
I RESPECTFULLY INVITE you to CALL.
J. WILKINSON, Proprietor.

PENNSYLVANIA HOUSE,
MRS. MARY PARKS, Proprietress,
Main Street,
Urbana,　　-　　-　　-　　Ills.

MILLINERY GOODS.

CARTER, MRS. S. L., Millinery & Fancy Goods, 45 Main st.

WILCOX & THROCKMORTON, Millinery, Dress and Cloak Makers. Changing, Pressing and Bleaching done on short notice and reasonable terms, 41 Main st. Established 1877.

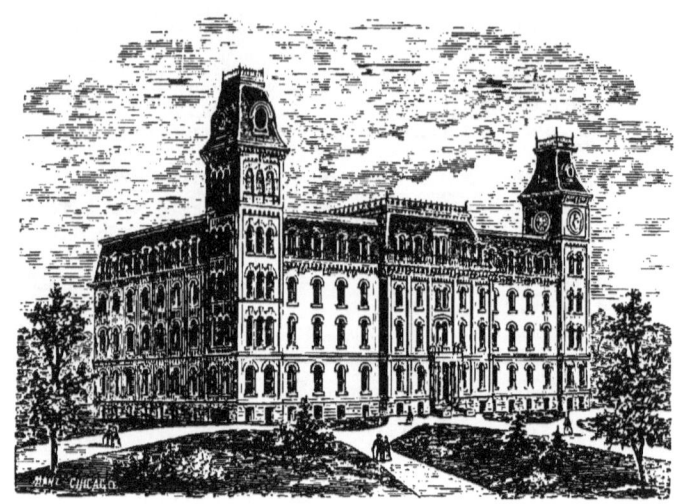

COURT HOUSE, BAY CITY, MICH.

ILLINOIS UNIVERSITY, URBANA, ILLS.

1872.

murdered by Mexican bandits, near Brownsville, Texas.

Aug. 12.—The Spanish iron-clad war-vessel Numancia arrives at this port, with yellow fever cases on board.

Aug. 13.—Mace and O'Baldwin arrested in Baltimore, and placed bonds not to fight in Maryland.

Aug. 19.—The Duke of Saxe, the son-in-law of the Emperor of Brazil, arrives in New York city.

The Third National Bank of Baltimore is robbed of $200,000 in money and securities.

Judge G. G. Barnard, of the Supreme Court, found guilty by the Court of Impeachment, at Albany, of high crimes and misdemeanors, removed from the bench, and declared ineligible ever to hold office in the State.

Aug. 20.—Prince Philip, of Coburg-Gotha, arrives in New York city, to join his brother, the Duke of Saxe.

Dr. Howard arrives in New York city from Cadiz, Spain.

Aug. 21.—Mace and O'Baldwin meet at Harmon's Creek, W. Va., to fight a prize fight, but failing to agree in the choice of a referee, back out.

Aug. 24.—The P. M. S. America destroyed by fire at Yokohama, Japan; sixty lives and a large amount of specie lost.

Aug. 26.—Arapahoe Indians massacre the guard of a government mule train, rob and burn the wagons, at Dry Creek, Colorado Territory, and end by scalping Mr. Bryant, the wagon master, while alive.

Mrs. Charlotte Lamb is arrested at Trimbelle, Wis., charged with having killed her husband, two children, and two neighbors, with poison.

Aug. 30.—The Providence and New York steamer Metis run into by a schooner, on Long Island Sound; the Metis soon breaks up, and 155 persons are compelled to trust their lives to the few boats and such floating material as they can secure; only 107 persons get to the shore in safety.

Sept. 1.—W. J. Sharkey, a New York ward politician, murders Robert Dunn, at No. 200 Hudson street.

Sept. 4.—Billy Edwards and Arthur Chambers fight on Walpole Island, on the Canadian frontier; after 26 rounds, lasting 1 hour 35 minutes, Chambers is awarded the victory, Edwards having bitten him.

Sept. 7.—Billy Forrester, the alleged murderer of Mr. Benjamin Nathan, is arrested in Washington, D. C.

Dr. Schoeppe acquitted of the charge of poisoning Miss Steinecke, at Carlisle, Pennsylvania.

The Cuban steamer Virginius escapes from the blockade of the Spanish war vessels at Puerto Cabello, Venezuela.

Sept. 14.—A riot occurs between a Grant and Wilson club, composed of negroes, and Democrats, in Pittsburgh, Pa.; several persons badly hurt.

The Geneva (Switzerland) Tribunal of Arbitration on the Alabama claims awards $16,250,000 to the United States.

Sept. 21.—In a political affray in Colum-

URBANA—*Continued.*

RESTAURANTS.

ROB'T BOWMAN,
Confectionery & Restaurant,
47 MAIN STREET.
Cigars & Tobacco a specialty. Est. 1871.

Thos. Madison,
RESTAURANT,
8 MAIN STREET,
URBANA.

TOBIAS, MRS. C., Dining Hall.
37 Main st.

TAILORS—MERCHANT.

J. H. HARTZELL,
MERCHANT TAILOR,
16 Main Street,
URBANA, - - - *ILLINOIS.*

H. STEWART,
MERCHANT TAILOR,
25 W. Main Street,
Established 1870. Urbana, Ills.

WATCHMAKER AND JEWELER.

RILEY, ALBERT, Watchmaker and Jeweler, Main st.

CHAMPAIGN, ILLS.

ATTORNEYS AT LAW.

GERE, GEO. W., Attorney at Law,
21 Main st.

PITTMAN, G. W. M., Attorney at Law, over First National Bank. Established 1874.

ROLAND & KNIGHT,
ATTORNEYS,
11 Main St., Champaign, Ills.
COLLECTIONS AND REAL ESTATE LAW MADE A SPECIALTY.

BAKERY AND CONFECTIONERY.

EBBERT, JACOB, Bakery and Confectionery, 53 First st.

BOARDING HOUSE.

DOYLE, JOHN, Boarding House and Liquors, cor. Main and Oak sts.

BOOTS AND SHOES.

WILLIAM ROYER, Manf'r & Dealer in
BOOTS & SHOES,
Neil st., three doors South of Post Office.
Repairing neatly done.

VOGEL, CONRAD, Manf'r and Dealer in Boots and Shoes, 84 University ave.

CHAMPAIGN—Continued.

BROOM MANUFACTURER.

STRAUB, E., B.oom Manufacturer,
90 University st.

CARPENTERS AND BUILDERS.

FLEMING, JESSE, Carpenter and Joiner, Church st. Established 1856.

MILLER, B. F., Carpenter and Builder, Market and Second sts., South.

DENTIST.

SHERMAN, A., Dentist,
51 Neil st., opp. Main.

DINING ROOMS.

Holton's New Dining Rooms,
E. G. HOLTON, PROP.,
Cor. Main and Fremont Sts., Champaign, Ills.

DRESS AND CLOAKMAKING.

COLEMAN, VINNIE, Dress and Cloakmaking, cor. Main and Walnut sts.

LOUISA HARRIS,

DRESS AND CLOAKMAKING,
57 Neil street, Champaign, Ills.

MISS S. E. LINEGAR,

DRESS AND CLOAKMAKING,
61 Neil street, Champaign, Ills.

DRUGGIST.

HUDDLESTON, R. H., M.D., Physician and Surgeon, 4 Main st.

DRY GOODS AND CARPETS.

E. MILLER,
Dry Goods, Notions & Carpets,
Est. 1860, under Miller & Toll; est. 1873, E. Miller.
7 MAIN-STREET.

C. S. MOREHOUSE,
Wholesale and Retail Dealer in

Dry Goods and Carpets,
Barrett Block. Established 1866.

WILLIS, G. C., Dry Goods, Millinery and Notions, 11 Main st.

DYEING ESTABLISHMENTS.

Champaign Steam Dyeing and Cleaning Establishment.

JULIUS MUELLER, DYER,
25 N. Walnut St.,
Silks, & Woolen Goods Dyed to any Color
Also Cleans Gentlemen's and Ladies' Wearing Apparel, Shawls, Curtains, Carpets, Gloves, etc.
All Premium Colors Warranted.

Souder's Steam Dyeing and Renovating Establishment.
Only Steam Dye House in the City.
Fremont st.   Established 1866.

1872.

bia, S. C.; J. D. Caldwell is shot dead and Major Morgan wounded, by George Tupper.

Sept. 22.—A terrible riot occurs between Irish and negro laborers, at Patenburgh, New Jersey; one Irishman and three negroes killed.

Sept. 24.—A force of U. S. cavalry, under Col. Mason, surprise a band of marauding Apache and Mojave Indians, in Arizona Territory; they kill about 40 of the band.

Sept. 26.—Ex-City Treasurer Marcer and Chas. F. Yerkes, convicted of embezzling the funds of the city of Philadelphia, pardoned by Governor Geary.

Sept. 30.—Baron Steuben monument unveiled at Steuben, N. Y.

Mrs. Laura D. Fair's second trial at San Francisco, for the murder of Judge Crittenden, results in her acquittal.

Oct. 7.—A riot between white Greeley men and negro militiamen occurs in Cincinnati, O.; several persons are wounded.

Oct. 8.—In an affray at Shreveport, La., Chief of Police Sherrod and Police Officer Sheppard kill R. J. Wright, clerk of the District Court of Shreveport, La., and his brother W. A. Wright; some friends of the Wrights immediately afterwards kill Officer Sheppard.

A great part of the business section of the town of Sing Sing, N. Y., destroyed by fire; loss, about $200,000.

Oct. 13.—Archbishop Bailey installed as Primate of the Catholic Church in the United States, at Baltimore.

A fire destroyed the rolling mill of the Cambria Iron Works, at Johnstown, Pa.; loss, $100,000.

Oct. 14.—The Saratoga County Bank, at Waterford, New York, robbed of $500,000 in money and bonds, the burglars gag and bind the family of the cashier, and compel him, by threats, to disclose the secret of the bank vault's lock.

Oct. 16.—The great race between Goldsmith Maid and Occident, at Sacramento, Cal., won by the former in three straight heats; best time, 2:20¼.

Mr. Froude, the English historian, delivers his first lecture on the History of Ireland, in New York.

Oct. 22.—Steamship Missouri, of the A. M. Steamship Line, burned at sea; 87 lives lost.

The Emperor William, of Germany, communicates his decision on the San Juan dispute to the representatives of England and the United States. It approves the claims of the United States Government.

Nov. 2.—The monument to Sir Walter Scott unveiled in Central Park, N. Y.

John Scannell shoots Thomas Donohue dead in Johnson's club rooms, cor. of 28th street and Broadway, N. Y.

Nov. 6.—The mutilated remains of Abijah Ellis are found in two barrels floating in the Charles river, at Boston.

Nov. 7.—A party of negroes in the Sixth ward, Baltimore, fire into a crowd of whites, and kill a boy and wound two other persons.

Nov. 9.—The greatest fire that ever raged

Deutsches Gasthaus.

Wir werden stets bemüht sein, unsern Gästen in jeder Hinsicht Zufriedenheit zu stellen.

Just opened and newly furnished with the best accommodation for the traveling public, very convenient to Depot. Eastern Prices—Eastern Management.

Price, $1.50 to $2.00 Per Day.
THE PALISADE HOTEL,
Corner 5th, & Bluff Sts., Kansas City.

H. FABER, Proprietor.

WE DYE TO LIVE!
NEW YORK STEAM SCOURING AND DYE WORKS,
No. 174 Massachusetts St., Lawrence, Kas.

Every description of Silk and Woolen Goods Dyed equal to any house East, and finished by Cylinders. Ladies' and Gentlemen's Wearing Apparel Renovated, and made to appear as new; such as Crape, Brocha and Cashmere Shawls; also, Cashmere, Merino and Silk Dresses.

Crape Shawls Dyed all Shades and Colors.

SOILED GLOVES AND PLUMES CLEANED.

GEO. W. PEEL, Prop'r.

Formerly PEEL & SONS' Boston Dye House, Cincinnati, Ohio. Established in 1812.

The New American Sewing Machine.
Lightning! Running! Self-Threading!
Ahead of all others in Improvements.

It is the lightest running! the simplest to learn to use! the most durable! and the best for all purposes! has the most room under the arm! self threading shuttle! and never skip stitches or breaks thread!

There is no machine which is so easily learned, and which combines lightness and durability. For these and other reasons the American Machines is the best in which to invest your money. Sold at a moderate price, and on terms to be within the reach of all. Warranted Five Years by the Company.

KENNEDY & MARTIN, Agents,
212 DOUGLASS ST., OMAHA. NEBRASKA.

ADVERTISEMENTS. 231

MISSOURI RIVER BEND, KANSAS CITY, MO.

ALOIS GATZ, MERCHANT TAILOR,
And Clothier, and Dealer in Gents' Furnishing Goods,
506 Maine Street, Between Fifth and Sixth, Quincy, Illinois.

1872.

in Boston breaks out early this evening, and continues all night.

Bowles Brothers, the American bankers in Paris, France, suspend their business.

Nov. 10.—The great fire in Boston is got under control about 3 p. m., after having burned over an era of 200 acres, in the business center of the city; again, at about 12 p. m. the flames appear near the place of origin of the first fire, and spread rapidly to buildings that had escaped them before; an explosion of gas produced this second conflagration.

Nov. 20.—A fire destroys Rand & Avery's printing establishment, No. 3 Cornhill, Boston; loss, $250,000.

Henry M. Stanley, the discoverer of Livingstone, arrives in New York from England.

Nov. 21.—The great fire occurs in Galva, Ill.; loss, $218,000.

A mob prevents Mrs. Fair from lecturing in San Francisco.

Nov. 22.—Jay Gould makes a "corner" in N. W. R. R. S. stock; great excitement in Wall street.

The Erie Railroad Co. begins an action against Jay Gould for the recovery of $9,726,551; Gould is arrested, but immediately after bailed in $1,000,000.

Dec. 10.—Mary Ann Foley, alias Maud Merrill, shot by her uncle, Robert P. Bleakley, at No. 10 Neilson Place, New York.

Dec. 11.—The Fifth Avenue Hotel New York fire; eleven servant girls are suffocated and burned to a crisp.

Dec. 17.—Jay Gould restores $9,000,000 worth of property to the E. R. R. Co., for the sake of peace.

Dec. 18.—The second trial of Edward S. Stokes, for the murder of James Fisk, Jr., commenced.

Dec. 24.—Barnum's museum and circus destroyed by fire; loss, $1,000,000.

A train on the Buffalo and Pittsburg Railroad falls through the trestle bridge, near Prospect Station, N. Y.; twenty passengers are killed or burned to death, the wreck having taken fire.

Andrew Strong, of Swamp Angel notoriety, is killed, at Eureka, N. C., by William Wilson.

Dec. 26. Great storm throughout the country and along the coast; many shipping disasters result.

The bark Kadosh wrecked in Massachusetts bay; seven lives lost.

Ship Peruvian lost on Massachusetts coast, and all hands, 25 in number, drowned.

1873.

Jan. 2.—Mrs. Mary Ann Lampley murdered in her house in Baltimore by Thomas R. Hollohan and Joshua Nicholson; the murderers executed for the deed, August 1st.

Jan. 4.—Edward S. Stokes convicted of the murder of James Fisk, Jr. Sentenced to death Jan. 6.

Jan. 6.—Larson, a young Swede, brutally murdered by rowdies in Chicago.

Jan. 11.—Lydia Sherman, the convicted murderess of her husband and several children, sentenced to imprisonment for life at New Haven.

Jan. 15.—Burning of Edwin Forrest's library in Philadelphia; $20,000 worth of books consumed.

CHAMPAIGN—Continued.

FARM MACHINERY.

SABIN, C. J. (Successor to Sabin Brothers,) Dealer in

Standard Farm Machinery,
Wagons, Buggies, Corn Shellers, Coal, etc.

FURNITURE.

L. W. WALKER,
Manufacturer of

Inside Furnishing for Dwellings, Banks & Offices
Turning, Mouldings, Scroll Sawing, Stair Work, General Jobbing, Wholesale Furniture,

CHAMPAIGN.

GROCERIES.

BOLLMAN, FREDERICK, Groceries and Provisions, 45 First st.

HOTELS.

CHAMPAIGN HOUSE, P. Coffey, Prop.
NEIL ST., Northwest of I. B. & W. Depot,

CHAMPAIGN, ILLS.

This Hotel is first-class in all its fittings, and no pains are spared for the comfort of guests. Good Sample Rooms for the accommodation of Commercial Agents. Rates Moderate. Baggage conveyed to and from all Trains. Travelers are invited to "stop and see me."

HOUSE FURNISHING GOODS.

LEWIS EMRY,
HOUSEFURNISHING GOODS,
34 NEIL STREET.

Repairing Clothes Wringers a Specialty.

CHAMPAIGN.

LAUNDRY.

CHAMPAIGN
Steam Laundry,
J. E. LUPTON, Proprietor,
FREMONT STREET.

LOAN BROKERS.

BURNHAM, TREVETT & MATTIS, Loan Brokers, 21 Main st.

LUMBER.

M. E. LAPHAM & CO.,
Dealers in
LUMBER, DOORS, BLINDS
Sash, Lime, Cement, Brick, Etc.,
CHAMPAIGN, - ILLS.
—:o:—
YARD, corner Market St. and University Ave.

CHAMPAIGN—Continued.

MILLINERY GOODS.

BLANCHARD, E. C., Dealer in *FASHIONABLE MILLINERY, RIBBONS, FLOWERS, FEATHERS ETC.,*
AGENT FOR BUTTERICK'S PATTERNS.
57 Neil street.

MISS M. HAINES, Dealer in

MILLINERY AND FANCY GOODS,
39 Neil st. Mourning Goods a Specialty.

NEWSPAPER.

The Champaign Journal

Only German Paper in the 14th Congressional District. JOHN BECKER, Editor & Prop.

PAPER STOCK.

LOCKE & SAXTON, Paper and Paper Stock,
Bet. Doane House & University ave.

REAL ESTATE.

REED, THOS. A., Real Estate and Loan Agent,
5 Main st.

TAILOR.

Established 1873.

WM. BOWEN,

Tailor and Draper,

No. 14 MAIN STREET,
Champaign Ills.

TOBACCO AND CIGARS.

SAMUEL EPPSTEIN,
Manufacturer of Cigars,
And Wholesale Dealer in Tobaccos, Pipes, etc.,
44 MAIN ST., CHAMPAIGN & URBANA.

WAGON MANUFACTURERS.

LINK, LUTHER, Wagon and Harrow Manufacturer, cor. Neil & Washington sts.

JOHN W. SPALDING,
Manufacturer of the
SPALDING WAGON
Shop on S. Neil & Walnut sts., opp. Jefferson & Son's Livery Stable. Estab. 1871.

WATCHES AND JEWELRY.

CORE, H. C., Watches, Clocks and Jewelry,
27 Main st.

EVANSTON, ILLS.

BARBER.

SMITH, J. P., Barber,
Davis street.

1873.

Jan. 17.—First Congregational Church of Chicago destroyed by fire.

Jan. 20.—The Modocs sanguinarily defeat United States troops.

Feb. 2.—Murder of Grace Mabel Love, and suicide of the father and murderer in Boston.

Feb. 13.—Fall of a bridge into the James River, at Richmond; four workmen perish, many injured.

Feb. 15.—The steamer Henry A. Jones burned at Galveston, Texas; twenty-one persons perish.

March 4.—Second Inauguration of President Grant.

March 30.—Wreck of the White Star steamship Atlantic, off the coast of Halifax; 700 lives lost.

April 8.—Thirty persons drowned on Genesee river, Rochester.

April 11.—Gen. Canby and Rev. Dr. Thomas treacherously murdered by the Modocs on the lava beds.

April 15.—Deadly collision between the blacks and whites at Colfax, La.

April 18.—Attack on the Modoc lava beds.

April 19.—A passenger train breaks through a bridge on the Stonington and Providence road; a large number of passengers killed and wounded.
Second battle with the Modocs.

April 26.—Arrest of F. L. Taintor, cashier of the Atlantic National Bank, New York, defaulter in the sum of $100,000.

April 27.—The Modocs surprise and destroy a detachment of troops.

May 10.—The Modocs evacuate the Lava-Beds.
The Mordecai and McCarty duel, Richmond, Va.

May 20.—Surrender of Hot-Creeks and Modocs to Gen. Davis.

May 22.—General McKenzie's excursion into Mexico.
Destructive tornado in Iowa.

May 30.—The great Boston fire No. 2.
Popular observance of Decoration Day.

June 1.—Modoc Jack's surrender.

June 3.—Mansfield Tracy Walworth shot to death by his son at the Sturtevant House, New York.

June 4.—McDonnel, the English forger, put on board a steamer for England.

June 17.—Indians attack the Northern Pacific surveying party; four Indians killed.

June 20.—The body of Col. Wm. O'Conner Sydney cast ashore on Staten Island.

June 27.—The work of laying the new Atlantic Cable completed.

July 1.—Judge W. H. Cooley killed in a duel by R. D. Rhett, Jr., at New Orleans.

July 3.—Discovery of the body of Thomas Munce, supposed to have been murdered, in the Schuylkill, Phila.

July 5.—Frank Walworth, for murdering his father in New York, sentenced to imprisonment for life.

EVANSTON—Continued.

BOOTS AND SHOES.
McKAY, E., Boots and Shoes,
    Davis st.

CROCKERY AND GLASSWARE.
PINGREE, J. G., (Established 1864.) Dealer in Crockery, Glassware, Toys, Stationery, etc.

DENTISTS.
MANSFIELD & FREEMAN, Dentists,
    Evanston, Illinois.

FURNITURE.
IREDALE, GEORGE, Furniture.
    Upholstering, and Repairing done to Order.

HARDWARE.
WIGREN, C. T., Dealer in Hardware and House Furnishing Goods.

MEAT MARKET.
BAILEY & PALING, Meat Market,
    Davis st.

PHOTOGRAPHER.
HESLER, A., Photo. Artist. Highest award received at World's Fair, 1853, & Centennial '76

TAILORS.
HALLSTROM, H.,
    Merchant Tailor and Gents' Furnisher.

THE EVANSTON TAILORING ASSOCIATION,
    Davis street.

TURNER, JOHN,
    Merchant Tailor and Gents' Furnishing Goods.

ALTON, ILLS.

ATTORNEY AT LAW.
BRENHOLT, JNO. L., Attorney at Law,
    Third st.

BAKERS AND CONFECTIONERS.

H. JOSTING & CO.

Confectionery and Ice Cream Saloon,
No. 11 BELLE STREET.

A. L. Daniels.   Geo. A. Bayle.   Wm. B. Pierce

Kendall Bakery.
DANIELS, BAYLE & CO.,
Cracker & Biscuit Manufacturers,
ALTON, ILLS.

BOOKSELLERS.

LEVERETT & CASTLE.
(Successors to M. I. Lee & Co.)

Wholesale & Retail Booksellers & Stationers,
20 Third St. Paper-hangings & picture fittings.

ALTON—Continued.

BAKERS AND CONFECTIONERS.

HENRY NEERMAN,
Baker and Confectioner,
And Dealer in Candies, Fruits, Nuts, &c. Also an Eating House attached.
Cor. of Bell & Fourth Sts.

BOOTS AND SHOES.
BERNER & GAISER, Manufacturer of Boots and Shoes, Belle st.

GERBIG, GEO., Manufacturer of Boots and Shoes, Belle st.

J. W. SCHMOELLER,
First-Class Custom
BOOT AND SHOE MAKER,
2nd St., bet Market & Alby Sts.

J. STILL,
Manufacturer of
Gents' Boots and Shoes,
STATE STREET.

COMMISSION MERCHANT.
OLDHAM, G. W., Commission Merchant and Dealer in Hides, Tallow, &c., State st.

DENTISTS.
ROBIDON, DR. J., Dentist,
    Belle street.

D.C. WHITE,
DENTIST,
2nd Street, Opp. City Hall.

DRUGGIST.

CHAMBERLAIN & HAGEE,
Wholesale & Retail Druggists
No. 11 THIRD ST., South Side.
Proprietors and Sole Manufacturers of Perline Tooth Powder, Wade's Camphor Ice, Wade's Hair Restorer. "Favorite" Cologne.

GROCERS.

JOSEPH CROWE,
Wholesale and Retail Dealer in
Family Groceries, Provisions
FRUITS, PRODUCE, &c.,
STATE ST., Bet. 3rd & 4th. Goods Delivered Free of Charge.

IMPORTANT EVENTS OF THE CENTURY.   235

Pennsylvania Commissioners' Building, Centennial Exposition, Philadelphia.—It is a wooden gothic building, 98 feet by 55 feet. It is surrounded by a tasteful piazza, six feet wide, and is ornamented with a central tower, flanked on each side by two smaller octagonal towers. The height to the eaves is 22 feet, to the peak of the roof 39 feet, and to the top of the central tower 65 feet. The main hall is 30 by 50 feet, on the right of which are two rooms 20 by 20 feet each, intended for ladies' and gentlemen's parlors, beautifully fitted up, and having dressing rooms and other conveniences attached. On the left are two committee rooms, 20 by 27 feet. The State of Pennsylvania appropriated $15,000 for its erection. It is the headquarters of the Pennsylvania State Commission.

ALTON—Continued.

GROCERS.

BLAIR & ATWOOD, Wholesale Grocers,
Second st., cor. Piasa.

NISBETT, T. P., & CO., Grocers,
2nd st., opposite City Hall

GUNSMITH.

WUERKER, F., Manuf'r of and Dealer in Guns,
Rifles, Pistols, State st.

HOTEL.

"EMPIRE HOUSE."
Hotel and Boarding House,
Kept by
THEODORE FRIES.
Third St., bet. Piasa and State.
Travelers and Farmers can lodge here cheaper than any other house.

INSURANCE.

WHIPPLE & SMILEY,
Insurance and Real Estate Agents,
Money to Loan. Office over First Nat. Bank.

LIME KILNS.

WM. ARMSTRONG & BRO.,
Wholesale and Retail Ice Dealers,
And Proprietors of
BLUFF LIME KILNS,
And Dealers in
Cement, Lime, Hair, Plaster Paris, Etc.,
Second St.

LIVERY AND FEED STABLE.

H. W. HART,
Livery and Feed Stable,
STATE STREET,
Opposite Alton National Bank.

MILLINERY.

GILMAN, & CO., Dealers in Millinery
Goods, 12 Belle st.

OYSTER SALOON.

KARL BETZ'S
NEW
RESTAURANT & OYSTER SALOON,
Choice Ice Cream, Nuts, Cigars. Tobacco, &c.
MEALS AT ALL HOURS.
Corner Belle and Fourth Streets.

SALOONS.

BRUCH & BLACKBORNE, Choicest Wines, Liquors and Cigars, Second st., opp. City Hall.

ALTON—Continued.

SALOONS.

MATT, FRANCIS, Bank Saloon. Choice Liquors
and Cigars. State st.

MIESSNER, PAUL. Wine and Beer Saloon, cor.
Second and Piasa sts.

OBEN, M. F., Wine and Lager Beer Saloon,
No. 6, Second st.

STEINHEIMER, B., Wine & Beer Saloon, 2d st.,
opposite City Hall.

TAILORS.

MORITZ, H. C. G., MERCHANT TAILOR, and
Dealer in Gents', Youths' and Boys'
Clothing and Gents' Furnishing Goods,
THIRD ST., bet. State and Piasa.

TANNERY.

WILLIAMS, R. A., Manufacturer of Sheepskins
and White Linings, Belle st.

UNDERTAKERS.

KLUNK & WILLS'
Undertaking Establishment,
Keeps constantly on hand a full assortment of
COFFINS, METALIC CASES & CASKETS,
STATE ST., opp. Third (over Platt & Hart's Livery Stable).
Prompt attention given to carpenter work of all kinds, and repairing furniture.

WINES AND LIQUORS.

BASSE & GRAY,
Dealers in Imported and Domestic
WINES, LIQUORS, ETC.
State st.

WAGON MAKERS.

JOHN H. KOEHNE,
Manufacturer of
Farm, Spring and Platform
WAGONS.
REPAIRING DONE AT LOW PRICES.
Belle St., bet. Fourth & Fifth.

GEORGE LUFT,
General
Blacksmith and Horseshoer,
Wagons of Every Description made to order.
BELLE ST. Established 1872.

DECATUR, ILLS.

BARBERS.

JAMES HOLLINGER,
BARBER AND HAIRDRESSER,
Cor. E. Main St. and Old Square.

ROGAN & CHAPMAN, Barbers and Hairdressers,
30 E. Main st.

IMPORTANT EVENTS OF THE CENTURY. 237

Perry's Flag Ship "Lawrence."—Our illustration is from a Photograph by Viers & Dunlap, Erie, Pa., and shows the condition in which she appeared, when raised in Misery Bay, Erie Harbor, after laying at the bottom of Lake Erie for 63 years. She was raised September 17, 1875, and was on exhibition in Philadelphia, during the Cetennial year, 1876.

1873.

July 8.—Michael Desmond kills his wife, and then commits suicide, in Boston.

July 15.—Ethelbert S. Mills, President of the Brooklyn Trust Company, drowned at Coney Island.

July 17.—The great Harvard-Yale regatta, on the Connecticut; Yale the victor.

July 20.—The whaling ship, Ravenscraig, alias Capt. Buddington and party (14 in all) from their boat in the Arctic sea, subsequently transferred to the whaler, Arctic.

July 25.—Destructive fire in Baltimore. Delia Corcoran outraged and murdered by a party of negroes, on the Hudson.

Aug. 1.—Execution of Thomas R. Hollohan, alias Whalen, and Joshua Nicholson, for the murder of Mrs. Lampley at Baltimore. Murder of Mrs. Schusretier by her husband, and suicide of the murderer, at Philadelphia.

Aug. 2.—Destructive conflagration at Portland, Oregon.

Aug. 8.—Burning of the steamboat, Wawasset, on the Potomac; fearful loss of life.

Aug. 12.—Two women killed instantly and four fatally injured by lightning, near Scranton, Pa.

Aug. 14.—Sanguinary battle between the Pawnees and Sioux in the Republican Valley, reported.

Aug. 16.—Terrible railroad disaster on the Chicago and Alton Railroad; eleven passengers killed and many wounded.

Aug. 22.—Michael C. Broderick stabs his son James to death, at 81 Carmine street, New York.

Aug. 25.—Railroad smash-up on the South Side R. R.; fifty passengers injured.

Sept. 9.—The settlement of the Geneva award consummated.

Sept. 13.—Assassination of Gen. E. S. McCook by P. P. Wintermate, at Yankton, Dakota Territory.

Sept. 15.—The propeller, Ironsides, founders on Lake Michigan, with great loss of life.

Sept. 18.—Failures on Wall street, New York—Jay Cooke & Co., and others. The Dundee whaling steamer, Arctic, arrives at Dundee with Capt. Buddington and rescued companions.

Sept. 23.—The McCool-Allen prize-fight, near St. Louis; Allen the winner in the ninth round.

Sept. 26.—Imposing dedication of a Masonic temple at Philadelphia.

Sept. 30.—Grand Masonic parade in Philadelphia; over 3,000 men in line.

Oct. 3.—Execution of the Modocs, Capt. Jack, Sconchin, Boston Charley and Black Jim, for the murder of Gen. Canby and Rev. Dr. Thomas, at Fort Klamath, Oregon. First business session of the Evangelical Alliance held.

Oct. 4.—Capt. Buddington and ten other survivors of the Polaris expedition, arrive in New York on the steam ship City of Antwerp. Gen. Ryan and seventy others embark on the steamer Atlas, bound for Cuba Libre.

Oct. 7.—Edward S. Stokes put upon his

ALTON—Continued.

BARBERS.

H. SINGLETON,
BARBER & HAIRDRESSER
Prairie st., near corner Water.

STEWART, D., Barber and Hairdresser, Central Block, Merchant t.

BOOKBINDER.

TOWLING, WM., Bookbinder, cor. Old square and Main st.

DENTIST.

R. C. DAWKINS, D.D.S.,
DENTIST,
Corner Water st. and Park Established 1865.

MILLINERY AND DRESSMAKING.

MRS. M. V. BRIGHAM,

DRESS AND CLOAKMAKER,

Cor. State St. and Park.

DELHOUSEN, MRS. L. P., Millinery and Fancy Goods, Post Office Block, Prairie st.

MRS. E. A. EASTMAN,

Dressmaker and Milliner,
41 Water st.

MISS L. M. EASTON,

DRESS AND CLOAKMAKER,

19 EAST MAIN ST.

HAMSHER, MRS. R. C., Millinery and Fancy Goods, 21 Central block.

LEIBY, MRS. A. M., Dress and Cloakmaker, Central Block, Merchant st.

MRS. M. L. M'DONALD,
Dealer in

MILLINERY,

Straw and Hair Goods,
26 MERCHANT ST.

MUSIC TEACHER.

A. GOODMAN,

MUSIC TEACHER,

And Leader of the

Goodman Orchestra and Brass Band,
39 WATER ST., BRAMERNAN'S BLOCK.

IMPORTANT EVENTS OF THE CENTURY.   239

DECATUR—Continued.

NEWSPAPER.

THE DECATUR REVIEW, W. H. Bayne, Proprietor, South side old square.

PHOTOGRAPHERS.

Established 1861.

MRS. T. H. BUTLER,

The Indian Lady

Photographer.

Copying old Pictures a Specialty.

COR. WATER ST. & PARK.

Established 1862.

Mrs. J. Haws'

CITY

Photograph

AND

GEM GALLERY.

Enlarging, by Solar Work, a Specialty.

15 E. Main st., Decatur, Ills.

LEFORGEE & PIPER, Photographers,
25 Water st.

Established 1856.

W. C. PITNER,

Photographic Artist,

Copying and Enlarging a Specialty.

13 WATER ST.

PHYSICIANS.

BUMSTEAD, DR. S. J., Occulist & Aurist,
12 E. Main st

CURTIS, IRA B., Occulist & Aurist,
25 N. Main st.

KILNER, GEO., M. D., Occulist & Aurist,
35 N. Main st.

TILE AND CROCKERY.

GILLEN, GEO., Tile & Crockery,
53 W. Main st.

SEWING MACHINES.

BLUME, GEO. P., Agt. Singer Sewing Machines,
26 Merchant st.

16

1873.

third trial for the murder of James Fisk, Jr., at the Grand Central Hotel.

Oct. 11.—The General Conference of the Evangelical Alliance hold their closing session.

Ex-Senator Pomeroy shot and wounded by Ex-Congressman Conway, in Washington.

Oct. 14.—The delegates to the Evangelical Alliance received at the White House by President Grant.

Oct. 21.—The new Foundling Asylum on 68th street, New York, opened.

Oct. 25.—Arrival of the sloop-of-war, Juniata, from her Polaris search.

Oct. 29.—Close of third trial of Stokes, in the Court of Oyer and Terminer, New York; he is found guilty of murder in the fourth degree.

Oct. 31.—Capture of the American steamship Virginius by the Spanish gunboat Tornado, off the island of Jamaica.

Nov. 1.—The Virginius and her captor arrive at Santiago de Cuba.

Nov. 4.—The Santiago de Cuba slaughter. Bernabe Verona, Pedro Cespedes, Jesus del Sol, and Gen. Washington Ryan, captured on the Virginias, shot at 6 a. m. by order of Gen. Burrier, commanding the Spanish troops at Santiago de Cuba.

Nov. 7.—Capt. Joseph Fry, an American-born citizen, commanding the Virginius when captured by the Spanish gunboat Tornado, and thirty-six of his crew, executed at Santiago de Cuba. Santa Rosa, an adopted American citizen, was among the number of these victims.

Nov. 8.—Twelve more of the Cuban patriots executed at Santiago de Cuba, among them Franchi Alfaro, who offered a million of dollars as ransom for his own and companions' lives.

Nov. 8.—(1872) Capt. C. F. Hall, commander of the U. S. Polaris expedition, died at Polaris Bay, lat. 81° 38', long. 61° 34'. Buried in Polaris Bay, Nov. 11, 1872.

Nov. 11.—Terrible boiler explosion at Harlem; seven persons killed and nine wounded.

Nov. 15.—Duncan T. Templeton shoots his wife, nee Miss Ida Babcock, on Eighth avenue, near 15th street, New York.

Nov. 18.—The Virginius arrives at Havana from Santiago de Cuba, under escort of the Tornado and other Spanish war vessels.

Nov. 19.—Wm. Tweed (Big Six), convicted in the Court of Oyer and Terminer on 204 counts, charging him with defrauding the City Treasury of New York.

Wm. J. Sharkey, convicted of the murder of Robert S. Gunn, escapes from the tombs in New York.

Fatal prize fight near Ottowa, Ill., between Jack Lewis and Jim Rogers. Lewis dies immediately after the 36th round.

Nov. 20.—Loss of the Anglo-American cable steamer Robert Lowe, bound for St. Johns, Newfoundland. Commander Tidmarsh and sixteen of the officers and crew drowned.

Nov. 22.—The French steamer Ville de Havre, Captain Surmont, collides with the

DECATUR—Continued.

SEWING MACHINES.

HUMPHREY & SON,
Dealers in the
IMPROVED
Howe Sewing Machine,
NEEDLES, OIL & ATTACHMENTS.
ALL KINDS of MACHINES REPAIRED

Opp. P. O. blk., 23 N. Main st.

BELLEVILLE, ILLS,

BOOKSELLER.

PITTMAN, L., Bookbinder & Bookseller,
Belleville.

CHINA, GLASS AND QUEENSWARE.

ROEDER, A., China, Glass & Queensware,
15 E. Main st.

CUTTER AND GRINDER.

LOOS, JNO. ADAM, Cutter & Grinder,
W. Main st.

DRY GOODS, ETC.

NEW YORK BAZAAR, Wm. Bauman, Sr., Agt.,
Notions & Dry Goods, W. Main st.

WILDING, J. & SON, Groceries & Dry Goods,
207 W. Main st.

HATS, CAPS AND FURS.

RIEDELL, F. C., Manufacturer and dealer in Hats, Caps, Furs, Gloves & Umbrellas, Main street, second block West of public square. Sign—The big Hat and Glove.

PLANING MILL.

STORCK & BRO., Cor. 1st North & Spring sts., Manufacturers of Sash, Doors, Blinds, Frames, Mouldings, Brackets, Scroll Sawing, Stair Railing, Balusters, etc. All kinds of Wood Turning done.

MARBLE WORKS.

VAUGHN & LORD, Marble & Granite Works,
Belleville, Ill.

WINES AND LIQUORS.

ANDEL, C. W. & CO., successors to Andel & Weber, RECTIFIERS OF SPIRITS, and Wholesale dealers in Wines and Liquors, 222 East Main st.

BLOOMINGTON, ILLS.

BARBERS.

HILL, GEO. A., Barber,
Old P. O. Stand, cor, Jefferson & Main sts.

BLOOMINGTON—Continued.

BARBERS.

FRED KESTING,
New Post Office Barber Shop,
SHAVING AND HAIR CUTTING
In the latest style. Cor. Centre & Front sts.

RICHARD BLUE,
BARBER,
104 S. Main st.

BOOK BINDER.

AMOS KEMP,
BOOK BINDER AND BLANK BOOK MANUFACTURER,
216 & 218 N. Centre st.

BILLIARD HALL.

HAKER, FRED, Beer & Billiard Hall,
Cor. Centre & Washington sts.

BILL POSTERS.

HOLLY, JOEL, & SONS, City Bill Posters,
205 W. Front st.

BROOM FACTORIES.

LEWIS, W. M., Broom Factory,
820 E. Washington st.

WHITE, W. F., Manf'r of Brooms & Brushes,
Bloomington, Ill.

BUSINESS COLLEGE.

"Evergreen City"
BUSINESS COLLEGE,
MARQUAM & BAKER, Proprietors,
114 S. Main St.

CONFECTIONER.

TIMERMAN, J. L., Confectioner & Fruiterer,
118 S. Main st.

CRACKER BAKERY.

GERKEN, W. A., Cracker Bakery,
118 E. Front st.

DENTIST.

Dr. G. D. Sitherwood,
DENTIST,
Office : S. W. cor. Square.

DRUGGISTS.

DYSON & CO., Chemists & Pharmacists,
Cor Main & Grove sts.

CATHOLIC TOTAL ABSTINANCE FOUNTAIN, PHILADELPHIA, CENTENNIAL GROUNDS.

Peters' Horse Protector,
Or Elastic Patented Tug-Link for Harness,
For Teamsters, Farmers, and Street Railway Companies.

The advantages gained by the use of this invention may be comprised as follows:
FIRSTLY. That the horses breasts and shoulders will not be liable to soreness from the harness by any overstrain.
SECONDLY. The horses will start and convey heavy loads with more ease and will therefore be able to do longer duty.
THIRDLY. The saving in Harness-repairs will be quite a consideration.
FOURTHLY. The entire strain of the start being obviated, horses will show less tendency to baulk, and actually baulky horses will be cured by the use of the Protector.

Peters' Patent Elastic Tug-Links are furnished at $2.50 per pair by

PETERS & CO., Manufacturers,
Office, 65 N. Clark St., Chicago.

☞AGENTS WANTED EVERYWHERE.

REFERENCES:

Field, Leiter & Co., Wholesale Dry Goods, Chicago. | N. K. Fairbanks & Co., Lard & Oil Works, Chicago
Busch & Brandt, Brewers, - - " | Chicago Fire Department, - - "
A. Fisher, Northwestern Flour & Feed Mills " | North side Chicago Omnibus Line, R. Rager, "
C. Gee & Bro., General Teamsters. - - " | North Chicago City Railway - - "

MISSISSIPPI VALLEY VINEGAR WORKS.
First Premium Awarded at Agricultural and Mechanical Exposition.

JOHN GLAB,
Proprietor and Manufacturer of

All kinds of Choice Vinegars,
ALSO, DESSELDORF and FRENCH MUSTARD,
Warranted Manufactured from Pure Brown Seed.

FACTORY & OFFICE, 313 IOWA St., DUBUQUE, IOWA.

BLOOMINGTON—*Continued.*

FANCY GOODS AND NOTIONS.

WALKER, JOSEPH, Fancy Goods & Notions,
209 N. Main st.

FOUNDRIES.

N. DIEDRICH,

Union Foundry
AND
MACHINE SHOP,
Manufacturer of the
Ruttan & Hawley Furnace,
407 S. Center st.

HARNESS AND SADDLES.

MOORE, M. L., Harness, Saddles, Trunks, etc.,
114 S. Main st.

HIDES AND LEATHER.

AGLE & SONS, Hides & Leather,
307 S. Center st.

HOTEL.

STEVENS HOUSE, Mrs. E. Stevens, Proprietress,
Cor. Main & Grove sts.

INSURANCE.

WAITE, M. C., Insurance Agent,
Cor. Centre & Washington sts.

MARBLE WORKS.

HOLDEMAN MARBLE WORKS,
301 S. Main st.

MOORE, W. B., Marble & Granite Worker,
311 W. Washington st.

MILLINERY.

DUNHAM & HOYT, Millinery & Fancy Goods,
106 N. Centre st.

ROBINSON, MISS M., Millinery & Fancy Goods,
406 N. Main st.

TAYLOR, MRS. S. A., Millinery,
408 N. Main st.

WALKER, JOSEPH, Millinery,
209 N. Main st.

BLOOMINGTON—*Continued.*

NEWSPAPERS.

DEMOCRATIC NEWS, only Democratic Paper in the co., Dudley Creed, pub., 116 W. Front st.

THE WESTERN ADVANCE, A. O. Grigsby, Editor, 113 W. Front st.

OIL MANUFACTURER.

WINSLOW, N. N., Manf'r of Oils, E. of Main st., near L. B. & M. Pass. Depot.

PIANOS AND ORGANS.

VAN SCHOICK & ANDRUS, Pianos & Organs, Lincoln Block, cor. Main & Jefferson sts.

PHYSICIAN.

Dr. A. S. Burrows,
CURAPATHIST
Treats Diseases in every Stage,
ACUTE OR CHRONIC;
Strains, Sprains, Bruises, Insanity, etc., without any DRUGS OR MEDICINE.
Office and residence:
420 NORTH MAIN ST.

SEWING MACHINES.

DALLIBA, J. B., Sewing Machine Repair Shop,
101 E. North st.

SOAP AND CANDLES.

WINSLOW, N. N., Manf'r of Soap & Candles, E. of Main st., near L. B. & M. Pass Depot.

UNDERTAKERS.

FLINSPACH & DENEEN, Undertakers,
Cor. Oak & Market sts.

MAYER, AARON & CO., Undertakers,
Front st. under new P. O.

SHEBOYGAN, WIS.

AGRICULTURAL IMPLEMENTS.

KOHLER & SILBERZAHN, Manf'rs of Pat, feed Cutters, Cast steel & Chilled Plows.

ADVERTISEMENTS. 243

Woman's Pavillion, Centennial Exposition, Philadelphia.—The building covers an area of 30,000 square feet; it is of wood, roofed over by segmented trusses. It exhibits a nave and transept, each 192 feet long and 64 feet wide, terminating in porches 8 by 32 feet. The center of the structure rises 25 feet above the exterior portions, and terminates with a cupola and lantern 90 feet from the ground. The whole cost of the building, including interial decorations, is about $40,000. Built by money raised by women.

Established 1863.

NORTH-WESTERN VINEGAR WORKS. { Established 1863.

JAMES CUSHING, Proprietor,

Factory the largest in the State. Capacity equal to any in the United States,

Located on Eagle Point Ave., and Valeria St., Dubuque, Iowa.

244   IMPORTANT EVENTS OF THE CENTURY.

1873.

British ship Loch Earn, Capt. Robinson, and immediately sinks in mid-ocean, with the loss of 227 lives.

Wm. M. Tweed sentenced to twelve years' imprisonment and to pay a fine of $12,500.

Nov. 26.—James H. Ingersoll and John D. Farrington, convicted of defrauding the City Treasury of New York, and sentenced, Ingersoll to four years; Farrington in the Court of Oyer and Terminer, to one year and six months in the State Prison.

Nov. 30.—The brig Mattano boarded by masked robbers in the Harbor, N. Y.; the captain, T. H. Connauton, fired at and wounded; the watchman bound and muffled, and the cabin despoiled of all the valuables belonging to the captain's wife and family; two of the robbers were subsequently sentenced, in the Court of General Sessions, to twenty years each at Sing Sing.

Dec. 9.—Ex-congressman M. Conway indicted for assault with intent to kill Senator Pomeroy.

Dec. 11.—Double murder and suicide in Boston. George W. Kimball murders his wife and daughter and then cuts his own throat.

Dec. 12.—The Virginius towed out of the port of Havana for Bahia Honda, the port of surrender to the United States.

Michael C. Broderick convicted of manslaughter in the fourth degree, in causing the death of his son.

Mob demonstration in Havana against the delivery of the Virginius. Captain-General Jovellar addresses the mob.

The centennial anniversary of throwing the tea overboard in Boston Harbor celebrated throughout the New England States.

Dec. 16.—Surrender of the Virginius at Bahia Honda, by the Spanish steamer La Favorita, to the United States steamer Dispatch, Captain Whiting. President Castellar conveys the news in person to Minister Sickles, at Madrid.

Repeal of the Bankruptcy Law in the House of Representatives.

The corner-stone of the proposed bridge to span the Hudson at Poughkeepsie laid with appropriate ceremonies.

Dec. 18.—One hundred and two of the survivors of the Virginius and Santiago de Cuba butchery delivered by the Spanish General Burrier to Commander Braine of the United States steamer Juniata.

Dec. 19.—Conviction of Henry W. Genet in the court of Oyer and Terminer, for fraud against the New York city government.

Dec. 21.—The First Baptist Church, corner Nassau and Liberty streets, New York, destroyed by fire.

Dec. 22.—Henry W. Genet escapes from Sheriff Brennan's officers at his house in Harlem, and effectually evades recapture.

The Broome Street Ryan tragedy: Nicholas and Mary Ryan, brother and sister, found with their throats cut at 204 Broome street, New York.

Dec. 26.—The resignation of the U. S. Minister to Spain, Gen. Sickles, officially accepted.

SHEBOYGAN—*Continued.*

ATTORNEY AT LAW.

SUMNER, GEO. T., Attorney at Law,
German Bank Building.

BAKERY AND CONFECTIONERY.

WAGNER, G. A., Bakery & Confectionery,
8th & Niagara sts. Established 1873.

BOOTS AND SHOES.

KEMPF, JACOB, Boots, Shoes, Gaiters, Rubbers, Slippers, etc., 8th st.

CIGARS AND TOBACCO.

WIEHN, HENRY, Manf'r and dealer in Cigars & Tobacco, 8th st. Established 1862

CIGAR BOX LUMBER.

A. LOOK.   C. BECHLY.

Look & Bechly,

Manufacturers of

CIGAR BOX LUMBER,

And all kinds of BOXES,

Ninth Street, Near City Park.

CLOTHING.

HOBERGS, J., dealer in Clothing, Boots and Shoes, 8th st. & Penn avenue.

CROCKERY AND GLASSWARE.

DESCOMBES, L. A., Crockery, Table Glassware, Plated ware & Cutlery, 8th st.

DENTIST.

DUCKETT, C. H., Dentist,
Eighth and New York ave.

DRUGGISTS.

BOCK, LOUIS & SON, Druggists, Eighth st., near City Park. Established 1876.

A. MAHLENDORF,

Dealer in

DRUGS, PAINTS, OILS,

Varnishes, Brushes, Window Glass, Looking-Glasses. Lamps, Mouldings, Stationery, etc.,

EIGHTH ST., NEAR CENTRE.   EST. 1864.

FLOUR AND FEED.

STEFFEN & JUCKEM, Wholesale and Retail Dealers in
Flour, Feed and Produce.
Green Peas and Clover Seed a specialty.
Sheboygan.

FURNITURE.

MATTOON, GEO. B., Furniture and Upholstered Goods, Eighth st.

C. RIEDEL, Manufacturer of
Furniture, Coffins, Etc., and General Undertakers,
Eighth st., above Beekman House. Est. 1862.

SHEBOYGAN—Continued.

HOMŒOPATHIC PHYSICIAN.

SQUIRE, H. D., M.D., Homœopathic Physician and Surgeon, Eighth st.

HOLLOW WARE.

J. J. VOLLRATH,
Manufacturer of
PORCELAIN LINED HOLLOW WARE,
In Gray & White, Pump Cylinders, etc.
Gray Enameled Ware warranted to be durable for stove use. Prices compare favorably with Eastern Manufactories Established 1874.
Cor. Sixth and Huron Streets.

HOTELS.

BEEKMAN HOUSE. $2.00 per day. Eighth st. Halsted & Stearns, prop's.

NATIONAL HOTEL, L. Rauffus, prop., Eighth st. Established 1876.

NEWHALL HOUSE, J. F. Antisdel, prop., Milwaukee.

PARK HOTEL, Fred Esllen, prop., Eighth st., opp. City Park. Established 1875.

MACHINIST.

JENKINS, DAVID, MACHINIST and Builder of Zufelt & Craig's
Patent Hub Machine and Bailey Lathe.
Dealer in Shafting, Pulleys, Hangers, etc., Sheboygan.

MARBLE DEALER.

ROOT, WM. M., Marble Dealer. Dealer and Livery Stable, 8th st., West of Turner Hall.

MINERAL WATERS.

BERTSCHY & THAYER, Sheboygan Mineral Water, 241 Eighth st.

PHOTOGRAPHERS.

GROH, G. M. & BROS, Photograph Parlors, cor. Eighth st. and Pennsylvania ave.

SHAVING AND BATHING SALOON.

BACH, C., Hairdressing and Shaving Saloon, Mineral Baths, Hot, Cold or Shower, 8th st.

WINE AND BEER SALOON.

HOBERGS, J., Wine and Beer Saloon, Eighth st. and Pennsylvania ave.

Sheboygan Business Houses.
WHEN ESTABLISHED.

LOOK & BECHLY, Cigar Box Lumber, 1871.
MAHLENDORF, D·uggist, 1864.
VOLLRATH, J. J., Hollow Ware, 1874.

RIPON, WIS.

ATTORNEYS AT LAW.

REED, L. E., Attorney at Law. Money Loaning. Collecting a specialty. Est. 1866.

1873.
The Virginius, in tow of the Ossipee, en route from Bahia Honda to New York, is abandoned off Frying-Pan shoals and sinks to the bottom.
The great strike among the engineers and firemen of the Pennsylvania and connecting railroads occurs.
James Gallagher, at 50 Pearl Street, Brooklyn, throws his wife down stairs, and believing that he has killed her, fatally shoots himself.
Jennie Griffin instantly killed, and several other girls injured by the falling of a floor in a house of ill fame, in Buffalo.

Dec. 27.—Seizure of the books of the mercantile firm of Jordan, Marsh & Co., at Boston. The firm charged with extensive revenue frauds against the government.

Dec. 28.—Arrival of the steamship Juniata in the harbor with 102 survivors of the Virginius from the Santiago de Cuba massacre.
Wholesale arrest of 200 young men and girls in a dance-house in Grand street, New York.

Dec. 29.—The steamer Ossipee, the convoy of the steamer Virginius from Bahia Honda to the sinking of the latter, arrives in the harbor.
A party of roughs enter the saloon of Wm. Hile, a German, in Washington, and attack and beat his wife. Hile fires at the party, shooting his wife and instantly killing her.
De Platte, an insane spiritualist, aged 64 years, stabs himself to the heart at No. 4 Cortlandt Street, N. Y.

Dec. 30.—The Emperor of Germany's gift of five bronze cannon to St. Matthew's Lutheran German congregation arrives at Baltimore.

Dec. 31.—The jury in the trial of Maggie Jourdan, charged with aiding the escape of Sharkey from the Tombs, disagree. Maggie is admitted to bail.

1874.

Jan. 3.—Franenthal's Opera House, Wilkesbarre, destroyed by fire.
W. C. Durgin murdered at Brandy Station by a negro.

Jan. 9.—Execution of Jacob Mechella in Jersey City, for the murder of U. S. Marshall Stephenson.
Great fire in Broadway, New York, loss $100,000.

Jan. 10.—The fugitive, Henry W. Genet, seen by an acquaintance in Belfast, Ireland.

Jan. 11.—Seizure of an illicit distillery on Barren Island by revenue officers and U. S. troops.
W. W. Hazard, proprietor of the Atlantic House, Newport, R. I., drowns himself in a cistern.

Jan. 13.—Workingmen's mass meeting at Tompkins Square, New York, dispersed by the police.
Fatal fire in the Stiner mansion, 24 East 60th street, New York. Mr. Jacob Stiner leaps from the flames to the yard and is almost instantly killed. Mrs. Stiner and Miss Deborah Stiner found dead in their apartment. The servant, Mary McGuire, seriously injured by leaping to the ground.
Terrible conflagration in Natick, Mass.—the town almost utterly consumed.

Jan. 17.—Edward Edmunds and H. N. Mason arrested, charged with robbery of

ADVERTISEMENTS.

RIPON—*Continued.*

DENTISTS.

LUTHER, T. G., Dentist, Pettibone's Block. Established 1864

S. R. PATTEN,
DENTIST,
East side of Public Square. Established 1875.

DRUGGISTS.

1866.   B. H. PHELPS & CO.,   1876.
Dealers in
DRUGS AND MEDICINES,
Books and Stationery, opp. First Nat'l Bank.

DRY GOODS.

MATTICE & GARY, Chicago Dry Goods Store, 18 Public Square.

PETTIBONE, A. W., Wholesale and Retail Dry Goods, N. E. cor. Public Square. Est. 1864.

PHOTOGRAPHERS.

BRADLEY, G. W., Photographer, Pettibone's Block. Established 1877.

LOCKWOOD, WM. M., Photographer, East side of Public Square. Established 1858.

REAL ESTATE AND INSURANCE.

LYLE, W. R., Insurance, Real Estate and Loan Broker, Main st. Established 1871.

TAILORS.

J. E. BROWN,
Merchant Tailor
And Dealer in
Gents' Furnishing Goods,

Hats, Caps, Trunks, Valises, etc.,

45 MAIN STREET.

CORBETT, JOHN, Merchant Tailor, Greenway Block.

ISAAC BROWN,
MERCHANT TAILOR
And Dealer in
Cloths & Cassimeres,
35 MAIN STREET.

WIND MILL.

THE HAZEN WIND MILL. Manufactured by S. Hazen & Son, Ripon, Wis. Estab. 1872.

Ripon Business Houses.
WHEN ESTABLISHED.

BROWN, J. E., Merchant Tailor, 1866.
BROWN, ISAAC, Merchant Tailor, 1876.

RIPON—*Continued.*

BUSINESS HOUSES.

CORBETT, JOHN, Merchant Tailor, 1859.
PHELPS, B. H., & CO., Druggist, 1866.

BERLIN, WIS.

ATTORNEYS AT LAW.

SILVER, O. F., Attorney at Law, Huron st. Established 1850.

WARING & RYAN, Attorneys at Law, Yates' Block. Established 1875.

BAKER AND CONFECTIONER.

SPENCER, H., Baker and Confectioner, Huron st. Established 1857.

BLACKSMITH AND CARRIAGES.

HITCHCOCK, W., Black-mith and Carriage Maker, Huron st. Established 1867.

WHEIGHTON, T. W., Blacksmith and Horse Shoeing, Wisconsin st. Established 1877.

DENTIST.

WIGHTMAN, P. B., Dentist, Pearl st. Established 1867.

DRUGGISTS.

F. H. & J. R. Brown,

AT THE
NEW "CENTRAL" DRUG STORE, BERLIN.

DODSON, N. M., Druggist, Huron st. Established 1855.

DRY GOODS.

KUETZING, F., Dry Goods, Groceries and Grassware, Huron st. Established 1874.

FLOUR AND FEED.

MORRIS, C. S., Flour and Feed Mill, Broadway. Established 1870.

FURNITURE.

CASE, C. I., Repairer and Finisher of Furniture, Market Square, N. Side.

KLEIN, C. H., Manufacturer and Dealer in Furniture, Huron st. Established 1856.

SMITH, J. E., All Kinds of Furniture, Huron st. Established 1876.

HARNESS AND SADDLES.

BASSETT, T. S., Harness and Saddle Maker, 14 Broadway. Established 1857.

LOUNSBERY, GEO. W., Harness and Saddle Maker, Huron st. Established 1857.

IMPORTENT EVENTS OF THE CENTURY. 247

New Hampshire State Building, Centennial Exposition, Philadelphia.—Like the other state buildings, it is constructed of wood, two-stories high with an attic. The first floor is surrounded with a portico. It is a roomy building, handsomely finished inside and outside. It contains all the conveniences necessary to make the Centennial visitors comfortable.

Newspaper Building, Centennial Exposition, Philadelphia.—The pavilion was sold for $520 to A. Wessels, Secretary of Bellevue Literary Association, to be erected Sixty-third and Vine streets as an institute.

1874.

bonds from the Treasury Department, Washington.

Jan. 23.—Lulu Terrence, actress, commits suicide by shooting, in San Francisco.

Alexander D. Hamilton, Treasurer of Jersey City, absconds with $50,000 of the public money.

Jan. 26.—Intelligence of the death of Livingstone (died May 1st, 1873) received.

Jan. 30.—The Olympic Theatre, Philadelphia, burned—two firemen killed and six seriously injured.

Feb. 6.—Gen Sickles takes official leave of the Spanish government.

Feb. 12.—Anniversary of the late President Lincoln's birth; celebrations in various parts of the country.

Eighty-third anniversary birth-day of Peter Cooper. He is feted by the Arcadian Club.

Feb. 17.—Terrible triple murder in Halifax, Mass.—a maiden lady, Mary Buckley, and Thomas and Simon Sturtevant, brothers, being the victims.

Feb. 18.—Supervising Architect Mullet has a fisticuff encounter with Henry Kessler in the streets of Cincinnati.

Feb. 19.—John E. Simmons sentenced to three years and six months for the killing of Nicholas W. Duryea in Liberty street, New York.

Feb. 23.—Stephen Lowery, last of the Swamp Angels, encountered and shot by his pursuers.

Feb. 28.—Ex-President Baez arrested in New York on a charge of false imprisonment.

March 7.—Reported surrender of three Cubans to the Spanish authorities by Captain Deaken of the steamship City of New York; two of them after reported as garrotted.

March 11.—Charles Sumner dies.

March 19.—The suicide of Second Lieutenant Fred. P. Ela, by jumping overboard from the steamer Great Republic, reported.

Robert E. L. Patton, of Philadelphia, drowns himself in the surf at Cape May.

March 21.—The State prison at Charlestown, Mass., takes fire: workshops and other property valued at $50,000 destroyed.

March 28.—Henry Ward Beecher acquitted by the Congregational Council.

April 5.—Charles Kingsley shot dead in the New York picture gallery, San Francisco, by one Cowden, who instantly after committed suicide.

April 9.—The Polar steamer, Tigress, explodes her boiler, killing twenty-one of her crew, including two engineers.

April 10.—Emil Lowenstein hanged at Albany for the murder of John D. Weston, one-armed peddler of Brooklyn.

April 13.—Sir Lambton Lorraine arrives in New York by the steamer Canima, from Bermuda.

April 15.—The remains of Livingstone arrive at Southampton.

BERLIN—*Continued.*

HOTELS.

AMERICAN HOUSE. H. B. Richards, Prop. Broadway.

EAGLE HOTEL. Aug. Buhler, Prop., Huron st. Established 1877.

MACHINIST.

JOHNSON, N., Machinist, Wisconsin st. Established 1874.

MARBLE WORKS.

NORTHWESTERN MARBLE WORKS.

J. E. GRIFFITHS,

Manufacturer of Italian and American

Marble Monuments, Headstones, Tablets, Etc,

MARKET SQUARE, Berlin, Wis.

Cheap as the cheapest; good as the best. Stones carefully boxed for transportation. Orders respectfully solicited.

MEAT MARKET.

ELLIS, S. J., Central Meat Market, Huron st. Established 1861.

PHOTOGRAPHERS.

HOLLY, M. S., Photographer, Huron st. Established 1867.

TAYLOR, S. M., Photographer, Huron st. Established 1871.

RESTAURANT AND CONFECTIONERY.

HATHAWAY & BELLIS, Restaurant and Confectionery, Huron st. Established 1870.

WATCHES AND JEWELRY.

HEANEY, J. M., Dealer in Watches, Clocks and Jewelry, Huron st. Established 1872.

WHIP MANUFACTURERS.

LUTHER, J. P., Patentee and Manufacturer of the Berlin Solid Leather Whip, Broadway.

J. N. MORRIS,

Manufacturer of and Dealer in the

Berlin Solid Leather Whip

AND SOLID LEATHER & BONE WHIP.

ALSO, BRAIDED & ROUND LASHES.

Berlin Business Houses,
WHEN ESTABLISHED.

BROWN, F. H. & J. R., Druggists, 1875.
GRIFFITHS, J. E., Marble, 1875.
MORRIS, J. N., Whip Manufacturer, 1876.

IMPORTANT EVENTS OF THE CENTURY.   249

LAC, WIS.

AT LAW.
Attorney at Law, 518
ed 1873.

JPERINTENDENT.

GREEN,
aperintendent,
SION ST.
l Estimates for Public
s carefully drawn.
Construction a Spe-
y.

DING.
kbindery, 463 Main st.

D SHOES.
.RBER,

SHOES,
rling's Block.
l Shoemaker,
585 Main st.

SCHOLL,

d Dealers in Fine

d SHOES
IN ST.
Boots and Shoes. Fine
ecialty. 556 Main st.

RNISHING GOODS.
ARNAHAN, Dealers in
ENTS' FURNISHING
TS, CAPS,
ES, TRUNKS,
ing Bags.

HISTS.
SON & CO.,
POTHECARIES,
street.
ion Druggist, 530 Main
7.

use in the City.

NDALL,
r in

gists' Sundries
Darling's Block.
, Apothecary. Prescrip-
98 Main st.

1874.

Gov. Baxter of Arkansas forcibly ejected; the executive chair usurped by Governor (?) Brooks.

April 18.—Destructive floods along the Mississippi; twenty-seven plantations overflowed.

April 21.—Julius P. Mason commits suicide in the Parker House, Boston.

Street conflict between the Baxter and Brooks factions in Little Rock, Ark.

April 22.—Horace Mullin, a young lad, shockingly murdered by young Edward Pomeroy, at Dorchester, near Boston.

Sir Lambton Lorraine presented with the freedom of New York city.

May 1.—Deadly encounter between the Brooks and Baxter factions; nine of the Brooks party killed and twenty wounded. Capture of Major General Churchill, commanding Baxter's militia.

May 2.—Judges of the Supreme Court of Arkansas seized and carried off by Baxterites.

May 16.—The Mill River Reservoir disaster near Northampton, Mass. Fearful loss of life.

May 21.—Marriage of Miss Nellie Grant to A. C. F. Sartoris.

May 23.—Henri Rochefort, the French Communist, arrives in San Francisco.

May 27.—The Ellsworth monument at Mechanicsville unveiled.

May 30.—Henri Rochefort arrives in New York.

Dedication of the Fiske monument at Brattleboro, Vt.

June 2.—President Grant lays the corner-stone of the American Museum of Natural History, Eighth avenue and 77th street, New York.

June 11.—Charles Anderson, a retired Swedish sea captain, robbed of $15,000 worth of diamonds on Broadway, New York.

June 21.—A strawberry festival disaster; a floor in the Central Baptist Church at Syracuse gives away; fourteen persons killed and 200 injured.

June 30.—James P. Sanders, a lawyer, shot in the court room, Yonkers, by August Lachanme.

July 1.—Coggia's comet; first appearance.

Abduction of Charley Ross.

July 3.—Mr. Jewell, minister to Russia, accepts the Postmaster-Generalship.

July 4.—President Grant and family arrive at Long Branch.

Destructive fire in Allegheny City; over one hundred houses destroyed.

July 5.—Sam. McDonald, Baltimore, the "millionaire murderer," stabs his friend.

July 12.—Blush Hollow reservoir on Middlefield Brook, near Chester, Mass., bursts; damage, $1,000,000.

July 14.—Disastrous fire in Chicago; 7 persons killed, 3 steamers burned, and numerous buildings destroyed.

July 18.—The great Saratoga regatta contest; the Columbia crew the victors; time,

FOND DU LAC—Continued.

DYEING AND SCOURING.

FOUNTAIN CITY
Steam Dyeing & Scouring
ESTABLISHMENT,

HENRY C. DITTMAR, Prop.,
28 W. DIVISION ST., West side of Bridge.

Silks, Woolens, Crapes and Merinos scoured and dyed all colors in the best style. Half Cotton Goods Dyed plain colors. Also Gentlemen's Clothing, Ladies' Cloaks and Mantillas, and Kid Gloves cleaned and Dyed. Old Velvet made up like new. Cleaning done on short notice.

FARM IMPLEMENTS.

SUSAN, G. L., Farm Implements, Field Seeds, etc., 16 E. Second st. Established 1873.

FILE WORKS.

FOND DU LAC
FILE WORKS,
HENRY SCHERER, PROP.

Files and Rasps of Every Description Re-cut.

28 JOHNSON STREET.

GROCERIES AND PROVISIONS.

WISNOM, A. & CO., Groceries and Provisions, Crockery, Glassware, 549 Main st. Est. '76.

WYATT, ROB'T, Groceries, Provisions, 7 and 9 Second st., cor. Main st.

HARNESS AND SADDLES.

O'CONNELL, P., Harness, Saddles, Collars, Bridles, Whips & Saddlery Hardware, 410 Main.

SULLIVAN, M. O., Manufacturer and Dealer in HARNESS, SADDLES, COLLARS,
Bridles, Whips.
Also Dealer in Uncle Sam's Harness Oil.
394 Main st.

HOTELS.

FOND DU LAC HOUSE, Wm. Koehme, Prop., Main and Fourth sts. Established 18 0.

NEW AMERICAN,
H. SHATTUCK, PROP.
COR. MAIN & COURT STS.
This Hotel was recently rebuilt and newly furnished throughout.

WISCONSIN HOUSE, M. Schumacher, prop., Main st. Established 1876.

LUMBER MERCHANTS.

HAMILTON & FINLEY, Lumber Merchants, Main st. Established 1855.

MARBLE WORKS.

CAMPBELL & HOLLEY, Manf'rs of Italian and American Monuments, 16 E. Second. Est. '67.

FOND DU LAC—Continued.

MEAT MARKETS.

COFFMAN & SERVATIUS, Fresh and Salt Meats, 419 Main st. Established 1871.

MURPHY, J. & C., Beef, Pork, Lard, Tallow, Cut Meats, etc., 8 Division st.

ROLOFF, WM., prop. of Central Market and Dealer in Fresh and Salt Meats, 8 Forest st.

D. D. TRELEVEN & CO.,
Dealers in
FRESH & SALT MEATS,
Lard, Butter, Eggs, Etc.
BEEF AND PORK PACKERS.
COR. MAIN AND THIRD STS.

PATENT RIGHTS.

HAZARD, GEO. R., Real Estate and Insurance Agent, Patent Rights and Patent Medicines, Darling's Block. Agents wanted.

PHOTOGRAPHERS.

DILLON, JOHN W., Landscape and Portrait Photographer, 493 Main st. Est. 1871.

MOODY, H. W., Photographer, Main st., opp. American House. Established 1862.

PRINTER.

BRYANT, THOS., Premium Plain and Ornate Printer, 493 Main st.

REAL ESTATE.

HAZARD, J. A., Real Estate and Insurance Agent, Darling's Block.

HORTON & CUDWORTH, Real Estate Exchange. Office, S. W. cor. Main & Second sts. Est. '75.

TAILORS.

JACOB DREIS,
Fashionable
Merchant Tailor
And Gents' Furnisher.
All work promptly done, and satisfaction guaranteed.
315 Main St., bet. Merrille and Rees.

EHRHART, P. C., Merchant Tailor, 597 Main st. Established 1857.

HUNDT & HABERKORN,
MERCHANT TAILORS,
Dealers in
Ready-Made Clothing, Hats, Caps and Gents' Furnishing Goods.
No. 463 MAIN STREET.

SCHNEIDER, PH. H., Custom Tailor, 503 Main st. Established 1857.

WEBER, JOHN, Merchant Tailor, 321 Main st. Established 1858.

The Pioneers of the City of Sheboygan, dedicated to public use, four acres of ground in the heart of the city, which is covered with the original forest growth of evergreens. The Water and Park Commissioners of the City have erected a beautiful fountain, at a cost of $1500, in the centre of the Park, and a tasty building, 65 feet high, surmounted with a bronze statue of Hebe.

The artistic embellishments added to the natural growth of the forest, makes this one of the finest Parks of its size in the country.

FOUNTAIN PARK, SHEBOYGAN, WIS.

GRANITE ROCK SPRINGS

The strongest mineral water in the State.

FREE FROM ORGANIC MATTER,

BERTSCHY & THAYER,
SHEBOYGAN.

PROF. CHANDLER,

f New York, finds 590 grains of medicinal salts in one gallon. PHYSICIANS find it cures **Piles, Dyspepsia, Urinary Derangements,** and **Sick Headache.**
The PEOPLE find it contains the elements of health and produces
SOUND AND REFRESHING SLEEP.
☞ Send 75 cents for sample two-gallon jug.

1874.

16 min., 42¼ sec. Wesleyans second, Cambridge third.

July 26.—Destructive rain-storm in Pittsburgh, Pa.; 200 persons drowned, hundreds of houses demolished.

July 28.—Theodore Tilton arrested on a charge of slander against Henry Ward Beecher.

Aug. 1.—Lord Gordon fatally shoots himself at Fort Garry, Manitoba.

Aug. 9.—The great Corinthian yacht race at Newport; the Idler the victor of the cup.

Aug. 11.—The Collier and Edwards light weight fight in Brook county, West Virginia; the latter the victor; eleven rounds in twenty-eight minutes.

Aug. 20.—Geo. C. Harding, editor and proprietor Indianapolis *Herald*, shoots Sol. Maritz; Miss Harding, seduced by Moritz, commits suicide. H. W. Burnside, brother of Gen. A. E. Burnside, hangs himself in a fit of insanity at Indianpolis.

Aug. 28.—The Trautz-Johnson great swimming match; 3 miles, Pleasure Bay: the latter wins.

Sept. 3.—The River Belle, Long Branch steamer, burned at her pier No. 8 North River, New York.

Sept. 4.—The town of Mokelumne Hill, Cal., totally destroyed by fire.

Sept. 5.—Balloon ascent at Philadelphia; six ladies among the voyagers.

Sept. 13.—Monument to General Lyon. killed at the battle of Wilson's Creek, inaugurated with appropriate ceremonies at St. Louis, Mo.

Sept. 14.—The Kellogg riot in New Orleans; eight Metropolitan police and eight White Leaguers killed; great number wounded. The Kellogg government temporarily overthrown.

Sept. 16.—The Irish rifle team—arrival of the first detachment by the Scotia.

Sept. 19.—The Granite Woolen Mills, Fall River, destroyed by fire; of the operatives, twenty were killed; injured thirty-eight, two fatally. A man named Salmond walks into the rapids at Niagara, and is carried over the falls.

Sept. 21.—A train of six cars breaks through a bridge on Waxahachie Creek; W. M. Boyd, ex-judge of the Supreme Court of Alabama, and an engineer, fireman, and several passengers killed.

Sept. 26.—The International rifle match at Creedmoor; the American team the victors. Lieut. Charles F. DeBorst, 71st regiment, falls from the cars on the return from Creedmoor, and is killed.

Sept. 28.—The Lord Mayor of Dublin and the Irish team entertained at a banquet in Brooklyn.

Oct. 1.—Army headquarters removed to St. Louis.

Oct. 2.—The Bennett prize in the long range contest at Creedmoor won by the Irish team.

Oct. 4.—A drove of Texas steers invade New York city; a great number of citizens se-

---

FOND DU LAC—*Continued.*

TURKISH BATHS.

DR. J. A. DANIELS,
Proprietor of the Celebrated

TURKISH BATH ROOMS,
Sheboygan Street,
Near Main.

WINES AND LIQUORS.

NICHOLSON, J., Dealer in Wines and Liquors, 517 Main st.

UNDERTAKERS.

GESSWEIN, FRED, General Furnishing Undertaker, 323 Main. Established 1857.

KAEDING, MARTIN, General Furnishing Undertaker, Sixth and Main sts. Est. 1876.

Fond du Lac Business Houses.
WHEN ESTABLISHED.

ANDERSON, H. B., Druggist, 1871.
DANIELS, DR. J. A., Bath Rooms, 1866.
DITTMAR, HENRY C., Dye Works, 1874.
DREIS, JACOB, Tailor, 1868.
GREEN, THOS. H., Architect, 1855.
HUNDT & HABERKORN, Tailors, 1866.
KENDALL, H. E., Druggist, 1876.
SCHERER, HENRY, File Manufacturer, 1867.
STONEHOCKER & CARNAHAN, Clothing, 1877.
SULLIVAN, M. O., Harness, Saddles, 1871.
TRELEVEN, D. D. & CO., Meat Market, 1866.
VENNE & SCHOLL, Boots and Shoes, 1871.

LA PORTE, IND.

ABSTRACTS OF TITLES.

DORLAND, GEO. C., Real Estate, Insurance, Abstracts of Title, & Agt. A. T. & S. Fe R. R.

AGRICULTURAL IMPLEMENTS.

Little Giant Agricultural Works.
WANDEL BROS., Proprietors,
Manufacturers of the

LITTLE GIANT SULKY PLOW,
To which one or more common Plows can be attached; also, manufacturers of all kinds of Castings. All orders promptly filled.
LA PORTE, IND.

ATTORNEYS AT LAW.

BLISS & VAN WIE, Attorneys at Law, Rooms 5 & 6 Alexander Block.

LA PORTE—*Continued.*

ATTORNEYS AT LAW.

FARRAND & TRAVER, Attorneys at Law,
• Main st.

MILLER, GEO. M., Attorney at Law, Real Estate & Insurance Agent, Main st.

OSBORN, CALKINS & WILE, Attorneys at Law, 39 Indiana avenue.

TRIPP, S. L., Lawyer, LaPorte & Chicago.
(Office with M. Nye, Esq.)

WEIR & BIDDLE, Attorneys at Law,
Cor. Jefferson st. & Indiana ave.

BILLIARD HALL.

Established 1857.

THE OLD RELIALBE

BILLIARD HALL,

HENRY ZAHRT, Proprietor,

35 Michigan Ave.

BOTTLERS.

LABES, CHARLES, Manufacturer of and dealer in all kinds of Soda and Seltzer Water, Ginger Ale and Champaign Cider. 42 Indiana avenue. All orders will receive prompt attention.

CARRIAGE MANUFACTURERS.

W. H. DREW,
Manufacturer of
CARRIAGES, WAGONS, SLEIGHS,
Etc., Adams st., near E. Main st.

WM. C. PITNER,
Manufacturer of Carriages and Wagons,
94 Monroe st., cor. Harrison st.

R. J. REESE,
Manufac'r of Carriages and Wagons,
Cor. State & Detroit sts.

CHAIR MANUFACTURERS.

LA PORTE CHAIR COMPANY,
Manufacturers of

Cane Seat Chairs

Cor. Indiana ave. & Washington st.

W. WILSON, President and Treasurer.

FANNING MILL.

MICHAEL, E. & CO., Manf'rs of Michael's Newly Improved Fanning Mill.

FURNITURE.

WEIR & CUTLER, Manuf'rs and dealers in all kinds of Furniture, Main st.

1874.

verely hurt, some of whom subsequently die from their injuries.

Oct. 5.—Fiftieth anniversary celebration of the 7th regiment. First annual meeting of the Church Congress of the United States.

Oct. 12.—Negro incendiaries burn the court house at Waresboro, Ware co., Ga.

Oct. 16.—Major Harry Larkyns shot and instantly killed by E. J. Maybridge, photographer, San Francisco.

Oct. 19.—F. T Sawyer, cashier of the Souhegan National Bank, Milford, and family, gagged by robbers, who robbed the bank of $100,000.

Oct. 23.—Aleck Hamilton, the fugitive defaulting treasurer of Jersey City, surrenders to the authorities.

Nov.—Kalakaua, King of the Hawaiian Islands, arrived in San Francisco, visited our chief ports, examined our industrial resources and capabilities, and endeavored to hasten the negotiations of a commercial treaty between his government and that of the United States.

Nov. 1.—James Leek and wife, of St. Pauls, attacked in the street and murdered.

Nov. 7.—Miss Cushman bids farewell to the stage---she is crowned with laurel, and receives a popular ovation.
Herman Schilling brutally murdered in a tannery in Cincinnati, O., and his body thrust into a furnace and consumed.

Nov. 18.—Major Arthur B. Leech and members of the Irish rifle team embark for home by the Russia.

Nov. 22.—Mr. McGahan, New York *Herald* special correspondent, and Mr. Buckland, of the New York *Times*, seized and imprisoned by the Spaniards.
Mrs. J. A. Judd, a well-known Parisian milliner, commits suicide at her home in Norwalk, Connecticut.

Nov. 25.—Shock of an earthquake experienced in Massachusetts.
Mr. Frederick G. Schneider, of Union Hill, N. J., commits suicide by shooting himself at the Grand Union Hotel.

Nov. 27.—George Simms (colored) executed at Covington, Ga.

Nov. 28.—J. A. McGahan, N. Y. *Herald* correspondent, set at liberty by the Spaniards.

Nov. 30.—Mayor Havemeyer, of New York, seized with a sudden illness, and in a few moments expires in his office in the City Hall.

Dec. 2.—S. C. Robinson. flour merchant, of 86 Broad street, New York, commits suicide at the Grand Pacific Hotel, Chicago.
John D. White, Republican Congressman elect from Kentucky, shoots and kills Harrison Cockerill, at Mount Sterling, Ky.

Dec. 6.—Booth's Theatre, New York, sold for $385,000 to Oliver Ames.

Dec. 7.—Seven hundred armed negroes attack Vicksburg; some twenty-five negroes and several whites killed.
Destructive fire at East New York. Eight houses and other property destroyed.
Edward Madden, editor of the Merced *Tribune*, shot and killed by H. Granise.

Dec. 10.—Destructive fire at Charleston, capital of West Virginia.

LA PORTE—Continued.

HOTEL.

MYERS HOUSE,
W. C. CHILDS, Proprietor,

LA PORTE, - - IND.

References: Commercial Men.

LIVERY AND FEED STABLE.

RATHBUN, E. D. & BRO., Proprietors of LaPorte Livery Stable, Indiana & State sts.

MACHINIST.

BROOKS, JAMES N., Machine Works, Turbine Water Wheels, & Mill Machinery a specialty.

PHYSICIANS.

BARNS, C. G., M. D., Treatment of Piles a specialty, cures warranted. Office: op. Myers h'se

COLLINS, DR. S. B., Painless Opium Antidote, Collins ave. Discovered in 1868.

Geo. M. Dakin., M. D.,
Chronic Diseases a Specialty,
Also Proprietor of
Dr. Dakin's Improved Catarrh Remedy.
Send For Circular.
LA PORTE, IND.

FAHNESTOCK, C. S., M. D., Surgeon & Homeopathist, opposite Court House.

WHITING, S. C., M. D., Homeopathic Physician & Surgeon, Jefferson st.

TOBACCO AND CIGARS.

WALTON, WM. M., Dealer in Tobacco & Cigars, 41 Michigan avenue.

WINES AND LIQUORS.

ITTICH, JOHN, Wines, Liquors & Cigars, 8 Michigan ave.

KOKOMO, IND.

ATTORNEYS AT LAW.

CONN, L. M., Attorney at Law. Special attention given to Collections. Walnut st.

GIDEON, F. M., Attorney at Law, Main st.

MAHAN & KIRK, Attorneys at Law, Office: in Armstrong, Pickett & Co.'s Block.

O'BRIEN, JAMES, Attorney at Law, Main st.

DENTIST.

PLEAS, M. E. Dentist, Rail Road st.

KOKOMO—Continued.

BANKES.

WALKER'S BANK.
Walker, Welsh & Co.,
Bankers, Real Estate & Insurance Agts.

Collections promptly made, taxes paid, rents collected, and real estate sold for non-residents. Business solicited.

GROCERS.

TATE & HULL, Wholesale & retail Grocers, 40 Rail Road st.

TITUS & CO., Groceries & Provisions, Rail Road st.

HOTELS.

Hote l'Clinton,
J. C. GILBERT, Proprietor.

Changed hands, re-furnished and thoroughly repaired. Good Sample Rooms.

Kokomo. - - Ind.

LINDLEY-BELL HOUSE, Mrs. S. A. Hiser, Proprietress, Walnut & Rail Road sts.

LIVERY AND FEED STABLE.

HINTON & LEACH, Livery & Feed Stable, dealers in Horses, Cattle & Hogs, Walnut st.

MACHINISTS.

BIRCH BROS. & CO., Stationery & Portable Engines, etc., near Rail Road Junction.

NEWSPAPER.

KOKOMO SATURDAY TRIBUNE. Established 1851. T. C. Phillips & Sons, proprietors. The largest paper in Howard co., and twice as many subscribers as any other.

PHOTOGRAPHER.

STRODE, J. M., Photographer, Rail Road st.

REAL ESTATE.

COX, ELIHU, Real Estate Agent, negotiates loans & pays taxes in all W. States, Main st.

STUART, W. A., Real Estate, Life & Fire Insurance Agent, S. E. cor. Public Square.

RESTAURANTS.

ROST, H. A., Restaurant & Confectionery, Rail Road st.

SCOFIELD, FRANK, Restaurant, Bakery & Confectionery, Main st.

SEWING MACHINES.

LAWSON, G. W., Mang'r Singer Sewing Machine Office, Howard Block, Main st.

1874.

Dec. 12.—King Kalakaua arrives in Washington.

Dec. 14.—William Mosher and Joseph Douglass, the supposed abductors of Charlie Ross, shot and killed by the Van Brunts in the commission of a burglary at Bay Ridge, Long Island.

Dec. 15.—Serious fire in Boston; loss over a million.

Dec. 17.—The Pacific mail steamer Japan destroyed by fire near Yokohama, Japan, with great loss of life.
The emigrant ship, Cospatrick, while in lat. 37 N., long. 11 W., destroyed by fire; 465 lives lost.

Dec. 20.—Police Captain Isaac S. Bourne, of the Brooklyn police, accidentally shot and instantly killed by John C. Pollock, a newspaper reporter.

Dec. 23.—King Kalakaua arrives in New York.

Dec. 25.—Amos Young, a notorious desperado, shot and instantly killed, at Chester, Ill.

Dec. 26.—D. C. Byerley, of the *Bulletin*, New Orleans, attacks Governor Warmoth in the street. The latter, in self-defense, stabs and killes Byrley.

1875.

Jan. 1.—Mutiny on board the school ship Mercury; sixteen boys escaped; a boatman stabbed.

Jan. 4.—Political riots in New Orleans.
Opening of the Tilton-Beecher case.

Jan. 12.—Thos. E. Bramlette, ex-Governor of Kentucky, dies at Louisville.

Jan. 23.—The East river spanned by an ice bridge.

Jan. 24.—St. Patrick's church, Hartford, Conn., destroyed by fire.
George Paris, tax collector of New Orleans, shoots and kills Wm. Weeks, ex-Assistant Secretary of State.

Jan. 25.—Steamer Lady of the Lake burned at her wharf, Norfolk, Va.
The Cumberland M. E. Church of Philadelphia destroyed by fire.

Jan. 30.—Louis A. Grill, an ex-captain in the army, shoots himself in the head at 126 East 13th street, New York.

Feb. 2.—Thomas Neilson Sanderson, familiarly known as "Nelse Seymour," the comedian, dies in New York city, aged 39 years.

Feb. 14.—Edward Spangler, noted as one of the assassinators of President Lincoln in 1865, dies near Baltimore, Maryland, aged 55.

Feb. 16.—The propeller E. A. Woodward, sunk by ice in the Sound.

Feb. 20.—John F. W. Thon, an ex-county Treasurer, commits suide at Wyandotte, Mich.

March 14.—The tow-boat R. A. Babbridge sunk near Cairo; George Ables, chief engineer, and two others, lost.

March 15.—Archbishop McClosky perconized Cardinal at Rome.

KOKOMO—*Continued.*

TOBACCO AND CIGARS.

PARKER, A. F., Confectionery, Ice Cream, Cigars & Tobacco. Main st.

WINES AND LIQUORS.

J. B. PARKER.   W. H. H. SAYLER.

Parker & Sayler,

Wholesale Dealers in

PURE KENTUCKY WHISKIES,

Wines, Brandies, Gin, Etc.

Fine Sample Room Attached.
RAIL ROAD STREET.

John L. Pegram,

WINES, LIQUORS.

Cigars and Billiards,

RAIL ROAD STREET.

WILSON, A. B., Tobacco, Cigars, Flour and Feed, Sycamore st.

MUNCIE, IND.

PHOTOGRAPHER.

JAS. M. BARNES,

PHOTOGRAPHER,

141 E. Main St.

Old Pictures copied and enlarged to any size.

PIANOS AND ORGANS.

Prof. M. Kuechman,

Dealer in

PIANOS, ORGANS,

And all kinds of small Instruments, Sheet Music, Merchandise, teacher of harmony vocal and instrumental music.
128 E. MAIN ST.

PUMP MANUFACTURER.

GIFT, C. W., Manf'r and dealer in Improved Wooden Pumps, 214 Jackson st.

CAMBRIDGE CITY, IND.

BOARDING.

PETTYCREW, MRS. ANNIE, Boarding by the day, week or meal. Church st. near depot.

DRY GOODS.

SHROYER, H. A., with John Kepler's Dry Goods House, 208 Main st.

CAMBRIDGE CITY—Continued.

GROCERIES.

HASTINGS, E. B., Groceries, Provisions, Queensware, Glassware, etc., South side Main st.

HOTEL.

CENTRAL HOTEL,

EUROPEAN PLAN,

WM. P. STAHR, Proprietor.

Good sample rooms and superior accommodations
Main st., Cambridge City.

SMALLEY, GEO. F., Prop'r Thurman House Restaurant & Dining Room, 1st door W. of Depot.

LIVERY AND FEED STABLE.

LACKEY, J. N., Livery, Feed, Sale & Training Stables, Foot st., South of Main.

SALOON.

STOBAUGH, FRANK, dealer in Whiskies, Wines, etc., 243 Main st.

TAILOR.

GRUSINGER, JACOB, Merchant Tailor. Established 1867. Cambridge City.

TOBACCO AND CIGARS.

GUNTER, J. L., Manf'r and wholesale and retail dealer in Cigars and Smokers' Articles.

WATCHES, CLOCKS AND JEWELRY.

KALB, W. C., The Jeweler, dealer in Watches, Clocks & Jewelry, 276 Main st.

SHELBYVILLE, IND.

ATTORNEYS AT LAW.

HARRISON, JAMES, Attorney at Law,
  Cor. Harrison & Franklin sts.

MAJOR & MAJOR, Attorneys at Law,
  Bank Building, W. Washington st.

CARRIAGE MAKERS.

CARITHERS, M., Carriage Maker,
  Cor. Broadway & Pike sts.

McGUIRE & JENNINGS, Carriage Makers,
  E. Washington st.

CARPENTER AND BUILDER.

SPRINGER, J. B., Carpenter & Builder,
  Cor. South and Pike sts.

CLOTHING.

AUERBACH, SOL., Clothier,
  Cor Washington st and Public Square.

DRY GOODS.

AULL, J. & CO., Dry Goods,
  South Side Public Square.

HOWARD, GEO. P., Dry Goods,
  Cor. Harrison and Public Square.

FURNITURE.

CONREY, WALLAR & DEPREZ,
Manufacturers of

ALL KINDS OF FURNITURE,
E. Washington st.

1875.

A rencounter takes place between James A. Cowardin of the *Dispatch* and Mr. A. Fulkerson, of the House of Delegates, at Richmond, Va.

March 16.—Steamer W. J. Lewis, from Vicksburg to St. Louis, burned to the water's edge; one of the crew drowned; others missing.

March 19.—Tiburcio Vasquez, the bandit, hanged at San. Jose, Cal.

Charles K. Landis (father of Vineland) shoots Mr. Carruth, editor of the Vineland *Independent*.

April 10.—Dan Bryant, the talented negro minstrel, dies in New York city, aged 42 years.

April 19.—Centennial of Concord and Lexington.

April 22.—John Harper, firm of Harper Bros., publishers, New York, dies, aged 78.

April. 23.—Three steamers burned at the New Orleans levee; 30 women and children lost.

April 24.—Daniel O'Leary, of Chicago, walks 115 miles in 24 hours.

April 26.—Railroad collision at the Navy Yard Tunnel, near Washington; several persons injured.

April 27.—Cardinal McCloskey invested with the beretta in St. Patrick's Cathedral, N. Y.

April 28.—Oshkosh, Wis., burned to the ground.

April 28.—Mrs. Sarah G. Conway, the noted actress and manageress of Brooklyn Theatre, dies in that city, aged 41 years.

May 1.—Archbishop Williams consecrated at Boston.

May 2.—Methodist church at Rockport, Mass., burned by an incendiary.

May 3.—The mutiny on board the schooner Jefferson Borden; the two mates killed.

The steamer St. Luke collides and sinks in the Missouri river at St. Louis; six passengers lost.

May 8.—The steamship Schiller wrecked off the Scilly Isles; 311 lives lost.

May 11.—Colonel D. R. Anthony, editor of the *Times*, Leavenworth, Kansas, shot by Wm. Embry, editor of the *Appeal*.

May 15.—The Ripley Opera House Block, Rutland, Vt., destroyed by fire.

May 20.—Hon. Jesse D. Bright, ex-member of Congress from Indiana, died in Baltimore, aged 63 years.

Gray Beard, head chief of the Cheyennes, killed while attempting to escape from his captors.

May 21.—Great fire in South Norwalk; loss, $150,000.

May 23.—The church belfry tragedy in Boston; Mabel H. Young murdered by Thomas Piper.

May 26.—A house in Boston blown to atoms; several persons killed and wounded.

May 27.—The French Catholic church at

BIRD & MICKLE,
LITHOGRAPHERS
—AND—
MAP PUBLISHERS,
REYNOLD'S BLOCK,

Cor. Main and Mechanic Sts., - *JACKSON, MICH.*

GEO. H. GALE,
—DEALER IN—

OPEN AND  TOP BUGGIES
Cutters, Lumber
WAGONS, HORSES, ROBES, BLANKETS, WHIPS,
FARMING TOOLS, ETC.

LIVERY AND SALE STABLES, MECHANIC STREET, OPP. P. O.,
JACKSON, MICH.

Established 1873.

F. WENTER,
MANUFACTURER OF
FANCY CABINET WARE,
Consisting of Parlor Brackets, Wall Pockets, Side and Corner Brackets, Music and Flower Stands, Toilet Cases, Clock Shelves, Etc.

Factory and Salesroom, 70 & 72 W. Washington St., CHICAGO, ILL.

G. C. KIMBALL.   G. L. DENHAM.   R. M. WHITEHOUSE

GENESEE IRON WORKS!
KIMBALL & CO.,
Manufacturers of all kinds of
MALLEABLE IRON, GREY IRON & COMPOSITION CASTINGS, STEAM ENGINES, &c,
FLINT, MICH.
G. L. DENHAM, Treas.   [Established 1869.]   *R. M. WHITEHOUSE, Supt.*

F. L. FURBISH,
Manufacturer of
FANCY CABINET WARE,
BRACKETS, &C.,
No. 42 & 44 Mill St.,
GRAND RAPIDS, - - - **MICHIGAN.**

State Capitol, Lansing, Mich.—Cost of Building $1,350,000. Complete building entirely fire proof; exterior, cut stone; height of dome 269 feet; length of building 420 feet; centre building 212 feet deep, height of building in centre, to top of pediment, 112 feet; height of cornice from ground on wings, 82 feet, 7 inches.

Carpenter's Hall, Philadelphia.—The hall is situated on Chestnut street, a few paces east from Fourth, Philadelphia. On the 5th of September, 1774, the first Continental Congress met in this hall, and begun their deliberations, which resulted in the Declaration of Independence, July 4th, 1776. The building is owned by the Carpenters' Company of Philadelphia, an organization which has maintained its existence since 1724 up to the present time. The hall was built in the year 1771.

1875.

Holyoke, Mass., burned; seventy-five lives lost.

May 28.—Paul Boynton swims across the English Channel.

May 30.—Destructive incendiary fire at Springfield, Mass.

June 2.—The New York Temple of Masonry dedicated.

June 5.—The American Rifle Team embark for Ireland.

June 6.—Kaiser William confers the order of Civil Merit on George Bancroft and Henry W. Longfellow.

June 12.—The steamer Vicksburg reported lost in the ice off St. John's, New Brunswick, May 31st.
The Boston express train thrown off the track at 178th street, Tenton; narrow escape of Vice-President Wilson.

June 13.—Seizure of the steamship Octavia.
Tom McGehan, of Vallandingham notoriety, shot and killed at Hamilton, O.

June 17.—The Bunker Hill Centennial Celebration.

June 21.—Loss of the United States steamer, Saranac, off Vancouver's Island.

June 24.—The jury retire in the Tilton-Beecher case.
The Aldine Printing Office, Liberty street, New York, destroyed by fire.

July 5.—Disaster on the Long Island Southern Railroad; 11 persons killed.

July 6.—Collision between the steamer Isaac Bell and the tug Lumberman in Hampton Roads; 10 lives lost.

July 13.—Saratoga regatta. The freshman contest won by Cornell.

July 14.—A portion of the City Hotel, Lynchburg, Va., falls; one person killed, several injured.

July 15.—The Donaldson-Grimwood fatal balloon ascension from Chicago.

July 23.—Isaac Merrit Singer, the inventor of the Singer Sewing Machine, dies in London, aged 64 years.

July 27.—Duncan, Sherman & Co. suspend payment.

July 31.—Hon. Andrew Johnson, U. S. Senator from Tennessee, and ex-President of the United States, dies at Carter's Depot, near Greenville, Tenn., aged 67.

Aug. 6.—An explosion at the Bridesburg Arsenal, Pa.; 1 killed and 19 wounded.

Aug. 17.—The body of Grimwood, Donaldson's companion, found at Montague, Lake Michigan.

Aug. 21.—The American Rifle Team home.

Aug. 28.—Courtney and Robinson win the double sculls at Saratoga.

Aug. 27.—Mr. W. C. Ralston, President of the California Bank, drowned while bathing.

Aug. 28.—The new post-office, New York, occupied.

Sept. 11.—Propeller Esquinox foundered in a storm on Lake Michigan, with 26 souls on

SHELBYVILLE—*Continued.*

HARNESS AND SADDLES.

BROWNING, W., Harness & Saddles,
South Side Public Square.

HOTELS.

INDIANA HOUSE, Daniel Deprez, Proprietor,
Cor. Noble & Washington sts.

JACKSON HOUSE, H. H. Jackson, Proprietor,
North Side Public Square.

REAL ESTATE.

MILLER, W. C., Real Estate & Insurance Agent,
Cor. Harrison & Jackson sts.

SALOONS.

DENNY, JOHN, Saloon,
Cor. Harrison st. & Broadway.

DEPREZ, GEORGE, Saloon,
South Side Public Square.

LOUDEN, DAVID, Saloon,
East Washington st.

NICHOLS, G. D., Saloon,
South Harrison st.

PHILLIPS, I. H., Saloon,
Cor. Washington & Noble sts.

STOVES AND TINWARE.

GRIFFEY & CO., Stoves & Tinware,
East Side Public Square.

WINES AND LIQUORS.

NICKUM & VANNOY, Wholesale Liquor Dealers,
North Side Public Square.

SILAS METZGER,

LIQUOR DEALER,

Sour Mash Bourbons,
California Wines,
Grape Brandies, Etc.

SAMPLE ROOM ATTACHED.

E. Washington St.

HUNTINGTON, IND.

AGRICULTURAL IMPLEMENTS.

PHINEAS T. BAKER,

Agent for the

Johnson Harvester, Eclipse Thresher,

PORTABLE ENGINES

And Agricultural Implements Generally,

Established 1873. HUNTINGTON.

PROVINES, J. S., Agricultural Implements and
Farm Machinery, Jefferson st.

ATTORNEYS AT LAW.

SPENCER & BEST, Attorneys at Law,
Jefferson st.

DRUGGIST.

DAVIES, JESSE, Wholesale and Retail Druggist,
Market st.

HARNESS AND SADDLES.

KOHL, JOHN, Manufacturer of Harness, Saddles, Collars, &c., cor. Jefferson & Franklin

HUNTINGTON—*Continued.*

HOTELS.

WM. CRATER,
Hotel and Restaurant,
MEALS AT ALL HOURS.

Jefferson St., Huntington,

HUBBELL HOUSE, A. A. Hubbell, Prop.
Cor. Market & Cherry sts.

Revere House.
(Formerly NATIONAL.)

GARDNER & COOK, Props.

Refurnished and Refitted. Good Accommodations for Drummers.

Cor. Market & Cherry Sts., Huntington.

JUSTICE OF THE PEACE.

PAULLUS, P. L., Justice of the Peace,
Jefferson street.

MILLINERY.

MISS PATTERSON & SISTER,
Fashionable Millinery
ALL WORK GUARANTEED.

Market St., One Door East of New Bank Building.

RADABAUGH & AGLER, Millinery and Notions,
Jefferson street.

PHOTOGRAPHER.

RADABAUGH, E. B., Photographer,
Jefferson street.

TAILOR.

SWICK, P. D., Merchant Tailor. Good fits guaranteed. Market st.

WAGON MAKERS.

BEAVER, HENRY, Blacksmithing, Jobbing and Repairing. Franklin st.

JACOB SCHEERER,
Wagon Manufacturer.
REPAIRING & NEW WORK.

Franklin St., Huntington.

RUSHVLLIE, IND.

ATTORNEYS AT LAW.

BIGGER, FINLEY, Attorney at Law,
16 Ruth st.

HALL, FRANK J., Attorney at Law,
Ruth st., opp. Court House.

1875.

board. Capt. Bain, of the schooner Onondago, swept overboard and lost.

Sept. 16.—The steamer Zodiac, from Nassua, burned at sea on the 6th inst.

Galveston, Texas, visited by a fearful storm of wind and rain; the city inundated.

Sept. 17.—The dry goods house of Jordan, Marsh & Co., of Boston, almost destroyed by fire; loss nearly $1,000,000.

Sept. 21.—Indianola, Texas, visited by a cyclone and almost entirely destroyed.

Sept. 27.—Edwin O'Baldwin, the Irish giant, shot by J. Cassidy, at 45 West street, N. Y.

Sept. 29.—Ned O'Baldwin, the Irish giant, dies in New York city, aged 35.

The earth's passage through the moon occurs.

Oct. 4.—Miss Josie Langmaid, school-girl of Suncook, N. H., murdered in the woods.

Oct. 9.—Fire at First and South Eleventh streets, Brooklyn. Loss, $100,000.

Oct. 7.—American ship Mayflower, Capt. W. S. Herrington, founders at sea.

Oct. 13.—John T. Huss, cashier of the First National Bank of Tiffin, Ohio, commits suicide.

Oct. 21.—Frederick Hudson, journalist, thrown from his carriage by a locomotive at Monument street railroad crossing, Concord, and killed.

Oct. 26.—The Dauntless and Mohawk ocean race; the Dauntless victor.

Conflagration in Virginia City, Nev. Loss, $8,000,000.

Oct. 28.—The Dauntless beats the Resolute in the great ocean race from Cape May.

Oct. 30.—Reported loss by fire of the American ship John Pascal, Capt. Tapley.

Oct. 31.—Fire in Philadelphia; loss, $500,000.

Nov. 2.—George Schmidt, hotel proprietor of Annapolis, Md., shot and killed by William Barber.

Nov. 3.—Robert Miner falls from the dome of the Memorial Building at Philadelphia, and is killed.

Nov. 9.—The steamer City of Waco burned off Galveston bar.

Nov. 17.—John C. Johnson, a Newark alderman, commits suicide by shooting.

Nov. 22.—Hon. Henry Wilson, Vice President of the United States, dies at Washington, D. C., aged 64 years.

Dec. 4.—Escape of Wm. M. Tweed.

Dec. 7.—The steamship Deutschland wrecked on the Galloper Sands; 50 lives lost.

Dec. 11.—The dynamite explosion at Bremmerhaven; 60 persons killed; the steamship Mosal injured and detained.

1876.

Jan. 1.—On Staten Island the Rev. Henry Boehm, the venerable patriarch of the Methodist church, dies, aged one hundred and one years.

Jan. 9.—In South Boston, Dr. Samuel

RUSHVILLE—Continued.

ATTORNEYS AT LAW.

HELM, JEFFERSON, JR., Attorney at Law and Real Estate Agent, 16 Ruth st.

POE, THOMAS, Attorney at Law, Masonic Hall, Main st.

SEXTON & CAMBERN, Attorneys at Law, Ruth st., opp. Court House.

THOMAS & SPANN, Attorneys at Law and Solicitors of Patents, 10 Ruth st.

DENTIST.

HAYS, DR. W., Dentist, Ruth st., Melodion Block.

HOTEL.

CAPP HOUSE.

F. A. CAPP, Prop:
Cor. Ruth & Morgan Sts.

TAILOR.

McCARTHY, P., Merchant Tailor, Ruth st., opp. Court House.

ELKHART, IND.

DENTIST.

CUMMINS, S. M., D. D. S., Office, Masonic Block, Main st.

FURNITURE.

WALLEY, CHAS., Furniture Dealer and Undertaker, Pigeon st.

GUNS, RIFLES, &c.

ROGERS, JOHN, Manufacturer of Guns & Rifles, and Dealer in Sporting Goods.

LIVERY AND SALE STABLE.

BUTTERFIELD, JAS. H., Prop of City Livery, Sale and Boarding Stable.

MUSICAL INSTRUMENTS.

ATTENTION, BANDS!

For Instruments of all Kinds, Music Etc.

Address C. G. CONN, Elkhart, Ind.

Subscribe for "TRUMPET NOTES," The only paper printed in the interest of Amateur Bands. Send for sample copy. Use the Elastic Rim Mouthpiece.

PAPER MANUFACTURERS.

A. Upp, Pres. J. W. Bliss, Sec. A. Work, Treas.

ELKHART TISSUE PAPER COMPANY

Manufacturers of

ALL KINDS OF TISSUES.

Copying Paper a Specialty

ELKHART, IND.

ELKHART—Continued.

REAL ESTATE.

HUTCHISON, J. H., Justice of the Peace. Conveyancer. Real Estate and Collecting Agent.

STARCH MANUFACTURERS.

Excelsior Starch Manufacturing Company

ELKHART, IND.

Manufacturers of the EXCELSIOR GLOSS STARCH. The strongest and best made. Excelsior Corn Starch, for Culinery use, has no equal. For sale by all first-class Grocers.

SOUTH BEND, IND.

ATTORNEYS AT LAW.

ARNOLD & CREED, Attorneys at Law. With Arnold's Abstracts of Title. 87 Washington st

GEORGE & PFLEGER, Attorneys at Law, Post Office Building.

TONG, L. G., Attorney and Notary Public, Arnold's Block.

BARBERS.

LOTT, J. B., Shaving and Hairdressing Parlors, 66½ Washington st.

Bath Rooms, Shaving & Hairdressing Parlors

HENRY SPETH, Proprietor.

57 Washington Street.

BRACKET MANUFACTURERS.

VARIETY BRACKET WORKS,

Wholesale Manufacturers

Brackets, Shelves, Frames, Etc.

Also Patent Toilet Brackets and Patent Album Frames.

Factory, Cor. St. Joseph & Washington Sts.

COAL, LIME AND PLASTER.

LANE, H. & J. W., Lime. Plaster, Coal. Plastering Hair Lath, Stucco Cement, &c., 87 Main

DENTISTS.

CUMMINS, D. E., Dentist, 96 Michigan st., over Wyman's.

MILLER, R. T., Dentist, 100 Michigan st.

ENGRAVER ON WOOD.

HOOVER, E. W., Designer and Engraver on Wood. Arnold's Block.

FURNITURE.

KNOBLOCK BROS., Furniture and Upholstered Goods, No. 75 Main st.

Photographic Studio, Centennial Exposition, Philadelphia.—
It is a very handsome structure of wood and plaster, and is of a highly decorative style of architecture. It is one story high, situated on a terrace three feet above grade. The front portion of the building is reached by a wide stairway, and comprises a wide vestibule and reception-room, and on each of the latter gallery 22 feet square, for the exhibition of photographs. There are public and private offices, dressing-rooms for ladies and gentlemen, and all the appurtenances of a first class photographic gallery on a large scale.

United States Mint, Philadelphia.—Was established in 1792. The present beautiful building, which is pure Ionic architecture, was completed in 1833, is situated on Chestnut street above 13th. The Mint, besides being a great money-coining establishment, also contains a museum or cabinet of coins, embracing the coined "legal tenders" from the earliest ages up to the present period.

J. B. PEABODY. GEO. W. ROBINSON.

PEABODY & ROBINSON,
PROPRIETORS

PEABODY HOUSE,
EAU CLAIRE, WISCONSIN,

First Class House. Commercial Sample Rooms Free. and on the Ground Floor.

SOUTH BEND—*Continued.*

HOTELS.

Central Hotel,
(Late ST. JOE,)
OPPOSITE POST OFFICE, SOUTH BEND, IND.
New Management and Newly Furnished Throughout. Best Table in the City.
GEO. DAVIS, Clerk.   C. C. HULSART, Prop.

DWIGHT HOUSE
SOUTH BEND, IND.
KNIGHT & MILLS, Proprietors.

GRAND CENTRAL HOTEL
114 & 116 MICHIGAN ST.
HENRY C. KNILL, Prop. Rates, $2.00 per Day.

NATIONAL HOTEL,
SOUTH BEND, IND.,
Near L. S. & M. S. R. R. Depot.
W. H. WANSBROUGH, Prop.   Rates, $1.50 per Day.
Commercial Men will find Good Accommodations.

LIVERY AND SALE STABLES.

IRELAND & SON, Proprietors of
Livery and Feed Stables,
54 Michigan st.
Hack line to and from all trains, or any part of the city.

REYNOLDS'
Livery, Sale and Feed Stable,
146 MICHIGAN ST.
Best Turnouts in the city.
Carriages furnished for Balls, Parties, etc.
Prices reasonable. Geo. W. Reynolds, Prop.

SOUTH BEND—*Continued.*

PHYSICIANS.

BARBOUR, O. P., M.D., Physician and Surgeon, office, 71 Washington st.

DENSLOW BROS.,
ECLECTIC PHYSICIANS,
Clairvoyant and Magnetic Healers.
TERMS:
Personal Examination,................$1 00
When lock of hair, with name and age is sent, 2 00
Piles and Fistula a Specialty. No Charge until Cured.
SOUTH BEND, IND.

HUMPHREYS, L., M.D., Physician and Surgeon, 61 Washington st.

DR. MAURER,
Botanic and Water Doctor.
Chronic Diseases a specialty.
Office, 107 Michigan st.

STURGIS, D. B., M.D., Physician and Surgeon, 122 Michigan st.

SCHOOL.

UNIVERSITY OF NOTRE DAME, Rev. P. J. Colovin, C. S. C., Pres., Notre Dame, Ind.

SLIDE-VALVE.

W. J. Westwood, Pres.   O. S. Witherill, Treas.
O. H. Palmer, Sec.
Westwood's Frictionless Slide-Valve,
For Locomotive, Stationary and Marine Engines.
Patented, Jan 25, 1876. Improved, Feb 13, 1877.

STOVES AND TINWARE.

SANDROVEL, HENRY, Stoves, Tinware and Housefurnishing Goods, 77 Main st.

TOBACCO AND CIGARS.

A. BAILEY,
MANUFACTURER
And Wholesale and Retail Dealer in
TOBACCO AND CIGARS,
87 MAIN STREET.

ADVERTISEMENTS.

Horticultural Hall, Centennial Exposition, Philadelphia.—The building is 383 feet long, 193 feet wide, and 72 feet high to top of the lantern. It is illuminated by 3,500 burners. Thirty-five acres of ground surround the building, which is devoted to horticultural purposes.

New Era Renovating Works,

MOTHS & BUGS
—FOR DESTROYING—
in Furniture, Carpets, Bedding, Furs and Clothing, by immersion in tanks of prepared liquid without the slightest injury.

Also, CARPETS, CLOTHING, CURTAINS, BLANKETS, PIANO COVERS, BEDDING, SHAWLS, AFGHANS, &c., cleaned from grease and dirt.

FLINT & COOK,
1215 State Street, CHICAGO.

1876.

Gridley Howe, the distinguished philanthropist, dies, aged 74 years.

Jan. 13.—The National Republican Committee decide to hold their Presidential Convention at Cincinnati June 14.

Jan. 14.—A bill appropriating $29,533,-500 for pensions passed by Congress.

Jan. 25.—The Centennial bill appropriating $1,500,000 was passed by the House. An amendment to the bill provides that the money appropriated shall be repaid to the United States before any dividends are made to stockholders.

Feb. 5.—In Cincinnati, the gallery in Robinson's Opera House, during a Sunday-school festival, gave way. Twelve lives lost, and between fifteen and twenty persons injured.

Feb. 7.—In Brooklyn, N. Y., Rear-Admiral Silas H. Stringham, U. S. N., dies in his seventy-eighth year.

Feb. 8.—Destructive fire on Broadway, New York city. Loss about $3,000,000.

Feb. 10.—In Annapolis, Md., the Hon. Reverdy Johnson, the distinguished jurist, dies in his eightieth year.

Feb. 11.—The Centennial Appropriation bill was passed by the Senate. The President, on the 16th, signed the bill with a quill from the wing of an American eagle shot near Mount Hope, Oregon.

Feb. 12.—Explosion in a colliery at West Pittsburg, Pa. Four men killed and several wounded.

Feb. 15.—The historic elm on Boston Common was blown down by a high wind Tuesday evening. It was above two hundred years old, and one of the most dearly prized landmarks of the city. An immense crowd of relic hunters have visited the place to secure pieces.

Feb. 18.—In Boston, Charlotte S. Cushman, the actress, dies, aged sixty years.

Feb. 23.—A sleeping-car was thrown from the track on the Harlem Railroad extension. The car was burned, and Mr. Bissel, of the Sherman House, Chicago, and his son, perished in the flames.

March 1.—A bill was passed by the House recommending the people of the several States to assemble in their respective counties or towns on the Centennial anniversary, and to cause to be delivered a historical sketch of the county or town from its formation, copies of which are to be filed in the county clerk's office and in the library of Congress, so that a complete record may thus be had of the progress of the Republic.

March 2.—Resolutions of impeachment against Wm. W. Belknap, Secretary of War, were passed by the House, and the Senate was notified of the appointment by the House of a committee to impeach him at the bar of the Senate. The ground of impeachment was the charge that General Belknap had profited by post-tradership appointments. General Belknap had already resigned his position, and his resignation had been accepted by the President.

March 6.—A freight train, with a passenger car attached, fell through a bridge on the

South Bend—*Continued..*

TOBACCO AND CIGARS.

W. H. LUCE,
Dealer in Tobacco and Cigars.
The best brands constantly on hand.
SOUTH BEND, IND.

WATER PIPE.

STONE AND PIPE MANUFACTURING CO., Manufacturers of
Concrete Water Pipe,
Guaranteed to stand any pressure required.
156 Lafayette st.

WINES AND LIQUORS.

Mozart Hall.
WM. BENDER, Prop.
Dealer in Wines, Liquors and Cigars,
115 Michigan st.

JOHN WAGENER, Dealer in
Wines, Liquors and Cigars,
71 Washington st.

URBAHNS, HENRY, Wines, Liquors and Cigars, 34 Washington st.

ANDERSON, IND.

BLACKSMITH.

EDWARD MULLIKIN,
HORSESHOEING, PLOW REPAIRING,
And Manufacturer of Harrows.
All kinds of Job Work done to order.
SOUTH MAIN ST.

BOOTS AND SHOES.

MADARA, P. B., Boot and Shoemaker. All work guaranteed. S. Main st.

CARPENTERS.

J. CRAIGHEAD & SON,
Saw Gummers and Filers,
And Agents for the "Victor Stock Scale,"
And General Repair Shop.
Office at the Shop, South end Main Street.
Sign of Big Saw. Proprietors of the New Lancaster Mill.

CARRIAGE AND WAGON MAKERS.

H. H. CONRAD,
Manufacturer of
Carriages, Buggies
Spring & Lumber Wagons,
NORTH MAIN STREET.

ANDERSON—Continued.

CARRIAGE AND WAGON MAKERS.

T. A. Loftus.   (Est. 1874.)   W. P. Watkins.

LOFTUS & WATKINS,
Manufacturers of
Buggies, Platform & Eleptic Spring Wagons,
Also, Lumber and Farm Wagons and Custom Work Generally.
ALL WORK WARRANTED.
SHOP, 106 AND 108 N. MAIN STREET.

MATHES, GEORGE, Manf'r of Spring Wagons, Heavy and Light Road Wagons, North of P. C. & St. L. R.R. Depot.

QUINN, H. W., Carriage Makers' Materials, Wood Works, Oil, &c., 98 & 104 N. Main st.

COAL AND LIME.

E. G. VERNON,
Dealer in
COAL AND LIME,
Lath, Shingles, Cement, Plaster of Paris,
Fire-Brick & White Sand.
Agent for the Terra Cotta and Pipe Works.
NORTH END OF MAIN STREET.

GROCER.

THE CASH GROCERY
—OF—
C. H. PRESTON
Is the Place to Buy Good Goods Cheap.
COR. BOLIVAR & MAIN STS.

HOTEL.

AMERICAN HOUSE. H. L. Trueblood, Prop., Main st.

LIVERY AND SALE STABLE.

WILLIAMSON & TUTTLE,
Proprietors of the
LIVERY, FEED AND SALE
STABLE,
(Stable formerly occupied by Baxter & Blake.)
SOUTH MAIN STREET.
Horses kept at reasonable terms. Good accommodation for Drummers.

MACHINIST.

HILL, J. N., Wrought Iron Works, Iron Railing, Fencing, etc. Shop on Benton st.

TOBACCO AND CIGARS.

DREFFER, N. J., Manufacturer and Dealer in Cigars and Tobacco, 7 S. Main st.

NILES, MICH.

AGRICULTURAL IMPLEMENTS.

CLELAND, A. J. & SON, Manf'rs of and Dealers in Agricultural Implements, 65 Second st.

1876.

Baltimore and Ohio Railroad, and 11 persons were killed.

March 7.—The Home for the Aged, in East Brooklyn, New York, was partly consumed by fire. Eighteen old men were burned to death.

March 22.—The House passed a bill prohibiting contributions to election funds by officers of the United States government and by Senators and Representatives in Congress. The second section of the bill makes punishable by fine and imprisonment any bribery or intimidation with a view to influence elections of United States officers or Congressmen.

March 30.—The reservoir of the water works at Worcester, Mass., gave way, depriving the city of water, damaging property to the amount of one million five hundred thousand dollars.

April 4.—The formal presentation to the Senate of the articles of impeachment against Gen. Belknap took place. On the 17th, the day fixed on which the process against the late Secretary was made returnable, Gen. Belknap's counsel interposed the plea of non-jurisdiction.

April 10.—In New York city, A. T Stewart died, aged 73 years. He was said to be one of the wealthiest merchants in the United States.

Bill passed Congress authorizing the resumption of specie payment, which went into effect during the present month.

April 12.—A new postal bill, relating to third-class matter, passed by the Senate. The new rate will be one cent an ounce for all packages weighing four pounds or under, without regard to the distance to which they are sent. The rate for transient newspapers and magazines, without regard to distance, is to be one cent for three ounces or fractional part thereof, and one cent for each two additional ounces or fractional part thereof. This law is to take effect, should it be accepted by the House, on the 1st of July next.

April 15.—Arrival of Dom Pedro, Emperor of Brazil; at New York. He declines a public ovation, and, in the habiliments of a private citizen, makes a tour of the United States.

April 18.—President Grant vetoed the bill passed by Congress reducing his successor's salary to $25,000 per annum.

The Gray Nuns Act of 1875 repealed by the New York Legislature. The especially obnoxious clause of the act was one authorizing the Superintendent of Public Instruction to issue a certificate of qualification as a teacher in the common schools to any graduate of its seminaries to whom the Roman Catholic Sisterhood of Gray Nuns may have awarded a diploma.

May 10.—Grand opening of the Centennial Exhibition. The first official conception of the Centennial Exhibition was an act passed by Congress, March 3, 1871, creating the United States Centennial Commission, under whose supervision the exhibition was carried to a perfect success. On July 5th, 1873, the Secretary of State sent official notifications to the various foreign nations of the intended exhibition, and of the thirty-nine nations so invited and notified, they not only accepted, but sent

ADVERTISEMENTS.

NILES—Continued.

BATTERY BELT.

WITHERELL & KIRKHAM, Manufacturers of the Celebrated Battery Belt.

CARRIAGE MANUFACTURER.

BROWN, W. H., Carriage and Wagon Maker Second st.

CARRIAGE PAINTER.

SCOVIL, A. J., Carriage Painter, Second st.

DENTISTS.

LOWRY, T. A., Dentist, cor. Main and Front sts., over Post Office.

ROWLEY, DR. C. R., Dentist, office, over Finley's Drug Store, 48 Main st.

HOTEL.

BOND HOUSE,

O. M'KAY, Proprietor.

NILES,   -   -   MICH.

LIVERY AND SALE STABLE.

R. P. & W. B. BUNBURY,

Prop's of Livery, Feed and Sale Stable,

Cor. Second and Cedar sts.

NEWSPAPER.

HORN, O. P., M.D., Editor and Proprietor of the Niles Democrat, 48 Main st.

MISHAWAKA, IND.

AGRICULURAL IMPLEMENTS.

ST. JOSEPH MANUFACTURING CO.,

Manufacturers of

Steel and Cast Plows, Double Shovel Plows,

Cultivators, Combined Riding and Walking Cultivators, Mishawaka Feed Mills, &c., &c.,

MISHAWAKA, IND.

BREWERS.

DICK & KAMM

Manufacturers of

LAGER BEER,

MISHAWAKA, IND.

HOTELS.

Milburn House, Mishawaka, Ind.

D. S. PEMBROKE, Prop.

Rates, $2.00 per day.

MISHAWAKA—Continued.

HOTELS.

ST. JOSEPH HOUSE, $1.00 per day. Kuhn & Schindler, Props., Main st., Mishawaka, Ind.

WINDMILL & AX CO.

P. C. Perkins, Pres.   J. C. Snyder, Vice-Pres.
A. Hudson, Sec. and Treas.

PERKINS WINDMILL & AX CO.,

Manufacturers of

WINDMILLS, PUMPS, AXES,

Edge Tools, Mill Picks, Stone Hammers, etc., etc.,

MISHAWAKA, IND.

PLYMOUTH, IND.

ATTORNEY AT LAW.

REEVE, J. S., Justice, Attorney at Law, Real Estate and Insurance Agent.

CARPENTER AND BUILDER.

M'CANCE, ROBERT, Architect, Carpenter and Joiner, E. La Porte st.

GRAIN ELEVATOR.

THAYER, H. G., Prop. Plymouth Steam Grain Elevator, Wholesale Dealer in Grain, Seeds, etc., on Pennsylvania R.R.

HOTEL.

PARKER HOUSE, U. S. Dodge, Prop.   Bus to and from all trains.

LUMBER DEALERS.

G. L. BRINK & SULT,

DRESSED & UNDRESSED LUMBER

Manf'rs of Mouldings, Brackets and all kinds of Scroll Work, Plymouth.

PATENT MEDICINES.

LIEBER'S

FEVER AND AGUE CURE,

In Liquid or Pills.

Cures the worst forms of Chills, Fevers, Dumb-Ague, Third-day Ague, or Fevers without Chills. Cures General Debility, Loss of Appetite, &c., &c.   Pershing & Co., Manf'rs, Plymouth.

SCHOOL FURNITURE.

SIMONS, W. H., Manf'r Plymouth Straightwood School Desk, Plymouth.

WATCHES, CLOCKS AND JEWELRY.

PHILPOT, A. R., Watches, Clocks, Jewelry, Silverware, Michigan st.

MICHIGAN CITY, IND.

FURNITURE.

BADER BROS., Dealers in all kinds of Furniture. Coffins a specialty. Franklin st.

ADVERTISEMENTS. 269

The Casino, Central Park, New York.—A handsome structure, situated near the Broadway entrance, in Central Park, New York.

COREY & GRIFFIN,

Managers for Nebraska, Wyoming & Dakota of the

Connecticut Mutual Life Insurance Company,

Organized 1846. Assets $47,000,000. Cor. 15th & DOUGLAS St., OMAHA, NEB.

SAMUEL J. HOWELL,

FIRE INSURANCE AGENT, REPRESENTS OVER $21,354,000.

London Insurance Corporation, Established by Royal Charter in 1720. $15,000,000
Niagara, New York, 1,500,000
American Central, St. Louis, 1,375,000
Hamburg, Bremen of Hamburg, Germany, 2,250,000
Manufacturer's Fire and Marine, Boston, 1,229,082
                                         $21,354,082

235 DOUGLAS ST., CALDWELL BLOCK, OMAHA, NEB.

1876.

goods in great profusion for the international display. Foreign industries make up three-fifths of the display in the Main Building, and, perhaps, four-fifths in the Art Department, and a large proportion in every other department.

The President and Cabinet, the Diplomatic Corps, the Senate and House of Representatives, together with Commissioners from every State in the Union, were present at the opening. Dom Pedro, the Emperor of Brazil, was present.

The Army and Navy were largely represented from the highest rank to the private in line.

It is estimated that over 300,000 persons were on the ground, and the receipts amounted to $75,000.

The following is a comparative statement of the space occupied by the different World's Exhibitions since 1850:

Munich, 1850, - - - - - 4.4 acres
London, 1851, - - - - - 18.6 "
New York, 1854, - - - - 4.2 "
Paris, 1855, - - - - - 22.1 "
London, 1862, - - - - - 23.0 "
Paris, 1867, - - - - - 31.0 "
London Crystal Palace, - - - 25.6 "
Vienna, 1874, - - - - - 56.5 "
Philadelphia, 1876, - - - 60.0 "

May 17.—Boiler explosion on the steamer Pat Cleburne, six miles below Shawneetown, on the Mississippi river; nine persons killed, including the Captain.

May 18.—The Greenback National Convention at Indianapolis, Ind., nominated Peter Cooper, of New York, for President, and Senator Booth, of California, for Vice-President.

May 28.—Near Cincinnati, Ohio, G. M. D. Bloss, one of the editors of the Cincinnati *Enquirer*, was killed while walking on the railroad track; aged fifty years.

May 29.—It was decided by a majority of 8, in the United States Senate, that that body had jurisdiction in the Belknap impeachment case.

June 16.—The National Republican Convention, at Cincinnati, nominated Governor Rutherford B. Hayes, of Ohio, for President of the United States, and the Hon. William A. Wheeler, of New York, for Vice-President.

June 17.—B. H. Bristow resigned his seat in the Cabinet as Secretary of the Treasury.

June 25.—Custer's disaster in his expedition against the Indians. Gen. Custer had been detached from Gen. Terry's command, with orders to follow the trail of the hostile Sioux in the direction of the Big Horn river, while Gen. Terry should ascend the Big Horn and attack the enemy in the rear. On the 25th, Gen. Custer came suddenly upon a large force of Indians. Without waiting for support, he attacked the enemy. He had twelve companies of cavalry. Four of these companies had been detached under Colonel Reno to make an attack from the other side upon the enemy. Gen. Custer's force was overpowered and annihilated. Gen. Custer, his two brothers and nephew were killed. Not one of the command escaped. Col. Reno's force was surrounded and sustained severe losses, but was finally rescued by Gen. Gibbon's command. The entire loss was 261 killed and 50 wounded.

MICHIGAN CITY—*Continued*.

HOTELS.

Grand Union Hotel,
Near Mich. C. R.R. Depot.

C. NICHOLS, PROP.,
MICHIGAN CITY, - - IND.

THIS HOUSE HAS BEEN RE-FITTED AND NEWLY FURNISHED.

ST. NICHOLAS HOTEL,
Michigan City, - Indiana.

AUG. SCHAUSTEN, PROP.

New, Elegantly Furnished and Centrally Located. Everything First-Class.

RATES $2.00 PER DAY.

LIVERY AND SALE STABLE.

A. F. EARL,

Livery and Feed Stable,
Cor. Michigan and Washington Sts.

INSURANCE.

HOPKINS, H. M., Justice of the Peace and Insurance Agent, Franklin st.

SASH, DOORS AND BLINDS.

J. S. & G. C. ORR,
Contractors and Builders, Manufacturers of SASH, DOORS, BLINDS, ETC., ETC., Michigan City.

PERU, IND.

ATTORNEYS AT LAW.

ASTRIM & BAILEY, Attorneys at Law, Broadway.

W. W. SULLIVAN,

ATTORNEY AT LAW.

Special attention given to examining titles of real estate. Broadway.

BOOTS AND SHOES.

HALE & BUTLER, Boots, Shoes, Hats and Caps. Broadway.

KOOB, JACOB, Boot and Shoemaker. Fine work a specialty. Broadway.

DRY GOODS.

EMSWILER & SON, Dry Goods, Groceries and Notions, Broadway, opp. Odd Fellows' Hall.

KILGORE, SHIRK & CO., Hardware, Dry Goods, Boots, Shoes & Clothing, Main & Broadway.

FURNITURE.

LENHART & SCHMITT, Undertakers and Dealers in Furniture. Broadway.

GROCERIES.

CAUCHER & WELMER, Groceries and Provisions, 71 Broadway.

ROSS BROS., Groceries, Queensware, etc., Main st., opp. Court House.

MICHIGAN CITY—*Continued.*

HOTELS.

BROADWAY HOUSE, Kirtley & Son, Prop's, Peru, Ind.

NATIONAL HOTEL
(FORMERLY KELLER HOUSE),

ANDREW WEY, PROP.,
PERU.

The above House has been newly refitted, and Guests will find in it all the comforts of a First-Class House. Free Bus to and from all Trains.

LIVERY AND SALE STABLES.

SEAGER, H. R. Training, Feed and Sale Stable, Broadway.

WALLACE, J. C. & B. E., Livery, Feed and Sale Stable, opp. National Hotel.

PHOTOGRAPHERS.

LAMOREAUX & LEAS, Photographers, Main and Broadway.

MOORE & JONES, Photographers, Broadway.

RESTAURANTS.

PELKEY, R., Restaurant and Confectionery, Broadway.

ROCHESTER, IND.

ATTORNEYS AT LAW.

CALKINS, E., Attorney at Law, Rochester.

HERMAN & ROWLEY, Attorneys at Law, Masonic Building

M'CLARY, T. J., Attorney at Law, Rochester.

SHRYOCK & CONNER, Attorneys at Law, Rochester.

SLICK, J. S., Attorney at Law, Rochester.

HARNESS AND SADDLES.

OSGOOD, O. P., Dealer in Harness, Saddles, etc., Main st.

STOCKTON, G. W., Harness, Saddles, Collars, Whips, etc., Main st.

HOTELS.

CENTRAL HOUSE, R. N. Rannells, Prop. Good sample rooms on 1st and 2d floors. Rochester.

WALLACE HOUSE, R. Wallace, Prop. Good sample rooms on the first floor.

MERCHANT.

GOULD, D. S., Dry Goods, Groceries, Boots, Shoes, Hats, Caps, etc., Main st.

PHOTOGRAPHER.

MOORE, M. H., Photographer, Main st.

PLANING MILL.

SAMUEL BARKDOLL.

Planing Mill,
Door, Sash and Blind Factory, Near Railroad Depot.

1876.

June 27.—The Democratic National Convention met at St. Louis, and, on the 28th of June, nominated Governor Samuel J. Tilden, of New York, for President, and Hon. Thomas A. Hendricks, of Indiana, for Vice-President.

July 4.—Terrific storm in Iowa. Forty-two persons drowned in the village of Rockdale.

July 5.—A bill was passed regulating the price of postage, allowing for all third-class mail matter, except unsealed circulars, to be transmitted at the rate of one cent for every two ounces, and one cent for every additional two ounces. The present rate of one cent per ounce for all merchandise remains unchanged.

July 9.—Castle Garden, New York City, destroyed by fire.

July 10.—Burning of the propeller St. Clair, on Lake Superior. Seventeen passengers and ten of the crew drowned.

July 16.—Congress unanimously passed the Senate joint resolution for the completion of the Washington Monument.

July 20.—Commodore Garner's yacht Mohawk, was capsized in front of the Club House of the New York Yacht Club, off Stapleton. Commodore and Mrs. Garner, Mr. Frost Thorne, Miss Adele Hunter and a cabin-boy were drowned.

July 26.—Argument in the Belknap impeachment case closed. The result was a failure to convict for a want of two-thirds majority.

Aug. 1.—President Grant issued a proclamation declaring Colorado to be a State of the Union.

Aug. 14.—The first wire stretched across East River for the great suspension bridge, which is to connect New York and Brooklyn.

Aug. 19.—The Hon. Michael C. Kerr, Speaker of the House of Representatives, died, aged fifty years.

Sept. 6.—The Lafayette statue was unveiled in Union Square, New York city.

Sept. 7.—William M. Tweed was arrested at Vigo, in Spain, where he had just arrived from Cuba. He was afterwards taken on board the U. S. steamer Franklin, and arrived in New York November 23d and was immediately conveyed to Ludlow-street jail.

Sept. 12.—Died, in Richmond, Va., General Henry A. Wise, aged 70 years.

Sept. 14.—The international rifle match at Creedmoor, resulted in a victory for the American team by twenty-two points. In the contest were teams from America, Scotland, Ireland, Australia and Canada. The Irish team came out second and the Scotch third. In a subsequent match, September 21, between the Irish and American teams, the latter won by eleven points.

Sept. 22.—At Black Lick Station, near Columbus, O., on the Pan Handle Railroad, four cars of an express train jumped the track and rolled down an embankment. Over thirty people were injured, four of whom were instantly killed.

Sept. 24.—Hell Gate, or the mine under

ROCHESTER, IND—Continued.

SUPERINTENDENT OF SCHOOLS.

MEYERS, E., Superintendent of Schools, Fulton Co., Rochester.

WATCHES, CLOCKS AND JEWELRY.

WOLF, C. C., Watches, Fine Jewelry, Silverware, Gold Pens, Musical Instruments, etc.

MARSHALL, MICH.

ATTORNEYS AT LAW.

GEER, W. S., Attorney at Law. The Law of Real Estate & Chancery Practice made a specialty.

RANDALL, IRA E., Attorney at Law, Marshall, Perfecting Titles to land and foreclosing of Mortgages throughout the State of Michigan made a specialty.

PORTER, WM. H., Attorney at Law, 141 State st.

BOOTS AND SHOES.

BUTLER, J. & R., Groceries, Provisions, Boots, Shoes, Crockery, etc., 78 State st.

HOTEL.

FOWLER HOUSE, Byron Lockwood, Proprietor, Marshall.

HOT AIR FURNACES.

DOBBINS, J. L., Phelps' Improved Hot Air Furnaces, Tinners.

LIVERY STABLE.

WARD, W. H., Livery & Feed Stable. Office in rear of Fowler House.

PATENT SOLICITOR.

B. F. WELLES,

Solicitor of American and Foreign Patents, Civil and Mechanical Engineer and Draughtsman, Marshall.

SHIFTING TOPS.

HUNT, F. A., Manf'r of Leather and Shifting Tops and Cushions, 14 State st.

BATTLE CREEK, MICH.

ATTORNEYS AT LAW.

BROWN & THOMAS, Attorneys at Law, Main & Jefferson sts. Established 1869.

BARBER.

EVANS, JOHN J., Tonsorial Barber, 1 East Main st. Established 1856.

BOOTS AND SHOES.

JEFFERSON, R., Manf'r & dealer in Boots and Shoes, 10 S. Jefferson st. Established 1871.

MARTIN, JULIUS, Boots & Shoes, repairing neatly done, 18 S. Jefferson st.

BUILDER.

PITTEE, LYMAN, Jobber & Builder, Sash, Doors & Blinds, S. Jefferson st.

BATTLE CREEK, MICH—Continued.

CONFECTIONERY.

WEEB, C. H. & CO., Confectionery & Restaurant, 31 E. Main st. Established 1873.

DENTISTS.

GRAVES, F. S., Dentist, Bet. 3 and 5 W Main st. Established 1863.

ROWE, W. H., Operative Dentist, 16 Main st. Established 1873.

E. B. WEEKS,

DENTIST.

A good set of Teeth for $10. Natural Teeth saved by filling, at 25 or 50 per cent. less than code prices, 3 East Main st.

DYEING AND SCOURING.

BRADLEY, T. J., Ladies' & Gents' garments neatly cleaned, dyed & press'd at 14 S. Jef'sn st.

HOTEL.

BRISTOL HOUSE, Carl A. Hodges, Proprietor, Battle Creek, Mich.

MEAT MARKET.

MARSH, H. N., all kinds of fresh and cured Meats, 8 S. Jefferson st. Established 1865.

MILLINERY.

STONE, ABELS & CO., N. Y. 99ct. Store, and dealers in Mil inery Goods, 5 W. Main st.

NEWSPAPERS.

REVIEW AND HERALD, Published by the Seventh Day Adventist Publishing Assoc'ion.

PHOTOGRAPHERS.

CRISPELL, T., Photographer, 7 N. Jefferson st. Established 1873.

J. F. MILLER,

Photographic Art Gallery,

5 East Main St.

Every style of Picture made, old Pictures copied and enlarged.

PUMP MANUFACTURER.

MILES, A., Manf'r of Wooden and Force Pumps, West Canal st.

GREEN BAY, WIS.

BOOTS AND SHOES.

ALBRIGHT & CO.,

Manufacturers and Wholesale and Retail

BOOTS & SHOES,

129 Washington St., cor. Cherry.

HOTELS.

WHITTINGTON HOUSE, H. Whittington, Proprietor. Cor. Washington & Crook sts.

THE OLD ELM, BOSTON COMMON, BOSTON, MASS.

The Union Hotel, Galesburg.

This truly elegant and first-class house which has been identified with the progress of Galesburg for years, is under the experienced and skillful management of Mr. C. Wormly, late of Kalamazoo, with "Judd" Gowdy as managing clerk. The whole house has been calcimined, redecorated and overhauled, and is now in the neatest and sweetest order, new carpets being laid down on all the corridors. The Union Hotel is not only holding its old reputation but is gaining new success under its present courteous and popular proprietor, who brings to his aid the assistance which money cannot buy, the refined taste of an affectionate wife and mother. The immaculate whiteness of the linen, the neatess of the furniture of all the house, its freedom from dust and smoke, all bear evidence of superior management in that department, where woman is at home. In fact the traveling public will receive every accommodation at the Union Hotel that is combined in the best hotels in the United States.

The Galesburg Thermæ.

THE TURKISH BATHS
—ARE GIVEN AT—
WRIGHT'S BATH ROOMS,
N. E. Corner of Prairie & Simmons Sts., - - - *Business College Building.*

Traveling men can find a first-class Turkish Bath at all times for $1.00. Those wishing treatment for all chronic diseases, can find board at a low figure at the place. The cure is permanent.

Mr. & Mrs. W. A. WRIGHT,
N. E. Cor. Prairie & Simmons Sts. Galesburg, Ill.

1876.

Hallett's Point Reef, Astoria, Long Island, was exploded by General Newton.

Sept. 27.—Died, at Galveston, Texas, Braxton F. Bragg, Confederate General, aged 64 years.

Oct. 12.—Explosion of a battery of boilers in a nail mill at Pittsburgh, Penn. Fifteen men killed and a large number injured.

Oct. 17.—President Grant issues a proclamation commanding the South Carolina rifle clubs to disband in three days. The same day the Secretary of War ordered troops to Columbia, S. C. to enforce the proclamation should it be disregarded.

Oct. 21.—Arrival of the whaling bark Florence, at San Francisco, with intelligence that twelve American whaling ships of the Arctic fleet have been wrecked in the ice, with immense loss of life.

Oct. 28.—Edward S. Stokes, convicted of shooting James Fisk, Jr., released from Auburn prison, N. Y., his term of sentence having expired.

Oct. 31.—Sumner's Opera House, Akron, Ohio, destroyed by fire, which includes Sumner's Hotel and several stores. Total loss, $75,000.

Nov. 7.—Election of President of the United States. On the night of the election, it seemed to be pretty generally conceded by both parties that Governor Tilden, of New York, the Democratic candidate, was elected, but later news during the following day rendered it extremely doubtful who was chosen. Governor Hayes, of Ohio, was the Republican candidate for President.

Nov. 10.—Closing of the great Centennial Exhibition, Philadelphia. The Exhibition was open 159 days. During that time the paid admissions were 8,004,325. The free admissions were 1,785,067. Total admissions, 9,799,392. The total receipts were $3,813,749 75. Money received from concess'ns $290,000; from per centages and royalties, $205,000; grand total, $4,307,749 75. The average daily total admissions were 61,568. The average daily receipts were $23,935 85.

The following is a comparative statement of the attendance, receipts and number of days open of the different international exhibitions held since 1855:

Year.	Place.	No. of Visitors.	Receipts.	Days Open.
1861	London	6,039,195	$2,530,000	141
1855	Paris	5,162,330	610,500	200
1862	London	6,211,103	2,360,000	171
1867	Paris	10,000,000	2,822,932	210
1873	Vienna	7,254,687	2,000,000	186
1876	Philadelphia	9,799,392	3,812,749	159

Nov. 18.—Fall of a crowded floor in the Opera House, Sacramento, Cal. The Peak family, the original Swiss Bell-ringers, were performing, and this was the opening night of the Opera House, when the floor gave way, killing seven persons, and four fatally injured, besides fifty persons were more or less seriously injured.

Nov. 21.—The Peoria Woolen Mills, at Peoria, Ill, destroyed by fire. Loss, $30,000.

Nov. 26.—Sperry & Barnes' pork-packing establishment, at New Haven, Conn., destroyed by fire. Loss, including building, stock and fixtures $200,000.

GREEN BAY—*Continued.*

GROCERIES.

JOANNES BROS.,
Wholesale & Retail
GROCERIES
128 WASHINGTON STREET.

LIQUOR DEALERS.

DIEKMANN & DREYER,
(Successors to Northam & Diekmann.)
WHOLESALE LIQUOR DEALERS,
No, 109 Washington Street.

MILLINERY.

SPRAGUE, MRS. S., Fashionable Millinery, Pine street.

PHYSICIANS.

BROOKS, DR. H. A., Physician and Surgeon, Adams & Cherry sts.

KING, DR. E. B., Physician, Fox Block, Washington st.

OLMSTED & SQUIRE,
HOMEOPATHIC PHYSICIANS,
OFFICE, SHAYLOR BLOCK.

SEWING MACHINES.

INGALLS, GEO. H., Agent for all kinds of Sewing Machines, Shaylor Block.

SOAP MANUFACTORY.

Fox River Soap Manufacturer,
290 & 292 WASHINGTON STREET, GREEN BAY, WIS.
SEND FOR CIRCULAR.

WATCHMAKERS AND JEWELERS.

E. ASIMONT,
WATCHMAKER & JEWELER,
173 Washington St., Green Bay, Wis.
Established 1857.

A. MICHAAL,
Dealer in Watches, Clocks and Jewelry,
German Accordions, Violins, Harmonicas, Spectacles, &c., 113 Washington st. All work promptly Repaired and Warranted.

MENASHA, WIS.

BAKERY AND CONFECTIONERY.

ARNOLD, G. M. F., Bakery, Confectionery and Ice Cream Saloon. Main st. Estab. 1872.

BOOTS AND SHOES.

STILP, JACOB, Boots and Shoe Maker, Main st.

DRY GOODS, GROCERIES, &c.

A. LANDGRAF,
Dry Goods, Groceries and Saloon,
Established 1876. BROAD STREET.

IMPORTANT EVENTS OF THE CENTURY. 275

NEENAH, WIS.

DRESSMAKER.

CLARK, MRS. S. T., Fashionable Dressmaker,
Cedar st., opp. P. O.

GROCERIES AND PROVISIONS.

JOHNSON & SON,
Groceries and Provisions,
Fruits, Vegetables and Produce,
NEENAH, WIS.

NEUDECK, EMIL, Groceries and Provisions,
Wisconsin ave.

RESTAURANT AND CONFECTIONERY.

LANSING, W., City Restaurant and Confectionery, Wisconsin ave.

FORT HOWARD, WIS.

FURNITURE.

OLDENBURG, A. G., Undertaker and Furniture
Manufacturer, 20 Main st.

HARDWARE.

HALL & BURNS, Hardware,
Main street.

HOTELS.

NORTHWESTERN HOTEL
GALLAGHER & DONOVAN, Props.
Broadway & Hubbard Sts., Fort Howard.

PLANING MILL.

PLANING MILL,
WATER STREET.
Send for Circular C. SCHWARTZ & CO.

EAU CLAIRE, WIS.

BARBER.

HALVORSON, A., Barber. 10 Shaves for $1.00.
Barstow st., North Side.

HARDWARE.

CHARLES LANG,
Dealer in

Stoves, Tin & Hardware
OPP. Gallaway House, Eau Claire.

HOTELS.

RITZINGER HOUSE,
GEORGE RITZINGER, Prop.
EAU CLAIRE STREET.

1876.

Dec. 4.—The bust of Horace Greeley, the philosopher and founder of the New York *Tribune*, presented to the friends of the deceased by the American printers and journalists, was unveiled at Greenwood Cemetery, New York, in the presence of about 1,000 people.

Dec. 5.—Brooklyn Theatre, Brooklyn, N. Y., destroyed by fire. This was one of the most terrible and fatal calamities that has ever occurred in the United States—far exceeding in horrors that of the burning of the Richmond (Va.) Theatre, Dec. 27, 1811 (see page 65). Over three hundred and fifty lives were lost, burned and buried in the ruins, disfigured so much that but few were in condition to be recognized, so completely charred and burned as to be impossible to tell whether they were male or female, human or animal. Many persons were seriously injured in their efforts to escape from the flames by jumping out of the windows, and some were killed outright. Others were crushed and mangled by the mad rush of human beings seeking egress from the theater by the main outlet on Washington street. Of the actors, two lost their lives—Harry S. Murdoch and Claude Burroughs. The play was the *Two Orphans*, with Miss Claxton as the heroine; and the fire occurred in the last act, and in five minutes more the play would have been concluded and the audience dismissed. The fire originated from a piece of canvass, out of which trees are made, which broke from its fastenings and fell over the border lights near the center of the stage. The curtain was then lowered, took fire and communicated the flames to the gallery, where the scene of alarm was something horrible to contemplate. There were 405 persons in the gallery; and, in the theatre altogether, including musicians, actors, subordinates, etc., about 1,050 persons.

Dec. 5.—First cremation in the United States was performed at Washington, Pa. It was the body of Baron De Palm, who was born in Augsburg, Southern Germany, in the year 1809.

December 12.—Ice broke on the Mississippi river in front of St. Louis, sinking four vessels of the Keokuk Packet Line and three others, besides inflicting great injury to other vessels. Loss supposed to be $200,000.

Dec. 14.—Destructive fire at Little Rock, Arkansas. Loss, $200,000.

Dec. 29.—Terrible railroad accident at Ashtabula, Ohio, over 100 lives lost. As the passenger train on the Lake Shore railroad was crossing the iron bridge at Ashtabula about 8 A. M., the bridge gave way, precipitating the cars down a frightful chasm sixty feet deep into the water and ice. Men, women and children lost their lives by being crushed, burned and drowned; and out of 185 passengers and employees but seventy were known to have been saved. There is no cause assigned for the breaking of the bridge unless from the effects of the extreme cold.

1877.

The monopoly of sewing machines ex-

EAU CLAIRE—Continued.

HOTELS.

PEABODY HOUSE. Peabody & Robinson, Proprietor. River and Gibson sts.

EAU CLAIRE HOTEL.

WM. NEWTON, Prop.

FIRST-CLASS.

Cor. Barstow & Eau Claire Sts.

INSURANCE.

WM. A. TEALL,

General Insurance Agent,

Music Hall Block, Barstow St.

MILLINERY AND DRESSMAKING.

MRS. C. CASE,

MILLINERY, FANCY GOODS

And Butterick's Paper Patterns,
BARSTOW STREET.

MISS M. A. ELDERKIN,

Chicago Millinery and Notion Store,
BARSTOW ST.

PHELPS, MRS. E., Dressmaking,
Barstow st.

PHYSICIAN.

NOBLE, J. H., Homœopathic Physician, Barstow st.

ROOFING.

P. ANDERSON,

Roofing & General Job Work,
Cor. River and Kelsey sts.

SALOONS AND RESTAURANTS.

E. J. BERG,
WINE & LIQUOR SALOON,
Barstow st., near Broadway (North side).

C. M. WALLER,
Saloon and Restaurant.
WATER ST.

TAILORS.

RADENSLEBEN & SCHROEDER,
MERCHANT TAILORS,
Old Eau Claire House, Eau Claire.

TOBACCO AND CIGARS.

E. M. KRETLOW,

MUSICIAN, AND

Manf'r and Dealer in Cigars, Tobacco, &c.,
Barstow and William sts., North side.

MADISON, WIS.

AGRICULTURAL IMPLEMENTS.

SHELDON, S. L., Reapers, Mowers and Threshing Machines.

BAKERY AND CONFECTIONERY.

HEILMAN, GEO., Madison Bakery and Confectionery, cor. Main & Webster sts. Est. '73.

BOOTS AND SHOES.

DAVIDSON, D. L., Manf'r of Boots and Shoes, 233 Main st. Established 1867.

BUSINESS COLLEGE.

BUSINESS COLLEGE, Ellsworth Block, Madison. Wis. Wilmot, Deming & Boyd. Prop's.

CARRIAGES AND SLEIGHS.

DAVIES, H. H., Carriage Maker, Webster st. Established 1875.

HANSON, CHRIS, Carriage and Sleigh Manf'r, Webster st., bet. Main and King sts.

DRUGGIST.

HILL, H. J., Druggist, Groceries, Provisions, 7 King st. Established 1875.

DRY GOODS.

FRIEDRICH, C. W., Staple and Fancy Dry Goods & Millinery. Hobbins' bl'k, Pinckney st.

FURNITURE.

CLARK, DARWIN, Manf'r and Dealer in Furniture, Upholstery Goods, &c , 213 Main st.

GROCERIES AND PROVISIONS.

WALWER & DEIKE, Groceries and Provisions, 9 King st. Established 1876.

HARNESS AND SADDLES.

BODENSTIEN, B., Manf'r of Harness and Saddles. Webster st. Established 1855.

BOEHMER, MALIGUS, Harness, Saddles and Trunks, 21 King st. Established 1876.

MARBLE WORKS.

MADISON MARBLE WORKS, Abijah Abbott, Main st., near Court House.

NEWSPAPER.

WISCONSIN STATE JOURNAL

Daily, Tri-Weekly and Weekly.

MADISON, WIS.

All kinds of Job Work and Stereotyping
at short notice and in good style.

OYSTERS AND FRUIT.

OPPEL, W. A., Oysters, Fruit, Game and Fish, 213 Main st. Established 1856.

SILVERSMITH.

GILBERSON, C., Gold and Silversmith, 214 Main st. Established 1874.

TIN, COPPER AND SHEET IRON.

HEYL, C. W., Tin, Copper and Sheet Iron Ware, 10 Webster st. Established 1857.

ADVERTISEMENTS. 277

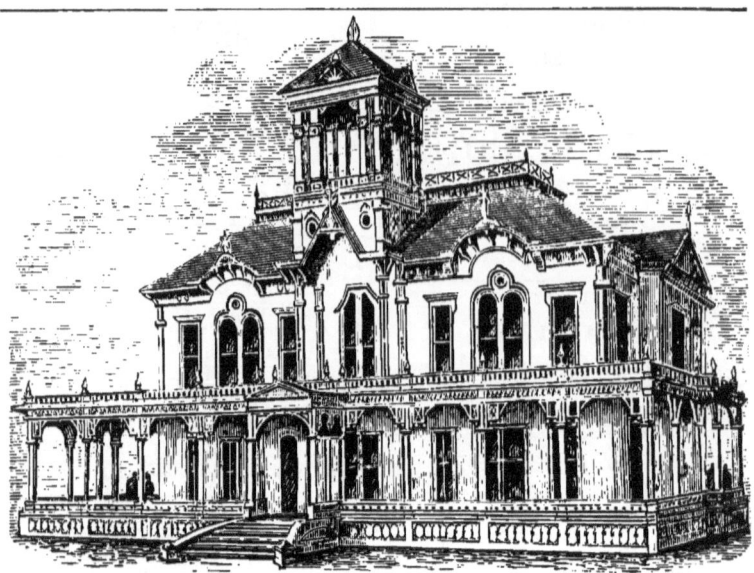

New York State Building, Centennial Exposition, Phila.—Is 30x60 feet, with spacious square bays in each end, which extend to roof, while a portico 13.6 wide extends across street front. The first floor contains two rooms one for ladies and one for gentlemen, with retiring and private consultation rooms, etc. In the hall a winding stair case ascends to second floor, which contains two parlors and several private apartments. From this floor the staircase continues to attic floor, thence to the cupola. The interior is decorated in soft gay colors, and with its many irregular features, ranks among the handsomest structures of its size on the ground.

JOHN G. WILLIS,

GENERAL

COMMISSION

MERCHANT,

No. 254 Dodge St., Omaha, Neb.

REFERENCES:
CALDWELL, HAMILTON & Co., Bankers.
A. J. SIMPSON, Omaha National Bank.
McCLURE & SMITH, Steam Cracker Factory.

Are prepared to make liberal advances on consignments. Prompt attention given to consignments. Send for Price Current.

S. A. WRIGHT,

General dealer in Sewing Machines, Needles, Attachments, Oil and Findings. Sole agent in Pettis Co. of the St. John Sewing Machines. Machines bought, sold and exchanged. Sewing machine repairing a specialty. 230 Ohio Street, Sedalia, Mo.

1877.

pired this year, reducing the price of these machines to about one-half their original cost.

The last of the troops that were left in the South, the result of the rebellion, were withdrawn this year from all the Southern States, and thus, virtually, these States became free for the first time since the rebellion.

Jan. 4.—Cornelius Vanderbilt died at his residence in New York city, aged 83 years. He was the richest man in the United States, his wealth being estimated at $80,000,000. He commenced life a poor boy and worked himself up to his great wealth by personal exertions. At the age of forty he commenced dealing extensively in Railroad stocks, and in 1849 he was known as Commodore Vanderbilt, on account of the great number of steamboat lines owned by him. At the time of his death he owned so much exclusively Railroad stock as to be denominated the King of Railroads.

Jan. 17.—House of Representatives ordered the arrest of the Louisiana Returning Board for refusing to furnish papers to the investigating committee in relation to the Presidential election in Louisiana.

Jan. 18.—The Congressional joint committee reported to both Houses, in the shape of a bill, a plan for counting the electoral vote. It makes the function of the President of the Senate purely ministerial, and the two kinds of objections likely to be raised when the certificates are opened, are to be settled as follows: First, when only one set of returns is presented from a state, any objection to their reception must be sustained by the concurrent vote of both Houses. Failing this, such return must be counted as the vote of the state. When two sets are presented, they are to be immediately referred to a commission composed of five Senators, five members of the House, and four of the Associate Justices of the Supreme Court, whose names are given—and one other justice selected by these four. The decision of this tribunal of fifteen is to be submitted to the two Houses assembled in joint session, and is to be final, unless both Houses agree to reject it.

Jan. 25.—Senate passed the Electoral Bill. Yeas 47; nays 17.

Jan. 26.—The House passed the Electoral Bill by a vote of 191 to 96.

Jan. 27.—Academy of Music of Indianapolis, Ind., destroyed by fire, involving a loss of nearly $100,000.

Jan. 29.—President signed the electoral bill. The President gave the following reasons for signing the bill: The country is agitated; it needs aid; it desires peace and quiet and harmony between all parties and sections. Its indus-

MADISON—*Continued.*

UNDERTAKERS.

FITCH, D., Undertaker and Manf'r of Coffins, Caskets. etc., Main st. Established 1850.

FRAUTCHI, CHAS., Undertaker and Dealer in Metallic Cases, Coffins, &c., 27 King. Est. '69.

WATCHES, CLOCKS AND JEWELRY.

MILLER, C., Watches, Clocks and Jewelry and Silver Plated Ware, 12 King st. Est. 1858.

RACINE, WIS.

ATTORNEYS AT LAW.

NELSON P. BROMLEY,

ATTORNEY AT LAW,
144 Main st.

FISH & LEE, ATTORNEYS AND COUNSELLORS AT LAW.

REFERENCES.
First National Bank, Racine; Manf'rs National Bank, Racine; Hon. Francis Bloodgood, Register in Bankruptcy. Milwaukee.

CHAS. H. SMITH,

Attorney at Law,
163 MAIN STREET,
RACINE

BAKERY.

SCHOUBOC, ANDREW, Copenhagen Cake Bakery, 32 State st.

BARBER.

LAUER, J. W., Shaving Parlor. Ladies' and Children's Hair Cutting a specialty. 80 Main st.

BILLIARD PARLOR.

CASE, R. & SON, Billiard Parlor, 163 Main st.

BIRD STORE.

ROBERTS, R. W., Bird Store, 30 College ave.

BOOKSELLER AND STATIONER.

JAMES J KAVENAUGH, Bookseller, Stationer and Newsdealer. All orders for Catholic Books promptly attended to; also, agent for all Catholic newspapers of the U. S., 152 Main st.

BOOTS AND SHOES.

BUCKINGHAM & SONS, Manf'rs and dealers in Boots & Shoes. 140 Main st.

JONES & WILLIAMS, Boots & Shoes, 13 6th st.

WELFL & KRAYNIK, Dealers in Boots and Shoes, Rubber Goods, etc., custom work done to order, and warranted to give satisfaction, 104 Main st. Established 1870.

ADVERTISEMENTS.

Fort Industry Block, Toledo, O.—Stands at the S. E. corner Summit and Monroe streets, fronting 80 feet on the former and extending at a like width to Water street. It was built in 1843 by Richard Mott, who now owns it, at a cost of some $14,000, and divided into four stores. In 1874 it was raised by being screwed up, making four roomy offices in the basement, the entire building being thoroughly overhauled and almost rebuilt at an expense of about $20,000.

DOWNING HOUSE,

EAST SIDE SQUARE,

F. L. DOWNING, · · · · *OSKALOOSA, IOWA.*

The Only First-class House in the City.

RACINE—Continued.

DENTIST.

LUKES, J. C., Dentist,
174 Main st. Established 1852.

FANCY GOODS.

MRS. H. S. CARY,
Dealer in Fine Steel Engravings, Chromo Lithographs, Picture Frames, Stationery, Brackets, Photograph Albums, Elias Howe Sewing Machines, etc. 171 Market Square.

FURNITURE.

BEFFEL, MATT, Furniture,
6th st., bet. Willow & Campbell sts.

JENNINGS, W. H., Furniture,
129 Main st.

GENERAL MERCHANDISE.

FREUDENFELD, JOS., Clothing & General Merchandise, 115 Main st.

GROCERIES.

HAAS, F. X., & CO., Groceries, Provisions, etc.,
66 Main st.

HANSEN, JAMES, Grocery,
140 State st.

MOHR, C. J., Grocery,
127 State st.

WEBER, ADOLPH, Groceries & Provisions,
71 6th st.

HARNESS MAKER.

SUTHERLAND, B., Harness Maker,
97 Main st.

HATS, CAPS AND FURS.

C. BROWN,

HATS, CAPS & FURS,

139 Main Street,

RACINE. - - WIS.

HOTELS.

WASHINGTON HOUSE.
Frank Schmit Proprietor, Foot of Main street, next Hotel to Western Union Railroad Depot and the Steamboat landing. Racine, Wis. Farmers, Travelers and Boarders will find good and cheap Board, clean Rooms and Beds. Good stabling for horses.

MILLINERY.

BURDICK, MRS. A. R., Millinery, etc.,
173 Main st.

PAINTER'S MATERIALS.

CARRE, WM., Painter's Materials,
Cor. State & Marquette sts.

PAINTER.

HASS, GEO. A., House & Sign Painter,
Wisconsin st. near 5th st.

PHOTOGRAPHERS.

E. T. BILLINGS,

Photographer,
Cor. Main and 5th sts.

RAPS, JOHN JR., Photographer,
117 Main st.

RACINE—Continued

PHYSICIAN AND SURGEON.

DR. TEEGARDEN,

Eclectic

PHYSICIAN AND SURGEON,

207 Main Street.

Office Hours—From 8 to 12, and 2 to 5.

TAILORS—MERCHANT.

F. ELMLINGER,

Merchant Tailor.

And dealer in Ready-Made Goods for Gentlemen's wear, 138 Main st.

FIELD, A., Merchant Tailor,
Cor. 4th & Main sts.

HETZEL, D., Merchant Tailor,
23 6th st.

HOERNEL, G., Merchant Tailor,
College ave. head of 5th st.

LAUF, JOSEPH, Merchant Tailor,
59 6th st.

RITTER & SCHMEISER, Merchant Tailors,
106 Main st.

ROBERTSON, C., Merchant Tailor,
105 Main st.

WINES AND LIQUORS.

JOHNSON, B. M., Wines & Liquors,
70 Main st.

CHAS. ROTH,
Wholesale Liquors & Cigars, also dealer in Chewing and Smoking Tobacco, Pipes, etc., 102 Main st.

ANN ARBOR, MICH.

COUNTY OFFICERS.

Register of Deeds—C. H. MANLEY.
Treasurer—MATTHEW GENSLEY.

AGRICULTURAL IMPLEMENTS.

McLAREN, S., Manf'r of and dealer in all kinds of Agricultural Implements, Detroit st.

BAKERY AND CONFECTIONERY.

WILLIAM CASPARY.

Bakery and Confectionery,
ICE CREAM AND SODA WATER,
28 East Huron St. *Established 1876.*

BOOTS AND SHOES.

BRENNAN, P., Estab 1866, Manf'r and dealer in Boots & Shoes, 17 4th st.

CARRIAGES AND BUGGIES.

HANDY & WURSTER, Estab. 1844, Buggies, Sleighs & Wagons, 21, 23 & 25 Detroit st.

SCHMIDT, ANDREW R., Established 1867, manufacturer of Carriages, Buggies, Wagons and Sleighs. I respectfully solicit your patronage and guarantee prices to correspond with the times. Shops, corner Detroit and North sts., Ann Arbor, Mich.

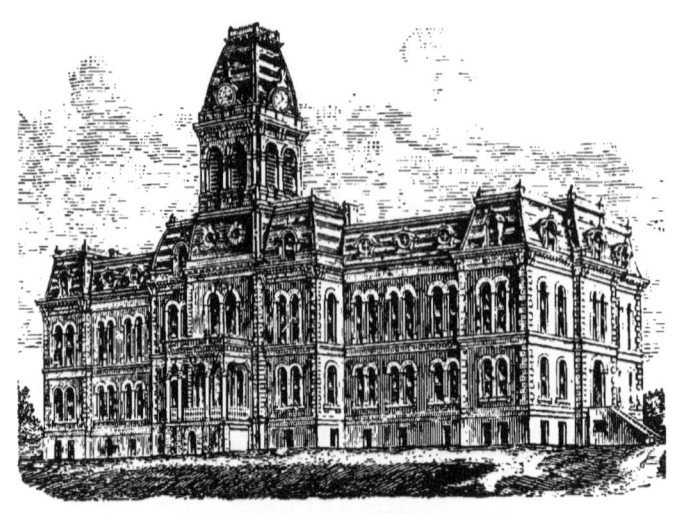

COURT HOUSE, LEAVENWORTH, KANSAS.

Iron Axles, Fifth Wheels, Spokes, Gearings, Wheels, Plow Steel Skeins, Axle Clips, Hubs, Bodies, Ducks, Springs, Malleables Etc. Felloes, Seats, Drills, Broadcloth, Top props, Lining, Nails, Etc.
LEAVENWORTH, KANSAS, SEND FOR PRICE LIST.

DOUBLE AND SINGLE ACTING POWER AND HAND

Pumps, Steam Pumps, Engine Trimmings,

MINING MACHINERY,

Belting Hose, Brass and Iron Fittings, Pipe. Steam Packing at Wholesale and Retail.

HALLADY WIND MILLS. CHURCH AND SCHOOL BELLS.

A. L. STRANG,
205 Farnam Street., Omaha, Neb

1877.

tries are arrested, labor unemployed, capital idle, and enterprise paralyzed by reason of the doubt and anx ety attending the uncertainty of a double claim to the Chief Magistracy of the United States. It wants to be assured that the result of the election will be accept d without resistance from the support ers of the disappointed candidate, and that its highest officer shall not hold his place with a questioned title or right.

Jan. 30.—The Senate and House each elected five members to serve on the Electoral Commission as follows: Senators Edmunds, Morton, Freelinghuysen, Thurman and Bayard, and Representatives Payne, Hunton, Abbott, Garfiel t and Hoar.

Jan. 31.—The four United States Associate Justices to serve on the Electoral Tribunal—Clifford, Miller, Field and Strong, chose as the fifth member of the Tribunal Justice Joseph P. Bradley, Colorado declared a state.

Feb. 1.—The joint convention to count the electoral vote assembled in the ha l of the House of Representatives. The vote of Florida was objected to, as there were three certificates presented from that state, and ref rred to the Electoral Commission.

Feb. 9.—The Electoral Commission, by a vote of 8 to 7, gave the vote of Flor da to Hayes and Wheeler, Judge Bradley voting with the Republicans.

Feb. 12.—Congress re-assembled in joint convention to count the electoral vote. When the state of Louisiana was reached its vote was referred to the commission, on account of the state presenting certificates from the Republicans and Democrats.

Feb. 16.—The Commission, by a vote of 8 to 7, decided the Louisiana vote for Hayes and Wheeler.

Feb. 15.—An attempt made to assassinate Gov. Packard, of Louisiana, while sitting in his room in the State House. W. H. Weldon, was the assassin. He claims to be the son of a Lutheran minister in Pennsylvania.

Feb. 21.—The joint convention refused to receive the vote of O egon, on account of two certificates from that state; but, on the 23d, the electoral tribunal decided by a vote of 8 to 7, that the vote of Oregon should be counted for Hayes and Wheeler.

Feb. 23.—Fox's New American Theatre at Tenth and Chestnut treets, Philadelphia, destroyed by fire. Total loss was about $250,000. It was built in 1870.

March 2.—The electoral count finished, and Hayes and Wheeler declared President and Vice-President of the United States.

ANN ARBOR—*Continued.*

DRUGGIST.

Established in 1843.
EBERBACH & SON,
Dealers in

Drugs, Medicines, Chemicals & Toilet

Articles, Chemical Glassware, Apparatus and Reagents. Agents for Tieman & Co.'s Surgical Instruments, 12 S. Main st., Ann Arbor, Mich.

FURNITURE.

BODWELL, A. M., Manf'r of Opera House Chairs, and Bodwell's Patent Folding Seat and Desk, 32 N. 4th st.

HARDWARE.

EBERBACH, C., Hardw re, Stoves, Tin and Sheet Ironware, 23 & 25 Main st.

HARNESS AND COLLARS.

BURKHARDT, J. C., E-t. 1866, Harness & Collars, send for price list, 3 Huron st.

HOTELS.

LEONARD HOUSE, B. J. Billings, Proprietor. First Class House.

LIVERY AND HACK LINE.

J. A. POLHEMUS, Proprietor of
LIVERY, HACK and BUS LINE, Cor. Main & Catherine sts.
Established 1863.

MARBLE WORKS.

EISELE, ANTON, Monuments, Grave & Building Stones, Detroit st. Established 1868.

NURSERY.

SMITH, R. G., Prop'r of the Celebrated Ann Arbor Nursery, West Liberty st.

PHOTOGRAPHER.

E. B LEWIS,
Established 1874.

Leading Photographer,

First Floor over Express Office,
6 Huron St., Ann Arbor, Mich.

SHAVING AND BATH ROOMS.

OWEN, O. G., (Student) Shaving Parlor & Mineral Bath Rooms, 9 N. Main st.

SHEWCRAFT, M. C., Prop'r of the Barber Palace, Gregory House, Ann Arbor.

IONIA, MICH.

ATTORNEYS AT LAW.

JENNINGS, L. H., Attorney at Law, Over First National Bank, Main st.

MITCHEL & PIATT, Attorneys at Law, Opp. Second National Bank, Main st.

WELLS & MORSE,
ATTORNEYS AT LAW,
Over First National Bank, Main st.

IMPORTANT EVENTS OF THE CENTURY. 283

Ohio State Building, Centennial Exposition, Phila.—It is the most substantial of the State buildings. It is built of Sandstone, furnished by the proprietors of the various quarries in Ohio. Some of the stones are very beautiful, and the colors are tastefully blended together. Each course of stone is from a different quary, and twenty-one quarries are represented in the like number of layers from the ground to the eaves. The building is two stories, with high roof. It is 60 feet wide and 58 feet deep, including the front porch. A varandah 12 feet wide runs on each side and in rear of the building, that on the east being covered with a porch without columns—the other porches having supporting columns. A hallway 9 feet wide and 46 feet long runs through the center of the building, on each floor, on each side of which are committee, reception, retiring and other suitable rooms. At a meeting of the Ohio State Board, a resolution was adopted donating their State building to the Philadelphia Park Commissioners.

Maryland State Building, Centennial Exposition, Phila.—Is constructed of wood, one story high, with an addition. It is divided off into four rooms, arranged for the convenience of visitors, Commissioners from that State, and reception room for ladies. It has on exhibition a variety of memorials from the State of Maryland.

ADVERTISEMENTS.

IONIA—Continued.

BANK.

SECOND NATIONAL BANK, (Established 1887.)
Main st., Ionia.

BILLIARD PARLORS.

HARLOW, J. M., Proprietor Billiard Parlors,
Sherman House.

HEALY, WM. M., Billiards and Restaurant,
Cor. Main & 3rd sts.

BOOKKEEPER.

RITTINGER, J. H., Bookkeeper. with Summ
& Co., Dexter street.

BREWER.

SUMM, GEO., JR., & CO., Brewer,
Dexter st. Established 1867.

CARRIAGE MAKER AND BLACKSMITH.

R. D. CAIN,
CARRIAGE MAKER & BLACKSMITH,
2nd St., Opp. Sherman House,

DRY GOODS.

HALL BROTHERS, Dealers in Dry Goods,
Sherman House Block, Main st.

GUNSMITH.

PICKETT, R. M., Gunsmith,
2nd st., opp. Sherman House.

HOTELS.

EAGLE HOTEL

D. WINTROWD, Prop.
Opposite D. L. & N. Depot.

Revere House,
R. W. PAGE, Proprietor.
Opposite D. & M. Depot.

SHERMAN HOUSE.

JOHN TOMPKINS, Prop.
Main Street.
IONIA, MICH.

MARBLE WORKS.

WHITING, TRUMAN, Proprietor Rutland Marble Works, opp. Baptist Church.

MEAT MARKET.

WILLIAM MARVIN,
Dealer in all kinds of Fresh and Salt Meats,
Hides and Pelts,
MAIN STREET.

PHYSICIAN.

ALLEN, T. R., Homeopathic Physician and Surgeon, No. 1 Main st.

IONIA—Continued.

POTTERY.

AMPHLETT, W. O., Proprietor of Ionia Pottery,
near D. & M. Depot.

WELL AUGER.

MUNN, L. D., Proprietor Well Auger,
Sherman House.

WINES AND LIQUORS.

FRANK SCHMUCKER,
Dealer in Wines, Beer and Liquors,
Cor. Main & Dexter Sts., Ionia, Mich.

LANSING, MICH.

BLACKSMITH.

COOKE, H. L., City Horse Shoer and General
Blacksmith, Michigan ave., near Bridge.

BUSINESS COLLEGE.

LANSING BUSINESS COLLEGE. H. P. Bartlett,
Principal. Established 1867. Lansing.

CIGAR MANUFACTURER.

Established 1874.
HENRY FIRTH,
MANUFACTURER OF FINE CIGARS
21 Michigan Ave., Lansing.

DRUGGIST.

BISBEE, JOHN B., Drugs, Medicines, Fancy and
Toilet Articles, 137 Washington ave.

EAVES-TROUGH AND TINWARE.

BALCH & LAWRENCE,
Manufacturers of
Eaves-Troughing, Spouting & Tinware,
Dealers in Stoves, White Lime, Water
Lime, Calcine Plaster, Etc.,
OPP. LANSING HOUSE, LANSING, MICH.

FURNITURE.

F. Carns. W. Wharfield.
CARNS & WHARFIELD,
Dealers in
New & Second-Hand Furniture.
Mattresses & Couches of all kinds made to Order.
Opp. Lansing House, Washington Ave., Lansing,
Mich. Repairing of all Kinds done on short
notice. Established 1876.

HARNESS AND SADDLES.

CANNELL & EDMONDS, [Established 1856,]
Harness, Saddles, Trunks, 114 Washington av.

HOTEL.

EVERETT HOUSE. W. H. Packard. Prop.
Cor. Main st. & Washington ave.

MARBLE WORKS.

KEYES, D. E., & CO., Marble Workers, Washington ave., opp. Lansing House. Estab. 1877.

Rhode Island State Building, Centennial Exposition, Phila.—
It 21 by 42 feet, with an addition to the rear of 6½ ft. by 19 ft, and an open porch in front 6 feet by 14 feet. There are in the building ladies' and gentlemen's waiting rooms, and a luggage room in the rear of entrance vestibule. It is built of solid timber, the frame-work showing on the outside. The roof is cove ed with Pennsylvania black slate. The interior is very plain, the rooms being sheathed with narrow boards, the joints running horizontally. The same material shows both inside and outside. No plaster has been used.

Arkansas State Building, Centennial Exposition, Phila.—
This building is a pavilion, with offices and retiring rooms, covering an area of over 5,000 square feet. The shape of the building is octagonal; the columns are placed in a circle, 82 feet in diameter; the ceiling is spherical, and an octagonal dome is placed on the top of the roof; the top of the dome is 50 feet above the floor line. The roof construction is of iron; the sides of wood and glass.

1877.

March 5.—President Hayes and Vice-President Wheeler inaugurated.

March 23.—Execution of John D. Lee, Mormon bishop, convicted of being the main instigator in the Mountain Meadows massacre in 1857. This massacre was one of the most atrocious fanatical religious murders of the last thousand years. One hundred and fifty men, women and children were assaulted, and all, save seventeen infant children, were murdered. Lee was shot to death by a file of United States soldiers, on the same spot where the massacre was committed. Lee's allies were Mormons and Indians.

April 2.—The Southwestern portion of Chicago was covered with water to the extent of nearly seven miles square. In some cases the water reached the first stories, and people were obliged to make their way in boats.

April 11.—The Southern Hotel, one of the largest and finest in St. Louis, destroyed by fire. The fire broke out shortly before two o'clock, and spread with such rapidity that in less than an hour the entire building was in ruins. The guests rushed from their beds frantically, but many were driven back to their rooms by the dense smoke which filled the hallways. Some were rescued by means of ropes and ladders, but others, becoming desperate, leaped from the upper windows and were instantly killed, or so badly mangled, that death resulted soon after. The number who lost their lives was fourteen. The loss will probably reach $750,000.

May 10.—Opening ceremonies of the Permanent Exhibition at Philadelphia, where over one hundred thousand persons assembled.

May 11.—The new Winnebago County Court House, Rockford, Ill., fell, burying the workmen in the ruins and killing nine men.

June 4.—Mount Carmel, Ill., nearly destroyed by a Tornado, over 20 persons were killed and nearly 200 wounded, over half a million dollars worth of property destroyed.

June 14.—The bridge across the Connecticut River between Northampton and Hadley, Mass., was blown down by a hurricane. Fifteen persons who had taken shelter there and a number of teams, went down in the ruins.

June 20.—St. John, N. B., nearly destroyed by fire, the main portion of the city burned, all the public buildings and business houses destroyed. 15,000 people homeless, no household effects were saved. 500 acres were burned over. Many lives were lost. Intense suffering among the people. Loss about $20,000,000.

July 16.—The firemen and brakemen of the freight trains on the Baltimore and

LANSING—*Continued.*

MEAT MARKET.

A. BERTCH,
Wholesale & Retail Dealer in

FRESH & SALT MEATS

Dried Beef, Hams, Sausages and Poultry,

118 WASHINGTON AVE.
Established 1859.

TAILOR—MERCHANT.

FRED. WRIGHT,
MERCHANT TAILOR,
BUTLER BLOCK,
Washington Ave., Lansing, Mich.

MUSKEGON, MICH.

ATTORNEYS AT LAW.

COOK, F. W., Attorney at Law, 87 Western ave.

BOOTS AND SHOES.

SMITH, B. H., Manufacturer and Dealer in Boots and Shoes, 185 Pine st.

CARRIAGES, WAGONS, &c.

ROBERT STITTS,
Manufacturer Buggies, Log Carts, Wagons, &c.,
CLAY AVE. & TERRACE ST.

CIGARS AND TOBACCO.

JIROCH, FRANCIS, Cigars and Smokers' Articles, Wholesale and Retail, 78 Western ave.

CLOTHES PINS.

BRITTON, J., Manufacturer of Clothes Pins and Wood Turning, Pine & Apple sts.

CLOTHING.

PICK, I., Star Clothing House, 51 Western ave.

DRUGGISTS.

BENNETT, J. R., & CO., Apothecaries and Druggists, Western ave.

BENSON, C., Wholesale and Retail Dealer in Drugs and Medicines, 73 Western ave.

VANDER LINDE, CHARLES, & BRO., Druggists and Chemists, 192 Pine st. Established 1877.

GROCERY AND BAKERY.

HOPSTRA, S. A., Crockery and Glassware, Grocery and Bakery, Hopstra Block.

HOTELS.

KEMPF HOUSE. Barbara Kempf, Prop. Pine st.

MUSKEGON—Continued.

THE OCCIDENTAL,

N. A. BARNEY, Prop.

Muskegon, Michigan.

PHYSICIANS.

W. H. DELAP, M. D.,
Confidential Physician and Surgeon.
Will Cure Cancer, or no pay. Twenty years Experience. 194 PINE STREET.

W. J. SLOAN, M. D.,
Physician & Surgeon
Proprietor of

SLOAN'S AGUE CURE,
192 PINE ST., Muskegon Mich.

REAL ESTATE,

WOOD, WESLEY F., Real Estate Dealer, Pine st.

SALOON,

MAHER, M., Saloon and Restaurant and Engineer, Pine st.

NEUMEISTER, GUSTAVE, Saloon, 137 Pine street.

STOVES AND HARDWARE.

MILLER, JOHN A., Stoves, Hardware and House Furnishing Goods, Western ave.

WINES AND LIQUORS.

KAICHEN, BEN., Imported and Domestic Wines and Liquors, 59 Western ave., Muskegon.

SCOTT, GEO. F., Dealer in Wines and Liquors, 52 Clay ave. Established 1875.

GRAND HAVEN, MICH.

BRASS AND IRON.

SNYDER, W. A., dealer in Brass and Iron Goods. 57 Washington st. Established 1875.

CARRIAGES AND WAGONS.

HUBERT, G. & CO., Carriage & Wagon Maker, 3d & Elliott sts. Established 1872.

FLOUR, FEED AND GRAIN.

JOHN T. PERCIVAL,
Wholesale and retail dealer in

FLOUR, FEED & GRAIN,
59 Washington St.

Goods delivered in the city free.
Established 1875.

1877.

Ohio Railroad at Baltimore, Md., and Martinsburg, Va., struck on account of reduction of wages.

July 17.—The railroad strikers at Martinsburg, V., attacked and fired on a train. The troops returned the fire, killing one of the rioters and wounding several.

July 18.—At the request of the Governor of West Virginia, President Hayes ordered federal troops to Martinsburg, Va., to quell the railroad riot.

July 20.—The strikes on the Baltimore and Ohio and Pennsylvania Railroads continue, and a strike took place on the Erie Railway, stopping all trains. A riot occurred at Baltimore, and the Sixth Maryland Regiment fired into the crowd, killing nine and wounding between forty and fifty. Troops were also called out in Pennsylvania and Ohio.

July 21.—A conflict occurred at Pittsburg, Pa., between railroad strikers and the military, during which a number of persons were killed, including Sheriff Fife, and many wounded, among the number being General Pearson. The mob sacked all the leading gun-stores, and late at night attacked the soldiers from Philadelphia who had been compelled to take refuge in the Round House at the outer depot of the Pennsylvania Railroad. Another riot also took place at Baltimore, Md., but no one was killed. President Hayes issued a proclamation, ordering all those engaged in these unlawful proceedings to desist and retire to their homes by 12 o'clock noon of the 22d.

July 22.—The railroad strikers continue their riotous work at Pittsburg. Early in the morning the mob set fire to and completely destroyed the round-house of the Pennsylvania Railroad Company, together with 125 first-class locomotives housed there, hundreds of loaded freight cars and other property, aggregating in value, according to a rough estimate, $3,000,000. The troops, who had been penned up in the round-house all night, were forced to attempt escape when the building was fired, and as they marched out hastily they were attacked by the strikers, who followed them as they doublequicked toward the Arsenal, firing shots and hurling all sorts of missiles at the soldiers, many of whom were badly hurt and others shot down and left in the streets. Once the military turned and fired into their pursuers, twenty or more persons being killed by the discharge. The commandant at the Arsenal refused to allow the troops admission, saying that he had but twenty men with him, and if he allowed them to enter he could not protect the place against the mob. They then hurried on to the bridge over the Alleghe-

R. G. LUTKE,
Manufacturer of all kinds of

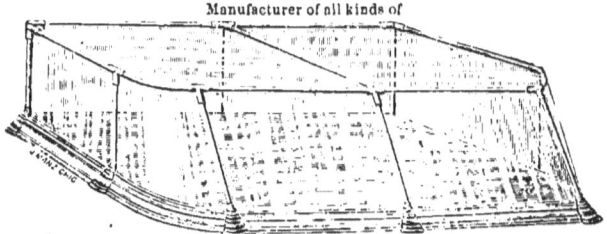

SHOW CASES,
215 HAMILTON ST. — — — — PEORIA, ILL.

E. PARSONS, M. D.,
Kewanee, Ill.

Treats Chronic Diseases with Vapor Baths, Turkish Vapors, Electric Baths, Hadfield's Equalizer, &c., and warrants a

CURE IN ALL CURABLE CASES.

MEDICINES MILD AND EFFECTUAL. DR. PARSONS HAS AN EXPERIENCE OF TWENTY-FIVE YEARS IN THEIR USE.

JOHN HERSCHBERGER,
Manufacturer of

SASH, DOORS AND BLINDS, MOULDINGS
Brackets, Window and Door Frames,

STAIR BUILDING, STAIR RAILS, BALUSTERS,

PACKING BOXES, ETC.

Planing, Matching and Scroll Sawing done to Order.
704 S. Washington St., near Chestnut St., — — PEORIA, ILL.

HERMAN FRIEDRICHS,

 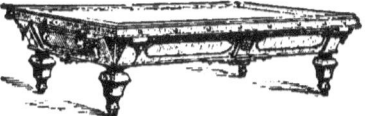

Commercial   Billiard

PARLORS,
116 & 118 South Jefferson Street, PEORIA, ILL.

The Choicest Foreign and Domestic Wines and Liquors, and Cigars at the Bar, Milwaukee Lager Fresh on Draught.

Court House, Peoria, Ill.—The building was begun in May, 1876, and is to be completed in May, 1878. It has a front of 184 feet by 164 feet in depth, is built of Amherst, Ohio, sandstone, 3 stories high, with a large dome in the centre, iron beams and brick arches for the floors, and is strictly fire-proof. It is being built by P. H. Decker, contractor, Chicago, and superintended by W. E. Elliott. The total cost of building will be $250,000.

Peoria Foundry and Machine Shop!

NICOL, BURR & CO.,
Manufacturers of

STEAM ENGINES!

Flour Mill and Distillery Machinery, Shafting, Pulleys and Hangers, Building Castings, &c. Agents for Stillwell's Patent Heaters and Lime Extractors.

☞ Judson & Gardner's Governor and Sturtevant's Blower. ☜

We also furnish Steam Engine Boilers, Steam Pipe and Fittings, Cocks, Valves, Steam Gauges, and all the requisites for the connection of Engines and Boilers complete.

CHASE ELEVATOR MACHINERY

Made a specialty; and in connection with the same we furnish belting, elevator buckets and bolts, and all of the necessary fittings. ☞Special attention given to repairing, day or night.

Cor. of Walnut and Water Streets,   -   -   PEORIA, ILL.

GRAND HAVEN—Continued.

DRUGGISTS.
GRIFFIN, H. & CO., Drugs, Medicines & Chemicals, Washington & 1st sts. Estab. 1856.

FURNITURE.
BARNS, J., Household Furniture, Coffins, etc., Washington st. Established 1867.

GROCERIES.
GALE & PFAFF, Groceries, Provisions & Crockery Glassware, 78 Washington st. Est. 1873.
STONER, J., dealer in Groceries, Fruits & Confectionery, 95 Washington st. Est. 1872.

MEAT MARKETS.
VAN ALLSBURG, A. R., dealer in Fresh Meats, 44 Washington st. Established 1873.
VANDE, SRINE D., dealer in Fresh Meats, etc., 93 Washington st. Established 1873.
VAN WEELDEN, G., dealer in Fresh Meats, 94 Washington st. Established 1870.

TAILOR—MERCHANT.
SANFORD, I. P., Merchant Tailor, & dealer in Stationery, 47 Washington st. Est. 1859.

WATCHMAKER.
COPPAGE, WM., Watchmaker for the Trade, 47 Washington st. Established 1875.

OSHKOSH, WIS.

ARCHITECTS.
BELL & COLE,
Architects and Builders, corner Pearl & Market streets. Stair Railing, Newel Posts, etc., furnished. Scroll sawing done to order.

BAKERY AND RESTAURANT.
HENRY SCHMIDT,
BAKERY and RESTAURANT,
11 Main st.

BARBER.
BLACK, ALFRED, Barber, Beckwith House.

BLACKSMITH AND CARRIAGES.
J. CORRIGALL,
Blacksmith and Carriage Builder,
221 & 223 Main st,

BOOTS AND SHOES.
BARTA, J. S., Maufr and dealer in Boots and Shoes, 92 Main st.

BUSINESS COLLEGE.
W. W. DAGGETT.   A. A. SPENCER.
Established September, 1867.
OSHKOSH
BUSINESS COLLEGE,
Cor. Main and Church sts.
Daggett & Spencer,   OSHKOSH.

OSHKOSH—Continued.

CIGAR MANUFACTURERS.
DERKSEN, H., Manf'r and dealer in Cigars, 152 Main st.

JOHN MESSNER,
CIGAR MANUFACTURER,
24 Main st.

CORSET MANUFACTORY.
ASKEN, MRS. C. V., Corset Manf'r and Milliner, 193 Main st.

DRUGGISTS.
WILLIAMS & FROEHLICH,
Wholesale & Retail
Druggists, Paints and Varnish,
59 Main st.

DRY GOODS.
E. L. HUGHES & CO.,
Dry Goods, Etc.,
105 Main st.

FLOUR AND FEED.
GITTINS, JOHN, dealer in Flour and Feed, 165 Main st.

FURNITURE.
SOPER, B. H., dealer in Furniture & Chromos, 37 Main st.

THOMPSON & YOUNG,
Furniture & Hand Rails,
7th & Nebraska sts.

R. J. WEISBROD,
Manufacturer and Dealer in
All Kinds of Furniture,
17 Main st.

GROCERIES.
JOSHUA DALTON,
Dealers in
GROCERIES AND PROVISIONS,
178 Main st.

HOLMES, & VAN DOREN, dealers in Groceries & Provisions, 15 Main st.

A. LICHTENBERGER & CO.,
—Dealers in—
CHOICE TEAS, GROCERIES AND PROVISIONS,
254 Main St.

WEITZEL, MATHIAS, Groceries, Provisions & Saloon, Tenth and Kansas st.

HARNESS AND SADDLES.
ALLEN, A. P., Harness & Saddles, agent for Elgin Watch, 74 Main st.
NEWMAN, JAMES, Manufacturer of Harness & Saddles, Kansas st

HOTELS.
FREY'S HOTEL, 308 Main st., $1 per day, $5 per week. Barbara Frey, Proprietress.

IMPORTANT EVENTS OF THE CENTURY.   291

Post Office, Custom House and Court House, Cincinnati, O.—
Occupies one-half of the square bounded by Fifth, Sixth, Main and Walnut streets. The exterior walls are to be of Granite, the basement and stylobate from the Red Granite quarries of Middlebrook, Mo. The building will be 354 by 164 feet, four stories in height above ground, exclusive of the attics and roof stories. To complete this building will cost, exclusive of the site, nearly $3,000,000.

Spanish Commissioners' Building, Centennial Exposition, Philadelphia.—Is a handsome structure, built in an octagonal form, 50 feet in diameter. It is occupied as the headquarters of the Spanish Engineers.

The road to wealth, happiness and prosperity, RUNS WEST, Passing through the most fertile portions of

CENTRAL MISSOURI,

AND IS KNOWN THE WORLD OVER AS THE **OLD RELIABLE**

Hannibal and St. Joseph R. R.

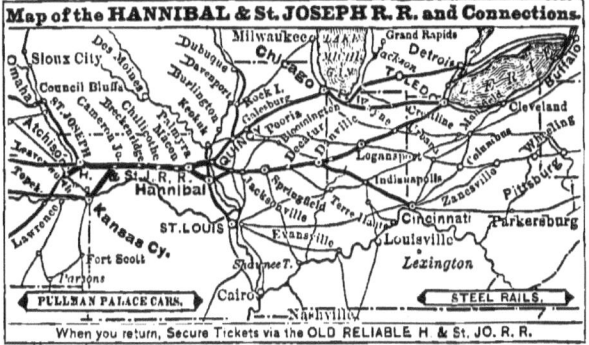

Twenty-five years ago the counties of Buchanan, Caldwell, Clinton, Linn, Livingston, Macon, Marion, and Shelby, through which this road passes, were nearly a wilderness; to-day, by a late census, it is discovered that the valuation of *personal and real estate* in these eight counties, is $83,100,000. The number of acres of improved land is 844,458. The farms are valued at $39,812,719. The farm products foot up an aggregate of $9,216,851. Bushels of corn, 5,535,161; wheat, 1,065,378; oats, 1,842,990. There are 114 counties in the State. The aggregate of corn in the whole State was 66,034,075 bushels; oats, 16,578,813; wheat, 14,215,926.

By these figures it will be seen that over 1-12 of the entire corn crop is gathered from those counties; over 1-14 of the wheat, and over 1-9 of the oats. Hay, potatoes, and the orchard crop, etc., bear an equally favorable comparison, and in some articles a very much better exhibit is made. Of the $84,285,273 worth of live stock in the State, $9,585,286 of the valuation is found in those counties. In those same counties there are 811 manufacturing establishments, with a capital of $2,793,880. The gross valuation of the products of these establishments was $8,202,286. The entire valuation of church property in the State was $9,909,358, $794,400 of which valuation is found in the counties traversed by the HANNIBAL & ST. JOE RAILROAD. It would be but fair to deduct the valuation of church property in the city of St. Louis from the remaining portion of the State, which is $4,940,-270. The entire valuation outside of St. Louis county would then be $4,969,088 nearly 1-6 of which will be found in those counties.

Of 324,348 attendants of the schools in the one hundred and fourteen counties of the State, about one tenth of the whole number is found in those counties along the line of the HANNIBAL & ST. JOSEPH RAILROAD. Now deduct the school-going population of St. Louis county (which would be fair,) and about one-eighth of the entire school attendance is found in these eight counties.

The same growth of country is now being repeated in Kansas, Nebraska, Colorado and New Mexico, and the immortal Greeley had this identical route and section of country in mind when he breathed those stirring words of wisdom, "*Young man, go West!*" Therefore, it is but natural that parties taking this advice should desire to pass over a road that has done so much for a great State, (especially as it offers the best facilities) and see for themselves. By the HANNIBAL & ST. JOSEPH R. R., through cars are run from Cleveland and Toledo, and through connections made from Cincinnati and Indianapolis, *via Quincy*, to St Joe, Atchison and Kansas City, and from Chicago to Kansas City, *without change*.

We are about to issue, in connection with our own, a County Map of Colorado and New Mexico, giving valuable information as regards time tables, routes, distances, altitudes, &c., which we will be pleased to furnish FREE, upon application in person or by letter addressed to

J. A. S. REED, 59 Clark St., Chicago, Ill.   T. PENFIELD, Gen'l Pass. and Ticket Agent, Hannibal, Mo.

ADVERTISEMENTS. 293

City Hall and Market House, St. Joseph, Mo.—It is a magnificent structure 70x170 feet, with its tower extending 112 feet high. The work on this building was commenced in September, 1873, and it was completed in June, 1874, at a cost of $50,000.

WILLIAM O'DONOGHUE,
Wholesale Commission Dealer,
FRUIT AND PRODUCE, Butter, Eggs, Poultry, Game, &c., &c.

Second St., South of Market Square, ST. JOSEPH, MO.

1877.

ny at Sharpsburg, after crossing which they separated in squads and took to the woods. The civil authorities were totally powerless, and thieves, who took advantage of the reign of terror, broke open and plundered the cars, and carried off the stolen goods with perfect impunity. The strike in Philadelphia was inaugurated at 6 o'clock P. M., by the men abandoning their places. Trouble occurred at Hornellsville, N. Y., on the Erie road, the strikers preventing trains departing.

July 23.—A mob of Erie Railroad men and canal men drove the men out of the New York Central stock-yards at Buffalo, N. Y., and prevented freight trains from going out. No one was injured. All trains were abandoned on the Cleveland and Pittsburg Railroad, and the same was the case with the freight trains on the Lake Shore and Southern Michigan road. The Vandalia Railroad men at Indianapolis, Ind., struck, as did also the Niagara division of the Erie Road employes. Trains resumed running at Baltimore, and the excitement was subsiding. The Twenty-third Regiment arrived at Hornellsville, N. Y., where all was reported quiet. The New York Central men struck, and all freight trains were stopped. The estimated number of killed and wounded at Pittsburg was, killed 54, wounded 109—163. A vigilance committee was organized at Pittsburg, for the protection of property. The trainsmen on the Eastern roads running out of St. Louis also struck. At Reading, Pa., troops fired upon rioters who were engaged in tearing up tracks, at least seven persons being killed and over thirty wounded. At Buffalo, N. Y., the strikers drove away about two hundred soldiers, a number of whom were pretty roughly handled. Citizens' organization maintained order at Pittsburg, and quiet prevailed at Baltimore, Md., and Hornellsville N. Y.

July 24.—Additional strikes took place in Ohio, Illinois, Pennsylvania, and New York; the New York Central, Delaware and Lackawanna, and all the roads centering at Chicago, Ill., being among the number. Vigilance committees and large bodies of police were organized in different cities and towns of Pennsylvania, Ohio, and other states, which action had great effect in restoring order.

July 25.—The strikers were joined by the Central New Jersey, Lehigh Valley and the Texas Pacific freight-men. Conflicts between the mob and police took place in Chicago, St. Louis and San Francisco; one man being shot and another dangerously wounded at the first-named place. President Hayes ordered to Baltimore and Louisville nearly all the troops in the South. The Erie strikers at Hornellsville, N. Y., surrendered to the rail

OSHKOSH—*Continued*

LUMBER DEALERS.

JAMES McNAIR,
(Successor to P. Sawyer & Son)
LUMBER DEALER,
W. Main St, & River.

C. N. PAINE & CO.,
PINE LUMBER,
Sash, Doors, Lath, Shingles, Pickets, &c.

MEAT MARKET.

UETZ, GEORGE, Fresh and Salt Meats,
167 Main st.

NEWSPAPER.

OSHKOSH TIMES, Fernandez & Glaze, Editors and Proprietors. O. F. Block, Main st.

PAINTS AND OILS.

SCHWALM, LOUIS, Dealer in Paints, Oils, Colors and Varnishes, 18 Main st.

PIANOS AND ORGANS.

PERRY & BARROW, Pianos, Organs and Musical Merchandise, 164 Main st.

FRANK WILLE,
Dealer in
Pianos, Organs & Sheet Music,
26 MAIN STREET.

REAL ESTATE & LOAN BROKERS.

COLTON, E. B., Attorney at Law; Agent for Real Estate; Money to Loan, 55 Main st.

O. H. HARRIS,
Real Estate & Loan Broker,
General Agent for buying and selling property,
136 Main Street.

RHEUMATIC HOSPITAL.

RHEUMATIC HOSPITAL, by Dr. M. Mellen,
35 Ceap st.

SEWING MACHINE.

WHEELER, W. C., Victor Sewing Machine Agt. Stencil Plates, 164 Main st.

STOVES AND TINWARE.

HASBROUCK & MONROE, Manufacturers of Tinware; Sheet Iron Work, &c.

TAILORING.

DUANE, T. J., Tailoring and Furnishing Goods,
111 Main st.

TRUNKS, VALISES, &c.

SCHMIT BROTHERS, Trunks, Valises, Travelling Bags, &c., 211 & 213 Main st.

WINES AND LIQUORS.

MASSE & BESNAH,

Wines & Liquors,
28 MAIN STREET.

WATERTOWN, WIS.

ATTORNEYS AT LAW.

TUTTLE & STEINER, Attorneys at Law. Collections of all kinds attended to promptly.

BLACKSMITHING.

AUG. KRAMP,
Blacksmithing and Manfg. Patent Straw Cutter.
Sixth Street.   Established 1862.

ZAUTNER. B., Blacksmithing and Carriage Maker, Sixth near Main.

BOOTS AND SHOES.

POHLMANN & DITTES, Boots and Shoes, Main st.

CONFECTIONERY, FRUIT, ETC.

WOODWARD & STONE, Mnfs. dealers Crackers, Confectionery, Fruits, Oysters, &c., Water st

DENTIST.

(Established 1874)

EUGENE GOELDNER,
DENTIST,
Second door East of Post Office.

DRY GOODS.

HABHEGGER, J., & CO., Dry Goods and Groceries, Third st.

TOELKE, AUGUST, Dry Goods, Notions, Groceries and Crock ry, Cole's Block.

WEBBER, JACOB, & SON, Dry Goods and Groceries, W. Water st

HARDWARE.

KUSEL, D., & F., Hardware, Stoves, Iron, Steel, Nails Glass and Tinware, Main st.

HARNESS AND SADDLES.

STEINMANN, W. C., Harness Maker and Sadler, Corner W. Water and Main st.

ZAUTNER, ALBERT, Harness Maker and Sadler, Main st.

HOTELS.

WASHINGTON HOTEL, Fred Kroniz, Main st.

WISCONSIN HOUSE, Louis Willam Krueger, Proprietor, Main and Fifth sts. Est. 1854.

INSURANCE AGENTS.

VOLKMANN, AUGUST, General Insurance Agent, Main st.

WEDEMEYER, H. A. Insurance Agent, Main and Fourth sts.

WHEELER, C. I., Insurance Agent, Main and Third sts. Est. 1876.

MILLINERY.

PARKER, MRS. M. E., Dealer in Fashionable Millinery, East end Main street Bridge.

PAINTERS' MATERIAL.

STRAW & MURPHY, Painting Material, Wall Paper, Frames, &c., 24 Main st.

PAINTERS.

BUNTROCK, CHAS., House, Sign and Carriage Painter, Main and Sixth sts. Est. 1869.

1877.

way officials, and those at Rochester, N. Y., agreed to go to work until such time as a conference could be had with Mr. Vanderbilt.

July 26.—Rioting took place in Chicago, Ill., the police and troops fighting the mob nearly all day. Fifteen persons were known to have been killed, and many wounded. Many of the rioters were arrested. Disturbance also took place at St. Louis, but no one was reported injured. Trains began running on the Erie Railway, the Delaware, Lackawana and Great Western, Morris and Essex, and the American Division of the Canada Southern Railroad. At San Francisco, incendiary fires were started by the rioters, but strong bodies of vigilants prevented the contemplated depredations or serious trouble. In Philadelphia, the police, in breaking up a disorderly meeting, became involved in a fight, which was desperately waged, a number of persons being badly hurt, and one boy, aged about 17, killed.

July 28.—Under the protection of troops, seven freight trains were sent away from Baltimore, and about 500 cars from Cumberland over the Ba timore and Ohio road. Governor Hartranft and staff, with about 4,000 United Sta es troops and militia—infantry, cavalry, and artil ery—arrived at Pittsburg and took peaceable possession of the Pennsylvania Company's territory there. At Johnstown a mob assailed the trains with missiles, some of which inflicted severe wounds. They likewise threw a train from the track, wrecking five cars, but fortunately not seriously injuring anyone. A revised list put the number of killed during the rioting in Chicago at twenty-one; wounded, about ninety, six of whom will probably die. One of the killed and eleven of the wounded were policemen. The authorities had the mob under control at St. Louis. The strikers at Fort Wayne, Ind., overpowered the authorities in two attempts to move trains on the Pittsburg, Ft. Wayne and Chicago road.

July 29.—The seven freight trains which were sent westward from Baltimore, Md., were stopped by strikers at Keyser, West Va., one of them being partially wrecked. Another attempt to move an engine out of the yard at Fort Wayne, Ind., was frustrated. A compromise with the firemen and brakemen on the Pittsburg, Fort Wayne and Chicago road was partially effected. Troops were concentrating at East St. Louis, Ill., in anticipation of an attack upon the bridge, and General Bates had caused the arrest of sixty-five strikers, who attempted to prevent a passenger-train from going out; trains were sent out on all the roads except the Toledo and Wabash Strikers in the Lackawanna, Pa., region destroyed an engine-house and other prop-

WATERTOWN—Continued.

PHOTOGRAPHERS.

MAY, JOHN B., Photographic Artist,
Main st.

REAL ESTATE.

WOODWARD & WHEELER, Real Estate Agency,
Main and Third sts. Est. 1877.

SEWING MACHINES.

FULLER, S. B., Agent, Singer Sewing Machines,
Watertown, Wis.

TAILORS.

BRUNNER, JACOB, Merchant Tailor and dealer
in Furnishing Goods, Main st. Est. 1868.

HIRSH, J. A. Jr., Merchant Clothier and Tailor,
Main st. Est. 1869.

THRESHING MACHINES.

J. B. BENNETT,

Iron Founder & Machinist,

—Manufacturer of—

THRESHING MACHINES, STEAM ENGINES,

First St., - WATERTOWN, WIS

TOBACCO AND CIGARS.

WIGGENHORN, BROS., Mnfrs. of and dealers in
Cigars and Tobacco, Pipes, &c., Main st.

WATCHES, CLOCKS AND JEWELRY.

SALICK, JOS., Clocks, Watches and Jewelry,
1 E. Main st Est. 1853.

WAGGERHORN, A., Watchmaker and Jeweler,
Main and First sts. Est. 1865.

WINES AND LIQUORS.

BLAIR, ADOLPHUS, Dealer in Wines and Liquors, Western av.

CECH, W., Dealer in Wines and Liquors.
Main st.

SEDALIA, MO.

AGRICULTURAL IMPLEMENTS.

BAKER, I. N., Agricultural Implements, Carriages & Sewing Machines, 208 E. Main st.

DAVID BLOCHER,
AGRICULTURAL IMPLEMENTS
And Singer Sewing Machines,
115 E. Main st.

HEROLD, W. W., Agricultural Implements, agt.
for McCormick Reaper, 304-6 E. Main st.

ATTORNEYS AT LAW.

FELIX & BRO., Lawyers, Sedalia, Mo.,
W. L. Felix & J. D .Felix.

CHARLES M. McCLUNG,
Attorney at Law, Smith's Hall Building. Collections solicited and all business promptly attended to.

SEDALIA—Continued.

Established 1866.
W. W. S. Snoddy. U. F. Short.
Notary Public.
SNODDY & SHORT, Sedalia, Mo.,

ATTORNEYS AT LAW.

BAKERIES AND RESTAURANTS.

PAUL BUHLER,
Bakery, Restaurant & Fancy Groceries, 202 E.
Main st. Meals 25cts.

HEYDINGSFELDER, J. G., Bakery & Restaurant,
114 Main st.

BARBERS.

HENRY BAUER'S

Shaving and Hair Cutting Parlors and Bath Room, Porter's Block.

LEECE, TONY, Shaving & Hair Dressing Saloon,
201½ Ohio st.

SAVAGE, JOHN, Shaving & Hair Dressing Saloon, 304 Ohio st.

DENTIST.

ELLIS, DR. L. O., Dentist,
54 Main st., up-stairs.

DRUGGISTS.

CLIFFORD, T. T., 107 Ohio st. Prescriptions
compounded by a German graduate.

ROLL, CHAS. & CO., Druggists and Chemists,
317 Ohio st.

FARMER'S MILLS.

ZIMMERMAN & HARTER, Farmer's Mills,
W. Main st.

FURNITURE.

S. B. COHEN,
Second-hand Furniture bought, sold and repaired. Chairs re-caned, and Picture frames made to order. Upholstering and Mattress making a specialty. Satisfaction guaranteed. E. Main st.

GROCERS.

S. GERYE,
Fruits, Vegetables, Produce and Groceries, fresh Fish and Game, 119 E. Main st.

WHITNEY, WM. A., Family Groceries,
Ohio st., bet. 6th & 7th sts.

CHARLES YOST,
Groceries, Provisions, Wood and Willow Ware, Flour and Feed,
232 Ohio st.

HAIR DEALER AND DRESSER.

Mrs. S. C. JOHNSON,
HUMAN HAIR WORK
Of Every Description,
121 E. MAIN ST.

HARDWARE.

THOMAS, W. R. & CO., Hardware & Cutlery,
117 W. Main st.

City Hall, Philadelphia.—The building is situated on Penn Square. It covers an area of nearly 4½ acres, and consists of one building, surrounding an interior court yard. The north and south fronts measure 470 feet; the east and west 486½ feet in their extreme length.

MASONIC TEMPLE, CORNER SIXTH AVE. AND 23D ST., NEW YORK.

SEDALIA—*Continued.*

HOTEL.

AMERICAN HOUSE,
W. W. Brown, Proprietor, corner Engineer and Third streets. Every attention paid to the comfort of guests.

LEROY HOUSE, E. Barrett, proprietor,
Cor. Ohio & 6th sts.

LINDELL HOTEL.
J. C. Pierce, proprietor, 321 West Main street, Rate, $1 per day, reduction by the week. Low prices, good accommodations.

SEDALIA HOUSE, Chas. Wentzelmann, proprietor 211 W. Main st.

UNION HOTEL, Mrs. C. Mathews, proprietress Engineer st.

INSURANCE.

KNAPP'S INSURANCE AGENCY,
210 Ohio st.

JUSTICE OF THE PEACE.

CLARK, LOGAN, Justice of the Peace & Mayor, 211 Ohio st.

MARBLE WORKS.

O'DONNELL, JAS. & CO., Marble Works,
14 W. Main st.

MILLINERY AND DRESS MAKING.

MRS. M. A. CROSS,

DRESS MAKING,

311 W. Main St.

Shirt and Underclothing making a specialty.

NORTON, MRS. G. B., Milliner,
118 Ohio st.

Established 1870.
Miss D. E. Thomas,
Fashionable

Milliner & Dressmaker
61 Main st.

HAIR WORKING,
Bridal Trosseau a Specialty.

PHOTOGRAPHER.

LATOUR, Photographer,
62 W. Main st. Established 1866.

REAL ESTATE.

BYLER, JAS. M., Real Estate Title, Abstract & Loan Office. Established 1865.

ROSS, W. H., Real Estate & Land Office,
234 Ohio st.

SALOONS.

HEALTH OFFICE SALOON,
Ed. Lyon, Proprietor,
Ilgen House, OHIO ST.

SEDALIA—*Continued.*

QUIN, TOM, Wines, Liquors & Cigars, 15 Ball Pool, 120 E. Main st.

Established 1870.
WINE HALL.
Hermann Schmitt, proprietor, corner Osage and Main sts. Wines, Liquors and Cigars.

PHYSICIAN.

ROGERS, JAS. S., M. D., hours, 9 to 12 A. M. and 2 to 6 P. M., Sedalia, Mo.

SEWING MACHINES.

WRIGHT, S. A., Sewing Machines,
230 Ohio st.

TAILORS.

BYRNE, OWEN, Merchant Tailor,
Ohio st.

S. C. JOHNSON,

TAILOR,
123 East Main St.
Cleaning and Repairing neatly done.

TELEGRAPH INSTITUTE.

Western Telegraph Inst'tute,
J. D. Brown, Manager. Young men and Ladies qualified as operators; good situations when qualified. Send for circular.

TOBACCO AND CIGARS.

KOBROCK, CHAS. & BRO., Manuf'rs of Cigars,
203 W. Main st.

WATCHMAKER AND JEWELER.

LANDES, JOHN S., Watchmaker & Jeweler,
111 Main st.

JEFFERSON CITY, MO.

AGRICULTURAL IMPLEMENTS.

JEFFERSON CITY
Agricultural Works,
DALLMEYER & FISCHER, Props.,
Manufacturers of
Mowers, Reapers, Grain Drills,
SULKY PLOWS AND RAKES,
109 Water st.

ATTORNEYS AT LAW.

EWING, A. W., Attorney at Law,
206 High st.

HOCKADY (late Attorney-Gen'l of Mo.) & SILVER, Madison & High sts.

HOUGH, A. M., Attorney at Law,
206 High st.

AUCTIONEERS.

SHOWERS & WAGNER,
General Auctioneers, Commission Merchants and Manufacturers' Agents, 215 E. High st.

Tootle's Opera House, situated in the center of the prosperous city of St. Joseph, Missouri, with a population of above 30,000. This House is one of the most elegant and commodious theatres in the West; has a seating capacity of 1,500, with patent folding chairs throughout the auditorium, and is otherwise supplied with all the modern improvements. The boxes, of which there are four, with seats for six, are superbly furnished and decorated. Large, nice dressing rooms adjoin the stage, which is in width 67 feet, and from front to rear 40 feet, the opening 35x34 feet. There is an ample supply of scenery, which has lately been retouched and increased. Stage furniture and a new "Steinway Grand Concert Piano," has been bought for use at Concerts, &c. The house will be let, licensed, lighted and warmed, with the usual stage attachees, to first class combinations, at reasonable rates. Sharing propositions, also, will be entertained, if preferred.

JULIUS CRONE, Agent.   MILTON TOOTLE, Proprietor.

F. F. CASE,
Builder, Jobber and Superintendent of All

Kinds of Work done in Wood,
—: SUCH AS :—

Scroll Sawing, Shaping, Slitting, Boring, Turning, &c. Show Cases, Desks, Table and Solid Counters, Etc., on Hand or Made to Order on Short Notice and Reasonable rates.

Office and Shop 907 Francis St., and Frederick Ave.

SAINT JOSEPH, MO.

Orders from the Country Solicited and Especially from Builders.

REFERENCES.

Tootle's Opera House. | Hamilton's, cor. Fifth and Felix Sts.
Hundley's, cor. Fourth and Felix Sts. | Senate Restaurant, cor. Fifth & Edmond Sts.

Earnst & Brill, Charles St.

1877.

erty, causing a suspension of work in the mines.

July 30.—Striking trainmen of the Lake Shore, Texas Pacific, Delaware, Lackawanna and Great Western Railroads, and of several lines centering at Pittsburg, Pa., went back to work at the reduced wages, the question of pay to come up for future discussion. Freight trains in large numbers were moved on the Pennsylvania and Baltimore and Ohio roads. At Galveston, Texas, the colored laborers struck. Regular trains were running on the Morris and Essex and New Jersey Central Railroads.

July 30.—No fresh outbreaks occurred on the railroads, and dispatches from various points indicated a speedy resumption of work. At Baltimore many of the old men were returning, more offering than could be made use of.

Aug. 3.—Eight or more girls lost their lives by the burning of a box-factory in Cincinnati.—The labor war was virtually at an end. Freight trains were running, or were about to be started, on all the roads. The striking miners in the coal regions of Pennsylvania were kept quiet by the presence of troops. The coroner's jury at Baltimore, Md., exonerated the Sixth Regiment from all blame for the riot.

Aug. 11.—News was received of a severe battle between General Gibbons' command and the Nez Perces Indians, on the Big Hole River, M. T., Aug. 9. The soldiers attacked an Indian camp, which they took after hard fighting, but were afterwards driven back, with the loss of nearly one-half their force. The Indians also suffered greatly. Among the killed were Capt. William Logan and Lieut. James H. Bradley, while Gen. Gibbon, Capt. Williams, and Lieutenants Coolidge, English and Woodruff were wounded.

Aug. 16.—The centenary of the battle of Bennington, Vt., was celebrated. A procession four miles long was witnessed by over sixty thousand people. Prof. Bartlett delivered the oration, a poem by W. C. Bryant was read by Prof. Churchill, and speeches were made by President Hayes, Secretary Evarts and others.

Aug. 18.—A. Gesner, E. T. Henderson and E. B. Weston were arrested at Chicago, Ill., charged with being members of an extensive gang of forgers, who during the past year have obtained more than $400,000 by means of raised checks and forgeries.

Aug. 29.—Brigham Young died at Salt Lake City. He had nineteen wives and was considered worth $6,000,000.—Railroad accident on the Chicago and Rock Island R. R., at Four Mile Creek seven miles from Des Moines. Sixteen persons killed and many injured.

JEFFERSON CITY—*Continued.*

BANKS.

JEFFERSON CITY BANK,
J. S. FLEMING, Prest.,
G. H. DULLE, Vice-Prest.,
J T SEARS, Cashier.
Special attention given to collections.
126 HIGH ST.

A. M. DAVISON,   J. G. SCHOTT,   W. Q. DALLMEYER,
President.   Vice-Prest.   Cashier.

1809.

First National Bank,

Dealers in Foreign Exchange. Capital, $75,000; Surplus, $18,000.
126 EAST HIGH ST.

BARBERS.

HEIDT, WM., Barber & Hair Dresser,
136 High st.

WATTS & HADEN, Barbers & Hairdressers,
206 High st.

BOOKS AND STATIONERY.

ROMMEL, FRED, Books, Stationery, Wall Paper, Picture Frames, etc., 122 High st.

BOOTS AND SHOES.

ANTWEILER, JOHN, Boots, Shoes, Saddles and Harnesses, 213 High st.

CARPENTERS AND BUILDERS.

SCHWARZOTT, HENRY, Carpenter and Builder,
31 Madison st.

CHINA, GLASS AND QUEENSWARE.

GOODRICH, R. M., China, Glass and Queensware, 121 High st.

CLOTHING.

GOLDMAN, J., Clothing and Gents' Furnishing Goods, 211 High st.

CONFECTIONERY.

McCARTEN, GEO. I., Confectionery and Ice Cream Saloon, 128 High st.

DRUGGISTS.

CITY DRUG STORE, Tennessee Matthews, M.D., Proprietor, 116 High st.

DRY GOODS.

(Established 1874.)
DALLMEYER, CRAVEN & CO.,
Wholesale and Retail Dealers in

Dry Goods, Groceries and Liquors,
208 & 210 E. HIGH ST., Jefferson City, Mo.
Goods sold at St. Louis prices for Cash.

LOHMAN, L. C. & CO., Dry Goods, Groceries, Hardware, etc., 102 High st.

OBERMAYER & CO., General Dry Goods and Gents' Furnishing Goods, High & Madison sts

JEFFERSON CITY—Continued.

FURNITURE.
STAMPFLI & KARGES,
Furniture Dealers & Undertakers,
312 MADISON STREET.

GROCERIES.
A. J. HOEFER,
Dealer in
Staple and Fancy Groceries, Hardware, Farm Implements, Etc.
222 HIGH STREET.

J. CHRIST LINHARDT;
—Dealer in—
GROCERIES AND PROVISIONS,
Jefferson, City.

HARDWARE.
WILSON, J. K. & CO., Hardware, &c, and Agricultural Implements, 107 W. High st.

HARNESS AND SADDLES.
SCHMIDT & HEISINGER,
—Manufacturers of—
HARNESS,
Saddles, Collars, Bridles, Nets, &c.,
224 E. High St., - JEFFERSON CITY, MO.

HOTEL.
CITY HOTEL,
Cor. High and Madison Sts.
J. B. KAISER, - - Proprietor.

Travelers are furnished with comfortable accommodations at reasonable rates.
A trusty Porter at all Passenger Trains.

LUMBER DEALERS.
BECKERS & BROOKS, Lumber, Sash, Doors and Blinds, Main and Madison sts.

MARBLE WORKS.

JEFFERSON CITY MARBLE WORKS,
VICTOR ZUBER, - Prop.
Manufacturer of and Dealer in
Monuments, Tombs and Headstones,
of Foreign and American Marble.
High st., between Jefferson and Washington.
Orders from a distance will receive prompt attention.

MILLINERY AND DRESSMAKING.
MRS. SUTER & BUCK,
Millinery & Dressmaking,
Also Fancy Goods and Hairdressing.
113 HIGH STREET.

SKETCHES
OF THE
PRESIDENTS.

(FIRST PRESIDENT.—TWO TERMS.)

George Washington was born on the Potomac river, in Westmoreland county, Virginia, February 22d, 1732, and died December 14, 1799. In 1754 he was made Lieutenant Colonel of the militia, and accompanied Braddock in his expedition against Fort Duquesne in 1755. In the same year he was made Commander-in-Chief of the military forces of the Colony of Va., and in 1787 he was unanimously chosen President of the Convention that met to frame a Constitution. He was inaugurated first President of the United States, April 30, 1789; and, being re-elected, he held the office until 1797. In 1788 and in 1792 he was again chosen President of the United States, but, conceiving it to be a dangerous precedent to serve more than two terms, he patriotically declined a third election. In early life he followed the occupation of an engineer. He was married to Miss Martha Custis, in January, 1759. Congress unanimously elected him commander of the revolutionary forces, and he took active command July 2, 1775, and held supreme military control throughout the strug-

JEFFERSON CITY—Continued.

PHYSICIANS.

YOUNG, DR. R. E., Office 216 High street, Residence, 516 E. Main.

PRINTERS.

L. S. HITCHCOCK,

Commercial Job Printer,

AND ADVERTISING AGENT,

Popp's Building, High St., Stairs at McCarten's Confectionery. Card, Bill, Letter-head and Circular Printing made a Specialty. Give us a call.

REAL ESTATE.

COX, S. W., Land Agent, Buy and Sell Lands on Commission. Pay Taxes. Redeem Lands sold for taxes in any County in the State. Agent Atchison, Topeka, and Santa Fe Railroad. Three million acres of Land for sale on eleven years' credit. Send for circulars and Maps, giving full and reliable information about Kansas.

STOVES AND TINWARE.

F. J. MAYER,
Dealer In

STOVES & TINWARE,
218 HIGH STREET.

TOBACCO AND CIGARS.

WENDELL STRAUB,

Manufacturer of and Wholesale Dealer in

CIGARS,

A Fine Assortment of Havana and Key West Cigars constantly on hand.

228 Madison St.,

All Orders promptly attended to.

WATCHES, CLOCKS AND JEWELRY.

N. GRIESHAMMER,
Dealer in

Gold and Silver Watches,

Jewelry, Silver and Plated Ware, Gold Pens and Holders, Spectacles, Clocks, &c. Watches, Clocks and Jewelry Repaired Promptly and Warranted.

No. 114 HIGH STREET.

WINES AND LIQUORS.

E. HOCHSTADTER.
Dealer in Fine

LIQUORS

Families Supplied at Reasonable Rates.

120 High Street,

KRAUP, F., Wines Liquors and Beer, under City Hotel, Cor. High and Madison sts.

JEFFERSON CITY—Continued.

JEFFERSON CITY BUSINESS HOUSES
WHEN ESTABLISHED.

COX, S. W., Real Estate, 1867.
DALLMEYER, CRAVEN & CO., Dry Goods, 1874.
FIRST NATIONAL BANK, 1867.
GRIESHAMMER, N., Jeweler, 1868.
HOCHSTADTER, E., Liquor Dealer, 1875.
HOEFER, A. J., Grocery, 1871.
JEFFERSON CITY BANK, 1874.
MAYER, F. J., Stoves and Tinware, 1862.
SCHMIDT & HEISINGER, Harness and Saddles, 1875.

BURLINGTON, IOWA.

ATTORNEYS AT LAW.

FEGAN W. SCOTT, Attorney at Law,
409 Jefferson st.

HALL & BALDWIN, Attorneys and Counsellors at Law. Parson's Block.

BAKERY.

KIESLING, GEO., Hawk-Eye Bakery,
514 Jefferson st.

BARBER.

GUNNELL, S., Shaving and Hairdressing and Bath Rooms, 208 N. Third st.

BOOTS AND SHOES.

BOTT, GEO., Manufacturer of McComber's Glove Fitting Boot, 403 N. Third st.

CLAYTON, A., Boot and Shoe Maker,
803 S. Main st.

SCHAFER, MARTIN, Boot and Shoe Maker,
205 Washington st.

ZIMMER, HENRY, Manufacturer of Fashionable Boots and Shoes, 221 Division st.

CHINA, GLASS AND QUEENSWARE.

PERKINS, A. A., China, Glass and Queensware,
314 N. Main st.

CIVIL ENGINEER.

H. I. CHAPMAN,
Civil Engineer,
321½ Jefferson Street.

DYE HOUSE.

BRUGGE, J. H. & SON, Burlington Steam Dye House and Tailoring. Third and Jefferson sts.

FURNITURE.

CHAS. BUETTNER,
— Manufacturer and Dealer in —

FURNITURE AND UPHOLSTERY,
Chamber Suites, Mattresses, &c. Picture Frames of all kinds.

520 JEFFERSON STREET.

IMPORTANT EVENTS OF THE CENTURY. 303

Vermont State Building, Centennial Exposition, Philadelphia.—This building presents a rather odd appearance in contrast with the other buildings on the Centennial grounds. It is constructed of wood, divided into fine large appartments for the convenience of visitors, male and female. The illustration above is a correct style of the architecture.

ENGLISH COMMISSIONERS' BUILDING, CENTENNIAL EXPOSITION, PHILADELPHIA.

gle for independence.
With George Washington for our first President, we began our new experiment in the manner of choosing rulers, taking the surest possible mode, as all the world then thought, of selecting a good man and the one best adapted to the position.

Washington was left fatherless at eleven years of age; his education was directed by his mother, a woman of strong character, who kindly, but firmly, exacted the most implicit obedience. Of her Washington learned his first lessons of self-command. His favorite amusements were of a military character; he made soldiers of his playmates, and officered all the mock parades. His inherited wealth was great, and the antiquity of his family gave him high social rank. On his Potomac farms he had hundreds of slaves, and at his Mount Vernon home he was like the prince of a wide domain, free from dependence or restraint. He was fond of equipage and the appurtenances of high life. Although he always rode on horseback, his family had a "chariot and four," with "black postillions in scarlet and white livery." This generous style of living, added perhaps to his native reserve, exposed him to the charge of aristocratic feeling. While at his home, he spent much of his time in riding and hunting. He rose early, ate his breakfast of corn-cake, honey, and tea, and then rode about his estates. He spent his evenings with his family around the blazing hearth, retiring between nine and ten. He loved to linger at the table, cracking nuts and relating his adventures. In personal appearance, Washington was over six feet in height, robust, graceful, and perfectly erect. His manner was formal and dignified. He was more solid than brilliant, and had more judgment than genius. He had great dread of public life, cared little for books, and had no library. Washington was a consistent christian, and a regular attendant of the Episcopal church, of which he was a communicant. He was a firm advocate of free institutions, but believed in a strong government and strictly enforced laws. As a President, he carefully weighed his decisions, but, his policy once settled, he pursued it with steadiness and dignity, however great might be the opposition. As an officer, he was brave, enterprising, and cautious. His campaigns were rarely startling, but they were always judicious. He was capable of great endurance. Calm in defeat, sober in victory, commanding at all times, but irresistible when aroused, he exercised equal authority over himself and his army. His last illness was very brief, and his closing hours were marked by his usual calmness and dignity. "I die hard," he said, "but I am not afraid to go." Europe and America vied in tributes to his memory. Said Lord Brougham, "Until time shall be no more, a test of the progress which our race has made in wisdom and virtue will be derived from the veneration paid to the immortal name of Washington." Washington left no children. It has been beautifully said, "Providence left him childless that his country might call him Father."

BURLINGTON—*Continued.*

LINDSTADT, JOHN P., Manufacturer of all kinds of Furniture, 513 Fifth st.

GROCERS.

BIKLEN, WINZER & CO., Wholesale Grocer, 110 Main st.

WEHMEIER & BRO., Groceries and Provisions, 409 & 411 Jefferson st.

HARNESS AND SADDLES.

STEYH, HENRY, Harness, Saddles, Bridles, Whips, &c., 221 Division st.

HOTELS.

BARRETT HOUSE, R. A. Barrett, Proprietor, Burlington.

PACIFIC HOUSE, Chas. Wahl, Proprietor, 418½ to 420 N. Main st.

MACHINIST.

L. THEO. FLODIN,

Machinist, and manufacturer of Models, Burning Brands in every style, and all kinds of light work in Steel, Iron, Brass, etc., 512 Jefferson st.

MEDICAL INSTITUTE.

DR. CHAS. LENGEL,
BURLINGTON
Medical and Surgical
INSTITUTE,
Devoted to the treatment of Special and Chronic Diseases, Strabismus, Hair Lip, Stricture, Catarrh, Fistula, Tumors, and diseases of the Urinary and Generative Organs. Medicine sent throughout the country. 111½ Main st.

MILLINERY AND FANCY GOODS.

MISS A. C. DETERICK,

Milliner and Dressmaker, and dealer in Millinery, Notions and Fancy Goods, 223 Division st. Hoop skirts made and repaired, and Stamping done to order

PAINTERS.

JENSEN & HEINZ, Decorative Painters, 618 Jefferson st.

MURPHY, E., House & Sign Painter, 307 Washington st.

PHYSICIAN.

DAVIS, W. H., Eclectic Physician, 413 Jefferson st.

PUMPS.

SWAN & FOSTER,

Manufacturers and wholesale dealers in Patent Elastic Rubber Bucket Chain Pumps, Copper and Iron Lightning Rods and Patent Roofing, 716 Jefferson st.

SALOON.

DREHER, CONRAD, Wine & Beer Saloon, 421 Jefferson st.

SEWING MACHINES.

TIBBLES, C. E., dealer in all kinds of Sewing Machines, 405 Jefferson st.

SHIRT MANUFACTURER.

GRIFFIN, A. F., Shirt manuf'r and Excelsior Steam Laundry, Vance Block.

BURLINGTON—*Continued.*

TAILORS.

HAWKINS, JOHN, Merchant Tailor,
N. Main st., opposite Barrett House.

KELLY & DAILY, Merchant Tailors, Tailoring in
all its branches, 321 N. Main st.

KANSAS CITY, MO.

AGRICULTURAL IMPLEMENTS.

BAKER, J. F., Agricultural Implements & Seeds,
417 Walnut st.

ATTORNEYS AT LAW.

ALLEN, SILAS F., Lawyer,
630½ Main st.

BROWN & WRIGHT, Attorneys at Law,
42½ Main st.

CAMPBELL, M., Attorney at Law,
Cor. 5th & Main sts.

HOLMES & DEAN, Attorneys at Law,
Rooms 1 & 2, 2d floor, 544 Main st.

LIPSCOMB, J. H., Attorney at Law,
Cor. 4th & Main sts.

MARK & JOHN WILLIAMS,
Attorneys. Prompt attention given to Collecting. Refer, by permission, to H. M. Holden, Prest. 1st National Bank, Kansas City; J. V. C. Karnes, Prest. Com. National Bank, Kansas City; J. Irving Pearce, Prest. 3d National Bank, Chicago; Field, Leiter & Co., Merchants, Chicago.

YOUNG, JAMES G., Attorney at Law, Rooms 10
& 12, Hart's Office Building, W. 4th st.

WOFFORD, JOHN W., Attorney at Law,
Hart's Office Building, 4th st.

AUCTION AND COMMISSION.

STEPHENS, J. H. & SONS, Auction & Commission Merchants, 561 Main st.

BARBERS.

H. FEARMAN,

**FASHIONABLE
BARBER AND HAIRDRESSER**
South Side Mo. Ave., bet. Main & Walnut sts.

THE O. K. BARBER SHOP, Andrews & Jordan
proprietors, 14 W. 5th st.

BILLIARD SALOON.

METROPOLITAN BILLIARD SALOON, Joseph
Loeffler, prop., cor. 15th st. & Grand Ave.

BLACKSMITHING.

LOGAN, THOMAS, Horseshoeing & Blacksmithing, cor. Independence & Sharlett aves.

E. JENKINS,
HORSESHOEING
AND GENERAL BLACKSMITHING,
Cor. 11th & Main sts.

BOOKSELLERS AND STATIONERS.

KANSAS CITY BOOK & NEWS CO., Booksellers
& Stationers, 720 Main st.

BOOTS AND SHOES.

BUNZ, JACOB, Boot & Shoe Maker,
513 Main st.

(SECOND PRESIDENT.)

John Adams was born in Braintree, Mass., October 1735, and died 1826. He graduated at Harvard College in 1755, and, abandoning the idea of becoming a minister of the gospel, was admitted to the bar in 1758. He was one of the delegates first sent to the Continental Congress from Massachusetts. In 1776 he was made President of th. Board of War, and went to France as a Commissioner in 1777. He served as President of the United States from 1797 to 1801. He was a member of the first and second Congresses, and nominated Washington as commander-in-chief. Jefferson wrote the Declaration of Independence, but Adams secured its adoption in a three-days' debate. He was a tireless worker, and had the reputation of having the clearest head and firmest heart of any man in Congress. In his position as President he lost the reputation he had gained as Congressman. His enemies accused him of being a bad judge of men; of clinging to old unpopular notions, and of having little control over his temper. They also ridiculed his egotism, which they declared to be inordinate. He lived, however, to see the prejudice against his administration give place to a more just estimate of his great worth and exalted integrity. As a Delegate to the Constitutional Convention, he was honored as one of the fathers of the republic. Adams and Jefferson were firm friends during the Revolution, but political strife alienated them. On their return to private life they became reconciled. They died on the same day—the fiftieth anniversary of American independence. Adams' last words were, " Thomas Jefferson still survives." Jefferson was, however, already lying dead in his Virginia home. Thus, by the passing away of these two remarkable men, was made memorable the 4th of July, 1826.

KANSAS CITY—Continued.

BRITTON, JAMES, Boot & Shoe Maker,
E. 6th st. near Main st.

RUDD & GREGOR, Boot & Shoe Maker,
424 Main st.

BUFFALO ROBES AND FURS.

A. C. KOOGLE,

PHILIP OLMSTED,

KANSAS CITY, MO.,
Manufacturer of Buffalo Robes, Fur Robes, Fur Overcoats, Gloves and Mittens.

CIGAR BOX MANUFACTURERS.

PENNINGTON & PALMER, Cigar Box Manufacturers, 907 Maine st.

CLOTHING, ETC.

Great Western Outfitting Store,
H. Silverman, prop., dealer in Clothing, Hats, Caps, Trunks, Valises, Boots, Shoes, Tents, Wagon Covers, etc., 9 E. Fifth street, opposite Market square.

John A. Poll & Co.,
Dealers in

CUSTOM MADE CLOTHING,

And Gentlemen's Furnishing Goods,
1021 Main st. bet. 10th & 11th,

KANAS CITY, - - MO.

J. E. J. GADDIS, Mang'r.

CONFECTIONERIES.

C. J. WALRUFF,
Dealer in all kinds of

CONFECTIONERY,

Fruits, Nuts, Toys, Fancy Goods, Etc.

Oysters and Game in Season.
528 MAIN ST.

KANSAS CITY—Continued.

FIELD, S. A., Confectioner,
802 Main st.

KASSIMER, A., Manf'r & wholesale dealer in Candies, 2119 Main st.

DAIRY.

ROCK SPRING DAIRY CO.,
1121 Main st.

DENTISTS.

LA VEINE, E. N., Dentist,
726 Main st.

TREGO, A. HOMER, Dentist,
712 Main st.

SCHELL, A. C., Dentist,
714 Main st., up-stairs.

STARK, J. K. & SON, Dentists,
548 Main st.

DYE HOUSE.

SCHMACK, CHAS., New York Dye House,
520 Main st.

FISH AND OYSTERS.

BEDGOOD, H. H., Wholesale & retail dealer in Fish, Oysters, Game, etc., 117 E. 4th st.

FLOUR AND FEED.

C. F. BAUER,
Dealer in all kinds of

FLOUR & FEED

N. E Cor. Main & 19th Sts.

DOSE, CHARLES, Wholesale and retail dealer in Feed, 904 Main st.

GROGGER & BROTHER,
Dealers in

WOOD, COAL, FEED & FLOUR,

1129 Main st.

W. L. PEAK,

FLOUR and FEED,

932 Main st.

ALSO, BOARDING AND FEED STABLE.

GRAIN DEALERS.

A. C. KEEVER & CO.,
Commission and Forwarding Merchants of Grain and Produce. Office: In Board of Trade Building, Kansas City.

GROCERIES AND PROVISIONS.

Established 1874.
J. P. BELL & CO.,
Dealers in

Produce & Groceries,

And all kinds of Game, Dressed and Live Poultry, Fresh Vegetables and Fruits,
N. E. COR. WALNUT ST. & MISSOURI AVE.

FOURTH STREET GROCERY, W. D. Oldham, Agent, 109 East 4th st.

HAX, GEO. L., Groceries and Provisions,
1201 Main st.

Court House, Quincy, Ills.—John S. McKean, Architect and Superintendent. Work on the foundation for this building was commenced in May, 1876, and by the 4th of July, 1877, the building was complete. It is 170 feet long by 105 wide, and 166 feet from the ground to the base of the flag-staff. The contract price for the building was $218,250. It is considered one of the finest buildings of its character, in the West.

On receipt of 25 cents to pay postage, I will send to any address samples of my choice

Flavors, Baking Powder,

—AND—

DRY HOP YEAST,

Enough for a good baking and a fair trial.

TRADE MARK

"GOOD LUCK."

ASK YOUR GROCER FOR GOOD LUCK.

I am to be found in all the Grocery Stores in pounds and ½ ℔ cans. I will keep any length of time in any climate, and retain my full strength. I have no equal in the market. Give me a trial and have Good Luck.

☞ Ask your Grocer for Good Luck.

JAS. E. WOODRUFF,

MANUFACTURER OF

Good Luck Dry Hop Yeast,

Good Luck Baking Powder, Choice Flavoring Extracts, Bluing, Aromatic Ginger Ale, &c., &c.,

808 Main St., QUINCY, ILL.

SKETCHES OF THE PRESIDENTS.

(THIRD PRESIDENT.)

Thomas Jefferson was born at Shadwell, Virginia, April 2d, 1743; and died July 4, 1826. After graduating from William and Mary College, he adopted the profession of the law. "Of all the public men who have figured in the United States," says Parton, "he was incomparably the best scholar and the most variously accomplished man." He was a bold horseman, a skillful hunter, an elegant penman, a fine violinist, a brilliant talker, a superior classical scholar, and a proficient in the modern languages. On account of his talent, he was styled "The Sage of Monticello." The immortal document, the Declaration of Independence, was, with the exception of a few words, entirely his work. He was an ardent supporter of the doctrine of State rights, and led the opposition to the Federalists. After he became President, however, he found the difficulty of administering the government upon that theory. "The executive authority had to be stretched until it cracked, to cover the purchase of Louisiana;" and he became convinced on other occasions that the federal government, to use his own expression, "must show its teeth." Like Washington, he was of aristocratic birth, but his principles were intensely democratic. He hated ceremonies and titles; even "Mr." was distasteful to him. These traits were the more remarkable to one of his superior birth and education, and peculiarly endeared him to the common people. Coming into power on a wave of popularity, he studiously sought to retain this favor. There were no more brilliant levees or courtly ceremonies as in the days of Washington and Adams. On his inauguration day, he rode down to Con-

KANSAS CITY—*Continued.*

LOHRER, C., Staple and Fancy Groceries,
911 Main st.

McCORD, NAVE & CO., Wholesale Grocers,
416 Delaware st.

C. A. ROLLERT,
GROCERY,
1316 MAIN STREET.

ROSS, MIKE, Grocer,
No. 57 First st., bet. Charlotte & Campbell.

SEEWALD, FRED., Dealer in Staple and Fancy
Groceries, 205 West 5th st.

THAYER, MRS. W., Groceries and Provisions,
No. 11 East 17th st.

WARINNER, GREGORY & CO., Wholesale Grocers, 51 & 53 Third st.

WISE, H. S., Grocer,
No. 5 Commercial st.

HARDWARE.

DUNCAN, WYETH & CO., Hardware, Cutlery
and Nails, 412 Delaware st.

HARNESS AND SADDLES.

ILES, WM., Saddler,
308 Main st.

HATS AND CAPS.

BIRD & HAWKINS,
Hats, Caps, Buck Gloves, Mittens, Fancy Roves, Etc. A so a full line of Ladies' Trimmed Hats, at Wholesale only.
310 DELAWARE STREET.

O. C. McWilliams. Brutus Crooke. David Russell.

McWilliams, Crooke & Co.
Wholesale
Hats, Caps, Gloves, &c.
ALSO FULL LINE STRAW GOODS.
308 Delaware St., Kansas City, Mo.

HOTELS.

BARNUM'S HOTEL, Cor. 4th & Main sts.
F. S. Bradbury & Co., Props.

BOYLE'S
HOTEL AND RESTAURANT,
N. W. COR. MAIN & 4TH STS.,
PETER BOYLE, Prop.   Kansas City, Mo.
Price, $1.50 per day Street Car Fare to and from the House free. Hot and cold Lunches at any time—paying only for what you get.

DAGGETT HOUSE, Cor. 6th & Walnut sts.
L. P. Swayne, Prop.

LINDELL HOTEL, Cor. 5th & Wyandotte sts.
J. H. Robertson, Prop.

Main Street Hotel.
J. P. BAUGHMAN, Prop.

No. 416 Main St., bet. 4th & 5th, Kansas City, Mo.
TERMS: Per Day, $1.50; per Week, $5.00.
Newly refitted and centrally located.

KANSAS CITY—*Continued.*

PACIFIC HOUSE, Cor. 4th & Delaware sts.
John Hall, Prop.
SOUTHERN HOTEL. S. J. Patton, Proprietress,
1609 Grand ave.
ST. JAMES HOTEL. L. C. Alexander, Prop.
Walnut st., near Mo. ave.

LIGHTNING RODS.

TRAIN, H. C., & SON, Lightning Rods,
828 Delaware st.

LIVERY STABLES.

CARTER, EUGENE, Livery and Sale Stables,
3rd st., bet. Main & Walnut.

LOOKSMITH AND BELL-HANGING.

BRUNNER, H. J., Locksmith and Bell-Hanger,
903 Main st.

LUMBER DEALER.

ANDERSON, JAMES, Lumber Dealer,
1324 Grand ave.

MACHINIST.

WITTE, AUGUST, Machine Shop and Brass
Works, West 7th st., near Delaware.

MARBLE WORKS.

KISER, JOHN F., Marble Works,
Cor. 9th & Walnut sts.

James F. Sheehy,
MARBLE WORKS,
BROADWAY, Bet. 10th & 11th Sts.

MATTRESSES.

Great Western Mattress Manufactory.
JOSEPH BAILEY,
Manufacturer and Dealer in Mattresses and Upholstery,
MAIN ST., Bet. 11th & 12th.

MEAT MARKET.

SINGER, JOS., Dealer in Fresh and Salt Meats,
1707 Grand ave.
STAMM, SAM., Dealer in Fresh and Salt Meats,
1507 Grand ave.
LAMBADER, WM., Dealer in Fresh and Salt
Meats, 1503 Grand ave.
MORLEY, L., Dealer in Fresh and Salt Meats,
419 W 5th st.

MERCHANDISE BROKER.

GORDON, DAVID S., Merchandise Broker,
14 W. Missouri ave.

MILLINERY AND DRESSMAKING.

MRS. G. H. BARNES,
DRESSMAKER
712 MAIN STREET.

HUSTADT, R., Millinery and Fancy Goods,
816 Main st.
MUCKE, MRS. EMMA, Dress and Cloak Making
and Millinery, 1403 Grand ave.
QUIGLEY, MRS. J., Fashionable Dress and
Cloak Making, 12th st., bet. Main & Walnut.
SACHS, MRS. R., Fashionable Milliner,
No. 608 Main st.

gress unattended, and, leaping from his horse, hitched it, and went into the chamber dressed in plain clothes, to read his fifteen-minutes' inaugural. Some of the sentences of that short but memorable address have passed into proverbs. The unostentatious example thus set by the nation's President was wise in its effects. Soon the public debt was diminished, the army and navy reduced, and the Treasury replenished. A man of such marked character necessarily made bitter enemies, but Jefferson commanded the respect of even his opponents, while the admiration of his friends was unbounded. The last seventeen years of his life were spent at Monticello, near the place of his birth. By his profuse hospitality, he had, before his death, spent his vast estates. He died poor in money, but rich in honor. His last words were, "This is the fourth day of July."

(FOURTH PRESIDENT,—TWO TERMS.)

James Madison was born in King George county, Virginia, March 16, 1751, and died in 1836. He graduated at Princeton College in 1778, after which he studied law; and from 1809 to 1817 he was President of the United States. In Congress in 1789 he became one of the strongest advocates of the Constitution and did much to secure its adoption. From his political principles he was obliged, though reluctantly, to oppose Washington's administration, which he did in a courteous and temperate manner. He led his party in Congress, where he remained till 1797. The next year he drafted the famous "1798-99 Resolutions," enunciating the doctrines of State rights, which, with the accompanying "Report" in their defense, have been the great text-book of the Democratic party. He was Secretary of

JOHN A. BUSH,

Manufacturer and Dealer in

Masonic, Odd Fellows,

and all other kinds of

REGALIA.

K. T. and I. O. O. F. Uniforms made to order at low figures. Banners for all societies made to order of any design. Jewels for Lodges furnished. Write for circular.

408 Main Street, PEORIA, ILL.

Peoria Novelty Wire Works!
PEORIA, ILL.,

H. R. VAN EPS,
Manufacturer of the Celebrated

Wire-Folding Card Rack, Fruit Baskets,

PHOTOGRAPH RACKS,
— and other useful and ornamental —
PLATED WIRE GOODS,

The Trade, Traveling Salesmen and Country Peddlers are requested to send for illustrated catalogue.

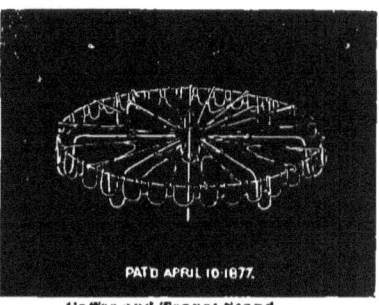

PAT'D APRIL 10 1877.

Coffee and Teapot Stand.

Daniel McFarland,

Attorney at Law,

AND SOLICITOR IN CHANCERY,

111 South Adams Street,

PEORIA, ILL.

Will practice in Peoria and adjoining Counties, and in the Federal and Supreme Courts of Illinois.

Prompt and Vigorous Attention Given to Collections.

Refers, By special permission, to the following Eminent Firms and Citizens of Peoria.

First National Bank, of Peoria.
Day Bros, & Co., Wholesale & Retail Dry Goods.
Zell & Francis, Distillers and Rectifiers.
Peoria Transcript Company.
D. J. Calligan, Wholesale and Retail Boots & Shoes

S. H. Thompson & Co., Wholesale Grocers.
Singer & Wheeler, Wholesale Druggists.
Col. John Warner, Mayor.
Gen'l D. W. Magee, Postmaster.
Howard Knowles, Collector of Internal Revenue.

ADVERTISEMENTS. 311

Chamber of Commerce, Peoria, Ill.—The erection of this building was completed in 1875, at a total cost of $93,000. It is built of brick, with Ohio sandstone trimmings; is 61 feet wide, and 145 feet long, three stories high, with Mansard roof surmounted with a tower. It is a very h ndsome building, as the engraving shows.

W. B. VANCE,

UNDERTAKER.

Wholesale and Retail Dealer in all Kinds of

Metalic AND Wood

CASES, COFFINS

502 Main St., near Post Office, Peoria, Ill.

Residence over Ware Room.
Telegraph orders promptly attended to, day or night.
Oldest UNDERTAKING Establishment in the city.

State to Jefferson. After his Presidential services, he retired from public station. Madison's success was not so much the result of a great natural ability as of intense application and severe accuracy. His mind was strong, clear, and well balanced, and his memory was wonderful. Like John Quincy Adams, he had laid up great store of learning, which he used in the most skillful manner. He always exhausted the subject upon which he spoke. "When he had finished, nothing remained to be said." His private character was spotless. His manner was simple, modest, and uniformly courteous to his opponents. He enjoyed wit and humor, and told a story admirably. His sunny temper remained with him to the last. Some friends coming to visit him during his final illness, he sank smilingly back on his couch, saying, "I always talk better when I lie." It has been said of him, "It was his rare good fortune to have a whole nation for his friends."

James Monroe

(FIFTH PRESIDENT.—TWO TERMS.)

James Monroe was born in Westmoreland county, Virginia, April 28, 1758, and died in the city of New York, July 4, 1831. He filled the office of President of the United States from the year 1817 to 1825. As a soldier under General Washington he bore a brave record, and especially distinguished himself in the battles of Brandywine, Germantown, and Monmouth. Afterward he studied law, and entered political life. Having been sent by Washington as Minister to France, he showed such marked sympathy with that country as to displease the President and his cabinet, who were just concluding a treaty with England, and wished to preserve a strictly neutral policy. He was therefore recalled. Under Jefferson, who was his warm friend, he was again

KANSAS CITY—*Continued.*

MRS. A. N. TAYLOR,
DRESSMAKER,
610 MAIN STREET.

MUSIC TEACHER.
H. BURMEISTER,
Academy of Music. Instructions given on Piano, Organ, and all String and Brass Instruments, also Repairing of all kinds of Musical Instruments. 1304 Grand Ave.

NEWSPAPER.
DAILY POST & TRIBUNE, Weekly. Westliche Volkezeitung, Wuerz & Lumpe, Proprietors. 908 Main st.

PAINTERS.
BENBOW, E. M., House, Sign and Ornamental Painter, No. 2 East Missouri ave.

BROOKE'S SIGN WORKS. Chas. Brooke, Jr., Prop. House Painting. 5th st., near Walnut.

A. STURGES & CO.
Painters, Kalsominers,
Paper-Hangers and Repairers.
JOB WORK PROMPTLY ATTENDED TO.
No. 1032 MAIN STREET,
Kansas City, Mo.

PAWN BROKER.
BAKER, S. S., Pawn Broker, 424 Main st.

PHOTOGRAPHER.
BOWER BROS., Photographers, 548 Main st.

PHYSICIANS.
BAKER, H. C., M. D., Homeopath, 708 Main st.

BOGIE, DR. M. A., Office. 902 Main st., Kansas City, Mo.

CADWELL, DR. J. W., Office, 902 Main st.; Residence, 1801 McGee st.

PIERCE & GREENO, Medical and Surgical Institute, 409 Delaware st.

SLOAN, DR. A. B., Office, 902 Main st.; Residence, N W. Cor. 13th & Delaware sts.

WILSON, JOHN, Physician and Surgeon, 804 Main st.

PIANOS AND ORGANS.
CONOVER BRO'S Dealers in Pianos and Organs, 613 M in st.

PLUMBERS AND GASFITTERS.
FARLEY BROS.
Practical Plumbers, Gas & Steam Fitters
Dealers in Pumps, Brass Goods, Engine Trimmings, Rubber Hose, Stone, Lead and Iron Pipes, Gas Fixtures, etc.
No. 315 MAIN STREET.
All work promptly executed and satisfaction guaranteed.

KANSAS CITY—Continued.

SHAW & BEWSHER, Plumbers and Gasfitters,
Cor. Ninth & Delaware sts.

PRINTERS.

S. D. MACDONALD, W. W. WATERS, PETER D. ETUE.

Macdonald, Waters & Etue,

COMMERCIAL PRINTERS, LITHOGRAPHERS
AND
Blank Book Manufacturers,
Office, 409 Delaware St. - - Kansas City, Mo.

Blank Books with or without printed headings, for Corporations or Firms, furnished in the best style at St. Louis prices. Book and Job printing execnted with promptness, and forwarded by mail without charge for transportation.

REAL ESTATE.

SWYGARD, JOHN P. & CO., Real Estate, Rental and Collecting Agents, 904 Main st.

WEBSTER, ED. H., Real Estate Agent,
603 Main st.

RESTAURANTS AND SALOONS.

CROWLEY & McRAE, Litt'e Church,
Cor. E. Main & Missouri ave.

DRIVING PARK EXCHANGE, John C. Simpson, Driver, Cor. Sixteenth and Grand ave.

KELSEY'S DINING ROOMS,
Cor. Fourth & Walnut Sts.,
EAST SIDE MARKET SQUARE,
MEALS AND LODGING 25 CENTS.
This house being centrally located, is convenient to all the principal business houses, commission merchants and street cars pass directly in front of the door.

M. KELSEY, - - Proprietor.

METROPOLITAN
Hotel and Restaurant,
IN NELSON BLOCK, Kansas City, Mo.
Meals at all hours, open Day and Night. JOHN McQUEENY, Proprietor.

GEO. G. SASS,
Farmers' Dining Rooms,
115 N. SIDE MARKET SQUARE.

SCHAEFER, PHILLIP, Saloon and Restaurant,
Cor. Levee & Grand ave

VIENNA GARDEN RESTAURANT, S. W. Cor. Missouri ave , and Walnut st., S. Caro, Prop.

SADDLERY HARDWARE.

ASKEW, W. W. & F., Leather and Saddlery.
Hardware, N. E. Cor. Third and Delaware sts.

sent to France in 1803, when he secured the purchase of Louisiana. He is said to have always taken particular pride in this transaction, regarding his part in it as among the most important of his public services. Soon after his inauguration as President, he visited the military posts in the north and east, with a view to thorough acquaintance with the capabilities of the country in the event of future hostilities. This tour was a great success. He wore a blue military coat of home-spun, light-colored breeches, and a cocked hat, being the undress uniform of a Revolutionary officer. Thus was the nation reminded of his former military services. This, with his plain, unassuming manners, completely won the hearts of the people, and brought an overwhelming majority to the support of the administration. Monroe was a man more prudent than brilliant. who acted with a single eye to the welfare of the country. Jefferson said of him: "If his soul were turned inside out, not a spot could be found on it." Like that beloved friend, he died "poor in money, but rich in honor," and like him also, he passed away on the anniversary of the independence of the country he served so faithfully.

J. Q. Adams
(SIXTH PRESIDENT.)

John Quincy Adams was born at Braintree, Mass., July 11, 1767, and died at Washington, February 23, 1848. He was President from 1825 to 1829.

John Q. Adams was a man of learning, of blameless reputation and unquestioned patriotism President he was hardly more successful t.... his father. This was, doubtless, owing greatly to the fierce opposition which assailed him from the friends of disappointed candidates, who at once combined to weaken his measures and prevent his re-election. Their candidate was Andrew Jackson, a

ADVERTISEMENTS.

KANSAS CITY—*Continued.*

SCHOOL DESKS.

GOOLMAN'S
Folding School Desk,
CHURCH AND HALL SEATS,
Patented, June 23, 1874.

GOOLMAN'S
Improved Standard Scales,
Patented May, 23rd, 1871. - Manufactured by

THE GOOLMAN CO.
Cor. Walnut & 20th Sts.,
KANSAS CITY, MO.

☞ All kinds of castings made to order and scales repaired.

SEEDS.

TRACY, H., Farm Machinery, Field and Garden Seeds, 415 Walnut st.

SEWING MACHINES.

MACELROY, J. G., Dealer in all kinds of Sewing Machines, 1030 Main st.

SHOW CASES.

A. R. JACKSON,
Manufacturer of all Kinds of
METAL & WOODEN
Show Cases,
A Large Assortment on Hand.
226 Main St., - KANSAS CITY, MO.

TAILORS.

BAUER, C., Cleaning and Repairing, Cor Fourth and Main, under Barnum's Hotel

GROSS, G., Merchant Tailor, Twelfth st., between Walnut and Grand ave.

NOOK, WILLIAM, Tailor, Scouring and Repairing done neatly, 20 Missouri ave.

RIEKEN, JOHN W., Merchant Tail r and Repairer, N. E. Cor. Ninth and Main sts.

TOBACCO AND CIGARS.

BEITMAN BROS., Manufacturers and Jobbers of Cigars, 1410 Grand ave.

BISHOP, C. G. & CO., Cigars and Tobacco, 420 Main st.

J. M. CONNOR & CO.,
Manufacturers of
CHOICE CIGARS,
And dealers in all kinds of
Cigars, Tobaccos, Pipes, Etc.
No. 525 Main Street,
Bet. Fifth & Missouri Ave., KANSAS CITY, MO.

KANSAS CITY—*Continued.*

DAVIDSON, B., Dealer in Cigars and Tobacco, 522 Delaware st.

JELLINECK, TONY A., Cigar Maker, 722 Main st.

MADICK, JOS., Cigar Maker, 610 Main st.

TRANSFER CO.

HOFFMAN, HARRY G., With R. R. Transfer Co. No 14 W. Missouri ave.

TRUNK MANUFACTURER.

GEORGE, LOUIS, Trunk Manufacturer, 558 Main st

TYPE FOUNDRY.

TYPE, ELECTROTYPES,
CARD & PAPER CUTTERS,
BRASS RULES, LEADS, SLUGS, &C.,
Presses, Cabinets, Cases, Stands,
Galleys, Inks, Bronzes, Roller Composition, &c.
205 W. FIFTH ST.,
J. T. RETON, - - - - Proprietor.

UNDERTAKER.

J. T. WELDEN,
UNDERTAKER
And Dealer in

Metalic Burial Cases and Caskets,
Also, Wooden Coffins of all Sizes. Embalming done with perfect success

No. 914 MAIN STREET.

WATCHES AND JEWELRY.

HAYTER, E., Watchmaker and Jeweler, 903½ Main st.

SEEGER, HENRY R., Jeweler and Instrument Maker, Missouri ave. bet. Main & Walnut.

WINES AND LIQUORS.

FEINEMAN, B. A. & CO., Wholesale Liquors, 414 Delaware st.

RYAN, JOHN, Wholesale dealer in Pure Kentucky Whiskies, 523 Main st.

KANSAS CITY BUSINESS HOUSES
When Established.

CONNOR, J. N. & CO., Cigar Manufacturers, 1875.
FARLEY BROS., Plumbers, 1873.
THE GOOLMAN CO., School Desk, 1870.
WEBSTER, ED. H., Real Estate, 1865.

W. KANSAS CITY, MO.

BARBERS.

EDWARDS, THOMAS, Barber, 1224 W. Ninth st.

Mississippi State Building.—This building has a front of 40 feet with a depth of 36, two stories high. The outside of the building is covered entirely with hickory bark, interspersed with panels laid in diagonal style. The roof is tin and the eaves are draped with bill moss from the State of Mississippi There are 68 different varieties of wood used in the building, all from the State it represents. It has four rooms, two for the use of male visitors, and two for ladies—one for a ladies' parlor and the other a dressing room.

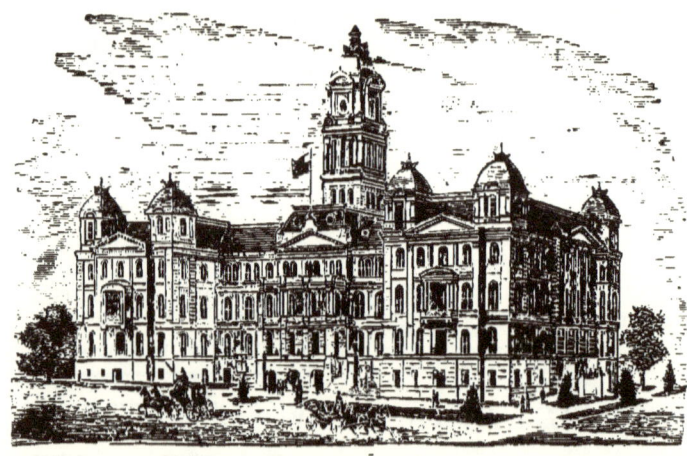

State Capitol, West Virginia.—The Capitol was changed temporarily from Charleston to Wheeling in 1874. The city of Wheeling offered to erect a building with ample accommodations, giving the use of it free as long as the state would occupy it as a capitol. Upon the acceptance of this generous offer the city erected the above building. It was completed in July, 1875. The building is 200 feet in length, each wing being 50x112 feet. The height of the main tower is 150 feet. The building cost $95,000.

man whose dashing boldness, energy and decision attracted the popular masses, and hid the more quiet virtues of Adams. To add to his perplexities, a majority of the House, and nearly one-half of the Senate, favored the new party; and his own Vice-President, John C. Calhoun, was also the candidate of the opposition, and of course committed to it. To stem such a tide was a hopeless effort. In two years Adams was returned to Congress, where he remained until his death, over sixteen years afterward. Ten years of public service were thus rendered after he had passed his "three-score years and ten," and so great was his ability in debate at this extreme age, that he was called "the old man eloquent." Like his father, he was a wonderful worker, and his mind was a complete store-house of facts. He lived economically, and left a large estate. He was the congressional advocate of anti-slavery, and a bitter opponent of secret societies. His fame increased with his age, and he died a trusted and revered champion of popular rights. He was siezed with paralysis while occupying his seat in Congress, after which he lingered two days in partial unconsciousness. His last words were, "This is the last of earth: I am content."

Andrew Jackson
(SEVENTH PRESIDENT.—TWO TERMS.)

Andrew Jackson was born in Waxhaw settlement, North or South Carolina, March 15, 1767, and died at the Hermitage, near Nashville, June 8, 1845. He served as President of the United States from 1829 to 1837.

The nomination of Presidential candidates by "Convention," as the term is now understood and applied, dates from the year 1832. At the first election Jackson was nominated by

W. KANSAS CITY—*Continued.*

WOODLAND, J. W., Barber,
Cor. Mulberry and Union ave.

BLACKSMITH.

MAGERS, PETER, Blacksmith & Wagon Maker,
9th and Hickory. Est. 1875.

O'KEEFE & DE FRIES, General Blacksmiths,
Eleventh near Liberty.

SEISS & VOGT,

BLACKSMITHS,

Santa Fe and Ninth Street,

Special Attention given to Dressing Mill Picks.

BOARDING AND LODGING.

PURVIS, MRS. M., Board and Lodging.
Cor. Ninth and Hickory sts.

BOOTS AND SHOES.

THOMAS DANLAN,

BOOT & SHOE MAKER,

St. Louis Avenue near Mulberry Street.

JOHN FECHT,

BOOT & SHOE MAKER,

Mulberry bet. Ninth & St. Louis ave.

SHAKESPERE, WM., Boot and Shoe Maker,
Cor. Twelfth and Liberty sts.

CEMENT AND PIPE CO.

FREAR STONE AND PIPE MANUFACTURING CO.
C. A. Brackett, Supt.

DRUGGIST.

SIMMS, H. A., Druggist,
Cor. Ninth and Mulberry st.

DRY GOODS.

BEE HIVE DRY GOODS STORE, John Lloyd,
Proprietor, Twelfth and Liberty st.

N. HOLZMARK,

Dry Goods & Clothing,

Ninth bet. Hickory & Mulberry,

ELEVATOR CO.

ADVANCE ELEVATOR CO.,
West Kansas City, Mo.

FLOUR AND FEED.

MILLIGAN & CURRY,

Jobbers in

Flour and Feed,

And all descriptions of Country Produce,
1220 UNION AVENUE,
WEST KANSAS CITY, MO.

GROCERIES.

MILLER, GEO., Family Grocery & Provisions
1321 Union avenue.

Delaware State Building, Centennial Exposition, Phila.—Is 54 by 34 feet in size, and two stories high. It is built on the Swiss Gothic style of architecture, composed of wood entirely from the State of Delaware. It is occupied by the State Commissioners, the first floor being used as reception rooms, while the second floor is devoted to business purposes.

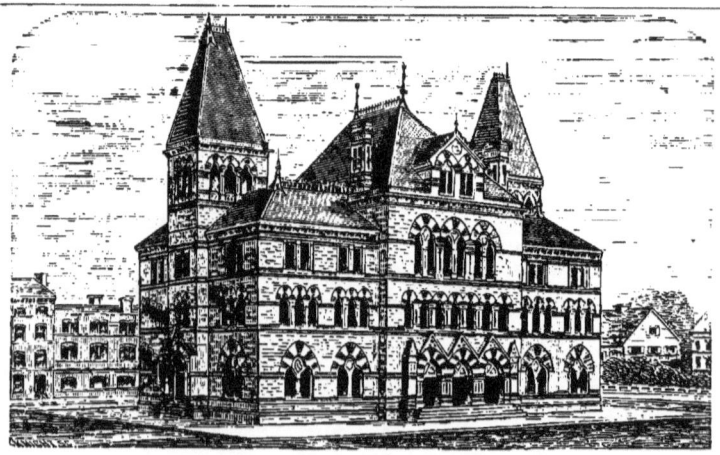

POST OFFICE, COVINGTON, KY.

W. KANSAS CITY—Continued.

MITCHELL, MRS. D., Grocery,
9th st., near Bell st.

MORIARTY, J. D., Groceries & Produce,
Cor. Bell & 9th sts.

McMAIN & CO.,

GROCERIES, FEED and GRAIN,
Cor. Mulberry & St. Louis sts.

NUGENT & FINUCANE, Groceries & feed,
1523 W. 12th st.

RUFF, GEORGE, Grocery & Restaurant.
9th bet. Mulberry & Santa Fe sts.

MEAT MARKETS.

BURNETT, WM., Meat Market,
9th & Mulberry sts.

A. ROGERS,

MEAT MARKET,

1408 12th st., W. Kansas City.

MILLINERY, ETC.

MRS. V. CHOUQUETTE,

MILLINERY & HAIR WORK,

West Kansas City, Mo.

PHOTOGRAPHER.

BOWER, H. C., Photographer,
1222 Union ave.

SALOONS AND RESTAURANTS.

CHICAGO HOUSE SALOON
J. W. CONKLIN, Proprietor,
1306 West Ninth street, West Kansas City.

J. M. HEAVEY,

SALOON.

Open day and night, free lunch at all hours,
Cor. Twelfth and Wyoming sts., W. Kansas City.

MINT SALOON,

LAWRENCE FLOOD, Prop.,

1196 West Ninth street, West Kansas City.

WM. O'CONNELL,

SALOON,

Cor. 9th & Wyoming sts., W. Kansas City.

JOHN PARETTI,

ST. JOHN RESTAURANT & SALOON,

Opp. Union Depot, W. Kansas City.

TIN, COPPER AND SHEET IRON.

J. S. HEALD,

JOB, TIN, COPPER AND SHEET IRON SHOP,
Cor. Mulberry st. & St. Louis ave.,
WEST KANSAS CITY.

W. KANSAS CITY—Continued.

TAILORS.

BERGER, S., Tailor & Repairer,
9th st., bet. Mulberry & Santa Fe sts,

PAULICH, L., Tailor & Repairer,
Hickory st., bet. Union ave. & 12th st.

TOBACCO AND CIGARS.

H. FALK,

CIGAR & TOBACCO MANF'R,

811 Santa Fe st., W. Kansas City.

LAWSON, JULIUS, Manuf'r of Cigars, W. Kansas
City, Mo. Established 1874.

GEORGE STEINMILLER,
Man'f of and dealer in

CIGARS AND TOBACCOS
Ninth street, bet. Mulberry & Santa Fe sts,
WEST KANSAS CITY, MO.

WATCHES AND JEWELRY.

O. C. SHULL,

WATCHMAKER AND REPAIRER,

West Kansas City.

WELL AUGER.

BROCKETT PATENT WELL AUGER, C. A.
Brockett & Co., W. Kansas City, Mo.

MILWAUKEE, WIS.

ATTORNEY AT LAW.

ERWIN, J. B., Attorney at Law & Solicitor of
Patents, Iron Block.

ARCHITECTS AND SUPERINTENDENTS.

G. COLDEWE,

ARCHITECT,

And Superintendent,

Opera House Block, Room 17, residence 831 6th st.

DAVELAAR, WM., Architect & Practical Building Superintendent, 452 E. Water st.

LANDGUTH, A. S., Architect,
279 3d st. cor. State st.

BAKERS AND CONFECTIONERS.

ARMSTRONG, S. W., Baker & Confectioner,
140 Mason st. Established 1873.

LANGE, CHAS., Confectionery,
521 E. Water st.

BELL-HANGER AND LOCKSMITH.

WM. FRANKE,

BELL-HANGER AND MANUF'R OF LOCKS

47 Oneida st.,
OPPOSITE GRAND OPERA HOUSE.

COURT HOUSE, MADISON, WIS.

Buetow & Schræger,

TAILORS

423 East Water Street,

MILWAUKEE,

WIS.

the Legislature of Tennessee and other States, as well as by several bodies of citizens and Conventions, but the first regularly constituted Convention of a party as an organized body, and fulfilling all the assumed functions of the old Congressional Caucus, met at Baltimore, on the 22d of May, 1832, and nominated Jackson and Van Buren as the Democratic candidates for President and Vice President. The Whig candidates, less "regularly" nominated, were Henry Clay and John Sergeant, of Pennsylvania, who were the anti-Masonic candidates. The leading issue of the campaign grew out of the question of the re-charter of the United States Bank, the Whigs favoring and the Democrats opposing it.

Jackson was of Scotch-Irish descent. His father died before he was born, and his mother was very poor. As a boy, Andrew was brave and impetuous, passionately fond of athletic sports, but not at all addicted to books. His life was crowded with excitement and adventure. At fourteen, being captured by the British, he was ordered to clean the commander's boots. Showing the true American spirit in his refusal, he was sent to prison with a wound on head and arm. Here he had the small-pox, which kept him ill for several months. Soon after his mother had effected his exchange, she died of ship-fever while caring for the imprisoned Americans at Charleston. Left entirely destitute, young Jackson tried various employments, but finally settled down to the law, and in 1796 was elected to Congress. His imperious temper and inflexible will supplied him with constant quarrels. Often they were passionate word-contests, sometimes they became hand-to-hand encounters, and on one occasion a formal duel was fought, in which he killed his adversary, himself being severely wounded. The scars he bore upon his person were of wounds received in private battles, some of which left a mark for life. Jackson first distinguished himself as a military officer in the war against the Creek Indians, which he made a signal victory. His dashing successes in the war of 1812 completed his reputation, and ultimately won him the Presidency. His nomination was at first received in many States with ridicule, as, whatever might be his military prowess, neither his temper nor his ability seemed to recommend him as a statesman. However, his re-election proved his popular success as a President. His chief intellectual gifts were energy and intuitive judgment. He was thoroughly honest, intensely warm-hearted, and had an instinctive horror of debt. His moral courage was as great as his physical, and his patriotism was undoubted. He died at the "Hermitage," his home near Nashville, Tennessee. Jackson and Adams were born the same year, yet how different was their childhood! One born to luxury and travel, a student from his earliest years, and brilliantly educated; the other poor, hating books, and seeking any kind of work to escape from want. Yet they were destined twice to compete for the highest place in the nation. Adams, the first time barely successful, was unfortunate in his administration; Jackson, triumphing the second, was brilliant in his Presidential career.

MILWAUKEE—*Continued.*

BASKETS AND WILLOW WARE.

SCHULZ, W. F., Manf'r and dealer in Brackets & Willow Ware, 148 Reed st.

BILLIARD AND POOL TABLES.

ERNST PLANER,
Manufacturer of Billiard & Pool Tables. (with Delany's Patent Steel Spring Cushion.) Importer and dealer in Billiard Goods, Trimmings, Ivory Balls, Cushion and Frame Bolts, Cues, etc., 607 Cedar st., Milwaukee. Particular attention given to orders in the country.

BOTTLER OF BEER, ALE, ETC.

WM. BUNTROCK,
Bottler of

Milwaukee Lager Beer

From Best and Schlitz Brewing Company's.

ALE AND PORTER.

417 and 443 East Water street, Milwaukee, Wis.

BOILER WORKS.

EVISTON, J. W., Boiler Works, 192 to 220 Broadway & 281 & 283 Chicago st.

BOOKSELLERS AND STATIONERY.

A. SULZER & CO.,

BOOKSELLERS,

289 Third street,

German & English Periodicals promptly delivered to any part of the city. School Books, Stationery, etc., always on hand. We call particular attention to our Antiquarian Department. We will purchase entire Libraries, as well as single Volumes.

BOOTS AND SHOES.

KOBLER, WM., Manuf'r and dealer in Boots, Shoes & Rubbers, 411 3d st.

SCHULTZ, F., Boot & Shoe Maker, 132 Mason st.

BRASS FOUNDER.

MELLEN, WM., Brass Founder. Brass castings made to order, 168 Clinton st.

CARRIAGES, BUGGIES AND SLEIGHS.

LANE & HEILE, Manf'r of Carriages, Buggies & Sleighs, 217 Broadway & 93 Chestnut st.

CARRIAGE WOOD WORK.

D. FORD,

Manuf'r of all kinds of

CARRIAGE AND SLEIGH WOOD WORK,

219 Milwaukee st.

Milwaukee, - - Wis.

Orders by mail promptly attended to.

CIGAR BOXES.

HARTMANN & SUHR, Manf'r of Cigar Boxes, 74 Biddle st. cor. Market st.

MILWAUKEE—*Continued*

E. STRUPPE,
Manuf'r of and dealer in
CIGAR BOXES
Edgings, Labels, Trimmings, Brands, Ribbons,
ETC., ETC.,
317 & 319 Mineral street, near Reed street.

CIVIL ENGINEERS.
CHAS. A. VON BORCKE.   FRANCIS BENZLER.

Chas. A. von Borcke & Co.,
CIVIL ENGINEERS,
Surveyors, Architects, Landscape Gardeners
AND DRAUGHTSMEN,
Room 14, Opera House Building, (Oneida st.)
MILWAUKEE.
Also, publishers of the New City Map of Milwaukee.

COMMISSION MERCHANTS.

R IGGS & CARY, Commission Merchants,
306 Broadway.   Established 1874.

CROCKERY AND GLASSWARE.

D USHEN, W., dealer in Crockery & Glassware,
317 & 319 Chestnut st.

HERMANN MARTIN,
Dealer in Crockery and Glassware,
415 Chestnut st,
Milwaukee, - - - *Wis.*

DENTIST.

E MMERLING, JOS. C., Dentist, Maier's Block,
164 & 166 Reed st.   Established 1864.

DRUGGIST.

C UTLER, FRANK W., Druggist,
352 Milwaukee st.

ENGRAVERS AND LITHOGRAPHERS.

K NAUBER, J. & CO., Lithographers, Engravers
& Printers, 1 Spring st.   Established 1867.

M ARR & RICHARDS, Designers & Engravers on
Wood, S. W. cor. E. Water & Wisconsin sts.

FURNITURE.

G MELIN, FRED, Manf'r & dealer in Furniture &
Upholstery, 517 Spring St.   Estab. 1875.

H. LINGELBACH,
Manufacturer of and dealer in
FURNITURE
Of Every Description,
60 Oneida st,
MILWAUKEE,   -   WIS.

☞ Orders promptly attended to. ☜

GUNSMITH.

B OLKENIUS, ALBERT, Gunsmith and Dealer in
Guns, Rifles, Pistols, 501 E. Water st.

(EIGHTH PRESIDENT.)

Martin Van Buren was born at Kinderhook, New York, December 5, 1782, and and died, at the same place, July 24, 1862. He studied law and was admitted to practice in 1803; was elected President of the United States, and served four years, from 1837 to 1841. He early took an interest in politics, and in 1818 started a new organization of the Democratic party in New York, his native State, which had the power for over twenty years. In 1831 he was appointed Minister to England, whither he went in September, but when the nomination came before the Senate in December it was rejected, on the ground that he had sided with England against the United States, on certain matters, and had carried party contests and their results into foreign negotiations. His party regarded this as an extreme political persecution, and the next year elected him to the Vice-Presidency. He thus became head of the Senate which a few months before had condemned him, and where he now performed his duties with "dignity, courtesy and impartiality."

As a President, Van Buren was the subject of much partisan censure. The country was passing throug a peculiar crisis, and his was a difficult position to fill with satisfaction to all. That he pleased his own party is proved from the fact of his re-nomination in 1840 against Harrison. In 1844 he was once more urged by his friends, but failed to get a two-thirds vote in the convention on account of his opposition to the annexation of Texas. In 1848 he became a candidate of the "Free Democracy," a new party advocating anti-slavery principles. After this he retired to his estate in Kinderhook, N. Y., where he died.

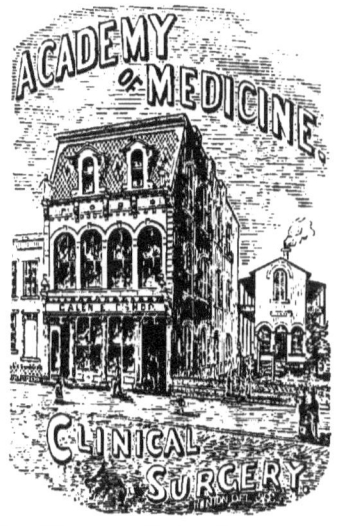

Cataract,
Gravel,
Hernia,
'Trephine'
Amputations,
Ovariotomy,
Tracheototomy,
Staphiloraphy,
Artificial Pupil,
Fistula-Lachrymalis,
Cross-Eye,

Hare-Lip, Varicocele,
Club-Foot, Hydrocele,
Wry-Neck, Phymosis,
Enlarged Tonsils, Fistula,
Pterygium, Piles,
Ectropion, Cancers,
Tumors, Ulcers,
Wens, Plastic Surgery,
Anurism, Artificial Eyes,
Tarix, And all other
Surgical Diseases of every kind.

Lung and Head Diseases, Scorbutus,
Scrofula, Epilepsy,
Syphilis, Neuralgia,
Tubercolisis, Paraligsis,
Dropsy, Chorea,
Ozena, &c., &c.

Perfect familiarity in the use of the Stethoscope, the Laryngoscope, and Rhinoscope, the Ophthalmoscope, and all other newly discovered and unimproved instruments for the diagnosis of the diseases of chest, throat, nose, eye and other organs.

Persons writing to me, will not forget to give their Postoffice, Town, County and State; and when ordering medicine by express, their express office always enclosing the old labels where medicine is to be repeated.

The best time for surgical operations is during the temperate Spring and Fall months, April, May and October, and more especially for operations on the eye, as cataract, artificial Pupil, &c.

I *put up* an Alterative, or remedy for Secondary and Tertiary Syphilis, called MEDICINA AMERICANA, and a remedy for Sexual Debility and Spermatorrhea, etc, called. KNOW NOTHING, a superior remedy. Another for Heart Diseases of valuable efficacy.— Any of which medicines can be sent by express in quantities of half dozen or more bottles.

For details send to me for circular.

GALEN E. BISHOP, M.D.,
ACADEMY OF MEDICINE, COR. 3D AND JULE STS.,

ST. JOSEPH, MO.

Established 1846.

IMPORTANT EVENTS OF THE CENTURY. 323

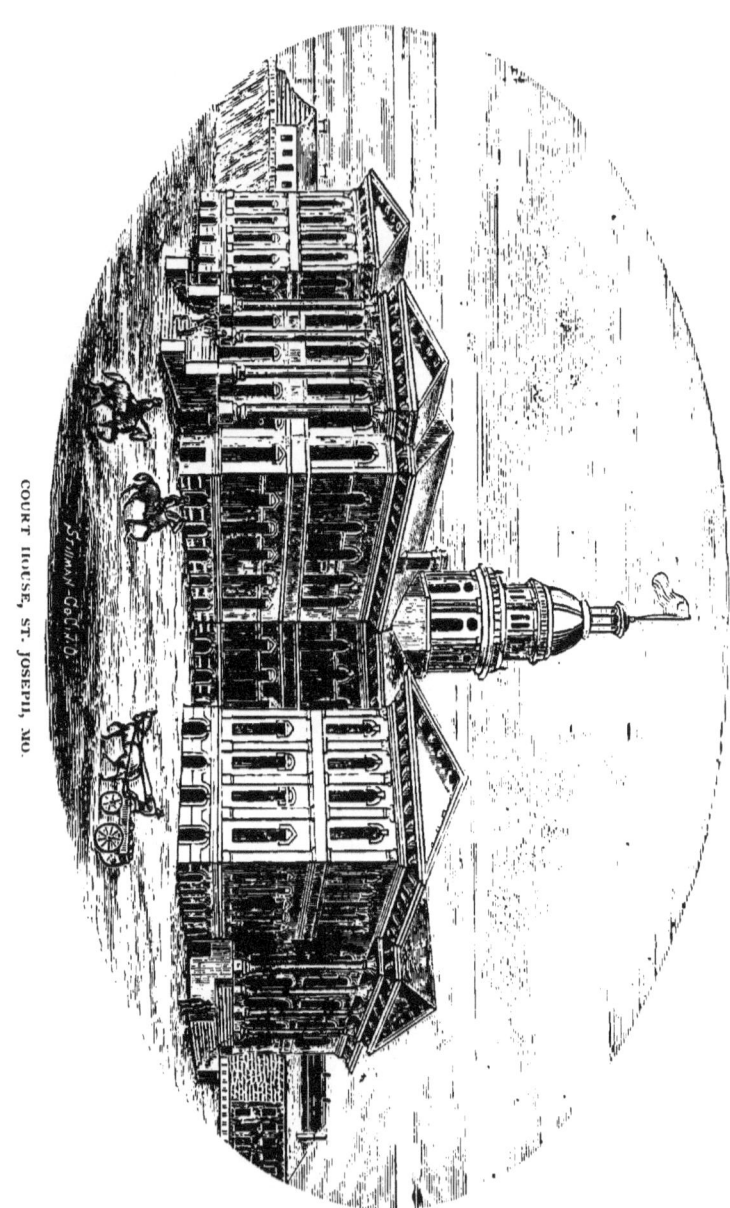

COURT HOUSE, ST. JOSEPH, MO.

(NINTH PRESIDENT.)

William Henry Harrison was born in Charles City county, Virginia, February 9, 1773. He entered the army in 1791, after graduating from Hampden-Sydney College. After reaching the grade of Captain he resigned in 1797; was chosen delegate to Congress from the North-western Territory in 1797; appointed governor of Indiana in 1801, and continued to 1813. He was elected President of the United States in 1840, and had scarcely entered upon the duties of his office when he died at Washington, April 4, 1841. In 1812 he distinguished himself during the war, especially in the battle of the Thames. His military reputation made him available as a Presidential candidate. His character was unimpeachable, and the chief slur cast upon him by his opponents was that he had lived in a "log cabin" with nothing to drink but "hard cider." His friends turned this to good account. The campaign was noted for immense mass-meetings, long processions, song-singing and general enthusiasm. "Hard cider" became a party watch-word, and "log cabins" a regular feature in the popular parades. He was elected by a very large majority, and great hopes were entertained of his administration. Though advanced in years, he gave promise of endurance. But "he was beset by office-seekers; he was anxious to gratify the numerous friends and supporters who flocked about him; he gave himself incessantly to public business; and at the close of the month he was on a sick bed." His illness was of eight days' duration. His last words were, "The principles of the government, I wish them carried out. I ask nothing more."

MILWAUKEE—*Continued.*

HARNESS AND SADDLES.

SCHAEFER, CHAS., Harness, Saddles, Whips, &c., 503 E. Water st. Estab. 1872.

HOTELS.

HASS' HOTEL, (Formerly "European Hof,") 553 & 555 East Water St., Milwaukee, Wis. This Hotel has been entirely renovated and travelers will find there a pleasant Home. Boarders taken. Good Stabling for Farmers.
J. C. HASS, Prop.

NEWHALL HOUSE. J. F. Antisdel, Prop. The most popular house in the city.

INSECT POWDERS.

BRUMMER'S
Infallible Insect and Vermin Destroyer

is the only perfect and successful Exterminator in this country, to make clean work of Bedbugs, Fleas, Flies, Ants, Cockroaches, Moths, Mosquitos, Lice on Canary Birds, Plants, Fowls and Animals. 205 SECOND STREET. Please send for circular.

IRON WORKS.

UNION IRON WORKS
BAYLEY & GREENSLADE,
Architectural Iron Work,

Castings of all Descriptions, Vault Doors, Roofs and Bridges. Cast and Wrought Iron Railings and Crestings, Etc. Jail and Court House work a specialty.
Established 1856. *MILWAUKEE.*

WENZEL TOEPFER,
Manufacturer of Iron Railings, Doors, Cells, Tanks
SMOKE STACKS,

Beer Coolers, Malt Kilns, Perforated Sheet Metals and all kinds of Iron Work,
Nos. 86 & 88 Menomonee St., bet. E. Water St. & Broadway Bridge, Milwaukee, Wis.

JULS. G. WAGNER,
(Successor to Hornbach & Wagner,)
Architectural Iron Works,
516, 518 & 520 MARKET ST., MILWAUKEE, WIS.

JEWELER—MANUFACTURER.

F. A. M. LEIDEL,
Manufacturing Jeweler & Diamond Setter
523 E. Water St., Milwaukee.

LAUNDRY.

ORIENTAL LAUNDRY,
MRS. J. COOKMAN, Proprietress.
197 E. WATER ST.
Work done in first-class style.

MILWAUKEE—*Continued.*

LETTER CUTTER.

CHAS. H. CLARKE,
LETTER CUTTER
Flour Brands and Seals a Specialty. 82 WISCONSIN ST.

LOCKS AND HOUSE TRIMMINGS.

Adam Loeffelholz. Robert Durr.

A. LOEFFELHOLZ & CO.
Manufacturers of
Locks, Silver & Nickel-Plated House Trimmings
Agents for Western Electric Burglar Alarms, Electric and Jackson's Hotel and Dwelling House Annunciators, Electric Call Bells. Sole agents for J. F. Wollensack's Transom Lifters. 84 Mason st.

MACHINISTS.

THOS. CORBETT & CO.
BUILDERS OF
Steam Fire Engines, Engines and Machinery.
Also Manufacturers of
Corbett's Automatic Governor and Variable Cut-Off.
135 & 137 FERRY ST.,
Office, 256 Lake St. MILWAUKEE, WIS.

KLEINSTEUBER, C. F., Machinist and Engraver, 318 State st.

MATHEMATICAL INSTRUMENTS.

WM. E. HUTTMANN,
PHILOSOPHICAL
Mathematical Instrument Maker.
Engineers' Transits, Levels, Theodolites, Compasses, Galvanic Batteries, Magnetic, Electric Machines, Ship Compasses and Spy Glasses Repaired. **397 EAST WATER ST.**

MAP PUBLISHERS.

Established 1846.

S. CHAPMAN & SON,
MAP PUBLISHERS
122 & 124 Grand Ave., Up-stairs.
Maps, Show Bills, Pictures Mounted to Order, Maps Drafted, Estimates Made, Map Paper for Sale, etc., etc.
S. Chapman. F. N. A. Chapman.

PAINTERS.

BIERBACH, GEO. E., Wagon and Carriage Painting, 110 Clybourn st.

ALEX. HARPER & CO.
House & Sign Painters
GRAINING & CALSIMINING.
415 Spring Street, Milwaukee.
Wall Painting and Tinting a Specialty.

John Tyler

(TENTH PRESIDENT.)

John Tyler was born in Charles City county, Virginia, March 29, 1790, and died at Richmond, Va., January 17, 1862. He studied law, and was elected to Congress in 1816, and served some five years; was elected U. S. Senator in 1827; re-elected in 1833, and was President of the Peace Convention at Washington in 1861.

Mr. Tyler became President upon the death of Mr. Harrison as his constitutional successor as Vice President of the United States. John Tyler was in early life a great admirer of Henry Clay, and is said to have wept with sorrow when the whigs in convention rejected his favorite candidate for the Presidency, and selected Harrison. He was nominated Vice-President by a unanimous vote, and was a great favorite with his party. In the popular refrain, "Tippecanoe and Tyler too," the people sung praises to him as heartily as to Harrison himself. The death of Harrison and the succession of Tyler, was the first instance of the kind in our history.

Tyler's administration was not successful. He opposed the measures of his party, and made free use of the veto power. His former political friends denounced him as a renegade, to which he replied that he had never professed to endorse the measures which he opposed. The feeling increased in bitterness. All his cabinet, except Webster, resigned. He was, however, nominated by a convention composed chiefly of office-holders, for the next Presidency; he accepted, but, finding no popular support, soon withdrew from the canvass. In 1861 he became the presiding officer of the peace convention in Washington. All efforts at reconciliation proving futile, he renounced his allegiance to the United States and followed the Confederate fortunes. He died in Richmond, where he was in attendance as a member of the Confederate Congress.

MILWAUKEE—*Continued.*

PATENT SOLICITOR.

SMITH, J. B., Solicitor of Patents,
19 Pfister's Block. Estab. 1856.

PATTERN AND MODEL MAKERS.

Giljohann & Dietrich,

PATTERN MAKERS,

216 East Water St., Cor. Chicago.

Models and Patterns made for Stoves, Ranges, Furnaces, Machinery Buildings, Etc.

H. F. KRAFT & CO.

Model and Pattern Makers

And Manufacturers of Fancy Goods, of Silver and Plated Ware, Fire Gilders, Gold, Silver and Nickel Platers. 228 & 230 Cedar st. Manufacturers of anything in fine machinery, from a Marine Chronometer to a two horse-power Steam Engine.

PHYSICIAN.

FLYNN, LYTTON, M. D.,
Office & Residence, 136 & 138 Grand ave.

PICTURE FRAMES.

WERNER, F., Manufacturer and Dealer in Picture Frames, 432 Broadway.

PHOTOGRAPHERS.

ADAM HEEB,

PHOTOGRAPHER

N. W. Cor. of 3rd & Chestnut Sts., (Sean's Block.)

BROADWELL, D., Palace Photographic Studio, 132 Mason st.

E. H. CANFIELD,

PHOTOGRAPHER,

224 & 226 GRAND AVE.

306 GRAND AVE. 306.

PHOTOGRAPHIC STUDIO.

F. LENZ, Proprietor. Burnished Photographs. $2.00 per Dozen. Satisfaction guaranteed.

J. S. PARR,

Gallery of Art & Photographic Studio,

421 E. WATER ST., Bet. Mason & Wisconsin.

PLATER.

DAVIS, H. N., Gold and Silver Plater, also Fine Gilding, 1 Grand ave.

PLUMBER AND GASFITTER.

OPAL, H. C., Plumber and Gasfitter,
207 Reed st.

MILWAUKEE—*Continued.*

PRINTER—BOOK AND JOB.

Established 1876.

AUG. M. FIELDBERG,

BOOK AND JOB PRINTER,

Nos. 164 & 166 Reed St., South Side.

The Only Place in the City where the Scandinavian Languages are executed. Translations: German, Swedish, Norwegian.

RESTAURANT.

HARTMANN, H., Grand Avenue Restaurant, Meals at all hours, 216 Grand ave.

SASH, DOOR AND BLINDS.

CONWAY, W. C., Sash, Blinds and Doors, 52 to 70 Third st. Est. 1855.

WILLER, WM., Sash, Doors, Blinds and Ornamental Wood Work, Est. 1866, 315-323 Cedar

SAW MAKER.

MILEY, A. N., Saw Maker and Repairer,
130 Clinton st.

STOVES, RANGES AND TINWARE.

J. D. PIERCE,
Manufacturer of

Sheet Iron & Tin Plate Work,

CONDUCTORS, GUTTERS, ROOFING,
In all styles and in best manner. Agent for

DUTCHER, VOSE & ADAMS.

Furnaces, Stoves, Ranges, Repaired, Cleaned and Put Up. Refrigerators and Filters Re-Packed as Good as new. All work warranted.
128 MASON STREET.

PETER POERTNER,
General Jobber in

ROOFS, GUTTERS, CONDUCTORS, ETC.

Stoves, Tin and Sheet Iron Work.

35 Oneida St., - - MILWAUKEE, WIS.

Repairing done at short notice. Second Hand Stoves Bought and Sold.

LOEBEL, GEO. A., Dealer in Hardware, Stoves, &c., 529 Chestnut st.

TAILORS.

BOLLAND, L., Merchant Tailor, Repairing neatly done. 381 Spring st.

BUETON & SCHRAEGER, Merchant Tailors,
423 E. Water st.

AUGUST FELDT.
FASHIONABLE

Merchant Tailor,

475 E. WATER STREET.

[Grand Opera House Block,]

MILWAUKEE, WIS.

HANSON, N., Merchant Tailor, Clothes Cut and Made to Order, 186 Reed st.

THRESHING MACHINES.

OWENS, E. E., Manufacturer of Threshing and Brick Machines, 171 Second st.

GLASS BUILDING, CENTENNIAL EXPOSITION, PHILADELPHIA.

THE STEVENS
ORIGINAL AND ONLY GENUINE MACHINE-MADE

LOCK STITCH BARB,
ALL STEEL
FENCE WIRE!

Light and Open Twist Provides for
Expansion and Contraction
BY HEAT AND COLD.

Both main strands and Barbs are of Bessemer steel Wire, and warranted superior to any Barbed Fence Wire known to the trade. For full particulars, address

DILLMAN & STEVENS,
PROPRIETORS,
JOLIET, ILLINOIS.

(ELEVENTH PRESIDENT.)

James K. Polk was born in Mecklinburg county, North Carolina, November 2, 1795, and died at Nashville, June 15, 1849. He graduated from the University of North Carolina in 1816, and studied law; was elected to Congress in 1825, and several terms subsequently; chosen Speaker of the House, 1835 and 1837, and Governor of Tennessee in 1839. Mr. Polk was very unexpectedly nominated for President, in Baltimore, on the 27th day of May, 1844. He pleased his party as a candidate, and justified their fondest expectations as a man well worthy and well qualified to fill the office of Chief Magistrate of the United States, who surrounded himself with an able cabinet of counsellors. He served as President from 1845 to 1849.

Mr. Polk was one of the most conspicuous opposers of the administration of J. Q. Adams, and a warm supporter of Jackson. In 1839, having served fourteen years in Congress, he declined a re-election and was chosen Governor of Tennessee. His Presidential nomination, in connection with that of George M. Dallas, of Pennsylvania, as Vice-President, had the effect of uniting the Democratic party, which had been disturbed by dissensions between the friends and opponents of Martin Van Buren. However, the Mexican war, which in many States was strongly opposed, the enactment of a tariff based on a revenue principle instead of a protective one, and the agitation caused by the "Wilmot Proviso," all conspired to affect his popularity before the end of his term. He had, however, previously pledged himself not to be a candidate for re-election. He died about three months after his retirement from office.

MILWAUKEE—*Continued.*

MILWAUKEE
Threshing Machine Works

C. F. RAVN, Proprietor, 619 Cedar st. bet. 6th and 7th, West Side, Milwaukee. Manufacturer of Milwaukee Pitts' Patent Separator and Horse Powers, also Pitts' 8 and 10 Horse Power, and Climax 1, 2, 4, 6, 8 and 10 Horse Powers. Mill Machinery, Boiler and Bridge Castings, Shafting and Repair Work Generally. Have all the old patterns of Kirby & Langworthy.

TIN AND SHEET IRON WORKS.

R**AHTE & ROMANG,** Job Tinners,
41 Oneida st.

W**ILLIAMS, JACOB A.** Tin and Sheet Iron Work cr. 583 E. Water st. Est. 1863.

TOBACCO AND CIGARS.

PETER GOEBEL,

Manufacturer of CIGARS and dealer in Tobacco, Snuff and Smokers Articles of all Kinds. No. 55 Oneida street, opposite Grand Opera House, Milwaukee.

TURNER.

JACOB HIRSCH,
FANCY TURNER,
IN WOOD, HORN, BONE, ETC.

A nice assortment of all kinds of Briar Pipes always on hand and made to order. Billiard Balls Turned and Colored. Meerschaum pipes reboiled. Repairing nice and cheap.
No. 45 ONEIDA STREET,
MILWAUKEE.

UNDERTAKER.

Z**ANDER, M. J.,** Furnishing Undertaker,
495 E. Water and 482 Eleventh sts

VETERINARY SURGEON.

HORSE INFIRMARY,
306 Milwaukee St., Milwaukee.

DR. C. C. TAYLOR, V. S., Veterinary Practitioner from England. For fifteen years has treated all diseases of Horses and Cattle. Makes diseases of the feet a specialty. Medicines snpplied for all diseases of the Horse, &c., at the Infirmary.

WINES AND LIQUORS.

W**EIMER, JOHN,** Distiller of Alcohol and Spirits, 225 Reed st. Est. 1868.

WIRE WORKS.

Established 1857.

C. A. WAPLER,
Manufacturer of WIRE WORK, MALT KILNS, Muzzles and Seives of every description.
606 CHESTNUT STREET.

MILWAUKEE BUSINESS HOUSES,
When Established.

CANFIELD, E. H., Photographer, 1872.
CORBETT, THOS. M. & CO., Machinist, 1872.

SKETCHES OF THE PRESIDENTS.

MILLWAUKEE—Continued.

EVISTON, J. W., Boiler Works, 1868.
EXCELSIOR MANUFATURING CO. 1877.
FELDT, AUGUST, Merchant Tailor, 1873
FIELDBERG, A. M., Book and Job Printer, 1876.
FORD, D., Carriage Wood Work, 1874.
FRANKE, WM., Bell Hanger, 1873.
GILJOHANN & DIETRICH, Pattern Makers, 1875.
GOEBEL, PETER, Cigars, 1865.
HARPER, ALEX. & CO., Painters, 1845.
HARTMANN & SUHR, Cigar Boxes, 1877.
HIRSCH, JACOB, Fancy Turner, 1874.
HUTTMANN, WM. E., Instrument Maker, 1870.
KLEINSTEUBER, C. F., Machinist, 1852.
KRAFT, H. F. & CO., Model and Pattern. Makers, 1855.
LANDGUTH, A. S., Architect, 1864.
LEIDEL, E. A. M., Manufacturing Jeweler, 1872.
LENZ, F., Photographer, 1868.
LINGELBACH, H., Furniture, 1854.
LOEFFELHOLZ, A. & CO., Lock Makers, 1857.
PIERCE, J. D., Tin and Sheet Iron Worker, 1862.
PLANER, ERNST, Billiard Table Manufacturer, 1869.
POERTNER, PETER, Tin and Sheet Iron Worker, 1877.
RAVN, C. F., Threshing Machines, 1868.
STRUPPE, E., Cigar Boxes, 1868.
TAYLOR, C. C., Veterinary Surgeon, 1874.
WAGNER, J. G., Iron Works, 1855.

GRAND RAPIDS, MICH.

AGRICULTURAL IMPLEMENTS.

CASTLE BROS.,

Dealers in Agricultural Implements, Sewing Machines, Field and Garden Seeds. Manufacturers of Castle's Three-horse Equalizers.
106 W. BRIDGE ST., & CONSTANTINE, MICH.

W. C. DENISON,

General Dealer in

FARM IMPLEMENTS AND MACHINERY,

OFFICE AND WAREROOMS,

90 & 92 South Division Street.

ARCHITECTS.

ROBINSON & BARNABY, Architects, Grand Rapids.
GRADY & WADDELL, Architects & Superintendents of Buildings, 38 N. Ionia st.

(TWELFTH PRESIDENT.)

Zachary Taylor was born in Orange county, Virginia, November 24, 1784. He entered upon the duties of President in 1849, and died at the Presidential Mansion July 9, 1850, after an illness of five days. Soon after his birth his parents removed to Kentucky. His means of education were of the scantiest kind, and until he was twenty-four years of age he worked on his father's plantation. Madison, who was a relative, and at that time Secretary of State, then secured for him an appointment in the army as lieutenant. From this he rose by regular and rapid degrees to a major generalship. His triumphant battles at Palo Alto, Resaca de la Palma, Monterey, and Buena Vista, won him great applause. He was the popular hero of a successful war. The soldiers admiringly called him "Old Rough and Ready." Having been offered the nomination for President, he published several letters defining his position as "a whig, but not an ultra-whig," and declaring that he would not be a party candidate or the exponent of party doctrines. Many of the whig leaders violently opposed his nomination. Daniel Webster called him "an ignorant frontier colonel." The fact that he was a slaveholder was warmly urged against him. He knew nothing of civil affairs, and had taken so little interest in politics that he had not voted in forty years. But he was nominated and elected. His nomination caused a secession from the whigs, resulting in the formation of the free-soil party. He felt his want of qualifications for the position, and sometimes expressed his regret that he had accepted it; yet he maintained as President the popularity which had led to his election, and was personally one of the most esteemed who have filled that office.

GRAND RAPIDS—Continued.

ATTORNEYS AT LAW.

Peter Doran,
ATTORNEY AT LAW,
Rooms 19 & 20 Pierce's New Block.

Bankrupt Cases and Collections a Specialty. Prompt action; Charges reasonable. References furnished when desired.

WM. E. GROVE.　　　GEO. W. THOMPSON.
Established 1859.
GROVE & THOMPSON,
ATTORNEYS AND COUNSELORS AT LAW,
28 Canal Street.

McBRIDE, JAMES E., Attorney at Law,
41 Monroe st.

JOHN M. NIEHAUS,
Attorney at Law and Notary Public,

Rooms: 10 & 11 *PIERCE'S BLOCK.*

WM. L. STOUGHTON,
Attorney and Counselor, 43 Pearl street. Practices in State and United States Courts.

STUART & SWEET, Counselors at Law,
45 Pearl st.

WESTFALL, W. O., Attorney at Law,
46 Canal st.

BAKING POWDER.

JUDD & DERRICK, Baking Powder,
28 S. Division st.

BAKERS AND CONFECTIONERS.

CURTIS, JOHN J., Baker & Carriage Trimmer,
56 Summit st.

PEOPLE'S BAKERY,
HENRY J. PESSINK, Prop'r.
Baker and Confectioner.
Cream and Wedding Cakes made to Order. Ornamental work done. Parties Furnished at Short Notice.
No. 37 W. DIVISION STREET.

BARBER.

George H. Wilson,
BARBER SHOP,
5 N. Division Street.

BOOTS AND SHOES.

GOEBELL, JOHN, Dealer in Boots & Shoes,
64 Bridge st.

GRAND RAPIDS—Continued.

STOVER, GEO., Dealer in Boots, Shoes and Rub-Rubbers, 106 Canal st.

WATSON, S. A., Dealer in Boots & Shoes,
34 Canal st. Est 1875.

BOTANIC PHYSICIAN.

DR. E. WOODRUFF,
Botanic Physician,
Office at his Root, Bark and Herb store, 44 Canal Street, where for 18 years every description of Acute, Chronic and Private Diseases have been successfully treated. Strictly on Botanic Principles. No Poison used. Over 300 Botanic Medicines constantly on hand. Counsel at office free.

BREWERIES.

George Brandt,
Proprietor of
UNION BREWERY,
87 S. Division St.

FREY BROTHERS,
Coldbrook Brewery,
Coldbrook st., near D.& M. R.R Depot.

C. KUSTERER,
Proprietor of
City Brewery,
And Dealer in Malt, Hops, &c.
60 *EAST BRIDGE STREET.*

PETER WEIRICH,
Proprietor of
MICHIGAN BREWERY,
296 Bridge street,
West Side, near the G. R.& I. R. R. Depot.

BURIAL CASES AND CASKETS.

POWERS & WALKER, Burial Cases and Caskets,
83, 84, 85, 86, 87 & 88 South Front st.

CABINET WARE.

FURBISH, F. L., Fancy Cabinet Ware,
42 & 44 Mill st.

CARPENTERS AND BUILDERS.

TRADEWELL & SON, Carpenters & Builders,
Ottawa & Lewis sts.

ESTABLISHED 1867.

HUBERMAN'S BLOCK,

A. ATKINSON,
—DEALER IN—

MILLINERY, FANCY GOODS AND LACES,

Pattern Bonnets and Fine Goods a Specialty. Orders by Mail will receive Prompt Attention.

ESTABLISHED 1867.

DOUGLAS STREET, Corner 13th, OMAHA, NEBRASKA.

Agricultural Hall, Centennial Exposition, Philadelphia.—The materials used for this building are glass and wood. The ground plan is a parallelogram, of 540 feet by 820 feet covering a space of about ten acres. It consists of a large nave, crossed by three transepts. Both nave and transept being composed of Howe trusses arches of a Gothic form. The nave is 820 feet in length by 125 feet in width, with a height of 75 feet from the floor to the point of the arch. The central transept is of the same height, and a breadth of 100 feet, the two end transepts 70 feet high and 80 feet wide. Sold to R. J. Dobbins for $13,105; original cost of the building, $375,000.

(THIRTEENTH PRESIDENT.)

Millard Fillmore, being elected Vice-President to President Taylor, became his constitutional successor, and served the unexpired term from 1850 to 1853. Very exciting questions arose during his term of office: among them the slavery question, the admission of California into the Union as a free State, and the passage of the Fugitive Slave Law—providing for the return to their owners of slaves escaping to a free State. During the debate of these questions, for a while it seemed as if the Union would be rent asunder. Mr. Fillmore treated them with dignity, if not with statesmanship, till finally conciliatory measures prevailed, and the questions were amicably settled. In every respect Mr. Fillmore discharged the duties of President as a conscientious, sensible man, thoroughly acquainted with legislative and general political principles.

President Fillmore was born in Cayuga county, New York, January 7, 1800, and died March 8, 1874. He had not a very liberal education, and, when young, served as an apprentice to the fuller's trade. In the year 1821, he was admitted to the bar, and practiced law with success. From 1832 to 1840 he was a member of Congress; in 1842 he was nominated by the Whigs of New York for Governor, and was defeated; and in 1856 the Native American party ran him for President, and he received only the electoral vote of Maryland.

Upon the death of President Taylor, the entire Cabinet resigned.

GRAND RAPIDS—Continued.

CANDY MANUFACTURER.

J. W. WRIGHT,

CANDY MANUFACTURER,
And dealer in

CONFECTIONERY & ICE CREAM
5 SOUTH DIVISION ST.

CARRIAGE AND WAGON MANUFACTURERS.

C. E. BELKNAP,
Manufacturer of

SPRING WAGONS,
Freight Trucks, Lumber Wagons, and Democrat Buggies, has facilities for doing a large amount of Repairing and Carriage Painting.
GRAND RAPIDS, MICHIGAN,
Cor. Front & First sts.

W. P. NOEL,

Carriage Maker and Blacksmith,
Repairing Promptly attended to.
29 HURON ST.

J. M. ROUSE, C. A. PARMALEE.

J. M. ROUSE & CO.,
Manufacturers of

BUGGIES,
WAGONS & SLEIGHS,
36 North Division Street,
GRAND RAPIDS, - - MICHIGAN.

SCHOLL, JOHN, Carriage-maker & Blacksmith, Furman st., near W. Bridge st.

WOOD, ARTHUR, Carriage-maker,
37 Waterloo st.

CHEMIST.

ARCTIC MANUFACTURING CO.
C. W. JENNINGS,

Manufacturing Chemist

AND PERFUMER,
Office and Laboratory, 15 South Division st.

DESIGNERS AND ENGRAVERS.

REED, W. A. & CO., Designers & Engravers on Wood, 25 Canal st.

DRUGGIST.

THUM, WM., Druggist & Apothecary,
84 Canal st. & 145 W. Bridge st.

GRAND RAPIDS—*Continued.*

DYE WORKS.
C. D. ROSE,
CHEMICAL
Steam DYE Works,
4 & 6 Pearl st., and 9 S. Division st.

Cleaning and repairing neatly done at reasonable Prices.

TETLEY, WM., Steam Dye Works,
Olmy st. Established 1856

EDGE TOOLS.
CHASE, HAWLEY & STONE, Ax and Edge Tool Works, Mill st., N. of Bridge.

FANCY GOODS.
LOETTGERT, F., Fancy Goods & Toys,
18 Canal st. Established 1866.

FLAVORING EXTRACTS.
FLAVORING EXTRACTS, C. W. Jennings, Manufacturer, 15 S. Division st.

FLOUR, FEED AND GRAIN.
DYKEMA, P. & SON, Flour, Feed & Grain, 134 Monroe st., & 45 S. Division st. Est. 1866.
SONKE & CO., Flour, Feed & Grain,
13 S. Division st. Established 1871.

FURNITURE.

A. A. LORD,
Dealer in

NEW AND SECOND-HAND FURNITURE,
And House-Furnishing Goods,
117 MONROE ST.

GROCERIES.
COLE BROS., Groceries, Provisions & Meats,
5 Granville ave.
FOX, S., Wholesale Grocer.
17 S. Division st. Established 1861.

GUN MANUFACTURER.
CHAS. LINDBERG,

Gun Manufacturer,
And dealer in all kinds of Gun Materials.
ALL ORDERS PROMPTLY FILLED.
61 CANAL ST.

HARNESS AND SADDLES.
BROWN G. L., Harness, Saddles, Trunks, &c.,
75 Waterloo st.
LAPPLEY, F. J., Man'f'r and dealer in Harness, Saddles, Collars, etc., 135 Canal st.

L. LOUWERSE
Manufacturer of and dealer in
HARNESS, TRUNKS, &c., &c.,
119 Monroe st.

(FOURTEENTH PRESIDENT.)

Franklin Pierce was born at Hillsborough, New Hampshire, on the 23d of November, 1804, and died in 1869. He graduated at Bowdoin College, Maine, in 1824; studied law and was admitted to the bar in 1827. He was President from 1853 to 1857.

Mr. Pierce had barely attained the requisite legal age when he was elected to the Senate. He found there such men as Clay, Webster, Calhoun, Thomas H. Benton, and Silas Wright. Nathaniel Hawthorn says in his biography of Mr. Pierce: "With his usual tact and exquisite sense of propriety, he saw it was not the time for him to step forward prominently on this highest theatre in the land. He beheld these great combatants doing battle before the eyes of the nation, and engrossing its whole regards. There was hardly an avenue to reputation save what was occupied by one or another of those gigantic figures." During Tyler's administration, he resigned. When the Mexican war broke out, he enlisted as a volunteer, but soon rose to the office of brigadier-general. He distinguished himself under General Scott, against whom he afterwards successfully ran for the Presidency, and upon whom, during his administration, he conferred the title of lieutenant-general.' On the question of slavery, Mr. Pierce always sided with the South, and opposed anti-slavery measures in every shape. In a message to Congress in 1856, he characterized the formation of a free State goverment in Kansas as an act of rebellion, and justified the principles of the Kansas and Nebraska Act. He, however, espoused the national cause at the opening of the civil war, and urged a cordial support of the administration at Washington.

GRAND RAPIDS—Continued.

NILSON, J. P., Manf'r and dealer in Harness Saddles, Bridles, etc., 12 N. Front st., W. Side

HOTELS.

COMMERCIAL HOTEL, W. F. Parish, prop., 53 Lyon st. Rates, $1.50 per day.

HOTEL WEBER,
Peter Weber, Prop.,
142 Canal St., GRAND RAPIDS, MICH.

MORTON HOUSE,
PANTLIND & LYON, Props.,
Grand Rapids, - Mich.

PRAIRIE STREET HOUSE,
M. M. QUARTEL, Proprietor.

Cor. Fulton and Ionia streets, one block North of Union R. R. Depot.

SWEET'S HOTEL, Lyon & Picking, Proprietors, Grand Rapids.

INKS AND BLUEING.

INKS AND BLUEING, ARCTIC MANUFACTURING Co., C. W. Jennings, prop., 15 S. Division st.

JEWELERS.

LOUIS J. BUCHSIEB,

PRACTICAL JEWELER & STONESETTER,
Room 8 Nellis Block, 23 Monroe st.

WINEMAN & YENTSCH,
PRACTICAL JEWELERS,
GOLD and SILVER PLATERS,
76 Ottawa st., near Monroe.

LEATHER AND FINDINGS.

THE CAPPON & BERTSCH LEATHER CO.,
Tanners and Dealers in

LEATHER & FINDINGS,
Hides, Pelts, Wool and Furs,
100 CANAL ST.

PERFUMERY.

JENNINGS, C. W., Perfumery Manufacturer,
15 S. Division st.

GRAND RAPIDS—Continued.

LIVERY AND BOARDING STABLES.

GILDERSLEEVE, GEO. H., Livery Stable,
56 Ionia st.

NATIONAL
Livery & Boarding Stables,
FRENCH & CO., Proprietors,
64 IONIA STREET.

PAINTERS.

C. Hetherington, Chas. M. Ellsworth,
(Formerly Partner with H. M. Goebel) SignWriter

First-Class House, Sign & Ornamental Painting
Plain and Decorative Paper-Hanging, Kalsomining, Gilding, Bronzing and Glazing. Estimates furnished and contracts taken on all kinds of Painting.
75 MONROE ST., under Patten & Hinsdale's.

BY. MORRISON,
SIGN PAINTER
36 CANAL STREET,
GRAND RAPIDS, MICH.

PAPER BOXES.

Established 1872.
T. C. PUTNAM,
Manufacturer of all Kinds of Paper Boxes
6 HURON STREET.

PEDDLERS' SUPPLIES.

CURTISS, J. A., & CO., Dealers in Peddlers' Supplies, 41 S. Division st. Estab. 1871.

PHOTOGRAPHERS.

HUTCHINSON & BAYNE, Photographers, Artists in India Ink and Water Colors, 75 Monroe st.

MERRILLS, C. L., Photograph and Gem Gallery, 72 Canal st.

L. V. MOULTON,
PHOTOGRAPHER
Special attention given to Solar Printing and Trade Photographing.
18 CANAL ST., McReynold's Block.

WYKES, WARREN, Photographic Gallery of Art, opp. Rathbun House.

PHYSICIANS.

AIKIN, N. J., M. D., Eye, Ear, Lung, Female, Nervous and all Chronic Diseases, 57 Monroe.

GRISWOLD, J. B., M. D., Physician and Surgeon. Ottawa & Pearl sts.

ADVERTISEMENTS. 335

THE ADAM MANUFACTURING CO.,

Manufacturers of the Best

GENERAL MANUFACTURERS.

WM. ADAM, President. F. G. STANLEY, Vice President. W. J. ADAM, Sec'y and Treasurer.

Carriage Building, Centennial Exposition, Philadelphia.—It is built of wood and iron, and lighted principally by skylights. It is 345 ft. long and 230 wide. The exhibits by American manufacture number over one hundred; English, 45; France, 36; and Germany and Italy each one. Was bought by R. J. Dobbins at public auction for $4,100.

FENCE  WIRE!

Bessemer Steel Barbed Cable

EITHER GALVANIZED OR JAPANNED.

This barb is curved (not bent) and is woven between the strands of the wire, and cannot be removed. Secured by letters patent, Nov. 21, '76. It is the cheapest, because the best. It sells at Sight.

Adam Manufacturing Company, - - - - JOLIET, ILLINOIS.

22

(FIFTEENTH PRESIDENT.)

James Buchanan was born in Franklin county, Pennsylvania, April 13, 1791, and died at Wheatland, June 1, 1868. He was a graduate of Dickinson College and was admitted to the bar in 1812. He was President from 1857 to 1861, and was so constantly in office from 1820 up to that time that he was known by the sobriquet of "Public Functionary."

The "bachelor-President," as Mr. Buchanan was sometimes called, was sixty-six years old when he was called to the executive chair. He had just returned to his native country, after an absence of four years as Minister to England, previously to that he had been well known in public life as Congressman, Senator, and as Secretary of State under President Polk. As Senator in Jackson's time, he heartily supported his administration. With Van Buren, he warmly advocated the idea of an independent treasury against the opposition of Clay, Webster, and others. Under Tyler, he was urgently in favor of the annexation of Texas, thus again coming in conflict with Clay and Webster. However, he cordially agreed with them in the compromise of 1850, and urged its favor upon the people. Much was hoped from his election, as he avowed the object of his administration to be "to destroy any sectional party, whether North or South, and to restore, if possible, that national fraternal feeling between the different States that had existed during the early days of the Republic." But popular passion and sectional jealousy were too strong to yield to pleasant persuasion. When Mr. Buchanan's administration closed, the fearful conflict was close at hand. He retired to his estate in Pennsylvania, where he died.

GRAND RAPIDS—*Continued*.

STEPHENSON, DR. H. C., & BRO., Medical and Surgical Institute, 29 Monroe st.

PLASTER MANUFACTURERS.

GRAND RAPIDS PLASTER CO., Land and Calcined Plaster. Wm. Hovey, Supt. & Agent, 16 Monroe st.

GRANDVILLE PLASTER CO., Manufacturers of Calcined & Land Plaster, 100 Monroe st. Est. '72

PLUMBERS AND GAS FITTERS.

JOHN McDERMOTT & CO.

Practical Plumbers, Gas and Steam Fitters,

99 OTTAWA, ST., Grand Rapids, Mich.

SPROUL & McGURRIN,

Practical Plumbers, Steam & Gas Fitters

And Dealers in all kinds of Plumbing and Gas Fitting Materials. Estimates given on heating Factories, Churches, Dwellings, etc. by Steam.

126 MONROE STREET.

REAL ESTATE AND INSURANCE.

DOOGE, L., Dealer in Real Estate, Office, 46 Canal st. Estab. 1851.

S. O. KINGSBURY,

General Land & Tax Agent.

Established in 1850.

Will attend to the purchase, sale and exchange of Real Estate. Particular attention will be given to the payment of Taxes, purchasing Lands sold at Tax Sales, examining Titles, reclaiming Lands sold at Tax Sales, and will take a general supervision of all Lands entrusted to his charge, and Agent for Mobile Underwriters. *64 CANAL ST.*

MILLER, H., Real Estate Dealer, 3 N. Division st. Estab. 1869.

VAN DIENSE, JOHN H. C., Real Estate and Insurance Broker, Monroe & Division st.

SALOONS AND RESTAURANTS.

HENRY WEIRICH,

Saloon and Restaurant

CHOICE CIGARS, TOBACCO AND ALL SMOKERS' ARTICLES.

No. 104 Monroe St.

WHITE, ERASTUS W., Saloon and Restaurant, 52 Summit st.

SAWS.

T. J. EVERHART.

SAW MAKER, REPAIRER

And Dealer in

H. DISTON & SONS' SAWS,

No. 45 WATERLOO ST.

PITTS, JAMES L., Manufacturer of Saws, Pearl & Campau sts.

GRAND RAPIDS—Continued.

SPRING BEDS.

E. B. Hill. Wm. H. Bennett. O. W. Horton.

E. B. HILL & CO.
Wholesale Manufacturers and Dealers in

Hill & VanValkenburgh's Patent Spring Beds
Office & Salesroom, 109 Canal St.; Factory, 28 Mill Street.

TOBACCO AND CIGARS.

D. J. DOORNINK,
Dealer in Cigars & Tobaccos, Books & Stationery
81 MONROE STREET.

UNDERTAKERS.

DURFEE, ALLEN, Furnishing Undertaker, 103 Ottawa st.

FARWELL, J. H., General Furnishing Undertaker, 16 Pearl st. Estab. 1866.

WATCHMAKER AND JEWELER.

EIKHOFF, JOSEPH, Watchmaker and Jeweler, 37 South Division st.

WINES AND LIQUORS.

BILLY AT HOME.
WM. ECHTERNACH,
Dealer in

Choice Liquors & Cigars
No. 111 MONROE STREET.

DeRUGTER, JOHN, Wholesale Liquor Dealer, 116 Canal st.

PULCHER, C. G., Dealer in Wines, Liquors and Cigars, 119 Canal st.

WIRE WORKS.

GRAND RAPIDS WIRE WORKS
EDWARD RACINE, Prop.
92 MONROE STREET.
Manufacturer of Plain and Ornamental

WIRE WORK
OF EVERY DESCRIPTION.

WOOD TURNERS.

BACHMAN & PRIESTLEY,
WOOD TURNERS
And Manufacturers of Eureka Croquet Sets, Base Ball Bats, Packing Boxes, &c., *MILL STREET.*

Grand Rapids Business Houses.
WHEN ESTABLISHED.

AIKIN, N, J., M. D., 1869.
BRANDT, GEORGE, Brewery, 1863

(SIXTEENTH PRESIDENT.)

Abraham Lincoln was born in Hardin county, Kentucky, on the 12th of February, 1809. He was elected President in 1860, and was re-elected in 1864, and had entered upon the duties of his office for the second time, when he was assassinated by John Wilkes Booth, April 14th, 1865, and died the following day.

His father was unable to read or write. Abraham's education consisted of ... ..'s schooling. When he was eight years old, his father moved to Indiana, the family floating down the Ohio on a raft. When nineteen years of age, the future President hired out as a hand on a flat-boat at $10 a month, and made a trip to New Orleans. On his return he accompanied the family to Illinois, driving the cattle on the journey, and on reaching their destination helped them to build a cabin and split rails to enclose the farm. He was now in succession a flat-boat hand, clerk, captain of a company of volunteers in the Black Hawk War, country store-keeper, postmaster, and surveyor, yet he managed to get a knowledge of law by borrowing books at an office, before it closed at night, and returning them at its opening in the morning. On being admitted to the bar, he rapidly rose to distinction. At twenty-five he was sent to the Legislature, and was thrice re-elected. Turning his attention to politics, he soon became a leader. He was sent to Congress; he canvassed the State, haranguing the people daily on great national questions; and, in 1858, he was a candidate for Senator, a second time, against Stephen A. Douglass. The two rivals stumped the State together. The debate, unrivalled for its statesmanship, logic and wit, won for Lincoln a national reputation. He lost the election in the Legislature, as his party was in the minority. After his accession to the Presidency, his history, like Washington's, is identified with that of his country. He was a tall, ungainly man, little versed in the refinements of society, but gifted by nature with great common

GRAND RAPIDS—*Continued.*

DENISON, W. C., Farm Implements, 1862.
DORAN, PETER, Attorney at Law, 1876.
DURFEE, ALLEN, Undertaker, 1871.
FURBISH, F. L., Cabinet Ware, 1874.
GRAND RAPIDS PLASTER CO., 1856.
GROVE & THOMPSON, Attorneys at Law, 1859.
HILL, E. B., & CO., Spring Beds, 1871.
HOTEL, WEBER, 1865.
KINGSBURY, S. O., Land Agent, 1850.
KUSTERER, C., Brewer, 1848.
LINDBERG, CHAS., Gun Manuf., 1870.
NIEHAUS, JOHN M-, Attorney at Law, 1876.
MOULTON, L. V., Photographer, 1863.
POWERS & WALKER, Wood Burial Cases, 1875.
ROBINSON & BARNABY, Architects, 1865.
STEPHENSON, DR. H. C., & BRO., Medical Institute, 1874.
THE CAPPON & BERTSCH LEATHER CO., 1875.
WEIRICH, PETER, Brewery, 1856.
WOODRUFF, DR. E., Physician, 1860.

MINNEAPOLIS, MINN.

BARBERS.

NICOLLET HOUSE BARBER SHOP,
LOUIS RASMUSEN, PROP.,
12 Nicollet Block.   Established 1875.

STERRETT & LUCAS, Shaving Parlor,
Cor. Nicollet & 2d sts. Est. 1875.

BILLIARDS.

DAILY & REED,
BILLIARD HALL & SAMPLE ROOM,
205 Nicollet ave.

BOOTS AND SHOES.

YOUNG, N. J., Boots & Shoes,
621 Washington ave., South.

BUSINESS COLLEGE.

CURTIS & HYDE, Business College,
Bridge Square.

BUTTER PACKAGES.

FINNEGAN, A. J., Manf'r of Butter Pakages,
30 Hennepin ave.

CARRIAGE WORKS.

NOVELTY CARRIAGE WORKS,
246 Second avenue South,
M. Roeller, Manufacturer of Carriages & Sleighs.
Repairing promptly attended to.
Established 1873.

MINNEAPOLIS—*Continued.*

CLOTHING.

BOSTON ONE PRICE CLOTHING STORE,
2 & 6 Academy of Music.

OFSTIL, JOHN, Clothing & Gents' Furnishing Goods, 227 Washington ave. S. Est. 1877.

CONFECTIONERIES AND BAKERIES.

CHAS. W. SYPHER,
CONFECTIONERY AND BAKERY,
217 Nicollet ave.

GAVEGAN & O'BRIEN,
Confectionery and Cigars,
115 Nicollet ave.

HUNT, M. P., Confectionery,
619 Washington ave.

NYBERG, NILS, Confectionery,
216 Hennepin ave.

PAHSON, OLIVER, Confectionery,
329 Washington ave.

CONTRACTORS AND BUILDERS.

LOVERIN, H. A., Wire Window & Door Screen
Manf'r, Cont'or & Builder, 307 Hennepin ave.

PATTERSON & DUNLAP, Contractors in Brick
& Stone, 310 Hennepin ave.

DENTISTS.

BOWMAN & GRISWOLD, Dentists.
West Falls Block.

FANCY GOODS.

LADIES' STORE.
WORSTEDS AND EMBROIDERIES,
Mr. & Mrs. L. E. WEITZEL,
401 Nicollet ave.

FISH AND OYSTERS.

JONES, R. F., Dealer in Fish & Oysters,
305 Hennepin ave.

FURS.

J. BRZEZINSKY,
MANUFACTURER OF FANCY FURS,
3 Academy of Music.

P. F. EICHELZER,
MANUFACTURER AND DEALER IN FINE FURS,
212 Nicollet ave.   Established 1872.

FURNITURE.

A. H. EDSTEN,
— Manufacturer and Dealer in —
ALL KINDS OF FURNITURE,
303 Washington ave. south. Estab. 1870.

GUN MANUFACTURERS.

BACHNER BROS.,
GUN MANUFACTURERS,
And dealers in Sporting Equipments,
206 Hennepin ave.

Post Office, Boston.—The corner-stone was laid on the 16th of October, 1871. Our sketch shows the post office as it is. It has a front of over two hundred feet on Devonshire street, occupying the whole square between Milk and Wa'er streets, and it is, sooner or la'er, to be extended to Congress street. The government has never before owned the building in which the Boston post office was located. The upper stories of the new post office are occupied by the sub-treasury. The building was completed and occupied early in 1875. The entire cost of the government exceeded $3,000,000.

City Hall, Boston.—The corner-stone was laid on the 22d of December, 1862—the anniversary of the landing of the Pilgrims at Plymouth. The amount first appropriated was $160,000, but before the building was occupied the actual cos' was more than half a million dollars. The building was completed and dedicated on the 18th of September, 1865. The tablet in the wall, back of the first landing, perpetuates in beautifully worked marble, the statement that the dedication took place on the 17th of September. This day would have been highly appropria'e for the ceremony, being the two-hundredth and thirty-fifth anniversary of the settlement of Boston, had it not fallen on Sunday. The ceremony was accordingly postponed until the following day.

LEE M. FITZHUGH.   EDWIN C. THORNTON.

L. M. FITZHUGH & CO.,
Wholesale Dealer in

TEAS, TOBACCO
And Cigars,
66 South Meridian Street,
INDIANAPOLIS.

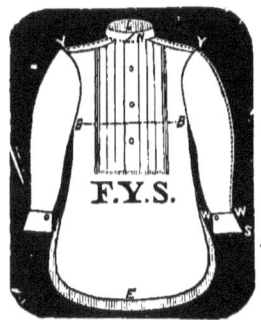

A. H. DEYO,
Manufactures to Measure the Celebrated

French Yoke Dress
AND NIGHT SHIRT.
ALSO COLLARS AND CUFFS OF ALL STYLES.

F.Y.S.

Light and Heavy Underwear Made to Order,

A Perfect Fit Guaranteed. Goods sent by Express to any part of the Country.

EAST SAGINAW, MICHIGAN.

ALEX. HURTUBISE,
IS MAKING THE

Best Cast Steel  **Pevys IN THE World.**

Poles, Cant-hooks and all kinds of River Work.
Which he sells at Wholesale or Retail for less money and warrants to give better satisfaction than any other work in the valley.

CHAMPION HORSE-SHOER,
Blacksmithing—Master of anything that can be forged under the hammer, iron or steel. Carriages, Wagons, Sleighs and Pevys. Wholesale and Retail. Cast-Steel Pevys a specialty. All kinds of Carriage Work, Painting and Trimming. All work Warranted.

Cor. Hamilton and Mackinaw Sts.,   -   -   **SAGINAW CITY, MICH.**

UNITED STATES BANK OF SWEETNESS.
Three Dollars will pay for a Nicer and better Cake at

JULIUS MIESSEN'S
CONFECTIONERY.
Ornamental Cakes, Pyramids, Ice Creams, Water Ice, Jellies, Charlotte Russe, and all kinds of Cakes will be made to order. Particular attention paid to

WEDDINGS AND PARTIES.
Manufacturer of Roses, Panorama Eggs and Hearts, Sugar Toys and Penny Toys, etc.

180 VIRGINIA AVENUE,
Indianapolis,   ▪   ▪   ▪   **Ind.**

Michigan State Building, Centennial Exposition, Philadelphia.—In the absence of any appropriation from the state, this building was erected mainly through the exertions of the Michigan State Centennial Board and Julius Hess, the architect, at a cost of about $15,000. It is constructed entirely of Michigan lumber, above the foundation. The inside as well as the outside of the building is highly decorative. The walls and ceilings inside the building are paneled, no plastering being used, and the floors of several rooms are inlaid to neat patterns.

Grand Rapids Plaster Company,

Manufacturers and Dealers in

LAND AND CALCINED PLASTER

WM. HOVEY, Supt. and Gen'l Agent.

16 Monroe St., Up Stairs.

GRAND RAPIDS, MICH.

ADVERTISEMENTS.

MINNEAPOLIS—Continued.

HAIR DEALERS AND DRESSERS.

PAGE, MRS. S. A., Hairworker & Ladies' Hair-Dresser, 31 South 4th st.

MADAME M. A. NICHOLS,
Manufacturer of
HUMAN HAIR,
And Ladies' Fashionable Hairdresser,
107 Washington ave. South. Established 1871.

HATTER.

P. F. EICHELZER,
FASHIONABLE HATTER AND FUR DEALER,
212 Nicollet ave. Established 1872.

MEAT MARKET.

FLETCHER & SCHULZE,
Wholesale and Retail Dealers in
FRESH & PACKED MEATS,
310 Nicollet ave. Established 1875.

MILLINERS AND DRESSMAKERS.

FRAZIER, MRS. M. F., Fashionable Dressmaker, 251 Hennepin ave.

LEGG, MRS. GEO. B., Millinery & Dressmaking, 314 Hennepin ave.

LONG, MISS. S. R., Dressmaking Establishment, 430 Nicollet ave.

NEWSPAPER.

THE MONDAY MORNING INDEX,
Dr. R. D'UNGER,
Editor and Publisher,
243 Hennepin ave. Established 1875.

NEWSDEALER.

HILLIKER, A. M., Postoffice News-stand, City Hall Building, Stationery, Cigars, etc.

PHOTOGRAPHERS.

FLOYD & POWER, Photographers, 430 Nicollet ave., cor. 5th st. Established 1875.

JOHN H. OLESON,
PHOTOGRAPHER,
307 Washington ave. South. Estab. 1874.

RAYMOND, J. F., Photographer,
223 Nicollet ave.

PHYSICIANS.

U. D. Thomas, M. D.,
ECLECTIC, MAGNETIC
AND CLAIRVOYANT PHYSICIAN.

All Diseases of the Blood and Nervous System uccessfully treated. Send or call for circulars.

108 Washington ave. south,

MINNEAPOLIS. - - - MINN.

MINNEAPOLIS—Continued.

BLECKEN, C. H., M. D., Eclectic Physician,
Over Gray's Drug Store.

MOYER, A., M. D., Eclectic Physician,
252 Hennepen ave.

PAINTER.

JOHN WEINARD,
FRESCO and SIGN PAINTER,
112 Washington Avenue South,
MINNEAPOLIS.

PIANOS AND ORGANS.

WILLSON, GEO. H., Pianos & Organs,
4 Academy of Music.

PRINTERS.

DAVISON & HENDERSON,
Ornamental Job Printers,
213 Hennepin ave. Est. 1876.

JOHNSON, SMITH & HARRISON, Printers & Lithographers, 21 2d st. south.

LAMB & WAY,
PLAIN and ORNAMENTAL
STEAM JOB PRINTERS,
Prices down to the bottom, and good work in ev ry case.
105 WASHINGTON AVE. SOUTH.
Established 1877.

REAL ESTATE AND LOAN AGENTS.

FINNEGAN, A. J., Real Estate, & Loan Insurance Agent, 310 Hennepin ave.

HAMLIN & BROWN, Real Estate & Insurance, 2d st., room 2, Center Block.

SMITH, C. B., Real Estate & Loan Agent,
242 Hennepin ave.

STATIONERY.

WILLIAMS, S. M., Stationery,
224 Hennepin av.

STENCIL WORKS.

LOY, ELLWOOD, Stencil Works,
214 Hennepin av.

TAILORS.

SHERMAN, H. P., Merchant Tailor,
111½ Washington av., So.

J. H. THOMPSON,
MERCHANT TAILOR,
188 HENNEPIN AVE.

TENTS AND AWNINGS.

JOHN HILL,
Manufacturer of
TENTS & AWNINGS,
105 Washington Ave., South. Est. 1874.

MINNEAPOLIS—Continued.

TURKISH BATHS.

A. S. ERVIN,
TURKISH BATHS,
405 Nicollet Ave., - Minneapolis.

WATCHES AND JEWELRY.

W. B. WOOLSEY,
Jewelry Store,
219 NICOLLET AVENUE.

WOOD DEALERS.

GROVE & ROWE,
Office, East Entrance City Hall. Dealers in all kinds of MILL AND HARD WOOD. We keep constantly on hand the largest and best stock in the City. Call and See Us.

MOLINE, ILLS.

BLACKSMITHS AND HORSESHOERS.

CANCELMANN, B., General Blacksmithing and Wagon Making, Cor. Main & Atkinson st.

ZEIGLER, N. R., Horseshoeing. Fancy shoeing a specialty. Lynde st.

BOOTS AND SHOES.

FREDRICKSON, J., Boot and Shoe Maker, Railroad av., opp. C. & R. I. Depot.

DRESS AND CLOAK MAKER.

HARRIS, M. A., Dress & Cloak Maker, Lynde near Main st.

DRUGGISTS.

W. G. MORRIS,
Dealers in
Drugs, Medicines, Perfumeries, &c.
Cor. WELLS AND LYNDE STREETS.

FLOUR AND FEED.

BROWN, R. L., Wholesale & Retail Flour, Feed and Ship Stuffs. 212 Main st.

GROCERIES.

McDONALD, J. A., Moline Grocery, Cor. Madison & Illinois sts.

S. WALKER & SON,
Dealers in Choice Family Groceries, Stone's Pure Flavors, Queensware, &c.
Cor. BASS AND WELLS STREETS.

HARDWARE.

(Established 1855.)
THOMAS DUNN,
Dealer in Hardware, Cutlery, Iron, Nails, Window Glass, &c. 117 & 119 Wells st.

HARNESS AND SADDLES.

MATZEN, H. C., Harness Manufacturer, Wells st.

SKETCHES OF THE PRESIDENTS.

sense, and everywhere known as "Honest Abe." Kind, earnest, sympathetic, faithful, democratic, he was only anxious to serve his country. His wan, fatigued face, and his bent form, told of the cares he bore and the grief he felt.

(SEVENTEENTH PRESIDENT.)

Andrew Johnson was born near Raleigh, North Carolina, December 29, 1808. He was Vice-President when Abraham Lincoln was assassinated, and by his death Mr. Johnson became the constitutional President of the United States. He died in 1875, while serving as United States Senator from Tennessee.

When only ten years of age, Mr. Johnson was bound apprentice to a tailor of Raleigh. Never having been a day at school in his life, he yet determined to secure an education. From a fellow-workman he learned the alphabet, and from a friend something of spelling. Thenceforth, after working ten or twelve hours per day at his trade, he spent two or three every night in study. In 1826, he went West to seek his fortune, with true filial affection carrying with him his mother, who was dependent on his labor for support. After his marriage at Greenville, Tenn., he continued his studies under the instruction of his wife, pursuing his trade as before by day. His political life commenced with his election as alderman. He was successively chosen mayor, member of the Legislature, Presidential elector, State Senator, twice Governor, and for fifteen years United States Senator. Remaining true to the Union when his State seceded, his loyalty attracted general attention. A life-time Democrat, he was elected on the Republican ticket as Vice-President, in reward for his faithfulness. Coming into office with a Republican Congress, it is not strange that his way was hedged with difficulties, and his Presidential career a most unhappy one.

Central Illinois Soap, Oil and Candle Works!

ESTABLISHED 1855.

N. N. WINSLOW,

MANUFACTURER OF AND DEALER IN

Soap, Candles!

LARD AND TALLOW OILS!

A FULL STOCK OF

Lubricating Oils,

ALWAYS ON HAND. ALSO

OIL BLACKING

Warranted superior to any other oil in use for HARNESS AND ALL KINDS OF LEATHER.

ESPECIAL ATTENTION CALLED TO SOAPS,

German Mottled, Spanish Lilly,

And other brands, which are the best in the market. Competition defied in quality of Goods and Prices.

ORDERS FROM THE TRADE SOLICITED.

CASH PAID FOR

Tallow, Lard and Grease!

OFFICE AND SALESROOMS:

East of Main Street, Near the L., B. & M. Passenger Depot,

BLOOMINGTON, ILLINOIS.

Court House, at Bloomington, McLean Co., Ill., was erected in 1870, at a cost of $400,000. It is built of handsome marble; joists and dome of iron. Spacious halls, with marble floor, and is considered fire proof. The dimensions of this beautiful structure are, 90 by 120 feet, and ranks among the finest buildings in the State.

JOSEPH WALKER,

—— DEALER IN ——

Millinery, Notions and Fancy Goods,

No. 209 NORTH MAIN STREET,

Directly East of Court House, Bloomington, Ill.

Grand Central Hotel,
OMAHA, NEB.
George Thrall, Proprietor.

The Leading Hotel
BETWEEN
Chicago and San Francisco.

(EIGHTEENTH PRESIDENT, TWO TERMS.)

Ulysses S. Grant was born at Point Pleasant, Clermont county, Ohio, April 27, 1822. He was very unwilling to follow his father's trade, which was that of a tanner, and, at seventeen, an appointment was secured for him at West Point. His name having been wrongly registered, Grant vainly attempted to set the matter right, but finally accepted his "manifest destiny," assumed the change thus forced upon him, and thenceforth signed himself "Ulysses Simpson," the latter being his mother's family name. Two years after completing his four years' course as cadet, the Mexican war broke out, in which Grant conducted himself with great gallantry, receiving especial mention and promotion. In 1847 he was made first-lieutenant, captain in 1853, and in 1854 he resigned his commission, and entered the leather and saddlery business at Galena, Illinois, in 1859, where he remained until the opening of the war in 1861, when he immediately offered his services in behalf of the Union. His modesty and diffidence delayed their acceptance, and Governor Yates, of Illinois, was the first to avail himself of them. Grant finally took the field as Colonel of the Twenty-first Regiment Illinois Volunteers. In February, 1862, he was made a major-general, and commanded the armies of the South-west. On the 12th of March, 1864, he was made lieutenant-general and put in command of all the armies, and took personal direction of the military operations in Virginia, and, on the 9th of April, 1865, General Lee surrendered the Confederate armies to him, at Appomattox Court House, and hostilities were ended.

He was nominated and elected by the Republicans President of the United States in 1868, and re-elected by the same party in 1872, and is now the present incumbent. His term expires in 1877.

MOLINE—Continued.

SMITH & CASSEL,
Dealers in Hardware, Stoves, House Furnishing Goods, Gas Fixtures & Tuning.
216 & 218 Main Street.

LIVERY STABLE.
HARWOOD, H., Livery Sale & Feed Stable.
Main st., near R dman ave.

MEAT MARKET.
GRANTZ, C. F., City Meat Market,
214 Main st.

PHOTOGRAPHER.
PEAL, CHAS., Photographer,
124 Wells st.

RESTAURANT.
PIERCE BROS., Restaurant,
232 Main st.

TAILORS.
OLESON & LOFQUIST, Merchant Tailors,
306½ Main st., near Reese Hotel.
OSTLUND, A., Merchant Tailor, Clothes Cleaned and Hats dressed, 200 Main st.
YOUNGBURG, L. J., Merchant Tailor,
Railroad ave., opp. C. & R. I. Depot.

WAGON MANUFACTURERS.

MOLINE WAGON CO.,
Manufacturers of the

Moline Wagon,
Farm & Spring Wagons, Buggies & Carriages.
NEAR C. & R. I. Depot.

WATCHES AND JEWELRY.
A. B. SHERMAN,
Watches, Clocks & Jewelry
240 MAIN STREET.

ROCK ISLAND, ILLS.

ATTORNEY AT LAW.
WM. W. RATHBUN,
Attorney & Counselor at Law & Notary Public,
S. W. Cor. Second ave., & 17th st.

BAKERY AND CONFECTIONERY.
WM. NEPKA,
Bakery and Confectionery, School Books, Toys and Notions.
1002 THIRD AVENUE.

BARBER.
HARDY, E., Tonsorial Artist,
4th ave., near 22d st.

ROCK ISLAND—*Continued.*

CARRIAGES AND BUGGIES.

GEORGE A. BAIN & CO.,
Manufacturers of
LIGHT, OPEN AND TOP BUGGIES,
Painting, Repairing, &c.
17TH ST., NEAR 3RD AV.

DRESSMAKER.

FRENCH, M., Modiste,
Rock Island.

DRUGGISTS.

E. BREUNERT,
Harper House Drug Store,
Wholesale & Retail Dealer in
Fine Drugs, Chemicals, Druggists Sundries, Paints, Oils, Paint Brushes, &c.

FANCY GOODS.

SOUTHARD, S. L., Ladies' & Gents' Variety Store, 1324 Third ave.

FLOUR AND FEED.

WM. A. PILGRIM,
Dealer in Flour, and Feed, Baled Hay and Straw, Fruits and Vegetables always on Hand.
1203 THIRD AVE, Cor. 12th ST.

FURNITURE.

G. A. DOELLINGER,
Parlor & Chamber Furniture,
1506 to 1510 SECOND AVENUE.

GROCERIES.

J. B. CARGILL,
Grocer and Commission Merchant, and Dealer in Fruits, Vegetables, Butter, &c.
Cor. THIRD AVE., & FOURTEENTH ST.

ZEIS, JUSTUS, Groceries & Provisions,
17th st., near 4th ave.

GUNSMITH.

WOLFF, CHAS., Gunsmith, and dealer in Guns & Sporting Utensils, 17th st., opp. P. O.

INSURANCE AGENTS.

Hayes & Cleaveland,
GENERAL INSURANCE AG'TS,
Office, Bengston's Block.

LIVERY STABLE.

JOHN EVANS,
LIVERY AND BOARDING STABLE,
18th st. bet. 1st & 2d ave.

POTTERY.

HAVERSTICK, L. M., Man'f'r of Yellow and Rockingham ware, 9th st.

[NINETEENTH PRESIDENT.]

Rutherford B. Hayes was born at Delaware, Ohio, October 4, 1822. He graduated at Kenyon College, Ohio. He commenced the practice of law in Cincinnati in his thirty-fourth year, when he received his first official position as City Solicitor, which he held till the war broke out in 1861. Very near its opening he enlisted in the Twenty-third Ohio volunteers, and served with the regiment till he received the command of a brigade in 1864. His first appointment was as Major, his first promotion came within less than a year, and in September of 1862 he held a commission as Lieutenant-Colonel, and was in command of his regiment, which he led into the battle of South Mountain. During the battles of the Army of Potomac, Colonel Hayes received a severe wound in the arm, but remained with his regiment to the last, and was the first officer whose command established a position at South Mountain. Two years later he had became Brigadier-General Hayes, and was elected to Congress from the second Ohio district by the Republicans. In the fall of 1866, Mr. Hayes was nominated and elected to Congress a second time by the Republicans, but Congress had held but one session, when he was nominated and elected Govenor of Ohio by the same party. During his political career, he was three times elected Govenor of Ohio, and twice a Member of Congress. A reference to the "Important Events" in 1876-77, will be found the particulars of his election to the Presidency of the United States in 1877. Mr. Hayes took the oath of office on Saturday the 3d of March, and was inaugurated President of the United States, Monday the 5th of March. Pending the time of the election and before the meeting of the electoral commission, the country was greatly agitated and seemed threatened with civil war, but immediately after his inauguration quiet and confidence was restored and peace reigned through out the United States.

ROCK ISLAND—*Continued.*

PUMPS.

CANDEE, AMES & CO.,
Manufacturers of Common Wood Pumps, also, Patent Porcelain Lined Pumps, 1st avenue, opposite St. Louis Depot. Correspondence solicited.

REAL ESTATE.

LEWIS CHRISMAN,
REAL ESTATE & LOAN AGENCY,
Farms and Farm Lands for sale or exchange,
17th st., near 3d ave.

RESTAURANT.

DRUBE, L., Restaurant & Ice Cream Rooms,
1816 2d ave.

SAWS AND SAUSAGE STUFFERS.

Established 1857.
D. DONALDSON,
Manufacturer of Saws, Sausage Stuffers and Rockers, plain and corrugated iron doors and shutters, 4th ave., near 16th st.

STOVES AND TINWARE.

O. M. GROSS,
Dealer in Stoves, Furnaces, Ranges, Tinware, House-furnishing Goods, Sheet-iron and Copper work, 1009 3d ave.

HOLDORF, Stoves & Tinware,
4th ave., near 21st st.

SAWYER, N. B., Manf'r and dealer in Glass and Tinware, 1618 1st ave.

TAILORS.

JOHN WOLLENHAUPT,
Custom Tailor,
1105 3d ave., near 11th st. Cloths, Cassimeres and Vestings, of latest styles, at Eastern prices, on hand.

ZIMMER & STEGEMANN, Merchant Tailors,
1903 Second ave.

UNDERTAKER.

MERRILL, L., Undertaker,
1504 2d ave.

WAGON MAKERS.

STECKFUS, B. & SON., Wagon Shop & Horse-shoeing. cor. 4th ave and 9th st.

WATCHES AND CLOCKS.

SCHMID, D., Watches, Clocks, Jewelry, etc,
1805 2d ave.

DAVENPORT, IOWA.

AGRICULTURAL IMPLEMENTS.

PARMELL & HURD,
Manufacturer's agents for the Archer Rake, and McSherry Seeder, for Iowa, Nebraska and Dakota, 314 Harrison st.

ARCHITECTS.

CLAUSEN, F. G., Architect,
207 W. 3d st.

DAVENPORT—*Continued.*

ABSTRACT AND CONVEYANCING.

BROWN'S
ABSTRACT and CONVEYANCING OFFICE,
230 Main st.

B. W. GARTSIDE,
Architect and Superintendent of Building,
N. E. COR. 3d & BRADY STS.

ATTORNEYS AT LAW.

CLARK & HEYWOOD,
ATTORNEYS AND COUNSELORS,
214 MAIN ST.

COOK & RICHMAN,
ATTORNEYS
—AND—
Counselors at Law,
N. W. COR. 3d & MAIN STS.

NASH, D. B., Attorney at Law, U. S. Com. & Reg. in Bankruptcy, 207 Main st.

PORTER, SAMUEL, Attorney at Law,
Room 7, Cutter's Block, Brady st.

TWOMEY & STUYVESANT, Attorneys at Law,
Cor. Brady & 2d sts.

BLACKSMITHS.

VILLWOCK & STRATHMANN, Blacksmithing,
822 W. 2d st.

BOOTS AND SHOES.

GRUENAU, P. H., Boots & Shoes, custom work a specialty, 408 W. 2d st.

PATO, F. E., Centennial Boot & Shoe Shop,
115 E. 2d st.

CEMENT PIPE WORKS.

DAVIS & CAMP, Cement Pipe Works, Marble & Granite Monuments, 234 E. 3d st.

COMMISSION MERCHANT.

HARDING, P. B., Com. Merchant and dealer in Barley, cor 2d ave. and Harrison st.

COOPER STOCK.

STEFFEN BROS., dealers in Cooper Stock,
528 W. 2d st.

DYEING AND SCOURING.

AUG. SEBELIEN'S
Iowa State Steam Dye and Cleansing Works and Repairing Establishment, 223 Perry street, between 2d and 3d sts.

ELASTIC HAND STAMP.

T. S. Buck & Co.,
Manufacturers of the Patent Improved
ELASTIC HAND STAMP,
128 EAST THIRD ST.

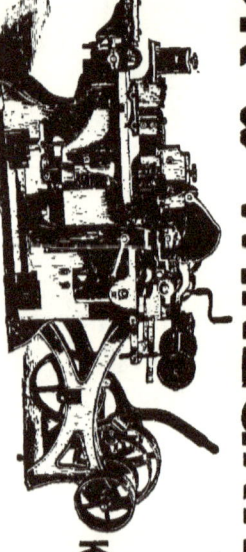

IMPROVED NINE INCH MOLDER.

KERRICK & WINEGARDNER,

Wood and Iron Working MACHINERY,
Of Every Description.

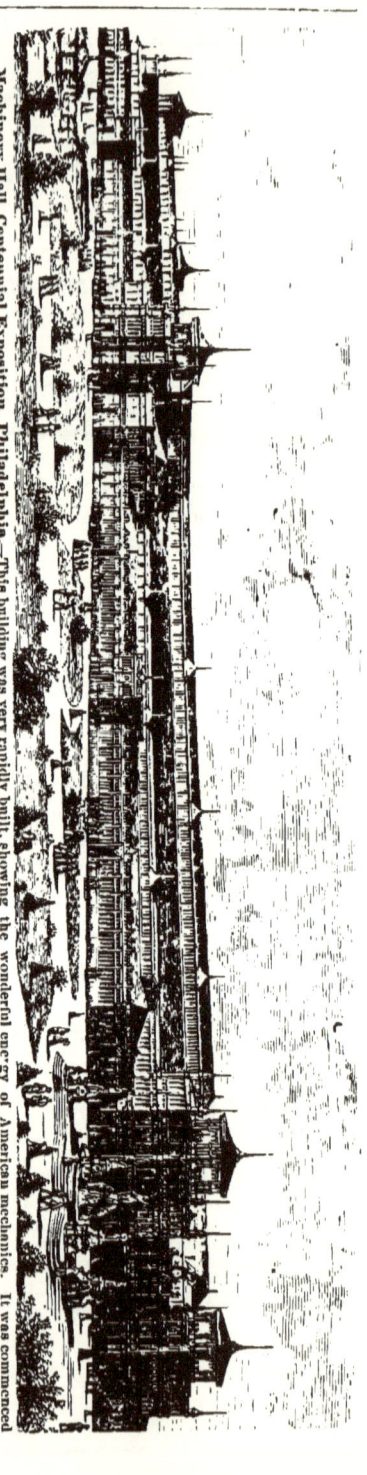

Machinery Hall, Centennial Exposition, Philadelphia.—This building was very rapidly built, showing the wonderful energy of American mechanics. It was commenced April 13th, 1875, and, on the 4th day of July following, it was so far completed as to enable a monster gathering of 50,000 people to assemble beneath its roof, to celebrate, in appropriate manner, the natal day of our independence. The building is 360 feet wide by 1,402 feet long, with an annex on the south side of 208 by 210 feet. The entire area covered is 558,440 square feet, or 1.32 acres, exclusive of the upper floors. Sixteen lines of shafting, running almost the entire length of the building, and counter-shafts introduced into the aisles, at almost every point, are placed in position. Twelve lengths of the shafting is run at a speed of 120 revolutions, and four lengths at a speed of 240 revolutions per minute. Cost of structure, $722,000.

WE DEFY COMPETITION.

SEND FOR PRICE LIST.

KERRICK & WINEGARDNER
63 and 65 West Maryland Street,
INDIANAPOLIS, IND.

DAVENPORT—Continued.

FURNITURE.

STEPHENSON, J., Man'f'r and Repairer of Furniture, 612 Brady st.

GROCERIES.

HOFFMANN, J. V., Groceries, Fruit & Vegetables, 510 W. 2d st.

TANK, R. H., Groceries, Spices, etc.,
502 Brady st.

GUNSMITH.

HENRY BERG,

GUNSMITH

And dealer in Muzzle and Breech-Loading Shot Guns, Rifles, Pistols and Sporting Apparatus, 230 3d st., cor. Harrison st.

HAIR WORK.

DE VINNY, R. E., MRS., Man'f'r of Hair Work and Hair Jewelry, 117 Main st.

HARDWARE.

SIEG & WILLIAMS, Iron & Heavy Hardware,
Cor 3d & Main sts.

HARNESS AND SADDLES.

G. G. HILLER,

329 Harrison street, Manufacturer of and dealer in Harness, Saddles. Collars, Bridles, Whips, Halters, Combs, Brushes, etc. All work warranted. Uncle Sam's Harness Oil always on hand.

HORSESHOEING.

BARRETT, PAT., Horseshoeing Shop,
325 Harr'son st.

METROPOLITAN HORSESHOEING SHOP,
302 Third st., cor. Rock Island st.,
Snyder & Shado, props. Particular attention paid to Diseased Feet, Interfering, Forging, Knee Cutting, etc.

INSURANCE.

NORTHWESTERN MUTUAL LIFE INS. CO., I. T. Martin, State agt. for Iowa and Nebraska.

LIVERY STABLE.

FISHER & HEBERT, Livery, Sale & Feed Stable,
209 to 213 W. 3d st.

MARBLE WORKS.

DAVIS & CAMP, Marble Works & Cement Pipe Works, 224 E. 3d st.

MILLINERY AND DRESSMAKING.

McCUTCHEON & SOLOMON,

DRESS AND CLOAK MAKING,
Stamping and Machine Embroidery,
312 PERRY ST.

SNYDER & CURTIS,

Millinery, Fancy Goods & Dressmaking,
309 BRADY ST.

PHYSICIANS.

BAKER, J. F., Physician and Surgeon,
Cor. 3d and Brady sts.

CANTWELL, A. W., Physician and Surgeon,
217 Brady st.

IMPORTANT INVENTIONS

AND

IMPROVEMENTS!

Achromatic Lens.—By Dolland, 1758.

Air Brakes.—Invented by George Westinghouse in 1869; improved by John W. Gardiner, 1872; by Henderson, 1872; by Carl Fogelberg, 1872. Prior to Westinghouse some inventions had been patented as air brakes in England, but his was the first successful and used air brake.

Air Engine.—Invented by Glazebrook in 1797; improved by Medhurst in 1799; by Ericsson, 1851; by Augin and Crocker, 1864; by Mowbray, 1864; by Pease, 1865; by Baldwin, 1865.

Air Gun.—Invented by Shaw in 1849.

Amalgamator.—Invented by Varney, 1852; improved by Hill, 1861; by Coleman, 1863; Wheeler, 1863; Heath, 1863; Dodge, 1864; Brodie, 1864; Moore, 1865; Peck, 1865; Charles, 1866; Staats, 1866.

Aneroid Barometer.—Invented by Conte in 1798.

Apple Parer.—Invented by Contes, 1803; improved by Gates in 1810; by Mitchell, 1838; by Pratt in 1853.

Argand Lamp.—Invented by Amie Argand in 1784.

Armor Plating for vessels and forts.—Invented by J. B. Love, 1861; improved by W. W. Wood, 1862; by J. L. Jones, 1862; by Heaton, 1863; by L. D. Carpenter, 1865.

Armstrong Gun.—Invented by Armstrong, 1855.

Battery Gun.—Invented by Gatling, 1861; by Hardy, 1862; by Taylor, 1871; by Dodge, 1856.

Bessemer Steel.—Invented by H. Bessemer in 1856, and improved by him in 1861 and 1862.

Blast Furnace.—Invented by Detmold in 1842; improved by VanDyke in 1860.

Electro-Magnet.—Invented by Sturgeon in 1825.

Beer.—Ale invented 1404 B. C.; ale-booths set up in England 728, and laws passed for their regulation. Beer first introduced into England 1492; in Scotland as early as 1482. By the statute of James I, one full quart of the best beer or ale was to be sold for one penny, and two quarts of small beer for one penny.

Boot Crimper.—Invented by Moore in 1812.

Bows and arrows introduced in 1066.

Breech Loading Fire Arms—Invented by Thornton and Hall in 1811; improved by C. H. Ballard in 1851; A. A. Chassepot, 1867.

Breech Loading Fire Arms.—Invented by H. Harrington in 1837; improved by I. Adams in 1838; by C. Sharp in 1848.

Bread.—First made with yeast in England in the year 1754; the quarter loaf was sold for

DAVENPORT—Continued.

E. H. HAZEN, M. D.,
SPECIALTY EYE AND EAR,
Office at his Infirmary, cor. 6th & Brady sts.
Established 1867.

REAL ESTATE AGENTS.

O CHS, JOHN & SONS, Real Estate Agents,
Cor. Harrison & 2nd sts.

RESTAURANT.

C ONKLIN, JOHN, Restaurant & Ice Cream Saloon, 109 Main st.

SEWING MACHINES.

E. W. ALLEN,
Wholesale and Retail dealer in the Wilson Shuttle Sewing Machines and all kinds of needles and attachments. All kinds of machines repaired. 209 MAIN STREET.

STOVES AND TINWARE.

F ROSCHLE, L., Stoves and Tinware,
219 W. Third st.

REIMERS & BRAUCH,
Dealers in
Stoves and House Furnishing Goods,
414 W. SECOND STREET.

TAILORS.

F REBERG, GUSTAV, Tailor, Cleaning and Repairing, 316 Perry.

P. A. HALLING,
Merchant Tailor,
310 PERRY STREET.

P ERRY, SAM, Merchant Tailor, Gents' Furnishing Goods. &c., 113 Brady st.

THOMPSON & BAHLS,
MERCHANT TAILORS,
And Dealers in Fine Cloths, Cassimeres and Vestings.   118 East Third Street.

TOBACCO AND CIGARS.
Established 1863.

RAMMELSBERG & PRIESTER,
Manufacturers and Wholesale Dealers in Tobaccos and Cigars.
406 West Second Street.

TURKISH BATHS.

THOMAS C. BAIRD,
TURKISH BATHS,
Cor. Fifth & Brady Sts.

WAGON MAKER.

T ECHENTIN, F. J., Wagon Maker. Repairing promptly done. 814 W. 2nd st.

WATCHMAKER AND JEWELER.

N EWBERN, J. F., Watchmaker and Jeweler.
107 W. 3 d st.

about 8 cents; three years after, it rose to about 20 cents, and in March, 1800, to about 34 cents, when new bread was forbidden, under the penalty of $1.20 per loaf, if the baker sold it until 24 hours old.

Bridge.—The first stone one, in England, at Bow, near Stratford, in 1087.

Buckles.—Invented about this time in 1680.

Calicos.—First made in Lancashire in 1771.

Carte de Visite.—(Photographic) first made by M. Ferrier, in Paris, 1857.

Carronades.—Invented by Gen. Melville in 1779.

Cast Iron Plow.—Invented by Newbold in 1797.

Cannon.—Invented in 1330, and were first used by the English in 1346; first used in England in 1445; first made of iron in England in 1547; of brass, in 1635. Cannon first used in ships of war in 1539.

Coal.—Was discovered in 1234 near Newcastle; first dug at Newcastle by a charter granted the town by Henry III.; first used in 1280 by driers, brewers, etc. In the reign of Edward I., began to use sea-coal for fire in 1350, and he published a proclamation against it in 1398 as a public nuisance.

Chimneys.—First introduced into buildings in the year of 1200. In England only in the kitchen, or large hall, where the family sat round a large stove, the funnel of which passed through the ceiling, 1300.

Collodion.—Use in photography. Originated by F. S. Archer in 1851.

Concrete Pavement.—Invented by Straub, 1863; improved by Prescott, 1872; Bellamy, 1875.

Corn Sheller.—Invented by Phinney in 1815; improved by James in 1819.

Cotton Gin.—Invented by Eli Whitney in 1793. The result of the invention was the making of cotton the great American staple. Improved by Whipple, 1840; by Parkhurst, 1845.

Circular Saw.—Invented by General Bentham, in England, in 1790; improved by Trotter, 1804; by Brunel, 1805 and 1809.

Curved Stereotype Plates.—Invented by Cowper in 1815.

Cutting Glass by Sand Blast.—Invented by B. C. Telghman, 1870.

Cut-off for Steam Engines.—Invented by Sickles in 1841.

Daguerreotype.—Definite experiments looking to the production of a picture by the action of light upon a sensitized surface were made as early as 1802, but the production of a permanent picture was not accomplished until 1838, by M. Daguerre, an optician of Paris, France, from whom such pictures were named.

Dahlgren Gun.—Invented by Admiral Dahlgren, U. S. Navy, 1801.

Davy Lamp, for miners.—Invented by Sir Humphrey Davy, in 1815.

Diving Bell.—Invented in 1838.

Drummond Light (Lime Light).—Invented by Lieut. Drummond in 1826.

Earth Closets.—Invented by Moule & Girdlestone in 1860.

Ebonite Hard Rubber).—Invented by Charles Goodyear in 1849.

MUSCATINE, IOWA.

AGRICULTURAL IMPLEMENTS.

RAFF, A. K. & CO., Standard Farm Machinery,
Cor. 2nd & Walnut sts.

ATTORNEYS AT LAW.

D. C. CLOUD,

ATTORNEY AT LAW,
IOWA AVENUE.   Established 1845.

(Established 1861.)
ALLEN BROOMHALL,
Attorney at Law and Examiner of Titles. Has Complete Abstract Books.

(Established 1857.)
D. M. LAMBERT,

ATTORNEY AT LAW,
REAL ESTATE BROKER,
Butler's Block.

H. J. LAUDER.   J. M. DORAN.
LAUDER & DORAN,
ATTORNEYS
MUSCATINE, IOWA.

J. E. STEVENSON,
Attorney at Law, will practice in Muscatine and Cedar counties; Examine and Furnish Abstracts of Titles; and attend to Conveyancing, Pay Taxes, making Collections, &c. Established 1872.

WESTERN BOUNTY AND PENSION AGENCY.
L. H. Washburn.
Attorney at Law and Solicitor for Pension and Bounty Claimants. Send stamp for pamphlet, showing who are entitled to pensions & Bounties.

BAKER AND CONFECTIONER.

CHRIS. RUCKDESCHEL,
Baker and Confectioner, Graham Block. Fresh Bread, Cakes and Pies. Ice Cream Room open at all reasonable hours; Oysters in their season. Full stock of Fresh Confectionery—the finest in the city.

BLACKSMITHING.

DAWSON, ELI, Horse-shoeing & Blacksmithing,
Cor. 2nd & Mulberry.   Est. 1873.

JACOB ELICKER,
General Blacksmithing and Carriage Ironing,
Cor. Third & Mulberry sts.   Established 1870.

FARRELL & SCHRODER,
Manufacturer of Farm Wagons and Buggies. Horse Shoeing a Specialty. General Blacksmithing done, and all work warranted.
S. W. COR. SECOND & MULBERRY STS.

MUSCATINE—*Continued.*

MACKEY & FAHEY, General Blacksmithing,
Third st,   Est. 1836.

BLANK BOOKS.

G. SCHMIDT & BRO.,
Dealers in Pianos, Organs, Melodeons, General Musical Merchandise, Blank Books, Stationery, Wall Paper, Curtain Goods, Chromos, &c. Blank Books made to order. Magazines, Music, &c., neatly bound. Second St., near Bridge. Est. 1862.

BOOKS AND STATIONERY.

(Established 1862.)
DEMOREST & COE,
Wholesale and Retail dealers in Books and Stationery, also Pianos and Organs,
170 SECOND STREET.

BOOTS AND SHOES.

SCHWARTZ, L., Boot & Shoe Maker,
Mulberry st.   Est. 1874.

BREWERY.

MRS. MARIA EIGENMANN,
Muscatine Brewery
COR. 7TH & MULBERRY STS.   Est. 1859.

BROOM MANUFACTURER.

HAGERMANN, HENRY, Broom Manufacturer,
Cor. Mulberry & 6th sts.

CARPENTERS AND BUILDERS.

PARVIN, D. J. & CO., Carpenters & Builders,
Cor. 3rd & Cedar sts.   Est. 1866.

CARRIAGES AND BUGGIES.

JOS. P. AMENT, JR.,
Manufacturer of
Carriages, Buggies & Phaetons,
THIRD STREET.

BLOCKERT, CHRISTIAN, Carriage and Wagon Manufacturer, Mulberry st.   Est. 1853.

GROSCHEL & KNOWLES, Manufacturers Carriages, Buggies, Spring Wagons, &c. Iowa av.

COMMISSION MERCHANTS.

J. J. & S. BOWMAN,
Auction and Commission Merchants and dealers in Dry Goods, Notions, Horses, Harness, Wagons, Buggies, Second-Hand Furniture, &c., &c.
SECOND ST., next door to Graham's Drug Store.

CONFECTIONERY AND FRUITS.

CARL, J. H., Confectionery, Oysters, &c.,
Mulberry st., under the Park House.

JAS. E. MARSHALL,
Wholesale and Retail dealer in Confectionery, Foreign and Domestic Fruits, Nuts, &c., Fine Cigars and Tobacco.
EAST SECOND STREET.

DENTISTS.

C. H. STERNEMAN,
Dentist. Particular attention paid to the preservation of the natural teeth.
184 Second Street.   Established 1847.

KULP, J. S., Dentist,
145 2nd st.   Est. 1857.

IMPORTANT EVENTS OF THE CENTURY. 353

Feneuil Hall, the "Cradle of Liberty."—This building was presented to Boston by Peter Faneuil. It was erected in 1742 destroyed by fire in 1761, and immediately thereafter was rebuilt by the vote of the town. In 1805 it was enlarged to its present size, and until 1822 all town meetings of Boston were held within its walls. The hall is 76 feet square and 28 feet high. It is never let for money, but is at the disposal of the people, whenever a sufficient number of persons, complying with certain regulations, ask to have it opened. By a provision in the charter of Boston, it is forbidden the sale or lease of the hall.

Brattle Square Church, Boston—Was first built in 1699, was taken down in 1772, and the building just demolished, erected on the same spot, was dedicated on the 25th of July, 1773. During the Revolution the pastor, who was a patriot, was obliged to leave Boston, services were suspended and the British soldiers used the building as a barrack. A cannon-ball from a battery in Cambridge, or from a ship of war in the Charles river, struck the church, and this memento of the glorious contest was afterwards built into the external wall of the church, above the porch. The old church was sold in 871, and the last services was held in it July 30th, of that year. The ancient pulpit, the organ, the old bell, the historic cannon-ball, and some other mementoes, were reserved at the sale. A large business block now occupies the site of the church.

THE INVENTORS'
SCIENTIFIC & COMMERCIAL WORLD.

PROSPECTUS.

The *Scientific and Commercial World* is devoted to the interests of popular science, the mechanic arts, manufactures, inventions, agriculture, commerce, history, and interspersed with humerous matter to make the solid articles more digestable. It is valuable and instructive not only in the workshop and manufactory, but also in the household, the library and reading room, and as an advertising medium can not be surpassed.

Terms of Subscription.

One copy one year $1.00
One copy six months . Post free. .75
One copy four months .50

Remit by postal order, draft or express. Canada subscribers must remit 25 cents extra to pay postage. Terms in advance. Address all orders to

Wolverton & Connor,

216 East Washington Street,

INDIANAPOLIS, IND.

Barret House,

RICHARD A. BARRET, - - **Owner and Proprietor.**

STRICTLY FIRST-CLASS AS TO CUISINE, ROOMS & APPURTENANCES
Five stories. Fire escapes perfect. Graduated prices—

$3.00, $2.50 & $2.00 PER DAY.

The favorite Hotel of Burlington. Every room is light, airy and well ventilated. *New Paint, New Paper, New Management. No Runners. Extensively repaired, remodeled and renovated.*

ADVERTISEMENTS. 355

Smithsonian Institution, Washington, D. C.—This building is constructed of red freestone, and has numerous towers. Its length from east to west is 447 feet, and breadth including carriage porch, 160 feet. The corner-stone was laid in 1847, and the building completed in 1856. It cost $450,000. The Institution is a bequest of James Smithson, an English gentlemen, who bequeathed $515,169 for the construction of the building. Here are deposited collections of all the exploring expeditions of the United States, besides all other sorts of curiosites, which would require weeks to examine.

MUSCATINE.—*Continued.*

H ARDMAN, JOSEPH, Dentist,
E. 2nd st., near Bridge. Est. 1851.

DRUGGISTS.

OLDS & REPPERT,
Druggists, dealers in none but strictly pure Drugs and Medicines.
Cor. 2nd St., & Iowa Ave.   Established 1877.

DRY GOODS.

F OWLER BROS., Staple and Fancy Dry Goods,
Old's Block, 2nd st.

GROCERIES.

J. W. BERRY,
GROCERIES AND PROVISIONS,
E. Second Street.   Established 1872.

MARTIN H. BITZER,
Dealer in Groceries, Rents Property and Makes Collections.
2nd St., Opp. National Hotel.   Established 1855.

G EISENHAUS, FRED., Groceries & Provisions,
216 Second st.

C. F. KESSLER,
Groceries and Provisions,
COR. MULBERRY AND FIFTH STS.

W ILSON, J. A., Groceries, &c.,
203 2nd st.   Est. 1851.

HARNESS AND SADDLES.

J. H. HERWIG
Manufacturer of Harness, Saddles and Collars,
EAST SECOND ST,

MUSCATINE—*Continued.*

HOTELS.

Commercial House,
J. W. VARNER, Agent,
J. M. Van Patten, Clerk.   MUSCATINE.

NATIONAL HOUSE,
JACOB BOWMAN, Proprietor,
Free Carriage to and from the house, also baggage free.
COR. SECOND AND WALNUT STS.

PARK HOUSE,
JAMES F. STEVENS, Proprietor,
Corner Fourth and Mulberry streets.

JUSTICE OF THE PEACE.

GEO. MEASON,
JUSTICE OF THE PEACE
145 Second st.   Established 1852.

LUMBER.

G ARLOCK, J. S., Lumber, Laths, Shingles,
Doors, Blinds, etc., 236 Second st.

MILLINERY AND DRESSMAKING.

D E MOSS, NELLIE, Dressmaker
E. Second st.   Established 1870.

H AWLEY, MRS. G. R., Dress & Cloakmaking,
E. Second st.

Electric Light.—Invented by Stalte & Petrie about 1846; improved by Jules Dubosq in 1855; by M. Lerrin, 1862; by Holmes, 1858; by Dumas & Benoît, 1862.
Electric Loom.—Invented by G. Bonelli, of France, 1853.
Electro-Magnetic Governor.—Invented by Phelps in 1858.
Electro-Magnetic Needle.—Invented by Oersted in 1819.
Elevated Railway.—Invented by Sargent in 1825; improved by Andrew in 1861.
Electrotype.—Invented by Spencer in 1837; improved by Prof. Jacobs in 1838; by Robt. Murray in 1840.
Fairbanks' Platform Scales.—Invented by Thaddeus Fairbanks, 1831.
Fairs and Markets.—First instituted in 886 in England by Alfred. The first fairs took their rise from wakes, when the number of people then assembled brought together a variety of traders annually on these days. From these holidays they were called fairs.
Gas Meter.—Invented by H. Robinson, 1831.
Gun Cotton.—Invented by M. Schonbein in 1845-46.
Gutta Percha Manufacture.—Invented by Dr. Montgomery in 1843.
Harvesters.—Invented by Palmer & Williams, 1851; improved by Cyrenus Wheeler in 1852; by Densmore, 1852; Dove, 1859; Kirby 1859; Mayall, 1859; Manny, 1875.
Hats.—First made in London in 1510.
High Towers.—First high towers or steeples erected on churches in 1000.
Howitzer.—Invented by Colonel Pacham in 1822.
Ice Making Machine.—Invented by Carre in 1860; improved by David Boyle, 1872; by Martin & Beath, 1872; by Beath, 1875.
Illuminating Gas (manufacture of).—Invented by L. Entros and W. Zigler in 1815; improved by Ward & Hall in 1821; by J. Boston in 1831.
India Rubber Manufacture.—Invented by Chaffee in 1836; improved by Charles Goodyear in 1844.
Inhaling Ether to Prevent Pain.—Discovered by W. T. G. Morton, 1846.
Jacquard Loom (for weaving figured fabrics).—Invented by Jacquard, of France, in 1800.
Knitting Machine.—Invented by Hooton in 1776; improved by Lamb, 1865.
Knives first made in England in 1563.
Lamp for preventing explosion by fire-damp in coal mines, first invented in 1815.
Lanterns first invented by King Alfred in 890.
Leaden Pipes for carrying water invented in 1236.
Life-boats invented in 1802.
Lead Pipe Machine.—Invented by T. Alderson, 1804; improved by Dobbs, 1820; by Hague, 1822.
Lightning Rods.—Invented by Benjamin Franklin, Patriot, Philosopher and Statesman, in 1752.
Liquid Meter.—Invented by Pontifex in 1824. Improved by Fice.

MUSCATINE—*Continued.*

MRS. WM. WHITE,
MILLINERY AND NOTIONS,
SECOND ST.

PAINTERS.

EMIL GROSCHEL,
CARRIAGE AND WAGON PAINTING,
Mulberry st., bet. 5th and 6th sts.

C. KIRSCH & BRO.,
House and Sign Painters, Grainers, Glaziers and Paper Hangers, shop on Cedar street, between 2d and 3d sts. The best material at the lowest possible prices. Mixed paints for sale cheap.

PHOTOGRAPHERS.

ALLEN & MULL,
PRACTICAL PHOTOGRAPHERS
E. Second st., over Burnett's Bookstore.

J. G. EVANS,
PHOTOGRAPHER,
Iowa ave. Large assortment of Stereoscopic Views of Muscatine and vicinity always on hand.

PHELPS, J. P., Artistic Photographer, Second st., over Post Office.

PHYSICIANS.

DEAN, H. M., Physician & Surgeon, cor. Second st. & Iowa ave., entrance on ave., Est. 1861.

FULLIAM, GEO. W., Physician,
194 Second st.

Dr. H. LINDNER,
German Physician,
SECOND STREET,
Two doors below National Bank. Est. 1854.

SMITH, CAL. W., Physician and Surgeon, Office, Masonic Building, 229 E. Second st.

PLUMBERS AND GASFITTERS.

N. BARRY & SON,
Plumbers, Gas and Steam Fitters,
E. SECOND ST., NEAR MULBERRY.

PUMPS.

MATHIS, C. W., Manf'r and dealer in Rubber Bucket Chain Pumps, E. Second st.

SMITH, R. A., Manf'r & wholesale dealer in Rubber Bucket Pumps, cor. 2d & Mulberry sts.

RESIDENCE

CADLE, CORNELIUS,
Front st., Block 16.

STOVES AND TINWARE.

PARVIN, WM. S., Stoves, Tinware, etc., Tin Roofing and Spouting, E. Second st.

TAILORS.

DELAHEN, JOHN, Tailor,
195 E. Second st. Established 1866.

IMPORTANT INVENTIONS AND IMPROVEMENTS. 357

MUSCATINE—Continued.

John G. Hoehl,
Fashionable **MERCHANT** Tailor,
E. SECOND ST., NEAR BRIDGE.
JOHN HOEHL, Jr., Cutter.

S CHOLTEN, D., Tailor,
E. 2d st. Established 1872.

TOBACCO AND CIGARS.

FERDINAND KAUFMANN,
Manufacturer of Cigars, and wholesale and retail dealer in Smoking and Chewing Tobaccos, Snuff, Pipes, and Smokers' Articles Generally, 200 Second st.

UNDERTAKERS.

J. P. FREEMAN & SON,
Undertakers, Cabinet Job Workers, and dealers in Metallic and Wooden Caskets, Second st., near Bridge st. Est. 1840.

WATCHES AND JEWELRY.

P. A. UMSTON,
Dealer in
Watches, Jewelry, Musical and
OPTICAL INSTRUMENTS, ETC.
☞ **Perfect Satisfaction Guaranteed.** ☜
E. Second Street, West side National House.
Established 1862.

LAWRENCE, KAS.

ATTORNEYS AT LAW.

C ORNING, CYRUS, Attorney at Law,
First National Bank Building.
E MERY, J. S., Attorney at Law,
134 Massachusetts st. Established 1857.
L AW OFFICE OF ALBERT KNITTLE, City Attorney, 95 Massachusetts st.
P ATTERSON, W. J., Attorney at Law,
National Bank Building. Established 1875.

BANK.

L AWRENCE SAVINGS BANK, Enoch Hoag, Prest.
John K. Rankin, Cashr, 32 Mass. st.

BARBERS.

A NTHONY, MARK, First-class Barber,
145 Warren st.
B RADLEY, E. L., Barber,
134 Massachusetts st. Estab. 1861.
M ITCHELL & JOHNSON, First-class Barbers,
Under National Bank.
T HOMAS, H. H., P. T. of F.,
136 Massachusetts st. Estab. 1876.

BLACKSMITHS.

DIMERY & SWEEZERY,
BLACKSMITHING,
Done in the best style, at low prices.
22 MASSACHUSETTS ST.
(Established 1875.)

Locomotive.—Invented by Trevethick in 1802. The improvements are too numerous to mention here.
Magic Lanterns.—Invented by Roger Bacon in 1252.
Magnifying Glasses.—Invented by Roger Bacon, in 1260.
Manufacture of Lampblack.—Invented by Mini in 1844.
Metallic Cartridge.—Invented by Cazalet in 1826; improved by Roberts, 1834; by Smith & Wesson, 1854-60.
Mettalic Washboards.—Invented by Rice, 1849.
Minie Rifle.—Invented by M. Minie, an officer in the French army, 1833.
Nail Machine.—Invented by Jeremiah Wilkinson in 1775; improved by Thomas Gifford in 1790; by Ezekiel Reed, 1786; by Benj. Cochran, 1794; by Haddock in 1870.
Needle Gun.—Invented by G. A. Blittkowskie and F. W. Hoffman in 1856.
Post-mark Stamp.—Invented by M. P. Norton in 1859.
Paper Bag Machine.—Invented by Francis Wolle in 1853; improved by E. W. Goodale in 1855; by Rice in 1857; by H. G. Armstrong in 1860.
Papier Mache.—Invented by Lefevre in 1740.
Parlor Skates.—Invented by Plympton in 1863; improved by Pollitt in 1870.
Parrott Gun.—Invented by Parrott in 1862.
Percussion Caps.—Came into use between 1820 and 1830, the inventor unknown.
Photolithography.—Invented by Osborn in 1861.
Rifle, Repeating.—Invented by C. Sharp in 1848; improved by G. Henry in 1852; by Spencer, 1848.
Planing Machine.—Invented by Woodworth in 1828; improved by Stover in 1861.
Power Loom.—Invented by Cartwright, 1785; improved by Bigelow, 1857; by Marshall, 1848.
Pneumatic Railway.—Invented by Pinkus in 1834; improved by Henry in 1845.
Puddling Furnace.—Invented by Henry Cort, about 1781; improved by Dank in 1875.
Reaper.—Invented by McCormick in 1834; improved by Hussey in 1847; Seymour in 1851, and numerous subsequent inventors.
Revolver.—Invented by Samuel Colt in 1836; improved by Sharp in 1850; Smith & Wesson, 1863; E. T. Starr, 1864; A. M. White, 1875; Kittridge, Palmer, Joslyn, Reynolds, Wood, 1864; Pettingill, 1859; T. Remington, 1863.
Rifle.—Invented by Whitworth about 1800.
R. R. Cars.—Invented by Knight in 1829; improved by Winans in 1834; by Imlay, 1873.
Scenes—First introduced into theatres 1533.
Seeding Machine.—Invented by Cahoon in 1857; improved by Brown, 1863.
Sewing Machine.—Invented by Thimmunier, a Frenchman, in 1834; improved by Elias Howe

LAWRENCE—Continued.

DR. W. S. RILEY,
Horseshoeing and Carriage Work
Neatly done. Veterinary surgeon.
52 VERMONT ST.

BOOTS AND SHOES.

HENRY FUEL,
BOOT

AND SHOE MAKER.

Custom Work made to order, repairing neatly done.

No. 10 Cor. Mass. and Pinkney sts.

MENGER, A. G., Boots & Shoes,
82 Massachusetts st. Estab. 1870.

CARPENTER AND BUILDER.

CRAMER, B. J., Carpenter & Joiner,
40 New Hampshire st.

CLOTHING.

HOUSE, J. & CO., Wholesale & Retail Clothiers,
79 Massachusetts st.

STEINBERG'S CLOTHING HOUSE, Men's, Youths' & Boys' Clothing, etc., 87 Massachusetts st.

COMMISSION MERCHANTS.

HOWARD BROS.,
General Commission Merchants,
And Shippers of Fruit and Produce,
157 Massachusetts st. Established 1876.

CONFECTIONERS.

MOORE BROS.,
MANUFACTUR'G CONFECTIONERS,
And dealers in Foreign & Domestic Fruits,
73 Massachusetts st. Established 1876.

WIEDEEMANN & SON, Confectioners, & dealers in Toys, 129 Massachusetts st. Est. 1868.

DENTIST.

WILSON, DR. F. H., Dentist,
135 Massachusetts st. Established 1871.

DRESSMAKERS.

MRS. NORA BALDWIN,
Emporium of Fashions, Patterns and Dressmaking Rooms, Agent for S. T. Taylor's System of Cutting Parisien Fashions & Styles.
133 Massachusetts St.

HUFFMAN, MISS S. E. & M., Fashionable Dressmakers, 127 Massachusetts st Estab. 1876.

LANHAM, MRS. L., Dressmaker,
117 Massachusetts st. Estab. 1877.

STARKWEATHER, MRS. M. J., Dressmaker,
135 Massachusetts st. Estab. 1871.

DRUGGISTS.

CHESTER, E. P., Druggist and Jeweler,
59 Massachusetts st. Estab. 1875.

LAWRENCE—Continued.

HENRY KELLERMAN,
DRUGGIST
149 Massachusetts St. Estab. 1875.

DYER AND SCOURER.

PEEL, GEO. W., Dyer and Scourer, (Established 1842,) 147 Massachusetts st.

FURNITURE.

HILL & MENDENHALL, Furniture Dealers and Undertakers, 46 & 48 Vermont st.

GOVERNMENT OFFICER.

NICHOLSON, WM., Superintendent of Indian Affairs, National Bank Building.

GROCERS.

CHAMBERLAIN, THOMAS, Grocer,
17 Massachusetts st. Estab. 1875.

GENTRY, ABRAM, Grocer and Dealer in Poultry,
171 Massachusetts st. Estab. 1874.

HENDERSON & WEIBER, Staple and Fancy Grocers. 43 Massachusetts st. Estab. 1876.

TUCKER, CHAS., Dealer in Groceries.
171 Massachusetts st. Estab. 1873.

GUNSMITH.

JAEDICKE, F. W., Manuf'r and Dealer in Breech and Muzzle-Loading Shot Guns, 74 Mass. st.

HARNESS AND SADDLES.

GROUT, A. D., Concord Harness Shop, Warren st., in rear of State Bank. Estab. 1877.

HARVESTING MACHINES.

I. N. VAN HOESEN,
McCormick's Harvesting Machines,
(ESTABLISHED 1866,)
160 MASSACHUSETTS ST.

HOTELS.

COMMERCIAL HOTEL, Cor. New Hampshire and Winthrop sts. $1.00 per day. J. A. Tilton, Prop.

DURFEE HOUSE
GEO. WELLS, Proprietor.
Price per Day, $2.00. Board by the Week at reduced rates.

GEO. WELLS,
ARCHITECT,
Public buildings a specialty. Plans and specifications furnished on short notice.

LIVERY AND SALE STABLE.

THOMAS, JOEL, Horses and Mules Bought and Sold, 166 Massachusetts st. Estab. 1856.

MARBLE WORKS.

PARNHAM & GRIGGS,
Dealers in Marble & Granite Monuments
180 Massachusetts St. Established 1867.

Canada Lumber Building, Centennial Exposition, Phila.—This building, as its name denotes, is built exclusively of Canada lumber, for the special purpose of displaying the lumber grown in that country. It is an open structure, supported by logs, within which is cut lumber, in almost every shape. In the center, as the illustration shows, is a large log from the pine forests of Canada, some seven feet in diameter.

LAWRENCE—*Continued.*

MILLINERY.

ORMES, MRS., Millinery Rooms,
133 Massachusetts st.

PAINTERS.

HARRIS & SNYDER, Painters, Graining, Glazing, Paper Hanging, &c., Winthrop st., near National Bank.

ROHR, A., Sign Painter and Pictorial Draughtsman, 11 Henry st.

PHYSICIANS.

ABDELAL, DR. A. G., Physician and Surgeon,
149 Massachusetts st. Estab. 1849.

DOBBINS, DR. R., Proprietor Turki h Bath and Electro-Medical Institute, 60 Vermont st.

RESTAURANTS AND SALOONS.

DELMONICO RESTAURANT.

Paul Suturius, Proprietor. No. 84 Massachusetts st. Boarding by Day or Week. Strangers supplied with good Lodging. Established 1872. On the European plan.

PERSON, OLOF, Bar-Room.
152 Massachusetts st. Estab. 1872.

LAWRENCE—*Continued.*

RUBBER GOODS.

SAGE, W. H., & CO., State Agents for Corey's Patent Elastic Expansion Rubber Pump Bucket, 159½ Massachusetts st. Established 1875.

VAIL, T. C., Dealer in Rubber Goods.
51 Massachusetts st. Estab. 1875.

STOVES AND TINWARE.

ROBERTS, S. A., Agent, Tinner, Steam Fitter and Plumber. 183 Massachusetts st. Est. 1869.

WATTS, SAM'L, & CO., Stoves, Tinware, &c.,
142 Massachusetts st.

TAILOR.

WEBER, A., Merchant Tailor,
134 Massachusetts st. Estab. 1870.

UPHOLSTER.

STRAFFON, R. J., Upholster,
Vermont st., bet. Henry & Warren.

VETERINARY SURGEON.

JAMES DAVIS,
HOSLER, FARIER AND BUTCHER,
No. 3 R. R. Stables, Massachusette St. Est. 1876.

in 1841; improved by Greenough, an American, 1842; by I. M. Singer, in 1850; by Elias Howe, in 1846; by A. B. Wilson, in 1851; by Grover and Baker, 1851; by T. E. Weed, 1851; Gibbs, 1857. Besides these there are on record the names of more than a thousand inventors of improvements in sewing machines.

Shoe Pegging Machine.—Invented by Gallahue, in 1858; improved by Standish and Miller in 1854; by Wardwell, 1854; by Batchelder, 1856; by Budlong, 1863; by Gallahue, 1853.

Shoes.—Of the present fashion first worn in England in 1633.

Sleeping Cars.—Invented by T. T. Woodruff in 1856; improved by Wheeler, 1859; by Field and Pullman, 1865; by Lucas, 1875.

Soda Water Apparatus.—Invented by North in 1775.

Spinning Mule.—Invented by Crompton in 1779, England.

Square Hole Auger.—Invented by Branch in 1826.

Spinning Jenny.—Invented by Hargreave, in 1764, England.

Steel Cannon.—First made by A. Krupp, 1849.

Steamboat.—Invented by Robert Fulton, in 1807, and his first trip was made in August of that year, from New York to Albany.

Steam Fire Engine.—Invented by Captain Ericsson, in 1830; and improved by him, 1842-43.

Steam Hammer.—Invented by James Nasmyth, in 1838.

Steam Plough.—Invented by John Fowler, 1864.

Steam Printing Press—Rotary.—Invented by Hoe, 1842; improved by G. P. Gordon, 1850; W. Bullock, 1867.

Steam Printing Press—Reciprocating Bed.—Invented by Seth Adams, 1830.

Steam Winding Watch.—Invented by T. Noel, in 1851.

Steel Pen.—Invented about 1820.

Stereoscope.—Invented by Charles Wheatstone, in 1838.

Stereotype Printing.—Invented by William Ged, a goldsmith, of Edinburgh, Scotland, in 1735.

Street Sweeper.—Invented by R. A. Smith, in 1855.

Tallow Candles.—First used in 1290, and were so great a luxury that splinters of wood were used for lights. There was no idea of wax candles in the year 1300.

Theater Seat (to turn up out of the way).—Invented by A. A. Allen, 1854.

Telegraph—Fire Alarm.—Invented by Farmer and Channing, about 1846; improved by John W. Gamewell, 1871; by M. G. Crane, 1875; by H. W. Spang, 1875; by L. H. McCullough.

Telegraph—Electro Chemical.—Invented by Baine, England, 1849.

Telegraph—Electro-Magnetic.—Invented by L. F. B. Morse, in 1837; improved by same, 1840; Edison (duplex), 1875.

Telegraph—Electric Needle.—Invented by Cooke & Wheatstone, 1837, England.

LAWRENCE—*Continued.*

WINES AND LIQUORS.

THEODORE HANSEN,
Successor to Rampendahl & Hansen, Wholesale dealer in Fine Bourbon, and Rye Whiskies, California Wine Dept.
185 Massachussetts St.,   Established 1870

LEXINGTON, MO.

BOOTS AND SHOES.

F. KLUG,
Fashionable
Boot & Shoe Maker,
Laurel St., - LEXINGTON, Mo.

DENTIST.

HASSELL, J. F. D. D. S., Surgeon Dentist,
Main st.

FEMALE COLLEGE.

BAPTIST FEMALE COLLEGE, A. F. Fleet, A. M., President. Lexington.

HOTEL.

BOURBON HOUSE,

T. S. CHANDLER, - - - Proprietor.

First Class Accommodations and Low Prices.
The Family Hotel of Lexington.
Terms, $1.50 per Day; $7 per Week.

MEAT MARKET.

ZEILER, JOHN W., Meat & Vegetable Market,
49 Main st.

NEWSPAPER.

THE LEXINGTON INTELLIGENCER
Official County Paper.

Only Democratic Paper in the County. Circulation Larger than any other Country Paper in the State. Lafayette County gives 2,500 Democratic Majority upon a Full Poll of the Vote.

PHYSICIANS AND SURGEONS.

BOLTON, T. L., M. D., Eclectic Physician Surgeon,
71 Main st.

(Established 1851.)

JAMES G. RUSSELL, M. D.,
Lafayette County Physician.

Physician and Surgeon.
Office Hours.
8 to 12 A. M.,   **45 MAIN STREET.**
1 to 6 P. M.

YOUNG, G. W., Physician and Surgeon,
Lexington, Mo.

IMPORTANT INVENTIONS AND IMPROVEMENTS. 361

LEXINGTON—*Continued.*

TAILORS.

CHARLES STUART,
MERCHANT TAILOR,
45 Main Street, . LEXINGTON, MO.

☞ Repairing and Cleaning neatly done.

GALENA, ILLS.

ATTORNEYS AT LAW.

ROWLEY, W. R. & L. A., Attorneys at Law, Abstract & Insurance Office, Main st. Est. 1872.

SPARE, E. O., Attorney at Law. Collections a Specialty, Main & Ferry sts. Est. 1875.

AGRICULTURAL IMPLEMENTS.

(Established 1847.)

JOHN ADAMS,
Manufacturer and Dealer in

PLOWS & AGRICULTURAL IMPLEMENTS
FRANKLIN STREET.

Established 1877.

JENKINS & PALMER,
Dealers in

FARM IMPLEMENTS
Musical Instruments, Wind Mills, Pumps, &c.,
256 MAIN ST., Opp. LOGAN HOUSE.

SPARE, J. C., Farm Machinery, Hides & Pelts, 209 Main st.

BAKERY.

CAILLE, GEO., Steam Bakery & Confectionery, 159 Main st.

BARBER.

SCHMITT, HERMAN, Tonsorial Parlor, Desoto House Block. Est. 1863.

BLACKSMITHING.

PARKER, HENRY, Gen'l. Blacksmithing, Horseshoeing, &c., 40 Main st.

BOOKS AND STATIONERY.

BRIDGMAN, H. N., Dealer in Books & Stationery, 100 Main st. Est. 1865.

BOOK BINDER.

ELCE, CHAS., Book Bindery & Paper Box Manufacturer, opp. Desoto House.

BOOTS AND SHOES.

HILGERT, J. P., Boots, Shoes & Gaiters, 181 Main st. Est. 1861.

NAGLE, JOHN, Manufacturer & Dealer of Boots & Shoes, 140 Main st. Est. 1850.

Telescopes.--Invented in 1549.
Telegraphing Musical Notes Apparatus.--Invented by E. Wilson, 1866; improved by Gray, 1875.
Telegraph--Printing.--Invented by R. E. House, in 1846; improved by Hughes, in 1856.
Threshing Machine.--First invented by M. Menzies, of Scotland, 1732.
Torpedo Shells.--Invented by Dr. Bushnell, in 1777.
Truss Bridge.--Invented by Price & Phillips, in 1841; by Whipple, 1841; improved by J. Barnes, in 1859; improved by F. C. Lowthrop, 1857.
Truss—for Rupture.--Invented by Robert Brand, in 1771.
Turning Irregular Forms—Machine for.—Invented by Blanchard, in 1820; improved by Gear, 1853.
Type Setting Machine.—Invented by Wm. H. Mitchell, 1854; improved by Alden, in 1857.
Vaccination.—Invented by Dr. Edward Jenner, in 1780.
Wood Paper.—Invented by Watts & Burgess, 1853.
Wood Pavements.--Invented by Samuel Nicholson, in 1854; improved by De Golyer, 1869; by Ballard, 1870; by Beidler, 1172.
Watches.—Said to have been invented at Nuremberg in 1477.
Window Glass.--First made in England in 1557.
Zinc White.--Jones, 1852.

CHRONOLOGY
OF THE
HEROES OF THE REVOLUTION
AND THE
WAR OF 1812.

James Otis was born at Barnstable, Mass., 1725. He was the leader of the Revolutionary party in Massachusetts at the beginning. He was wounded by a British official in 1769, and never entirely recovered. He was killed by lightning in 1772.

Samuel Adams was born in Boston in 1722. He was one of the signers of the Declaration of Independence; was afterwards Governor of Massachusetts, and died in 1803. It is also believed that he was one of the leaders of the patriots in the Boston massacre, March 5, 1770.

Charles Thomson was born in Ireland in 1730, and came to America when he was only eleven years of age. He settled in Pennsylvania, and was Secretary of Congress perpetually from 1774 until the adoption of the Federal Constitution, and the organization of the new government in 1789. He died in 1824 at the age of 94.

GALENA—Continued.

CARRIAGES AND WAGONS.
GRIMM, L. & C., Manufacturers of Wagons, Carriages & Sleighs, Franklin st. Est. 1875.

CLOTHING.
CORWITH, H. P., Clothing Manufacturer, Main st. Est. 1847.

DENTIST.
HOWARD, G. O., Dentist, 129 Main st. Est. 1868.

DRUGGISTS.
CRAWFORD, S. & CO., Druggists, Paints, Oils & Dye Stuffs, 131 Main st. Est. 1846.
HOFFMANN, J. P., Wholesale & Retail Druggist, Paints, Oils, &c., 108 Main st.

DRY GOODS.
SCHMOHL, LENA, Est. 1852, Dry Goods, Notions & Millinery, 132 & 134 Main st.

FURNITURE.
SAUER, MICHAEL, Manufacturer and Dealer in Furniture, 118 Main st. Est. 1842.
SCHEERER, ARMBEUSTER & CO., Furniture, Caskets & Cases, 183 Main st. Est. 1865.

GROCERIES.
FRIESENECKER, M., Groceries & Provisions, Tobacco, Cigars, &c., 120 Main st. Est. 1865.
HARRIS, JAS. M., Wholesale & Retail Grocer, 177 Main st. Est. 1877.
HELLMAN, J. H., Wholesale Grocer, 130 Main st. Est. 1846.
MOORE, JOHN, Dealer in Groceries & Provisions, Broadway. Est. 1867.

GUNS AND CUTLERY.
BURKHARD, J. J., Importer of Guns, Cutlery, &c., 143 Main st. Est. 1852.

HARDWARE.
COURTAD, JOHN & BRO., Hardware, Copper and Sheet Iron Work. 79 Main st.
MEUSEL, JOHN A., Hardware, Stoves,&c., Glass & Crockery Ware, 203 Main st.

HARNESS AND SADDLES.
RODDWIEG, A., Harness & Saddles, Repairing neatly done, 225 Main st. Est. 1874.

HATS AND CAPS.
BRENDEL, J. P., Hats, Caps, Furs & Gents' Furnishing Goods, 197 Main st.

HOTELS.
DE SOTO HOUSE, W. H. Blewitt, Prop., Main st.
LAWRENCE HOTEL, John J. Hassig, Prop. Market square. Est. 1873.
MISSISSIPPI HOUSE, Jas. Dirnberger, Prop. Opp. National Bank. Est. 1874.

(Established 1872.)

UNITED STATES HOTEL,

J. C. INGRAM, Prop.,
193 Main street,
RATES - - - $1.50 per Day.

GALENA—Continued.

VAN EMBDEN, L., European Hotel, 141 & 143 Main st. Est. 1874.

HOUSEFURNISHING GOODS.
BUTCHER, C. L., Dealer in Housefurnishing Goods, Main st. Est. 1870.

LIVERY STABLE.
COMSTOCK, S. P., Livery & Sale Stable, Commerce st.

MACHINISTS.
JAMES WESTWICK.
Established in 1855.
FOUNDRY AND MACHINE SHOP,
Steam Engines and Machinery of all Descriptions. Pumps and Pump machinery a specialty. General repairing of machinery. All work warranted and work done on short notice. Foundry and Machine Shop on Meeker street, opposite Barrows, Taylor & Co.'s Mill.

GALENA FOUNDRY.
(Established 1852.)

JOHN WESTWICK, Prop.

Manufacturer of *STEAM ENGINES* and all style of *Iron Fences, Pumping Machinery* and *Iron Mills*, for farmers, shelling and grinding corn. Castings of all kinds of Machinery in General.

CLAUDE ST., near MEEKER.

MILLINERY AND DRESS MAKING.
RHOTON, MRS. B. W., Millinery & Dressmaking, Notions, &c., 163 Main st.

MARBLE WORKS.
FRANKLIN MARBLE WORKS. R. & J. Mannell, Proprietors. Diagonal st. Established 1872.

MEAT MARKET.
KUHN, E., Meat Market. Fresh and Salt Meats, 235 Main st. Established 1869.

NEWS DEALER.
BENNETT, J. T., News Dealer, Stationery, Confectionery, Cigars, &c., 139 Main st.

PAINTER.
G. & W. ETHERLY,
HOUSE & CARRIAGE PAINTING,
Franklin St., near Catholic Church. Orders from the country will receive prompt attention. All work done promptly & in a workmanlike manner.

PHOTOGRAPHERS.
JAMES, J. E., Photographic Studio, Main & Perry sts. Established 1865.
POOLEY, J. H., Art Gallery, Oil Miniatures, &c. 133 Main st.

PHYSICIANS.
FOWLER, B. F., Physician and Surgeon, Office, 133 Main st., Galena, Ills. Est. 1860.
LOWES, J. S., Eclectic Physician, Office & Residence, over Birmingham's Store

German Empire Building, Centennial Exposition, Phila.—It was a handsome brick structure, containing offices for the German Commissioners, and a reading room where German papers were constantly kept for the convenience of visitors, together with facilities for receiving and writing letters.

GALENA—*Continued.*

PUMPS.

KEMPTER, FRANK, Manufacturers of Sheet-Iron, Miners' Pumps, 112 Main st. Est. 1858.

REAL ESTATE.

BRAND, ROBERT, Auctioneer and Real Estate Agent, 114 Main st. Established 1850.

SALOON.

FECKEY, JOHN, Billiard Hall and Sample Room, 217 Main st., Galena, Ills.

SASH, DOOR AND BLINDS.

FRITZ, JOHN, Sash, Doors, Blinds, Mouldings, Market Square. Established 1873.

TAILORS.

BRENDEL, JOHN, & SON, Merchant Tailors, Main st. Established 1842.

MARS, G. H., Merchant Tailor and Gents' Furnishing Goods, 128 Main st. Estab 1836.

TOBACCO AND CIGARS.

HELLER & BIESMANN, Manuf'rs Cigars, Dealers in Smoking Articles, &c., 107 Main st.

GALENA—*Continued.*

WATCHES, CLOCKS AND JEWELRY.

COATSWORTH, J., & SON, Manuf'rs of Jewelry, Watches, Clocks, Musical Instruments, 147 Main street.

LEBRON, L. M., & SON, Watchmakers and Jewelers, 128 Main st. Established 1851.

SCHNEIDER, H., Manufacturing Jeweler, Watches, Clocks, &c., 165 Main st.

DUBUQUE, IOWA.

AGRICULTURAL IMPLEMENTS.

CONRICK, E. P., Agricultural Implements, 142 Locust st. Established 1867.

HALE, FAHERTY & CO., Agricultural Implements, 225 to 229 Main st. Estab. 1874.

ATTORNEYS AT LAW.

CULVER, JAMES C., Attorney at Law and Solicitor of Patents 510 Main st.

ENGELMAN & CHARLES, Attorneys at Law, Main st., cor. 5th. Estab. 1877

William Prescott was born at Groton, Mass.; was a colonel at the battle of Bunker Hill, and served under Gates until the surrender of Burgoyne, when he left the army. He died in 1795.

Joseph Warren was born at Roxbury, Mass., in 1740. He was killed by a musket ball at the battle of Bunker Hill, while retreating, and was buried where he fell, near the redoubt. The tall Bunker Hill monument stands on the very spot where he fell, commemorates his death, as well as the patriotism of his countrymen. He was a physician, and was 35 years of age when he died. His remains now rest in St. Paul's Church, Boston. A statue to his honor was inaugurated on the 17th of June, 1857.

Patrick Henry was born in Hanover county, Virginia, in 1736. He appeared suddenly in public life when almost thirty years of age. He was an active public man during the Revolution, was Governor of Virginia, and died in 1799.

Richard Schuyler was born in Albany, N. Y., in 1733, and died in 1804. He was a captain under Sir William Johnson, and was in active public service until the Revolution. He was a general in the patriot army, and was a legislator after the war.

Richard Montgomery was born in Ireland in 1737. He was with Wolfe at Quebec, in 1759; afterward married and settled in the State of New York. He was a general in the patriot army, and was killed at the battle of Quebec, in 1775.

Ethan Allen was a colonel in the patriot army. He was born in Litchfield county, Conn. He attacked the English at Montreal, was defeated, taken prisoner, and sent to England in irons. He was never engaged in active military service after his capture. He died in Vermont, in 1799, and his remains lie in a cemetery two miles from Burlington.

General Thomas was a native of Plymouth, Mass., and was one of the first eight brigadiers appointed by Congress in 1775. He died with the small-pox in 1776, at Chambly, in Canada.

Charles Lee was born in Wales in 1731. He was a brave officer in the British army. He settled in Virginia in 1773, and was one of the first brigadiers of the Continental army. He was arrested and tried by a court-martial for disobedience of orders and disrespect to Washington at the battle of Monmouth. He was found guilty, and was suspended from command for one year. He never entered the army again, and died in obscurity in Philadelphia, in 1782.

William Moultrie was born in South Carolina in 1730, and died in 1805. He was a general in the Revolution, and an active officer until made prisoner in 1780, when for two years he was not allowed to bear arms.

Richard Henry Lee was born in Westmoreland county, Virginia, in 1732. He was much in public life, signed the Declaration of Independence, was a U. S. Senator, and died in 1794.

John Hancock was born at Quincy, Mass., in 1737. He was an early and popular opponent of British power, and was chosen the second President of Congress. He was afterwards Governor of Massachusetts, and died in 1793.

DUBUQUE—*Continued.*

BAKERY AND CONFECTIONERY.

CARROLL, MARTIN, Dublin Bakery, 129 Main st., Dubuque. Estab. 1852.

MEHLIN, A. G., Bakery and Confectionery, 1072 Main st. Estab. 1874.

BARREL WORKS.

ATHERTON, S. A., Key City Barrel Works, 248 Iowa st. Established 1867.

BILLIARD HALLS AND SALOONS.

BREWERS' HEADQUARTERS. M. Blumenauer, Prop. 531 Main st., Dubuque, Ia. Est. 1877.

GRAND CENTRAL BILLIARD HALL. P. T. Wagner, Proprietor, 629 Main st.

JAEGER, NICHOLAS, Julian House Billiard Hall.

BOOTS AND SHOES.

AUGUSTIN, F. E., Manuf'r and Dealer in Boots and Shoes, 763 Main st. Estab. 1859.

GREAT BANKRUPT SHOE STORE, 737 Main st.

HANCOCK, ED., Dealer in Boots and Shoes, 892 Main st. Estab. 1857.

McLAUGHLIN, M., Manufacturer Boots and Shoes, 120 First st., Dubuque, Iowa.

WINBERG, F., Boot and Shoe Maker, 1072 Main st.

BRASS FOUNDERIES.

ANDREW DREES,
Coppersmith and Brass Founder
Manufacturer of
Soda Water Apparatus,
901 to 905 WASHINGTON ST.
Apparatus tested to 500 pounds pressure and warranted. Send for Circular. Estab. 1864.

C. W. Farley.   Sam'l Hatfield.
FARLEY & HATFIELD,
Proprietors of the
Key City Brass Foundry,
No. 831 CLAY ST., Bet. 8th & 9th.
Manufacturers of all kinds of Brass Goods. Railroad Work and Brass Castings a specialty. Cash paid for old Copper, Brass, Zinc, &c.

DUBUQUE BRASS FOUNDRY.
O. F. HODGE,
Manufacturer and Dealer in
Brass Goods
Of every Description. Brass Castings made a Specialty. CLAY ST., bet. 8th & 9th. The highest cash price paid for old Metals.

BROOMS AND BRUSHES.

MILLER, F. A., Manuf'r of Brooms and Brushes. Fourth st., bet. Clay & White. Estab. 1871.

CARRIAGES AND WAGONS.

PARKER & KENNA, Carriage and Wagon Manufacturers, 40 Eighth st. Established 1877.

HEROES OF THE REVOLUTION.

DUBUQUE—*Continued.*

HILL, THOS., Manufacturer of Carriages and Wagons, 38 Eighth st. Established 1870.

CLOAK MAKING.

RAGUE, J. F., Cloak Making, Cloths, Trimmings, Laces, &c., 153 Main st. Estab. 1862

COMMERCIAL COLLEGE.

BAYLIE'S COMMERCIAL COLLEGE. Founded 1858. Incorporated 1859. 7th & Main sts. Send for circular.

COMMISSION MERCHANTS.

RYDER & FRY, Commission Merchants, Dealers in Produce, Grain and Wool, 135 Main st.

CONFECTIONERY.

HYDE, C. H., Confectionery, Cigars, Tropical Fruits, &c., 771 Main st. Established 1877.

DENTIST.

KING, J. WADE, Dentist, N. E. Cor. Main & 8th sts. Estab. 1863.

DRY GOODS.

GREAT REVOLUTION STORE, Dry Goods, Notions and Job Lots, 635 Main st. D. Conigisky, Prop. Established 1877.

ELECTRICAL HEAD BATHS.

Ch. Vath's Electrical Head Bath.
The only Preparation known to clear the Head of Dandruff, and clean the Hair thoroughly without injury. One application will relieve the most intense Headache. For sale by all Druggists and first-class Barber Shops. Price, 50 cents per bottle. Discount to the Trade. J. C. VATH, Manufacturer and Proprietor, 861 Main St. Estab. 1856.

FLOUR MILLS.

HOSFORD & WALTERS, Proprietors of Rockdale Flour Mills. Established 1875.

GROCERIES.

BECKER, HENRY, Groceries, Provisions, Wines, Liquors, etc., 123 Main st. Estab. 1877.

FRITZ & WELSH, Teas, Staple & Fancy Groceries, 797 Main st., Dubuque, Est. 1876.

MEYER, H., Groceries and Provisions. 241 Main st. Established 1852.

PETTIBONE, B., Groceries & Provisions, Main & 11th sts. Established 1862.

WESTERCAMP, B., Groceries, Teas a specialty, S. W. cor. Locust & 8th sts. Est. 1876.

HARNESS AND SADDLES.

GILMORE, S., Manf'r Saddles, Bridles, Collars, etc., 385 Main st., Dubuque

PFIFFNER & KRIEBS, Carriage Trimmers and Harnessmakers, 46 8th st. Est. 1876.

HORSESHOERS.

LAGEN & CLAIR, Horseshoers & Blacksmiths, 532 Locust st. Established 1862.

HOTELS.

TREMONT HOUSE, W. W. Pyne, proprietor, Cor. 8th & Iowa sts.

General Putnam was born at Salem, Mass., in 1718. He was a very useful officer during the French and Indian war, and was in active service in the Continental army, commencing with the battle of Bunker Hill until 1779, when bodily infirmity compelled him to retire. He died in 1790 at the age of 72.

William Alexander Stirling was a descendant of the Scotch Earl of Stirling. He was born in the city of New York in 1726. He became attached to the patriot cause and served as a faithful officer during the war. He was made prisoner at the battle of Long Island. He died in 1783.

Hugh Mercer, a general in the Continental army, was killed at the battle of Princeton. He was a native of Scotland, and was practicing medicine in Fredericksburg, Va., when the Revolution broke out. He was 56 years of age when he died.

General McDougal was born in Scotland, and came to America in early childhood. He rose to the rank of major-general, was a New York State Senator, and died in 1786.

Marquis de La Fayette was born in France in 1757. He was an active patriot during the Revolution, and contributed men and money to the patriot cause. He was commissioned major-generrl by the Continental Congress July 31, 1777. He died in France in 1834, at the age of 77.

Arthur St. Clair was a native of Scotland, and came to America in May, 1755. He served under Wolfe, and when the Revolution broke out he entered the American army. He served as a general during the war, and died in 1818 at the age of 84.

Zebulon Butler was born in Connecticut in 1731. Served in the Revolution as a colonel, and died in Wyoming in 1795.

Baron Steuben came to America in 1777, and joined the Continental army at Valley Forge. He was a veteran from the armies of Frederick the Great of Prussia. He was made Inspector General of the American army. He died in the interior of New York in 1795.

Benjamin Lincoln was born in Massachusetts in 1733. He was a farmer. He joined the Continental army in 1777, and rose rapidly to the position of major-general. He died in 1810.

John Ashe was born in England in 1721, and came to America when a child. He was engaged in the Regulator war in North Carolina in 1771, and was a general in the Continental army. He died of small-pox in 1781.

Anthony Wayne was born in Pennsylvania in 1745. He was a professional surveyor, then a provincial legislator, and became a soldier in 1775. He was very active during the whole war, and was successful in subduing the Indians in the Ohio country in 1795. He died on his way home, at Erie, Pa., near the close of 1796.

George Rogers Clarke was a native of Virginia, and was born in 1752. He was one of the most accomplished and useful officers of the Western pioneers during the Revolution. He died near Louisville, Ky., in 1848.

DUBUQUE—Continued.

Established 1856.
WILLIAM LUTHER,
Proprietor of

EUROPEAN HOTEL,

229 to 243 SEVENTH ST.

ICE COMPANY.

Z OLLICOFFER LAKE ICE CO., Fl›cher, Wheeler & Co., Third & Iowa sts. Estab. 1857.

IRON WORKS.

N OVELTY IRON WORKS, Manf'rs of Steam Engines, etc., 10th and Washington sts.

IOWA IRON WORKS.

Rouse, Dean & Co.,
IRON BOAT BUILDERS,
Manufacturers of

STEAM ENGINES, BOILERS,

Architectural Iron Work & General Machinery. Send for Catalogue. Largest Stock of Patterns in the State. Est. 1851.

C. W. SCHREIBER. F. STRINSKY.
SCHREIBER & STRINSKY,
Proprietors of the

KEY CITY IRON AND BRASS WORKS,

Builders of Portable and Stationery Engines and Boilers. Steamboat and Mill Work. Steam Fitters and Machinists. Shop 8th st., bet. Iowa and Clay sts.

LAUNDRY.

D UBUQUE LAUNDRY, 155 8th st., F. E. Ormsby, proprietor. Established 1877.

LINIMENT.

CALL FOR
Collet's Liniment.
It is the only radical cure for Rheumatism, Pain in the Back, Sprains, Swellings, Bruises, Nervous Headache, Chilblains, Stomach Cramp, Neuralgia, Cuts, and Open Sores. Kept by all druggists, and manufactured by F. C. COLLET, 453 Main st., Dubuque Iowa. Price, 25cts, 50cts and $1.00 per bottle. Established 1874.

LIVERY AND SALE STABLES.

G IBBS & CO., Livery and Sale Stable, 139 4th st. Established 1876.

L AGEN & SON, Livery & Sale Stable, 136 4th st. Established 1861.

W ASHINGTON SALE AND LIVERY STABLE, O'Brien & Byene Bros., props., 129 7th st.

MEAT MARKET.

W ILKINSON, JAMES, Dealer in all kinds of Fresh Meats, 156 5th st. Established 1874.

MILLINERY.

G ILLEAS, MRS. M., Millinery, Notions, etc., 709 Main st., Dubuque. Established 1876.

DUBUQUE—Continued.

MUSICAL INSTRUMENTS.

G ABLE, L. L., Musical Instruments, 131 8th st. Established 1877.

PAINTERS.

S MITH & PITSCHNER, House and Sign Painters, 5th st., bet. Main & Iowa sts.

PHOTOGRAPHERS.

B ILBROUGH, J. E., Artistic Photographer, S. W. cor. Main & 8th sts. Estab. 1860.

C UTTER, E., Photographic Studio, Main & 5th sts. Estab. 1853.

S. ROOT,

PHOTOGRAPHER,

MAIN & EIGHTH STREETS.

Established 1851.

PHYSICIANS.

F OWLER, S. M., Physician and Surgeon, 15 8th st., Dubuque. Established 1872.

M ILLAR, WM. S., Physician & Surgeon, Edinburgh & Paris, 1853, Main and 8th sts.

PIANOS AND ORGANS.

F AUST, J. S., Dealer in Organs & Pianos, 1086 Main st. Established 1875.

RESTAURANT.

U PTON'S, SAMUEL, American Restaurant, 583 Main st. Established 1857.

SEWING MACHINES.

S COTT, ANDREW, Dealer in Sewing Machines, 69 8th st. Established 1877.

SPICE MILLS.

A LDEN, H. L., Key City Spice Mills, Dubuque. Established 1861.

TAILORS.

K ABAT, JOS., Merchant Tailor, Cloaks Cut and Made to order, 537-Main st.

S TAMMEYER, JOSEPH, Merchant Tailor & Gents' Furnishing Goods, 545 Main st. Est. 1853.

TIN AND SHEET IRON.

P AINE, J. C., Tin and Sheet Iron Worker, 846 Main st. Established 1873.

Y ATES, R. G., Tin and Sheet Iron Worker, 132 Main st. Established 1876.

TOBACCO AND CIGARS.

A NDRES, H. M., Tobacco, Cigars and Pipes, 708 Main st. Established 1862.

L UNGWITZ, E. A., Cigars, Tobacco & Smokers' Articles, 299 Main st. Estab. 1865.

TURKISH BATHS.

G EE, R. S., Remedial Institute and Turkish Baths, 970 to 982 Main st.

VINEGAR WORKS.

G LAB, JOHN, Manf'r of all kinds of Choice Vinegars, 313 Iowa st.

K AISER, A., Excelsior Vinegar Works, 9th st. Estab. 1856.

N ORTHWESTERN VINEGAR WORKS, Jame Cushing, prop.. Eagle Pt. ave. & Valeria s

ADVERTISEMENTS.

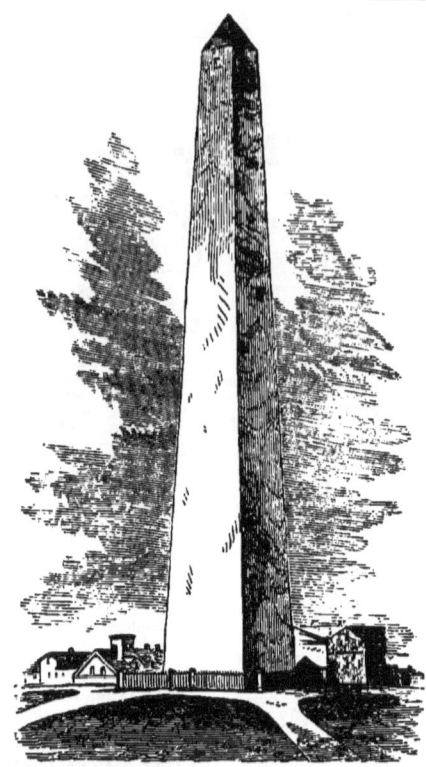

Bunker-Hill Monument, Charleston, Mass.—Marks the spot where the first real battle of the Revolution was fought. It is 221 feet high. The corner stone was laid by Gen. Lafayette, June 17, 1825, and Daniel Webster delivered one of his most memorable orations on the occasion. The monument was completed in 1842, and was dedicated June 17, 1843, in the presence of the President of the United States ; nd his Cabinet.

L. C. Daemicke

(The Old Stand)

Established 1865.

508 STATE ST.

(Cor. Taylor,)

CHICAGO, ILL.

Furnaces
AND
Kettles,

From 15 to 220 Gallons.

Headquarters for

Butchers, Coopers, Packers, and Ice-Makers.

Tools and Machines,

Stoves. Ranges, Etc.

John Sullivan was born in Maine in 1740. He was a delegate to the first Continental Congress in 1774, and was one of the first eight brigadiers in the Continental army. He resigned his commission of general in 1779; was afterward member of Congress and Governor of New Hampshire, and died in 1795.

James Clinton was born in Ulster county, N. Y., in 1736. He was a captain in the French and Indian war, and an active general in the Revolutionary army. He died in 1812.

John Paul Jones was born in Scotland in 1747, and came to Virginia in boyhood. He entered the American navy in 1775, and served as commodore during the war. He was an intrepid and daring officer. He was afterwards rear-admiral in the Russian service. He died in Paris in 1782.

John Rutledge was born in Ireland, and came to South Carolina when a child, and was Governor of that State in 1780. After the Revolutionary war he was made a judge of the Supreme Court of the United States, and also chief justice of South Carolina. He died in 1800.

Horatio Gates was a native of England, and was educated for military life. He was the first adjutant-general of the Continental army, and was made major-general in 1776. He retired to his estate in Virginia at the close of the war, and finally took up his abode in New York, where he died in 1806 at the age of 78 years.

Thomas Sumpter was a native of South Carolina, and was early in the field. Ill health compelled him to leave the army just before the close of the war in 1781. He was afterward congressman and died on the high hills of Santee, S. C. in 1832, at 98 years of age.

Baron de Kalb was a native of Alsace, a German province ceded to France. He had been in America as a secret French agent, about fifteen years before. He came to America with Lafayette in 1777, and congress commissioned him a Major-General. He died of wounds received at the battle of Camden in 1780.

Benedict Arnold was a native of Norwich, Conn., where he was born in January, 1740. He fought nobly for freedom until 1778, when his passions got the better of his judgment and conscience, and he became a traitor and joined the British army. He went to England after the war, and died in London, June 14, 1801.

Nathaniel Greene was born of Quaker parents, in Rhode Island, in 1740. He was an anchorsmith, and was pursuing his trade when the Revolution broke out. He hastened to Boston after the skirmish at Lexington, and from that time until the close of the war he was one of the most useful generals in the army. He died near Savannah in 1786, and was buried in a vault in that city. His sepulchre can not be identified.

Daniel Morgan was born in New Jersey in 1736, and was in the humble sphere of a wagoner when called to the field. He had been a soldier under Braddock, and joined Washington at Cambridge in 1775, and became a general. He was a farmer in Virginia after the war, where he died in 1802.

DUBUQUE—*Continued.*

WINES AND LIQUORS.

PRATT, PAUL & CO., Wholesale dealer in Wines & Liquors, 521 Main st. Est. 1874.

WIRE CLOTH.

DUDDY. T. C., Manf'r of Wire Cloth, Wire Work Riddles & Screens, 38 9th st. Est.1869.

DUBUQUE BUSINESS HOUSES,

WHEN ESTABLISHED.

DREES, A., Soda Water Apparatus, 1864.
EUROPEAN HOTEL, 1856.
GLAB, J., Vinegar Works, 1873.
HODGE, O. F., Brass Goods, 1868.
KEY CITY BRASS FOUNDRY, 1877.
KEY CITY IRON AND BRASS WORKS, 1877.
NORTHWESTERN VINEGAR WORKS, 1863.
ROUSE, DEAN & CO., Steam Engines, 1851.

RED WING, MINN.

BAKERY AND CONFECTIONERY.

ANDERSON, M., Restaurant, Ice Cream Saloon & Confectionery, 53 Main st.

BIXBY, T. & CO., Bakery & Confectionery, 73 & 75 Main st.

BARBER.

OBRECHT, C., Barber, 86 Main st.

BOOTS AND SHOES.

HEFFELFINGER, HOWELL & CO., dealers in Boots & Shoes, 85 Main st.

CARRIAGES AND WAGONS.

ERICKSON, PETERSON & CO., Manf'rs of Wagons, Carriages, Sleighs, etc., 5th & Plum sts.

CLOTHING.

EISENBRAND, W., Clothing House & Furnishing Goods, 83 Main st.

LEVI, E. A., Clothing, 80 Main st.

POOR MAN'S FRIEND CLOTHING STORE, 89 Main st.

WING, J. S. & T. M., Clothing, Hats, Caps, Trunks, Gloves, Mittens, etc., Plum st.

COLLECTION AGENT.

BALDWIN, DWIGHT M., General Collection Agent, 67 Main st.

DRESSMAKING.

BISSONETT, MRS., Dressmaking, 94 Main st.

DRUGGISTS.

JOHNSON BROS., Druggists, 72 Main st.

RED WING—*Continued.*

DRY GOODS.

SIMMONS, J., Dry Goods, etc.,
82 Main st.

FURNITURE.

ERICKSON & SWANSON, Red Wing Furniture Manf'y, Salesrooms on Plum st.

McDONALD & KELLOGG, Furniture,
76 Main st.

GROCERIES.

CARLSON & ANDERSON, Groceries, Provisions, Flour, Feed, etc, 87 Main st.

KEMPE, J. & CO., Groceries, Crockery, Flour, Feed, etc.. Plum st.

LINDHOLM, A. T., Groceries, Provisions, Chinaware, etc., 19 Plum st.

SEXTON, J., Groceries & Provisions,
3d & Plum sts.

HARDWARE.

BETCHER, CHAS. & CO., Hardware,
70 Main st.

MARTINSON & ANDERSON, Hardware, Stoves & Tinware, 55 Main st.

HARNESS AND SADDLES.

KRUGER, T., Harness, Saddles & Collars, Manf'r & dealer in, Plum st.

WUNDERLICH, G., Harness & Collar Manf'r, Main st.

WATSON, E. P., Novelty Harness Works,
Bush st.

HOTELS.

CENTRAL HOUSE, Gus Knight, prop.,
Plum st.

HICKMAN HOUSE, H. Hickman, prop.,
Bush st.

IRON WORKS.

DENSMORE BROS.,
Red Wing Iron Works.

LIVERY STABLE.

McLEAN, JOHN, Livery Stable,
3d st.

PAINTS AND OILS.

HAWKINS, W. E., Paints, Oils & Wall Paper,
Bush st.

PHOTOGRAPHERS.

KELLOGG, J. D., Photographer,
Main & Plum sts.

MESSER,
The Photographer,
WE AIM TO PLEASE,
RED WING, 88 Main st.

SALOONS.

GERKEN, P., Billiard Hall & Saloon,
84 Main st.

HARTMAN, GEO., Wine & Liquor Saloon,
Plum st.

STEEGE, K. E., Saloon,
64 Main st.

SASH, DOOR AND BLINDS.

D. C. HILL,
Manf'r of Sash, Doors, Blinds, Cornices, Etc.,
MAIN & BLUFF STS.

John Eager Howard, of the Maryland line, was born in Baltimore county in 1752. He went into military service at the commencement of the war. He was a colonel, and was in all the principal battles of the Revolution; was chosen Governor of Maryland in 1778, and was afterward a United States Senator. He died in 1827.

William Washington, a relative of the General, was born in Stafford county, Va. He entered the army under Mercer, and greatly distinguished himself at the South as a commander of a corps of cavalry. Taken prisoner at the battle of Eutaw Springs, he remained a captive until the close of the war, and died in Charleston in 1810. In a personal combat with the British Colonel Tarleton, at the battle of the Cowpens, Washington wounded his antagonist in the hand. Some months afterward, Tarleton said, sneeringly, to Mrs. Willie Jones, a witty American lady, "that Colonel Washington, I am told, is illiterate, and can not write his own name." "Ah! Colonel," said Mrs. Jones, "you ought to know better, for you bear evidence that he can *make his mark*." At another time he expressed a desire to see Colonel Washington. Mrs. Jones' sister instantly replied, "Had you looked behind at the Cowpens, you might have had that pleasure."

Henry Lee was born in Virginia in 1756. He entered the military service as a captain of a Virginia company in 1776, and in 1777 joined the Continental army. At the head of a legion, as a colonel, he performed extraordinary services during the war, especially in the South. He was afterward Governor of Virginia, and a member of Congress. He died in 1818.

Andrew Pickens was born in Pennsylvania in 1739, and served as a general in the Revolution. In childhood he went to South Carolina, and was one of the first in the field for liberty. He died in 1817.

Thomas Mifflin was born in Philadelphia in 1744. He was a Quaker, but joined the patriot army in 1775, and rapidly rose to the rank of major-general. He was a member of Congress after the war, and also Governor of Pennsylvania. He died in January, 1800.

John Jay was a descendant of a Huguenot family, and was born in the city of New York in 1745. He was early in the ranks of active patriots, and rendered very important services during the Revolution. He retired from public life in 1801, and died in 1829, at the age of 84 years. His residence was at Bedford, Westchester county, N. Y.

William Bainbridge (Commodore) was born in New Jersey in 1774. He was the captain of a merchant vessel at the age of 19, and entered the naval service in 1798. He was distinguished during the war of 1812, and died in 1833.

Stephen Decatur was born in Maryland in 1779. He entered the navy at the age of 19. After his last cruise in the Mediterranean he superintended the building of gunboats. He rose to the rank of commodore, and during the war of 1812 he was distinguished for his skill and bravery. He afterward humbled the Barbary powers, and after returning home he was killed in a duel with Commodore Barron, in March, 1820.

ACADEMY OF ST. FRANCIS.
COUNCIL BLUFFS, IOWA.

Conducted by the Sisters of Charity of the B. V. M.

The Scholastic Year, which is divided into two sessions of five months, each, begins THE FIRST MONDAY IN SEPTEMBER, AND ENDS THE LAST WEEK IN JUNE.

TERMS—Board and Tuition, per session of five months, $75. Piano, organ, guitar, vocal music, painting, drawing, languages, etc., are extra. For prospectuses, containing further particulars, address

SISTER SUPERIOR,
St. Francis Academy,
COUNCIL BLUFFS, IOWA.

G. C. OWENS,

CONTRACTOR & BUILDER,

Cor. Sixth and Walnut Streets,

DES MOINES, IA.

SASHES, BLINDS, &C
Constantly on Hand.

SCALES !
S. S. Hitchcock's
NEW PATENT.

Mr. H. is one of the oldest scale makers in the world, having got up the Truss Lever Scales 32 years ago, and made and sold the same 23 years at Rochester, N. Y., and Chicago, Ills. It being the same, that is called Fairbank's scales. Then I got up the Chicago scale, and sold to my partner, Wm. W. Nutting. Then I got up the Des Moines Scale Co., and sold out two years ago. Now I have got up a NEW PATENT, of the greatest importance,

Which will Neither Freeze nor Get out of Order.

My scales have taken 216 medals, diplomas, and transactions over all others. In Albany, N. Y., in 1850, I took diplomas, medals and transactions over eight manufacturers, all were there, except the Pittsburg scales, it not being represented. And there have been over 8,000 sold, of my improved stock or hay scales. I have got up a

NEW BUSHEL BEAM,

Improved, January, 1877, weighing 20 different kinds of bushels, adapted to 4, 6, or 10 ton scales. Manufactory,

WEST COURT AVENUE, 3d FROM BRIDGE.

Repairs of every description to order. Address all communications to,

S. S. HITCHCOCK,
DES MOINES, - IOWA.

BIGGS HOUSE.

W. L. BIGGS,
Proprietor.

COUNCIL BLUFFS, IOWA.

The Best Accommodations at all times.

Strangers will consult their best interests, by stopping there.

TO THE AFFLICTED!

Any person, Male or Female, suffering with that terrible life destroyer,
TAPE WORM, by calling on me at my residence on
MAIN ST., - COUNCIL BLUFFS, IOWA,
Can have the same entirely removed from the body in from one to three hours. Consultation Free.

W. L. BIGGS,

C. GEISE,
—Proprietor of—

STEAM BREWERY
AND MALT HOUSE,

Council Bluffs, - - IOWA.

Special attention given to Orders.

Bryant House

E. S. WIBLEY,
Proprietor.

Middle Broadway, Council Bluffs,
IOWA.

TERMS - - $2.00 PER DAY.

ADVERTISEMENTS.

U. P. DEPOT, COUNCIL BLUFFS, IOWA.

Pacific House,

G. W. FURGASON & SON,

Proprietors.

COUNCIL BLUFFS, IOWA.

(Two doors from Banks.)

First Floors, - - - $2.50 per day.

Second and Third Floors, $2.00 per day.

1st and 2nd Floors, $3 per day.   Upper Floors, $2 per day.

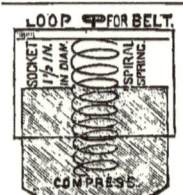

RUPTURED
ARE YOU?!!

Why wear the old SPRING MAN-KILLING TRUSS that is daily destroying you, causing you to suffer from DYSPEPSIA, PARALYSIS, General Debility, etc. Order at once "Howe's SPRING PAD FELT TRUSS," for the treatment and cure of RUPTURE or HERNIA, invented and patented by the Rev. Howe for his own use, after having tried all kinds for twenty years. The HOWE TRUSS is endorsed by physicians all over the United States, including Dr. Gregory, principal of St. Louis Medical College. It has cured a five years' rupture in five weeks. Send $3 for sample Truss, circulars, endorsements, etc., or 10 cents for our Weekly Truss Paper. We make trusses for men, women and children. We also manufacture the best FEMALE SUPPORTER KNOWN, for falling of the womb. Send names of ruptured friends to "HOWE TRUSS CO.,"

Box 1110,   COUNCIL BLUFFS, IOWA.
FOR SALE BY ALL DRUGGISTS.   AGENTS WANTED.

Metropolitan Hotel,

L. D. HARRIS, Proprietor.

LOWER BROADWAY.

Board, $2 Per Day.

COUNCIL BLUFFS, IOWA.

HALL & BANTA,

WHOLESALE AND RETAIL

Grocers, Produce and Commission Merchants,

Butter, Eggs, Green Fruits and Vegetables a Specialty.

South Main Street, Council Bluffs, Iowa.

Aaron Burr was born in New Jersey in 1756. In his twentieth year he joined the Continental army, and accompanied Arnold in his expedition against Quebec. Ill health compelled him to leave the army in 1779, and he became a distinguished lawyer and an active public man. He died on Staten Island, N. Y., in 1836.

Robert Fulton, the inventor and discoverer of steam navigation, was born in Pennsylvania, and was a student of West, the great painter, for several years. He had more genius for mechanics than for the fine arts, and he turned his efforts in that direction. He died in 1815, soon after launching a steamship-of-war, at the age of 50 years.

Henry Dearborn was an officer of the Revolution, and, in the war of 1812, was appointed major-general and commander-in-chief of the armies. He was born in New Hampshire. He returned to private life in 1815, and died at Roxbury, near Boston, in 1829, at the age of 78 years.

William Hull was born in Connecticut in 1753. He rose to the rank of major in the Continental army. Though severely censured for his surrender of Detroit in 1812, he was a good man, and distinguished for his bravery. He was appointed governor of the Michigan Territory in 1805. After the close of his unfortunate campaign he never appeared in public life. He died, near Boston, in 1825.

Isaac Hull was made a lieutenant in the navy in 1798, and in 1812 was commodore, in command of the United States frigate, Constitution. He died in Philadelphia in February, 1843.

Isaac Shelby was born in Maryland in 1750. He entered military life in 1774, and went to Kentucky as a land surveyor in 1775. He engaged in the war of the Revolution, and was distinguished in the battle on King's Mountain, in October, 1780. He was made Governor of Kentucky in 1792, and soon afterward retired to private life, from which he was drawn in 1813. He died in 1826.

James Winchester was born in Maryland in 1756. He was made a brigadier in 1812; resigned his commission in 1815, and died in Tennessee in 1826.

Green Clay was born in Virginia in 1756, and was made a brigadier of Kentucky volunteers early in 1813. He commanded at Fort Meigs, in 1813. He died in 1826.

Zebulon M. Pike was born in 1779. While pressing towards the capture of York (Toronto), in 1813, the powder magazine of the fort blew up, and General Pike was mortally wounded. He was carried on board the flagship of Commodore Chauncey, where he died, with the captured British flag under his head, at the age of 34 years.

John Chandler was a native of Massachusetts, and served as a general in the war of 1812. Some years after the war he was a United States Senator from Maine. He died at Augusta, in that State, in 1814.

General Wilkinson was born in Maryland in 1757, and studied medicine. He joined the Continental army at Cambridge, in 1775, and continued in service during the war. He died near the city of Mexico, in 1825, at the age of 68 years.

RED WING—*Continued.*

SEWING MACHINES.

PAULSON & HIMMELMAN, Sewing Machines, Pianos & Organs, 78 Main st.

SPRAKE, O. M., Singer Sewing Machines,
Bush st.

TOBACCO AND CIGARS.

JELLINECK, FRANCIS, Manf'r of Fine Cigars,
67 Main st.

RHINER, AUGUST, Manf'r of Cigars,
Music Hall Block.

VETERINARY SURGEON.

McCART, DR. T. S., Northwestern Veterinary Stable, Bush st.

ROCHESTER, MINN.

AGRICULTURAL IMPLEMENTS.

EDGAR & HYMES, Gen'l dealer in Farm Machinery, Wagons, Main & Zumbro sts.

BAKERIES AND CONFECTIONERIES.

HOPKINS, F. A., Ice Cream Saloon, Bakery and Confectionery, Main & Zumbro sts.

JARGO, MRS. N. C., Bakery, Confectionery and Ice Cream, Broadway.

BARBERS.

EARL, CHAS., Hairdressing & Shaving Saloon,
3d st. & Broadway.

MURRAY, J. B., Climax Barber Shop,
Broadway near 3d st.

RENSLOW, L., Shaving & Hairdressing Rooms, under Stebbins & Co.'s Hardware store.

BLACKSMITHS AND HORSESHOERS.

McNAMEE, JOHN, Practical Horseshoer,
Main st. bet. College & 3d sts.

SPAULDING & MADISON, Blacksmiths & Horseshoers, foot of 3d st.

WAGONER & STREETER, Blacksmiths & Horseshoers, 4th & Main sts.

BOOTS AND SHOES.

LARSON, L., Boot & Shoe Maker,
3d st. West of Broadway.

MEYETTE, J. C., Boot and Shoe Maker,
Broadway, near 4th st.

CARRIAGES AND WAGONS.

OLESON & LARSON, prop's of the Northwestern Wagon & Carriage Works, Broad'y & 5th sts.

CONFECTIONERY.

GOULD, WM., Ice Cream, Confectionery, Cigar Store and Restaurant, Broadway.

COOPER.

MEDBERRY, W. D., Cooper, manuf'r of Barrels, Firkins, etc, Main st.

DRESS AND CLOAK MAKERS.

ARIES, MISSES A. E. & C. N., Fashionable Dress and Cloakmakers, Broadway.

BECKWITH, MISS JENNIE, Fashionable Dress & Cloakmaker, 3d st. & Broadway.

BENTLEY, MRS. C. C., Dress & Cloakmaker,
Broadway.

CANFIELD, MRS. M. E., Fashionable Dressmaker Masonic Block.

ROCHESTER—*Continued.*

DRUGGISTS.

HARGESHEIMER, G. & CO., Practical Druggists & Chemists, 1 Masonic Block.

FLOUR AND FEED.

HUMASON, J. S., Flour, Feed, Grain & Green Fruits, Broadway.

FURNITURE.

BERG, L. H., Upholsterer & Furniture Manf'r, Broadway. near R. R. bridge.

OWEN, T. C. & CO., Furniture dealers & Undertakers, College st., bet. Broadway & Main st.

GROCERIES.

BARBER, R., Fancy Groceries, Provisions, etc., Broadway.

CASHEL, J. L., staple & fancy Groceries & Provisions, Broadway.

HALL, A. M., Groceries. Crockery, Flour, Provisions, etc., Broadway.

SEHL, WM., Groceries, Boots & Shoes. East side of Broadway.

ZIMMERMAN, J. G. & CO., Groceries, Boots, Shoes, Crockery, etc., Broadway.

HAIR DEALERS AND DRESSERS.

WORDEN, MISS L. N., Hair Manf'r and Ladies' Hairdresser. Masonic Block.

HARNESS AND SADDLES.

SPORNITZ, W. A., Harness, Saddles, Collars, Whips, etc., 3d st. & Broadway.

HOTELS.

BRADLEY HOUSE,
ROCHESTER, MINN.
Bath and Billiard Rooms Attached.

Free Omnibus and Baggage Wagon to and from Cars. $2.00 per day.

J. D. BRADLEY, Proprietor.

NORTON HOUSE, P. Norton, Proprietor, Zumbro st.

REMONDINO HOTEL, A. G. Remondino, propr., Cor. Broadway & College st.

LIVERY STABLES.

CLARK, R. B. & SON, Railroad Sale & Livery Stables, Broadway, one block East of Depot.

COOK BROS., Livery & Boarding Stables, Cor. College st. & Broadway.

MEAT MARKETS.

BAIHLY, GEO., Butcher, Fresh & Salt Meats, etc. Broadway.

PROCTER, G. W., Fresh & Salt Meats, Poultry, Game, etc., Zumbro st. & Broadway.

THE ROCHESTER MEAT MARKET,
Broadway, bet College & 3d sts.,

F. ROMMELL & BRO., Proprietors,
FRESH & SALT MEATS,
Poultry, Fish and Game. Highest price paid for Cattle and Hides.

General Armstrong was born in Pennsylvania in 1758; served in the war of the Revolution; was Secretary of the State of Pennsylvania; Minister to France in 1804; Secretary of War in 1813, and died in Duchess county, N. Y., in 1843.

General John Coffee was a native of Virginia. He did good service in the war of 1812, and in subsequent campaigns among the Indians. He died in 1834.

James Lawrence was a native of New Jersey, and received a midshipman's warrant at the age of 16. He is remembered by every American as the author of those brave words: "Don't give up the ship." On this occasion he was wounded while commanding the United States frigate Chesapeake, and the engagement took place in 1814. He died four days after receiving the wound, at the age of 31 years.

Commodore David Porter was among the most distinguished of the American naval commanders. He was a resident Minister of the United States in Turkey, and died, near Constantinople, in March, 1843.

Jacob Brown was born in Pennsylvania in 1775. He engaged in his country's service in 1813, and soon became distinguished. He was made major-general in 1814. He was commander-in-chief of the United States army in 1821, and held that rank and office when he died, in 1838.

George Izard was born in South Carolina in 1777. He was a general, and made military life his profession. After the war he left the army. He was Governor of Arkansas Territory in 1825, and died at Little Rock. Ark., in 1828.

Thomas McDonough was a native of Delaware, and a commodore in the navy. He was 28 years of age at the time of the engagement at Plattsburg. The State of New York gave him one thousand acres of land on Plattsburg Bay for his services. He died in 1822, at the age of 39 years.

Commodore Barney was born in Baltimore in 1759. He entered the naval service of the Revolution in 1775, and was active during the whole war. He bore the American flag to the French National Convention in 1796, and entered the French service. He returned to America in 1800, and took part in the war of 1812, and died at Pittsburgh in 1818.

Samuel Smith, the commander of Fort Mifflin in 1777, was born in Pennsylvania in 1752. He entered the Revolutionary army in 1776; served as a general in command when Ross attacked Baltimore in 1814; afterward represented Baltimore in Congress, and died in April, 1839.

Henry Clay was born in Virginia in 1772. He became a lawyer at Richmond, and at the age of 21 he established himself in his profession at Lexington, Ky. He first appeared in Congress, as Senator, in 1806, and from that period his life was chiefly devoted to the public service. He died in Washington City, while United States Senator, in 1852.

Henry Atkinson was a native of South Carolina, and entered the army as a captain in 1808. He was retained in the army after the war of 1812, was made adjutant-general, and was finally appointed to the command of the Western army. He died in Jefferson Barracks, in June, 1842.

Rheumatic Hospital,

—: BY :—

DR. M. MELLIN,

35 Ceape Street - - *OSHKOSH, WIS.*

For reference and particulars send for circular.

ROCHESTER—*Continued.*

MILLINERY AND FANCY GOODS.

STEWART, MRS. A. E., Millinery & Fancy Goods Store, Broadway.

MUSIC TEACHER.

LEFLER, MRS. M. B., Music Teacher, Bank Block, Broadway.

PAINTERS.

CLARK, JOHN, Wagon, Carriage & Sign Painter, Broadway.

DATE, S. H., House and Sign Painter, Broadway and 5th st.

FANKHAUSER BROS., House Painters, Paper Hangers, etc., Main and Zumbro sts.

PHYSICIANS.

ALLEN & MOSSE, Homœopathic Physicians and Surgeons, Leland's Block.

MARTINITZ, DR. ST. V., Physician and Surgeon, Office at 13 Broadway. Established 1872.

PUMP MANUFACTURERS.

F. HOLMES,

MANUF'R OF PUMPS, WIND & FEED MILLS,

6th st. and Broadway, ROCHESTER.

SALOONS.

KENNEDY, P. S., Wine, Liquor and Beer Saloon, Cor. College st. and Broadway.

STOVES AND TINWARE.

LOVELL & DYSON, Stoves, Tin and Sheet-Iron Worker, Broadway.

HASTINGS, MINN.

AGRICULTURAL IMPLEMENTS.

VAN SLYKE, J., Farm Machinery & Implements, Edison's Block.

BARBERS.

OVERALLS, A. J., Fashionable Hairdressing and Shaving Parlor, 241 2d st.

TAYLOR, WESLEY, Tonsorial Parlor, 265 2d st.

HASTINGS—*Continued.*

BOARDING HOUSE.

FREAS, JO., Boarding House, Second st.

BOOTS AND SHOES.

CHASE, N. M., Boots & Shoes, 262 2nd st.

KALKES, P., Boots & Shoes, 72 Vermillion st.

LAUB, NIC., Boot & Shoe Manufacturer, 241 2nd st., up-stairs.

DRUGGISTS.

ATHERTON, W. E., Druggist, 2d & Vermillion st.

FINCH & SON, Druggists, Pharmacists, Pure Wines & Liquors, 257 2nd st.

DRY GOODS.

EYRE BROS., & OLIVER, Dry Goods & Clothing 254 2nd st.

GILLITT, H., Dry Goods, Clothing, Hats, Caps, Boots & Shoes, 268 2nd st.

GROCERIES.

DAVIS, B. F. & SON, Groceries & Provisions, 2nd & Ramsey sts.

MATHER, CHAS., Groceries, 250 2nd st.

REED, WM., B. & CO., Groceries, 274 2nd st.

HARDWARE.

McHUGH, J. P., Hardware, Tinware, Stoves, &c. 2nd & Vermillion st. Est. 1861.

HORSESHOERS.

KANE & TRACY, Horseshoers, Cor. 5th & Vermillion sts.

HOTELS.

FARMER'S HOTEL, Andrew Noble, Prop. Cor. Vermillian & 1st sts.

YEAGER, C., American House, 224 Second st.

LUMBER DEALER.

DUDLEY, JOHN, Dealer in Lumber, Flour, Feed &c., Vermillian st.

MACHINIST.

WARSOP, A., Star Iron Works and General Machinist. Lower Levee.

MARBLE WORKS.

KOPPES, PETER, Marble & Granite Works, 235 2nd st.

Main Exhibition Hall, Centennial Exposition, Philadelphia.—This is in the form of a parallelogram, extending east and west 1,880 feet in length, and north and south 464 feet in width. The framework is of iron. The foundations consist of 672 stone piers. The larger portion of the structure is one story in height, and shows the main cornice upon the out-side at 45 feet above the ground, the interior height being 70 feet. Upon the corners of the building there are four towers 75 feet in height, and between the towers and the central projections or entrances there is a lower roof introduced, showing a cornice 24 feet above the ground. Small balconies or galleries of observation, have been provided in the four central towers of the building, at the heights of the different stories. This edifice cost $1,420,000, exclusive of drainage, water-pipe, plumbing, painting and decoration. It was sold at public auction at the close of the exhibition to the Permanent Exhibition Company for $250,000. It is to remain on the grounds as a permanent Exhibition Hall.

— H. T. DAEMICKE.

PAUL J. DAEMICKE.   G. F. DAEMICKE.

DAEMICKE BROTHERS,

HARDWARE, STOVES AND RANGES,

Butcher's Tools and Machines, Iron Kettles
And Furnaces, all Sizes. OUR SPECIALTY is Mechanical Tools of all Kinds.
GRATES, BRICKS, AND PIECES FURNISHED FOR ALL STOVES MADE.

☞ Orders and information by MAIL promptly attended to. ☜

The New Firm in the Old Established Long Frame Shanty.

912 State Street, - - - - CHICAGO, ILL.

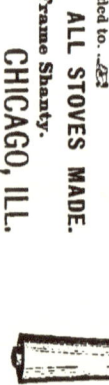

Alexander Macomb was born in Detroit in 1782, and entered the army at the age of 17 years. He was made a brigadier in 1814. In 1835 he was commander-in-chief of the armies of the United States, and died in 1841.

Edmund P. Gaines was born in Virginia in 1777. He entered the army in 1799, and rose gradually until he was made major-general for his gallantry at Fort Erie in 1814. He remained in the army until his death, in 1849.

Thomas S. Jesup was born in Virginia in 1778. He was a brave and useful officer during the war of 1812, and was retained in the army. He was breveted major-general in 1828, and was succeeded in command in Florida by Colonel Zachary Taylor in 1838. He died in Washington City.

Daniel Webster was born in Salisbury, New Hampshire, in 1782. He was admitted to the bar in Boston in 1805. He commenced his political career in Congress in 1818. He was in public employment a greater portion of the remainder of his life, and was the most distinguished statesman of his time. He died at Marshfield, Mass., in October, 1852.

Major Brown was born in Massachusetts in 1788; was in the war of 1812, and was promoted to major in 1843. He was wounded in the Mexican war by the bursting of a bombshell, and died on the 9th of May, 1846. He was 58 years of age.

William J. Worth (General) was born in Columbia county, New York, in 1794; was a gallant soldier during the war of 1812; was retained in the army, and for his gallantry at Monterey, during the Mexican war, he was made a major-general, by brevet, and received the gift of a sword from Congress. He was of great service during the whole war with Mexico. He died in Texas, in May, 1849.

John Ellis Wool (General) was a native of New York. He entered the army in 1812, and soon rose to the rank of lieutenant-colonel, for gallant conduct on Queenstown Heights, in 1812. He was breveted brigadier in 1825, and for gallant conduct at Buena Vista, in 1847, was breveted major-general.

Winfield Scott was born in Virginia in 1786. He was admitted to law practice at the age of 21 years. He joined the army in 1808, was made lieutenant-colonel in 1812, and passed through the war that ensued with great honor to himself and his company. He was breveted major-general in 1814, and was made general-in-chief of the army in 1841. His successes in Mexico greatly added to his laurels, and he was considered one of the greatest captains of the age. He was made lieutenant-general in 1855. He died May 29, 1866, at West Point, aged 80 years.

Stephen W. Kearney was a native of New Jersey. He was a gallant soldier in the war of 1812. He was breveted a brigadier in 1846, and major-general in December the same year, for gallant conduct in the Mexican war. He died at Vera Cruz, in October, 1848, at the age of 54 years.

David E. Twiggs was born in Georgia in 1790. He was a major at the close of the war of 1812, and was retained in the army. He was breveted major-general after the battle of Monterey, and for his gallantry there he received a gift of a sword from Congress.

HASTINGS—*Continued*.

MEAT MARKET.

ZEISZ & REIGEL, Meat Market,
200 Second st.

MILLINERY GOODS.

MOORHOUSE, S. E., Millinery, Fancy & Ladies' Furnishing Goods, 261 2nd st.

PHOTOGRAPHERS.

SCOTT, ALEX. A., Photographer,
One door west of Tremont House.

PRINTERS.

DUFFY & FREEMAN, Job Printers,
Post Office Block.

NEWSPAPER.

HASTINGS NEW ERA. The Boss Job Office of Dakota County. 268 Second st.

SALOON.

REUTER, M., Saloon,
276 Second st.

SEWING MACHINES.

BEELER, JAMES M., Agent Singer Sewing Machine, 46 Vermillion st.

TAILORS.

BOOR, V., Merchant Tailor,
Ramsey st., near Foster House.

FIESELER, H., Merchant Tailor,
46 Vermillion st.

SCOTT, P., Merchant Tailor,
280 Second st.

WAGON MAKER.

BECKER, D., Wagon Builder, Blacksmith and Horseshoer, Vermillion & 4th sts.

ST. PAUL, MINN,

BARBERS.

LEININGER, L., Hair Dressing and Shaving Saloon, 75 Robert st. Est. 1866.

SIGO, M., Barber,
113 Jackson st.

BOOKS AND STATIONERY.

DAVENPORT, JAMES, Bookseller & Stationer,
20 W. 3rd st.

MILHAM, E. H., Books & Stationery,
169 E. 7th st.

BOOTS AND SHOES.

ANDEREGG, C., Boots and Shoes,
95 Jackson st.

BARWISE, THOMAS, Fashionable Boot and Shoe Maker, 45 Robert st.

STRUTZELL, JOHN, Boot & Shoe Manufacturer,
49 Robert st.

BRIDGE BUILDER.

SHERWOOD, GEO. W., Bridge and Trestle Work Builder, &c., 80 Robert st.

DRESSMAKING.

CLARK, MRS. M. J., Dressmaking,
13½ W. 3rd st.

ST. PAUL.—*Continued.*

FANCY GOODS.

MUELLER, AUGUST, Fancy Goods, Zephyrs, &c., 129 E. 7th st.

FUR DEALER.

RYDER, M., Ladies' and Gents' Fur Goods, 55 Jackson st.

GROCERS.

FONTAINE, L., Groceries, Boots & Shoes, Feed, &c., 61 Robert st.

HARVESTER MANUFACTURER.

ST. PAUL HARVESTER WORKS,

Manufacturers of the Elward Harvester,
H. L. PILKINGTON, · · · Sec. & Treas.
COR. FOURTH & ROBERT STREETS.

IRON AND STEEL.

ROTHWELL, JOSEPH, Reliance Steel and Iron Works, 6th and Robert sts.

MARBLE WORKS.

THOMAS BOWER,

MARBLE & GRANITE WORKS,

Cor. SEVENTH & CEDAR STS.

MEAT MARKET.

WENTWORTH, G. W. & CO., Excelsior Meat Market. 47 Robert st.

PHOTOGRAPHER.

DERAGON, J. B., Photographer, 71 Robert st.

SALOONS.

FRANK WERNER'S Place, 120 W. Third st. Est. 1863.

GOTTFRIED ELBEL'S

Saloon, Wines, Liquors & Cigars,

182 W. THIRD STREET.

KAUFMAN, D. F., Wine, Beer and Liquors, No. 77 & Res. 91 Robert st.

SHIRT MANUFACTURER.

BRIGGS & MERRILL,

Troy Shirt Manufacturer,

● 34 Jackson Street.

STOVES AND TINWARE.

WOLTERSTORFF BROS., Stoves, Tinware and Wind Mill Dealers & Manfs., 123 E. 7th st.

TAILORS.

CONNOR, M., Fashionable Tailor, 55 Robert st.

WM. GEISENHEYNER,

Merchant Tailor

99 W. THIRD STREET.

MEYER, C. & CO., Merchant Tailors, 115 E. 7th st.

ADDENDA

TO

Important Improvements and Inventions.

Automatic Corn-Sheller—Invented by A. V. Cleland, 1874.

Barbed Fence—Invented first by Wm. E. Hunt, in the year 1867, improved by Scutt & Watkins in 1874, and by H. B. Scutt, in 1876.

Beach Patent Shifting Seat Carriage Bodies—Patented by S. W. Beach, in 1870.

Cash Register—Invented by W. J. Ripley, 1875.

Circle Tracking Wagon—Patented July 1, 1876, by L. W. Frederick Hall.

Combinaton Lock for drawers, etc.—Patented 1876 or 1877.

Combined Plum and Squares Level and Conformator for measuring for coats and vests—Invented by Fred Wright, 1877.

Combined Pad and Collar Fastener—A. Racine, 1875.

Concrete Water Pipe—Invented by T. Millen, 1877.

Corbett's Automatic Variable Cut-off Governor, for steam engines—Invented by Thos. M. Corbett, 1875.

Crescent Fluid, non-explosive—A. F. Beattie, 1876.

Double-acting, Anti-freezing Force Pump—Invented by H. M. Wyeth, in 1876.

Eccentric Brake (for cars or wagons)—Patented by W. M. Groze.

Economical Pump Sucker—Patented Feb. 23, 1875, and —— 1877, by J. M. Springer.

Electric Clasp Switch—Invented by A. H. Freeman, in 1871.

Electric Burglar Alarm—Improved by A. H. Freeman, in 1876.

End and Side Bar Spring—Patented and invented by H. M. Curtis, 1876.

Escapement for Clocks Compound Pendulum—Invented by J. E. Wolverton, in 1876.

Excelsior Hod Elevator—Patented June 30, 1874, by C. Bradford.

Fastening for Trunks (without straps or buckles)—Invented by C. C. Taylor, 1867.

Glass Wheel Electric Pendulum Clock—Invented by J. E. Wolverton, in 1876.

Horse-Hoof Paring Machine—Geo. W. Schaefer, 1873.

Howe's Spring Pad Belt Truss (for the treatment and cure of Rupture or Hernia)—Patented and improved by "Howe Truss Co.," Council Bluffs, Iowa, May 17, 1870, March 14, 1871, and March 23, 1875.

Ink Keg—Invented by F. A. Redington, 1876.

Ink Vent—Patented and invented by F. A. Redington, Feb. 15, 1876.

Insect Powder Blower—Patented June 5, 1877, by W. T. Brummer.

Interfering Horse Shoe (to prevent horses from hurting themselves)—Invented by Joseph Stanton.

Information worth Thousands To Those out of Health.

THE *Electric Quarterly* contains valuable information for invalids and those who suffer from Nervous, Exhausting and painful diseases. It treats upon the laws of hygiene and physical culture, and shows how perfect bodily health and energy may be fully enjoyed by means of

PULVERMACHER'S
ELECTRIC BELTS AND BANDS
THE BEST KNOWN CURATIVE AGENT.

These highly perfected Curative Appliances supply to the body mild and continuous currents of Electricity, and in so effective a manner that the most stubborn and complicated diseases yield to their magnetic influence after every other plan of treatment has failed. They are applicable to either sex, the young and old; and although applied externally by the patient himself, exert a beneficient and recuperative influence throughout the entire economy. The Electric action begins at once, as soon as the Belt or Band is applied, and the beneficial effects are perceptible almost from the start. Cases regarded incurable, and of years standing, yield to their mild but wonderful influence. In no case can the application be attended with the least harmful effects. The action penetrates every bodily organ, and thus promotes Digestion, Excretion, Nutrition and Circulation, restoring health and vigor to the debilitated constitution.

Their many invaluable qualities and adaptation for medical purposes, obtained for them at once full recognition from scientists and the *elite* of the medical profession at home and abroad. They combine in the utmost degree efficiency, comfort in application, and economy, and are *self-applicable by the patient himself*, for the speedy and effectual cure of Nervous, Chronic and functional Diseases. Among others, the following:

Rheumatism,	*Nervous Debility,*	*Spermatorrhœa,*
Neuralgia,	*Liver Complaint,*	*Epilepsy,*
Dyspepsia,	*Kidney Disease,*	*Paralysis,*
Constipation,	*Female Complaints,*	*Spinal Diseases,*
Sciatica,	*Skin Diseases,*	*Catarrh,*
Lumbago,	*Nervousness,*	*Deafness,*
Aches and Pains,	*Trembling,*	*Nervous Complaints,*
General Debility	*Indigestion,*	*General Ill-Health,*
Head Troubles,	*Diseases of the Chest,*	*Decline, &c.*

☞ *Descriptive Pamphlet and Electric Quarterly, an eight-page illustrated Journal containing valuable information and full particulars mailed free.*

ADDRESS

PULVERMACHER GALVANIC CO.

292 Vine St., Cincinnati, O.

ADVERTISEMENTS.

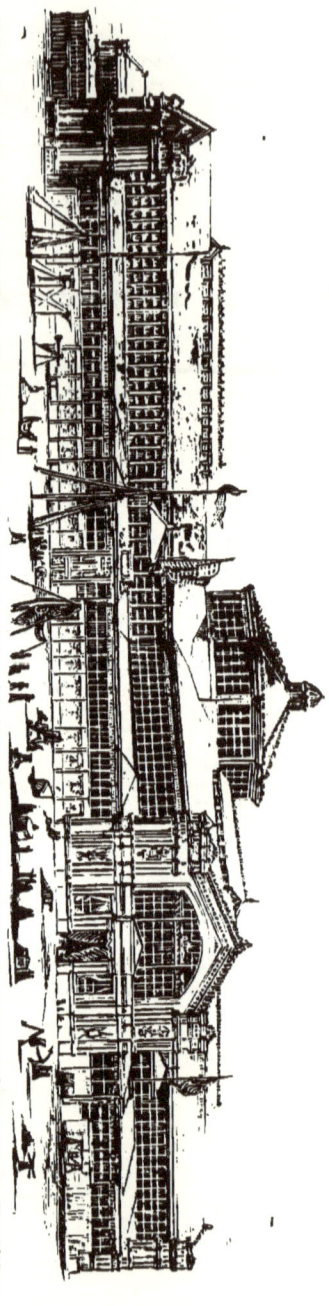

United States Government Building, Centennial Exposition, Philadelphia.—It is 480 feet long by 346 feet wide, and covers more than two acres. It exhibits a complete display of the progress of the government. In the manufacture of arms, ammunition, and accoutrements since the earliest days of the Republic until the present time. In fact, in this building will be revealed to the visitor the practical working of nearly every department of the government, together with illustrations and comparisons of former times with the present, and a large collection of treasures and curiosities from both sea and land.

CONRAD HAASE,
UPHOLSTERER,
—AND—
Mattress Manufacturer.

Main St., bet. 7th and 8th, near R. R. Depot,
EVANSVILLE, IND.

The Accommodation Glove Store.
H. JENSEN,
FRENCH GLOVE MAKER.

We measure the hand. A perfect fit guaranteed.

652 State Street, Chicago, Ill.

All kinds of Gloves repaired. Ordered Gloves promptly attended to by sending number of size worn.

St. Paul—Continued.

TOBACCO AND CIGARS.

J. P. LEITNER,
CIGARS, TOBACCO, PIPES, SNUFF,
26 W. THIRD STREET.

VINEGAR MANUFACTURERS.

SPINK & SON,
Vinegar   Manufacturers,
95 E. Seventh Street.

WATCHMAKER AND JEWELER.

MAX WITTELSHOFER,
Jeweler and Watchmaker,
36 Jackson Street.

WINONA, MINN.

BARBERS.

EIEKEMEYER, W. C., Barber,
63 E. 2nd st.

SCHMITT, J., Barber,
Cor. Main & 3rd st.

BILLIARD HALL.

LICHTENSTEIGER, T., Billiard Hall, Restaurant and Saloon, 55 E. Second st.

BOOKSELLER AND STATIONERY.

DOYEN, F. E., Bookseller and News Dealer,
13 E. Third st.

BOOTS AND SHOES.

BARTLETT & PIERCE,
Ladies' and Gents' Furnishing Goods,
BOOTS AND SHOES.
COR. SECOND AND CENTER ST.

CUMMINGS & VILA, Dealers in Boots & Shoes,
17 E. Third st.

HABERLE, LOUIS, Boots & Shoes,
Cor. Third and Lafayette sts.

FLADELAND, JOHN G., Boots and Shoes, Gloves and Mittens, 24 E. Second st.

JANSON BROS., Boots and Shoes,
77 E. Third st.

SCHERER, C. JR., Boots & Shoes,
56 E. Second st.

SCHUMACHER, F. P., Boots and Shoes,
70 E. Second st.

CABINET MAKER.

GOETZE, E. F., Cabinet Maker,
Lafayette bet. 2nd & 3rd sts.

CLOTHING.

ARNOLD, W., Clothing, Boots and Shoes,
13 E. Second st

FOX & FOREST, Clothing and Furnishing Goods, 26 E. Second st.

CROCKERY AND GLASSWARE.

GREGORY & CO., Crockery and Glassware,
39 E. 2nd st.

Winona—Continued.

DENTISTS.

PENEGRINE, J. S., Dentist,
Cor. 2nd and Main st.

WELCH, A., Dentist,
11 E. Third st.

DRUGGISTS.

KENDALL, I., Drugs and Medicines, Paints and Oils, 17 E. Second st.

A. O. SLADE,
CITY DRUGSTORE
22 East Third Street.

WEDEL, DR. H. R., Druggist and Apothecary,
Cor. Second and Lafayette sts.

DRY GOODS.

CHOATE, H., Dry Goods,
Center & 3d st.

RHEINBERGER BRO.,
DRY   GOODS,   NOTIONS   AND   FANCY   GOODS,
CENTER Bet. SECOND & THIRD STS.

THE POOR MAN'S FRIEND CLOTHING STORE,
Dry Goods and Gents' Furnishing Goods,
No. 4 Simpson Block, Second Street.

FURNITURE.

THRUNE, A. & CO., Furniture,
42 E. 2d st.

GROCERIES.

CURTIS, E. F., Grocer,
24 E. Third st., cor. Center st.

DURAND, GEO. W., Grocery Clerk,
Hubbard Block.

GREENES & VILLAUNICE, Groceries, Crockery, Glass, Wood & Willow Ware, 52 E. 3d st.

HASKIN, GEO. E., Grocer,
44 E. Second st.

GROCERY AND COMMISSION HOUSE,
G. L. HALLOWELL.
3d St., bet. Main & Johnson.

LATSCH, J., Grocer,
103 W. 2d st.

GUN MAKER.

FELSTED, T. I., Gun Maker,
Lafayette st., bet. 2nd & 3rd.

HARDWARE.

ELMER & WILCOX, Hardware,
16 E. 3rd st.

HARNESS AND SADDLES.

ROBT. CROSSGROVE,
Harness, Saddles, Whips, &c.,
COR. WALNUT & THIRD STS.

HOTELS.

EUROPEAN HOTEL
GEORGE ROBINSON, Proprietor.
67 East Third St.

The Washington Elm, Cambridge, Mass.—Not far from the college grounds stands one of the famous trees of the country—the Washington Elm—the only known survivor of the ancient forest that originally covered this part of Cambridge. It was under this tree that General George Washington took command of the Continental army, on the morning of July 3, 1775. A neat fence surrounds this giant of the ancient forests, and an inscription commemorates the important event, which was the most interesting in its centuries of existence.

WINONA—*Continued.*

ISWELL HOUSE.
JAMES LAW, Prop.
COR. JOHNSON & SECOND STS.

MERCHANTS' HOTEL. M. Schweitzer, Prop. Terms, $2.00 per day, Cor. Walnut & 2nd sts.

INSURANCE AGENT.

DIXON, A. C., Fire, Life and Accident Insurance Agency, 2nd, Nat Bank Building.

JEWELRY STORE.

MORGAN, S. W., Watchmaker and Jeweler, 15 E. 2nd st.

LIVERY STABLES.

J. B. MOREHEAD,
LIVERY STABLE,
THIRD & WALNUT STS.

SCHNEIDER BROS., Livery, 97 W. 2nd st.

MILLINERY GOODS.

MURPHY, MRS. P. J., Millinery and Fancy Goods, No. 51 E. 2nd st.

MUSICAL INSTRUMENTS.

ROOT, JULIUS M., Musical Instruments, 13 East 3rd st.

WINONA—*Continued.*

PHOTOGRAPHERS.

DEN CHAMBERLAIN,
PHOTOGRAPHER
—AND—
Inventor of Photographing in Natural Colors,
13 EAST SECOND STREET.

HOARD & TENNEY,
PHOTOGRAPHERS
18 CENTER STREET.

SALOON.

BEER AND BILLIARD HALL, 2nd st., bet. Lafayette & Walnut. Gust. Henrichs, Prop.

TAILORS.

BARRIE, J., Tailor and Dealer in Sewing Machines, 14 E. 2nd st.

KASIMOR & VOTRUBA, Merchant Tailors, 12 East 2nd st.

UPHOLSTERER.

SIMON, P., Upholsterer and Cabinet Maker, Lafayette, bet. 2nd & 3rd sts

Metallic Support for Trunk Tops—Invented by C. C. Taylor, 1867.
Movable Fronts for Buildings—Invented by John Murphy, 1875.
Oil Can—Invented by Bartels, 1877.
Original Inventors' Manufacturing Association, established 1876; first and only one.
Padlock Improvement—By Geo. R. Cutbirth, 1875.
Perkins Wind Mill—Invented by P. C. Perkins, 1868; improved 1869.
Piano Forte Pedal Attachment—Invented by L. C. Whiting, 1875.
Reagan's Patent for Flanging Flue-Holes in Boiler Heads—E. Reagan, Patentee, Indianapolis, Ind.
Rotary Morticing Machine—Invented by J. A. Peabody, 1855; improved, Improved, 1868.
Seamless Shoes—Patented Sept. 26, 1876, and ———— 1877, by H. Brossel.
Sickle Grinder—Patented by H. S. Stevens, Oct. 31, 1876, and improved by him April 3, 1877.
Taylor Horse-Sweep Powers—Patent bearing date December 22, 1874; manufactured by Taylor, Mack & Smith, 189 La Salle Street, Chicago, Ill.
The Automatic Gold Condensing Mallet (for filling teeth)—Invented and improved by Morrison, in 1864-65 and '68.
The Eclectic Heater—Invented, 1871; improved, 1873, by Servoss, Northen & Co.
The Morrison Burring Engine (for drilling teeth for filling)—Invented by M. Morrison, 1871.
Westwood Slide Valve—Invented by Westwood in 1876; improved, 1877.

LA CROSSE, WIS.

ARCHITECT AND SUPERINTENDENT.

C. F. STRUCK,
Architect & Superintendent,
68 MAIN STREET.

AUCTION AND COMMISSION.

ANDERSON, S. S., Auction and Commission House, 22 N. 3rd st.

BILLIARD HALL.

H. LIVERMAN,
Proprietor of
Harry's Place and the Metropolitan Billiard Hall
26 NORTH THIRD ST.

BOOTS AND SHOES.

HEIL, HENRY, Dealer in Fine Boots and Shoes, 33 Main st.

CONFECTIONERY.

BARNES, R. R., Confectionery, Ice Cream Parlors, cor. State & 3rd sts.

LA CROSSE—*Continued.*

CROCKERY WARE.

J. W. TOMS & CO.,
Importer of Crockery
38 MAIN STREET.

DRESSMAKING.

THOMPSON, MISS M. A., Fashionable Dress and Cloak Maker, 68 Main st.

DRUGGIST.

H. HEYERDAHL,
LION DRUG STORE
23 South Third Street.

DRY GOODS.

MARCUS ANDERSON,
Dry Goods, Notions, Fancy Goods, &c.
THIRD AND MAIN STS.

SUNDE, HAROLD, Dry Goods and Furnishing Goods and Auction Prices, 29 Main st.

FURNITURE.

GANTERT, S., Furniture, 14 S. Third street.

GROCERIES.

FREISE, WM., Commission Merchant and Grocery, Provision and Seed Dealer, 64 Main st.
HOGAN, THOS., Wholesale Dealer in Groceries, cor. Main & 2nd sts.
ROTH, ANDREW, Groceries and Provisions, Alzinger. Jos. Liquors and Cigars, 88 Main st.

C. B. SOLBERG,
Wholesale Grocer,
COR. PEARL & THIRD STS.

STEVENS, A. A., & SON, Groceries and Provisions, 93 Main st.
TAYLOR, G. H. & W., Cash Grocery Store, 31 N. 3rd st.
TURNER, W. J., Groceries, Confections, Fruits, Game. &c., 4th & Main sts.
WATSON, A. M., Choice Family Groceries, 5th & Main sts.
WILLING, JOHN, Groceries, Dry Goods, &c., 18 S. 3rd st.
WILSON, E. A., Groceries and Provisions, 15 S. 3rd st.

HARDWARE.

KRONER, FRED., Hardware and Stoves, Agricultural Implements, 16 S. Third st.

HATS AND CAPS.

LUTZ, PAUL, Manuf'r of Hats, Caps and Ladies' and Gents' Furs, 27 Main st., La Crosse, Wis.

JEWELRY STORE.

PATZ, A., Jewelry Store, 67 Main st.

MEAT MARKETS.

JEHLEN, DOMINIC, Proprietor of the Cedar Market, 66 Main st.

LA CROSSE—Continued.

VOIGHT, GUSTAVUS, Court House Meat Market, 3rd st., bet. State & Vine.

NEWSPAPER.

Established in 1852.

THE
Morning Liberal Democrat,

SYMES & USHER, Editors & Props.

LA CROSSE.

The leading Newspaper of Western Wisconsin. Widely circulated in Wisconsin and Minnesota.

PAINTER.

D. B. HARRISON,
Painter, Grainer, Paper-Hanger, &c.
MAIN ST., Bet. 5th & 6th Sts.

PHOTOGRAPHER.

MYERS, MRS. E. M., Photographer, 86 Main st.

WINES AND LIQUORS.

MUELLER, FRED., Wholesale Dealer in Liquors and Cigars, bet. Main & State sts.

KEOKUK, IOWA.

ARTISTS.

LIFE SIZE PORTRAITS.
H. A. SMITH,
Portrait Artist,
Studio in Ayres & Son's Building, Main st., bet. 5th and 6th sts.

UPP, GEO., Artist, Portrait and Landscape Painting, Estes House Block.

ATTORNEYS AT LAW.

ALLYN, FRANK, Attorney at Law, 5th st., bet. Main & Blondien.

BALLINGER, M. A., Attorney at Law, 132 N. Main st.

BROWNE, GIBSON, Attorney and Counselor at Law, 3 N. 5th st.

COCHRAN, WM. J., Attorney at Law, Estes House Block.

DRYDEN & DRYDEN, Attorneys at Law, 5th st., bet. Main & Blondien.

HOWELL, H. SCOTT, Counselor at Law, 5th st., bet. Main and Blondien.

MARSHALL & SONS, Attorneys and Counselors at Law, Cor. 3d and Main sts.

McCRARY, HAGERMAN & McCRARY, Attorneys at Law, Gate City Building.

REID, J. M., Attorney at Law and U. S. Claim Agent, 5th st.

AUCTION AND COMMISSION MERCHANTS.

BROWN & TYLER,
General Auction & Commission Merchants,
152 Main st., Keokuk Iowa.

FICTITIOUS NAMES
OF
STATES, CITIES, NOTED PERSONS, &c.

Albany Regency.—A name popularly given in the United States to a junto of astute Democratic politicians, having their headquarters at Albany, N. Y., who controlled the action of the Democratic party for many years, and who had great weight in national politics. The effort to elect Wm. H. Crawford President, instead of John Quincy Adams, was their first great struggle.

Badger State.—A name given to Wisconsin.

Bay State.—A popular name of Massachusetts, which, previous to the adoption of the Federal Constitution, was called the Colony of Massachusetts.

Bayou State.—A name sometimes given to the State of Mississippi, which abounds in bayous or creeks.

Bear State.—A name by which the State of Arkansas is sometimes designated on account of the number of bears that infest its forests.

Battle of the Kegs.—The subject and title of a mock heroic poem, by Francis Hopkinson. This ballad, very famous in Revolutionary times, was occasioned by the following incident: Certain machines in the form of kegs, charged with gun powder, were sent down the river to annoy the British shipping then at Philadelphia. The danger of these machines being discovered, the British manned the wharves and shipping, and discharged their small arms and cannons at everything they saw floating on the river during the ebb tide.

Blue Hen, The.—A cant or popular name for the State of Delaware. This soubriquet is said to have had its origin in a certain Captain Caldwell's fondness for the amusement of cock-fighting. Caldwell was an officer in the 1st Delaware regiment in the war of the Revolution, and was greatly distinguished for his daring and bravey. He was exceedingly popular in the regiment, and its high state of discipline was generally conceded to be due to his exertions; so that when officers were sent on recruiting service to fill vacancies occasioned by death or otherwise, it was a saying that they had gone home for more of Caldwell's game-cocks; but as Caldwell insisted that no cock could be truly game unless the mother was a Blue hen, the expression Blue Hen's chickens was substituted for game-cocks.

Bluff City.—A descriptive name applied to the city of Hannibal, Mo.

Boston Massacre.—A name popularly given to a disturbance which occurred in the streets of Boston, on the evening of March 5th, 1770, when a sergeant's guard belonging to the British garrison fired upon a crowd of people who were surrounding them, and pelting them with snow-balls) and killed three men, besides wounding several others. The leader of the town-people was a black man, named Crispus Attucks.

Boston Tea Party.—A name given to the famous assemblage of citizens in Boston, December 16, 1773, who met to carry out the non-importation resolves of the colony, and who, disguised as Indians, went on board three

STALLMAN & CO.

ENGRAVING ON WOOD

N.W. COR. FRONT & VINE
CINCINNATI OHIO

Best of Reference Furnished if Desired. Wood Cuts of

Stoves, Machinery, Furniture, Buildings, Labels,
AGRICULTURAL IMPLEMENTS, LANDSCAPES, &C.,

GOT UP IN THE BEST STYLE AT

REASONABLE PRICES.

ADVERTISEMENTS.

Illinois State Building, Centennial Exposition, Phila.—This building is a handsome structure, and reflects great credit on the State. Its dimensions are 40x60 feet, a story and a half high, with a French roof. It is the headquarters for visitors from Illinois, and offers a welcome to strangers from all parts of the country.

S. RICKE & CO.,

MANUFACTURERS OF ALL KINDS OF
PARLOR FURNITURE & FRAMES,
265 DIVISION STREET,

Take either the Clybourn Ave., or Larrabee Street Cars at Clark and Madison Streets to Division.

FACTORY, ON VEDDER ST., near CLYBOURN AVE.,   **CHICAGO, ILL.**

Catalogues will be sent on application.

ships, which just arrived in the harbor, and destroyed several hundred chests of tea. The British Parliament retaliated by closing the port of Boston.

Brother Jonathan.—A sportive collective name for the people of the United States, originating as follows: When General Washington, after being appointed commander of the army, went to Massachusetts to organize it and make preparations for the defense of the country, he found a great want of ammunition and other means necessary to meet the powerful foe he had to contend with, and great difficulty in obtaining them. If attacked in such conditions, the cause at once might be hopeless. On one occasion, at that anxious period, a consultation of the officers and others was had, when it seemed that no way could be devised to make such preparation as was necessary. His Excellency Jonathan Trumbull, the elder, was then Governor of Connecticut, and, as Washington placed the greatest reliance on his judgment and aid, he remarked, "We must consult Brother Jonathan on the subject." He did so, and the Governor was successful in supplying many of the wants of the army. The origin of the expression being soon lost sight of, the name Brother Jonathan came to be regarded as the national sobriquet.

Buckeye State.—The State of Ohio, so-called from the Buckeye tree, which abounds there.

City of Brotherly Love.—Philadelphia is sometimes so-called, this being the literal signification of the name.

City of Churches.—A name popularly given to the city of Brooklyn, N. Y., from the unusually large number of churches which it contains.

City of Elms.—A familiar denomination of New Haven, Connecticut, many of the streets of which are thickly shaded with lofty elms.

City of Magnificent Distances.—A popular designation given to the city of Washington, the capital of the United States, which is laid out on a very large scale, being extended to cover a space of four miles and a half long, and two miles and a half broad, or eleven square miles. The entire site is traversed by two sets of streets from 70 to 100 feet wide, at right angles to one another, the whole again intersected obliquely by fifteen avenues from 130 to 160 feet wide.

City of Rocks.—A descriptive name popularly given in the United States to the city of Nashville, Tenn.

City of Spindles.—A name popularly given to the city of Lowell, Massachusetts, the largest cotton manufacturing town in the United States.

City of the Straits.—A name given to Detroit, which is situated on the west bank of the river or strait connecting Lake St. Clair with Lake Erie. Detroit is a French word, meaning "strait."

Corn-Cracker.—A popular nickname or designation for the State of Kentucky. The inhabitants of the State are often called Corn-crackers.

Cow-boys.—A band of marauders in the time of American revolution, consisting mostly of refugees who adhered to the British side, and who infested the so-called "neutral grounds," lying between the American and British lines,

KEOKUK—*Continued.*

BAKERY AND CONFECTIONERY.

ZERR, CHAS., Bakery, Confectionery and Ice Cream Saloon, South Side Main st.

BANKERS.

H. G. BOON & CO.,
Bankers, do a general Banking and Exchange Business. Prompt attention given to collections and remittances. Special attention given to the purchase and sale of City and County Bonds, and other Western securities, office, 4th st., bet. Main and Johnson.

BARBERS.

CABUS, GEO., Shaving and Hairdressing Room, 73 Main st.

ELDORADO HAIRDRESSING SALOON

Shaving, Dying and Shampooing done to the latest tip of the Wing, 3d street, bet. Main and Johnson, Prof. W. H. Jones, Tonsorial Artist.

MICHAELIS, OTTO, Barber, and Manf'r of all kinds of Hairwork, 114 Main st.

PRETTYMAN, GEO. H., Shaving and Hairdressing Saloon, N. Main st.

ROHDE, ADALBERT, H. F., Barber shop, E. side of 3d st., bet. Main & Johnson sts.

BOOKBINDER.

PEARCE, I. W., Blank Book Manf'r & Binder, 2d st., near Main.

BONNET BLEACHERY.

EMERSON, C. H., Stocking Factory and Bonnet Bleachery, 4th & Blondien sts.

BOOKSELLER AND STATIONER.

WESTCOTT, SAM'L C., Bookseller & Stationer, 167 Main st.

BOOTS AND SHOES.

SCHWARZ, J. F., Fashionable Boot & Shoe Maker, cor. Main and 7th sts.

BRASS FOUNDRY.

RIBYN, MATT., Miss. Brass Foundry, Brass, Copper and Tin Work, Main st., near 10th st.

CARRIAGES AND BUGGIES.

WORLEY, S. T., Manf'r of Carriages, Buggies, etc., cor. 1st and Main st.

CLAIRVOYANT.

ORR, MRS. M. M., Clairvoyant, Johnson st., near 3d st.

CONFECTIONERY.

ESSIG, J. A., Candy Manf'r, wholesale and retail, 112 & 154 N. Main st.

MILWARD, D. E., Manf'r and dealer in Confectionery, 187 Main st.

CONTRACTORS AND BUILDERS.

DURFEE & BRAY, Contractors & Builders, also, Durfee & Lowry, Family Groceries, Johnson st. bet. 7th & 8th sts.

DENTIST.

J. B. BENNETT,

DENTIST,

Office, over 141 Main st.

KEOKUK—Continued.

DRUGGISTS.

R. HEISER,
Druggist, and dealer in Paints, Oils, Varnishes, Window Glass and Glassware, Coal Oil Lamps, Chimneys, Shades, etc., 206 Main st.

Wilkinson, Bartlett & Co.,
Wholesale and Retail
DRUGGISTS,
COR. 4th & MAIN STS.
☞ Sign of the Golden Eagle and Mortar. ☜

DRY GOODS.
BOSTWICK, H. N., wholesale and retail dealer in Dry Goods, 102 and 104 Main st.

DYE HOUSE.
BLANK, B., Steam Dye House,
Main st., bet. 6th & 7th sts.

FURNITURE.
LINQUIST, L. F., Manuf'r of Furniture, Writing Desks, etc., 203 N. Main st.
SCHARDELMANN, H. A., Manf'r and dealer in Furniture, Mattresses, etc., 198 Main st.

GENTS' FURNISHING GOODS.
HUMPHREY, J. E., Gents' Furnishing Goods, Varieties & Notions, 183 Main st.

GROCERIES.
BARTLETT, H. D. & SON, Staple & Fancy Groceries, 71 Johnson st., bet. 2d & 3d sts.
BEADLE & GARGAS, Fancy Groceries, Fruits, Nuts, etc , 57 Johnson st., near 2d.
MEGART, JOHN, Groceries & Produce, 177 Main st., bet. 7th & 8th sts.
PETERSON, DANIEL & CO., dealers in Groceries, Produce & Provisions, 179 Main st.

HAIR DEALER.
WAY, MRS. C., Manf'r and dealer in Human Hair, 4th st.

HARNESS AND SADDLES.
GRIFFEY, J. C., Manf'r of Harness, Saddles, Collars, etc., 3d st., near Main st.
LEOPOLD, A. V., Harness Manf'r,
North side Main st.

HORSESHOEING.
MAHONEY, DANIEL, Horseshoeing & Blacksmithing, 3d st., bet. Johnson & Exch'ge sts.
MULLIN, PETER, Horseshoeing & Blacksmithing, 3d st., opp. Patterson House.
WOLF & ALTON, Horseshoers, and Iron Fence Railings, general repairing, N. Main st.

HOTELS.
EAGLE HOTEL, John Menz, prop.,
1st & Johnson sts.
HARDIN HOUSE, E. Hardin prop ,
2d & Johnson sts.
PATTERSON HOUSE, W. A. & J. C. Patterson, props, 3d & Johnson sts.

HOUSE-FURNISHING GOODS.
COMSTOCK, E. C., dealer in House-furnishing Goods, 77 Main st.

---

plundering all those who had taken the oath of allegiance to the Continental Congress. (*See Skinners.*)

Cradle of Liberty.—A popular name given to Faneuil Hall, a large public edifice in Boston, Mass.; celebrated as being the place where the orators of the Revolution roused the people to resistance to British oppression.

Creole State.—A name sometimes given to the State of Louisiana, in which the descendants of the original French and Spanish settlers constitute a large proportion of the population.

Crescent City.—A popular name for the city of New Orleans, the older portion of which is built around the convex side of a bend of the Mississippi river. In the progress of its growth up stream, however, the city has now so extended itself as to fill the hollow of a curve in the opposite direction, so that the river front presents an outline resembling the character S.

Empire City.—The city of New York, the chief city of the western world, and the metropolis of the Empire State.

Empire State, The.—A popular name of the State of New York, the most populous and the wealthiest State in the Union.

Excelsior State.—The State of New York, sometimes so called for the motto "Excelsior" upon its coat of arms.

Falls City.—Louisville, Kentucky, popularly so called from the falls which at this place, impede the navigation of the Ohio river.

Father of Waters.—A popular name given to the Mississippi river, on account of its great length (3,160 miles) and the very large number of its tributaries, of which the Red, the Arkansas, the Ohio, the Missouri, the Illinois, the Des Moines, the Wisconsin, and the St. Peters or Minnesota, are the most important. The literal signification of the name, which is of Indian origin, is said to be *Great River.*

Fern, Fanny.—A pseudonym adopted by Mrs. Sarah P. Parton (born 1811), a popular American authoress.

Flour City.—A popular designation in the United States of the city of Rochester, N. Y. A place remarkable for its extensive manufactories of flour.

Flower City.—Springfield, Illinois, the capital of the State, which is distinguished for the beauty of its surroundings.

Forest City.—1. Cleveland, Ohio—so called from the many ornamental trees with which the streets are bordered. 2. A name given to Portland, Maine, a city distinguished for its many elms and other beautiful shade trees.

Freestone State.—The State of Connecticut; sometimes so called from the quarries of freestone which it contains.

Funk, Peter.—A person employed at petty auctions to bid on articles put up for sale, in order to raise their prices; probably so called from such a name having frequently been given when articles were bought in. To *funk*, or *funk out*, is a vulgar expression, meaning to *slink away;* to *take one's self off.* In some localities it conveys the added notion of great fear.

Garden City.—A popular name for Chicago; a city which is remarkable for the number and beauty of its private gardens.

BEEMER BROTHERS,

Dealers in all kinds of

FURNITURE,

Bedding, Carpets,

OIL CLOTHS, STOVES, Etc

54 West Madison St.,
CHICAGO.

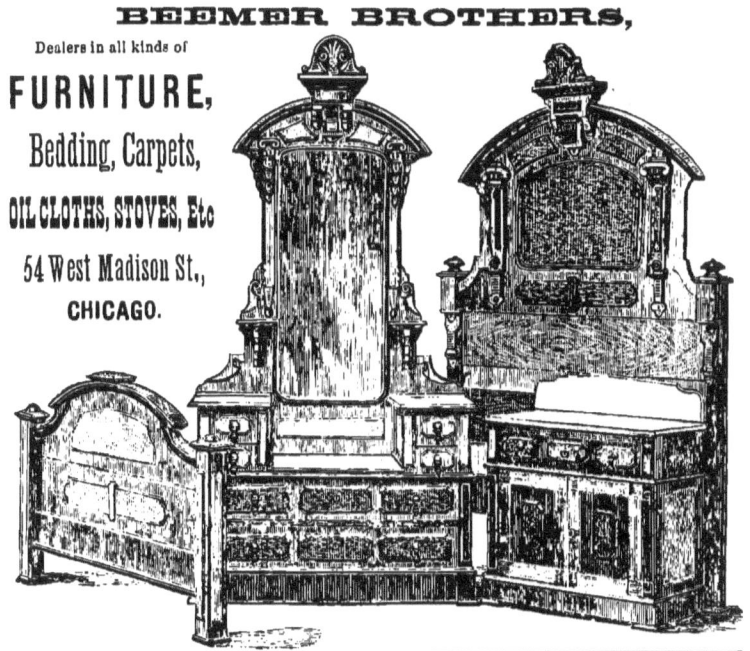

JOHN BECHAM,

DEALER IN ALL KINDS OF

Green and Flint Hides.

CORRECT WEIGHTS GUARANTEED,

AND HIGHEST MARKET PRICES PAID.

WEST WALNUT ST., - DES MOINES, IOWA.

ADVERTISEMENTS. 389

STATE CAPITOL, JEFFERSON CITY, MO.

HENRY BLOOM,
MANUFACTURER OF

Buggies, Spring Wagons and Road Wagons.
REPAIRING NEATLY DONE AT LOW PRICES.

318 Second Street, DES MOINES, IOWA.

KEOKUK—Continued.

IMPERIAL MILLS.

THE IMPERIAL MILLS, B. F. Hambleton, prop., Levee, bet. Main & Johnson.

INSURANCE.

W. H. CAREY,

FIRE AND LIFE INSURANCE,

132 MAIN ST.

THE IOWA LIFE INSURANCE CO.,
Cor. 5th & Main st.

JEWELRY.

AYRES, T. R. J. & SONS, Jewelry & Music,
130 Main st.

JUSTICE OF THE PEACE.

LYNCH, JAMES, Justice of the Peace,
5th st., cor. Blondien.

LIVERY AND SALE STABLE.

HILL & MILLER,

LIVERY & SALE STABLE,

COR. 8th & MAIN STS.

TITUS, I. B., Livery Stable,
Cor. 11th & Main sts.

MEAT MARKET.

CHARNIER, LOUIS B., Jr., Butcher, & dealer in Fresh & Cured Meats, W. side 4th st., n'r Main.

McDONALD & McMANUS, Fresh Fish and Pork House Meats, Main st., cor. 7th.

NARRLEY WALSMITH, Butchers, & dealers in Fresh, Salt and Smoked Meats, 157 Main st.

MILLINERY AND DRESSMAKING.

SOMERS, MRS. KATE, Dressmaking,
8th st., bet. Main & Blondien.

VORREITER, MRS. AUGUSTA, Millinery, Hair Goods & Harper's Bazar Patterns, 163 Main st.

NEWSPAPERS.

Daily and Weekly Keokuk Constitution
And Job Printing House, cor 6th and Main sts., Smith, Clendenin & Rees, props. The best advertising medium in Southern Iowa. Official paper of Lee county.

THE GATE CITY DAILY AND WEEKLY,

HOWELL & CLARK, Props.

5th street, bet. Main and Blondieu sts.

PAINTERS.

PRICE, W. M. & SONS., Wall Paper, House and Sign Painters, 182 N. Main st.

PATENT MEDICINE.

BAKER, DR. S. F. & SON., Manuf'rs of Proprietory Medicines, 5th and Blondieu sts.

PHYSICIANS.

BERTRAM, DR. W., late Brigade Surgeon & Med ical Director U. S. A., over 206 Main st.

COLLINS, DR. M. F., Physician and Surgeon,
Cor. 6th and Main sts.

SEIDLITZ, G. N., Physician, 3d st., near Main, residence, High st., bet. 6th & 7th sts.

KEOKUK—Continued.

DR. JOHN T. WILKINSON,

Specialist and Confidential Physician,

In the treatment of

CHRONIC AND LONG-STANDING DISEASES

Of Either Sex, either Hereditary or Acquired.
Office, cor. 3d & Main sts.

PLUMBERS AND GAS FITTERS.

T. BOWDEN & SON,

PLUMBERS & GAS FITTERS,

and dealers in Wrought Iron Pipe & Fittings,
3d ST., NEAR MAIN ST.

RESTAURANTS.

GOOD SAMARITAN COFFEE HOUSE, Mrs. L. Robertson, 65 Main st.

THE SENATE, First-class Restaurant, D. E. Crocker, propr., 156 N. Main st.

ROOFING.

SAMUELS, M. C., Galvanized Iron Cornices, Tin and Slate Roofing.

SEEDS.

WICKERSHAM & LOURIE, Garden, Field and Flower Seeds, Farm Machinery, etc., 159 Main.

SEWING MACHINES.

GAMPERT, W., Singer Sewing Machines,
166 N. Main st.

THOMAS, A. D., agt. for the unequaled St. John's Sewing Machine, runs either way without change of stitch. 169 Main st.

SODA WATER MANUFACTURERS.

BURK & BEMOLL, Manf'rs of Mineral & Seltzer Waters, North side Main st.

TOBACCO AND CIGARS.

KORNER, GEO., Manf'r and dealer in Tobacco & Cigars, 151 Main st.

NATIONAL CIGAR FACTORY, Edward Rube, prop., 136 Main st.

REIMBOLD & EISENHUTH, Cigar Manf'rs and dealers in Tobacco, Main st., bet. 6th & 7th sts.

TURKISH AND RUSSIAN BATHS.

MARSHALL HAMMONS,

Russian, Vapor and Turkish Baths. Chronic Diseases cured by Eclectic Treatment. Fifth st., near Main.

UMBRELLAS.

SCOTT, DR. SAMUEL, Visits the Sick and repairs Umbrellas, Main st., bet. 9th & 10th sts.

UNDERTAKERS.

PACKARD & MAJOR, Undertakers,
15 2d st.

JOHN T. PERKINS,

UNDERTAKER,

Open day and night, funerals promptly attended to, 15 3d st.

New Jersey State Building, Centennial Exposition, Phila.—This building is a frame structure, with tile roofing. Its dimentions are 82 ft. in length by 4? in width, and two stories in height, with attic and observatory. Cost of building $8,000

KEOKUK—*Continued.*

WAGON MAKERS.

LIST & HICKS,
Manufacturers of all kinds of Wagons, General Repairing and Blacksmithing, Johnson st., bet. 2d and 3d sts.

WINES AND LIQUORS.

AUWERDA, JOSEPH, Foreign & Domestic Liquors, 188 N. Main st.

YEAST.

BACHMAN, J. H., Manf'rs of the I. X. L. Dry Hop Yeast & Magic Washing Fluid, 5th near Main.

SPRINGFIELD, ILLS.

ATTORNEYS AT LAW.

BRADLEY & BRADLEY, Attorneys & Counselors, 117 S. 5th st.

SPRINGFIELD—*Continued.*

PALMER, JOHN M. & JOHN MAYO, Attorneys at Law, 510 S. 5th st.

ROGERS, H. H., Attorney at Law, 105 S. 5th st.

BOOKBINDERS.

R. RODERICK,

BOOK-BINDER,

—AND—

Blank Book Manufacturer,

221 S. 5th STREET.

Particular attention given to Ruling and Blank Book Work. Music Books, Magazines, Papers, etc., bound and rebound.

DRS. PIERCE & GREENO'S
MEDICAL AND SURGICAL INSTITUTE,
409 Delaware St., Kansas City, Mo.

THROAT AND LUNG DISEASES a leading specialty. Catarrh and Bronchitis treated by Electro-oxygen Compound Inhalation. Home treatment furnished to parties from distance. Cancers and Tumors treated without the use of Knife or Caustics. We guarantee cures in every case.

CORRESPONDENCE SOLICITED.

H. G. GRIFFITH,
Hair Goods, Silk Embroidery!
FOREIGN AND DOMESTIC FANCY GOODS,
211 South 5th Street, 5 Doors South of Bunn's Bank,
SPRINGFIELD, ILLINOIS.

MURPHY & WADE,
Hat and Bonnet Bleachers,
23 THIRD STREET, SPRINGFIELD, ILL.

Particular attention given to

GENTS' STRAW AND MANILLA HATS,
FELT HATS IN THEIR SEASON.

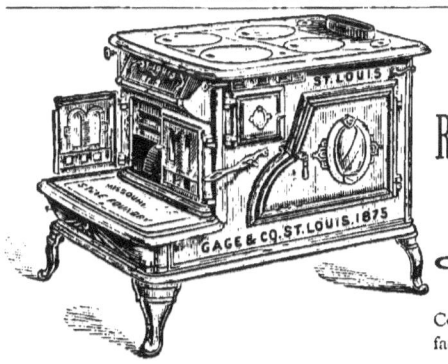

H. BERTHOLD & TROSSIN,
STOVES,
Ranges and Furnaces,
Tinware, Crockery and Glassware.

183 DOUGLAS STREET,

OMAHA, NEB.

Agents for Bonanza and St. Louis Co.'s Stoves. Guaranteed better satisfaction than the Charter Oak.

ADVERTISEMENTS.

KANSAS CITY IN 1855.

J. H. GIVEN, Superintendent Plow Department.

H. C. HARRIS, President.
R. W. CROSS, Secretary.

SAMUEL GREEN, Vice-President.

DES MOINES PLOW CO.,

Successors to J. H. GIVEN & CO., Manufacture

Breaking, Stirring, Single and Double Shovel Plows, Field Rollers, Cultivators, Revolving and Joint Harrows.

Special attention given to Miners and Millers' Tools.

WORKS, COR. VINE & SECOND STS.,

DES MOINES, IOWA.

Garden of the West.—A name usually given to Kansas, but sometimes applied to Illinois and others of the Western States, which are all noted for their productiveness.

Garden of the World.—A name frequently given to the vast country comprising more than 1,200,000 square miles which is drained by the Mississippi river and its tributaries—a region of almost unexampled fertility.

Gate City.—Keokuk, Iowa—popularly so-called. It is situated at the foot of the lower rapids of the Mississippi river (which extends twelve miles with a fall of twenty-four feet), and is the natural head of navigation. A portion of the city is built on a bluff one hundred and fifty feet high.

Gotham.—A popular name of the City of New York, first given to it in " Salmagundi" (a humorous work by Washington Irving, and William Irving, and James K. Paulding), because the inhabitants were such wiseacres.

Granite State.—A popular name for the State of New Hampshire, the mountainous portions of which are largely composed of granite.

Green Mountain State.—A popular name of Vermont, the Green Mountains being the principal mountain range in the State.

Grundy, Mrs.—A person frequently referred to in Morton's comedy " Speed the Plow," but not introduced as one of the *dramatis personœ*. The solicitude of Dame Ashfield, in this play, as to what *will Mrs. Grundy say?* has given the latter great celebrity, the interrogatory having acquired a proverbial currency.

Hamilton, Gail.—A pseudonym adopted by Miss Mary Abigail Dodge, of Hamilton, Mass., a popular American writer of the present day.

Hawkeye State.—The State of Iowa: said to be so named after an Indian chief, who was once a terror to voyagers to its borders.

Hoosier State.—The State of Indiana, the inhabitants of which are often called Hoosiers. This word is a corruption of *husher*, formerly a common term for a bully throughout the West.

Hub of the Universe.—A burlesque and popular designation of Boston, Mass., originating with the American humorist, O. W. Holmes.

Iron City.—A name popularly given in the United States to Pittsburgh, Pa., a city distinguished for its numerous and immense iron manufactures.

Ketch, Jack.—A hangman or executioner; so called in England, from one John Ketch, a wretch who lived in the time of James II., and made himself universally odious by the butchery of many brave and noble victims, particularly those sentenced to death by the infamous Jeffreys during the "Bloody Assizes." The name is thought by some to be derived from Richard Jacquett, who held the manor of Tyburn, near London, where criminals were formerly executed.

Keystone State.—The State of Pennsylvania; so called from its having been the central State of the Union at the time of the formation of the Constitution. If the names of the thirteen original States are arranged in the form of an arch, Pennsylvania will occupy the place of the keystone.

King Cotton.—A popular personification of the great staple production of the Southern

SPRINGFIELD—*Continued.*

LUSK, D. W., Bookbinder & Blank Book Manf'r
618 Washington st.

ROKKER, H. W., Bookbinder,
309 S. 5th st.

BOTTLERS.

A. AMMANN,
Wholesale dealer in

CINCINNATI LAGER BEER,

Bottling a Specialty,
220 SOUTH FIFTH STREET.

JOERGER, JACOB, Bottler of Beer & Ale,
617 Monroe st.

J. A. KELLEHER,

City Bottling Works,

Dealer in

BOTTLED LAGER and ALE,
217 MONROE ST.

SCHWAB, HENRY, Bottler of Beer & Ale,
416 E. Monroe st.

BUSINESS COLLEGE.

SPRINGFIELD BUSINESS COLLEGE, S. Bogardus, prop., 6th & Washington sts.

BUTTER AND EGGS.

BUCKLEY, H. P., Butter & Eggs,
7th st., bet. Washington & Adams sts.

CARRIAGE AND WAGON MAKERS.

BRAND, AUG., Carriage & Wagon Maker,
Cor. 9th & Washington sts,

KESSBERGER, A., Carriage & Wagon Maker,
1st st., opposite Gas Works.

McDONALD, J., Carriage & Wagon Maker,
8th st., bet. Washington & Adams sts.

DENTISTS.

FRENCH, A. W., D.D.S. Established 1848.
S. W. cor. 5th and Adams sts.

SPURRIER, MRS., Dentist,
120 S. 6th st.

DRY GOODS.

McGRATH, THOS., Dry & Fancy Goods,
207 S. 5th st.

FANCY GOODS AND NOTIONS.

GRIFFITH, H. G., Fancy Goods & Notions,
211 S. Fifth st.

HAIR DEALERS AND DRESSERS.

MRS. EUNICE BUTLER,

Hairdressing & Millinery,

519 MONROE STREET.

GRIFFITH, H. G., Dealer in Hair Goods,
211 S. Fifth st.

SPRINGFIELD—Continued.

HARNESS AND SADDLES.

J. O. RAMES,

Manufacturer of and Dealer in

Harness, Saddles, Collars

—AND—

HORSE CLOTHING.

Fine Harness a Specialty.

213 S. FIFTH STREET.

Springfield, Ills.

JOSEPH SAUL,

Manufacturer and Dealer in Harness, Saddles and Horse Clothing.

515 MONROE STREET.

WALSH, JAS. J., Harness & Saddles, 110 N. Fifth st.

HAT AND BONNET BLEACHERS.

MURPHY & WADE, Hat & Bonnet Bleachers, 231 Third st.

HOTELS.

CHENERY HOUSE, J. W. Chenery, Prop., 4th & Washington sts.

LELAND HOTEL, H. S. Leland & Co., Props., Springfield.

REVERE HOUSE, S. E. Johnson, Manager, 4th & Washington sts.

ST. NICHOLAS HOTEL, John McCreery, Prop., 4th & Jefferson sts.

INK MANUFACTURERS.

ROKKER, H. W., Banner Ink Co., 309 S. Fifth st.

LAUNDRY.

CAPITAL STEAM LAUNDRY,

D. HICKOX, Prop.,

510 E. Monroe street.

MARBLE WORKS.

BAUM, JACOB, Marble Worker, 323 E. Jefferson st.

MILLINERY.

McGRATH, THOS., Millinery, 207 S. Fifth st.

MISS K. C. HAYES,

Dealer in

HAIR GOODS, MILLINERY,

Toilet and Fancy Articles,

ALSO

Dress and Cloak Maker,

221 E. MONROE ST., near CAPITOL.

States of America. The supremacy of cotton seems to have been first asserted by the Hon. James H. Hammond, of South Carolina, in a speech delivered by him in the Senate of the United States, on the 4th of March, 1858.

Kitchen Cabinet.—A name sportively given, in the United States, to the Hon. Francis P. Blair and the Hon. Amos Kendall, by the opponents of President Jackson's administration. Blair was the editor of *The Globe*, the organ of the President, and Kendall was one of the principal contributors to the paper. As it was necessary for Jackson to consult frequently with those gentlemen, and as, to avoid observation, they were accustomed, when they called upon him, to go in by a back door, the Whig party styled them, in derision, the "Kitchen Cabinet," alleging that it was by their advice that the President removed so many Whigs from office and put Democrats in their place.

Lake State.—A name popularly given to the State of Michigan, which borders upon the four lakes—Superior, Michigan, Huron, and Erie.

Land of Steady Habits.—A name by which the State of Connecticut is sometimes designated, in allusion to the moral character of its inhabitants.

Learned Blacksmith.—An epithet sometimes applied to Elihu Burritt (born 1811), who began life as a blacksmith, and afterward distinguished himself as a linguist.

Lion of the Sea.—A name formerly given to the Cape of Good Hope.

Little Giant.—A popular sobriquet conferred upon the Hon. Stephen A. Douglass, a distinguished American statesman (born 1813, died 1861), in allusion to the disparity between his physical and intellectual proportions.

Little Magician.—A sobriquet conferred upon the Hon. Martin Van Buren, President of the United States from 1837 to 1841, in allusion to his supposed political sagacity and talent.

Lone Star State.—The State of Texas, so called from the device on its coat of arms.

Lumber State.—The State of Maine, the inhabitants of which are largely engaged in the business of cutting and rafting lumber, or of converting it into boards, shingles, scantling, and the like.

Mad Anthony.—A sobriquet of Maj. Gen. Anthony Wayne, distinguished for his military skill and impetuous bravery in the war of the Revolution.

Mason and Dixon's Line.—A name given to the southern boundary of the free State of Pennsylvania, which formerly separated it from the slave States of Maryland and Virginia. It lies in latitude 49° 43' 26.3'', and was run, with the exception of about twenty-two miles, by Charles Mason and Jeremiah Dixon, two English mathematicians and surveyors, between Nov. 15, 1763, and Dec. 26, 1767. During the exciting debates in Congress in 1820, on the question of excluding slavery from the State of Missouri, the eccentric John Randolph, of Roanoke, made great use of the phrase, which was caught up and re-echoed by every newspaper in the land, and thus gained a celebrity which it still retains.

Mill-boy of the Slashes.—A sobriquet conferred upon Henry Clay (1777-1852), a distin-

SPRINGFIELD—Continued.

NEWSPAPERS.

ILLINOIS FRIER PRESS, Fredrick Gerbing, Editor, 108 N. Sixth st.
ILLINOIS STATE GAZETTE, D. W. Lusk, Prop.,
618 Washington st.

PAPER HANGINGS.

P. F. KIMBLE,

Dealer in

WALL PAPER,

Window Shades, Paints, Oils, Varnishes
424 Adams Street.

PHOTOGRAPHERS.

ANDERSON, L. S., Photo Studio,
121 S. Fifth st.
JORNES, G. W., State Art Gallery,
111 S. Fifth st.
PIETZ, H., Photographer,
117 S. Fifth st.
PITTMAN, J. A. W., Photographer,
511 & 513 Washington st.

PRINTERS—BOOK AND JOB.

LUSK, D. W., Book and Job Printer,
618 Washington st.
ROKKER, H. W., Printer & Publisher,
300 S. Fifth st.

SPRINGFIELD PRINTING CO.,

W. H. BOOTHROYD, Supt.
PRINTERS AND BOOK BINDERS.
115 Fifth St., West Side Square.

TAILORS.

ANDERSON, G. W., Merchant Tailor,
S. W. cor. 4th & Washington st.
WELDON, J. D., Merchant Tailor,
502 E. Adams st., south side Square.

UNDERTAKERS.

RABENSTEIN & FOSTER,

Furnishing Undertakers,

615 E. Washington St., Bet. 8th & 9th.

SMITH, THOS. C., Furnishing Undertaker,
325 S. Fifth st.

UPHOLSTERERS.

DIRKSEN, A., Mattress Maker & Upholsterer,
408 E. Washington st.
MILLER, J. H., Upholsterer & Furniture dealer,
126 N. 5th st.

WINES AND LIQUORS.

JOHN P. FIXMER,

Manufacturer of Bonekamp Stomach Bitters, and Wholesale Liquor Dealer,
131 E. JEFFERSON STREET.

MUELLER, H. E., Wholesale Wines & Liquors,
Cor. 6th & Jefferson sts.

ST. JOSEPH, MO.

ATTORNEYS AT LAW.

COLLINS, T. W., Attorney at Law and Real Estate Agent, 216 Francis st.
HILL, E. O., Attorney at Law,
326 Francis st.

JUDSON & MOTTER,

Attorneys and Counsellors.
SAINT JOSEPH, MO.

LANCASTER, L. R., Attorney at Law,
505 Felix st.

A. A. OLDFIELD,

ATTORNEY AT LAW

Short Hand Reporter and Notary Public.

OFFICE, 410 FRANCIS STREET.

(With JUDSON & MOTTER.)

SALTZMAN, A., Attorney at Law, Justice of the Peace and Notary Public, City Hall Building.
THOMAS, J. P., Attorney at Law,
328 Francis st.

BANK.

STATE SAVINGS BANK,
S. E. Cor. 4th & Felix sts.

BARBERS.

HENRY ABERLE,

Shaving and Hair Cutting Saloon,
206 THIRD STREET.

EICHENLAUB, FRANK, Barber-Shop,
717 Felix st.
MAY, HENRY, Barber-Shop,
cor. 4th & Felix sts.

BIRDS AND BIRD CAGES.

SINGING BIRDS.

HERMAN HEGER, Importer of German Canaries, keeps on hand all kinds of Singing Birds and Bird Food, all kinds of Bird Cages, Gold Fishes, &c. Orders from the country promptly attended to.

No. 322 FRANCIS ST., Bet. 3rd & 4th.

KELL, WM., Bird Fancier, Dealer in Cigars, Tobacco and Fruit, 227 Edmond st.

BLEACHERY.

UNION STRAW & FELT WORKS

No. 613 FELIX STREET.

R. B. SINCLAIR,
Straw Bleacher and Presser.

Ladies' Straw Hats and Bonnets Bleached, Altered, Dyed and Refinished in the latest Style. Ladies' Felt Hats Cleaned, Dyed and Reshaped. Gents' Straw, Panama and Felt Hats Cleaned, Colored and Retrimmed. All work guaranteed to give satisfaction.

ADVERTISEMENTS.

BIRD'S EYE VIEW, CENTENNIAL GROUNDS, PHILADELPHIA.

B. F. FITCH,

DEALER IN

PAPER HANGINGS, WINDOW SHADES,

Paints, Oils, Glass, White Lead, Zinc, Varnishes, Brushes, &c.   Paper hung at reasonable rates.   Curtains made to order.

176 TWENTY-SECOND STREET, - - - - CHICAGO, ILLS.

ST. JOSEPH—*Continued.*

BOILER MAKER.

ZIPH, GEO. H., Boiler Maker and Sheet-Iron Worker, cor. 5th & Patee sts.

BOOK STORE.

FUELLING, CARL, German Book Store. Periodicals, Newspapers, &c., 321 Edmond st.

BOOTS AND SHOES.

BELLER, A., Manuf'r and Dealer in Fashionable Boots and Shoes, 512 S. 6th st.

BROOMS AND BRUSHES.

MUEHLENBACHER, PHILIP, Manufacturer of Brooms, Brushes, &c., cor. 15th & Mitchell av.

CONTRACTORS AND BUILDERS.

CASE, F. F., Builder and Superintendent, 907 Francis st.

WILLIAM P. WHITE,
CARPENTER,
Builder & Contractor
222 SECOND STREET.

CARRIAGE MANUFACTURERS.

MILES, GIDEON, Carriage Manufacturer, Charles st., bet. 2nd & 3rd.

PRAWITZ, & HAEGELIN, Carriage Manufactory, Charles st., bet. 3rd & 4th.

CHINA, GLASS AND QUEENSWARE.

JOHN PINGER,
Queensware, Glassware, French China,
SILVER PLATED WARE, MIRRORS, LAMPS & CHANDELIERS, BAR GOODS, &c.,
121 SOUTH THIRD STREET.

CLOTHING.

BIRD & BYRNE, Clothing, Hats, Caps, Trunks, &c., 103 E. side Market Square.

COAL AND WOOD.

S. H. RICE & CO.,
Coal, Charcoal, Wood, Baled Hay, Corn, Oats, Bran, &c.,
402 SOUTH FOURTH ST.

H. J. SEIP & CO.
Dealers in
COAL
Office, Cor. 6th & Olive Sts.

CONFECTIONERY AND BAKERS.

DIETZ, JACOB, Delmonico Confectionery and Fruit Store, 213 Francis st.

ST. JOSEPH—*Continued.*

NEIDINGER, C., Bakery and Confectionery, cor. 8th & Felix sts.

WASHINGTON & HAWKINS, Confectioneries, cor. Francis st. & Frederick ave.

DRESSMAKING.

HAFFNER, MRS. ROSA, Dressmaking and Masquerade Suits, 6th st., bet. Edmond & Felix.

WEAVER, MISS ORVIL, Dressmaking, cor. 6th & Felix sts., Up-stairs.

DRUGGISTS.

EWING, FRED. C., Druggist, cor. Francis & 5th sts.

SCHEIBE, F., Druggist and Apothecary, cor. N. 3rd & Franklin sts.

WADE, JOHN W., Druggist, intersection of Felix & 8th sts. with Frederick ave.

DRY GOODS.

DREIS, PETER, Dry Goods, Groceries, Boots, Shoes, &c., 10th & LaFayette sts.

NEW YORK STORE, Dry Goods and Notions. N. Stone, Prop. 6th and Felix sts.

NORRIS & PAYNE, Dry Goods. Boots, Shoes, Clothing and Groceries, Penn and 11th sts.

SKILES & TROXELL, Dry Goods, Groceries, &c., cor. 11th and Penn sts.

TOWNSEND, J., & CO., Dry Goods and Notions, 319 Felix st.

DYE WORKS.

TURNER, THOS. W., Proprietor New York Dye Works, 230 Edmond st.

ENGRAVER.

HINTON, GEO. W., Engraver on Wood, 408 Felix st.

FANCY GOODS.

GOLDBERG, A., Notions and Fancy Goods, 414 Felix st.

FISH AND OYSTERS.

ELLSWORTH, W. M., Fresh Fish, Oysters and Game, 316 Edmond st.

FLOUR MANUFACTURERS.

SAXTON & CO. EAGLE MILLS, Manufacturers of Fancy Fall Wheat Flour, 7th and Olive sts.

FURNITURE.

FELLING, T. J., New and Second-Hand Furniture, 914 east side Frederick ave.

LOUIS G. EGGERT,
New and Second-Hand

Furniture, Show Cases and Mattresses.
FURNITURE REPAIRED TO ORDER.
Cor. Sylvanie & 4th Sts.

PUMPHREY, MARY M., Second-Hand Furniture and Notions, 10th and LaFayette sts.

FURRIER.

LUEDERITZ, C., Furrier, cor. Felix and 7th sts.

GROCERIES AND PROVISIONS.

BERNARD, JOSEPH, Groceries, cor. 4th and Isabell sts.

DREIS, JOS., Groceries and Provisions, Flour, Feed, &c., cor. 14th st. and Mitchell ave.

New Masonic Temple, Philadelphia—Is situated northeast corner Broad and Filbert streets. The corner-stone was laid June 24, 1868, and was dedicated to the brethren of the order, September 26, 1873. The building is 250 feet long by 150 feet wide, in style of the Norman school, two stories and entresal, with pinnacles and towers. Main tower 240 feet from the base; foundation 31 feet below the level of the street. The cost of building the Temple was $1,540,000.

F. L. PEIRO, M. D.,
No. 90 Washington St., Chicago, Illinois.

Is exclusively engaged in the special treatment of **Catarrh, Coughs, Consumption, "Minister's Sore Throat," Hay Fever, Bronchitis, Asthma, Diphtheria,** and all other diseases of the **Throat** and **Lungs.** Special care given to children afflicted with such diseases whether **Acute** or **Chronic.** Enlarged Tonsils removed without pain. Remedies mild and efficacious. Patients can be treated at a distance. Medicines sent by mail.

Office Hours, 10 A. M. to 3 P. M.

Enclose stamp for reply. Address

**DR. F. L. PEIRO,
CHICAGO, ILLINOIS.**

400   ADVERTISEMENTS.

ST. JOSEPH—*Continued.*

GIBSON & KENNARD, Groceries and Provisions, cor. 9th and Olive sts.

GRAFF, JOHN, Staple and Fancy Groceries, 2112 S. 6th st.

HOGAN, M., Dealer in Groceries and Provisions, 1220 S. 6th st.

HARNESS AND SADDLERY HARDWARE.

LANDIS, ISRAEL, Wholesale Saddler Saddlery Hardware, 114 4th St.

MICHAEL McGEE,

Manufacturer of Saddles Harness, Collars, &c.

110 SECOND STREET.

HIDES AND WOOL.

JAMES H. CURTIS,

Hides, Wool, Pelts & Furs,

120 N. SECOND STREET.

H. MARKS & CO.,
Dealers in

HIDES, WOOL, PELTS & FURS,

46 & 48 Third Street.

HOMŒOPATHIC PHARMACY.

DR. W. G. HALL'S

Homœopathic Pharmacy,

Francis St., bet. 4th and 5th Street.

HORSESHOERS.

SOMERS & COBURN,

Blacksmithing. Horseshoeing a specialty. Also Manufacturers of Mill Picks. Dressing Picks a Specialty. All work warranted.
Cor. FIFTH & MESSANIE STREETS.

TULLAR & KINNEY,

HORSE-SHOERS,

Charles St., bet. 3d and 4th Sts.

Particular attention given to all diseased feet, hoof-bound and interfering or cutting horses, Trotters and Runners a specialty.

HOTELS.

GARRETT HOUSE, Mrs. E. F. Garrett, Proprietress. 6th and Edmond sts.

FINNEY HOUSE,

S. H. FINNEY, Prop.,

Cor. 4th &'Sylvanie Sts. Terms, $1.00 per Day; 25 cents per Meal. Accommodations for Man and Beast.

IOWA HOUSE, Hotel & Saloon, Geo. Aeschelman, Prop., 8th & Olive sts., opp. Depot.

PACIFIC HOTEL, Gilkey & Abell, Prop., Francis & 3rd sts.

SAUNDERS HOUSE, Moore & Stahl, Proprietors.

SCHWEIZER HAUS, Rudolph Bodtke, Prop., 10th st., bet. Olive & Lafayette.

ST. JOSEPH—*Continued.*

INSURANCE AGENTS.

ALBIN & BEACH, Insurance Agents, Cor. 4th & Felix sts.

LIVERY STABLE.

PACIFIC LIVERY STABLE, Henry Fish, Prop., Cor. 5th & Edmond sts.

MEAT MARKETS.

HITIGAN, T. F., Meat Market, Cor. 3d & Franklin sts.

PADBERG, E., Pork Packer and Dealer in Fresh & Salt Meats, 512 Edmond st.

ROSENBLATT, S., Wholesale Butcher and Live Stock Broker, 8th & Messanie sts.

MILLINERY GOODS.

MRS. L. RIETHMULLER,

Manufacturer, Importer and Jobber of

Millinery, Straw, Fancy

AND HAIR GOODS.

No. 418 FELIX STREET.

MUSICAL INSTRUMENTS.

WESTERN DEPOT OF MUSIC, M. S. Huyett, Prop., Pianos, Organs Musical Merchandise, 105 Fourth st.

MUSIC TEACHER.

BEHR, OTTO, Music Teacher, Cor. 7th & Felix st.

NEWSPAPERS.

DAILY AND WEEKLY CHRONICLE, Francis st., bet. 2nd & 3d sts. Chronicle Printing Co.

DAILY ST. JOSEPH VOLKSBLATT, H. Brunsing & Co., Publishers. $9.00 per annum.

PAINTERS.

C. T. GAUGH & SON.

House, Sign and Ornamental Painters, Grainers and Paper Hangers. Particular attention to Frescoing and Decorating.
324 FRANCIS ST., near FOURTH.

WILSON, C. F., Makes a specialty of re-painting Carriages, Buggies, &c, Charles street.

PHOTOGRAPHERS.

GRAND CENTRAL GALLERY, W. J. Rea, Cor. 4th & Edmond sts.

LOZO, ALEX., Photographer, Cor. 5th & Felix sts.

PHYSICIANS.

BISHOP, GALEN E., Physician and Surgeon, Academy of Medicine, 3d st.

DONELAN, E. A., M. D., Office hours 7 to 9 a. m., 1 to 3 p. m., 7 to 9 p. m. 309 5th st.

THOS. H. DOYLE, M. D.,

Graduate of the University of the City of New York, Physician and Surgeon,
Cor. FOURTH & EDMOND STREETS.

WM. G. HALL, M. D.,

Homœopathic Physician & Surgeon,

Office Hours : 8 to 9 a. m., 1 to 3 & 7 to 8 p. m.

St. Joseph—Continued.

PRODUCE DEALER.

O'DONOGHUE, WM., Wholesale Produce Dealer, Second st.

RAGS AND METALS.

STRAUS, J., Rags, Old Iron, Copper, Brass, &c., 43 Second st.

RESTAURANT.

STEWART, E. B., Restaurant and Confectionery. Warm Meals at all Hours, 903 8th st.

REAL ESTATE AGENTS.

JOHN DONOVAN, Attorney at Law.   A. M. SAXTON, Pres. State Savings Bank.

DONOVAN & SAXTON,
REAL ESTATE AGENTS,
Office, Fifth St., Bet. Felix & Francis.

Buy and sell Real Estate on commission, negotiate loans, make collections, and transact all business pertaining to a General Agency.

READ, S. H. & CO., Real Estate, 408 Felix st.

SALOONS.

BASSING, W., Harmonial Hall & Bar, 10th st., bet. Olive & Lafayette.

THE MINT,
BRADLEY & BLONDEAN, Props.,
Wines, Liquors, Segars, Ale and Beer. Fine Kentucky Whiskies a Specialty.
112 N. SECOND ST.

CLOW, JOHN E., Saloon, 310 Felix st.
HOFFMEISTER, H., Wine & Beer Saloon, Cor. 8th & Frederick ave.
MITCHELL, C. C., Mitchell's Sample Room, 416 Francis st.
ULLNAR, JOHN L., Saloon, 201 Felix st.
VALENTINE, WM., Wine & Beer Saloon, 222 Edmond st.

SEWING MACHINES.

CROSS, A. M., General Sewing Machine Agent, 604 Felix st.
DENNING, WM. L., Sewing Machine Repairer, 6th bet. Felix & Francis.

SHOW CASES.

H. C. WALLER & CO.,

SHOW CASE & MATTRESS Manfs. 207 THIRD STREET.

STOVES AND TINWARE.

C. H. BOLLER,
Wholesale and Retail Dealer in STOVES, TIN & JAPANNED WARE, Tin Plate, Sheet Iron, and Tinners' Stock.
510 EDMOND STREET.

---

guished American orator and statesman, who was born in the neighborhood of a place in Hanover county, Virginia, known as the *slashes* (a local term for a low, swampy country where there was a mill, to which he was often sent on errands when a boy.

Monumental City.—The city of Baltimore, so called from the monuments it contains.

Mormons.—The last of a pretended line of Hebrew prophets, existing among a race of Israelites, principally the descendants of Joseph, who are fabled to have emigrated from Jerusalem to America about six hundred years before Christ. This imaginary prophet is said to have written the book called "The Book of Mormon," which contains doctrines upon which the "Mormons," as "Latter Day Saints," found their faith; but the real author was one Solomon Spalding, (born 1761 and died 1816) an inveterate scribbler, who had in early life been a clergyman. The work fell into the hands of Joseph Smith, who claimed it as a direct revelation to himself from heaven, and, taking it as his text and authority, began to preach the new gospel of "Mormonism."

Mother of Presidents.—A name frequently given to the State of Virginia, which has furnished six Presidents to the Union.

Mother of States.—A name sometimes given to Virginia, the first settled of the thirteen States which united in the Declaration of Independence.

Mound City.—A name given to St. Louis on account of the numerous artificial mounds that occupied the site on which the city is built.

Nutmeg State.—A popular name for the State of Connecticut, the inhabitants of which have such a reputation for shrewdness that they have been jocosely accused of palming off wooden nutmegs on unsuspecting purchasers, instead of the genuine article.

Old Bullion.—A sobriquet conferred on Colonel Thomas H. Benton (1782-1852), a distinguished American statesman, on account of his advocacy of a gold and silver currency as the true remedy for the financial embarrassments in which the United States were involved after the expiration of the charter of the national bank, and as the only proper medium for government disbursements and receipts.

Old Colony.—A name given to that portion of Massachusetts included within the original limits of the Plymouth colony, which was formed at an earlier date than the colony of Massachusetts Bay. In 1692 the two colonies were united in one province, bearing the name of the latter, and at the formation of the Federal Union became the State of Massachusetts.

Old Dominion.—A name given to the State of Virginia.

Old Hickory.—A sobriquet conferred upon General Jackson, in 1813, by the soldiers under his command.

Old Hunkers.—A nick-name applied to the ultra-conservative portion of the Democratic party in the United States, and especially in the State of New York.

Old Ironsides.—A title popularly conferred upon the United States frigate Constitution, which was launched at Boston, September 20, 1797. She became greatly celebrated on ac-

ST. JOSEPH—Continued.

SCHOOLS.

YOUNG LADIES' INSTITUTE, Cor. 5th and Antoine sts. Chas. Martin, President.

DERSCH, H. & BRO., Stoves & Tinware,
803 N. 3d st.

TAILORS.

J. F. DERGANCE,
Merchant Tailor,
414 FRANCIS STREET.

A. L. GILKISON,
Merchant Tailor,
424 Francis Street,

HAMERSTINE, S., Tailor, Cleaner & Repairer,
Francis st., next door to P. O.

CHRISTIAN MAYER,
Merchant Tailor
Cleaning and Repairing Neatly Done.
504 Third Street.

PHIPPS, D., Tailor,
426 Francis st.

READY, T., Tailor, Cleaning and Repairing Neatly Done, Cor. 5th & Edmond sts.

TOBACCO AND CIGARS.

VOLLMER, GUSTAV, Cigar Manufacturer,
3d st., bet. Franklin & Pauline.

UNDERTAKER.

SEIDENFADEN, WM., Undertaker,
Cor. 4th & Messanie sts.

UPHOLSTERER.

FREDERICK, JOHN A., Upholsterer
Edmond st., bet. 6th & 7th.

VALLEY PACKING CO.

VALLEY PACKING CO.,
Office, cor. 3d & Francis sts.

VETERINARY SURGEON.

WASHBURN, Z. D., Veterinary Surgeon and Horseshoer, 813 Frederick ave.

WATCHES AND JEWELRY.

MOSER, FREDERICK, Practical Repairer of Watches, Clocks & Jewelry, 115 4th st.

PAAR, H., Watchmaker & Jeweler. Man'fug. & Repairing, 4th st., bet. Sylvania & Charles.

WINES AND LIQUORS.

HARTWIG, H. R. W. & CO., Wholesale Liquor Dealers, 212 Third st.

WORSTED GOODS.

WORSTED STORE,
Mr. P. Rahmann,
Will keep on Hand All Kinds of
WORSTED CANVAS.
And will make any kind of Fancy work to order. Also Clean Kid Gloves, Velvets, Silks and Ladies' Dresses of every Description. Laces done up and repaired. Charges Reasonable.

Francis st., between Third and Fourth.

ST. JOSEPH—Continued.

St. Joseph, Mo., Business Houses,
WHEN ESTABLISHED.

BISHOP, GALEN E., M. D., Physician & Surgeon, 1846.
CASE, F. F., Builder, 1865.
DONOVAN & SAXTON, Real Estate Agents, 1868.
EGGERT, LOUIS G., New and Second-Hand Furniture, 1877.
O'DONOGHUE, WM., Wholesale Produce, 1874.
PINGER, JOHN, Glassware, &c., 1865.
RAHMANN, MR. P., Worsted. 1871.
RIETHMULLER, MRS. L., Millinery, 1874.
SEIP, H. J. & CO., Coal, 1869.
WALLER, H. C. & CO., Show Cases & Mattresses, 1865.
WHITE, WM. P., Contractor & Builder, 1872.

LEAVENWORTH, KAS.

AGRICULTURAL IMPLEMENTS.

JULIUS AMBRUN,
—Manufacturer of—
AGRICULTURAL MACHINERY
Patentee of Hay and Straw Cutting Machine,
308 7th ST., NEAR CHEROKEE.

ATTORNEYS AT LAW.

CLOUGH, E. N. O., Lawyer and Notary Public,
113 N. 5th st.

ENT, M. L., Attorney at Law,
S. W. Cor. 5th & Delaware sts.

BARBERS.

MADUSKA & KEITH, Barbers,
427 Shawnee st.

ROUSE, JOHN, Barber,
418 S. 5th st.

BLACKSMITHS.

CHAS. CONRAD,
Old Reliable Blacksmith.
712 CHEROKEE ST.

G. V. KUHN,
BLACKSMITH,
First-class work guaranteed.
732 CHEROKEE ST.

BOOTS AND SHOES.

BEELER, O. C., Boot and Shoemaker,
228 Shawnee st.

ADVERTISEMENTS. 403

W. Virginia State Building, Centennial Exposition, Phila.
—Has a front of 59 feet, and depth of 90 feet, which includes an exhibition room in the rear for the special display of the products of West Virginia. The building contains four rooms. Two on the first floor intended for business purposes and the reception of visitors, and two on the second floor for the accommodation of ladies. It is built entirely of wood, representing nine different varieties from the State of West Virginia.

LEAVENWORTH—*Continued..*

ANDRE GALEND,
BOOT AND SHOE MAKER,
Best fits and material guaranteed,
626 CHEROKEE ST.

COLFER, PATRICK, Boot and Shoe Maker,
    Cor. 5th & Seneca sts.
DETWILER, S. C., Boot and Shoe Maker.
    113 S. 3d st.
DOBLER, FREDERICK, Boot and Shoe Maker,
    703 Cherokee st.
HEMMERLE, JACOB, Boot and Shoe Maker,
    215 N. 5th st.
LONGMOOR, JOSEPH, Boot and Shoe Maker,
    409½ Shawnee st.
MACKEL, P., Boot and Shoe Maker,
    212 Delaware st.
WISSLER, D., Boot and Shoe Maker,
    414 Shawnee st.

LEAVENWORTH—*Continued.*

F. W. OTTO.
BOOT AND SHOE MAKER,
Good fit and best material guaranteed. Call on me, cor. 5th & Miami sts.

J. F. WEDERBROOK,
BOOT AND SHOE MAKER,
Good Fit and Good Materail Guaranteed,
745 SHAWNEE ST.

BRASS FOUNDRY.

GEO. KAUFFMAN & CO.,
Brass Foundry and Railing Shop, Locksmiths and Bellhangers, 304 Shawnee st., bet. Third and Fourth. All work warranted.

LEAVENWORTH—Continued.

CABINET MAKER.

J. W. ROBERTSON,
CABINET MAKER AND FINISHER,
Especial attention given to Repairing and all Kinds of Job Work, 207 Shawnee st.

CARRIAGES AND WAGONS.

BUCKEYE CARRIAGE WORKS,
JOHN CRETORS, Prop.
First-class work. Repairing and re-painting promptly attended to. A full line of Light Carriages, Buggies, RoadWagons, etc., 417 to 423 Cherokee st.

WILLIAM GATES,
Wagon Maker and General Repairing,
☞ Best of work guaranteed. ☜
753 Cherokee st.

JOSEPH WALTER,
BLACKSMITH, CARRIAGE AND WAGON
MAKER.
And General Repairing Done,
112 N. 4th ST., COR. SENECA ST.

CARRIAGE MATERIAL

STEVENS & GARRIGUES, Wagon & Carriage Material, 206 Delaware st.

CLOTHING.

WOLLMAN, J., Clothier,
Cor. 5th & Delaware sts.

CONFECTIONERY.

R. BEIGA,
Dealer in Confectionery, Fruits, Nuts, etc., also Cigars and Tobacco, 310 Delaware street, bet. 3d and 4th sts. Fresh Oysters and Ice Cream in their season.

BEIGA, A., Confectioner,
422 Delaware st.

W. T. CREAGER,
CANDY MANUFACTURER,
Fine assortment of Candies always on hand.
207 N. FIFTH STREET.

DRESSMAKING.

Mrs. Mary E. Blakslee,
STAMPING, BRAIDING, DRESSMAKING,
—AND—
Fancy Goods,
402 S. FIFTH STREET.

BURKE, MRS. ANNIE, Dressmaker,
725 Miami st.

McGRAW, MRS. JAMES, Dressmaker.
706 Shawnee st.

LEAVENWORTH—Continued..

MRS. MUSE & HARRISON, Fashionable Dressmakers, 410 Shawnee st., up-stairs.

Mrs. M. Webster,
STAMPING, EMBROIDERING,
—AND—
DRESSMAKING,
309 Delaware Street, Up-Stairs.

DRUGGISTS.

EGERSDORFF, THEO., Druggist,
Cor. 4th & Shawnee sts.

ROBERT PARHAM,
Dealer in
Drugs, Medicines & Fancy Articles,
TRUSSES AND SUPPORTERS,
Cor. 4th and Delaware Streets.

FILES AND SAWS.

AUSTIN, W. H., Files, Saws, etc.,
506½ Shawnee st.

FRUITS AND PRODUCE.

B. M. TANNER,
Wholesale dealer in
DOMESTIC FRUITS,
Produce, Etc.,
215 DELAWARE ST.
☞ Goods received on consignment.

FURNITURE.

GEO. A. FOY,
Dealer in new and second-hand Furniture, and Housefurnishing Goods, at the lowest figure. Call and see for yourself, at the old place, 202, 204 and 206 North 5th st.

GENTS' FURNISHING GOODS.

CRANSTON, M. P., Gents' Furnishing Goods,
427 Delaware st.

GROCERIES.

FRANKE, M. E., Groceries, Provisions & Fruits, 308 S. 5th st.

GENUIT, AUGUST, Groceries and Liquors,
526 Shawnee st.

E. GWARTNEY,
GROCER
☞ Best of Provisions on hand. ☜
310 S. SEVENTH St.

HENRY KREZDORN,
Dealer in Groceries, Provisions, China Ware, Liquors and Wines, cor. Second & Pottawatomie streets.

PHELAN, MICHAEL, Groceries and Provisions, Teas & Flour a specialty, cor. 5th & Seneca sts.

LEAVENWORTH—Continued.

JOHN VOGEL,
GROCER and SALOON-KEEPER
Best of Provisions and Liquors,
753 SHAWNEE ST.

WETHERILL, GEORGE, Wholesale & retail Grocer, S. E. cor. 5th and Cherokee sts.

WITTENBERG, H., Groceries and Provisions, Cor. 4th & Osage sts.

GUNSMITHS.

JACOB BAUER,
Practical Gunsmith, and dealer in Guns, Revolvers, Ammunition, etc., 225 Shawnee st. Repairing done on short notice.

JOHN BIRINGER,
Gun and Locksmith, and dealer in all kinds of Guns, Pistols, Ammunition, Fishing Tackle, Pocket Cutlery, etc., corner Shawnee and Sixth sts.

HARDWARE.

RICHARDS, J. F. & CO., Hardware, 301 Delaware st.

HARNESS AND SADDLES.

B. S. RICHARDS,
Manufacturer of and dealer in Saddles, Harness, Whips, Collars, Spurs, etc., 417 Delaware street. Call and see me before purchasing elsewhere.

HOTELS.

ANNIE WEISMAN,
"LEAVENWORTH HOUSE,"
Best of board and accommodations. Fine Liquors at the bar. 218 Cherokee st.

COMMERCIAL HOUSE,
Deutsches Gasthaus, 216 Cherokee street, between 2d and 3d streets, Emil Wetzel, proprietor. Express wagon for the benefit of travelers.

LEONARD, THOMAS, Mansion House, Cor. 5th & Shawnee sts.

PRZYBYLOWICZ, MICHAEL, Continental Hotel, 4th st., N. W. cor. Cherokee st.

PLANTERS HOUSE, J L. Rice & Co., Main st., N. E. Cor. Shawnee st.

St. JAMES HOTEL,
A. HAUG, Proprietor,
CORNER SHAWNEE AND SECOND STS.

THE ST. LOUIS HOUSE,
COR. SEVENTH & CHEROKEE STS.,
Has been thoroughly renovated, and is now ready to furnish guests with accommodations equal to any house in the city. Board $1.00 per day. Best of Wines, Liquors and Cigars at the bar.

M. J. McCARTHY, Prop'r.

count of the prominent part she took in the bombardment of Tripoli, in 1804, and for the gallantry she displayed during the war of 1812. She is still in service.

Old North State.—A name by which the State of North Carolina is sometimes known.

Old Public Functionary.—A name given to James Buchanan, fifteenth President of the United States. He first applied the expression to himself in his annual message to Congress, in the year 1859. Sometimes humorously abbreviated O. P. F.

Old Wagon.—A sobriquet given to the frigate United States, which was launched at Philadelphia, in 1798, and was afterward rebuilt on the original model. She got her nick-name previous to the war of 1812, from her dull sailing qualities, which were subsequently very much improved.

Old-style Jonathan.—A nom de plume of Washington Irving, under which he contributed, in 1842, to the *Morning Chronicle*, a Democratic journal of New York City.

Palmetto State.—The State of South Carolina, so called from the arms of the State, which contain a palmetto.

Panhandle, The.—A fanciful and cant name given to the most northerly portion of the State of West Virginia, a long narrow projection between the Ohio river and the Western boundary of Pennsylvania.

Partington, Mrs.—An imaginary old lady whose laughable sayings have been recorded by the American humorist, B. P. Shillaber. She is distinguished, like Smollett's "Tabitha Bramble," and Sheridan's "Mrs. Malaprop," for her amusing affectation and misuse of learned words.

Pathfinder of the Rocky Mountains.—A title applied to Major-General John C. Fremont, who conducted four exploring expeditions across the Rocky Mountains.

Pennsylvania Farmer.—A surname given to John Dickinson (1732-1808), an American statesman and author, and a citizen of Pennsylvania. In the year 1768 he published his "Letters from a Pennsylvania Farmer to the Inhabitants of the British Colonies." These were republished in London, with a preface by Dr. Franklin, and were subsequently translated into French and published in Paris.

Pine Tree State.—A popular name of the State of Maine, the central and northern portion of which are covered with extensive pine forests.

Poor Richard.—The feigned author of a series of almanacs (commenced in 1732 and continued for twenty-five years) really written by Benjamin Franklin, and distinguished for their circulation of the prudential virtues, as temperance, frugality, order, justice, cleanliness, charity, and the like, by means of maxims or precepts, which, it has been said, "are as valuable as anything that has descended from Pythagoras."—See *Saunders, Richard.*

Prairie State.—A name given to Illinois in allusion to the wide-spread and beautiful prairies, which form a striking feature of the scenery of the State.

Puritan City.—A name sometimes given to the city of Boston, Massachusetts, in allusion to the character of its founders and early inhabitants.

LEAVENWORTH—Continued.

LIVERY STABLE.

VANTUYL, C. A., Propr. of Livery Stable,
Cor 3d & Seneca sts.

LOCAL EDITOR.

JOYCE, M. E., Local Editor of "Public Press,"
Near cor. Main & Delaware sts.

MEAT MARKETS.

KIRRMEYR, JO., Butcher.
Cor. 3d & Shawnee sts.

VEITH, J. D., Butcher & Sausage Maker,
213 Shawnee st.

VOLZ, JOHN, wholesale & retail dealer in Fresh and Salt Meats, 738 & 740 Shawnee st.

VOLZ, F. H., Butcher,
219 Cherokee st.

FREDERICK WARTHWINE,
Wholesale and retail dealer in all kinds of

Fresh Meat, Hams, Bacon, Lard, Poultry, Etc.,
731 CHEROKEE ST.

MILLINERY GOODS.

MRS. W. WEBER,
Fashionable

AND STRAW GOODS,
609 SHAWNEE STREET.

PAINTER'S GRAINING TOOLS.

HO PAINTERS! $20 day made clear at GRAINING. Send for Circulars, etc. J. J. CALLOW, Cleveland, O.

PAINTERS.

CHAS. LINDNER,
House, Sign and Ornamental Painter,
Call at his Saloon, 616 Cherokee street.
Best of Liquors on hand.

SCOTT & BRO.,
Painters and Paper Hangers,
And Dealers in Wall Paper,
224 SHAWNEE ST.

PATENT MEDICINE.

BROWN MEDICINE MANUFACTURING CO.,
LEAVENWORTH, KAS.,
Proprietors of

Brown's Popular Medicines,
Suitable for diseases of the Old and New West. Manufacturers of Comp. Ext. Sarsaparilla, Dandelion and Iodide Potassium, Medicated Elixirs, Flavoring Extracts, Perfumery, etc.

I. H. FERGUSON,
Photographer,
West Side 5th St., bet. Shawnee and Delaware.

LEAVENWORTH—Continued.

PHOTOGRAPHERS.

NOBLE'S PHOTOGRAPH PARLORS,

328 Delaware St, LEAVENWORTH, KAS.
Patent Permanent Chromotypes are only made at this Gallery.
C. B. NOBLE, Proprietor,
A. ST. CLAIR, Operator & Chromotypist.

PLUMBERS AND GAS FITTERS.

DENNIS CROWLEY,
Plumber, Gas and Steam Fitter, 117 Delaware st., bet.2d and Main sts. Pumps and Lead and Iron Piping, Agent for Moline and Climax Wind Mills. Old Gas Fixtures re-bronzed. Jobbing done at short notice and moderate charges.

RAGS AND METALS.

KOHN, GEORGE, dealer in Rags, Metals and Bones, 612 Cherokee st.

SALOONS.

DEITZ, GEORGE, Saloon,
403 Delaware st.

ALEXANDER DOERLE,
SALOON,
Best of Liquors and Cigars on hand. Call and see him, 424 Cherokee st.

KIHM, O., Saloon Keeper,
614 Cherokee st.

ANDRE MUNSCH,
SALOON,
Best of Wines and Liquors,
CORNER SECOND AND SHAWNEE STS.

SCHMITT, GEORGE, Saloon-keeper,
117 N. 3d st.

CHRIST SCHUBERT,
TURNER'S HALL SALOON,
Best of Wines, Liquors and Cigars,
CORNER BROADWAY & SHAWNEE STS.

McCARTHY, TIMOTHY, Saloon.
217 Cherokee st.

SEWING MACHINES.

HARTOUGH, C. S., Wheeler & Wilson Sewing Machines, 114 S. 5th st.

STOVES, TIN, COPPER AND SHEET IRON.

STOVES AND TINWARE.

B. Korman, dealer in all kinds of Stoves, Tin, Copper and Sheet Iron Ware, Roofing and Guttering, 417 Shawnee st.

GEO. RUSSELL,
Wholesale & retail dealer in

Tinware, Cooking & Heating
STOVES, ALSO DEALER IN
TINNER'S STOCK
309 DELAWARE ST.

Masonic Temple, Cincinnati, Ohio.—Is situated on the northeast corner of Third and Walnut streets; is one of the finest buildings in the city; is built of stone; its style is Elizabeth gothic, 115 by 66 feet; from base to roof it is 80 feet in height.

LEAVENWORTH—*Continued*

G. H. LUDOLPH,
Dealer in Heating and Cooking Stoves, and Queensware, and manufacturer of Tin, Sheet Iron and Copper Ware, 226 Shawnee street.

R. H. VARNEY,
Manufacturer of
Heavy Sheet Iron Work, Hot Air Furnaces, Tin Copper and Sheet Iron Ware,
321 CHEROKEE ST.

TAILORS.

A. M. BONEZKOWSKI,
TAILORING & CUTTING,
Cleaning and Repairing,
413 SHAWNEE ST.

ECKERT, AUGUST, Tailor, 4th st., bet. Delaware & Cherokee sts.

MITTELBACH, CHRIST., Practical Tailor, 213 Delaware st., bet 2d & 3d sts.

TOBACCO AND CIGARS.

BAXMAN, J. H., Cigars & Tobacco, 109 S. 5th st.

LEAVENWORTH—*Continued.*

C. CARPLES,
Dealer in Imported, Key West and Domestic Cigars, 105 Delaware st. A full line of Smokers' Fine Articles.

GIRARD & LANITZ, Cigars and Tobacco, 202 S. 5th st

DANIEL D. OLIVE,
Manufacturer of and Dealer in Cigars, Tobacco, Snuff, Pipes, Smokers' Articles, etc., etc.
No. 213 North 5th St., bet. Seneca & Miami.

EMIL WETZEL,
Manufacturer of and Dealer in Domestic and Havana Cigars.
No. 119 Cherokee Street.

WATCHES AND JEWELRY.

HENRY DECKELMAN,
Manufacturer and Dealer in Watches and Clocks, Jewelry and Silverware, Musical Instruments, Toys, Fancy Goods, &c. Watches and Jewelry Carefully Repaired and Warranted.
320 Shawnee Street.

JOHN DECKELMAN,
Manufacturing Jeweler. Watches and Jewelry carefully Repaired and Warranted.
208 Delaware Street, bet. 2nd and 3rd.

PATENTS Obtained
BY
Knight Bros.,
INFORMATION Free of Charge.
Send for Circular.
317 Olive St., St. Louis, Missouri.

EMPIRE
PATENT AGENCY.
J. E. BRYAN,
MANAGER,
602 NORTH FOURTH ST. - **ST. LOUIS, MO.**

Patentees having rights to sell, or desiring to have articles manufactured on royalty, or sold through Agents, are invited to correspond with us.
We employ Agents all the time on good commissions.

Established since 1865.

Wm. H. Lotz,
Mechanical and Consulting Engineer and Solicitor of

AMERICAN AND FOREIGN PATENTS.
Manager of Mechanics and Inventors Association of Detroit, Michigan.

OFFICE : ROOMS, - - 27 & 28, Staats Zeitung Building
93 FIFTH AVE.,
CHICAGO, ILLINOIS.

ADVERTISEMENTS. 409

Patent Office, Washington, D. C.—The Patent Office covers two squares from 7th to 9th streets, and from F to G streets, northwest. It measures 410 feet from east to west and 275 feet from north to south. The building was commenced in 1837, and was not entirely completed, as it now stands, until 1864. It cost $2,700,000. In this building are many articles which belonged to Gen. Washington possessing historical interest, and here is to be seen the original Declaration of Independence. Here, also, are on exhibition all the models of every patent issued since 1836. Those issued prior to that time were destroyed by fire in the destruction of the old building. Those destroyed were the accumulation of 46 years.

A. KUPSCH,

PATTERN

—AND—

MODEL MAKER,

—IN—

WOOD AND METAL

Manufacturer of

Railroad Locks and Light Machinery of all kinds, making Inventions of Patented Articles a Specialty.

LOCATION ON

Illinois St. Louis Bridge,

North Side, West Approach,

ST. LOUIS,   -   -   MO.

Having a long experience and acquired a good knowledge of this business, I claim to give entire satisfaction in price and quality, and desire your patronage.

LEAVENWORTH—*Continued.*

JOHN BATH,

Manufacturer and dealer in Cigars, Tobacco, Pipes, Snuff, etc., 117 North Fifth Street.

HERSHFIELD, R. N., Manufacturing Jeweler. 219 & 221 Delaware st.   Est. 1856.

HOFFMANN, H., Watchmaker and Jeweler. 212 N. 5th st.

HOFFMAN, L., Jewelry and Furnishing Goods. 429 Shawnee st.

KALBFLEISCH, HENRY, Watchmaker & Jeweler, 115 3rd st.

JOSEPH STERLING,

Practical Watchmaker and Dealer in Watches, Clocks and Jewelry. Repairing fine Watches a specialty.

409 Delaware Street.

WINES AND LIQUORS.

COUCH, S. A., Dealer in Fine Old Whiskies and Wines, 429 Cherokee st.

WOOD DEALER.

H. L. BICKFORD,

Contractor and Dealer in

Wood, Hardwood Lumber,

TIES, POSTS, &c.,

Office, 326 SHAWNEE ST., bet. 3rd & 4th.

TOPEKA, KANSAS.

ATTORNEYS AT LAW.

ARCHER, THOS., Attorney at Law, 183 Kansas ave. P. O. Box 200.

BRIER, DAVID, Attorney at Law & Justice of the Peace, 191 Kansas ave.

BROWN, W. S., Attorney at Law, 175 Kansas ave.

DOUTHITT & McFARLAND, Attorneys at Law, 185 Kansas ave.

SEARLE, JOHN G., Attorney at Law, 185 Kansas ave.

SHEAFER & SHEAFER, Lawyers, Practice in the Federal and State Courts, 108 Kansas ave.

BANKERS.

KNOX, JOHN D. & CO., Bankers, 202 Kansas ave.

BARBER.

DILLARD, H. W., First-class Barber, 118 Kansas ave.

BLANK BOOKS.

CRANE, GEO. W., Blank Book Manufacturer, 187 Kansas ave.

BOOTS AND SHOES.

BALDWIN, W. J., Boot and Shoe Maker, 155 Kansas ave.

NATTSEN, CHARLES, Fashionable Boot & Shoe Maker, 134 Kansas ave.

CONFECTIONER.

GERARD, PETER, Confectioner, 172½ Kansas ave.

CONTRACTORS AND BUILDERS.

GRIFFITH, W. H., Contractor and Builder, 186 Kansas ave.

WHITE, HOLCOMB & COUNCIL, Carpenters, Contractors & Builders, 238 Kansas ave.

CORNICES AND ROOFING.

SVENSSON, C. L., Man'fr. of Galvinized Iron Cornices, Tin Roofing, &c., 129 Kansas ave.

DRESSMAKING.

FAWLES, MRS. J. L., Dressmaking Establishment, 210 Kansas ave.

WHITNEY, MRS. MARY A., Fashionable Dress and Cloak Making, 191 Kansas ave.

DRUGS AND STATIONERY.

PARKER & KNEELAND, Drugs, Stationery, Fine Perfumeries, &c., 201 Kansas ave.

DRY GOODS.

CHARLES F. KENDALL,

Dry Goods, Carpets and Yankee Notions, Wholesale and Retail,
137 KANSAS AVENUE.

FURNITURE.

CAPITOL FURNITURE HOUSE,

W. M. Dignon & Co., Furniture Manufacturers, Upholsterers and Dealers in all kinds of Furniture.
232 KANSAS AVENUE.

TOPEKA—Continued.

GRAIN DEALER.

KEEVER, A. C., Dealer in Grain and Produce, 118 6th ave.

GROCERIES.

EWING, E. E., Wholesale and Retail Grocer, 227 Kansas ave.

RIPLEY, A. A. & SON, Grocers, Teas, Coffees, &c , 243 Kansas ave.

WARREN, W., Groceries, Provisions, &c., 110 Kansas ave.

HARDWARE.

THOMPSON, BROS., Hardware, Stoves and Tinware, 245 Kansas ave.

HOTELS.

GALT HOUSE,

Cor. Fifth & Jackson Sts.

The Best Dollar a Day House in the West. Boarding by the Day or Week.

By A. J. RYAN, the old Kansas Excursionist.

GORDON HOUSE,

(TOPEKA.)

J. C. GORDON, Proprietor,

105 KANSAS AVE.

LOAN AND TRUST COMPANY.

T. B. SWEET, Pres., A. C. BURNHAM, V-Pres.
GEO. M. NOBLE, Sec., Champaign, Ills.,

KANSAS LOAN & TRUST COMPANY,

Incorporated April, 1873. Devotes its entire attention to negotiating desirable loans, secured by first mortgage upon improved real estate in Eastern Kansas and Western Missouri.

MARBLE DEALERS.

STOUT, J. W. & CO., Foreign and American Marble, 108 Sixth ave.

MILLINERY.

HUTCHINSON, MRS. E. E., Fashionable Millinery, 195 Kansas ave.

MARMONT, MADAME, Millinery, 128 Kansas ave.

METCALF, MRS. E. C., Millinery, agent for Mme. Demorest's Patterns, 210 Kansas ave.

PATENTS.

MARTIN & BROWN, General Dealers in Patents throughout the West, 175 Kansas ave.

PHYSICIANS.

MARTIN, S. E., M. D., 110 Sixth ave., res. Fifth & Topeka ave.

SHELDON, S. E., Physician & Surgeon, 183 Kansas ave.

TOPEKA—Continued.

PRINTERS.

CUMMINGS, J. F., Printer, 101 Kansas ave.

SHAWNEE MILLS.

SHELLABARGER, GRISWOLD & CO., Proprietors of Shawnee Mills, Topeka.

STONE AND PIPE WORKS.

TOPEKA CARBONATED STONE & PIPE WORKS, S. P. Spear & H. Willis, Proprietors. Manufacturers of Building Stone, Pavements, Drain and Sewer Pipe, Well Tubing and all kinds of Chimney Flues. Kansas av., bet. 2nd & 3rd Sts.

STOVES AND TINWARE.

NEVANS, JOHN, Tinner and Dealer in Stoves, 237 Kansas ave.

TOBACCO AND CIGARS.

KRAEMER BROS., Manufacturers of Cigars, 150 Kansas ave.

MOESER, E., Manufacturer and dealer in all kinds of Cigars, 170 Kansas ave.

WYMAN, CHAS., Manufacturer of Cigars, Dealer in Tobacco, 133 Kansas ave.

UNDERTAKER.

STOKER, J. W., General Furnishing Undertaker, 127 Kansas ave.

WAGON MAKER.

WILSON, J. N., Wagon Maker, 126 Kansas ave.

WATCHMAKERS AND JEWELERS.

BAKER, OLIVER H., Watchmaker, formerly with Elgin National Watch Co., 201 Kansas ave.

BEAR, S. R., Watches, Clocks, Jewelry, &c., 185 Kansas ave.

HAYDEN, JAS. B., Practical Watchmaker and Jeweler, 212 Kansas ave.

ATCHISON, KANSAS.

BLACKSMITHS.

MILLER & SPOTTZ, Blacksmith & Wagon Maker & Wind. Mill Man'fs., Cor. 8th & Commercial.

BOARDING HOUSE.

HELD, GEO., Boarding House, 709 Commercial st.

BOOTS AND SHOES.

BARKOW, H. W., Dealer in Boots & Shoes, 533 Commercial st.

SENNINGER, D., Shoemaker, 721 Commercial st.

DENTIST.

BOWEN, W. H., Surgeon Dentist, 412 Commercial st., up stairs.

DRY GOODS.

STETTER, N., Dry Goods, Boots, Shoes, &c., 317 Commercial st.

RESTAURANT.

MILLER'S Restaurant, 211 Commercial st., opp. Otis House.

Quaker City.—A popular name of Philadelphia, which was planned and settled by William Penn, accompanied by a colony of English Friends.

Queen City.—A popular name of Cincinnati; so called when it was the undisputed commercial metropolis of the West.

Queen City of the Lakes.—A name sometimes given to the city of Buffalo, N. Y., from its position and importance.

Railroad City.—Indianapolis, the capital of the State of Indiana, is sometimes called by this name, as being the terminus of various railroads.

Rail-splitter.—A cant designation of Abraham Lincoln, the sixteenth President of the United States, who is said to have supported himself for one winter, in early life, by splitting rails for a farmer.

Red-Coats.—The name given by the Americans in the Revolutionary War to the British soldiery, in allusion to their scarlet uniform.

Regulators.—The popular name of a party in North Carolina, which arose in 1768, and had for its object the forcible redress of public grievances.

Rhody, Little.—A popular designation of Rhode Island, the smallest State in the Union.

Rough and Ready.—A sobriquet given to General Zachary Taylor (born 1790—died 1850), twelfth President of the United States, as expressive of prominent traits in his character.

St. Nicholas.—The patron saint of boys. He is said to have been Bishop of Myra, and to have died in the year 326. The young were universally taught to revere him, and the popular fictions which represent him as the bearer of presents to children on Christmas Eve is well known. He is the Santa Claus (or Klaus) of the Dutch.

Sam.—A popular synonym in the United States for the Know-nothings or Native American party. The name involves an allusion to *Uncle Sam*, the common personification of the United States Government.

Sambo.—A cant designation of the negro race. No race has ever shown such capabilities of adaptation to varying soil and circumstances as the negro. Alike to them the snows of Canada, the hard, rocky land of New England, or the gorgeous profusion of the Southern States. *Sambo* and Cuffy expand under them all.

Saunders, Richard.—A feigned name under which Dr. Franklin in 1732, commenced the publication of an Almanac—commonly called "Poor Richard's Almanac," of which the distinguishing feature was a series of maxims of prudence and industry in the form of proverbs.

Scarlet Woman, The.—In the controversial writings of the Protestants, a common designation of the Church of Rome, intended to symbolize its vices and corruptions. The allusion is to the description contained in Revelation, chapter xvi: 1-6.

Seven Sleepers.—According to a very widely diffused legend of early Christianity, seven noble youths of Ephesus, in the time of the Decian persecution, who, having fled to a certain

ATCHISON—Continued.

RAILROAD TICKET AGENT.
FARNSWORTH, D. E., Ticket Agent,
207 Commercial st.

SALOON AND BILLIARD HALL.
KAFFER, JOHN, Commercial Billiard Hall and Bar. 415 Commercial st.

TOBACCO AND CIGARS.
BRANDON, GUSTAVE, Cigar Maker,
412 Commercial st.

CLINTON, IOWA.

ATTORNEYS AT LAW.
STEPHEN, JAMES, Attorney at Law,
Room 4, P. O., Block. Est. 1875.

BOAT BUILDER.
JUCKETT, F. H., Boat Builder,
Ferry-boat Landing. Est. 1872.

BOILER WORKS.
CLINTON BOILER WORKS, John Alfred, Propr.,
Office, 2nd st. Est. 1870.

CLOTHING.
STAR ONE PRICE CLOTHING HOUSE, 208 5th av.,
Childs & Baer Proprietors. Est. 1875.

CONFECTIONERY.
SHERMAN, J. L., Restaurant and Confectionery.
Cigars, &c., 512 Second st. Established 1874.

CROCKERY, CHINA AND GLASSWARE.

Z. M. FRITH,
Wholesale & Retail Dealer in

Crockery, China, Glassware
And House Furnishing Goods,
206 FIFTH AVE.
Established 1877.

GROCERIES.
RIES & GODSKESEN, Wholesale and Retail Dealers in Groceries, 700 2nd st. Est. 1875.

HOTEL.
CENTRAL HOTEL, First and Fourth sts.
Bent & Cottrell, Props. Estab. 1876.

IRON WORKS.

UNION IRON WORKS.
Gang & Circular Saw Mills
Gang Edgers and Lumber Trimmers. Engines and Boilers of all Sizes made to Order.
Established 1872.   *CLINTON, IOWA.*

MEAT MARKET.
PIPPING, FRANK, Fresh, Salt and Smoked Meats, 5th ave. Established 1876.

CLINTON—Continued.

MILLINERY GOOODS.
MILLER, MISS TILLIE, Millinery and Fancy Goods, 211 Fifth ave, Established 1872,

NEWSPAPER.
DAILY HERALD. Waldo M. Potter, Editor and Proprietor. Established 1857.

PAPER MILL.
CLINTON PAPER CO., Manufacturers and Dealers in Paper. Established 1868.

PHYSICIAN.

NORTHWESTERN,
Surgical & Medical Institute
DR. M. E. BROWN, Principal.
CLINTON, IOWA.
Established 1875.

SASH, DOOR AND BLINDS.
CURTIS BROS., Sash, Doors and Blinds,
cor. 2nd and 13th ave. Estab. 1866.
HARADON, L. P., Sash, Doors and Blinds,
2nd st.; Factory, cor. 1st and Elm sts.

TIN, COPPER AND SHEET IRON.
KETTERER, JOHN H., Tin, Copper and Sheet Ironware, first door N. of Revere House. Established 1877.

TOBACCO AND CIGARS.
PULFORD, C. D., Manufacturer and Dealer in Cigars and Tobacco. 414 2nd st. Estab. 1874.

LYONS, IOWA.

FOUNDRY.
LYONS FOUNDRY AND MACHINE SHOP.
J. Moeszinger, Prop. Main and 2nd sts.

DENTIST.
PATERSON, JOHN, Surgeon Dentist,
Masonic Temple.

GROCERIES.
MILLER, WM., Grocer, Manuf'r of German Mustard, &c., Lyons. Estab. 1871.

FULTON, ILLINOIS.

COLLEGE.

Northern Illinois College,
Fulton, Whiteside Co., Ill., on the Mississippi. Preparatory, Collegiate. Normal and Musical Departments. Also ☞ Griffith's College of Reading and Oratory. Stammerers cured and taught to read and speak. Both Sexes admitted. Splendid Chapel, Library, Chemical and Philosophical Apparatus and Rooms. A School and Home for 250 Students. Full Faculty. Address,
ALLEN A. GRIFFITH, A. M., President.

Post Office and Custom House, Cleveland, O.—This building was erected about twenty years ago. Its exterior is composed entirely of stone and presents a very handsome appearance. It is located on the east side of Monumental Park, north of Superior street. In it are most of the government offices.

FULTON—*Continued.*

HOTEL.

Revere House

MRS. R. S. SAYER, Proprietress.

FULTON, ILLS.

Established 1877.

PIPE MANUFACTORY.

Fulton Pipe Manufactory,

GERTEN BROS.

Manufacturers of

CLAY PIPES

Estab. 1869.   *FULTON, ILLS.*

PEORIA, ILLS.

ARCHITECTS.

C. MEHLER,
ARCHITECT & SUPERINTENDENT,
325 MAIN STREET,

PEORIA—*Continued.*

QUAYLE, WM., Architect and Superintendent, 31 Chamber of Commerce. Estab. 1870.

ATTORNEYS AT LAW.

CUTRIGHT, JAS. M., Attorney at Law, 327 Main st.

GABLE, GEO. W., Lawyer. cor. Main & Adams sts., Peoria, Ill.

McFARLAND, DANIEL, Attorney at Law and Solicitor. 111 S. Adams st.

TURNER, THOS. H., Attorney and Counsellor at Law, cor. Main & Adams sts.

BARBERS.

ERION & WARKLE, Tonsorial Parlors, 214 Main st. Estab. 1865.

BILLIARDS.

FREIDRICH, HERMAN, Commercial Billiard Parlors, 116 & 118 S. Jefferson st.

BLEACHING.

DONIGAN, P. T., Hat and Bonnet Bleachery, 304 LaFayette st.

MRS. E. A. SCHULTZ.
Hat and Bonnet Bleachery and Dealer in Millinery and Fancy Goods, Notions, &c.,
No. 800 N. ADAMS ST.

BOOK BINDER.

REUS, E. C., Book Binder and Paper Hanger, 325 S. Adams st.

PEORIA—*Continued.*

BOOTS AND SHOES.

CHARVAT, J., Custom Boot and Shoe Maker, 207 Fulton st.

GREEN, J. C., & SON, Dealers in Boots & Shoes, 431 & 423 S. Adams st.

WEISBRUCH, JOSEPH, Manuf'r and Dealer in Boots and Shoes, 400 S. Washington st. Established 1857.

BUILDERS AND LUMBER DEALERS.

MILLER, JOSEPH, & SON, Builders and Dealers in Lumber, Lath, Shingles, Timber, Brick and Fire Wood, cor. Washington & Walnut sts. Estab. 1849.

CARRIAGES AND WAGONS.

SCHROEDER, J., Manuf'r Plows, Wagons and Buggies, 205 Bridge st.

SMITH, G. W., & SONS, Carriage Manufacturers, 303 to 307 Fulton st.

CIGAR BOXES.

HOKLAS & TORTAT,

Manufacturers of

CIGAR BOXES

No. 217 Harrison Street.

CRACKERS AND CONFECTIONERY.

KELLOGG & DAVIS, Manufacturers of Crackers and Confectionery, 6th & Franklin sts.

DENTIST.

MARTIN, W. C., Dentist, 307 Main st. Estab. 1876.

DRESSMAKING.

BEDEL, JULIA, Dressmaking, 504 Main street.

CALKINS, MRS. E. B., Dressmaking and Tailoring, 608 Main st.

CLAUSER, MRS. A., Dressmaker, 211 S. Adams st.

DRUGGISTS.

ALLAIRE, WOODWARD & CO., Pharmaceutical Chemists, cor. Water & Hamilton sts.

DAVIS, ROBT. S., Druggist, cor. Main & Washington sts. Est. 1872.

DRY GOODS.

EPPSTEINER, D., Staple and Fancy Dry Goods, 305 S. Washington st.

FLOUR DEALERS.

BONHAM, W. M., & CO., Wholesale Flour Dealers and Comission Merchants, 308 Bridge.

FURNITURE.

PEORIA FURNITURE CO.

Manufacturers of Fine & Medium

FURNITURE

SALESROOMS: FACTORY:
Nos. 104 to 110 Main St.   Nos. 107 & 109 N. Water St

SPECIAL DESIGNS MADE TO ORDER.

PEORIA—*Continued.*

GRAIN AND COMMISSION MERCHANTS.

ELDER & McKINSEY, Grain Commission Merchants, Room 20, Chamber of Commerce. Established 1869.

GERDES & SIEBERN, Grain Commission Merchants, 315 S. Washington st.

GRIER & CO., Grain Commission Merchants, Chamber of Commerce Building. Est. 1865.

MARTIN, ROBERT S., Dealer in Grain and Feed, 109 Liberty st.

MORGAN, B. H., & CO., Grain and Commission Merchants, 115 Liberty st.

GROCERIES.

EBERLE, C. F., Groceries and Provisions, 625 N. Adams st.

MULLER, JACOB, Groceries and Provisions, 212 Bridge st.

SCHIMPFF, R. A., Groceries, Fruits, Poultry, &c., 203 South Madison st.

ULRICH, VAL., Wholesale Groceries and Liquors, 109 S. Washington st.

GUN AND WHITESMITHS.

BOURDEREAUX, G., Practical Gunmaker, 208 Liberty st.

MULLER, F. W., Gun and Whitesmith, 223 Bridge st.

SCHNEIDER, JOHN, Whitesmith & Gunsmith, 410 Fulton st.

C. WHITTEMORE,

WHITESMTH and GUNSMITH,

306 Fulton st., bet. Adams & Jefferson sts.

HARDWARE.

PFEIFER, M., Hardware, Ammunition, Farming Implements, 232 Bridge st.

HARNESS AND SADDLES.

SAUPE, H., Harness Manufacturer, 208 Bridge st.

HATS AND CAPS.

KORSOSKI, JOHN, Hats, Caps & manf'r of Furs, cor. Adams & Fulton sts.

HOTELS.

CENTRAL HOTEL,

PHILLIPS & CRAWFORD, Props.,

CORNER WATER & HARRISON STREETS.

Rates, $2.00 per day. Free Bus. Good Stabling, Carriage House and Yard.

PEORIA HOUSE,

E. Corner Public Square.

CHAS. H. DEAN, Propr.

Rates reduced to $2.00, $2.50 and $3.00 per day, according to location and size of room. Under same management since March, 1867.

ADVERTISEMENTS. 415

City Hall, Cleveland, O.—Is situated on the north side Superior street, corner Wood. It was built by Leonard Case, at an estimated cost of $800,000, and leased to the city for public purposes for 25 years, at an annual rental of 36,000. It fronts 217 feet on Superior street, is five stories high, besides a basement under the whole. It was completed February, 1875. It is a very handsome building, as the engraving shows.

PEORIA—*Continued.*

ICE DEALER.

DETWEILLER, HENRY, dealer in pure Lake Ice, 108 S. Adams st. Established 1870.

INSURANCE AGENTS.

BILLS & BACON, Gen'l Ins. Ag'ts for Fire, Marine, Life & Accident, 108 & 110 S. Adams st.

IRON WORKS.

ADAM LUCAS,
Manufacturer of Fire-Proof Safes, Bank Vaults, Burglar-Proof Locks, Iron Shutters, Doors and Jail Work, 211 Fulton street.

JUSTICE OF THE PEACE.

FIELDER, WM., Notary Public and Justice of the Peace, cor. Main & Adams sts.

LIVERY AND SALE STABLES.

GABLE, JOHN M., Livery & Sale Stable, Rear 214 Com. Alley.

SCHLINK, J. P., Livery & Sale Stable, 528 S. Adams st.

WARNER, B. O., Livery & Sale Stable, 110 & 112 N. Washington st.

PEORIA—*Continued.*

MACHINISTS.

NICOL, BURR & CO., Manf'rs of Steam Engines & Machinery, cor. Water & Walnut sts.

MUSIC TEACHER.

TRAUTVETTER, C., Teacher of Music. 226 S. Adams st.

PHOTOGRAPHER.

COLE'S
ART & PHOTOGRAPHIC
STUDIO,
On Hamilton st., one square above Peoria House.

PHYSICIAN.

MARTIN, L. R., Physician, 303 Main st.

REGALIAS.

BUSH, JOHN A., manf'r and dealer in all kinds of Regalia. 408 Main st.

THE
Chicago, Burlington & Quincy
RAILROAD!

"BURLINGTON ROUTE,"

Will Continue to Run the Celebrated

SIXTEEN WHEEL DINING CARS

—BETWEEN—

Chicago & Omaha,

Giving you all the luxuries of the season that the markets afford.

As the proprietors of all FIRST-CLASS HOTELS make their DINING SALON the great feature of their houses, so the management of the "GREAT BURLINGTON ROUTE," having the COMFORT, PLEASURE and LUXURY of their patrons solely in view, do not use their CELEBRATED DINING CARS for Passage Traffic, or sleeping purposes (as is the case of the so-called Hotel Cars); hence they are always kept sweet, neat and clean, for eating uses only. Their ventilation is superb, and no disagreeable fumes from the kitchen permeate the air. The moderate charge of 75 cents only, is made for each meal, and the Menu is ample to satisfy the epicurean taste of the most fastidious.

Great care should be taken not to confuse these CELEBRATED DINING CARS with the Hotel Cars used on some Railways, where the Passengers Eat, Drink, Sleep and Bathe in the same Coach. The Dining Cars run on the "GREAT BURLINGTON ROUTE" are PULLMAN'S longest 16 WHEEL SALOON COACHES, used for eating purposes only. The well-known PULLMAN SIXTEEN WHEEL DRAWING ROOM SLEEPING COACHES (these Cars are just from the shops, having been refitted and refurnished throughout, with a MAGNIFICENT DRAWING ROOM built within, for families or select parties traveling together), are run on THIS ROUTE ONLY, between CHICAGO and OMAHA.

CHICAGO WATER WORKS.

H. C. PERKINS & CO.,
Repair Reapers, Mowers and Lawn Mowers.
Have for Sale Lawn Mowers,
ALSO BUY AND SELL

Second-Hand Reapers, Mowers and Lawn Mowers,
125 W. Randolph St., Cor. Desplaines, CHICAGO, ILLS.

PEORIA—*Continued.*

RESTAURANTS.

ANTON L. THEILIG,

Confectionery & Ice Cream Parlors,

Ladies' and Gentlemen's Restaurant,

352 MAIN ST. Established 1869.

RE-OPENED,
Merchant's Restaurant,
319 MAIN ST.,
☞ "Do not forget it." Call and see me.

CHAS. H. GAINES.

THE ST. ELMO RESTAURANT,
Cor. Adams & Hamilton sts.,
R. S. FLETCHER, Proprietor.
The Dining Rooms have been re-fitted and put in complete order.

SALOON.

CHAS. E. GILLIG,

WINE & BEER HALL,

214 & 216 Fulton St.

Established 1854.

SASH, DOOR AND BLINDS.

BUSH, H. A., Window Blinds, Sash & Doors, 716 Washington st.

HERSCHBERGER, JOHN, Manf'r of Sash, Doors & Blinds, 704 S. Washington st.

SEWING MACHINES.

SCHMUCK & BENNETT, Wheeler & Wilson Sewing Machines, 304 Fulton st.

SHOW CASES.

LUTKE, R. G., manf'r of Show Cases, 215 Hamilton st.

STARCH MANUFACTURERS.

PEORIA STARCH CO., E. S. Wilcox, Supt., Foot of South st. River Bank.

STOVES, TIN AND COPPER.

EHLEN, H. J., Tin, Copper and Sheet Iron, 600 S. Adams st.

HUNTER & CO., Cooking and Heating Stoves, Tinware, etc., 111 S. Adams st.

TOYS.

GILLIG, KARL G., Books, Stationery & Toys, 303 S. Adams st.

UNDERTAKER.

VANCE, W. B., Undertaker, Metallic Cases and Wood Coffins, 502 Main st.

PEORIA—*Continued.*

UPHOLSTERERS.

HOFFMAN & STOCK, Upholsterers & House-furnishers, 215 S. Madison st.

KELLY, JOHN, Upholsterer & House-furnisher, 426 Fulton st.

WIRE WORKS.

VAN EPS, H. R., Manf'r of useful & ornamental Wire Goods, 313 Halo st.

WRAPPING PAPER.

HARSCH & CO.,
Wholesale dealers in

WRAPPING PAPER, PAPER BAGS,

Building Paper, Carpet Lining, Twines, Etc,
316 BRIDGE STREET.
Cash paid for Paper Stock & old Metals.

PEORIA BUSINESS HOUSES.

WHEN ESTABLISHED.

BUSH, JOHN A., Society Regalia, 1856.
COLES, H. H., Photographer, 1850.
FRIEDRICHS, HERMAN, Billiards, 1858.
GAINES, CHAS. H., Restaurant, 1877.
HERSCHBERGER, JOHN, Doors and Blinds, 1865.
LUTKE, R. G., Showcases, 1867.
NICOL, BURR & CO., Machintsis, 1850.
PEORIA FURNITURE CO., 1873.
PHILLIPS & CRAWFORD, 1858.
VAN EPS, H. R., Wire Works, 1873.
VANCE, W. B., Undertaker, 1849.

JACKSONVILLE, ILLS.

BOOK BINDERS.

W. B. PEARSON,

Book Binder

WEST MORGAN ST.,
1st door West of Conservatory Block.

WARD BROTHERS, Booksellers & Bookbinders, Marble Block, S. side square.

BOOKS AND STATIONERY.

CATLIN & CO., Books, Stationery, Music, etc., 3 Opera House, S. side square.

WARD BROTHERS, Booksellers & Blank Book manfrs. Marble Block, S. side square.

BOTTLER.

KERSHAW, ALBERT, Manf'r Soda Water, also Bottler, N. W. Cor. square and Sandy st.

JACKSONVILLE—Continued.

CARRIAGES AND WAGONS.

MIDDLETON & DAVISON, Carriage & Wagonmakers, N. Sandy st.

CONSERVATORY OF MUSIC.

ILLINOIS CONSERVATORY OF MUSIC, W. D. Sanders, supt., South Sand st., near square.

FEMALE COLLEGE.

ILLINOIS FEMALE COLLEGE, Rev. M. F. Short, pres't., East State st.

JACKSONVILLE FEMALE ACADEMY, E. F. Bullard, Princp. cor. Church st. & College ave.

HOTELS.

DUNLAP HOUSE, W. F. Dunlap, propr, West State st.

PARK HOTEL, Cap. Smith, propr, Public Square.

SOUTHERN HOTEL, B. Hocking, Prop., College ave.

MILLINERY.

MRS. P. ALKIRE,

Millinery,

AND DRESSMAKING,

EAST SIDE SQUARE.

HILLERBY, MRS. B., Milliner and Dressmaker, E. Morgan st.

MRS. E. MILES,

Milliner

AND BONNET BLEACHER,

Cor. College Ave. and Mauvisterre St.

MUSIC DEALERS.

BARROWS, CHAS. S., Music Dealer, W. Morgan st., near square.

CATLIN & CO., Music & Musical Instruments, 3 Opera House, S. side square.

PHOTOGRAPHERS.

CADMAN, A. W., Photographer, S. Main st., P. O. Block.

CLENDENON & NICHOLS, City Photographic Gallery, King's Block, E. side square.

HOFMANN, J., ECKHARDT, Photographer, cor. E. State st. & square.

TAILORS.

HUNTOON, GEO. H., Merchant Tailor, 2 W. State st.

LEWINSON, M. S., Merchant Tailor, N. side East State st.

WATCHES, CLOCKS AND JEWELRY.

BAKER, FRANK W., Watchmaker, Jeweler and Engraver, 1 W. Morgan st.

---

cavern for refuge, and having been pursued, discovered, and walled in for a cruel death, were made to fall asleep, and in that state were miraculously kept for almost two centuries. Their names are traditionally said to have been, Maximican, Malchus, Martinian, Denis, John, Scrapton, and Constantine. The Church has consecrated the 27th of June to their memory. The Koran relates the tale of the seven sleepers, deriving it probably from the same source as the Christian legend, and declares that out of respect for them the sun altered his course twice a day that he might shine into the cavern.

Seven Wonders of the World, The.—A name given to seven very remarkable objects of the ancient world, which have been variously enumerated. The following classification is one of the most generally received: 1. The Pyramids of Egypt; 2. The Pharos of Alexander; 3. The walls and hanging gardens of Babylon; 4. The Temple of Diana at Ephesus; 5. The statue of the Olympian Jupiter; 6. The Mausoleum of Artemisia; 7. The Colossus of Rhodes.

Skinners.—A name assumed by a predatory band in the revolutionary war, who, professing allegiance to the American cause, but influenced by a desire to plunder, roamed over the "neutral ground," lying between the hostile armies, robbing those who refused to take the oath of fidelity.

Slick, Sam.—The title and hero of various humorous narratives, illustrating and exaggerating the peculiarities of the Yankee character and dialect, written by Judge Thomas C. Haliburton, of Nova Scotia. Sam Slick is represented as a Yankee clockmaker and peddler, full of quaint drollery, unsophisticated wit, knowledge of human nature, and aptitude in the use of what he calls "soft sawder."

Smoky City.—A name sometimes given to Pittsburgh, Pa., an important manufacturing city. The use of bituminous coal occasions dense volumes of smoke to fill the air in and around the place, soiling the garments of passengers, and giving the buildings a dark and sooty appearance.

Stonewall Jackson.—A sobriquet given, during the American civil war, to Thomas Jonathan Jackson (born 1824, died 1863), a general in the service of the Confederate States. This famous appellation had its origin in an expression used by the Confederate General Bee, on trying to rally his men at the battle of Bull Run, July 21, 1862—"There is Jackson standing like a stone wall." From that day he was known as *Stonewall* Jackson, and his command as the Stonewall Brigade.

Sucker State.—A cant name given in America to the State of Illinois, the inhabitants of which are very generally called *Suckers* throughout the west. The origin of this term is said to be as follows : The western prairies are in many places full of the holes made by the crawfish (a fresh-water shell-fish, similar in form to the lobster), which descend to the water beneath. In early times, when travelers wended their way over these immense plains, they very prudently provided themselves with a long hollow reed, and when thirsty thrust it into these natural artesians, and thus easily supplied their longings. The crawfish well generally contains pure water, and the manner in which the traveler drew forth the refreshing element gave him the name of *Sucker.*

NEBRASKA CITY, NEB.

ATTORNEYS AT LAW.

HAYDEN, D. T., Att'y at Law & Notary Public, colc'ns promptly attended to, Rottman's Blk

IRELAND, F. P., Attorney & Counselor at Law, 177 Main st.

MOREHOUSE, S. S., Att'y at Law, Notary Public & Real Estate Agent, 230 Main st.

AUCTION AND COMMISSION.

SCOTT, WM., Auction & Commission. Merchandise Bought & Sold, Main & 6th sts.

WHITE & WATSON, Auction & Commission, Furniture, Groceries, &c., 201 Main st.

BLACKSMITH.

KRESEN, CHARLES, Blacksmithing, also grinding & Polishing Plows, Main & 15th sts.

BOOKSELLERS.

HARDING, N. S. & CO., Booksellers, General Insurance Agents, 179 Main st.

COAL AND WOOD.

CORNUTT, L. F., Coal, Wood, Lime, Hair, Cement and Plaster Paris, Otoe & 8th sts.

CONFECTIONERY.

THOMAS, G. H., Dealers in Confectionary Cigars & Tobacco, 187 Main st.

DENTIST.

CHADDUCK, DR. J. N., Dentist, Nitrous Oxide Gas administered, 228 Main st.

DRUGGISTS.

HEMINGER, P., Druggist, 193 Main st.

REED, JAMES & BRO., Drugs, Paints, Oils, Varnish, Brushes, &c , 135 Main st.

O. A. THURMAN,
Druggist and Apothecary,
158 MAIN STREET.

FURNITURE.

FARIS, S. J., Dealer in Furniture, Undertaking a specialty, 166 Main st.

GROCERS.

DAVIES, S. T., Staple Dry Goods, Teas, Groceries, &c , 185 Main st.

JOHNSON & STRINE, Family Grocery, Confectionery, Nuts, Fruits, &c., 161 Main st.

LLOYD & WHITE, Dealers in Dry Goods & Family Groceries, Grand Central Block.

NORTHCUTT, J. B., Staple and Fancy Groceries, Cor. 13th & Main sts.

C. H. SCHEUCH,
Dealer in Staple and Fancy
GROCERIES,
Provisions, Liquors and Cigars, Wooden and Willow Ware, etc..
Corner of Fifth and Main Streets.

SIMPSON, D. W., Dealer in Groceries & Provisions, Flour & Feed, 174 Main st.

STRAUB & STAHLHUT, Dealers in Staple and Fancy Groceries, Cor. 7th & Main sts.

NEBRASKA CITY—Continued.

GROCERS.
J. W. WALDSMITH,
Groceries and Provisions, Confectionery, Tobacco and Cigars,
145 MAIN STREET.

GUN AND LOCKSMITH.

DEFIBAUGH, L., Gun & Locksmith, also General Job Work, Main bet. 8th & 9th.

HARDWARE.

BISCHOF & ZIMMERER, Hardware, Branch Houses at Edward & York, 179 Main st.

HAWLEY, E. S. & CO., Hardware, Stoves & Tinware & Agricultural Implements, 137 Main st.

HARNESS AND SADDLES.

KLEPSER, JACOB, Dealer in Harness, Saddles & Bridles, 180 Main st.

HOTELS.

BARNUM HOUSE, G. A. Wilcox, Prop., Leading Hotel in the city, Cor. Main & 8th sts.

FARMER HOUSE, Thos. Wymond, Prop., $2.00 per day House, Cor. Main and 7th sts.

GERMAN HOTEL, Joseph Brand, Prop., Finest of Wines, Liquors & Cigars, Cor Main & 9th.

GRAND CENTHAL HOTEL, J. Strine, Prop., Terms $1 to $2 per day, Cor. 10th & Main sts.

INSURANCE.

HAYNES, J. E. JR., Fire Insurance Agency, Office, Rottman's Block.

IRON WORKS.

NEBRASKA CITY IRON WORKS, John Wale, Prop., 6th st., near Otoe.

LIVERY AND SALE STABLES.

MONROE & LEVI, Elephant Stable, Livery, Feed & Exchange, Cor. 9th & Main st.

LUMBER DEALERS.

BALDWIN, FRANK T., Proprietor of Saginaw Lumber Yard. opp. Court House.

CADY, HENRY F., Wholesale and Retail dealer in Lumber, 205 Main st.

MILLINERY.

ADLE, MRS. E. G., Dealer in Millinery & Fancy Goods, 156 Main st.

FORSCUTT, MRS. W. H., Dealer in Millinery, Hair-work and notions, 182 Main st.

PATENTS.

DILL, J. A., Patents Bought and Sold, Agents Wanted to Sell Territory, 10th and Main sts.

PHOTOGRAPHERS.

MADISON, J. H., Photographer, Oil Photographs, Enlarging Pictures, &c., 151 Main st.

PHILLIPS, C. W., Photographer, 177 Main st.

PHYSICIAN.

HERSHEY, D. W., M. D., Physician and Surgeon, 212 Main st.

New Court House, Cleveland.—The above is a view from Seneca street. The centre has a front of 75 feet on Seneca street, and a depth of 92. The north wing is 34 feet front and 84 deep, the South wing 49 feet front, with a depth of 284 feet, surmounted with a tower 120 feet high. The building is three-stories high above the basement. The Court House and Jail are built entirely of Iron.

NEBRASKA CITY—*Continued.*

PLUMBER AND GASFITTER.

J. M. TAYLOR,

Gasfitter and Plumber, Dealer in Pumps, Gas Pipe, Engine Trimmings, Gas Fixtures and Fittings.

184 MAIN STREET.

REAL ESTATE.

GROAT, GEO. W., Real Estate and Collecting Agent and Notary Public, 230 Main st.

RESTAURANTS.

EBHARDT, CHRIST, Proprietor of the Erhardt Restaurant & Boarding House, Main & 9th.

SALOONS.

CLINGIN, GEO. W., Billiard Saloon, Finest of Wines, Liquors & Cigars, 149 Main st.

FASS BROS., Saloon, Finest of Wines, Liquors and Cigars, Grand Central Block.

JAHNS, F., Wine & Beer Saloon, 208 Main st.

SEWING MACHINES.

SINGER SEWING MACHINE CO., A. R. Newcomb, Agent, Main st.

NEBRASKA CITY—*Continued.*

STOVES AND TINWARE.

H. AIRD & CO.,

Manufacturers and dealers in Stoves, Tinware, Copper, Sheet Iron, Roofing, Spouting, &c..

186 Main Street.

TAILORS.

FIELDS, S. H., Merchant Tailor, 151 Main st.

HILL, R. M., Merchant Tailor. Main st.

TOBACCO AND CIGARS.

KOEHLER & KARSTENS, Manufacturers and dealers in Fine Cigars, 232 Main st.

WINES AND LIQUORS.

KEEGAN, CHARLES, Importer of Foreign and dealer in Wines, Liquors & Cigars, Main & 8th

HANNIBAL, MO.

BARBERS.

SCHNITZER, J. L., Barber Shop, 102 S. Main st.

HANNIBAL—Continued.

DRESSMAKING.

FOLEY, ANNIE, Dressmaking, 119 N. Main st.

MEEK, MRS. M. L., Dressmaking, 314 Broadway.

DRUGGIST.

SALLEE, R. C., Druggist, 125 Market st.

GROCERS.

OWENS, H. H., Groceries, Staple and Fancy, 710 Broadway.

RAZON, P., Grocer and Baker, 118 Market st.

WALLER, W. D. & CO., Grocer & Provisions, 409 Broadway.

HOTELS.

NATIONAL HOTEL, 315 Front st., G. A. Kettering, prop.

PLANTER'S HOUSE, Carl C. Riker & Co., props. Main st.

PAPER DEALER.

WEST, H., Bags and Wrapping Paper, 112 S. Main st.

PRINTERS.

WINCHELL & EBERT,

Printing & Lithographing Company,

JOB PRINTERS, BINDERS AND MANUFACTURING STATIONERS,

First-Class Work at Fair Prices.

HANNIBAL, - - - MO.

SOAP AND CANDLES.

SCHNIZLEIN, Manf'r. of Soap and Candles, Plank Road near Toll Gate.

STOVES AND TINWARE.

BROWN, W. G. & CO., Housefurnishing Goods, Stoves and Tinware, 116 S. Main st.

TAILORS.

POWELL, H. & CO., Merchant Tailor & Gent's Furnishing Goods, 114 S. Main st.

TOBACCO AND CIGARS.

ADAMS, J., Excelsior Billiard Hall and Cigars & Tobacco, 122 S. Main st.

DREYER, G. W., Cigar Manufacturer, 303 N. Main st.

ROMBERG, WM., Cigar Manufacturer, 201 Broadway.

GALESBURG, ILLS.

BARBERS.

SWANSON, & CO., Barbers, Hair cutting for Ladies and Children, 39 Main st.

BOOTS AND SHOES.

WENQUIST & JOHNSON, Manf'rs. of Fine Boots & Shoes, 66 Main st.

GALESBURG—Continued.

CONFECTIONERY.

ANDREW NELSON,

Confectionery, Notions, &c.,

63 MAIN STREET.

DENTISTS.

DAVIS, E. F., Dentist, 35 Main st. Est. 1851.

DAVIS, J. A. W., Dentist, 14 Main st.

DRESS AND CLOAK MAKING.

D. W. HAWKINS,

Dress and Cloak Making,

28 MAIN ST., - - Established 1870.

MRS. B. PALLAFOX,

DRESS & CLOAK MAKING

53 Main Street,

DYE WORKS.

HURLBURT, F. R., Proprietor of STEAM DYE WORKS, cor. Main and Kellogg sts. Ladies' Dresses and Gentlemen's Clothes Cleaned and Dyed; also Kid Gloves and Shoes Cleaned, and Plumes Cleaned, Curled and Dyed. All work warranted to give satisfaction. First-class Tailoring and Repairing done to order.

HOTELS.

AMERICAN HOUSE,

JAMES POLING, Proprietor. Terms, $2.00 per Day, Good Sample Rooms. Within two minutes walk of Depot, very desirable location for Commercial Travelers.

UNION HOTEL, C. Wormley, prop.

LIVERY AND SALE STABLE.

LIVERY, FEED & SALE STABLE,

JAS. O'CONNOR, Prop.,

Corner Simmons and Cherry Streets.

MILLINERY.

YOUNG, MRS. E. M., Millinery, 47 Main st.

MEAT MARKET.

J. W. ANDERSON,

MEAT MARKET,

Main Street.

GALESBURG—Continued.

NEWSPAPER.

GALESBURG PRINTING CO.,
Publishers of the Daily and Weekly "Republican-Register" and General Job Printers.
EAST SIDE PUBLIC SQUARE.

PHOTOGRAPHERS.

I. D. SMITH,

PHOTOGRAPHER,

Prairie Street.

PHYSICIAN.

PILES! Dr. Bell, successor to J. W. Mitchell, M. D., makes the treatment of piles a specialty. He does not use the kni e, caustic or ligature. Relief immediate and cure permanent. Patients giving security for fee, will not have to pay anything until a cure is completed. Call or address with stamp, Dr. S. T. Bell, Lock Box, 38, Rooms adjoining H. W. Carpenter's Insurance Office.

M. HERRMANN,

Physician & Surgeon,

PRAIRIE ST., Opp. CITY OFFICES.

TURKISH BATHS.

THE GALESBURG THERMÆ, Turkish Baths, N. E. cor. Prairie & Simmons st.

PEKIN, ILLS.

ARCHITECT.

J. P. HALL,

ARCHITECT & SUPERINTENDENT,
Cor. Capitol & St. Mary's Sts. Est. 1838.

DENTIST.

BUSH, GEO. L., Dentist, Over 307 Court st. Est. 1877.

FURNITURE.

SCHILLING & BOHN, Manufacturers & dealers in Furniture, &c., 425 Court st. Est. 1859.

HARDWARE, STOVES, &c.

(Established 1877.)
HENRY HEISEL,
Dealer in Hardware, Stoves, Tinware and Housefurnishing Goods.
514 COURT STREET.

Swedish Nightingale.—A name popularly given to Jenny Lind (Madame Goldschmidt, born 1821), a native of Stockholm, and the most celebrated of female vocalists.

Tammany, St.—The name of an Indian Chief who, in the United States, has been popularly canonized as a saint, and adopted as the tutelary genius of one branch of the Democratic party. Tammany was of the Delaware nation, and lived probably in the middle of the seventeenth century. He resided in the country which is now Delaware until he was of age, when he moved beyond the Alleghanies, and settled on the banks of the Ohio. He became chief sachem of his tribe, and being always a friend of the whites, often restrained his warriors from deeds of violence. His rule was always discreet, and he endeavored to induce his followers to cultivate agriculture and the arts of peace rather than those of war. When he became old he called a council to have a successor appointed, after which the residue of his life was spent in retirement, and tradition relates that "young and old repaired to his wigwam to bear him discourse wisdom." His great motto was, "Unite in peace for happiness, in war for defense." When and by whom he was first styled *saint*, or by what whim he was chosen to be the patron of Democracy, does not appear.

Tippecanoe.—A sobriquet conferred upon Gen. William H. Harrison, afterward President of the United States, during the political canvass which preceded his election, on account of the victory gained by him over the Indians in the battle which took place on the 6th of November, 1811, at the junction of the Tippecanoe and Wabash rivers.

Topsy.—A young slave girl in Mrs. Stowe's novel, "Uncle Tom's Cabin," who is made to illustrate the ignorance, low moral development and wild humor of the African character, as well as its capacity for education.

Turpentine State.—A popular name for the State of North Carolina, which produces and exports large quantities of turpentine.

Uncle Sam.—A cant or vulgar name of the United States Government. Immediately after the last declaration of war with England, Elbert Anderson, of New York, then a contractor, visited Troy, on the Hudson, where was concentrated and where he purchased a large contract of provisions, beef, pork, etc. The inspectors of these articles, at the place, were Messrs. Ebenezer and Samuel Wilson. The latter gentleman (invariably known as "Uncle Sam") generally superintended in person a large number of workmen, who, on this occasion, were employed in overhauling the provisions purchased by the contractors of the army. The casks were marked E. A.—U. S. This work fell to the lot of a facetious fellow in the employ of the Messrs. Wilson, who, on being asked by some of his fellow-workmen the meaning of the mark (for the letters U. S. for United States were then almost entirely new to them), said he did not know, unless it meant Elbert Anderson and "Uncle Sam," alluding exclusively to the said "Uncle Sam" Wilson. The joke took among the workmen, and passed currently; and "Uncle Sam" himself being present, was occasionally rallied by them on the increasing extent of his possessions. Many of these workmen, being of a character denominated "fond of powder,"

D. H. HODGES,
—CHEAP—
Dry Goods, Fancy Goods, and Notion
STORE,
No. 298 Massachusetts Avenue,
INDIANPOLIS, INDIANA.

J. CAYLOR,
DEALER IN
HARDWARE, CUTLERY, NAILS
Glass, Edge Tools, &c.

No. 296 MASSACHUSETTS AVENUE,
INDIANAPOLIS, INDIANA.

DAVIS & BRO.,
PRINTERS,
Established 1866.
Book Binders, Blank Book, Wood and Paper Box Manufacturers,
78 & 80 Clinton Street,
FORT WAYNE, IND.

JOHN N. MANNING.   G. S. MANNING.
JOHN N. MANNING & CO.,
Manufacturers and Contractors for
Steam Heating and Ventilating Apparatus

For Public and Private Buildings. Dealers in Wrought Iron Pipe, Fittings, Brass Goods, Boilers, Radiators, Pumps, etc., etc. Steam Fitting and General Jobbing. Specifications and Plans prepared, and Estimates furnished free of charge.

80 & 82 North Clinton Street, CHICAGO, ILL.

ADVERTISEMENTS.

Shoe and Leather Building, Centennial Exposition, Philadelphia.—Its size is 160 feet wide and 31½ feet deep. In shape the building forms a parallelogram. The materials of its construction are wood, glass, and iron, and the style of architecture strictly American. The interior of the building presents an open space 256 feet long and 160 feet wide. The roof is supported by columns 16 feet apart. The central section being a curve 80 feet wide, of the Howe truss pattern, over which is a Louvre ventilator 20 feet wide, and running the entire length of the building, and 39 feet above the ground. The flagstaffs are 80 feet high, and the pavilions respectively 20 and 30 feet in height. The building was bought by D. J. Dobbins for $3,000. The original cost was $30,750.

WOOD CARPET AND INLAID FLOORS,

For Halls, Parlors, Dining Rooms, Kitchens, Bath Rooms, Offices, Etc.

Inlaid or Parquet Floors. Beneficial to health. Wainscoting, of different designs. We are prepared to lay floors at short notice in any part of the city. Also, to ship goods in any quantity, and furnish all necessary information for laying, finishing, &c. All our work is fully guaranteed.

J. DUNFEE, No. 100 Washington Street, CHICAGO.

(SEND FOR CIRCULAR.)

ULICK BOURKE,

DEALER IN

Furniture, Bedding,

Crockery, Glassware, Stoves, Carpets, Oil Cloths, &c.,

92 West Madison Street, CHICAGO.

Everything in the line of Housekeeping Goods, Sold on easy Payments.

PEKIN—Continued.

HOTELS.

BEMIS HOUSE, Cor. Court & Front sts.,
T. K. Bemis, prop.

WHITE HOUSE,
A. W. WHITE, Proprietor,
New House, Newly Furnished, Everything First-Class, Established 1877.

LEATHER AND SHOE FINDINGS.

WAGENSELLER, J. & SON, Leather Shoe Findings & Saddlery Hardware, 120-122 Court st. Est. 1837.

SALOONS.

DIETZ & BERRY, Saloon & Billiard Hall,
Cor. Capital & Court sts. Est. 1857.

GDATOP, CHARLES, Saloon & Billiard Hall,
338 Court st. Est. 1875.

VALK, FRED. A., Wine and Beer Hall,
317 & 319 Court st. Est. 1873.

LEHMANN, OTTO, Saloon & Restaurant,
307 Conrt st. Est. 1874.

STOVES AND TINWARE.

JAECKEL, H. J., Stoves, Tin, Copper & Sheet Iron Ware, Court bet. 2nd & 3rd sts.

TOBACCO AND CIGARS.

H. O. STEIN,
Manufacturer of FINE CIGARS and dealer in all kinds of Smokers Articles,

312 COURT ST., - - Established 1853.

WATCHES AND JEWELRY.

ZUCKWEILER, H., Watches, Clocks, Jewelry. Engraving neatly done, 238 Court st., Est. 1859.

LA SALLE, ILLS.

BLACKSMITS AND HORSESHOERS.

HAYDEN, DAVID, Horseshoeing Shop,
Cor. 2nd & Gooding sts.

HAWES, C. N., Blacksmithing and Jobbing, Horseshoeing a specialty, Marquette, bet. 1st & 2nd sts.

CARPENTERS AND BUILDERS.

CHISHOLM, J. B., Carpenter and Builder,
Cor. Wright & 2nd sts.

GILBERT, V., Carpenter and Builder,
Gooding st., bet. 5th & 6th.

FLOUR, FEED AND GRAIN.

TREVETT & COLLINS, Dealers in Flour, Grain & Feed, First st. third door West of P. O.

FURNITURE.

VOLLMER, M., Furniture, Upholstery & Undertaking, First st., near Bank.

GUNMAKER.

P. P. SINGER,
Gunmaker and dealer in Guns, Pistols. Ammunition, Fishing Tackle, &c.; also Stencil Cutting and Key Fitting.

First St., bet. Joliet and Hennepin.

LA SALLE—Continued.

HARNESS AND SADDLES.

KNAPP, JACOB, Harness, Saddles, Collars, &c.,
First st., bet. Joliet & Marquette.

HOTELS.

HARRISON HOUSE,
WELCH & CORCORAN, Proprietors.

N. E. Cor. Wright & First Sts.,

Bus to and from all trains day and night.

Pacific House,
By C. Breutigam, Corner of Third and Wright Sts. Regular and transient Boarders accommodated at Reasonable Rates.

LAUNDRY.

BENNER, HENRY, La Salle Laundry and Shirt Factory, Marquette st., bet. 2d & 3d.

MARBLE WORKS.

P. F. MADDEN,
La Salle Marble Works, Foreign and American Marble Monuments, Head Stones and all kinds of Furniture Work.
Cor. Gooding and Second streets.

MEAT MARKET.

OSINGER, FRED. L., Butcher, Fresh and Cured Meats, Cor. 2nd & Gooding sts.

PAINTERS.

COULTER, R. K., House, Sign, Ornamental Painter & Grainer, 2nd & Marquette sts.

SEWING MACHINES.

SANDERSON, R. L., First-class Sewing Machines, Attachments, Needles, &c., Repairing done, First st.

TAILORS.

COFFEY, JOHN, Tailor, Cloths, Cassimeres and Vestings, First & Gooding sts.

DONNOVAN, EDWARD, Merchant Tailor,
1st near Joliet st.

WERNER, GUSTAV, Tailor and Agent for John Wannamaker, Phil., 1st st., opp., City Meat Market.

PERU, ILL.

BLACKSMITHS AND HORSESHOERS.

CONCELMAN, J., Horseshoeing & General Blacksmithing, Water st., opposite City Mills.

NEIMKE, H., all kinds of Blacksmithing, cor. 4th & Fulton sts.

SHEPPARD, A. M., General Blacksmithing and Steel Work, Water st.

BOOTS AND SHOES

HANSON, LEWIS, Man'fr of Custom Boots and Shoes of all kinds, Water st.

PERU—Continued.

CARRIAGES AND WAGON MAKERS.

GRAFF, LOUIS. Jr., Carriage & Wagonmaker, 4th st, W. of Four Corners.

DRUGGISTS.

METZGER, M. C., Druggist, prescriptions prepared at all hours, Orths' Bldg, Water st.

SEEBACH, B. C., Homœopathic Medicines, Cases and Books.

FURNITURE.

HAAS, C., & BARTELS, Furniture dealers, Upholsterers & Undertakers, Water st., near P. O.

GROCERIES.

CAHILL, JAMES, Gen'l Merchandise, Groceries, Dry Goods, etc., Water st.

LOCK AND GUNSMITH.

ACKERMANN, H., Lock & Gunsmith, Toolmaker, etc., Water st., opp. Young's Mill.

PHOTOGRAPHER.

EVEN, JOSEPH, Photographer, Picture Frames, Albums, etc., Water st.

STOVES AND TINWARE.

DENNY, B., Stoves, Tin, Hardware and House-furnishing Goods, Water st.

GMELICH, G., Stoves, Tin, Copper & Sheet Iron Ware, Water st., opposite Bridge.

TAILORS.

BRAUN & SON, Merchant Tailors, Clothing and Gents' Furnishing Goods, Water st.

WOOD, J. W., Tailor, Water st., over P. O.

TAXIDERMIST'S SUPPLIES.

SEEBACH, B. C., Bird & Animal Eyes & Taxidermist's Supplies of every kind.

TOBACCO AND CIGARS.

GRABOW, JOHN, Peru Cigar Manf'y, Tobaccos & Smokers' Artic's, Water st., opposite bridge.

UTHOFF, WM., Manf'r & dealer in Tobaccos, Cigars, Pipes, etc., Water st.

WATCHES AND JEWELRY.

LINNIG, H., Watches, Clocks, Jewelry, Musical Instruments, etc., Water st.

MORRIS, ILL.

BLACKSMITHING.

TETLOW, T., Wagon Manf'ry, Horseshoeing & Blacksmithing, Jefferson & Liberty sts.

BOOTS AND SHOES.

HIGHT, O. R., Manf'r of Boots & Shoes, Cor. Liberty & Jefferson sts.

CARRIAGES AND WAGONS.

McNOWN, FLYNN & GORMAN,

Carriage Manuf'y and General Blacksmithing.
JEFFERSON & LIBERTY STS.

DENTIST.

STEINER, M. W., Dentist, Goold's Block, Liberty st.

---

were found, shortly after, following the recruiting drum, and pushing toward the frontier lines, for the double purpose of meeting the enemy and of eating the provisions they had lately labored to put in good order. Their old jokes accompanied them, and before the first campaign ended, this identical one first appeared in print; it gained favor rapidly till it penetrated, and was recognized in every part of the country, and will, no doubt, continue so while the United States remain a nation.

Underground Railroad, The.—A popular embodiment of the various ways in which fugitive slaves from the Southern States were assisted in escaping to the North, or to Canada; often humorously abbreviated U. G. R. R.

Wagoner Boy, The.—A sobriquet of the Hon. Thomas Corwin (born 1794), a distinguished American Statesman. While yet a lad, Harrison and his army were on the Northern frontier, almost destitute of provisions, and a demand was made on the patriotism of the people to furnish the necessary subsistence. The elder Corwin loaded a wagon with supplies, which was delivered by his son, who remained with the army during the rest of the campaign, and who is said to have proved himself "a good whip and an excellent reinsman."

Western Reserve, The.—A name popularly given to a region of country reserved by the State of Connecticut at the time of the cession of the Northwest Territory to the United States. Dispute arose, after the war of the Revolution, between several of the States respecting the right of soil in their territory which were only allayed by the cession of the whole to the United States, Connecticut reserving a tract of 3,666,921 acres near Lake Erie. In 1800, jurisdiction over this tract was relinquished to the Federal Government, the State reserving the right to the soil to settlers, while the Indian titles to the rest of the soil were bought up by the general government. In 1799, the North-western Territory, over which Congress had exercised jurisdiction since 1787, was admitted to a second grade of territorial government. Shortly after, Ohio was detached from it, and erected into an independent territory, and in 1803 it was received as a State into the Union.

White House, The.—In the United States a name properly given to the executive or presidential mansion at Washington, which is a large building of freestone, painted white.

Wicked Bible.—A name given to an edition of the Bible published in 1632 by Baker & Lucas, because the word *not* was omitted in the seventh commandment. The printers were called before the High Commission, fined heavily, and the whole impression destroyed.

Wolverine State, The.—The State of Michigan; popularly so called for its abounding with wolverines.

Yellow Jack.—Among sailors a common personification of the yellow fever. Although used as a proper name, it is probable that the original meaning of the appellation was nothing more than *yellow flag*; a flag being termed *jack* by seamen, and *yellow* being the color of that customarily displayed from lazarettos, or naval hospitals, and from vessels in quarantine.

Young America.—A popular collective name for American youth, or a personification of their supposed characteristics.

L. M. ANDREWS,
Wholesale Tobacconist
No. 6 N. Wells St.,
CHICAGO, ILL.

ANDREW'S DURHAM A SPECIALTY.

W. T. Blackwell's lower than any other place in the city; Spalding & Werrick's Fine Cut; F. F. Addams Goods.

Carte Blanche in my own Brand.   Lorillard's Plug all Sizes.

---

198 to 202   N. Clark St.

SERVOSS, NORTHEN & CO.
MANUFACTURERS OF AND DEALERS IN

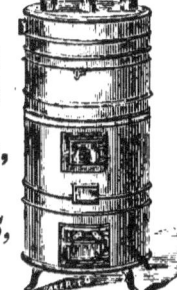

The Justly **"ECLECTIC** Celebrated **HEATER,"**

Cooking Ranges, *HOT AIR FLUES,* **Parlor Stoves,** *REGISTERS, VENTILATORS,*

NORTH SIDE,   **CHICAGO, ILL.**

REFERENCES.

Racine College, Wis.
Theological Seminary of The N. W., Chicago.
Lincoln Park Church, Chicago.
Tabernacle Church, Chicago.
Chas. L Way, Iron Inspector, Evanston.
E. G. Jackson, Real Estate, Rogers Park.
Gen. J. A. Lathrop, Elmhurst.
John P. Reynolds, Exposition, Chicago.
Edward Burling, Architect, Chicago.
N. H. Barnes, Ft. Agt. C. & N. W. R.R., Chicago.

Wm. J. Davis, Real Estate, Chicago.
Augustus Bauer, Architect, Chicago.
Gen. W. E. Strong, Pres. Peshtigo Co., Chicago.
Geo. E. Adams, Attorney, Chicago.
Wm. C. Dow, Rental Agent, Chicago.
Rev. Robert Collyer, Unity Church, Chicago.
James Otis, Capitalist, Chicago.
Carille Mason, Excelsior Iron Works, Chicago.
A. T. Galt, Attorney, Chicago.
Geo. L. Otis, Commercial Nat. Bank, Chicago.

Geo. H. Watson & Co.,
—Sole Agents—
FOR THE NORTHWEST OF THE CELEBRATED

MAGEE FURNACE CO.'S

Standard, Portable, and Brick Set Ranges, Standard Base Burner, and Standard Wrought Iron Furnace.

The Best in the World.   Send for Cuts and Prices.

272 and 274 State St.,   -   **CHICAGO, ILL.**

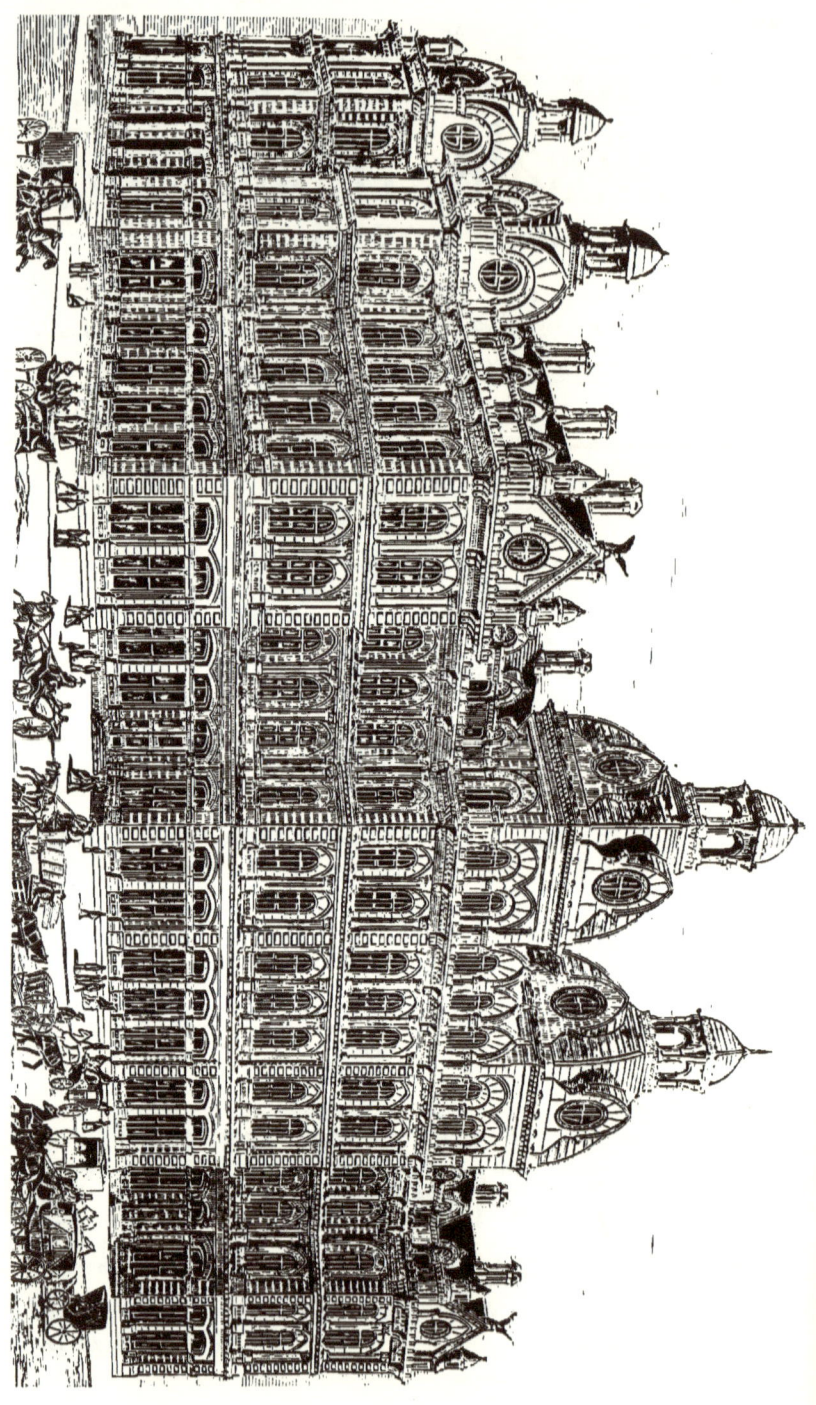

ADVERTISEMENTS.

MORRIS—*Continued.*

MORRIS CLASSICAL INSTITUTE.

Morris Classical Institute.

This Institution is a Thorough, well-conducted, Scientific and Classical School,

A. W. BULKLEY, *B. A.,* } Principals.
A. A. BEATTIE, *B. E.,* }

MUSIC DEALER.

E. L. BARTLETT,

MUSIC DEALER.

Every description of Musical Instruments, Sheet Music and Music Books, Washington st.

PHOTOGRAPHER.

J. B. BLANCHARD,

Photographer, and J. A. Reed, India Ink and Water Color Artist, rooms, Liberty st., between Jefferson and Jackson sts.

PUMPS AND WIND MILLS.

HITCHCOCK, B. C., all kinds of Pumps & Wind Mills, Washington st., near Express Office,

E. ROBINSON,

Agt. for Halliday's Wind Engine, and manufacturer's agent for Wood and Iron Pumps of all kinds, also, Iron Pipe, Hose and Steam Fittings, 92 Liberty st.

RESTAURANT AND BAKERY.

SHAW, THOMAS, Restaurant & Bakery, meals at all hours, Washington st., next door to P. O.

WATCHES AND JEWELRY.

BUTLER, J. P. M., Watches, Clocks, Jewelry & Silverware, Washington st.

MAYO, F. C., Watchmaker and Jeweler, Liberty st.

CEDAR RAPIDS, IOWA.

AGRICULTURAL IMPLEMENTS.

HAMILTON & AMIDON, Seeds and Farm Machinery, 50 Iowa ave. Established 1868.

BOOKS AND STATIONERY.

GRAVES, J. G., Books & Stationery, Iowa ave and Washington st. Est. 1867.

BOOTS AND SHOES.

GATES, JOHN, Manuf'r & dealer in Boots and Shoes, 15 S. Commercial st. Established 1865.

OTTMAR, M., dealer in Boots & Shoes, 17 Iowa ave. Established 1869.

RENCHIN & KOUBA, Manf'rs & dealers in Boots & Shoes, 28 N. Commercial st, Estab. 1873.

ROBINSON BROS., & GIFFORD, Wholesale dealers in Boots & Shoes, 51 Iowa ave. Est. 1870.

CEDAR RAPIDS—*Continued.*

BREWERIES.

Established 1859.

EAGLE BREWERY
—AND—
MALT HOUSE.

Lager Beer, Ale, Porter, Hops and Malt, C. Magnus, Proprietor, cor. of VanBuren and Johnson sts.

☞ In connection with the above is a Bottling Department of Lager Beer, Ale and Porter.

Established 1874.

GEO. WILLIAMS & CO.,
Proprietors of the

CEDAR RAPIDS BREWERY
Manufacturers of
FIRST PREMIUM LAGER BEER.

COAL AND WOOD.

BROCK, R. G., Coal & Wood, Washington & Linn sts. Established 1872.

COMMISSION MERCHANT.

NYE, J. A., Commission Merchant, Commercial st. & Park ave.

COOPER.

DANIELS, J. S., Cooper, S. Commercial st. Established 1877.

DENTISTS.

DENNIS, A. B., Dentist, office in Mansfield's New Block, S. Washington st. Est. 1875.

EBE, E., Dentist, 7 S. Commercial st. Established 1865.

MINOR, A. K., Dentist, 47 S. Commercial st, Established 1857.

DRUGGISTS.

BLISS, E., Druggist, Iowa ave, and Washington st. Established 1872.

BRASH, A. H., Drugs, Chemicals, etc., 12 North Commercial st. Established 1869.

ROE, DR. T. C. & CO., Manf'rs & dealers of Roe's Family Medicines, 50 S. Com. st. Est. 1875.

DRY GOODS.

DEVENDORF & MANN, dealers in Dry Goods, Carpets, etc., Com. & Eagle sts. Est. 1867.

WITOUSEK, F., dealer in Dry Goods and Notions, 27 Iowa ave. Established 1867.

EGG PACKERS.

MORIN, J. R. & CO., Egg Packers, S. Commercial st. Established 1874.

FURNITURE.

KREBS, T. J. & SON, Picture Frames, Furniture & Underclothing, S. Wash'ton st. Est. 1871.

GROCERIES.

EMERY, I. C., Groceries, Provisions, Fruits, &c., 42 S. Washington st. Established 1877.

KEYES, A. C., Wholesale Grocer, 23 S. Commercial st. Established 1856.

SMITH, W. W., Groceries, Toys, Notions and Children's Carriages, 20 S. Com. st. Est. 1865.

GUNS, PISTOLS, ETC.

COLLMAN, JOHN, Guns, Pistols, and Sporting Goods, 14 Iowa ave. Established 1873.

TUERK'S HYDRAULIC MOTOR FOR RUNNING

THE DEPARTMENT OF PUBLIC COMFORT, CENTENNIAL EXPOSITION, PHILADELPHIA.

Dental Machinery, Jewelers and Watchmakers' Lathes, Electric Machines, Sewing Machines, Scroll and Jig Saws, Revolving Signs, Washing Machines and Churns, House Cream, Dumb Elevators, Coffee and Spice Mills, Bellows, Shoe and Harness Machines, Ventilators and Blowers, Gas Machines, Meat Choppers, Lathes, Paint Mills, Ice Cream Freezers and Ice Crushers, Church Organs, Brick and Mortar Elevators, Coal Elevators, Printing Presses (all sizes), Quartz Mills and Ore Crushers, Passenger and Freight Elevators, etc., etc. (Secured by U. S. and Foreign Patents.) Patented 1874 and 1877.

Awarded two Centennial Medals at the World's Exhibition at Philadelphia, 1876, and two Diplomas of Merit for "Economy of Water," etc.

It requires considerable exertion and hard work for an operative to average 400 to 500 stitches per minute with the use of the treadle, when as, with a Motor, over 1000 stitches per minute can be obtained, and success ully worked with perfect ease. Thus it will be seen that a Motor w ll pay its own cost in a few weeks, besides saving the health and strength of the operator. These water wheels are Motors as well as Meters; water cannot get through them, without turning the wheel and performing a corresponding amount of work. The proportion of all the forces in the water netted by this Motor is 95 per cent. The inside wheel of the 4 inch Motor, weighing nearly 2 lbs , can be driven 40 r, volutions with one breath. These Motors are made of the best and most durable metals, of very fine and accurate workmanship, equal to that of a clock or watch, and will outwear any machinery they will ever be put to. Equal results can be obtained, with this Motor, in the upper as well as in the lower floors of a building, as the di-charge (waste water) being confined, creates a vacuum or suction in the pipe equal to the atmospheric pressure. These Motors are all highly finished and painted, and are an ornament to a house as much as a Sewing Machine itself. Send for circular.

TUERK BROS., Manufacturers, 163 Lasalle St., CHICAGO, U.S.

CEDAR RAPIDS—Continued.

HARDWARE.

HEIGLEY & BRO., dealers in Hardware, Stoves, etc, 9 & 11 S. Commercial st. Est 1874.

JONES & EATON, Shelf and Heavy Hardware, 48 Iowa ave. Established 1864.

LARIMER, E. K., dealer in Heavy Hardware, 24 S. Commercial st. Established 1869.

SWAB, J., Hardware, Stoves and Tinware, 3 S. Commercial st. Established 1871.

HARNESS AND SADDLES.

EGERMAYER, JACOB J., Harness, Saddles, Collars, etc, 40 S. Commercial st. Est. 1873.

FIESELER & KOUBA, Manf'rs & del'rs in Light & Heavy Harness, 16 N. Com'cial st. Est. 1870.

HOTEL.

BROWN'S HOTEL,
S. Commercial st.

MARBLE WORKS.

CEDAR RAPIDS MARBLE WORKS, Searles & Baxter props., 8 Commercial st. Est. 1871.

PREMIUM MARBLE WORKS, J. W. Fellbaum, propr., 15 Eagle st. Established 1871.

PAINTER AND CARRIAGE TRIMMER.

TISDELL, D., Carriage Trimmer and Painter, Commercial st. and Park ave. Est. 1867.

PLUMBERS AND GAS FITTERS.

Established 1873.

MILLER & CO.,

Practical

Plumbers, Gas and Steam Fitters,

Wholesale and retail dealers in Gas, Water & Steam Fittings, and Brass Goods, Cedar Rapids, Iowa. Lock box, 349.

STONE AND PIPE WORKS.

CARBONIZED STONE & PIPE WORKS, Mackintosh & Burness, props., Adams & Johnson sts. Established 1876.

TAILORS.

LORENSTEIN, L., Tailor, and del'r in Mens' and Boys' Clothing, 6 S. Commercial st. Est. 1863.

OUDKERK, H., Merchant Tailor, cor. Washington st. & Iowa ave. Established 1867.

TIN AND JAPANNED WARE.

J. R. BILLINGS,

Manufacturer and dealer in Plain Tinware, and dealer in Pressed Japanned Goods and Table Glassware. Iowa ave. Established 1875.

TOBACCO AND CIGARS.

COE, O. B., Tobacco, Cigars, Pipes, etc., Washington st. opposite P. O.

WATCHES AND JEWELRY.

DIXON, CHAS. & CO., Watches, Clocks & Jewelry, 31 Iowa ave. Established 1875.

MOLL, JOSEPH, Watches, Clocks & Jewelry, 24 N. Commercial st. Estab. 1866.

CEDAR FALLS, IOWA.

ATTORNEY AT LAW.

TOLLERTON, J. J., Attorney and Counselor, at Law, over Knapp's Bank. Estab. 1866.

BOOTS AND SHOES.

MORK, N. C., & CO., dealers in Boots, Shoes and Rubbers, Main st. Established 1872.

PIERCE, D. R., dealer in Boots, Shoes, Hats and Caps, Main st. Established 1874.

BUTTER, EGGS AND POULTRY.

BATES, J. E., dealer in Butter, Eggs & Poultry, Main & 2d sts. Established 1872.

DENTIST.

STURDEVANT, J. W., Dentist, Est. 1873, office over First National Bank.

DRUGGISTS.

SEVERIN, S. H., Drugs, Paints, Oils, etc., Main st Established 1867

WISE & BRYANT, Druggists & Booksellers, Main st. Established 1867.

DRY GOODS.

CABLE, A. & CO., Dry Goods, Notions & Millinery, Main st. Established 1877.

B. THORPE, JR., Dealer in

Dry Goods, Notions, Hats, Caps, Boots, Shoes
AND GROCERIES.
Main street. Established 1870.

WILSON & WILLIAMS, Dealers in Dry Goods, Notions, etc., Main & 2d sts. Est. 1877.

GALVANIZED IRON CORNICES.

BOEHMLER, THEO., Cedar Falls Galvanized Iron Works, Main st. Established 1876.

GROCERIES.

BAKER, E., dealer in Groceries & Provisions, Main st. Established 1872.

JUDD & CARTER, Groceries, Boots & Shoes, Main & 2d sts. Established 1877.

McNALLY, JACK, Groceries, Provisions, Boots & Shoes, Main st. Established 1867.

HARNESS AND SADDLES.

KRASSMAN, C., Harness, Saddles, Collars and Whips, Main st. Established 1874.

POOLER, O. C., Harness, Saddles, Whips and Collars, 2d st., near Main st. Estab. 1863.

SARSEN, JAS. P., Harness, Saddles, Collars and Whips, Main & 3d sts. Established 1874.

HOTELS.

Commercial Hotel,
CEDAR FALLS, IOWA.

Free bus to and from all trains. Everything new and first-class. Good sample rooms. Nearest hotel to Burlington depot.

C. VAN HOOSER, Prop'r.

CEDAR FALLS—Continued.

HOTEL.

J. E. HUNT.   GEO. A. SNOW.

Monitor House,
CEDAR FALLS, IOWA.

Free bus and baggage to and from all trains. Good sample rooms on first floor.

HUNT & SNOW, Props.

MEAT MARKETS.

JENNINGS, J. B., all kinds of Fresh Meats, Main st. Established 1860.

SCHINDLER, F. R., all kinds of Fresh Meats, Main st. Established 1875.

MARBLE WORKS.

CEDAR FALLS MARBLE WORKS, Warren Lewis, propr., Main st. Established 1874.

NOVELTY WORKS.

F. G. WYNKOOP,
Proprietor of the

NOVELTY WORKS,

And Jobbing Manufactory, and general Contractor of Wood Work, Main st. near the river. Established 1876.

PHOTOGRAPHER.

JORDAN, H. A., Artistic Photographer, Main st. Established 1876.

PHYSICIAN.

PETTIT, W. H., Homœpathic Physician & Surgeon, Main & 2nd sts. Established 1873.

TAILOR.

WYTH, J., Merchant Tailors, & dealer in Gents Furnishing Goods, Main st. Est. 1863.

WIND MILL.

E. A. MUNGER,
Proprietor of

CEDAR FALLS WIND MILL WORKS,

Also, manufacturer of Brass and Iron Cylinder Pumps, office and Factory, Main st., near the river. Established 1876.

WATERLOO, IOWA.

AGRICULTURAL IMPLEMENTS.

CASCAN, THOS., General dealer in Farmers Implements, Fourth st. Established 1873.

WHITAKER & EDGINGTON, Agricultural Implements, 4th st., E. side. Est. 1876.

Important Events Commencing with the Christian Era.

4. Leap year corrected having formerly been every third year.
19. The Jews banished from Rome.
40. The name of Christians first given at Antioch, to the followers of Christ.
49. London founded by the Romans.
60. Christianity about this time first preached in Great Britain.
64. Nero sets fire to the city of Rome, and throws the blame on the Christians.
68. Nero, the Roman emperor, commits suicide.
70. Vespasian, who was appointed by Nero, in the year 66, to wage war against the Jews, was now declared emperor by the army, and was acknowledged all over the East: in the beginning of whose reign Jerusalem is taken by the Romans under Titus, and all the awful predictions of our Lord, as well as those of the ancient prophets, are exactly accomplished. The city is desolated; the temple destroyed, so that not one stone was left on another; 1,100,000 persons perished miserably in the siege, and the remnant of the Jews are scattered to all nations.
107. The first creditable historian among the Chinese.
167. A plague prevails all over the known world.
179. Reign of Lucius, the first Christian king of Britain, and in the world.
189. The capitol of Rome destroyed by lightning.
191. Rome nearly destroyed by fire.
193. The Roman empire is bought at auction by Eidius Julianus, who is put to death by order of the Senate.
251. Monastic life begins about this time.
A. D.
274. France, Spain, and Britain reduced to obedience to Rome. Silk first brought from India. The manufacture of it first introduced into Europe by some Monks, in 551; first worn by the clergymen in England, in 1531.
330. Fearful persecution of Christians in Persia, lasting forty years.
340. One hundred and fifty Greek and Asiatic cities destroyed by an earthquake.
373. The Bible translated into the Gothic language.
394. Complete downfall of paganism.
419. Many cities in Palestine destroyed by an earthquake.
432. St. Patrick preaches the gospel in Ireland.
433. A part of Constantinople destroyed by fire.

C. F. KLEINSTEUBER,
MACHINIST AND ENGRAVER,

Manufacturer of all kinds of

Models, Small Machinery and Brass Castings.
Official Seals in Superior Presses, Medals,
Door-plates, Stencils, Brands, etc., etc.

318 STATE ST., MILWAUKEE.

Agent for the WEED and ÆTNA
SEWING MACHINES.

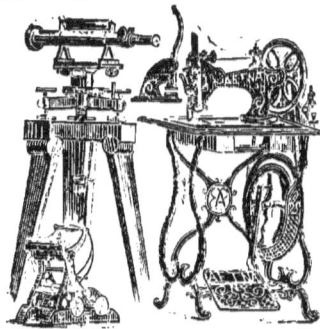

A. S. LANDGUTH,
ARCHITECT,
279 THIRD ST., COR. STATE,
Milwaukee, Wis.

Will furnish new Designs for Churches, Hotels, Country Residences, Country Villas, Cottages, Warehouses, Factories and Buildings for any purpose. You are invited to call at my office and examine my work.

Designed by A. S. Landguth

Milwaukee Steam Boiler Works.
J. W. EVISTON,
MANUFACTURER OF
High and Low Pressure Steam Boilers, Britchens,

Smoke Stacks, Lard, Oil, and Water Tanks, of Every Description,

192, 216 & 220 Broadway, 281 & 283 Chicago Street, MILWAUKEE, WIS.

☞ All kinds of Boiler, Plate and Sheet Iron Work. Repairing of all kinds promptly attended to. Orders solicited, and especial attention paid to the same.

AGENTS
SUPPLIED WITH
Chromos and Frames
AT BOTTOM PRICES.

Send for Circulars, Publisher of "THE ATLANTIC WEEKLY." $4.00 a year, with two large Chromos free.

ALBERT DURKEE & CO., 112 Monroe Street, Chicago, Ill.

ADVERTISEMENTS. 435

COURT HOUSE, MILWAUKEE, WIS.

BARNES' FOOT POWER MACHINERY.
INSURED BY TEN PATENTS.

Six years ago, comparatively little attention was given to foot power machinery. Its utility was supposed to be limited to the narrow capacity of the old crank and treadle motion which had followed along down unchanged from the times of the ancient Egyptians. Good mechanics, being well aware of the defects of this old motion in driving machinery, knew, that they could not accomplish anything in actual business to pay for the expense of such machines.

About that time, the Barnes' machines were offered to those having use for foot-power machinery. These new machines were an entire surprise to all who tested them. Such was their power and facility, that the accurate statements given by those using them were not at first credited. Only the actual trial would convince; and thus always ended doubt. The old established prejudice now begins to yield everywhere, to the fact that the new foot power, **without dead centers**, is a success in actual business.

To day **Twenty thousand** can testify to the merits and efficiency of these machines. Starting with the simple scroll saw, they now describe some **fifteen** machines and combinations constructed to answer to the calls sent from those using first, only the scroll saw.

With all these machines in use, and with the thousands who have seen them, reporting their work to others, it is no wonder that foot-power machinery now has a large increase of attention, and is eagerly inquired after. Many learn in a general way of this success, and are prompted to buy without careful investigation. Thus they are caught by advertisers of the old faulty style of construction, who have found it possible, in such cases to sell their wares on the reputation of these new machines. The result, of course, is only disappointment to those who, by their own carelessness have failed to get these radically new and successful machines.

Therefore, be sure to know what you are buying and carefully examine the description of our Machinery and the facts given of its power, utility and profit. We will be pleased to send our 48 page descriptive Catalogue FREE to any desiring it.

Address: Saying where you read this. Respectfully,
W. F. & JOHN BARNES, **ROCKFORD, WINNEBAGO CO., ILL.**

WATERLOO—Continued.

BOOTS AND SHOES.

HOOT, S. J., Boot & Shoe Maker, Fourth street, E. side. Established 1873.

LAMPE, H., Boot & Shoe Maker, Fourth street, E. side. Established 1874.

VOORHEES, M. H., Boots, Shoes, Hats, Caps, etc., S. Bridge st., W. side. Established 1877.

CARRIAGE AND WAGON MAKERS.

HALE, ADAMS & CO., Carriage & Wagonmakers, Lafayette st., E. side. Established 1870,

HITT, E. R., Manuf'r of Carriages, Commercial st., W. side. Established 1870.

CONFECTIONERY AND RESTAURANT.

SINDLINGER, W. M., Confectionery, Fruits, Cigars' etc., Commercial st., W. side. Est. 1867.

STOESSIGER, FRANK, Restaurant & Confectionery, 4th st., E. side.

DRY GOODS.

TRACY & DUNSHEE, Dry Goods, Notions, etc., 4th st., E. side. Established 1877.

FOUNDRY AND MACHINE SHOP.

ROBINSON, W. S., Foundry and Machine Shop, Commercial st., W. side. Es ab. 1875.

FURNITURE.

PARTRIDGE, M., all kinds of Furniture, 4th st., E. side. Established 1869.

GROCERIES.

CHAFFEE, P. M., Groceries and Provisions, 4th & Lafayette sts., E. side. Estab. 1870.

SMITH, J. H., Groceries and Provisions, 4th st., E. side. Established 1874.

GUN AND LOCKSMITH.

COLE, C. O., Gun and Locksmith, 4th st., E. side. Established 1876.

HARDWARE.

COLBY, L. W., Hardware, Stoves and Tinware, 4th st., E. side. Established 1876.

HOTELS.

CENTRAL HOUSE, J. H. Williams, propr., Commercial st., W. side.

COMMERCIAL HOUSE, C. Brubacher, propr., 5th and Commercial sts., W. side. Estab. 1877.

LOGAN HOUSE, Wm. Barrett, proprietor, 4th st., E. side.

JUDGE OF COURT.

BAGG, S., Judge of the Circuit Court, Commercial st., W. side. Established 1858.

LIVERY AND SALE STABLE.

COBB, W. S., Livery and Sale Stable, foot of 5th st., W. side. Established 1872.

MUSICAL INSTRUMENTS.

BENEDICT, D. R., Musical Instruments, 4th st., E. side. Established 1873.

WATERLOO—Continued.

PAINTERS.

RICKERT, HENRY F., House, Sign, Carriage Painter. Water st., east side. Estab. 1872.

WORCESTER & TURPENING, House, Sign and Carriage Painters, 4th st., E. side. Est. '54.

PHOTOGRAPHERS.

BARER, T. S., Photographer. Commercial st., W. side. Estab. 1872.

KING, J. P., Photographer, 4th & Water sts., E. side. Est. 1874.

TAILORS.

ERCANBRACK, S., Merchant Tailor, 4th st., E. side. Est. 1866.

KINSTLER, B., Merchant Tailor, Commercial st., W. side. Est. 1874.

SALZ, JOHN J., Cutter and Tailor, 4th st., west side.

TOBACCO AND CIGARS.

WICHMAN & McINTYRE, Manuf'rs and Dealers in Fine Cigars, 4th st., E. side. Est. 1875.

WATCHES AND JEWELRY.

BALLIET & WELD, Watches, Clocks, Jewelry, Logan House Block. Est. 1871.

FORT MADISON, IOWA.

BARBER.

BUCHHOLZ, FERD., Barber, Dealer in Cigars, Tobacco, &c., Front st.

COFFEE HOUSE.

ROTH, J. F., Coffee House, Front street.

FURNITURE.

SCHOTT, WM., Furniture Manufacturer, Undertaker, &c. Front st.

GROCERIES.

LINDEMUTH, H., Groceries and Notions, Front st.

HOTEL.

Established 1875.

GEO. ANTHES,
PROPRIETOR

Central Hotel,

Opposite Railroad Depot. First-Class Sample Rooms for Traveling Agents. Free Baggage to and from Hotel.

FORT MADISON, IOWA.

QUINCY, ILLS.

ATTORNEYS AT LAW.

WM. H. BENNESON,
ATTORNEY AT LAW,
534 MAIN ST., Up-Stairs.

BERRY, WM. W., Attorney at Law, 522 Maine st.

IMPORTANT EVENTS.

QUINCY—Continued.

ATTORNEYS AT LAW.

J. F. CARROTT,
Attorney & Counselor at Law
Office with Hon. O. H. Browning. Collections and Bankruptcy Business made a Specialty.

DAVIS & POLING, Attorneys at Law,
No. 9 North 5th st.

James E. Purnell.   John M. Grimes.
PURNELL & GRIMES,
ATTORNEYS AT LAW
Room 3, No. 9 North Fifth St.

THOMPSON, J. C., Attorney at Law,
5 6 Hampshire st.

WARREN & GILMER, Attorneys at Law,
cor. 5th & Hampshire sts.

BAKING POWDER.

TRADE MARK
See Page 307.

BARBERS.

GIEFING, FRANK, Barber, Cigars, Pipes and Tobacco, 612 & 1022 Hampshire st.

HILD, ADAM, Barber,
510 Hampshire st.

KOCH, GEO., New York Barber Shop,
611 Maine st.

TEIGELER, BARNEY, Barber,
612 Hampshire st.

WOLF, PHILIP, Barber,
836 Maine st.

ZOLLER, DAVID, Barber,
516 Hampshire st.

BLACKSMITH.

LONGRESS, J., General Blacksmithing and Horse Shoeing, 230 Maine st.

BOILER WORKS.

GRIMM BROS., Manuf'rs of all kinds of Boiler and Sheet Iron Works, Front & Delaware sts.

BOOTS AND SHOES.

FENTON, W. W., Boot and Shoe Maker,
25 South 5th st.

OSTERHOLD, C. C., Boot and Shoe Maker,
77 South 5th st.

RINNEBERG, S. G., Boot and Shoe Maker,
715 Hampshire st.

ZOLLE, PETER, Boot and Shoe Maker,
324 Hampshire st.

BRASS FOUNDRY.

WILLIAMSON & HAGEN, General Brass Founders, north-east cor. 6th & York sts.

A. D.

447. Attila, "The scourge of God," with his Huns, ravages the Roman empire and attempts to form an immense empire from China to the Atlantic. He died suddenly on the first night of his nuptials, in 453.

468. The principal established that every accused person shall be tried by his peers or equals.

476. Rome taken by Odoacer, King of the Heruli. This terminates the existence of the Roman Empire, and is the commencement of the Kingdom of Italy under Odoacer.
Odoacer's sack of Rome was the great event which preceded the middle or "dark ages." The form of the old Roman Government remained—the Senate, the Consuls, etc., but Italy, ravaged by a succession of wars, plagues, famines, and every form of public tyranny and domestic slavery, was nearly a desert.

480. An earthquake, lasting forty days, destroys the greater part of Constantinople.

493. Theodoric introduces the architecture of Greece to improve the buildings of Italy.

508. Prince Arthur begins his reign over the Britains.

511. A great insurrection in Constantinople; 10,000 killed.

516. Computation of time by the Christian era introduced by Dionysius, the monk.

525. Two hundred and fifty thousand persons destroyed by an earthquake at Antioch.

531. Chess introduced into Persia from India.

541. The reign of Totila, who twice pillages Rome, and reduces the inhabitants to such distress that the ladies and people of quality are obliged to beg for bread at the doors of the Goths. This continues till 542.

542. Plague at Constantinople. During three months from 5,000 to 10,000 die daily.

551. The manufacture of silk brought from India into Europe by monks.

557. A terrible plague all over Europe, Asia and Africa, which lasted nearly fifty years.

569. The Turks first mentioned in history.
581. The city of Paris destroyed by fire.
605. Use of bells introduced into churches.
607. The burning of candles by day.
609. The Jews of Antioch massacre the Christians.
612. Mohammed publishes his Koran.
617. First code of laws published in England.
632. Death of Mohammed, aged 63 years.

ST. LOUIS ELECTRIC MANUFACTURING COMPANY.

HEISLER'S

House, Hotel, Elevator Annunciators and Call Bells, Fire, Police and Private Telegraph Lines, Dial & Printing Instruments, WATCHMAN'S Time Recorders,

Low-water, Steam, Heat and Burglar Alarms, Physicians,' Laboratories and School Apparatus, Telegraph Instruments, Wires, Batteries and Supplies.

OFFICE & FACTORY:

309 CHOUTEAU AVE.,

ST. LOUIS, MO.

FRONT DOOR BELL.   ROOM KEY.

P. H. O'NEILL,
HORSE SHOER,

Removed from 1019 North Fifth Street, to

1007 Broadway.   (Under the Sherman House,)   **ST. LOUIS, MO.**

PROPRIETOR OF THE "O'NEILL PATENT RUBBER HORSE SHOE,"

Patented April, 1874. The O'Neill Patent Rubber Heel Horse Shoe cures Corns, Quarter Cracks, Sore Shoulders, and breaks the jar and concussion on hard roads whilst traveling.

GEO. WM. SCHAEFER'S

Patented Machine.   **Horse hoof Paring.**

This Invention facilitates the paring of Horses' Hoof preparatory to shoeing whereby that operation is performed with greater safety to the foot, and with greater ease to the operator, than when done in the ordinary manner. It pares the in and outside without endangering the frog of the hoof, and requires no burning to get a good, even foundation for the shoe, and the operator can pare the hoof so with it, that interfering becomes an impossibility. This machine speaks for itself, is well recommended by the best and prominent Horse Doctors and Horse Shoers of this city, and will give satisfaction in every respect. The machine took the first premium at the St. Louis Fair in 1873. State and County rights and single machines for sale by or other purposes.

GEO. W. SCHAEFER, Inventor and Patentee,

616 North Sixth Street,   East of Lindell Hotel.   ST. LOUIS, MO.

IMPORTANT EVENTS OF THE CENTURY. 439

United States Capitol, Washington, D. C.—The corner-stone of the Capitol was laid with Masonic ceremonies, September 18, 1793, by Master Mason, George Washington, President of the United States. In 1814 the British burned out the two wings. The space now occupied by the rotunda, up to that period, was only a wooden scaffolding, which united the two portions of the building. The foundation of the present Rotunda was laid March 2, 1818, and was considered finished in 1827. The corner-stone of the extension was laid July 4, 1851. The cost of the Capitol up to the present time has been $13,000,000. The whole Capitol covers an area of three and a half acres.

QUINCY—Continued.

BUSINESS COLLEGE.

GEM CITY BUSINESS COLLEGE, D. L. Musselman, Principal. 506, 508 & 510 Maine st.

CLOTHING.

J. D. LEVY & CO.
CLOTHIERS,
Cor. Third St. and Market Square.
Mnfr's of Men's, Youths' and Boys' Clothing.

COMMISSION MERCHANTS.

A. J. SIGSBEE & CO.
COMMISSION MERCHANTS
And Dealers in Flour, Feed, Grain, Fruits and Produce, 1024 & 1026 Maine St. Consignments solicited.

CONTRACTORS.

HAUWORTH, ORR & HODGDON, Contractors & Builders and Planing Mill, 58 N. 4th st.

MENKE, F. W. & CO., Contractors for Cut and Machine Sawed Stone, Front st., bet. State and Ohio.

CRACKERS AND CONFECTIONERY.

UNVERZAGT, H., Confectioner, 512 York st., near cor. 5th.

JOHN WESSELS,
Manufacturer of Crackers and Confectionery,
Wholesale Dealer in Fruits, Nuts, Oysters, Cheese, &c., 525 Hampshire St.

DENTIST.

SMITH, HENRY J., Dentist, 506 Maine st.

DRESSMAKING.

BECK, MISS E. C., Dressmaking, over 20 N. 4th st.

DRY GOODS.

DOERR, A. & BRO., Dealers in Dry Goods and Notions, 600 Maine st.

GEESING, WM., Dry Goods and Groceries, cor 11th & Hampshire sts.

RUFF, HENRY, & CO., Dry Goods, 20 N. 4th st.

DYE WORKS.

Chemical Steam Dye Works
COR. FIFTH & JERSEY STS.
Ladies' Silks and Woolens Dyed or Cleaned. The cleaning is done by a new process and Dresses need not be ripped. Kid Gloves cleaned and Ostrich Feathers dyed or cleaned. Feather Beds renovated and Carpets and Blankets cleaned. Gentlemen's Clothing dyed, cleaned and repaired in a superior manner. Give us a call. CHARLES SCHUETTE & CO., Successors to S. M. Tucker.

TUCKER'S
CHEMICAL
DYEING & CLEANING
ESTABLISHMENT,
No. 28 S. FIFTH ST., Adjoining the Church.

QUINCY—Continued.

DYE WORKS.

QUINCY CITY STEAM DYE WORKS,
610 Main Street. A. M. Stewart, Proprietor. Silk and Wool Dyer and Scourer. Gents' Coats, Vests and Pants are Dyed, Cleaned and Repaired by my great Chemical Process. Every spot of grease, paint, wax and tar, together with all other blemishes to which the above garments are liable, are entirely removed, and I warrant the spot not to reappear. If they fail to please you, no charge will be made. N. B.—Ladies' Shawls, Ribbons, Silk and Woolen Dresses, Kid Gloves, &c., a specialty. Feathers Cleaned, Dyed and Curled. All colors warranted fast. Remember the place: 610 Maine St. ☞All goods sent by Express will receive prompt attention.

WIEGAND, HERRMAN, Dyer and Cleaner, 1016 Maine st.

FANCY GOODS.

Misses L. A. & L. F. BARKER,
Dealers in
EMBROIDERY MATERIALS,
Star Braids, Soutaches, Chenilles, Flosses, Canvas and Bergman's Berlin Zephyrs. Also Manufacturers of Worsted Articles of any Pattern Desired. 608 Maine Street. ☞ Particular attention given to Stamping of all kinds. Orders respectfully solicited.

FISH AND OYSTERS.

VAN FRANK, C. D., Fresh Fish and Oysters, Levee, foot Broadway.

FURS, WOOL, &c.

SWIMMER, H., Dealer in Hides, Furs, Wool, &c. 316 Hampshire st.

GROCERIES.

J. H. BROWN,
Dealer in Staple and Fancy Groceries,
No. 626 MAINE STREET.

KELLER, WM., Grocer, cor. 5th & State sts.

MATHES, JOSEPH, Grocer, cor. 5th & Kentucky sts.

GUNSMITHS.

J. C. PIPINO,
GUNSMITH
618 HAMPSHIRE ST.

TOBIAS, F., Guns with, Rifles, Pistols, and Breech-Loaders for sale, 628 Hampshire st.

HAIR WORK.

CHATTEN, MRS. L., Ornamental Hair Work, 504 Hampshire st.

HARNESS AND SADDLES.

THOS. E. DURANT,
Manufacturer of Saddles, Harness, Collars, Whips, &c.
Nos. 507 and 509 Hampshire St.

H. MESSERSCHMIDT,
HARNESS & SADDLE MAKER,
328 HAMPSHIRE STREET.

IMPORTANT EVENTS. 441

QUINCY—Continued.

HOTELS.

AETNA HOUSE. J. W. Pearce, Prop.,
625 & 627 Maine st.

TREMONT HOUSE. Louis Miller, Prop.,
Quincy, Ill.

QUINCY HOUSE. Pampel & Moor, Props.
Quincy, Ill.

ICE AND WOOD.

JAMES JARRETT,
Wholesale and Retail Dealer in Ice and Wood,
Office, No. 7 Front Street.

INSURANCE AGENT.

BISHOP, JAMES M., General Insurance Co.,
cor 5th & Maine sts.

IRON AND STEEL.

LEMLEY BROTHERS,
Dealers in

IRON & STEEL,
Wagon and Carriage Material,
New Building: 217, 219 & 221 Maine St.,
Between Second and Third.

JUSTICES OF THE PEACE.

JOHN A. ALLEN,
MAGISTRATE,
COR. FIFTH & HAMPSHIRE STS.,
Up-Stairs.

JOHN HUTTON,
Justice of the Peace and Collecting Agent,
No. 25 NORTH FIFTH ST.

LEATHER AND FINDINGS.

SELLNER, CHAS., Leather and Shoe Findings,
636 Hampshire st.

LETTER CUTTER AND ENGRAVER.

J. G. BENTON,
General Letter Cutter and Engraver,
518 HAMPSHIRE ST.

LIME AND CEMENT.

A. ROSENKOETTER & CO.
Wholesale & Retail Dealers in
Lime, Cement, Plaster Paris and Hair,
FOOT OF JERSEY ST.

MACHINISTS.

EAGLE FOUNDRY.
SMITH, HAYNER & CO.,
General Machinists & Foundrymen
Steam Engines with Variable Cut-off, Semi-Portable Engines, Hand and Steam Elevators, Mill Machinery, Shafting Hangers and Pulleys, etc.
COR. FIFTH & OHIO STS.

A. D.
632. Africa and Asia, with the churches of Jerusalem, Alexandria and Antioch, lost to the Christian world by the progress of Mohammedanism.
636. Christianity introduced into China.
640. The library of Alexandria is burnt by the Saracens.
643. The temple of Jerusalem converted into a Mohammedan mosque.
644. Pope Martin I. ordains celebacy of the Roman Catholic Clergy.
660. Organs first used in churches.
664. Glass brought into England by Benalt, a monk.
685. The Britons, after a struggle of nearly one hundred and fifty years, are totally defeated by the Saxons, and driven into Wales and Cornwall.
711. The custom of kissing the Pope's foot first introduced.
716. The art of making paper brought from Samarcand by the Arabs.
726. Image worship being forbidden by the emperor, Leo. causes great excitement and many disturbances. The Greek possessions in Italy were lost on this account.
727. In Britain the King of Wessex begins the tax called Peter's pence, to support a college at Rome.
730. The Iconoclasts, or image breakers, commence their work of destruction.
746. A dreadful pestilence over Europe and Asia prevails for three years.
748. The computation of time from the birth of Christ first used in historical writings.
780. Leo IV, emperor of Rome, is succeeded by his wife Irene and his son Constantine VI.
781. Irene, queen mother, restores image worship.
786. Constantine imprisons his mother for her cruelty.
788. Pleadings in courts of justice first practiced.
794. Masses first said for money.
797. Irene murders her son, and reigns alone in Rome.
813. Insurrection at Rome against the Pope.
814. Germany separated from France.
826. The Danish prince, Harold, is dethroned by his subjects for being a Christian.
843. The Danes Ravage Great Britain, and burn the city of London.
844. Persecution of Christians in Spain.
846. An earthquake prevails over the greater part of the known world.
863. The certain history of Denmark now commences with the reign of Gormo the Old, who subdued Gutland and united all the small Danish States under his scepter till 920.
872. Clocks first brought to Constantinople from Venice.

CHICAGO AVENUE PICKLE AND VINEGAR WORKS.

G. J. GROSS,
MANUFACTURER OF
PICKLES AND ALL KINDS OF VINEGAR

Also Catsup and Sauerkraut,

No. 313 West Chicago Avenue,
CHICAGO, ILL.

FRANK HEINIG,
DRAPER & TAILOR.

FIREMEN'S and Police Regulation Uniforms

A SPECIALTY.

No. 281 Milwaukee Ave., CHICAGO, ILL.

H. PIETZ'S
Photographic Parlors,

NO. 117 SOUTH FIFTH STREET, WEST SIDE OF SQUARE,

SPRINGFIELD, - - - ILLINOIS.

PERFECTION
Coffee and Tea Pot.

PATENTED OCT. 5TH, 1875.

Something entirely new. The best and cheapest Coffee and Tea Pot ever made. Useful for Families, Restaurants, Boarding Houses and Hotels. It saves time and money and gives better flavored Tea and Coffee than any other pot in use. Send for Circular.

M. J. DEWALD,
340 North Ave., CHICAGO, ILL.

CHAMBER OF COMMERCE, CHICAGO, ILL.

N. BARSALOUX,
DEALER IN
Furniture

CARPETS,
OIL-CLOTHS,
Stoves, Crockery,
And everything in the Line of
HOUSEHOLD GOODS.
60 W. Madison St.,   CHICAGO, ILL.

J. E. GLENN
DEALER IN
Trunks
VALISES,

Traveling Bags, &c.

62 West Madison St.,

CHICAGO, ILL.

QUINCY—Continued.

MEAT MARKET.

F. OHLENDORF,
MEAT MARKET,
322 HAMPSHIRE STREET.

WERNETH & BARTH, Meat Market,
606 Hampshire st.

MILLERS.

GOVE & GWIN,
Manufacturers of the Celebrated
Gem City Mills Flour,
COR. BROADWAY & 25th STS.
Orders also received at 24 N. Seventh St.

WM. HUNERWADEL,
Manufacturer of
THE FAVORITE
CITY SPRING MILLS
FAMILY FLOUR,
105 S. Sixth St., bet. York & Kentucky.

NOTARY PUBLIC AND REAL ESTATE.

BERNARD, J. C., Notary Public & Real Estate Agent, 534 Hampshire st., up-stairs.

ORGANS.

OLOF MAGNUSSON,
Manufacturer of
GEM CITY ORGANS.
King's Building, Cor. 5th & Hampshire Sts.

PAINTER.

J. H. RICKENBERG,
House, Sign and Ornamental Painter, Paper Hanger, Grainer and Glazier. Calcimining, Wall Coloring, &c., done to order on short notice. Orders by mail promptly attended to.
1031 & 1263 HAMPSHIRE STREET.

PAPER AND CIGAR BOXES.

Gem City Paper & Cigar Box Factory.

H. G. SCHWARZBURG,
Manufacturer of
PAPER & CIGAR BOXES,
S. E. COR. MAINE & FIFTH STREETS.
Up-stairs.
All orders promptly attended to.

PHOTOGRAPHER.

SPARKS, JNO. T., Photographist,
423 Hampshire st

PHYSICIANS.

BLAISDELL, J. M., Homœopathic Physician and Surgeon, Office, 632 Maine st., Res. 413 Jersey st.

QUINCY—Continued.

PHYSICIANS.

A. J. CHAPEL, M. D.,
GYNÆCOLOGIST,
Office : 503 Hampshire Street. Residence: 503 Locust Street.

ELGIN, DR. W. W., Physician & Surgeon,
Office. 613 Maine st.

KENDALL, H. W., Physician & Surgeon,
514 Maine st.

PLUMBERS AND GAS FITTERS.

J. R. BUNTING & CO.,
Plumbers, Steam & Gas Fitters,
23 NORTH SIXTH STREET.

RESTAURANTS.

Bingham's Restaurant,
COR. FOURTH AND MAINE STS.,
BINGHAM & LOVELACE, Props.
Regular Meals 25 Cents.
Breakfast from 6½ to 9 A. M.; Dinner from 12 to 2 P. M.; Supper from 6 to 7½ P. M.

COLLAN, J. B., Union Depot Dining Hall, good square meal 50 cents, Union Depot.

HOLSKE, WM., Restaurant & Oyster Saloon,
325 Hampshire st

ROOFING.

SCHUPP, BEN., Tin & Slate Roofing,
N. E. cor. 11th & Hampshire sts.

SALOONS.

GEO. ERNST'S
SALOON & BILLIARD HALL,
The best Wines and Liquors always on hand.
No. 524 HAMPSHIRE STREET.

ILLINOIS HOUSE AND SALOON.
S. OTTO BAUMGARTNER, Proprietor.
Best of Liquors and Cigars.
513 HAMPSHIRE STREET.

JARAND, F. C., Saloon,
533 Hampshire st., northwest cor. of 6th.

SILAS S. KELLER,
FARMERS' HOME SALOON AND BOARDING HOUSE,
Corner 9th and Hampshire Street.

LANING, JOHN, Saloon,
719 Maine st.

J. H. MEYER,
GEM ART HALL
AND SALOON,
Choice Wines, Liquors and Cigars.
No. 528 Maine Street.

QUINCY—Continued.

SALOONS.

MICHEL, ANDREAS, Saloon,
Cor. 5th & York sts.

REUSER, LOUIS, Saloon,
615 Maine st.

SCULPTOR.

C. G. VOLK,
SCULPTOR,
322 MAINE STREET.

SEWING MACHINES.

SNITJER, D., Agent for the Singer Sewing Machine, 634 Maine st.

SHIRT MANUFACTORY.

J. GRAFFTEY & SON,
Manufacturers of

326 MAINE STREET.

STAIR BUILDER.

HEITLAND, J. H., Stair Builder,
5th st., bet. Hampshire & Vermont.

STOVES AND TINWARE.

THOMAS CLARK,
Dealer in
STOVES AND TINWARE,
Tin Roofing a Specialty.
54 NORTH SIXTH STREET,
Between Hampshire and Vermont.

TAILORS.

GATZ, ALOIS, Merchant Tailor and Clothier,
506 Maine st.

GROSCH & KRONENBERG, Merchant Tailors,
320 Maine st.

OLSSON, M. & CO., Merchant Tailor,
609 Maine st.

SCHROEDER, A. H., Merchant Tailor,
502 Hampshire st.

IMPORTANT EVENTS.

A. D.
- 879. Carles III, of Germany, was the first sovereign who added "in the year of our Lord" to his reign.
- 890. Alfred, the Great, establishes a regular militia and navy, and the mode of trial by jury; he also institutes fairs and markets.
- 900. England divided into counties, hundreds and tithings.
- 912. The patronage of the papal chair is now in the hands of harlots.
- 931. Mere children elevated to the highest offices in the church.
- 941. Arithmetic brought into Europe by the Saracens. Manufactories of linens and woolens in Flanders, which becomes the seat of western commerce.
- 955. Hungarians driven out of Germany.
- 959. Wolves expelled from England and Wales in consequence of a reward being offered for the purpose by the king. Violent disputes between the Monks and Clergy, St. Dusten, Archbishop of Canterbury, attempts to reform the church by enforcing clerical celibacy.
- 981. Greenland discovered by the Norwegians.
- 986. Louis V, the Indolent of France, poisoned by his wife, Blanche, and in him ended the race of Charlemagne.
- 1002. Massacre of all the Danes in England, on St. Brice's day, upon which Sweyn, king of Denmark, lands a large armament and brings war and all its miseries upon the country.
- 1004. All old churches rebuilt, about this time, in the Gothic Style.
- 1005. A pestilence raged all over Europe and lasted three years.
- 1010. St. Adalbert arrives in Prussia to preach Christianity, but is murdered by the Pagans. His death is afterward revenged by Boleslaus, a Poland, with fearful ravages.
- 1013. The Danes, under Sweyn, become masters of England.
- 1015. A law is passed in England forbidding parents to sell their children.
- 1017. Rain of the color of blood fell for three days in Aquitaine.
- 1024. Musical scale, consisting of six notes, invented by Guido Aretino.
- 1028. Romanus III, of Rome, a patrician, becomes emperor of the East by marrying Zoe, the daughter of the late monarch.
- 1034. Zoe, after prostituting herself to a Paphlagonian money-lender, causes her husband, Romanus, to be poisoned, and afterward marries her favorite, who ascends the throne under the title of Michael IV.

ADVERTISEMENTS.

QUINCY—Continued.

TAILORS.
WILLCOCKS, J. E., Merchant Tailor, 709 Maine st.

TOBACCO AND CIGARS.
BADER & HARTUNG, Cigar Manufacturers, 508 Hampshire st.
BLUNCK, NICHOLAS, Cigars & Tobacco. 40 North Front st.
GEM CITY TOBACCO WORKS, Manf's. of Plug Tobacco. Foot of Delaware st.

S. KINGSBAKER & BRO.,
Eclipse Cigar Manufactory,
331 HAMPSHIRE STREET.

TOBACCO DRUMS AND PAILS.
POTTER, JOHN, Manf'r Tobacco Drums & Pails. Front st., bet. Washington & Jefferson.

UNDERTAKERS.
WM. T. BENNESON,
FURNISHING UNDERTAKER,
No. 19 North Sixth Street, East Side.

FREIBURG, J. & F., Undertakers, 811 Maine st.

VETERINARY SURGEON.
R. WATKINS,
VETERINARY SURGEON.
QUINCY, ILL.

WAGONS AND PLOWS.
Established 1838.
W. T. & E. A. ROGERS,
Manufacturers of
WAGONS AND PLOWS,
And dealers in all kinds of
Agricultural Implements,
Office & Salesrooms, 24, 26 & 28 N. Sixth Street.
Factory, Cor. 4th & Oak Sts.

WALL PAPER AND WINDOW SHADES.
HAUBACH, C., Dealer in Wall Paper, Upholstery, etc., 429 Hampshire st.

J. H. KOST,
Dealer in Wall Paper, Window Shades, Paints, Oils and Window Glass. House Painting, Paper Hanging.
101 SOUTH FIFTH STREET.

WATCHMAKERS AND JEWELRS.
ANDREWS, J. F., Watchmaker, &c., One door East P. O Building. Hampshire st.
BENNESON, JAS. A., Watchmaker & Jeweler, 50½ Hampshire St.

QUINCY—Continued.

WATCHMAKES AND JEWELERS.
GAGE, W. H., American & Swiss Watches, Jewelry, Silverware, etc., cor. 5th & Maine sts.
WAHL, CHRIS., Watchmaker & Jeweler, 707 Maine st.

QUINCY BUSINESS HOUSES,
WHEN ESTABLISHED.

GATE, ALOIS, Merchant Tailor, 1875.
GRAFFETY, J., & Son, Shirt Makers, 1860.
LEMLEY BROTHERS, Iron & Steele, 1864.
STEWART, A. M., Steam Dye Works, 1876.

OMAHA, NEB.

ATTORNEYS AT LAW.
JOHN McBRIDE,
Attorney at Law,
Office with General Strickland, west entrance Caldwell Block, 231 Douglas Street.
Collections promptly attended to.

(Established 1867.)
MORTON & McLAUGHLIN,
ATTORNEYS AT LAW & CONVEYANCERS,
Real Estate & Commercial Brokers,
491 TENTH STREET.
Money Loaned and Collections made.

VAN ETTEN, D., Attorney at Law. Collections promptly attended to, Omaha, Neb.

BOOTS AND SHOES.
DOHLE, HENRY & CO., Boots & Shoes, 210 & 227 Farnham st.

J. H. HENGEN,
MANUFACTURER OF

And Dealer in
BOOTS, SHOES AND GAITERS,
150 FARNHAM STREET.

C. J. SCHMIDT,
Manufacturer of all Kinds of
Boots, Shoes
AND GAITERS,
263 DODGE ST.

ADVERTISEMENTS. 447

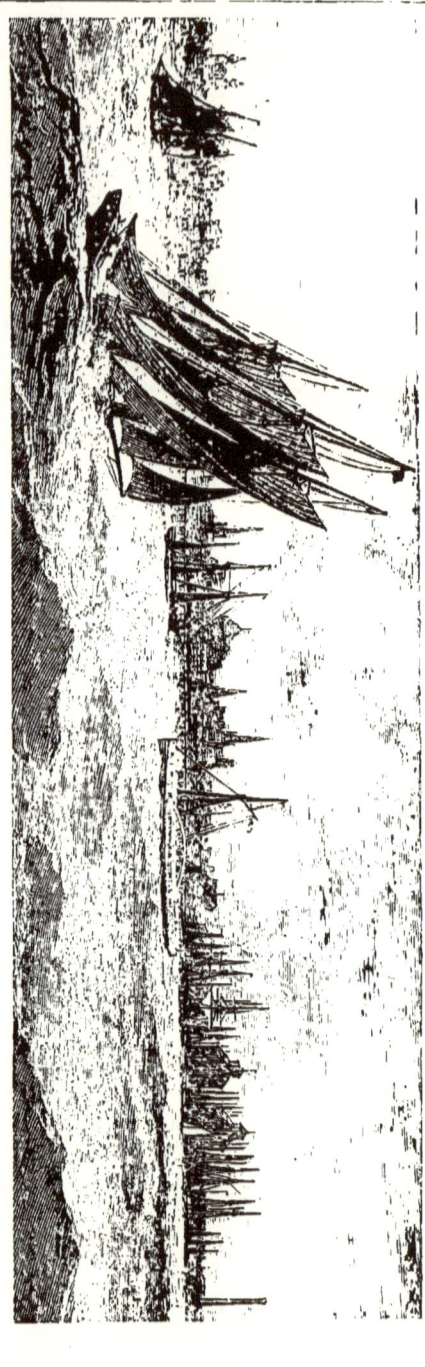

LAKE VIEW OF ERIE, PENNSYLVANIA.

ESTABLISHED 1872.

I. W. SPRINGER.   J. THAYER.   E. S. GREGORY.

SPRINGER, THAYER & CO.,
MANUFACTURERS OF

THE CELEBRATED IXL WIND MILL,

Also Wholesale and Retail Dealers in all kinds of IRON, WOOD AND BRASS PUMPS.

109 E. State Street, ROCKFORD, ILL.

ADVERTISEMENTS.

OMAHA—Continued.

BOOTS AND SHOES.

LANG, PHILLIP, Manufacturer and dealer in Boots & Shoes, 236 Farnham st.

BUTTER, EGGS AND CHEESE.

Longprey Bros.,
Wholesale and Retail Dealers in

EGGS, BUTTER & CHEESE
& General Commission Merchants,
No. 505 12th Street, near Farnham.
Goods delivered to all parts of the City free of charge.

COMMISSION MERCHANTS.

FRIEDMANN & BEHRENS,
Commission Merchants,
and Jobbers in Fruit,
512 TWELFTH STREET.

E. MORONY,
Produce and General

Commission Merchant,
493 TWELFTH STREET.

REFERENCES:
State Bank of Nebraska, Steele & Johnson, Whitney, Clark & Co., Pundt, Mayer & Raapke

WILLIS, JOHN G., Commission Merchant, 251 Dodge st.

CRACKER MANUFACTURERS.

McCLURE & SMITH,
Manufacturers of all Varieties of

CRACKERS,
185 HARNEY ST., Bet. 11th and 12th.

DENTISTS.

BILLINGS & NASON,
Dentists. Dentist's Material on Hand and for Sale. Nitrous Oxide Gas administered.
No. 234 FARNHAM STREET.

DR. JAMES S. CHARLES,
 DENTIST,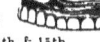
232 FARNHAM ST., bet. 14th & 15th.

Preservation of the natural Teeth made a Specialty.
☞ Oldest Practicing Dentist in the City.

PAUL, C. H., Dentist, 509 13th st.

DYER AND SCOURER.

JOHN BOEKHOFF
STEAM DYER & SCOURER
Ladies' and Gents' Garments a Specialty.
485 TWELFTH STREET.

OMAHA—Continued.

GUNSMITH.

SUTPHEN, D. C., Guns & Ammunition. 211 Farnham st.

HARNESS AND SADDLES.

KELLY, ALFRED, Saddles, Harness, Horse Equipments, &c., 254 Farnham st.

HOTELS.

ATLANTIC HOTEL

CHARLES HEINRICHS, Prop.,

Cor. Tenth and Howard Sts.,

Five minutes walk from Depot and Business Center of the City. $2.00 per Day. Reduction by the week.

GRAND CENTRAL HOTEL, George Thrall, prop., Cor. Farnham & 14th sts.

METROPOLITAN HOTEL,
Corner Douglas and 12th sts.

DR. A. VAN NAMEE, JR., Proprietor.

Located two blocks from Post Office and one from Academy of Music.

INSURANCE.

COREY & GRIFFEN, agts. Connecticut Mutual Life Ins. Co., cor. 15th & Douglas sts.

HOWELL, SAMUEL J., Insurance Agent, 235 Douglas st

JUSTICE OF THE PEACE.

LUTHER R. WRIGHT,
Justice of the Peace,
231 DOUGLAS ST.
Established 1875.

MACHINIST.

T. M. TREVETT,

Machinist and Boiler Maker, Jail work, Vault work and Shutters, Engraver of Seal Presses, and Stencil Cutter, Omaha.

MILLINERY.

ATKINSON, A., Millinery, Cor. Douglas & 13th sts.

NEWSPAPER.

OMAHA DAILY BEE, E. Rosewater, editor & prop., circl'n 4,000, $8 per year; weekly $2 per year circulation 3,500

IMPORTANT EVENTS. 449

OMAHA—*Continued.*

PATENT MEDICINES.

S. H. KENNEDY'S
Hemlock Remedies:
Pinus Canadensis,
Hemlock Liniment,
and
Hemlock Sheep Dip,

C. H. GOODMAN,
Wholesale Agent.

PHOTOGRAPHERS.

EATON, E. L., Photographer, & dealer in Photographic Materials, 248 Farnham st.

PHYSICIANS.

E. W. ALDRICH, M. D.,
Eclectic Physician and Surgeon,
254 FARNHAM ST.
Diseases of Women and all Female Complaints a specialty.

VICTOR H. COFFMAN, M. D.,

PHYSICIAN & SURGEON,
241 Farnham st.   Established 1867.

PRINTER.

F. C. FESTNER,
PRINTER, BOOK BINDER,
And Blank Book Manufacturer,
193 & 195 FARNHAM ST.

PUMPS.

STRANG, A. L., Pumps,
205 Farnham st.

SALOONS.

ALHAMBRA SALOON.
SAM. GARDNER, Proprietor.
Imported Wines and Liquors,
201 DOUGLAS STREET.

ANCHOR SALOON. George Peterson, Prop. Wines, Liquors and Segars. 185 Douglas st.

STOVES AND RANGES.

BERTHOLD, H., & TROSSIN, Stoves,
184 Douglas st.

FRANK H. GODDARD,
STOVES, FURNACES, RANGES
AND TINWARE.
Sole Agents for the Northern and Western States of the Wilmot Oil Stove.
227 DOUGLAS ST.

A. D.
1038. The Pope, for his scandulous conduct, driven from Rome, but re-established by the emperor, Conrad. Earthquakes and famine at Constantinople.
1039. Hardicanute, the third Anglo-Danish monarch of England, taxed England like a conquered country, was a glutton and drunkard, and died of apoplexy.
1042. Zoe and her sister Theodora, are made sole empresses of Rome by the populace, but after two months Zoe, though sixty years old, takes her third husband, Constantine X, who succeeds.
     The Danes expelled from England.
1053. The Welsh and Irish several times invade England, but are repulsed.
1062. Seventy thousand Europeans are killed or made prisoners by the Turks in Palestine.
1065. Jerusalem taken by the Turks.
1070. Popery at the height of its power, claiming supreme dominion, temporal and spiritual, over all the States of Christendom.
1072. Surnames first used among the English nobility.
1073. Booksellers first heard of.
1076. Justices of peace first appointed in England.
1080. Doomsday book began to be compiled from a general survey of the estates of England, and finished in six years.
1087. After the capture of Jerusalem by the Turks, the Christian pilgrims are insulted, robbed and oppressed, which gives rise to the crusades. Great struggle between Christianity and Mohammedans.
1091. The Saracens of Spain, beset on all sides by the Christians, call in the aid of the Moors, from Africa, who seize the territory they came to protect, and subdue the Saracens.
1059. Peter, the Hermit, preaches against the Turks in all the countries of Christendom.
1096. The first Crusade; Peter, the Hermit, and Walter, the Penniless, set out with a rabble, 300,000 of whom perish before the warriors are ready to start. There were 6 0,000 warriors, and 100,000 cavalry.
1099. Jerusalem taken by the crusaders on July 15th, when 70,000 infidels were put to the sword.
1110. Writing on paper made of cotton rags, commence about this time.
1137. A pretended Messiah in France.
1138. A pretended Messiah in Persia.
1147. Alphonsus of Spain, as-isted by a fleet of Crusaders on their way to the Holy land, takes Lisbon from the Moors.

ESTABLISHED 1865.

ED. H. WEBSTER,
Real Estate & Loan Broker,
No. 603 Main Street, KANSAS CITY, MO.

Special attention given to the interest of non-residents. Rents collected, taxes paid, money loaned, titles examined, all manner of written instruments carefully prepared and notarial business promptly attended to.

IRWIN, ALLEN & CO.,
LIVE STOCK COMMISSION MERCHANTS,
Office Rooms, 1 & 2 Live Stock Exchange Building, Kansas City Stock Yards, Kansas City, Mo. References: Bankers and Business men of Kansas City, Mo., and stock men generally. All sales cash on delivery. Remittances made promptly.
J. A. HUGHES, Bookkeeper.

KINGSBERY & HOLMSLEY, Live Stock Commission Merchants, Kansas Stock Yards, Kansas City, Mo. With correspondents at all Eastern Markets. References: Banks, Stock Dealers, Business men.

WHITE & HOLMES,
LIVE STOCK COMMISSION MERCHANTS,
Kansas Stock Yards, Kansas City Mo.

F. S. BRADBURY & CO., Proprietors.

A. E. DAVIDSON, Book keeper.

Barnum's Hotel,
COR. FOURTH & MAIN STS.,
Kansas City, - - Mo.
Terms: $2,00 Per Day.

Street Cars pass the door every ten minutes for all parts of the City.

S. F. ENSMINGER,
DEALER IN
Stoves, Staple Hardware,
Tinware, Cutlery, Nails, &c.

Manufacturer of TIN, COPPER, AND SHEET IRON WARE.

Particular attention paid to Roofing and Galvanized Iron Work. Job work solicited.

129 Second Street, DES MOINES, IOWA.

The Stock Exchange Building, Kansas City, Mo.—Has a frontage of 105 feet and is 127 feet deep, is three stories in height. The first floor is occupied by The Stock Yard Co. Offices, two banks, saloon, restaurant, barber shop and bath-rooms, and three large fire-proof vaults. The second floor contains twenty-four offices, occupied by Commission firms doing business at these yards. The third story contains offices and sleeping rooms.

Kansas City Stock Yard.—The Yards contain 114 pens, with capacity of 431 cars of cattle; 75 covered pens with capacity of 100 cars of hogs; 40 covered pens with capacity of 40 cars of sheep; 80 stalls with capacity of 100 head of horses; 113 chutes for loading and unloading stock; 7¾ miles of alleys and 8 miles of supply pipe and drainage for water from K. C. Water Works. One set of 80,000 lbs., one of 60,000 lbs., one of 50,000 lbs., and one of 8,000 lbs. Fairbanks' Scales. President Chas, F. Adams, Jr., Boston, Mass.; Secretary and Treasurer, C. Merriam, Boston, Mass.; General Manager, G. H. Nettleton, Kansas City; Superintendent, L. V. Morse, Kansas City; Ass't Sec'y and Ass't Treas., E. E. Richardson, Kansas City.

C. L. NEAGER,

Manufacturer and Dealer in

American and Italian

Marble Monuments,
—AND—
HEAD STONES.

LOWER BROADWAY,
COUNCIL BLUFFS, IOWA.

OMAHA—Continued.

SEWING MACHINES.

KENNEDY & MARTIN, Sewing Machines.
212 Douglas st.

TAILORS.

J. H. THIELE,
Merchant Tailor,
484 THIRTEENTH ST.

WINES AND LIQUORS.

HENRY HORNBERGER,
Wholesale and retail Wines, Liquors and Cigars. Fine old Kentucky Whiskies and Imported Goods a specialty, 239 Douglas street.

Omaha, Neb., Business Houses.
WHEN ESTABLISHED.

ATKINSON, A., Millinery, 1867.
BERTHOLD, H., & TROSSIN, Stoves, etc., 1876.
CHARLES, JAS. S., Dentist, 1866.
GODDARD, FRANK H, Stoves, 1873.
GRAND CENTRAL HOTEL, 1873.
HENGEN, J. H., Boots & Shoes, 1873.
HOWELL, SAMUEL J., Insurance Agt., 1874.
KENNEDY & MARTIN, Sewing Machines, 1877.
LONGPREY BROS., Com. Merchants, 1877.
McBRIDE, JOHN, Attorney at Law, 1874.
MORONY, E., Com. Merchant, 1874.
MORTON & McLAUGLIN, Attys, 1867.
SCHMIDT, C. J, Boots & Shoes, 1873.
WILLIS, JOHN G., Com. Merchant, 1877.
WRIGHT, LUTHER R., Justice of the Peace, 1875.

COUNCIL BLUFFS, IA.

ATTORNEYS AT LAW.

ROSS & FINKBINE, Attorneys at Law,
Over Pacific National Bank.

BARBERS.

ADAMS, W. H., First-class Barber,
336 Broadway.
SCHICKETANZ, CONRAD, First-class Barber,
14 S. Main st.

BOOK AGENT.

H. M. STEVENS,
Gen'l agt. for

Sunday School Supplies, Bibles, Standard Subscription Books, Maps, Charts, PICTURES, ETC.,
376 Middle Broadway,   AGENTS WANTED.

COUNCIL BLUFFS—Continued.

BLACKSMITH.

EVINS, JOHN, Blacksmith,
N. Main st.

BOOTS AND SHOES.

RANDALL, WILLIAM, Fashionable Boot and Shoe Maker, 328 Broadway.
RILEB, S. L., Boot and Shoe Maker,
Upper Broadway.

BREWERY.

GEISE, C., Steam Brewery & Malt House,
Upper Broadway.

CONTRACTOR AND BUILDER.

IMBRIE, J. M., Contractor & Builder,
246 Broadway.

GROCERS.

DICKEY, J. & SON, dealer in Groceries & Provisions, 461 Broadway.
HALL & BANTA, Wholesale & retail Grocers,
S. Main st.
LASKOWSKI, E., dealer in Groceries & Provisions, 320 Broadway.

HARNESS AND SADDLES.

KNABE, Manf'r of & dealer in Harness, Saddles, Collars, etc., Middle Broadway.
WALTERS, C. D., Manf'r of & dealer in Harness and Saddles, 328 Broadway.

HOTELS.

BIGGS HOTEL, W. L. Biggs, proprietor,
S. Main st.
BRYANT HOUSE, E. S. Wibley, proprietor,
Middle Broadway.
CRESTON HOUSE, opposite the court house, S. Main st., Max Mohn, prop.
KIEL & HOLIF, Hotel, cor. Main & Dodge sts., opposite court house.
METROPOLITAN HOTEL, Lower Broadway.
L. D. Harris, propr.
OGDEN HOUSE, upper Broadway, Council Bluffs Iowa, Geo. T. Phelps, propr.
PACIFIC HOUSE, G. W. Furgason & Son, props,
Council Bluffs.
TREMONT HOUSE, Lower Broadway. F. B. Daniger, propr   Terms, $1.50 per day.

LIVERY AND SALE STABLE.

JEFFERIS & NEWTON, Livery, Feed and Sale Stable, Lower Broadway.

MARBLE WORKS.

NEAGER, C. L., Marble Monuments and Headstones, Lower Broadway.

MEAT MARKETS.

CHICAGO MEAT MARKET, Evers & Schroeder, props., Meats, Sausage, Lard, Dried Beef, etc.,
South Main st.
DAWSON, H., Star Meat Market, Butcher, and dealer in Stock, 330 Middle Broadway.
SCHUMAKER & HUTH, First-class Butchers,
445 Broadway.

MILLINERY.

EITMAN, MRS. L., Dressmaker,
S. Main st.
HORTON, MRS. L. A., Fashionable Milliner,
N. Main st

COUNCIL BLUFFS—Continued.

MATTRESSES, ETC.

MORGAN, R., Manufacturer of and dealer in Mattresses, etc., Middle Broadway.

PHOTOGRAPHER.

GO TO SHERRADEN'S GALLERY, 347 Middle Broadway, for fine Photographs.

PHYSICIANS.

PATTON, DR. W. L., Physician & Occulist, Office, N. Main st.

RICE, R., M. D., Chronic Diseases a specialty, Middle Broadway, over Savings Bank, residence, N. E. Cor. Centre and Wall sts.

RESTAURANTS.

BRADLEY, J. N., Restaurant & Ice Cream Parlor, Confectionery, Oysters, etc., 236 up'r B'y.

MAIN STREET DINING ROOMS, bet. Court and Willow. Board $3.50 per week, meals, 25cts.

SHORT, JOHN, Wines, Liquors, Cigars and Restaurant, Broadway.

SCHOOLS.

ACADEMY OF ST. FRANCIS, conducted by the Sisters of Charity, of the B. V. M.

STOVES AND TINWARE.

DEVOL, P. C., Stoves, Stamped Tin & Japanned Ware, 416 Broadway.

TAILORS.

REITER & PETER, Merchant Tailors, nearly opposite City Building, 322 Broadway.

TAPE WORM DESTROYER.

BIGGS, W. L., Tape Worm Destroyer, Main st., Council Bluffs.

TRUSS CO.

VAUGHAN, W. R., Howe Truss Co., Council Bluffs, Iowa.

LINCOLN, NEB.

ATTORNEYS AT LAW.

BLODGETT & BRO., H. H. Blodgett and G. M. Blodgett, Att'ys at Law, over State Nat'l B'k

MONTGOMERY, M. & SON, Attorneys at Law, 9 Academy of Music Block.

PALMER, A. L., Attorney at Law, Office, Opera House

PHILPOT, J. E., Attorney at Law, Cor. O & 10th sts.

SESSIONS, M. H., Attorney at Law, 8 Academy of Music.

BANKERS AND BROKERS.

OWEN & OAKLEY, Bankers & Brokers, Money loaned on approved security, Academy of Music Block.

FURNITURE.

HOFFMAN & EISSLER, Man'f're and dealers in Furniture & Upholstery, 11th st., bet. N & O.

GROCERIES.

JOHNSON, J. D., Groceries, Grain. Flour, Feed, Cigars & Tobacco, 10th st., bet. N & O sts.

IMPORTANT EVENTS. 453

A. D.

1163. London bridge, consisting of nineteen small arches, first built of stone.

1167. English commerce confined to the exportation of wool.

1172. Henry II., King of England, takes possession of Ireland, which from that period is governed by an English Viceroy or Lord-Lieutenant.

1176. Dispensing of justice by circuits first established in England.

1178. Pope Alexander, by a special act, relieves the clergy of Berkshire from keeping the archdeacon's dogs and hawks during his visits.

1178. The Waldenses spread over the valley of Piedmont. They circulated the Scriptures; they were the forerunners of Protestantism; were condemned by the eleventh general council and severely persecuted.

1180. Glass windows begin to be used in private houses in England. Bills of exchange used in commerce.

1181. Digest of the laws of England made about this time by Glanville.

1189. Great massacre of the Jews at the coronation of Richard I.

1196. The Jews become the principal bankers in the world.

1199. The power of the Pope supreme; Rome mistress of the world, and kings her vassals.

1204. Jews of both sexes imprisoned; their eyes or teeth plucked out, and numbers inhumanly butchered, by King John, of England. The Inquisition established by Pope Innocent III.

1206. Reign of Genghis Khan, first Emperor of the Moguls and Tartars, one of the most bloody conquerors of the world. Fourteen millions of the human race perish by his sword, under the pretense of establishing the wor.hip of one God. He dies in 1227.

1208. London incorporated and obtained its first charter from King John.

1210. Ireland completely subdued, and English laws and customs introduced, by King John.

1213. The Pope declares King John, of England, a usurper, and John submits to hold his crown as a vassal of the Pope.

1214. Period of the Troubadors in France, the Minstrels in England, and the Minnesengers in Germany.

1217. Jerusalem taken by the Turks, who drove away the Saracens.

1229. The Scriptures forbidden to all laymen.

1233. The houses of London and other cities in England, France and Germany still thatched with straw.

JOSEPH WOLF,

Traveling Agent for the

Crystal Pebble Spectacles,

AND DEALER IN

Watches, Jewelry and Fancy Goods.

Orders Solicited and Promptly Attended to.

365 DIVISION STREET, CHICAGO, ILL.

Geo. H. Watson & Co.,

—Sole Agents—

FOR THE NORTHWEST OF THE CELEBRATED

MAGEE FURNACE CO.'S

Standard, Portable, and Brick Set Ranges, Standard Base Burner, and Standard Wrought Iron Furnace.

The Best in the World. Send for Cuts and Prices.

722 and 274 State St., - CHICAGO, ILL.

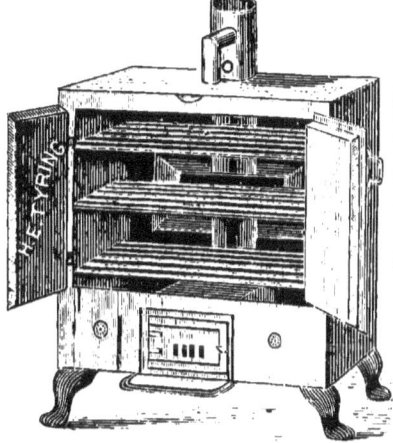

H. E. TYRING,
—DEALER IN—
STOVES, HARDWARE, &c.
Manufacturer of Galvanized Iron.
PORTABLE BAKE OVENS.
No. 66 W. Madison St., Chicago, Ills.

JOHN C. MEYER,

Manufacturer of and dealer in

all kinds of

VINEGAR

—AND—

Pickles.

56 N. Desplaines St.,

CHICAGO, ILL.

ADVERTISEMENTS. 455

COURT HOUSE, CHICAGO, ILL.

E. SMITH & CO.,

MANUFACTURERS OF WIRE SIGNS

AND

WIRE GOODS,

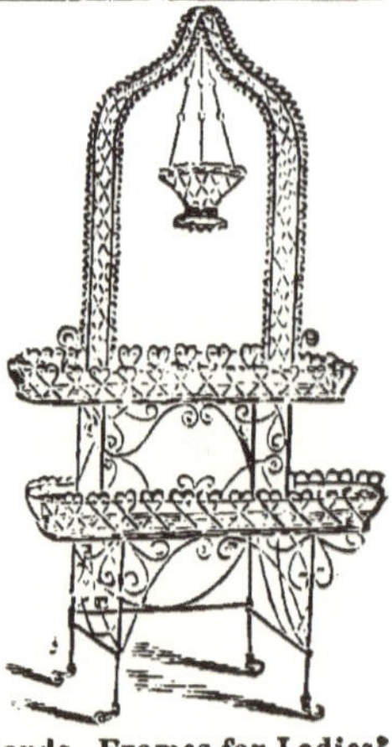

170 East Madison Street,
CHICAGO, ILL.

Railings, Guards, Coal Screens, Sand Screens, Flower Stands, Frames for Ladies' and Gents' Clothing. Sponge Baskets, Milliners' Trees and Stands, &c.

LINCOLN—Continued.

HOTELS.

BURLINGTON HOUSE,
F. M. LONG, Proprietor.
Best second-class house in the city. Terms, $1.00 per day. Convenient to all depots. 65 O street.

COMMERCIAL HOUSE, J. J. Inhoff, propr., Cor. P & 11th sts.

METROPOLITAN HOTEL, Jacob Snyder, propr., cor. O. & 8th sts.

PLUMBER AND GAS FITTER.

NICOL, ANDREW, Gas and Steam Fitter, dealer in Gas pipes, Fittings & Fixtures, Commercial Block, on 9th st.

SALOON.

WHIPPLE, C. W. & CO., props. of Commercial Sample Room, cor O & 9th sts.

GALVA, ILLS.

BAKERY AND RESTAURANT.

CLAUS HASS,
BAKERY AND RESTAURANT,
GALVA.

CARPENTER AND BUILDER.

PETERSON, P. S., Carpenter & Builder, Galva.

DENTIST.

SHEETZ, N. I., successor to C. A. Kitchen, Dentist, office in Olson Block.

DRUGGISTS.

EK, L. P., Druggist & Apothecary, 20 Exchange st., Galva. Established 1874.

SEELY, ISAAC B., Druggist, opposite Albro House, Galva. Established 1862.

FARM MACHINERY.

SMALLEY, C. O., Farm Machinery, Agricultural Implements, &c. Est. 1869. Galva.

FURNITURE.

CURTISS, F. J., dealer in Furniture, also General Undertaker. Church st. Est. 1856.

PETERSON & HERDIEN,
Dealers in
Furniture and General House-Furnishing Goods,
26 EXCHANGE STREET.

GROCERS.

GASTER, JAMES, Groceries & Provisions, Galva. Est. 1873.

KELSEY, N., Groceries, &c., Galva. Est. 1856.

HARDWARE.

SOPER, W. R., Hardware, Tinware, Stoves, Groceries, &c., Galva. Est. 1856.

HOTELS.

CITY HOTEL,
J. M. WICK, Proprietor.
Best accommodations for the traveling Public. F. Wyman, Porter. Galva.

GALVA—Continued.

LIVERY AND SALE STABLE.

D. W. SMALLEY,
LIVERY, FEED AND SALE STABLE,
Galva, Illinois. Carriages furnished with careful drivers to all points.

MILLINERY AND DRESSMAKING.

GOLDEN, MRS. L. J., Fashionable Dressmaker, Galva. Est. 1874.

UPDIKE, MRS. F. W., Millinery & Dressmaking, Galva.

STATIONERY AND TOYS.

PAINE, MRS. J. C., Stationery, Toys, Notions' &c., Church st. Est. 1860.

WAGONS, ETC.

PALMER, C. C., Wagon and Farm Implements repaired, Galva.

KEWANEE, ILLS.

AGRICULTURAL IMPLEMENTS.

O. H. LOOMIS & SON,
Dealers in
AGRICULTURAL IMPLEMENTS.
Salt, Lime, Cement, Field and Garden Seeds, &c. Cor. TREMONT & WILLARD STREETS.

FURNITURE.

JACKSON, S. H., dealer in Furniture & General Undertaker, 3d st.

HARNESS AND SADDLES.

GEO. D. ELLIOTT,
Manufacturer and Dealer in
Saddles, Bridles, Harness, Fly Nets, Whips, &c.,
KEWANEE, ILL.   Est. 1875.

MARBLE WORKS.

CROSS, W. T., Excelsior Marble Works, Est. 1864. Kewanee.

PICTURE FRAMES.

WILSON, L. P., Picture Frame Manfr. & General Job Work. Kewanee. Est. 1867.

TAILOR.

SCHRODER, JOHN C., Merchant Tailor, Third st.

TURKISH BATHS.

PARSONS, E., Vapor & Turkish Baths for all Chronic Diseases, Kewanee.

STERLING, ILLS.

AGRICULTURAL IMPLEMENTS.

BURKHOLDER, C., dealer in Farm Machinery of all kinds, Est. 1877.

IMPORTANT EVENTS. 457

STERLING—Continued.

ATTORNEY AT LAW.

ALLEN, E. G., Law and Collection Office. References. First National Bank and Sterling Mercantile Company.

AUCTION AND COMMISSION.

ROCK D. BARD, Auction & Commission. Dealer in bankrupt stocks, 109 Mulberry st. Est.1872.

BAKERY AND CONFECTIONERY.

BON TON, Geo. A. Allen, prop., Oysters, Ice Cream & Cigars, 482 3d st. Est. 1876.

EISELE, C., Bakery, Confectionery and Ice Cream Parlors, 512 3d st. Est. 1866.

FYFE, ALEX. L., Bakery and Confectionery, Fruits, Oysters and Ice Cream, 119 Mulberry st. Est. 1874.

BILLIARD PARLOR.

GAULT HOUSE BILLIARD PARLOR, S. C. Grubb, prop., under Gault House. Est. 1877.

BOOK-BINDERS.

MEDIN & LINDFELT, Book-binders, 497 3d st. Est. 1876.

CARPET WEAVER.

BOYLE, JOHN, Carpet Weaver, 513 3d st. Est. 1874.

COOPERAGE AND BUTTER TUBS.

SCHIFFMACHER, VICTOR, Manf'r. and dealer in Cooperage & Butter Tubs. Est. 1860.

DENTIST.

POLLOCK, D. J., Dentist. 490 3d st. Est 1873.

DISTILLERS.

MILLER, J. S. & CO., Distillers, Sterling. Est. 1864.

DRY GOODS.

COLE, D. & A., Chicago Cheap Store, 495 3d st. Est. 1877.

EAVE TROUGH HANGER.

EUREKA EAVE TROUGH HANGER CO., Manfr's of Eureka Eave Trough Hanger, C. T. Metzner, panteutee. Est. 1877.

FOUNDERS AND MACHINISTS.

WILLIAMS & ORTON, Manufacturing Co., Founders & Machinists, Mill Machinery of all kinds. Est. 1865.

FURNITURE.

CRUSE, CHAS. & SON, Furniture, Looking Glasses & Coffins, 451 3d st. Est. 1858.

STERLING SCHOOL FURNITURE CO., Manfrs. of all kinds School and Church Furniture. Est. 1869.

GENERAL WAREHOUSE.

KREIDER & BEDNAR, Grain, Coal. Salt. Lime, Cement, Plasterer's Hair, &c. Est. 1876.

GROCERS.

PEEBLES BROS., Grocers, 481 3d st. Est. 1865.

GUN AND LOCKSMITH.

CREIDER, S. S., Practical Gun, Lock and Sewing Machine Repairer, under Gault House. Est. 1873.

A. D.

1234. They circumcise and attempt to crucify a child at Norwich; the offenders are condemned in a fine of 20,000 marks.

1247. The first concordance of the Bible was made under the direction of Hugo de St. Charo, who employed as many as 500 monks upon it.

1254. The Jews persecuted everywhere.

1257. Certain record of the first gold coin in England.

1260. Kublia Khan builds Pekin, China, and makes it his capital.

1264. The Commons of England first summoned to Parliament.

1268. No Pope for about three years.

1269. Statute passed in England that no Jew should be allowed to enjoy a freehold.

1274. Every Jew lending money on interest compelled to wear a plate on his breast signifying that he was a usurer, or to quit the realm of England.

1277. First Nepotism. Pope Nicholas III, enriching his family at the expense of the church, introduces Nepotism. Two hundred and sixty-seven Jews hanged and quartered for clipping coin, or cutting pieces from silver and gold.

1279. The Tartars subdue China.

1282. The Sicilians massacre the French throughout the whole island of Sicily, without respect to sex or age, to the number of 8,000, on Easter day, the first bell for vespers being the signal. This horrid affair is known in history by the name of "Sicilian Vespers."

1287. Fifteen thousand, six hundred and sixty Jews are apprehended in one day and banished from England.

1289. England pays her last tribute to the Pope.

1291. End of the crusade to recover Jerusalem. It cost the lives of 2,000,000 men.

1293. From this year there is a regular succession of English Parliaments.

1 97. Sir William Wallace, Sir William Douglas, Robert Bruce and other chiefs head a rebellion against the English.

1298. Silver-hafted knives, spoons and cups a great luxury at this time. Tallow candles so great a luxury that splinters of wood were used for lights.

1300. University of Lyons founded. Rapid advance in civilization. Revival of ancient learning; improvements in the arts and sciences, and progress of liberty.

1303. Vacancy in the Papal chair nearly eleven months, with the papal power on the decline.

STERLING—Continued.

HARNESS AND COLLARS.

HANEY, FRANK, Manufacturer of Harness and Collars, Wholesale and Retail, 519 Third st. Est. 1877.

IRON SHUTTERS.

PERKINS & SON, Manufacturers of Fire-proof Iron Shutters, 433 3d st. Est. 1875.

IRON WORKS.

STERLING IRON WORKS, Cavert & Eastabrooks props., Est. 1875.

LAUNDRY.

WALTER, G. A., Shirt Manufacturer and Laundry, 114 Locust st. Est. 1875.

LIVERY AND SALE STABLE.

ADAMS, R., Livery, Feed and Sale Stable, 3d & Bridge sts. Est. 1873.

MEAT MARKET.

SCHMOEGER, S. A., Sterling Meat Market, 454 3d st. Est. 1875.

YOUNG, PETER, Variety Meat Market, Fresh & Salt meats always on hand, 458 3rd st. Est. 1867.

MUSICAL INSTRUMENTS.

HARDEN, JAS. & SON, Musical Instruments of all kinds, under Gault House. Est. 1867.

NEWSPAPER.

STERLING GAZETTE, Steam Printing House, Eastman & Jenne. Est. 1854.

PHOTOGRAPHERS.

ADAMS, J., Photographic Art Gallery, 478 3d st. Est. 1871.

HOUSER, MRS. E. F., Photographic Art Studio, Cor. 3d and Mulberry sts. Established 1873.

McLEOD, D., Photograph Parlors, 490 3d st. Established 1875.

PHYSICIANS.

ANTHONY, J. P., Physician & Surgeon, 123 Mulberry st. Established 1851.

PLUMBERS & GAS FITTERS.

FACEY, T. K. & SON, Plumbers, Steam and Gas Fitters, 522 3d st. Established 1856.

JOHNSTONE, J. S., Practical Plumber Steam & Gas Fitter, Locust-t., und. Galt H. Est. 1877.

PUMPS.

SHEAFFER, J. W., Manufacturer of Pumps, Repairing, etc., 4th & Elm st. Estab. 1865.

TAILOR.

EISELE, JACOB, Merchant Tailoring and Gents Furnishing Goods, 455 3d st. Estab. 1873.

TANNERS.

STREET & UNTERREINER, Manf'r of Leather, Hides, Tallow & Plastering Hair. Est. 1875.

WAGONS AND BUGGIES.

TREASHER, JACOB, Manf'r of Wagons, Buggies, etc. Shoeing & Repairing a specialty. Est. 1870.

VAN-DE-MARK, A., Manf's of Wagons, Buggies, etc. Established 1871.

WATCHES AND JEWELRY.

HAGEY & SON, Watchmakers and Jewelers, 485 Third st.

STERLING—Continued.

WATCHES AND JEWELRY.

KISTLER, C., Jeweler, dealer in American and Imported Goods, 524 3d st. Estab. 1873.

WINES AND LIQUORS.

ANNAS & LEDERER, Whol. Dealers in Choice Wines, Liquors & Cigars, 463 3d st. Est. 1877.

STEIN & MAAS, Imp. and Dealers in Wines Liquors, Mulberry st. Established 1875.

ROCK FALLS, ILL.

CORN PLANTER.

PATTERSON, J. A., Manufacturer of Sterling Corn Planter. Estab. 1875.

HOTEL.

CLIFTON HOUSE, J. N. Kern, Proprietor, Cor. Main and Gray sts., Rock Falls.

FLOURING MILLS.

GLOBE MILLS, J. Zollinger, Merchant & Custom Miller. Established 1871.

MITTENS AND GLOVES.

HUBBARD, WARD & CLARK, Patent calf-faced Sheep Mittens, Gauntlets & Gloves. Est. 1876.

DIXON, ILL.

BAKERY AND CONFECTIONERY.

PFISTERER, GEORGE, Bakery, Confectionary & Ice Cream Parlors, Main st. Est. 1875.

SMITH, WM., Baker & Confectioner, Restaurant, etc., Main st. Established 1861.

BOOKS AND STATIONERY.

MEAD, JAMES C., Books, Stationery, Wall and Window Paper, Musical Instruments, etc., Galena st. Established 1854.

BOOTS AND SHOES.

DIMICK, A. S., Dealer in Boots and shoes. Main st. Established 1860.

DRUGGISTS.

TILLSON, A. H., Druggist, Galena st. Established 1868.

DRY GOODS.

VAN EPPS & BRUBAKER, Dry Goods, Grocerie® and Crockery, Main & Galena sts. Est. 1854.

WICKES & LOVELAND, Dry Goods, Main st.

FILE WORKS.

STANLEY, JOHN, Proprietor of Dixon File Works, Peoria st. Estab. 1866.

FLOUR AND GRIST MILLS.

SCHATZMANN, VICTOR, Farmers Mills, Flour, Feed and all kinds of grinding, Water st. Established 1871.

SMITH & CATE, Flour, Grist and Woolen Mills, Water st. Established 1876.

Post-Office Department, Washington, D. C.—The building occupies the whole square between 7th and 8th and E and F streets, northwest, and is opposite the Patent Office. It is built of white marble. It measures 300 feet north and south, and 204 feet east and west. It cost up to 1876; $1,855,889.59. A portion of the present site was originally intended for a hotel, the corner-stone for which was laid in 1793; but failing to complete the building, it was put up at a lottery and was drawn by two orphan children. It was here the first theatrical entertainment was given in Washington. In 1810 it was bought by the Government. December 15, 1836, it was destroyed by fire, and in 1839 the erection of the present building was commenced.

DIXON—*Continued.*

GUN AND LOCKSMITH

DREW, H. J., Practical Gun and Locksmith and all kinds sport'g material, Galena st. Est. 1856.

HARNESS AND SADDLES.

AYRES, D. B., Manufacturer and Dealer in Harness, Saddles and Turf Goods, Galena st. Established 1862.

HOTEL.

CENTRAL HOUSE, Kentner & Bacon Proprietors, Galena st. Established 1877.

NEWSPAPER.

TELEGRAPH & HERALD CO., B. F. Shaw Proprietor, Galena st. Established 1851.

PLUMBERS.

DIXON PUMP AND PIPE CO., Wind Mills, Pumps, Pipe Fittings, etc., Main st. Est. 1876.

SASH, DOOR AND BLINDS.

FLETCHER, JAMES, Manf'r of Sash, Doors and B.inds, Water st. Established 1868.

TAILORS.

CAHILL, M., Merchant Tailor, Wedding Suits a specialty, Main st. Established 1868.

DIXON, F. F., Merchant Tailoring of all kinds, Opp. Dixon National Bank. Estab. 1869.

DOLAN, THOS., Merchant Tailor, Galena st., Opp. Opera House. Established 1870.

TOBACCO AND CIGARS.

SCOTT'S PLACE, T. S. Bowles Proprietor. Cigars, Tobacco and Smoking Articles, Main st. Established 1877.

UNIVERSITY.

ROCK RIVER UNIVERSITY, Established 1875 Rev. McKendree Tooke, D.D., Chancellor.

DIXON—*Continued.*

WATCHES AND JEWELRY.

DODGE, S. S., Jeweler, Galena st. Established 1868.

SUSSMILCH, E H., Watches, Clock and Jewelry, Millinary & Fancy Goods. Main st. Est. 1864.

MENDOTA, ILL.

BOOTS AND SHOES.

LEISER, GEORGE, Manf'r & Dealer in Boots and Shoes, Washington st.

CARPET WEAVING.

JOHN EGLI.

Carpet Weaving, &c.

WASHINGTON, ST.

FURNITURE.

HESS, JOHN, Furniture and Undertaker, Washington st.

SALOON.

ROBER, PETER, Saloon, etc., Main st.

STOVES AND HOUSE-FURNISHING GOODS.

DAWSON, J. B., Stoves and House-furnishing Goods, etc. 25 Washington st.

PRINCETON, ILL.

BLACKSMITHING.

ISAAC AVERY.

General Blacksmithing.

PERU STREET.

PRINCETON—*Continued.*

BLACKSMITHING.

BLACKSMITHING,
J. W. HUNTINGTON,
And all kinds of MACHINE REPAIRING.
Mower Guards Ground on Short Notice for $2.00 per Bar, also Plows Repaired, Ground & Polished.
Shop Cor. PERU and MAIN Sts.

BOOTS AND SHOES.

BUSCH, FRED, Boots and Shoes, Main st.

NELSON, N. J., Manf'r Boots and Shoes, Main st.

RESTAURANT.

STECHER, EDWARD, Restaurant, etc., 8 Main st.

DES MOINES, IOWA.

BAKERY.

FERGUSON, J. A., Proprietor Western Bakery
815 Walnut st.

BARBERS.

DINMEN, E. R., First-class Barber,
West Walnut st.

LEWIS, JOHN H. V., First-class Barber,
201 cor. Court ave. & 2nd st

BOOTS AND SHOES.

GENTRY, PAUL, Fashionable Boot and Shoe Maker, Court ave., bet. 3rd & 4th sts.

NORRIS SCHRADER,
Fashionable Boots & Shoes Made to Order
FIFTH STREET.

BUTTER.

SEEBURGER, R., Butter Packer.
424 cor. 5th & Walnut sts.

THE HAWKEYE BUTTER WORKER. Clow & Rhoads., Props. Pat. April, 1877. 102 Court av.

CARPET MANUFACTURER.

SCHWARTZ, SAM'L, Manf'r of Home-Made Carpets, 215 6th st., near cor. of Walnut.

CARRIAGE AND WAGON MANUFACTURERS.

BLOOM, HENRY, Manufacturer of Buggies, Wagons, &c., 318 2nd st.

CONFECTIONER.

MARSHALL, DAVID, Confectionery and Fruit Stand, N. 2nd st.

CONTRACTORS AND BUILDERS.

J. A. CROTHERS,
CONTRACTOR & BUILDER
Estimates for all classes of Buildings Furnished Free.
710 W. WALNUT STREET.

DES MOINES—*Continued.*

CONTRACTORS AND BUILDERS.

C. W. OWENS,
Contractor & Builder
All Estimates for Buildings Furnished Free.
WEST WALNUT ST.

OWENS, G. C., Contractor and Builder,
cor. 6th & Walnut sts.

RANSOM CREWS, Jr.
Contractor and Builder
THIRD ST., DES MOINES, IOWA.
Estimates Free.

DENTIST.

EDWARDS, S. L., Dentist,
Attorney Block, 5th st.

DRESSMAKER.

GOULD, MRS. H. A., Fashionable Dressmaker,
308 4th st, Up-stairs.

SAUNDERS, MRS. E., Fashionable Dressmaker,
Fancy Hair and Wax Work, 216 Sixth st.

DYER AND SCOURER.

Compressed Steam Dye Works.
Established 1871. D. L. Mutchlar, Prop. Cor. Locust and Third Sts., Des Moines, Iowa.
Dyes Silks, Silk Velvets, Merinos, Alpacas, &c. Gents' Clothing Cleaned and Dyed.

FISH AND OYSTERS.

JOHN HARTLEY,
Sole Agent for Fick & Chase's Maryland Brand Raw Oysters, Wholesale Commission Dealer in Fresh Fish, Foreign and Domestic Fruits, &c.,
306 WALNUT STREET.

OTIS, C. D., Fish, Oysters, Game, Fruits, Vegetables, &c., 611 W. Walnut st.

FOUNDRY.

S. GREEN, Proprietor
HAWKEYE FOUNDRY
104 & 106 SECOND ST.
Manufacturer and Dealer in Building, Bridge and Stove Castings.

FURNITURE.

BATTLE & KNIGHT,
Manufacturers of all kinds of Furniture and Office Fixtures. Offices Fitted up and Furniture Repaired in the neatest Style. at reasonable rates. Fancy Picture Frames, &c., 219 Sixth st.

GALVANIZED IRON CORNICE.

CLIFFORD NEWTON,
Manufacturer of Galvanized Iron Cornices,
Dormer Windows, Door and Chimney Caps. Finials, Gutters, Spouting. &c. Tin Roofing and General Job Work. 604 Walnut St.

DES MOINES—Continued.

GROCERY AND RESTAURANT.

TODD, MORRIS, First-Class Restaurant and Dealer in Groceries, Confectionery, &c., 104 2nd street.

GUNSMITH.

SMITH, C. L., Gunsmithing. Ribs, Handles, &c., for Parasols and Umbrellas. 323 Walnut st.

HARNESS AND SADDLES.

HAMILTON, JAS. G., Manufacturer and Dealer in Harness, Saddles, &c., 217 6th st., near cor. of Walnut.

HIDE DEALER.

BECHAM, JOHN, Dealer in Green and Flint Hides of all kinds, W. Walnut st.

HOTELS.

ABORN HOUSE.
G. B. Brown, Proprietor.

GRAEFE HOUSE, 214 Walnut st.
Henry Graefe, Proprietor.

MORGAN HOUSE, Directly opposite and West of Rock Island Depot. E. E. Long, Prop.

SAVERY HOUSE, Fred C. Macartney, Proprietor.

LIVERY AND SALE STABLE.

WELLS, L. J., Livery, Feed and Sale Stable, Fourth st., south of Allens' Bank.

MACHINIST.

LAING, JAMES, General Machinist, and dealer in Pumps, Iron Pipes, etc. 111 Court Ave.

MEAT MARKET.

BAKER, S. L., First-class Butcher Shop, sixth st., Bet. Mulbery and Walnut.

MILL WRIGHT.

JOHNSON & JARRETT, Practical Mill Wrights, 100 Court Ave.

PAINTER.

LUNN, GEO., House and Sign Painter, Shop 211 sixth st.

PLOW MANUFACTURER.

DES MOINES PLOW CO.
Works, cor. Vine & 2nd sts.

PHYSICIAN.

BROOKS, DR. R., Offers his services to the citizens of Des Moines, Office Cor. 4th and Walnut st.

SALOON.

DUTCHER, J. A., First-class Bar and Billiards, 125 third st.

SCALE MANUFACTURER.

HITCHCOCK, S. S., Manufacturer of Scales, W. Court Ave., 3d door from bridge.

STAMPS AND STENCILS.

Des Moines Stencil & Rubber Stamp Co.
L. & L. E. ROSSALL, Proprietors.
Dealers in
All kinds of Stencil Material, Checks Legal Seals, Brands. Rubber Stamps of all kinds, Visiting and Business Cards, Job Printing, neatly done.
All orders by mail promptly filled.
210 Walnut St.

IMPORTANT EVENTS.

A. D.
1305. Sir William Wallace of Elderslie, the Scottish hero of the 13th century, is betrayed to the English King by Sir John Menteith, and at London put to death in this year, aged about 30.

1306. In Scotland Robert Bruce is declared King and is obliged to flee; but, on the death of Edward, of England, resumes his position.
Edward II., of England, a weak King, was murdered in Berkeley Castle, by order of the Queen's paramour.
Isabella, daughter of the King of France, married Edward II. Her favorite, Mortimer, died by the gibbet, and she was confined for the rest of her life in her own house at Risings, near London.

1310. Chimneys first used in domestic architecture.

1312. Knight Templars wholly suppressed by the Pope and the King of France.

1314. Battle of Bannockburn between Edward II. and Robert Bruce, which establishes the latter on the throne of Scotland, July 25.

1314. The Cardinals meet in Italy, and not agreeing in the election of a Pope they set fire to the conclave and separate, by which the Papal chair is left vacant for two years.

1315. A famine prevails in England so dreadful that the people devoured the flesh of horses, dogs, cats and vermin.

1316. Pope John XXII. imposes taxes upon all countries of Europe to enrich the treasury of the church.

1317. Massacre of the Jews at Verdun, by the peasantry; five hundred defend themselves in a castle where, for want of weapons, they throw their children at their enemies, then destroy one another.

1319. Dublin University established.

1324. John Wickliff, the first English reformer, is born. He studied at Oxford, and is justly called "The Morning Star of the Reformation," as he led to the truth under Luther and the other reformers of the 16th century. He died in 1384.

1336. Giotto, a celebrated Florentine painter, who studied with Cenubue, was only a shepard's lad. He was a friend of Dante and Petrach, and is said to be the first who produced life-like portraits. He died at this time, aged 60.

1337. First comet observed whose course is described with exactness.

1337. Europe infected with locusts.

1340. Gunpowder invented by Swartz, a Monk of Cologne.

DES MOINES—Continued.

STOVES AND TINWARE.

ENSMINGER, S. F., Dealer in Stoves, Staple Hardware etc., 129 Second st.

RITCHHART, JOHN, Jr Tinsmith, 129 2nd st.

TAILOR.

LUETZENSCHWAB, ANTON, Tailor, 308 Fourth st. Perfect fits guaranteed.

VETERINARY SURGEON.

RAY, DR. W. C., Veterinary Surgeon, 521 Mulberry St. Treats all diseases of the horse.

VINEGAR WORKS.

MENNIG & SLATER, Manf's of pure Cider and White Wine Vinegars, 110 Second st.

WATCHMAKER AND JEWELER.

WM. DOUGLAS.
Watchmaker & Jeweler,
Fine Watch repairing a specialty. All work warranted. Chronometer work of every description repaired and adjusted to heat, cold and position.
Methodist Church Block,
209 FIFTH ST.

FLINT, MICH.

HOOPSKIRTS AND CORSETS.

MRS. ANNA WILLIAMS,
Manufacturer of
HOOP-SKIRTS AND CORSETS,
FIRST STREET.

IRON WORKS.

GENESEE IRON WORKS, Kimball & Co., Proprietors, Saginaw st., N. S. of River.

WINES AND LIQUORS.

SHAULTERS, DAVID, Wines, Liquors & Groceries, Saginaw street. Established 1875.

OTTUMWA, IOWA.

BAKERY.

AMBORN, PETER, Dealer in Confectionery, Oysters & Bakery, Main & College sts.

MEAT MARKETS.

REIFSNYDER, CHAS., Dealer in Fresh and Salt Meats, Vegetables, etc. East Main st.

SALOONS.

BOARD OF TRADE, all kinds of Refreshments. L. Schlotter & Co., A. N. Auwerda, Prest. Market st.

BLACK HAWK HOUSE, Bob. Swann, Proprietor, Choicest Wines, Liquors & Cigars. 2d st.

STOVES AND TINWARE.

MILLER, C., dealer in Stoves and Tinware and House-Furnishing Goods, Main st.

ROCKFORD, ILLS.

BOLT WORKS.

ROCKFORD BOLT WORKS,
Water Power. Est. 1802.

BOOTS AND SHOES.

EMMET & SON, Boots & Shoes, Notions, West State st. Est. 1877.

BREWERIES.

Established 1860.

A. KAUFFMAN,
Proprietor of the

South Rockford Brewery,
820 S. MAIN ST., S. ROCKFORD, ILL.

ROCKFORD BREWERY,
J. PEACOCK, Prop.
Brewer of
Cream Pale & Amber Ale.
Established 1849. N. MAIN ST., E. SIDE.

CARRIAGES AND WAGONS.

NEUMEISTER ANTON, Manufacturer of Carriages and Wagons. 119 N. Main St., W. S. Established 1858.

NEUMEISTER, A., Manufacturer of Carriages and Wagons, 212 and 214 E. State St. Est. 1860.

CIDER PRESS SALOON.

SCHMALZ & MAYER, New Cider Press Saloon, 108 W. State St. Est. 1870.

FOOT POWER MACHINERY.

BARNES BROS., manufacturers of Foot Power Machinery. Water Power. Est. 1870.

FURNITURE.

McNAUGHTON, O., dealer in all kinds of Furniture. 213 E. State St. Est. 1876.

ROBERTS, C., dealer in all kinds of Furniture. 215 E. State St. Est. 1855.

HOTELS.

COMMERCIAL HOUSE, G. H. Sperbeck, Prop., W. Bridge St. Est. 1876.

HOLLAND HOUSE, J. R. Starr, Prop., S. Main St.

WHITE'S HOTEL, Rockford, Ill. Established 1866.

PATENT SOLICITOR.

FORD, G. W., Solicitor of Patents. 221 E. State St. Est. 1860.

PATTERN AND MODEL MAKERS.

SAVAGE & LOVE, Pattern and Model Makers. Water Power. Est. 1873.

ADVERTISEMENTS. 463

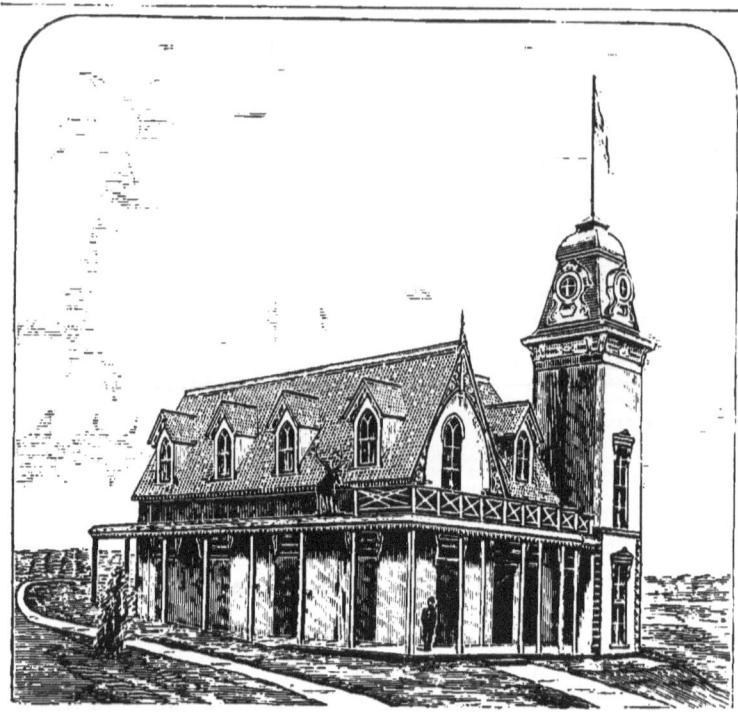

Missouri State Building, Centennial Exposition, Phila.—This building is constructed of wood, and o.her building materials. It is one story high with an attic and flag staff. It has fine large commodious apartments, arranged for the use of visitors, ladies' reception room, and a place for the Missouri State Centennial Commissioners. Altogether it is one of the handsomest state buildings on the ground.

RULE MANUFACTURER.

SMITH, E., Man'f of Waterbury's Combined Extension Rule. Pat. Oct. 24, 1876. Water Power. Est. 1877.

SEWING MACHINES.

COLE, J. J., General Sewing Machine Agent and Repairer. 217 E. State St. Est. 1870.

TAILORS.

BLOMQUIST, L. M., Merchant Tailor, Main and State St. Est. 1872.

RYMAN, JOHN, Merchant Tailor, and dealer in Gentlemen's Suitings. 217 E. State St.

UNDERTAKER.

LAGUE, WM., General Furnishing Undertaker, 502 E. S'ate St. Est. 1861.

WATCHES AND JEWELRY.

LUND, LOUIS, Watches, Clocks and Jewelry, 311 E. State St. Est. 1870.

ROCKFORD WATCH CO., H. P. Holland, Sec'y. S. Main St., Rockford, Ill.

WIND MILLS AND PUMPS.

CROOK, W. F., Mufr of Wind Mills and Pumps. 201 E. State St. Est. 1874.

SPRINGER, THAYER & CO., mfr's of I X L Wind Mills. 109 E. State St. Est. 1872.

WIRE CLOTH.

LOCKWOOD & LYMAN, Mf'rs of Wire Cloth. Water Power. Est. 1873.

ROCKFORD BUSINESS HOUSES,

When Established.

BARNES, BROS., Foot Power Machines, 1870.
LOCKWOOD & LYMAN, Wire Cloth Manufacturer; 1873.
NEUMEISTER, ANTON, Carriage Manufactory, 1858.
ROCKFORD BOLT WORKS, 1862.
SPRINGER, THAYER & CO., Wind Mills, 1872.

FREEPORT, ILLS.

BED RENOVATOR.

WIMERS, WM., Bed Renovator, Stephenson st. Est. 1877.

FREEPORT—Continued.

BAKERY AND CONFECTIONERY.

ROIIKAR, II., Bakery and Confectioner,
57 Stephenson st. Est. 1852.

BOOKS AND FANCY TOYS.

BAUMGARTEN, C., Books and Fancy Toys,
Galena st. Est. 1873.

BREWERIES.

Established 1860.

FREEPORT BREWERY,

BAIER & SEYFARTH,

Brewers of

LAGER BEER,

Corner Adams and Jackson Streets.
FREEPORT, ILL.

(Established 1864.)

JOSEPH MILNER & BRO.,

Brewers of

PALE, STOCK & CREAM ALE,

LAGER BEER & PORTER.

Chicago Street.

CARPETS AND COVERLETS.

BOYER, J., Dealer in Carpets and Coverlets,
139 Stephenson st. Est. 1877.

GROCERIES AND PROVISIONS.

A. LITMIS,

Dealer in

Groceries, Flour and Feed,

GALENA ST., Established 1867.

RUSTON, GEO., dealer in Butter & Eggs,
155 Stephenson st.

WINSLOW, F. S., Groceries and Provisions,
161 Stephenson st. Est. 1875.

HARNESS AND SADDLES.

FREIDAG & MOLTER, Harness, Saddles, Collars,
59 Stephenson st. Est. 1870.

LOOS, N. B., Harness, Saddles & Collars,
118 Stephenson st. Est. 1868.

REINEKE & OTTO,

Manufacturers & Wholesale & Retail Dealers in

Harness, Saddles

Bridles, Collars, Whips, Robes, Blankets, Brushes, Combs, Fly Nets, Trunks, Valises, &c
Cor. Galena & Van Buren Streets,
Freeport, Ill.

Repairing promptly attended to. The celebrated Vacuum Oil Blacking always on hand. Est. 1870.

SCHULTE, D. B., Harness, Saddles & Collars.
88 Stephenson st. Est. 1851.

HARDWARE.

ARNDT & LEEMHUIS, dealers in Hardware,
Stoves and Ranges, Galena st. Est. 1873.

KEHER, N., dealer in Hardware, Stoves, Ranges,
Galena st. Est. 1862.

HOTELS.

BRACKHAHAN, E. A., European Restaurant,
Stephenson st. Est. 1877.

FREEPORT—Continued.

HOTELS.

BREWSTER HOUSE,
Stephenson st., Freeport.

PENNSYLVANIA HOUSE, J. S. Zartman, prop.,
Stephenson & Walnut sts.

MEAT MARKETS.

LICHTENBERGER BROS., dealers in Fresh and Salt Meats, Chicago st. Est. 1861.

RHODES, B., dealer in Fresh and Salt Meats,
119 Stephenson st. Est. 1861.

METZ, HENRY, dealer in Fresh & Salt Meats,
Galena st., Est. 1857.

MAYER, M. M., dealer in all kinds of Fresh and Salt Meats, 86 Stephenson st.

PHOTOGRAPHER.

KASTEN, W., Photographic Artist,
87 Stephenson st. Est. 1865.

PLUMBER AND GASFITTER.

PERKINS, J. R., Plumber & Gasfitter,
1 Chicago st. Est. 1869.

SALOONS.

JANSSEN & MORGAN, Cincinnati Hall,
Chicago & Stephenson sts. Est. 1876.

KAUFMAN & GILBERT, Billiard & Pool Saloon,
90 Stephenson st.

SCHMICH & MERCK, Centennial Saloon,
Galena st. Est. 1875.

TAILOR.

STINE, ISAAC, Merchant Tailor & dealer in Gents' Furnishing Goods, 92 Stephenson st.

BELOIT, WIS.

BAKERY AND CONFECTIONERY.

CORCORAN, C. M., Bakery & Confectionary, and Groceries. School st.

BOOTS AND SHOES.

STARMER, J., Dealer in Boots and Shoes, Bridge st. Established 1875.

BROOM MANUFACTURERS.

BROWN, A. R. & S. A., Broom Manufacturers,
State st. Established 1876.

CARRIAGES AND WAGONS.

TRIPP, HERRICK & CO., Manufacturers of Carriages & Wagons, W. Bridge st. Est. 1877.

DENTIST.

CLARK, E. N. DR., Dentist, State st. Established 1847.

DRUGGISTS.

FENTON, F. S. & CO., Dealers in Drugs, Paints,
Oils, W. Bridge st. Est. 1862.

SMITH, E. R., Druggists, E. Bridge st. Estab.
1872.

GROCERIES.

BROWN, H., Groceries, Provisions and Crockery
W. Bridge st. Est. 1873.

HATCH, J. B., Groceries, Provisions & Crockery
W. Bridge st. Established 1868.

BELOIT—*Continued.*

HARDWARE.

WINSLOW & ROSENBERG, Dealer in Hardware, Stoves, etc., State & School sts. Est. 1866.

HARNESS AND SADDLERY HARDWARE.

YOUNG, A. W., Harness and Saddlery Hardware, State st. Est. 1877.

HOTEL.

GOODWIN HOUSE, S. J. Goodwin & Son, Proprietors, School and State sts.

MEAT MARKETS.

FINE, H. J., Dealer in all kinds of Fresh & Salt Meats, E. Bridge st. Est. 1875.

RITSHER, JOHN, Dealer in all kinds of Fresh and Salt Meats, Bridge st. Est. 1860.

BELVIDERE, ILL.

CARRIAGE AND WAGON MANUFACTORY.

WING, J. V., Carriage and Wagon Manf'r, Mechanic and Van Buren sts. Est. 1849.

COOPER.

CHURCH, CHAS., Cooper, North State st. Est. 1866.

HOTELS.

ANDERSON HOUSE, Wm. Anderson Proprietor. N. State st. Free Bus.

ESTABLISHED 1865.

JULIEN HOUSE

TOUSLEY & SHELDON, Props.,
Belvidere, Illinois.

The comfort of our Guests shall be our first consideration. We guarantee more for the money than any other hotel in the country.
Livery furnished & good stabling attached.

PIANOS AND ORGANS.

KELSEY, C. E., Pianos, Organs and Job Printer, N. State st. Est. 1864.

PUMP MANUFACTURER.

ROBERTSON, C. D., Pump Manufacturer, Mechanic st., S. Side. Est. 1877.

TAILOR.

BRADY, J. J., Merchant Tailor, S. State st., Est. 1876.

CHICAGO, ILL.

ADJUSTABLE SPRINGS.

LITTLEFIELD & SHERIDAN,
Patentees and Manufacturers of the
ADJUSTABLE FLAT STEEL SPRINGS
For Car Seats, Buggies and Spring Beds,
54 N. WELLS ST.

ADJUSTER OF TAX TITLES.

GAGE, ASAHEL, Adjuster of Tax Titles, 14 Portland Block, Chicago.

IMPORTANT EVENTS.

A. D.
1344. The first creation to titles by patents used by Edward III.
1348. 1,500,000 Jews are massacred in Europe, on suspicion of having poisoned the springs during a fatal distemper.
1349. The order of the Garter first instituted in England by Edward III.
1352. The Turks first enter Europe.
1357. Coal first brought to London.
1362. Law pleadings made in English, by favor of Edward III, instead of French, which had continued from the time of the Conqueror.
1365. Collection of Peter's pence forbidden by the English Government.
1368. A striking clock in Westminster.
1369. John Wickliff, the English reformer, begins to be publicly known by his disputes with the Friars.
1370. A perfect clock made at Paris, by Vick.
1378. Louis, of Hungary, dies, and the history of Hungary now presents a frightful catalogue of crimes. Charles Duras is murdered; Elizabeth, Queen of Louis, is drowned, and King (Hungarian queens reign with the title of king) Mary, their daughter, marries Sigismond, Marquis of Brandenburg, and causes the rivers of Hunry to flow with blood.
1381. Bills of exchange first used in England.
1383. Cannon first used by the English in the defense of Calais.
1384. Persia invaded by Tamerlane, a Tartar, who made pyramids of the heads of the slain.
1385. Linen weavers from Netherlands first establish business in London.
1391. Playing cards were first invented in France to amuse the king.
The English forbidden to cross the sea for beneficies.
1392. Charles, of France, seized with madness.
1394. The Jews banished from France by Charles VI.
1399. Tamerlane, in command of Mogul Tartars, takes the city of Delhi, defeats the Indian Army, conquers Hindostan, and butchers 100,000 of its people.
1400. A wonderful canal completed in China about this time.
1402. Battle of Angora, in which Bajazet I, King of the Turks, is taken prisoner by Tamerlane. Bajazet was exposed in a large iron cage, which he had destined for his adversary, and dashed his head against the bars and killed himself. At this defeat the Persian empire fell under the control of Tamerlane.

ADVERTISEMENTS.

CHICAGO—Continued.

AGRICULTURAL IMPLEMENTS.

BRISTOL, E. S., & CO., Farm Machinery and Seeds, 30 & 32 S. Canal st.

PERKINS, H. C., & CO., Reapers, Mowers and Lawn Mowers, 125 W. Randolph st., cor. Des-Plaines.

TAYLOR'S HORSE-SWEEP POWER. Taylor, Mack & Sm'th, Dealers in Agricultural Implements, 189 La Salle st.

ARCHITECTS.

AUSTIN, J., Architect. Rooms 23 & 24 S.W. cor. Dearborn & Madison sts.

S. E. CHAMBERLAIN,

191 So. Clark St., Chicago, Ill.

DAVIS, D. & H., REHWOLD & CO., Architects and Superintendents, 193 Washington st., Room 2.

P. HALE,

ARCHITECT

Cor. Clark & Washington Sts.

Established 1877.

HANSEN, C. O., Architect and Superintendent, S. E. cor. Clark & Madison sts., Room 34.

MERIAM, J. L., Architect and Superintendent, Room 12. No. 169 E. Madison st.

MEYER & BROOKES, Architects and Superintendents, Room 74, 116 Washington st.

S. M. RANDOLPH,

ARCHITECT

87 Washington St.,

U. S. Ex. Co.'s Bldg., Rooms 16 & 17. Est. 1871.

STRIPPELMAN & ENDER, Architects and Superintendents, Room 60, 159 & 161 La Salle st.

ARTIST.

FRISBIE, W. H. H., Artist,
 3 N. Clark st.

ATTORNEYS AT LAW.

BALDWIN & GRAHAM, Attorneys and Counselors, 197 Madison st., Room 11. Notary Public.

BRADLEY, FORDYCE G., Attorney at Law,
 188 Madison st.

BROWNE, HENRY, Attorney at Law,
Office. Ro m 19, 175 La Salle st., cor. Monroe.

BURGESS, W. J., Attorney at Law,
 97 S. Clark st.

CARUTHERS & PIERCE, Attorneys at Law,
 128 & 130 S. Clark st.

COWAN, DAVID, Marine and Chancery Lawyer, Room 25 Nixon B'lock, 175 La Salle st.

CHICAGO—Continued.

ATTORNEYS AT LAW.

DALE, JOHN T., Attorney at Law, Tribune Building, Chicago. Real Estate and Loans a specialty.

DECKER, HENRY, Attorney at Law, 92 La Salle st., Rooms 45 & 46. Collection a specialty.

ELLIOTT & CASS, Attorneys and Counse ors at Law, 146 Madison st.

B. F. FELCH,

Attorney & Counselor at Law & Notary Public

181 W. MADISON STREET.

FLOWER, JOHN F., Attorney and Counselor at Law. Collections a specialty, Room 12, 179 La Salle st.

HOYNE, PHILIP A., U. S. Commis-ioner and Commissioner of Deeds for every State and Territory for over 23 years, 157 La Salle st.

MARSHALL C. KELLEY,
Attorney & Counselor at Law,
Room 1, No. 146 Madison st. Notary Public, Abstracts Examined and all Legal Papers carefully drawn. Money Invested.

KING, SIMEON W., Attorney, U. S. Commissioner, Commissioner of Deeds for all the States and Territories, No. 3 Methodist Church Block.

LOWELL, F. W., Attorney at Law and Collection Agent, 116 E. Washington st.

D. W. MANCHESTER,
ATTORNEY AT LAW,
59 North Clark Street, Room 3.

MATTHEWS, H. M., Attorney and Counselor at Law, 152 La Salle st.

E. B. PAYNE,
ATTORNEY AT LAW,
25 North Clark Street, Room 10.

SCATES, HYNES & ROBINSON, Attorneys at Law, Room 53 Major Block.

SMITH & BURGETT, Attorneys at Law, Room 18, 175 La Salle St.

STEELE, HENRY T., Attorney and Counselor at Law, 86 Washington st., Room 10.

THE NATIONAL LAW & COLLECTION ASSOCIA tion, 121 Lake st. J. Stratton McKay. Manager.

VAN FLEET, A. B., Attorney at Law,
 1002 W. Madison st.

WILSON, EDGAR M., Attorney at Law, Room 61 Major Block, S. E. cor. Madison & La Salle streets.

BAKERY AND CONFECTIONERY.

J. B. BLAESY,
Bakery and Confectionery,
299 WEST RANDOLPH ST.

BRADY, SCOTT & CO.
Wholesale
Bread & Cake Bakers
702 West Lake Street.

CHICAGO—Continued.

BAKERY AND CONFECTIONERY.

ALDRICH, J. E., Magnolia Bakery,
199 Blue Island ave.

MRS. H. S. CANFIELD,
Bakery, Confectionery and Ice Cream Parlor
881 MILWAUKEE AVE.

CASE & MARTIN, Manufacturers of Connecticut Pies, cor. Wood & Walnut sts.

HULTON, J. W., Dealer in Fruit, Meat and Fish Cakes, Coffees, Spices, Syrups, &c., No. 148 W. Indiana st.

JOSEPH V. IRMOND,
BAKERY, CONFECTIONERY & RESTAURANT,
163 W. Randolph Street.

NEUFFER, WM., Bakery & Confectionery,
758 W. Madison.

BARBERS,
M. M. CHAPMAN,
SHAVING & HAIR-DRESSING ROOMS,
266 W. Randolph Street.

J. H. DIGGS,
SHAVING
—AND—
Hair-Dressing Parlors

Hair brushed by machinery. Ladies' and Gents' Bath Rooms. 122 S. Halsted.

DOERGE, AUGUST, Barber and Hair Dresser,
3921 Wentworth st.

FORD, A. J., Centennial Barber Shop,
307 W. Madison.

HANDY, PETER, Shaving and Hair-Dressing Rooms, 551 W. Madison.

QUINN, J. S., 590 Lake st., Tonsorial Artist. Estab. 1873.

VALERII'S, PAUL, Hair-Dressing room. Choice brands of Cigars. 422 W. Madison.

BELL-HANGING.

PORTER, H. B., 146 S. Dearborn st., Electric and Mechanical Bell-Hanging, Speaking Tubes, &c.

BITTERS.

HOWARD'S BOTANIC BITTERS, the great stomach and liver regulator. 165 W Van Buren.

BLACKSMITHS AND HORSESHOERS.

S. F. ENGLISH,
PRACTICAL HORSESHOER,
817 W. Lake.

Chas. Jirjahn and L. Meiser,
HORSESHOERS AND WAGONMAKERS,
285 Cottage Grove Ave. General Blacksmithing.

SHOMMER, P., Blacksmith, 253 W. Chicago Ave.

TORPE, AUGUST, General Blacksmith,
177 Madison st.

IMPORTANT EVENTS. 467

A. D.
1409. At the council of Pisa for the election of a Pope, Gregory and Benedict were disposed of, and Alexander V elected. Neither of them would yield, so there were three Popes at once.
1410. Joan of Arc born, sometimes called the Maid of Orleans, a peasant girl of France. She was sold to the English and after the formality of a trial, was burnt alive as a witch in 1431.
1415. John Huss and Jerome Prague, Bohemians, two of the first reformers, are burnt for heresy at Constance, which occasions an insurrection, when Sigismund, who betrayed them, is deposed and the Imperialists are driven from the Kingdom.
1420. Paris taken by the English who held it fifteen years.
1428. Joan of Arc, the Maid of Orleans, compels the English to raise the siege of that town. Wickliffe's remains burnt and his ashes thrown into the swift waters. Giovanni de Medici, one of the greatest merchant princes of Florence, died, and his son, Casmo de Medici, carried on the work his father begun. He induced artists and scholars to take up their abode in Florence. He died in 1461.
1429. Joan of Arc raised the siege and entered Orleans with supplies April 29, and the English, who were before the place from Oct. 12 preceding, abandoned the enterprise the following May. She captured several towns in possession of the English, whom she defeated in a battle near Patay, June 10.
1431. Joan of Arc was taken at the seige of Compeigne, and to the great disgrace of the English, was burnt for a witch five days after at Rouen in the 22nd (some say 29th) year of her age.
1438. Fifty thousand persons died of famine and plague in Paris during this year, when the hungry wolves entered the city and committed great desolation.
1440. The great invention of printing is due to Guttenberg, who was assisted in improving it by Schaeffer and Faust.
1442. The beginning of the negro slave trade.
1444. The earliest edition of the Bible was commenced this year by Guttenberg and finished in 1460.
1446. The sea broke in at Dort, Holland, and over 100,000 people were overwhelmed and perished, 300 villages were overflowed, and the tops of their towers and steeples were for

CHICAGO—*Continued.*

BITTERS.

WEST & COBBAN, Practical Horseshoers, 323 State st., bet. Harrison and Congress.

BLANK BOOK MAKERS.

McDONALD & JOHNSON, Blank Book Makers and Book Binders, 158 S. Clark st.

BOARDING HOUSE.

THIERRY, MRS. KATE, First-class Boarding House, 11 Blue Island Ave.

BOILER WORKS.

SHIELD & GODDARD, Star Boiler Works, 250, and 252 S. Clinton st.

BOOK-BINDERS.

DONOHUE & HENNEBERRY, Book-Binders, 105 Madison st.

GEIGER, J. J., Book, Binder and Picture Framer, 440 North Wells st.

P. RINGER & CO,

General Book-Binders,

137 and 139 S. State Street.

BOOKS AND STATIONERY.

BOOK FREE Book Agents or those wishing to procure a copy FREE of "Secrets of Life unveiled; or, Book of Fate,—550 pages—address M. A. Parker & Co., 163 & 165 Clark st.

Established 1865.

HARRIS' LIBRARY.

BOOKS, STATIONERY,
Newspapers & Magazines
TOYS AND FANCY GOODS,
637 Lake Street.

JONES BROS. & CO., Subscription Books, 76 and 78 Monroe st.

BOOTS AND SHOES.

Blonquist & Brother,
Manuf'rs of

Men's Boots & Shoes,
922½ Cottage Grove Ave.

BOLDT, J., Boots and Shoes, 457 W. Chicago Ave. Est. 1866.

EDW. BRABAND,
— Manufacturer and Dealer in —

BOOTS & SHOES,
221 NORTH AVENUE.
Repairing neatly done. Custom Work a specialty.

DATTELZWEIG, MRS. F., Boots, Shoes Notions, &c., 208 North ave.

DICKINSON & TREAT, C. O. D. Shoe and Boot Store, 191 W. Randolph st.

CHICAGO—*Continued.*

BOOTS AND SHOES.

DOENICH AUGUST, Boot and Shoe Maker, 88 S. Clinton st.

GIBSON, STEPHEN G., Rain-Bow Seam Shoe. Pat. applied for. 232 W. Randolph st.

LADIES'
Broad Sole Boots
Made under the supervision of
DR. KAHLER, CHIROPODIST,
191 Wabash Ave, Chicago.
All ailments of the feet successfully treated.

MULLER, PHILLIP, North Side Boot and Shoe Store, 373 Milwaukee ave.

OLSON, A. M., manuf'r and dealer in Boots and Shoes, 793 W. Madison st.

ROGAN, WILLIAM, Fashionable Boot & Shoe Maker, 3 Blue Island ave.

SILVER, G. & D., Fine Boots and Shoes. New York office in Chicago. W. J. Fleming.

VAN DOOZER A., 500½ W. Lake st., Custom Boot & Shoe Maker. Established 1875.

WEHL'S One Price Boot & Shoe House. 245 W. Madison st.

WOELFING, GEO., Manufacturer & dealer in Boots & Shoes, 35 E. Kinzie st.

WOLLER, AUGUST, Manfr. & dealer in Boots & Shoes, 418 W. Chicago ave.

YUNKER & SCHAEFFER, Premium Boot & Shoe Makers, 81 Dearborn st.

BROKER—NOTE AND BOND.

REED, ALBERT C., dealer in Notes & Bonds, 81 Washington st.

BRUSHES.

H. PAULSEN,
BRUSH MANUFACTURER,
Brushes of every description made to order.
58 WEST RANDOLPH STREET.

CABINET MAKERS AND UPHOLSTERERS.

W. DAVIES,
PRACTICAL CABINET MAKER & UPHOLSTERER
73 Twenty-second street.

Fine Upholstering, Mattress Renovating, Furniture made to Order, Repairing, Carpets Cleaned and Laid and Wire Screens made to order. All work warranted.

JOHN W. HEAL,
Cabinet Maker.
415 State Street (basement).
Furniture of all kinds made and repaired to order, Upholstered and Varnished at short notice.

L. Pottinger,
Manufacturer of
COUNTERS, SHOW CASES AND SHELVING.
589 W. LAKE STREET.

WENTER, F., Manf'r. of Fancy Cabinet Ware, Brackets, &c., 70 & 72 W. Washington st.

CHICAGO—Continued.

CAN MANUFACTORY.

MASON, E. T. & CO., Manf'rs. of Shipping and Plain Cans, 253 & 255 E. Lake st.

CARPENTERS AND CONTRACTORS.

BUTTON, THOMAS, Carpenter & Builder,
895 Cottage Grove ave.
DECKER, P. H., Contractor and Builder.
1408 Butterfield st.

C. GINGENBACH,

CARPENTER AND CONTRACTOR,
Stores and Offices Fitted Up. Jobbing promptly attended to.
406½ *STATE STREET.*

PIERCE, C. C., Carpenter & Joiner, Jobbing a specialty, 127¾ & 129 W. Madison st. Est. 1865.
SOEFFKERTHILE & CO., Contractors & Builders, 488 La Salle st.

CARRIAGE PAINTER.

GUDERIAN & WOLTER,

CARRIAGE AND WAGON PAINTING,

Rear 335 Blue Island Avenue.

CARRIAGES AND WAGONS.

EUREKA CARRIAGE AND WAGON WORKS,
311 East Division Street.
C. F. Bilhorn, prop. Repairing and Painting done at short notice. All work warranted.

JOSEPH HESTER,
Manufacturer of all kinds of

WAGONS & BUGGIES

All kinds of Blacksmithing and Jobbing done to order.

151 WEST RANDOLPH STREET,

Near Union.

CHRIST HEUSER,
Manufacturer of

Buggies, Wagons, Trucks, &c.,
129 Clybourn ave., cor. Rees.
Repairing and painting.

P. M. PETERSON & CO.
Manufacturers of
Buggies, Express Wagons, &c.,
703 W. LAKE STREET.
Repairing a specialty.

J. MILES STANDISH,

Carriage Manufacturer,

219, 221 & 223 W. LAKE STREET.

A. D.
1446. ages after to be seen rising out of the water. The inundation arose in the breaking down of the dykes.
1450. Insurrection in England by Jack Cade, calling himself Mortimer.
1453. "Civil wars of the Roses" occurs in England about this time, when the house of York began to aspire to the crown and by their ambitious views to deluge the whole Kingdom in blood.
1457. Glass first manufactured in England.
1460. Engraving and etching on copper invented.
An almanac in Lambeth palace written at this time.
1460. James II. of Scotland was killed by the bursting of one of the badly made guns as he was besieging the English in Roxburgh. He was succeeded by his son James III.
1461. Edward IV. succeeded Henry VI., having waged against him a civil war for six years. This was the war of the Roses, as the struggles between the houses of York and Lancaster were called.
1462. Mentz taken and plundered and the art of printing in the general ruin is spread to other towns.
Ivan the Great, of Russia, throws off the Mogul yoke, and takes the title of Czar.
1466. Faust dies at Paris, whither he journeys twice to sell his Latin Bible.
1468. John Guttenberg died aged 68. He was the inventor of movable types in printing, and was a partner of the famous Faust at Mentz.
1471. Warwick, Richard Nevil, the "King Maker," was the most distinguished actor in the wars of the Roses. He was slain at the battle of Barnet, Easter day, over whom Edward IV gained a decisive victory.
Richard III married Anne, daughter of Warwick and widow of Edward, prince of Wales, whom Richard had murdered.
King Henry, of England, is murdered in the Tower, aged 50 years.
1474. The foundation of the present monarchy of Russia commenced.
1476. Certain persons obtain license from Edward IV, to make gold and silver from mercury.
1477. Watches are said to have been first invented at Nuremberg.
1483. The Severn overflowed during ten days, and carried away men, women and children in their beds, and covered the tops of many mountains. The waters settled upon the lands, and were called the Great Waters for 100 years.
1484. Æsop's Fables, printed by Caxton, is supposed to be the first book with its leaves numbered.

BUSINESS ESTABLISHED 1858.

ANTON NEUMEISTER,
MANUFACTURER OF

FINE CARRIAGES,
Buggies, Sleighs, Phætons and Wagons.
Good Work and Reasonable Prices my Motto. Repairing promptly and neatly executed.

Salesroom and Factory, No. 119 North Main Street, EAST ROCKFORD, ILL.

Reaper City Wire Works,
LOCKWOOD & LYMAN, Props.,

MANUFACTURERS OF

Wire Cloth and Wire Goods, Flower Pots, Stands, Window Guards, Bank and Counter Railings, Asylum Windows, Doors, &c., &c., Brass, Wire Cloth for Paper Makers use, a full stock always on hand, of the best quality. Goods shipped promptly.

Rockford, · · Illinois.

S. J. GOODWIN.   CHAS. D. GOODWIN.
ESTABLISHED 1869.

GOODWIN HOUSE,
BELOIT, WIS.

S. J. GOODWIN & SON, Proprietors.

Frank Saxton, Chief Clerk.   Robert Martin, Night Clerk.

$2.00 PER DAY.
First-Class in all its Appointments.

The Butter, Cream and Milk used at the Goodwin House is brought daily from Goodwin's celebrated Maplewood Farm.

S. B. WILKINS, Pres't.   C. R. WISE, Sec'y.

ROCKFORD BOLT WORKS.
Manufacture to order all kinds of

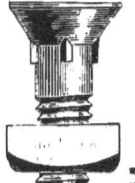

BOLTS,

For Agricultural Implements.
Established 1862.   Incorporated July, 1877.

ROCKFORD, · · ILLINOIS.

IMPORTANT EVENTS. 471

FOOT PASSAGE WAY, LA SALLE STREET TUNNEL, CHICAGO, ILL.

ENTRANCE FOR VEHICLES, LA SALLE STREET TUNNEL, CHICAGO, ILL.

472　　　ADVERTISEMENTS.

CHICAGO—*Continued.*

CARRIAGES AND WAGONS.

AUGUST THIELE,
WAGON MANUFACTURER
201 Blue Island Avenue.

CARRIAGE TRIMMER.

AUGUST, H., Carriage Trimmer. Repairing neatly done, 100 W. Adams st.

CARVER AND DESIGNER.

MARTENS, JOHN F., Art Furniture Carver and Designer, 74 W. Washington st. Est. 1872.

CHAIR MANUFACTURERS.

FORD, J. S., JOHNSON & CO., Manfrs. of Chairs, 255 & 257 Wabash ave.

SHAW, JOSEPH, Manf'r. of Cane & Wood Seat Chairs, 315 W. Randolph st.

CHEESE.

NEUMEISTER, GEO., dealer in Cheese & manf'r. of German & French Mustard, 16 S. Clark st.

CHEMIST.

BLANEY, JAS. R., Analytical and Consulting Chemist. room 20, 81 South Clark st.

CHINA DECORATING.

THE WESTERN DECORATING WORKS,
Decorating and Lettering on China, Glass, and Earthenware. Amateurs supplied with Colors, etc.; and firing done. Send for color price list. Grunewald & Schmidt, Proprietors, 84 Dearborn Street.

CHROMOS AND FRAMES.

DURKEE, ALBERT & CO., Chromos & Picture Frames. Agents Wanted. 112 Monroe st.

KELLY, WM. W. & CO., Chromo & Frame dealers, 135, 137, 139 & 141 Madison st.

CHIROPODIST.

KAHLER, DR. CHAS., Chiropodist. Lasts made to suit the Irregularity of the Feet. 194 Wabash ave.

CLAIRVOYANT & MAGNETIC PHYSICIANS.

BLADE, MRS. KATE, 51 S. Halsted st., bet. Washington and Madison sts., Spirit Phenomena' Messages for Tests, Business, etc., etc. Also, Examinations of Diseases and Disordered Conditions, with Magnetic Treatment. Independent Slate Writing a Specialty. Hours: 9 a. m., to 5 p. m.

MADAM DeVILLE,
BUSINESS AND MEDICAL CLAIRVOYANT,

121 W. Madison St.

DE WOLF, MRS., Business Clairvoyant & Test Medium, 263 West Madison st.

GRAY, PROF. M. M., Clairvoyant Magnetic Physician. Healing Institute, 243 West Madison st., near Peoria. Examination, $1; Treatment, $1 to $3. Office hours from 8 a. m., to 3 p. m.

CHICAGO—*Continued.*

CHIROPODIST.

DR. JOHN KRESS,
Magnetic   Healing   Medium,
Old Sores a Specialty.
313 WEST RANDOLPH STREET.

MRS. M. E. OWENS,
Magnetic and Electic Physician,
272 WEST RANDOLPH STREET.

MME. ROSA,
CLAIRVOYANT & MAGNETIC HEALER,

While unconscious will reveal to her visitors their most profound secrets.

241 West Madison Street

MRS. M. E. SUYDAM,
Business & Test Medium,
449 WEST MADISON STREET.

WITHERFORD, E. J., Materializing Medium. Private sittings daily, also public seances, 231 West Madison st., near Peoria.

N. VAN WERT,
MAGNETIC HEALER
334 West Madison St.

CLOTHING.

SAMUEL FRIEDMAN,
Manufacturer of
MEN AND BOY'S CLOTHING,
124 N. Wells St.
Residence 448 Dearborn Ave.

MRS. F. M. ROPER,
SHIRTS AND BOYS' CLOTHING
Cut and Made to Order.
217 BLUE ISLAND AVE.

COAL AND WOOD.

CONKEY & CO.,
Dealer in
COAL, WOOD, COKE,
Charcoal and Kindling.
Office & Yard 93 N. Clark St.

DARCHE, T., Dealer in Hard and Soft Coal. Office and Yard. 345 State st.

F. M. HALE & CO.,
COAL
AT LOWEST MARKET PRICE. OFFICE. 6 N. Clark St., Dock, N. Pier.

PALMER, SILAS, Coke, Coal and Wood, 1000 and 1002 West Lake st.

WOODROW, W., Coal, Wood, Coke & Kindling, 110, 112 & 114 W. Adams st.

IMPORTANT EVENTS. 473

CHICAGO—Continued.

COMMISSION MERCHANTS.

CAMPBELL, H. R., Commission Merchant, Dealer in Field Seeds, 134 E. Kinzie st.

CROSS, G. A. & CO., Fruit and Commission Merchants, 6 & 8 State st.

FANT, W. W., Commission Merchant and Dealer in Grain and Provisions, 159 Washington st. Rooms 7 and 8.

CONFECTIONERY.

R. W. DYBALL,

Confectioner and Caterer,

278 W. MADISON St.

GOOD, VICTOR, Confectioner, Cigars and Tobacco, 1½ Blue Island Ave.

SMITH & DRAKE, 632 W. Lake st. Manufacturer and dealer in Confectionery & Ice Cream.

THOMAS, L. M., Wholesale Confectioner. Chicago.

CONSERVATORY OF MUSIC.

CHICAGO

MUSICAL COLLEGE,

493 Wabash Avenue.
295 W. Madison.
480 North LaSalle.

WEST SIDE

Conservatory of Music.

MRS. MINNIE A. PHELPS, Prop't's.

372 W. Randolph st., Chicago.

COSTUMER.

MRS. T. SCHMITZ,

Masquerade Costumer

127 WEST MADISON ST.

CORSET MANUFACTURER.

The Combination Shoulder Brace

AND

Adjustable Bust and Skirt Supporter.

Also the Abdominal Corset will be fitted at 44 South Main St.
Agents wanted for city and country.

A. D.
1485. Richard III, King of England, and last of the Plantagenets, defeated and killed at the battle of Bosworth August 22d, by Henry VII, which puts an end to the civil wars between the houses of York and Lancaster. The crown of Richard was found in a hawthorn bush on the plain where the battle was fought, and Henry was so impatient to be crowned, that he had the ceremony performed on the spot with that very crown.
1488. James IV of Scotland, succeeded James III, who fell in a brawl with some of the barons.
1492. 500,000 Jews are banished from Spain, and 150,000 from Portugal.
1503. Shillings first coined in England.
1508. Negro slaves imported into Hespaniola.
1511. Cuba conquered by 300 Spaniards.
1514. Cannon bullets of stone still in use.
1517. Europeans first arrive in Canton, China. First patent for importing negroes to America granted by Spain.
1524. Some of the states of Europe were alarmed by the prediction that another general deluge would occur, and arks were everywhere built to guard against the calamity; but the season happened to be a very dry one.
1529. The name of Protestant given to those who protested against the Church of Rome at the diet of Spires, in Germany.
1537. Papal bull declares the American natives to be rational beings.
1539. Cannon first used in ships.
1543. Silk stockings first worn by the French king.
1547. First law in England establishing the interest of money at 10 per cent.
1548. Formal establishment of Protestantism in England.
1552. Books of geography and astronomy destroyed in England, as being infested with magic.
1553. Lady Jane Grey, daughter of the Duke of Suffolk, and wife of Lord Guilford Dudley, was proclaimed Queen of England on the death of Edward VI. Ten days afterwards returned to private life; was tried November 13, and beheaded Feb. 12, 1554, when but seventeen years of age, with her husband and his father.
1553. Elizabeth Croft, a girl of eighteen years of age, was secreted in a wall and with a whistle made for the purpose uttered many seditious speeches against the Queen and Prince of England, and also

CHICAGO—Continued.

CROCKERY CHINA AND GLASSWARE.

FORTIN, A., Dealer in China, Glass and Queensware, 95 Blue Island Avenue.

JOHNSTON, R. S., Crockery, Glassware, Lamps, Fancy Goods, etc., 744 W. Lake & 742 W. Madison.

THE PEOPLE'S
Crockery, Glassware
AND
LAMP STORE.
Lamp Burners a Specialty.
93 WEST MADISON St.
Lamps repaired and rebronzed.
H. HIRSCH, Prop.

DENTISTS.

ALBAUGH, WILLIAM, Dentist, 21 S. Halsted st. Office hours 9 A. M. to 4 P. M.

ELLSWORTH, P. J., Dentist, 81 N. Clark.

J. H. REINHARDT,
DENTIST,
204 SOUTH HALSTED SREET,
Rooms 1 and 2

WILDER, D. R., Dental Parlors, No. 213 State st., Cor. Jackson, Room 7.

YOUNG, J. H., Dentist, Room 5, No. 209 State street.

DENTISTS MATERIALS.

JUSTI, D. H., Manf'r and Dealer in Dentists Materials, 66 E. Madison st.

DETECTIVE AGENCY.

Wm. S. Beaubien,
NIGHT PATROL & DETECTIVE
POLICE FORCE AGENCY,
181 W. MADISON ST.

DRESS MAKERS.

MRS. E. D. ALLEN,
Dress and Cloak Maker,
CUTTING & FITTING.
326 W. Twelfth St.

BEESON, MISS EMMA, Room 9, No. 636 W. Lake st., Dressmaker. Est. 1876.

Mrs. R. H. Buckingham,
Dress and Cloak Making,
665 WEST LAKE ST.

MRS. E. B. CLARK,
Dress and Cloak Making,
739 West Lake St.

MRS. J. K. DeLANO,
"Le Bon Ton"
DRESS AND CLOAK MAKING,
No. 11 S. ANN STREET.
Ladies suits made to order. Cutting and Fitting a Specialty.

MRS. M. M. DOVEY,
DRESSMAKING,
SHIRTS MADE TO ORDER.
915 W. Lake St.

CHICAGO—Continued.

DRESS MAKERS.

MISS K. A. DYER,
DRESS & CLOAK MAKING
266 West Madison Street.

MRS. P. FITZGERALD,
Dressmaking and Patterns
141 West Van Buren Street.

GILSON, MISS C., Dressmaker, 155 22nd street.

MISS. H. M. GLEASON,
Dress & Cloak Maker
No. 327 State St.
Especial Attention Paid to Fitting.

HAAS, MRS. M., Dressmaking and Teacher in Needle Work, 135 Clybourn ave.

MRS. A. HART,
DRESSMAKING
94 S. Desplaines Street.

MRS. HAWKINS.
Fashionable Dressmaker
From London, England,
330 WEST RANDOLPH STREET.

MISS M. HOFFMANN,
Fashionable Dress and Cloak Maker,
723 MILWAUKEE AVE.

KEATING, MISS N., Dressmaking, 264 West Madison st.

MRS. M. KINSET,
DRESSMAKING
231 BLUE ISLAND AVE.

M. A. KIRKMAN,
Fashionable Dressmaking
254 WEST MADISON ST.

MRS. P. A. LLEWELLYN,
DRESS AND CLOAK MAKING
243 State St., Cor of Jackson, Howe Building.
Children's clothes a specialty.
A perfect fit guaranteed.

Miss M. E. McCafferty,
DRESSMAKING,
376 WEST MADISON STREET.

MISS D. MICHAUD,
Fashionable Dress and Cloak Maker,
669 COTTAGE GROVE AVE.

CHICAGO—Continued.

DRESS MAKERS.

E. C. MOORE.
Dress and Cloak Making
685 WEST LAKE ST.

MRS. MYRON,
DRESSMAKING
744 S. STATE STREET.

MISS. C. E. PAYNE,
DRESSMAKING,
757 West Madison Street.

MRS. KATE SALLSBURY,
DRESSMAKING
117 NORTH CLARK ST.

MRS. R. W. STEELE,
DRESSMAKER
322 STATE STREET.

Mmes. Bra Ziee & Wilmeroth,
MODISTES
171 North Clark St., Rooms 5 & 6.

DRUGGISTS.

Established 1874.
A. C. BRENDECKE,
Druggist
465 W. Chicago Ave., near Ashland Ave.

DAWSON & BAXTER, Druggists, 324 State street.

HARTWIG, CHAS. F., Apothecary, 410 Milwaukee ave.

KRAFT, HERMAN F., Apothecary & Druggist, 641 W. Madison st. Established 1875.

MATHISON & BUCHAN, Pharmacists & Chemists, 886 State st., near cor. 18th st.

EMIL OHRWALL'S
PHARMACY,
269 E. Division St.

This house was built and opened within ten days after the great fire of '71.

C. F. CLASS, DRUGGIST,
280 E. Division st. Established 1837.

O. W. TURNER,
Druggist, Dealer in every variety of Drugs and Chemicals, Patent Medicines, Fancy and Toilet Articles, Brushes, Perfumery, etc., 57 W. Randolph st. English and German prescriptions compounded at all hours.

C. B. WILSON,
APOTHECARY,
628 W. LAKE ST.

A. D.
1553. against the mass and confusion for which she was sentenced to stand upon a scaffold at St. Paul's Cross during sermon time, and make public confession of her imposture. She was called the Spirit of the Wall.

While Servetus, the founder of the Unitarian sect, was proceeding to Naples, through Geneva, Calvin induced the magistrates to arrest him on charge of blasphemy and heresy, and, refusing to retract his opinions, he was condemned to the flames, which sentence was carried into execution Oct. 27.

1554. The wearing of silk forbidden to the common people of England.

1554. The Company of Stationers of London is of great antiquity, and existed long before printing was invented; yet it was not incorporated until the second year of Philip and Mary.

1560. Minstrels continued until this time. They owed their origin to the gleemen or harpers of the Saxons. Queen Elizabeth, of England, was presented with a pair of black silk stockings, by her silk woman, and she never wore cloth ones any more.

1561. Philip II. commences his bloody persecutions of the Protestants.

1563. Captain, afterwards Sir John Hawkins, was the first Englishman, after the discovery of America, who made a traffic of the human species.

1564. William Shakspeare, the great poet and dramatist, was born at Stratford-on-Avon, to which place he returned from London and lived till 1616.

1568. Battle of Langside, between the forces of the regent of Scotland, the Earl of Murray, and the army of Mary Queen of Scots, in which the latter suffered a complete defeat on May 15. Immediately after this fatal battle, the unfortunate Mary fled to England, and landed at Workington, in Cumberland, May 16, and was soon after imprisoned by Elizabeth.

1571. Battle Lepanto. The great naval engagement between the combined fleets of Spain, Venice and Pius V., and the whole maritime force of the Turks. The Christian fleet for a time prostrated the whole naval power of Turkey.

1572 Massacre of St. Bartholomew. 70,000 Huguenots, or French Protestants, throughout the kingdom of France were murdered under circumstances of the most horrid treachery and cruelty. It began at Paris in

CHICAGO—Continued.

DRY AND FANCY GOODS.

BARRON, A. F., Fancy Dry Goods, Millinery & Jewelry, 250 North ave.

FOWLER, J. H., Dry Goods, & Ladies' & Gents' Furnishing Goods, 544 W. Madison st.

KATZ, J. P., 658 W. Lake st., Dry Goods, Notions, etc. Estab, 1865.

MRS. S. LOHMUELLER,
Embroidery and Stamping, also, dealer in all kinds of Wools, 167 W. Randolph Street.

SACHS, SIGISMUND, Oriental Bazaar and Fancy Goods, 193 S. Clark st.

SHIREK, S., Bankrupt Stock, N. E. cor. 22d & State sts. Established 1874.

MRS. C. THUMSER, Dealer in
Zephyrs, Fine Yarns, Canvas Chenilles, Silk Embroideries, Toilet Articles, etc., 655 W. Madison st.
Established 1872.

DYEING AND SCOURING.

C. E. CARLSTROM,
Stockholm Dye House, 276 E. Division st. All kinds of Ladies' and Gentlemen's Clothing received for Dyeing and Cleaning without ripping the seams of the garments or spoiling their shape.

GARDEN CITY STEAM DYE WORKS, J. H. Yerbury, prop., 395 W. Van Buren st

L. HARDING,
STEAM DYEING AND CLEANING ESTABLISHMENT,
Dyeing and Cleaning of Kid Gloves a specialty.
169 & 314 W. MADISON ST.

INTERNATIONAL DYE WORKS, Rau & Rehm, props., 413 6th ave. and 213 State st.

ELECTRIC WORKS.

CHICAGO ELECTRIC WORKS,
188 Madison st. Room 10,
A. H. Freeman & Co. Dwellings fitted up with Electric Burglar Alarms, House, Hotel and Elevator Annunciators, Check-boy Calls, Servant Calls and Signal Bells. N. B.—By our improved method dwellings furnished or unfurnished can be fitted up without marring or defacing the premises. All work warranted.

ELECTROTYPERS & STEROTYPERS.

BLOMGREN BROS., & CO., Electrotype and Sterotype Foundry, 162 & 164 S. Clark st.

SCHNIEDEWEND & LEE, Electrotypers, 200 & 202 S. Clark st.

ZEESE, A., & CO., Sterotypers and Electrotypers, 144 Monro st.

EMPLOYMENT OFFICE.

Mrs. S. LAPRISE,
LADIES' INTELLIGENCE OFFICE,
384 W. Madison st., Chicago.

MRS. SCHMIDT,
EMPLOYMENT OFFICE.
ALWAYS RELIABLE.
416 Wabash ave.

CHICAGO—Continued.

ENGINE BUILDERS.

AMES'
Portable & Mounted Engines
Three to forty horse power,
Forsman's Flouring & Feed Mills,
CORN SHELLERS, BELTING, ETC.,
14 S. Canal st. Collins Eaton, Gen'l West'n Agt.

ENGRAVERS—WOOD.

BERNHARD & CO., Designers & Engravers on Wood, room 5, N.W. cor. Madison & Clark sts.

MANZ, J. & CO., Engravers, 92 LaSalle st., cor. Washington. Send for estimates.

ENVELOPE MANUFACTURERS.

SEWELL, ALFRED L., Envelope Manufacturer and Stationer, 158 Clark st.

FARM BUREAU.

BUREAU for the sale of Farms on commission, E. P Hotchkiss, 142 LaSalle st.

FLAVORING EXTRACTS, PERFUMERY, ETC.

T. J. MOORE,
Manuf'r and dealer in
Flavoring Extracts
Perfumery and Toilet Articles.
No. 245 West Madison street, rooms 7, 8 and 9,

FLORISTS.

COOKENBACK & CO.,
FLORISTS,
860 West Lake st.

UNION PARK GREEN HOUSE, R. P. Larson, Florist, 556 W. Lake st. Established 1876.

FLOUR, FEED AND GRAIN.

MEYER, ADAM, Flour & Feed.
341 North ave.

North Avenue Feed Mills.

KEMPER & BRO.,
Wholesale dealer in
Grain, Flour & Feed
NO. 201 NORTH AVENUE.

FRINGES, CORDS AND TASSELS.

FRIEDLER, A. B., man'fr of Fringes, Cords, Tassels, Gimps, etc., 56 State st., & 449 & 451 N. Wells st.

CHICAGO—*Continued..*

FISH DEALER.

SJOBERG & CHAPMAN,

Dried, Salt and
FRESH FISH, ETC.
258 E. Division Street.

FURNITURE.

B ARSALOUX, N., Furniture & Household Goods,
60 W. Madison.

J. S. BAST,
270 & 272 N. Clark st., designer & manf'r of Unique Furniture, in walnut, ebonized or fancy woods. Also Wire Screens, Weather Strips, Picture Frames, Dumb Waiters, Moldings, Store & Office Fixtures, Dressed Lumber, Hardware, etc., etc. General House Repairing promptly attended to.

B EEMER BROS., Furniture dealers,
54 West Madison st.

B ERRY BROS., Furniture Made, Repaired and Upholstered, 729 West Madison st.

B OURKE, ULICK, dealer in Furniture, &c.,
92 West Madison st.

JOHNSON, ELLERSON & CO.,
Manufacturers of

Furniture,
Bureaus, Centre Tables, Sideboards, Bedsteads, &c.,

179 S. Clinton St., near cor. Jackson.
Scroll work of every description solicited.

G LENN, J. E., dealer in Furniture,
62 W. Madison st.

T. P. GLODY,
Architect & Superintendent,
Office, 682 Archer Avenue.

Furniture Dealer.

JOHN W. HEAL,
Furniture Manufacturer,
415 STATE ST., Established 1866.

F. X. MARTIN,
Designer and Constructor of Art Furniture,
90 SIXTEENTH STREET.

R ICHTER, HERMAN, Wholesale Furniture,
75 Clybourn ave.

R ICKE, S. & CO., Wholesale manf'rs. of Parlor Furniture & Frames, 265 Division st.

P HŒNIX FURNITURE CO., Fine and Medium Furniture, 672 W. Lake st. A. Schrock, Prop.

A. D.
1572. The night of the festival of St. Bartholomew, August 14, by secret orders from Charles IX., King of France, at the instigation of the queen dowager, his mother.
1585. Sextus V. rose from a shepherd boy to be Pope, is active and energetic, corrects abuses in the church and restores the Vatican Library.
1587. Mary, Queen of Scots, during the reign of Elizabeth, was beheaded in Fotheringay Castle, in which she had been long previously confined, February 8, after an unjust and cruel captivity of almost nineteen years, in England.
1589. Coaches first introduced into England,
1592. Massacre of the Christians at Croatia by the Turks, when 65,000 were slain.
1603. 30,578 perished of the plague in London alone in this and the following year. It was also fatal in Ireland.
1604. The celebrated religious conference held at Hampton Court Palace, in order to effect a general union between the prelates of the Church of England and the dissenting ministers. This conference led to a new translation of the Bible which was executed in 1607-1611, and is that now in general use in England and the United States.
1605. The memorable conspiracy in England, known by the name of the Gunpowder Plot, for springing a mine under the house of parliament, and destroying the three estates of the realm, king, lords and commons, was discovered Nov. 5. This diabolical scheme was projected by Robert Catesby and many high persons were leagued in the enterprise. Guy Faux was detected in the vaults under the House of Lords, preparing the train for being fired the next day.
Hugh Calverly, having murdered two of his children and stabbed his wife in a fit of jealousy, being arraigned for his crime at York assizes, stood mute, and was therefore pressed to death in the castle, a large iron weight being placed upon his breast.
1606. Demetrius Griska Eutropeia, a friar, pretended to be the son of Basilowitz, czar of Muscovy, whom the usurper Boris had put to death, but he maintained that another child had been substituted in his place, he was supported by the armies of Poland. His success astonished the Russians who invited him to the throne and delivered into his hands Fedor, the reigning czar

CHICAGO—Continued.

FURNITURE.

J. L. SECOMB & CO.,
Manufacturer's Agents, dealers in all kinds of Fine, Common and Medium Furniture.
Repairing neatly done.
694 WEST LAKE STREET.

JOHN UBER,
Dealer in all kinds of

FURNITURE,
Sofas, Lounges, Mattresses, Etc.,
306 Milwaukee avenue.

ZIELKE & ZIERCKE,
Practical Upholsterers. Manufacturers and Dealers in Furniture,
541 W. Madison street.

GLASS WARE.

R. G. BACHMANN,
Manufacturer of

CHEMICAL GLASSWARE,
33 W. Washington street.

GLOVE MANUFACTURERS.

CENTEMERI, P., Kid Gloves & Silks, 125 State st.

JENSEN, HANS, Glovemaker, 652 State st.

GROCERIES.

BERG, H., Dealer in Groceries and Provisions, 303 State st.

BLOOM, A. L., 364 East Division street, Staple and Fancy Groceries and Provisions. A Full supply of First-class Groceries and Provisions always on hand, which are sold for cash only. Call and see us.

P. E. Bolster & Co.,
Wholesale and Retail Dealers in

GROCERIES,
Teas, Fruits, St. Louis and Michigan Flour,
No. 430 STATE STREET.

COLE & STEWART, Wholesale & Retail Grocers and Tea dealers, 586 Archer ave.

GLENN, W. T., Choice Family Groceries. 829 W. Lake st.

KELLY & SMITH,
Dealers in

GROCERIES and PROVISIONS,
Crockery and Glassware,
719 WEST LAKE STREET, CHICAGO.
Goods delivered to any part of the city.

CHICAGO—Continued.

GROCERIES.

KASTNER BROS., Groceries, Flour, Feed, Liquors, Tobacco, Cigars, etc., 770 Archer ave.

LAW, ROBERT, Groceries & Provisions, 151 S. Clinton st., cor. Adams.

M. E. McDONOUGH,
Wholesale and retail dealer in choice Fancy and Staple Groceries, Provisions, etc. Flour at Jobbers' prices. Teas and Coffees a specialty. Country orders promptly filled. 112 W. Madison st. and 84 S. Desplaines st.

GUNSMITH.

RUDOLPH GRIMM,
Manufacturer & dealer in

Guns, Pistols, Powder and Shot,
107 W. RANDOLPH ST.
All repairs neatly and promptly done.

HAIR DEALERS AND DRESSERS.

MISSES C. & R. COHEN,

HAIR WORK,
324 W. TWELFTH ST.

MRS. H. FARNUM,
Manuf'r of Hair Goods and dealer in Machine Needles and Oils,
118 TWENTY-SECOND ST.

HULL, MRS. HATTIE M., Human Hair and Madame Demorest's Patterns, 270 W. Madison

MRS. CARRIE E. LEE,

HAIR PARLORS,
All kinds of Hair Work done to order. Combings made up. 707 W. Madison.

LEWINSOHN, L., manuf'r and dealer in Human Hair Goods, 130 E. 12th st.

MISSES J. MOELLER & A. THOMAS,
Dress Making and Hair Dressing Parlors,
Photo-Enamel and Wax Work also made to order.
428 Division street.

MUELLER, MRS. J., Ladies' Hair Store, 106 W. Madison st.

James Taite,
Importer of

HUMAN HAIR,
Switches, Braids, Curls, & Hair Jewelry,
256 W. Madison.

HARDWARE.

ALEX. BOOME,

Hardware, Stoves, Copper Tin
Galvanized and Sheet Iron Work.
139 EAST CHICAGO, AVE.

CORBLEY, J. F. & CO., Builder's Hardware, Carpenter's Tools, 296 State st.

ADVERTISEMENTS.   479

French Restaurant, Centennial Exposition, Philadelphia.—
Contains two dining halls, 100 feet by 50 feet, and a number of private saloons. All modern languages spoken, and the service entirely Parisian. Meals are furnished from bill of fare (*a la carte*) at specified charges. From an upper balcony a fine view of the grounds and buildings can be obtained.

CHICAGO—*Continued.*

HARDWARE.

DAEMICKE BROTHERS, Hardware, Stoves and Ranges, 914 State St.

DAEMICKE, L. C., Hardware, Stoves, Tools, etc., 508 State st.

DEWALD, M. J., Stoves, Hardware, Tools, Cutlery, etc., 340 North Ave.

MICHLITZ, THEO., Manf'r Tin, Sheet Iron and Copper Ware, 646 State st. Est. 1857.

ORR & LOCKETT, Hardware, Fine Cutlery, Tools, Butchers' Tools & Machinery, 170 S. Clark st.

PAUL, JOSEPH, Hardware and Carpenters Tools, 97 N. Clark st.

TYRING, H. E., Dealer in Hardware, Stoves, etc 66 W. Madison st

HARNESS AND SADDLES.

BIRR, F., Saddle and Harness Maker, 382 West Chicago Ave.

BOHNE, AUGUST, Saddle and Harness Maker, 344 N. Wells st.

C. ECKEBRECHT,
Harness Manufacturer
218 NORTH AVE.

ISLE, GEO. H., Saddle and Harness Maker, No. 70 35th st.

CHAS. H. KROETER,
Manf'r & Wholesale and Retail Dealer in
Harness, Whips, Blankets, &c.,
437 MILWAUKEE AVE.

31

CHICAGO—*Continued.*

HARNESS AND SADDLES.

G. LAAS,
Manufacturer and Dealer in
HARNESS AND HORSE CLOTHING,
663 West Lake Street.

E. SCHMIDT,
HARNESS AND SADDLE MAKER,
398 Milwaukee Ave.

GEO. G. STEYING,
Manufacturer and Dealer in
Harness, Saddles, Collars, Whips,
Brushes, Curry Combs, etc.
Fine work a specialty. Repairing neatly done,
46 NORTH WELLS ST

HASSOCKS AND OTTOMANS.

J. B. RUNGE,
Manufacturer of
Hassocks and Ottomans,
AWNINGS AND WINDOW SCREENS,
102 E. Van Buren St.
Carpets Fitted and Laid.

HATTERS.

KORF, JOHN F., Hats Dyed, Remodeled and Cleaned. 6 N. Clark st.

JULIUS MEYER,
HATS, CAPS AND FURS,
267 East Division St.

WALLASTER & MURPHY, Silk Hat Manufacturers. 197 E. Madison st., Cor. 5th Ave. up stairs.

CHICAGO—*Continued.*

HATTERS.

T. S. PORTSMOUTH,
Hat Manufacturer & Remodeler
25 S. HALSTED ST.
Soft Hats Cleaned, Dyed and Repaired.

HEALTH LIFT.

HAINSWORTHS' HEALTH LIFT, Patented and Manufactured by F. Hainsworth & Son, 192 5th Ave. Price $25 to $40.

HORSE PROTECTOR.

PETERS & Co., Manufacturers of Horse Protector, 65 N. Clark st.

HORSE-HOOF COOLERS AND EXPANDERS.

FURLONG'S PATENT FOOT COOLERS AND EXpanders, E. B. Draper, 103 E. Washington.

HOTELS.

ATHERTON HOUSE, E. A. Bacheldor Propr., 973 Wabash Ave.

BILLINGS HOUSE.
Cor. Jackson & Halsted Sts.,
J. D. BILLINGS, Prop.
Board by the week $6.00 to $10.00. House new and Elegantly Furnished.

BISHOP COURT HOTEL,

Patrick Brady, Prop..

511 W. Madison Street.

BURDICK HOUSE, Cor. Wabash ave., & Adams st., John A. Dewitt, Manager.

GALENA HOTEL AND RESTAURANT,
50 NORTH WELLS ST., Chicago, Ill.
Terms, $1.50 to $2 per Day; Meals, 50 cents. Mrs. Ellen Loftus, Proprietress.

GRAND PACIFIC, Cor. Clark & Jackson sts

MATTESON HOUSE, Cor. Wabash ave., & Jackson st.

METROPOLITAN HOTEL,
26 & 28 NORTH WELLS STREET.
G. E. Smith & C. A. Nesbet, Props. Opposite Depot Chicago & Northwestern Railroad. Terms, $2.00 per Day.

PALMER HOUSE, Cor. Monroe & State sts.

SAND'S HOTEL, Cor. Madison and Wabash ave.

SHERMAN HOTEL, Cor. Clark & Randolph sts.

ST. CHARLES HOTEL, 15 & 17 S. Clark st. $1.50 per Day. Rooms 75 cents per day. R. D. Kelly, Proprietor.

Windsor Hotel,
(Late Eastern House)
26 and 28 WEST MADISON ST.

Room and Board, $1 per Day. Room and Board $4 to $6 per Week. Commutation Tickets, 21 Meals $3. Single Meals, 20 cents.

E. Cockell,   -   Proprietor.

CHICAGO—*Continued.*

HYDRAULIC MOTOR.

TUERK BROS., Manf'rs. of Tuerk's Hydraulic Motor, 163 La Salle st.

INSURANCE AGENTS.

CASE, CHAS. H., Fire Insurance Agent, 120 La Salle st.

MONTGOMERY & TALLMADGE, Fire Insurance Agents, 134 La Salle st.

MOORE & JANES, Insurance Agents, 119 & 121 La Salle st.

INSTRUMENT AND SAMPLE CASES.

GEIGER, J. J., Manf'r. of Instrument and Sample Cases, 140 North Wells st.

LACE GOODS.

MRS. H. LONG,
Curtains and Fine Laces of every description, Black and White, Cleaned, Repaired and Transferred. Dresses and Fine Fluting.
516 Wabash ave., bet. Eldridge & Harmon Courts.

LAUNDRIES.

Hayward's American Laundry,
Goods called for and delivered free of charge, Special rates for hotel work.
226 W. WASHINGTON STREET.

HIGGINS & COLE,

Sheffield Laundry,
301 W. MADISON ST.,
Work Called for and Delivered Free of Charge. Family washing a specialty.

JUSTIN LOOMIS,
Proprietor of
LOOMIS' LAUNDRY,
193 & 195 W. Monroe street. Est. 1869.

PAULSON, A., Phœnix Laundry, 189 Milwaukee ave.

RICHHOLD'S LAUNDRY, Mrs. G. Richhold, proprietress, 199 W. Madison st.

VANDERPOOL, J., Chicago Laundry, 330 W. Randolph.

MRS. C. WHITE,
LAUNDRY,
Goods called for and delivered, all orders promptly attended to. 357 State st.

LEAD PIPE AND SHEET LEAD.

GARDEN CITY LEAD PIPE AND SHEET LEAD Co., cor. Jackson & Clinton sts.

LEATHER AND FINDINGS.

P. KIRKEBY, Dealer in
Leather, Findings & Shoemaker's Tools
38 CLYBOURNE AVENUE.

OLSEN, E., Leather & Findings, 131 Milwaukee ave.

SMITH, J. H. & CO., Brokers in Hides & Leather 184 E. Kinzie st.

CHICAGO—Continued..

LITHOGRAPHERS AND ENGRAVERS.

L. R. BROMLEY,
Lithographer, Engraver, Printer,
And Manufacturer of
CIGAR BOX LABELS AND BRANDS,
167 South Clark Street.

LOTT & ZEUCH, practical Lithographers & Engravers, 182 & 184 S. Clark st.

THE HATCH LITHOGRAPHIC CO., W. S. Pottinger, mang'r, 97 S. Clark st., room 8.

LIVERY AND SALE STABLE.

HENDRICKSON, S. F., Boarding & Sale Stable, 804 & 806 W. Madison st.

Northwestern Tattersall Livery, Boarding & Sale Stables,
138, 140, 142 & 144 N. WELLS ST.

SIOFFORD & MURPHY, P'rs

LOCKSMITHS AND BELL HANGERS.

COLE, W. L., Locksmith & Bell Hanger, 349 State st.

PARKER & RYTHER, Locksmithing, Bell Hanging and Speaking Tubes, 122 Dearborn st.

SACKRESON, JOHN P., Locksmith & Bell Hanger, 106 E. 12th st.

CHAS. WHITTINGHAM,
LOCKSMITH AND BELL HANGER,
Unpickable Bank and Safe Deposit Locks.
176 WEST MADISON ST.

LOOKING GLASS AND PICTURE FRAMES.

W. CALVERT,
MANUFACTURER OF PICTURE FRAMES,
Passe-Partouts and Mats. Display mats of every description made to order. 291 Wabash ave.

FOSTER, R. C., Looking Glass Manufacturer, 258 State st.

LAHODNY, W., Manf'r of Looking Glasses, 141 S. Clinton st.

MUTHER, JNO. C., Manf'r of Picture Frames, Mouldings, Easels, etc., 306 State st.

LUMBER.

GEO. SCHMID & SON,
Dealer in
GEORGIA YELLOW PINE
LUMBER
Office; Room 18, Uhlich Blk, No. 33 N. Clark st.

MACHINIST.

HARRIS, SAMUEL, Manf'r of Small Machinery and Tools for amatuer mechanics. 15 S. Canal street.

JEFFERY, T. B., Experimental Machinery. Working Models for Patent Office and for Exhibition, 253 & 255 S. Canal st.

A. D.
1606. and all his family, whom he cruelly put to death, his imposition being discovered, he was assassinated in his palace.
1611. 200,000 persons perished of a pestilence at Constantinople.
1619. Harvey discovers or confirms the circulation of the blood.
1620. Battle of Prague between the Imperialists and Bohemians of Germany. The latter, who had chosen Frederic V. of the Palatine, for their king, were totally defeated. The unfortunate king was forced to flee with his family into Holland, leaving all his baggage and money behind him. He was deprived of the hereditary dominions, and the Protestant interest ruined in Bohemia.
1624. George Fox, born, the founder of the society of Friends or Quakers. He was clad in a perennial suit of leather and wandered in solitude seeking some light to guide him, studying the Bible and himself. He died in 1690.
1628. The discovery of the circulation of the blood by Dr. Harvey, furnished an entirely new system of physiological and pathological speculation.
1629. St. Peter's Church at Rome completed, having been commenced about the middle of the 15th century.
1632. Battle of Lutzengen, or Lutze Called also the battle of Lippstadt. In this battle Gustavus Adolphus, king of Sweden, the most illustrious hero of his time and the chief support of the Protestant religion in Germany, and in alliance with Charles I. of England, was foully killed in the moment of victory.
1633. The art of preserving flowers in sand discovered.
1647. The tyranny of the Spaniards leads to an insurrection at Naples, excited by Maraniello, a fisherman, who in fifteen days raises an army of 200,000 men. The insurrection subsides and Maraniello is murdered.
1648. Eighty-one Presbyterians expelled from the English Parliament, which received the name of "the Rump."
1650. Quakers or Friends. Originally called Seekers, from their seeking the truth. Justice Bennett, of Derby, gave the society the name of Quakers at this time because Fox (the founder) admonished him and those present with him to tremble at the word of the Lord.

CHICAGO—Continued.

MANUFACTURER.

CHICAGO SCRAPER & DITCH CO., 34 Metropolitan Block.

MANUFACTURER'S AGENT.

MALLETTE & WALMSLEY, Manf'r's Agents.
197 E. Randolph st.

MAP MOUNTER.

TERRY, G. W., Map Mounting and Coloring,
Room 26, 79 Dearborn st.

MARBLE AND GRANITE WORKS.

NORTH SIDE MARBLE WORKS.
SCHMIDT & BAUER,
Manufacturers of

MONUMENTS,
Headstones, Mantels, Grates, and Plumber's Slabs,
53 CLYBOURN AVENUE.

THE HINSDALE-DOYLE GRANITE COMPANY,
91 Dearborn st., 658 Broadway N. Y., 1119 Olive st., St. Louis.

VOLK, J. H., Granite and Marble Monuments,
office cor. Dearborn & Randolph sts.

MATRRESS MANUFACTURER.

H. B. CRAWFORD,
Dealers in
FEATHERS, MATTRESSES,
Manf'r of the Eureka Mattress. Renovating by steam. 38 E. Adams St.
Pleasant Amick, Agt.

MEAT MARKET.

AURICH BROS., Fresh and Salt Meats,
25 & 62 Archer ave.

DAVIDSON, ROBT., Fresh and Salt Meats, Oysters & Fish & Game in season, 20: South Desplaines st.

SADLER, ROBERT, Meat Market,
108 E. 12th st.

MEDICAL ELECTRIC BATTERIES.

GEIGER, J. J., Repairer of Medical Electric Batteries, 440 N. Wells st.

METAL SIGNS.

FISHER, C. L. & SON, Metalic Sign Works, Patent Models, Movers, etc., 159 E. Van Buren st.

FRANK R. GROUT,
Glass, Board and Improved Metal Signs, Plain and Artistic Sign Painting, of every description, Unsurpassed facilities.
184 E. Madison.

WELCH, J. A., Manf'r of Engraved Metal Signs, Stencils, etc., 273 Mad son st.

MILL MACHINERY.

FARGUSSON, J., Mill Machinery and Furnishings. 56 S. Canal st.

MILLINERY AND FANCY GOODS.

BLACKWELL, MRS. N. E., Millinery and Fancy Goods, 193 Milwaukee ave.

CHICAGO—Continued.

MILLINERY AND DRESSMAKING.

BLAKE & FISHER, MRS., Milliners,
637 West Madison st. Established 18;2.

MRS. BRUCE,
Millinery, Dress and Cloak Making,
238 WEST RANDOLPH ST.

DALLMANN, MISS M., Fancy Millinery,
125 S. Halsted st.

DEVOY, MRS. T. J., Flowers, Feathers, Millinery and Straw Goods, 104 W. Madison st.

MRS. ELLIOTT,
Millinery and Dressmaking
755 West Madison St.

HOOKER, JOSIE H., Fashionable Mil iner and Dressma cr. 229½ E. Division st. Hats Pressed and Dyed.

MRS. C. E. JAMES,
286 W. Indiana St., Chicago.

Millinery & Ladies' Suits, Hair Goods, Notions, Etc.
Dressmaking, Stamping & Pinking done to Order.

MISS BESSIE A. KIRK,
MILLINERY.
Mourning Orders a Specialty.
969 WEST LAKE STREET.

MAGNAN, MDE., French Millinery and Fancy Goods. 685 W. Madison st. Est. March, 1876.

MARTIN, MISSES A. & E., French Millinery,
No. 7 Blue Island ave.

MISS M. MAVIS,
Millinery and Dressmaking,
426 WEST 12TH ST., Opp. Jesuit Church.

MORAN, MISS ELIZA, Millinery and Notions.
677 W. Madison st. Established 1877.

MRS. CATH. OEHM,
Millinery, Masquerade Costumes, Ladies' Fancy Goods, Etc
294 SOUTH STATE STREET.
Established 1856.

SCHWARZ, MRS. P., Fancy Millinery, Fancy Goods, Notions and Laces, 163 Milwaukee ave.

MRS. J. W. WELLS,
Millinery, Fancy Goods, Ladies' Furnishing Goods and Dressmaking,
843 WABASH AVE.

MRS. V. A. WILCOX,
Millinery & Dressmaking
964 WABASH AVE.

MRS. R. WILHARTZ,
Fashionable Milliner,
550 SOUTH HALSTED ST.

WOLF, MRS. E., Millinery and Ladies' Furnishing Goods, 305 East Division st.

CHICAGO—Continued.

MODEL AND PATTERN MAKERS.

C. W. CRARY,
MODEL & PATTERN MAKER,
Die and Press Work,
BRASS FINISHING, GEAR CUTTING, Etc.
Small Gears a specialty.
53 W. Randolph St.

DURKEE, GEO. B., Mechanical and Consulting Engineer, 253 & 255 S. Canal st.

STENBERG & MALMGREN, Machinists. Die and Model Makers, 211 E. Randolph st., Room 10.

A. WEAVER,
Pattern and Model Maker. Architectural, Furnace, Stove, Engine and Machinery Patterns. Inventors' and Patent Office Models, both in Wood and Brass. 60 S. Canal st.

MOULDING MANUFACTURERS.

F. BRACHVOGEL & CO.,
MANUFACTURERS of MOULDINGS,
364 NORTH AVENUE.

MUSIC DEALER.

UNGER, CHAS., West Side Music Store, all kinds of Instruments, 10 N. Halsted st.

MUSIC TEACHERS.

FREIBERG, FRED & BRO., Musicians, office, 132 E. 12th st. & 95 S. Clark st.

JOSEPH SINGER,
Teacher of Violin and Piano,
255 W. MADISON ST.

Annie B. Stewart,
MUSIC TEACHER,
934 South State Street.

NEWS DEPOT.

O'KELLY, J. H., 665 W. Madison st., Cigars, Tobaccos, Stationery & Periodicals. Est. 1871.

NEWSPAPER.
1872.
"EULENSPIEGEL,"
Illustrated Comic Weekly,
By M. Langeloth
CIRCULATION, 6,500.
The sprightliest German paper in the West. Office, 55 W. Randolph st., Chicago, Ill.

OIL STOVES.
THE CHICAGO OIL STOVE. Manufactured by F. Hainsworth & Son, 192 5th ave.

OPTICIAN AND OCULIST.
PHILLIPS, DR. JOHN, Optician and Oculist, 144 Dearborn st., 3 doors South of Madison st.

IMPORTANT EVENTS. 483

A. D.
1652. First war between the English and the Dutch.
1656. James Naylor personated our Savior; he was convicted of blasphemy, scourged, and his tongue bored through with a hot iron on the pillory by sentence of the House of Commons under Cromwell's administration.

The plague brought from Sardinia to Naples, being introduced by a transport with soldiers on board, raged with such violence as to carry off 400,000 of the inhabitants in six months.

1662. Charles II. is said to have first encouraged the appearance of women on the stage of England, but the queen of James I. had previously performed in a theatre at court.

An earthquake throughout China buries 300,000 persons at Pekin alone.

1663. The first idea of a steam engine was suggested by the Marquis of Worcester in his "Century of Inventions" as "a way to drive up water by fire."

1665. Memorable plague in London which carried off 68,596 persons.

1666. Great fire in London, Sept. 2, destroying 80 churches, including the Royal Exchange, the Custom House, Sion College, and many other public buildings, besides 13,200 houses, laying waste 400 streets. This conflagration continued three days and nights, and was at last only extinguished by the blowing up of houses.

Chain-shot to destroy the rigging of an enemy's ships invented by the Dutch admiral, DeWitt.

1667. The method of preparing phosphorous from bones discovered by Charles William Scheele, an eminent Swedish chemist.

1669. Candia or Crete obtained from the Venetians by the Turks after a siege of 24 years, during which more than 200,000 people perished.

1672. White slaves were sold in England to be transported to Virginia; average price for a five years' service $25, while a negro was worth $125.

1674. John Milton, one of the chief poets and greatest men of England died, aged 66 years. His task in writing two "Defenses of the People of England" totally destroyed his already impaired vision. He afterward fulfilled the prediction uttered in one of his former books by bringing out the great English epic "Paradise Lost."

In his domestic life Milton endured much trouble. Deserted for

CHICAGO—Continued.

OYSTERS AND FISH.

CURTIS, H. M., Packer, and wholesale dealer in Oysters & Fish, 18 S. Clark st.

PAINTERS.

WM. ADAMS.
HOUSE AND SIGN PAINTING,
Graining, Glazing and Calcimining. 628 Cottage Grove ave., (basement.) Jobbing promptly attended to.

BAILEY O. L., Painting, Graining and Calcimining, 959 W. Lake st.

BECKWITH, R. F., House & Sign Painter. Calcimining & Frescoing, 181 West Washington st. Est. 1866.

BIRSHOFF, A., Carriage Painting. 321 & 223 Division st.

ELLSWORTH, H. M., Sign Writer, with Waggoner, Gifford & Co., 8 Market st.

WM. J. EVANS,
House, Sign & Ornamental Painter
91 WEST MADISON STREET.

DAHNDEN & SCHRODER, Painters and Paint Dealers, 201 Milwaukee ave.

J. E. DUFFY,
—Practical—
HOUSE AND SIGN PAINTER.
Graining, Calcimining, &c. Glass Gilding and Signs of every Description.
85 WEST MADISON STREET.

(Established 1854)
GEORGE HOWARD,
House and Sign Painter,
Gilding, Graining, Glacing, Etc.,
100 W. LAKE ST.,
Wagons, Etc., Painted and Lettered. Wall Lettering a Specialty.

PERKINS BROS., House & Sign Painters, also dealers in Wall Paper, &c., 126 S. Halsted st.

J. D. ROBERTS,
PAINTER. All branches of Painting done to order. Sign Painting, Calcimining, Graining, Glazing, Paper Hanging. Work Warranted. Sign of the Golden Paint Pot, 314 W. Van Buren St.

SMITH, T. F. & SON, House and Sign Painters, Paints and Oils, 116 Blue Island ave.

WALL, WM. H., Artist and Ornamental Sign Writer, 54 West Madison st.

WRIGHT & IRISH, House and Sign Painters, 215 W. Madison st.

PAINTS AND OILS.

WM. SWISSLER,
Dealer in Paints, Oils, Varnishes, Brushes, Window Glass, Etc.
200 W. RANDOLPH ST.   Estab. 1857.

WILLIAM WILSON,
Dealer in Paints, Oils, Glass, Wall Paper, Window Shades, &c. House and Sign Painting, Calcimining, Graining and Glazing.
875 COTTAGE GROVE AVENUE.

CHICAGO—Continued.

PAPER MANUFACTURERS.

CLEVELAND PAPER CO.,
Manufacturers of

104 & 106 MADISON STREET.

PAPER BOXES.

MILLER, JOHN C., Manuf'r. of Plain and Fancy Paper Boxes, 187 & 189 E. Washington st.

SCHNEIDER, J. B., Manuf'r. of Paper Boxes, 141 South Water st.

PAPER HANGINGS.

FITCH, R. F., dealer in Paper Hangings & Window Shades, 176 22d st.

PATENT SOLICITORS.

LOTZ, W. H., Consulting Engineer, Solicitor of American and Foreign Patents, 93 Fifth ave.

D. STONER,
Patent Solicitor,
ATTORNEY & NEGOTIATOR,
EXCHANGE BUILDING,
116 WASHINGTON STREET.

PAWN BROKERS.

P. LICHTENSTADT,
Pawn Broker
93 W. RANDOLPH ST.
Liberal advances made on all goods of value. All jewelry kept in burglar and fireproof safes.

North-Western Loan Office,
89 W. RANDOLPH ST.
H. FRANKS & SON, Proprietors.

M. D. ROSENBACH,
HAY MARKET LOAN OFFICE.
All goods of value kept in fire and burglar-proof Safes. 111 & 117 West Randolph St. The highest cash price paid for Ladies' and Gents' cast off Clothing.

PERFUMERS.

BALDWIN, D. B., & CO., Manufacturing Perfumers, 7 West Randolph st.

PHOTOGRAPHERS.

ABBOTT'S CARD PICTURE, $3.00 per Dozen. Ten Pocket Portraits. 50 cents. 150 State st.

Berlin Photographic Art Studio,
679 WEST MADISON ST., Near Wood.
We give our Customers the privilege of two sittings, in different positions, so that a choice can be made therefrom. Proof can be seen before leaving the rooms. Satisfaction guaranteed.   J. M. LENZ.

IMPORTANT EVENTS.   485

CHICAGO—Continued.

PHOTOGRAPHERS.

BROWN, H. J., Photographer,
165 W. Madison St.   Est. 1872.

HOUGH, J., Photographer,
135 Chicago ave., cor. Market st.

WM. MORRISON,
Photographic Art Gallery,
57 WEST MADISON STREET.

A. PANNEBERG,
(Successor to George Schneider,)

PHOTOGRAPHER
219 & 221 NORTH AVE.

RIDER & GEHRIG, Gallery of Photographic and Fine Arts, 335 W. Madison st.

WHITING, S. H., 622 W. Lake st..
Photographic Art Studio. Estab. 1872.

PHOTO-ENGRAVERS.

SHAW & DRUMMOND,
MECHANICAL PROCESS

PHOTOGRAPHERS
No. 148 STATE STREET.
Photo-Lithographic Transfers and Photo-Engraving Plates. Wood Block Printing and Negatives for the various processes a specialty. A. J. Drummond, formerly Supt. Photo-Engraving Co., of Chicago.

PHOTOGRAPHERS' SUPPLIES.

BEARD, J. P., & CO., Photographers' Supplies, Picture Frames, &c., 230 Wabash ave.

PHYSICIANS.

BECKER, AUGUSTA, Physician,
75 N. Clark street.

L. E. CALKINS,
PHYSICIAN
943 WEST LAKE STREET.

DECKER, DR. H. G., Physician, 226 Blue Island ave. Est. 1847.

GRASMUCK, LOUIS, Homoepath. Consultation English and German, rooms 13 & 14 cor. Randolph and Halsted.

DR. L. A. HARCOURT,
PHYSICIAN,

Special attention given to obstetrics and diseases of women. Office hours, 8 to 9 a. m., 1 to 2 and 6 to 7 p. m. Graduated in Buffalo Medical College in Feb. 1869. 258 W. Madison st., cor. Sangamon

JUSTIN HAYES, M. D.,
Specialty treatment of

NERVOUS AND CHRONIC DISEASES,

With the best means of the profession, including electricity and care of patients, at 167 Wabash ave, Palmer House Block.

A. D.
1674. a while by his first wife, he saw no relief but in divorce. His daughters, in his old age and blindness, treated him with notorious want of love. His universal fame now rests on his poems, which were hardly known and not at all appreciated During his day.
1680. A comet appeared, and from its nearness to the earth alarmed the inhabitants. It continued from Nov. 3 to March 9 following.
1684. The first idea of a telegraph on the modern construction was suggested by Dr. Robt. Hook, a celebrated English mathematician and philosopher.
1686. An inundation at Yorkshire, when a rock opened and poured out water to the height of a church steeple.
1689. Peter I. the Great became sole ruler of Russia.
Assiento, a contract between the King of Spain and other powers, for furnishing the Spanish dominions in America with negro slaves. It was vested in the South Sea Company, 1713.
The memorable act to exclude Roman Catholics from ascending the throne of Great Britain was passed, and the crown of England was settled upon the present royal family by the act of June 12, 1701.
1690. Battle of Boyne gained by William III. over James in Ireland, July 1.
1691. The horrible Glencoe massacre of the unoffending inhabitants, the Macdonalds, merely for not surrendering in time to King William's proclamation. About 38 men were brutally slain, and women and children were turned out naked in a dark and freezing night, and perished by cold and hunger. This black deed was perpetrated by the Earl of Argyle's regiment.
1692. Earthquake at Jamaica which totally destroyed Port Royal, whose houses were swallowed 40 fathoms deep, and 300 persons perished.
1693. An earthquake in Sicily which overturned 54 cities and towns and 300 villages. Of Catania and its 18,000 inhabitants, not a trace remained. More than 100,000 lives were lost. Syracuse destroyed by an earthquake, with many thousands of its inhabitants.
First public lottery drawn.
1696. Plate, with the exception of spoons, was prohibited in England at public houses.
1701. Frederick III. in an assembly of the States, put a crown upon his own and upon the head of his consort, and is proclaimed King of Prussia

CHICAGO—Continued.

PHYSICIANS.

HELEN A. HEATH, M. D.,
136 NORTH CLARK ST.

HESS, W. W., Physician,
45 S. Clark st, rooms 4 & 5.

KOEHLER, G. C., Physician, 197 E. Madison st.

A. LAKAY,
PHYSICIAN,
373 North ave.

H. MEYER,
PHYSICIAN,
360 North Ave.

OLIN, A. G., Physician and Surgeon in all chronic diseases of either sex, 187 Washington st.

PALMER, H. B., Physician, treats cancers and all chronic diseases, 125 S. Clark st.

PEIRO, F. L., Throat & Lung Diseases a specialty, 90 Washington st.

PHELON, W. P., Physician, 75 E. Madison st., treats opium and liquor habits successfully.

MRS. L. F. SAWYER, M. D.,
195 North Clark St.

SMALL, A. E., Physician. Office, room 7, Kentucky Block, 201 S. Clark st.; residence 588 Wabash ave.

SPERRY, C. C., Physician, 173 N. Clark st.

F. W. STREICH,
PHYSICIAN,
147 N. CLARK ST.

TOWNSEND, DR. D. F., 183 S. Clark st. Office hours from 8 a. m. to 8 p. m. Consultation free.

VON TAGEN, CHAS. H., Surgeon (Graduate 1858.) Room No. 8, Kentucky Building, 201 S. Clark st.

DR. G. B. WALKER, M. D.
Specialty Cancers & Female Diseases.
Call or address 125 Clark st.
The afflicted who suffer from that terrible disease known as cancer should not delay application to Dr. G. B. Walker, M. D., whose renown in curing this disease warrants the utmost trust in his ability and experience. without the use of the knife or loss of blood. Dr. Walker's "Health Journal" sent free on application.

PIANO FORTES.

W. T. REED,
Manufacturer of and dealer in
Piano Fortes,
262 State st. Tuning and repairing a specialty.
Established in 1857.

CHICAGO—Continued.

PLASTERERS.

McCARTHY, I. C. & G. VOGT., Ornamental Plasterers, 571 State st. Orders by mail attended to.

PLATERS.

A. T. ANDERSON,
Manufacturing
SILVER SMITH,
Gold and Silver Plater.
Society Jewels & Emblems a Specialty.
190 South Clark St., 4th Floor.

COLBY BROS., Nickle Platers and Machinists. Polishing neatly done. No. 6 Calhoun Place.

PURTELL & HANNAN,
SILVER PLATERS
60 South Canal Sreet.
Manufacturers of Fine Gold. Silver and Nickle Harness Mountings, Plated Stairs and Balcony Railings, Plated and Iron Window Sash Bars, Door Plates, Carriage Irons, etc. Sleeping Car Plating a Specialty.

SILVER AND NICKEL PLATING, BELL HANGing, Iron and Silver Plated Sash Barrs. Baldwin & Co., 150 State st.

PLUMBERS AND GAS FITTERS.

JOHN BLAKE.
Plumbing, Gas and Steam Fitting,
No. 535 State Street.
Near Harmon Court.

BROOKS BROS., Plumbing and Gas Fitting Works, 427 W. Madison st.

CHAS. F. GRIFFITHS,
Plumber and Gas Fitter,
885 WEST LAKE ST.

HALLAREN, JAMES, Plumber and Gas Fitter, 1207 South State St.

HAMBLIN, JOHN J. & CO., Plumbing and Gas Fitting, 366 Ogden Ave. Est. 1857.

R. J. JOHNSON,
PLUMBER AND GAS FITTER,
714 West Lake Street.

NAP. O'BRIEN
PLUMBER AND GAS FITTER,
607 W. Lake St.

W. & J. RANKIN,
PLUMBERS & GAS FITTERS,
461 W. Madison St., Cor. of Ada.

ROTH, J. H., Plumber and Gas Fitter, 39 Blue Island Ave.

David Whiteford,
Practical Plumber and Gas Fitter,
346 W. RANDOLPH ST. & LAWNDALE.

W. W. Boyington, Architect, Chicago.   EXPOSITION BUILDING, CHICAGO, ILL.   P. H. Deckr, Builder, Chicago.

CHICAGO—*Continued.*

PORK PACKERS.

Established 1856.
S. CURTIS & CO.
Packers of Provisions,
Clear Pork and Mess Pork, Hams
and Shoulders
KETTLE-RENDERED LEAF LARD.
Ham, Beef, Extra Plate Beef Extra Mess and Mess
Beef, Dried Beef Tongues, Smoked Hams and
Shoulders.
Packing House, 790 State St.

PORTRAIT PAINTER.

SIBLEY, BENJ., Portraits in Oil, Water Colors
and India Ink, 089 W. Madison st.

PRINTING INK.

WOOD, JASON P., Agent for Queen City Printing Ink, 45 La Salle st.

PRINTERS.

ALEXANDER, W. R., Commercial Book and Job Printer, 157 Washington st.

BLAIR, GEO. W., Commercial Job Printer. Satisfaction guaranteed in price and work. 182 S. Clark st.

BLAKELY & BROWN, Book and Job Printers, 151 & 153, 5th Ave.

BURROUGH, C. J. & CO., Job Printers. Fine work, 192 & 194 Clark st.

DRAKE, J. C., Book & Job Printer, 181 & 183 W. Madison st.

GREGORY & STAIGER, Job & Pamphlet Printers. 55 N. Clark st.

GUILBERT & CLISSOLD, 188 Madison st., Job Work of every description.

PERCY HARRISON,

Commercial Job Printer, 81 Metropolitan block, (N. W. corner Randolph and LaSalle sts.) Take elevator. Visiting cards 60cts per 100,

JOHNSON, W. H., Tag Manufacturer and Job Printer. 178 Madison st.

JONES, T. T. Book & Job Printer, 799 W. Madison st.

McCALLASTER, H. & CO., Printers, 81 S. Clark st. Country orders solicited, Specimens free.

SCHELL, GEORGE, Stationer & Job Printer. 059 W. Madison st. Established 1877.

J. K. SCULLY & CO.,
Printers,
70 Metropolitan Block, corner Randolph and LaSalle sts.

WHITMAN, H., Artistic Printer, Room 9, 75 E. Madison st.

PRIVATE RESIDENCES.

KLEINMAN, J. J., 79 Walnut st.

WILSON, MRS. ADDIE, 1195 W. Madison st.

PUBLISHERS.

FACTORY & FARM—Illustrated Monthly—Fox, Cole & Co. Publishers, 177 LaSalle st.

LANE, M. T. & CO., Publishers & Booksellers, 167 & 169 Washington st.

STOELKER, W. H. & CO., Publishers, 35 Clark st. Send for sample copy, price 25 cts.

CHICAGO—*Continued.*

PUBLISHERS.

WARREN MOSES., publisher of Books by subscription, 103 State st. Agents wanted, send for circulars.

WESTERN FIRE MAP PUBLISHING CO., Room 59, Rep. Life Ins. Bldg, Chas. Rascher, M'gr

WORKINGMAN'S ADVOCATE, A. C Cameron, editor and propr., 151 & 153 S. Clark st.

RAILWAY SUPPLIES.

BREWER, JOHN S., Railway Supplies, 156 & 158 Lake st.

REAL ESTATE.

BOYD, T. B., Real Estate & Exchange Broker, 179 E. Madison st.

BROWN, IRA, 142 LaSalle st., deals only in his own property on the monthly instalment plan.

CHICAGO REAL ESTATE OFFICE. Est. 25 years, S. H. Kerfoot & Co. Correspondence solicited. 61 Dearborn st.

GOODRICH, HENRY J., Real Estate dealer and Loan Agent, (est. 1865) 125 Dearborn st., room 8.

KERFOOT, WM. D. & CO., 90 Washington st., Real Estate bought, sold & gener'y managed,

KNAUER BROS.,
Oldest north side Real Estate and Loan
Agents,
Office: Cor. CLARK & KINZIE STS.,
Rooms, 10 and 12.

MILLS, D. W., Real Estate dealer & Broker, 145 Clark st., cor Madison.

PROUDFOOT, W. S. & CO., Real Estate and Loan Agents. 170 Madison st.

SCOTT, T. A., Real Estate and Loans, 97 Clark st.

WHIPPLE, H., Real Estate and Loan Agent, 14 Methodist Church Block, 104 Washington st.

RENOVATORS.

FLINT & COOK, Furniture, Clothing & Carpet Cleaning, 1215 State st.

RESTAURANTS.

CENTRAL RESTAURANT, A. B. Olson, prop., 283 E. Madison st.

HENDRICH, R., Ladies' & Gents' Dining Rooms & Restaurant, 101 E. Kinzie st.

C. HOLMES,
RESTAURANT
83 W. RANDOLPH ST. - Est. 1876.

JOSEPH'S DINING ROOMS, Opposite Northwestern Railroad Depot, 55 E. Kinzie st.

LAVEZZI, JOS., 650 West Lake st., Confectionery, Ice Cream, Oysters, &c.

ST. CHARLES HOTEL RESTAURANT, No. 15 S. Clark st. Meals 25 cts. Raggio Bros., props.

THE LITTLE SHERMAN, Oyster Parlors & Dining Rooms, Barkers, props., 163 E. Lake st.

RUBBER STAMPS.

HOLDERNEES, S., Rubber Stamps of every description. 133 E. Madison st., room 8.

C. F. JONES & CO.,
Manufacturer of
RUBBER STAMPS,
No. 188 Madison Street.

TENNEY & REESE, Manfrs. of Rubber Stamps, 70 E. Madison st. Buy the Best.

CHICAGO—Continued.

SALOONS.

CREGAN, JOHN, Dealer in Wines, Liquors, Cigars & Tobacco, 49 Blue Island ave.

JOHN FEHN,

LAGER BEER HALL,

121 & 123 North Clark Street.

RAYMOND, H. W., Wine, Beer & Billiard Saloon. 13 Cottage Grove ave.

MAX ROMER,
WINE AND BEER HALL,
No. 45 North Clark Street.

SCHAEFER, DANIEL, Saloon, 67 Archer av.

ZIMMERMANN, JOHN, Saloon. Wines, Liquors, Cigars and Tobacco, 80 Blue Island ave.

SHIRT MANUFACTURERS.

CONE, S. F., Fine Shirts to Order. Send for blanks for self measurement. 150 State st.

NISSEN, C., Manufacturer of Shirts and Shirt Fronts, 381 North Clark st.

SPECTACLES.

WOLF, JOSEPH, Agent for the Hoosier State Spectacle Manf'r Co., 365 East Division st.

SPRING BEDS.

BARRETT, J. F., Dowell Spring Bed. 140 best Steel Springs. Price, $10.00. 86 State st.

W. F. HUNTINGTON,
AGENT FOR THE VICTOR SPRING BED,
Also the Huntington Spring Beds and Cots, 325 State Street.

LEWIS, H. H., Manufacturer of Bed Springs, 219 & 221 W. Randolph St.

STAINED GLASS.

MISCH, GEO. & BRO., Manufacturers of Stained, Enameled, Embossed, Cut and Ground Glass, 217 East Washington St.

STARCH MANUFACTURERS.

CHICAGO STARCH WORKS, Incorporated 1876. Office 73 S. Water St., H. Colberg, Agent, S. W Allerton, Pres't, E. H. Pray, Treas.

PEERLESS STARCH DEPOT, Amory Biglow, Agent, 105 South Water St.

STENCILS AND STAMPS.

KOCH GUSTAV, 73 Dearborn Street, Burning Brands, Stencil Dies & Seal Rubber Stamps.

STEREOSCOPIC VIEWS.

LOVEJOY & FOSTER, Stereoscopic Views of Chicago; Frames, Chromos, Albums, Photographs, &c., 88 State St.

STOVES, HEATERS, RANGES & TINWARE,

BARTHOLDY, N. C., Stoves and Hardware, 340 Milwaukee Ave., 238 W. Chicago Ave.

DIETRICH, PETER, 606 W. Lake St., dealer in Stoves and Tinware. Established 1865.

A. D.

by the title of Frederick I.
1703. The man of the Iron Mask died after a long imprisonment.
1718. Siege of Frederic's Hall, rendered memorable by the death of Charles XII. of Sweden, who was killed before its walls, and while in the trenches leaning against the parapet examining the works.
Lady Mary Wortley Montague introduced inoculation for the smallpox from Turkey, her own son having been inoculated with perfect success.
1729. The Methodists may be said to have appeared formally, if not originally, at Oxford.
1730. The large body of Christians called Wesleyan Methodists, was founded by John Wesley.
1735. Stereotyping is said to have been suggested by William Ged, of Edinburgh.
1738. Kouli Khan orders a general massacre and 150,000 people perish.
1770. Ann Lee imprisoned for her religious belief. Born in Manchester, England, Feb. 29, 1436. In 1758, "led by a vision and inspiration," she joined the society of James and Jane Wadley, followers of the French prophets, and who had been associated both with the Friends and the Methodists, she became the founder of the Shakers, who claim a real advent of Christ on the earth at this date.
1778. Invasion of Bohemia by Frederick II. of Prussia, and commencement of the "Potatoe War; (so-called on account of the numerous petty skirmishes and maneuvers respecting the convoys.)
1787. James Whitaker, first Shaker preacher, died at Enfield, Conn., aged 36 years. He was born at Oldham, England.
1789. Destruction of the Bastile by the French populace.
The police at Versailles attacked by the French populace, and the King Queen compelled to proceed to Paris.
The title King of France altered to the King of the French.
1790. Abolition of hereditary nobility and titles of honor in France.
1793. Louis XVI imprisoned in the Temple and brought to trial, is condemned to death and beheaded in the Palace de Louis Quinze. Thus perished at the age 39, after a reign of sixteen years and a half, passed in endeavoring to do good, the best but weakest of monarchs.
The first English church erected in Australia.

490 ADVERTISEMENTS.

CHICAGO—Continued.

STOVES, HEATERS, RANGES & TINWARE.

JOHN BEDAU,
Manufacturer of
Furnaces and Heating Pipes, Tin, Copper and Sheet Iron Ware,
And dealer in Stoves and Hardware, 110 East Division Street.

CHARLES W. GANSZ,
Dealer in Stoves, Tin and Hardware, Manufacturer of Tin, Copper and Sheet Iron Ware, 264 Division Street, Near Bremer.

ERNST HAUCK,
DEALER IN
STOVES, TIN & HARDWARE,
Also manufacturer of Tin, Copper and Sheet Iron Ware, 380 Division St., Cor. Franklin, Roofing, Guttering and Jobbing done to order.

KELLEY, H. C., Tin, Copper and Sheet Iron Work Patentee of Kelley's Lanterns, 184 E. Madison St.

MANNING, JOHN N. & CO., Steam Heating and Ventilating Apparatus, 80 & 82 N. Clinton st.

Multog & Becker,
Dealers in
STOVES, TIN & HARDWARE,
Manufacturers of Tin, Copper and Sheet Iron Ware.
177 W. RANDOLPH STREET.

OLENDORF, F., & SON, Stoves, Tin & Hardware, 278 W. Chicago ave.

POWERS, F. P., dealer in Hot Air Furnaces, 200 State st.

SERVOSS, NORTHEN & CO., Manf'r. of Furnaces, Ranges, &c., 198 to 204 N Clark st.

STUCKART, HENRY, Stoves and Ranges,Tin,Copper and Sheet Iron Ware, 717 Archer ave.

The Cheapest Place in Chicago to Buy

TINWARE
is 26 BLUE ISLAND AVENUE. Established 1863.

WATSON, GEO. H. & CO., dealer in Stoves and Furnaces, 273 & 274 State st.

WILKS, S., Manf'r. & dealer in Hotel and Car Ranges, 113 State st.

TAILORS.

CARROLL, JOHN, Merchant Tailor. Clothes Cleaned, Dyed and Repaired, 181 E. Madison st., in basement.

HEINIG, F., Draper & Tailor. Firemen's and Police Uniforms a specialty, 281 Milwaukee ave.

HERMANN, S., Merchant Tailor, 234 W. Randolph st.

A. JOHNSON,
MERCHANT TAILOR,
and Gentlemen's Furnishing Goods,
367 W. INDIANA STREET.

CHICAGO—Continued.

TAILORS.

JAMES JOHNSTON,
TAILOR & DRAPER,
59 W. RANDOLPH ST. · Second Floor.
The best of work at lowest prices.

KREIS & SCHAFER,
MERCHANT TAILORS,
No. 106 MONROE STREET,
3d door from Cor. Dearborn.

LACY, WM. J., Merchant Tailor. A first-class fit guaranteed, 317 W. Randolph st.

HERMAN LEUPPEN,
FASHIONABLE MERCHANT TAILOR.
61 West Madison Street.

N. LINDSTROM,
DRAPER AND TAILOR,
879 COTTAGE GROVE AVENUE,
Between 38th and 39th Streets.

LUNDQVIST, JOHN, Merchant Tailor, 898 Cottage Grove ave.

MARTIN, A., Merchant Tailor. 121 W. Madison st.

WM. McMASTER,
MERCHANT TAILOR
516½ W. MADISON ST.

CHARLES MUELLER,
Merchant Tailor,
164 KOSSUTH ST.

NELSON, M. J., Merchant Tailor, 201 W. Madison st.

NITSCHKOWSKY, L., Merchant Tailor, 51 State st.

PRICE, W., Merchant Tailor, 86 S. Clinton st., rear Madison st.

SADLER, L., Fashionable Tailor & Shirt Manf'r, 236 W. Washington st.

SAUER, G. E., Merchant Tailor, 110 E. 12th st.

SOLTOW, A. C., Fashionable Merchant Tailor, Cloths cleaned & repair d 81½ N. Wells st'

SIMON, PHILIP, Tailor. Scouring. Cleaning, Dyeing and Repairing. 1362 State st.

UNION PARK CLOTHING HOUSE.

VEIT & AARON,
Merchant Tailors
Manufacturers of Ready-made Clothing, and dealers in Hats, Caps and Furnishing Goods, 630 West Lake Street.

F. E. WHITE,
Merchant Tailor, and Manufacturer of Ready-Made Clothing,
710 W. LAKE ST.

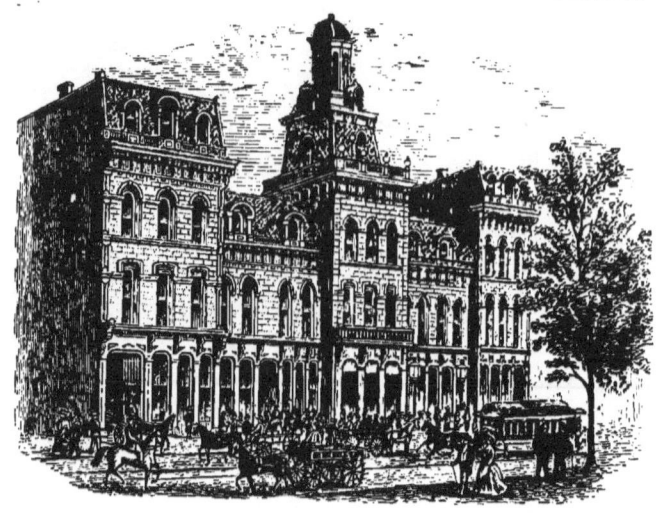

PUBLIC LIBERY BUILDING, LOUISVILLE, KY.

CHICAGO—Continued.

TEAS AND COFFEES.

ASSAM TEA CO.,
157 W. MADISON ST.
☞ Teas in Caddies at Wholesale Prices. ☜
GEO. PEAT, Proprietor.

BLACKALL, A. H., Imported Teas and Coffees, 49 Clark st. & 186 W. Madison st.

TEAS AT IMPORTER'S PRICES.

Great Atlantic and Pacific Tea Company, 219 West Madison st., 116 West Washington st., and 148 Twenty-second st.

TEA PACKERS.

OLENDORF, JOHN & CO., Tea Packers.
41 State st.

TOBACCO AND CIGARS.

An Invtation to visit
JULIUS HAMMERSCHLAG'S
West Side Cigar Palace and Manufactory,
343 WEST MADISON STREET.

ANDREWS, L. M., Wholesale Tobacconist, Andrew's Durham a specialty, 6 N. Wells st.

Established 1868.

D. CASTRO,
298 & 300 W. Madison St
SECOND FLOOR,
Cuban Cigar Factory.

CHICAGO—Continued.

TOBACCO AND CIGARS.

HULVEI BROS., Stationery, Fine Cigars and Tobacco, 210 W. Madison st.

MACE, E. W. & SON, Manf'r and dealer in Cigars & Tobacco, 95 22d st.

H. D. NELSON,
Dealer in Stationery, Cigars, Tobaccos, Candies
Toys, Baby Carriages, 99 E. Chicago ave.

OTT, THOMAS, manf'r of Cigars and dealer in Tobacco, Pipes, etc., 636 Archer ave.

TOYS AND BABY CARRIAGES.

MEYER, CASPER, Toys, Baby Carriages and Willow Ware, 991 & 993 State st.

ST. NICHOLAS TOY CO., manf'r of Velocipedes, Toys, &c., 790 to 794 W. Madison st.

UMBRELLAS AND PARASOLS.

HENRY SANDER,
Manufacturer and repairer of
Umbrellas and Parasols,
Special attention given to re-covering,
463 W. Madison st.

UNDERTAKERS.

FOLEY & CORRIGAN,
UNDERTAKERS,
And Embalm'rs, 166 W. Indiana st., cor. Sangamon. Horses and carriages furnished to order.

CHICAGO—Continued.

VINEGAR AND PICKLES.

Chicago Ave. Pickle and Vinegar Works.
G. J. GROSS,
Manufacturer of
PICKLES,
and all kinds of
VINEGAR,
Also Catsup and Sour Krant, No. 313 West Chicago ave.

MEYER, JOHN C., Vinegar and Pickle Manufacturer, 56 N. Desplaines st.
WISWELL, W. H. & CO., Manf'r of Pickles, Chicago, Ill.

WATCHES, CLOCKS AND JEWELRY.

ANDERSON, H., Watchmaker & Jeweler, Gold and Silver Plating, 181 E. Chicago ave.

FRED. BAIER,
Watchmaker & Jeweler,
230 Blue Island ave.

BOYNTON, A. P., Watchmaker & Jeweler, 582 State st.
DEY, S. L., JR., Wholesale & Retail Jeweler, 785 W. Madison st.

W. G. HARDS.
WATCHMAKER & JEWELER,
No. 37 N. Wells st. Repairing neatly done. All work warranted.

IMELLE, R. S., Watchmaker & Jeweler, 522 W. Indiana st.
JUERGENS & ANDERSON, Manufacturing Jewelers, N. E. cor State & Madison sts.
KNIGHT, C. H. & CO., Wholesale Jewelers, 125 & 127 State st.

G. C. KNOLL,
Watches, Clocks and Jewelry
109 W. Randolph st.

VOSS, WM., Watchmaker and Jeweler, 684 Milwaukee Ave.

WINES AND LIQUORS.

BARKLEY, L., Dealers in Wines, Liquors, Cigars and Tobacco, 119 W. Adams st
BROWN, L. A. & CO., Importers and Wholesale Liquor Dealers, 47 N. Clark st.
DOOLEY, M., Imported Wines, Liquors, Cigars and Tobacco, 108 W. Polk st.
ALTMAN, MICHAEL, Dealer in Imported Wines and Liquors. 594 Archer Ave.
RYAN, MICHAEL, Dealer in Wines and Liquors, 69 Blue Island Ave.
SHAWCROSS, EDWARD, Wines, Liquors, and Cigars, 75 W. Madison st.
TOOMEY, J. E., Dealer in Fine Wines, Liquors and Cigars, 415 Archer Ave.

WIRE WORKS.

Garden City Wire Works.
C. A. NIEBUHR,
Manufacturer of
FLOWER STANDS, BIRD CAGES,
WINDOW SCREENS,
393 Division St. Bet. Wells & Franklin Sts.

CHICAGO—Continued.

WIRE WORKS.

BLAIR, W. E., Sole Manf's Patent Wire Signs, 171 and 173 E. Madison st.
GREAT WESTERN WIRE WORKS, T. Spangenberg, Manf'r of all kinds of Wire Works 177 Madison st.
LOCKWOOD, CHAS. R., Brass and Wire Stands, Forms, etc., 198 E. Madison st.
MITCHELL'S WIRE WORKS, Manf'r of all kinds of Wire Goods, 284 Madison st.
NOVELTY WIRE WORKS, Edward Leger, Manufacturer of Stove Fixtures and Wire Frames, 127 State st.
SCHLEGEL, FRANCES T., Manufacturer of Wire Works and Wire Signs, 148 and 150 Madison st.
SMITH E. & CO., Manufacturers of all kinds of Wire Goods, 170 E. Madison st.
STARKE, WM., Manf'r. all kinds of Wire Springs, 107 W. Randolph st,

WOOD CARPET.

DUNFEE, J., Wood Carpet & Inlaid Floors, 100 E. Washington st.

WOOD AND WILLOW WARE.

FELIX, MARTON & BLAIR, Wooden and Willow Ware, 55, 57 and 59 South Water st.
SEYDELL, M., Manf'r. of Willow Ware, 825 Cottage Grove ave.

YEAST.

SPENCER, A. E., Manf'r. of Laprulice Yeast Gems, with Steele & Price, 11 S. La Salle st.

CHICAGO BUSINESS HOUSES,
When Established.

BRABAND, EDW. Boots & Shoes, 1872.
CONKEY & CO., Coal, Wood & Coke, 1870.
CRARY, C. W., Model and Patern Maker, 1869.
DAEMICKE BROS., Hardware, 1865.
DAEMICKE, L. C., Hardware, 1865.
DUNFEE, J., Wood Carpet, 1868.
DRAPER, E. B., Horse Foot Cooler, 1877.
DURKEE, ALBERT & CO., Chromos and Picture Frames, 1874.
GRAY, M. M., Physician, 1849.
GRIMM, RUDOLPH, Guns, 1872.
HALL, WARREN & CO., Manufacturers of Whips, Stocks & Lashes, 1870.
HARCOURT, L. A., Physician, 1868.
HAUCK, ERNST, Stoves, 1875.
KEMPER & BRO., Flour & Feed, 1873.
KNIGHTS, C. H. & CO., Jewelry, 1877.
MANNING, JOHN N. & CO., Steam Heaters, 1877.
MULTOG & BECKER, Stoves, Tinware, etc., 1869.
NELSON, M. J., Tailor, 1864.
PERKINS, H. C., & CO., Reapers and Mowers, 1874.
PORTSMOUTH, T. S., Hat Manufacturer, 1870.
PEIRO, F. L. M. D., 1873.
SERVOSS, NORTHEN & CO., Eclectic Heater, 1873.
STONER, D., Patent Solicitor, 1859.

BLAKELY & BROWN,

NEWSPAPER,

BOOK & JOB

PRINTERS.

Special attention given to Fine work.

Facilities large and Satisfaction guaranteed. Estimates for any section of the country promptly forwarded on application.

Nos. 151 & 153 Fifth Ave.,

CHICAGO.

www.ingramcontent.com/pod-product-compliance
Lightning Source LLC
Chambersburg PA
CBHW051234300426
44114CB00011B/733